1 MONTH OF
FREE
READING

at
www.ForgottenBooks.com

By purchasing this book you are eligible for one month membership to ForgottenBooks.com, giving you unlimited access to our entire collection of over 1,000,000 titles via our web site and mobile apps.

To claim your free month visit:
www.forgottenbooks.com/free93858

ISBN 978-1-5285-7256-9
PIBN 10093858

REPORTS OF CASES

DETERMINED IN

THE SUPREME COURT

OF THE

STATE OF NEW MEXICO

From May 17, 1913
to April 20, 1914

JOHN R. McFIE
REPORTER

VOLUME XVIII

SANTA FE, N. M.
NEW MEXICAN PRINTING CO.
1915

TABLE OF CASES REPORTED

(In Volume XVIII.)

The following cases were disposed of by the court in the case of Wood-Davis v. Sloan, p. 291, and no separate decisions were filed:

TABLE OF NEW MEXICO CASES CITED.

TABLE OF CASES REPORTED IN PACIFIC REPORTER.

CITATION

OF

CONSTITUTIONAL AND STATUTORY PROVISIONS.

NEW MEXICO STATUTES.

THE SUPREME COURT

OF THE

STATE OF NEW MEXICO

HONORABLE CLARENCE J. ROBERTS.......Chief Justice

HONORABLE RICHARD H. HANNA......Associate Justice

HONORABLE FRANK W. PARKER.......Associate Justice

HONORABLE FRANK W. CLANCY.......Attorney General

JOSE D. SENA......................................Clerk

HARRY W. CRONENBERG.........................Bailiff

The Supreme Court of the State of New Mexico begins its regular term on the second Wednesday in January and continues during the entire year, at Santa Fe, New Mexico. the seat of government.

Sessions of the January term, for oral argument, will be held on the second Wednesday in January, and on the first Mondays in March, May, September and November of each year.

UNITED STATES
DISTRICT COURT
FOR THE
District of New Mexico

HONORABLE WILLIAM H. POPE..District Judge Presiding
Santa Fe, N. M.

HONORABLE SUMMERS BURKHART.............
...............................United States Attorney
Albuquerque, N. M.

HONORABLE A. H. HUDSPETH.....United States Marshal
Santa Fe, N. M.

HARRY F. LEE......................................Clerk
Santa Fe, N. M.

At Santa Fe, on the first Mondays in April and October.
Special terms elsewhere as ordered by the Presiding Judge.

THE DISTRICT COURTS

OF THE

STATE OF NEW MEXICO

DISTRICT JUDGES.

FIRST DISTRICT.....Hon. Edmund C. Abbott, Santa Fe.
SECOND DISTRICT..Hon. Herbert F. Raynolds, Albuquerque
THIRD DISTRICT....Hon. Edward L. Medler, Las Cruces
FOURTH DISTRICT..Hon. David J. Leahy, Las Vegas
FIFTH DISTRICT....Hon. John T. McClure, Roswell
　　　　　　　　　Hon. Granville A. Richardson, Roswell
SIXTH DISTRICT....Hon. Colin Neblett, Silver City
SEVENTH DISTRICT.Hon. Merritt C. Mechem, Socorro
EIGHTH DISTRICT..Hon. Thomas D. Leib, Raton

DISTRICT ATTORNEYS.

FIRST DISTRICT.　　　Alexander Read, Santa Fe.
SECOND DISTRICT.　　Manuel U. Vigil, Albuquerque.
THIRD DISTRICT.　　　Humphrey B. Hamilton, Carrizozo.
FOURTH DISTRICT.　　Charles W. G. Ward, Las Vegas.
FIFTH DISTRICT.　　　Kenneth K. Scott, Roswell.
SIXTH DISTRICT.　　　James R. Waddill, Deming.
SEVENTH DISTRICT.　Edward D. Tittman, Socorro.
EIGHTH DISTRICT.　　George E. Remley, Cimarron.

TERMS OF STATE DISTRICT COURTS.

FIRST DISTRICT.

Hon. Edmund C. Abbott, Judge, Presiding.

Santa Fe County:	First Monday in March and Second Monday in September, (at Santa Fe, M. A. Ortiz, Clerk.)
Rio Arriba County:	First Monday in June and Third Monday in November, (at Tierra Amarilla, M. A. Gonzales, Clerk.)
San Juan County:	First Monday in April, Second Monday in October, (at Aztec, W. B. Wagner, Clerk.)

SECOND DISTRICT.

Hon. Herbert F. Raynolds, Judge, Presiding.

Bernalillo County: Third Mondays in March and September, (at Albuquerque, A. E. Walker, Clerk.)

McKinley County: Third Mondays in May and November, (at Gallup, F. W. Myers, Clerk.)

Sandoval County: First Monday in February and Fourth Monday in August, (at Bernalillo,. Abelino L. Lucero, Clerk.)

THIRD DISTRICT.

Hon. Edward L. Medler, Judge, Presiding.

Dona Ana County: Third Monday in February and Fourth Monday in August, at Las Cruces, C. O. Bennett, Clerk.)

Lincoln County: Second Monday in March and First Monday in October, (at Carrizozo, Albert H. Harvey, Clerk.)

Otero County: Second Monday in April and Fourth Monday in October, (at Alamogordo, Charles E. Thomas, Clerk.)

Torrance County: Fourth Monday in March and Third Monday in September, (at Estancia, Julian Salas, Clerk.)

FOURTH DISTRICT.

Hon. David J. Leahy, Judge, Presiding.

San Miguel County: Third Mondays in May and November, (at Las Vegas, Lorenzo Delgado, Clerk.)

Guadalupe County: First Monday in April and Fourth Monday in September, (at Santa Rosa, Geo. Sena, Clerk.)

Mora County: Fourth Mondays in April and October, (at Mora, Tito Melendez, Clerk.)

FIFTH DISTRICT.

Hon. John T. McClure, Judge, Presiding.
Hon. Granville A. Richardson, Judge, Presiding.

Chaves County: Second Monday in April and First Monday in November, (at Roswell, R. F. Ballard, Clerk.)

Curry County: Second Monday in February and Fourth Monday in September, (at Clovis, Walter C. Zerwer, Clerk.)

Eddy County:	Second Monday in January and First Monday in September, (at Carlsbad, A. R. O'Quinn, Clerk.)
Roosevelt County:	Second Mondays in March and October,(at Portales, C. P. Mitchell, Clerk.)

SIXTH DISTRICT.

Hon. Colin Neblett, Judge, Presiding.

Grant County:	First Mondays in March and September, (at Silver City, E. B. Venable, Clerk.)
Luna County:	Fourth Mondays in April and October, (at Deming, C. R. Hughes, Clerk.)

SEVENTH DISTRICT.

Hon. Merritt C. Mechem, Judge, Presiding.

Socorro County:	Third Mondays in March and September, (at Socorro, Edward L. Fortune, Clerk.)
Sierra County:	First Mondays in May and November, (at Hillsboro, Andrew Kelly, Clerk.)
Valencia County:	First Mondays in March and September, (at Los Lunas, Jesus M. Luna, Clerk.)

EIGHTH DISTRICT.

Hon. Thomas D. Leib, Judge, Presiding.

Colfax County:	First Mondays in May and December, (at Raton, John L. Boyle, Clerk.)
Quay County:	First Mondays in April and October, (at Tucumcari, D. J. Finnigan, Clerk.)
Taos County:	First Monday in June and Second Monday in November, (at Taos, A. A. Rivera, Clerk.)
Union-County:	First Mondays in March and September, (at Clayton, Juan Duran, Clerk.)

REPORTER'S EXPLANATORY NOTE.

1. The page reference beneath each paragraph of the syllabus indicates the page on which the holding of the Court is to be found.

2. The Black Letters in the margin of the cases reported in this volume, indicate the paragraphs of the syllabus of corresponding number.

3. The Black Letters are placed at the paragraph of the opinion where the holding of the Court, as stated in the syllabus, is most concisely stated.

4. The Index to this volume contains a double reference citation; the page number to the left, and immediately following the title of the case, refers to the page on which the case reported commences; the numbers on the right indicate the black letters of the syllabus, in the margin of the case, and the page on which the respective paragraphs of the syllabus is succinctly stated by the Court. In a long case this black letter citation will be found most convenient.

REPORT OF CASES

DETERMINED IN THE

SUPREME COURT

OF THE STATE OF NEW MEXICO

JANUARY TERM, 1913

[No. 1528, May 17, 1913.]

FARMERS DEVELOPMENT COMPANY, Appellant, v. RAYADO LAND & IRRIGATION CO., Appellee.

SYLLABUS (BY THE COURT).

1. Assignments of error that "the court below erred in affirming the decision of the Board of Water Commissioners," and that "the court below erred in rendering judgment herein in favor of said appellee, affirming the said decision of the Board of Water Commissioners," are not sufficiently specific to present any question for review.

P. 6

2. Under chap. 49, S. L. 1907, from any act or refusal to act of the state engineer, the aggrieved party may appeal to the Board of Water Commissioners, and may likewise appeal from the decision of said board to the district court. The statute contemplates a hearing or trial de novo before each board or tribunal, and not a review of the order or decision of the inferior tribunal. An assignment of error, in such a proceeding, upon appeal from a judgment of the district court, that "the court below erred in finding and adjudging that the said Board of Water Commissioners had and was possessed of the right, warrant and authority to review the discretion of the said state engineer in the matter of the approval of permits to appropriate," is therefore not well taken, because the record in this case fails to show that the district court so held, or that any such issue was presented, or could have been involved in the case.

P. 7

Appeal from District Court, Colfax County; Thomas D. Leib, District Judge; appeal dismissed.

JULIUS C. GUNTER, Denver, Colo., HENRY L. LUTZ, Denver, Colo., and H. L. BICKLEY, Raton, N. M., for appellant.

Act creating office of Territorial Irrigation Engineer. Ch. 102, laws of 1905; chap. 104, laws of 1905; sec. 28, chap. 102, laws of 1905; Young and Norton v. Hinderlider, 110 Pac. 1045; sec. 63, chap. 102, laws of 1905.

JONES & ROGERS, for Appellee.

Record proper is not part of the transcript of record because not properly certified. Sec. 66, chap. 49, laws of 1907; Territory v. McGrath, 16 N. M. 202; U. S. v. Sena, 106 Pac. 383; U. S. v. Lesnet, 9 N. M. 373; 2 Cyc. 1074; Archibeque v. Miera, 1 N. M. 160; Romero v. Luna, 6 N. M. 440.

Assignments of error are insufficient to raise any issue in appellate court. Cevada v. Miera, 10 N. M. 62; Mellina v. Freig, 15 N. M. 455; Pierce v. Strickler, 54 Pac. 748; Schofield v. Territory, 56 Pac. 303; McRae v. Casson, 110 Pac. 574; Territory v. Clark, 13 N. M. 59; Candelaria v. Miera, 13 N. M. 360; Maxwell v. Tufts, 8 N. M. 396.

Questions not properly raised in lower court may not be assigned as error on appeal. Daily v. Fitzgerald, 125 Pac. 625; Territory v. Mills, 120 Pac. 325; Chavez v. Lucero, 13 N. M. 368; Clelland v. Hostetter, 13 N. M. 43; Gillett v. Chavez, 12 N. M. 353.

Errors invited, waived or immaterial are not available in appellate court. Chaves v. Myers, 68 Pac. 917; Jung v. Myers, 68 Pac. 933; U. S. v. Adamson, 106 Pac. 653; Conway v. Carter, 11 N. M. 419; Lund v. Ozanne, 13 N. M. 293; R. R. Co. v. Rodgers, 113 Pac. 805; Territory v. McGrath, 114 Pac. 364; Gillett v. Chavez, 12 N. M. 353; 3 Cyc. 243; 3 Cyc. 250.

There was no error in assuming jurisdiction. Elliot on

Development Co. v. Land & Irrigation Co., 18 N. M. 1.

Appellate Procedure, sec. 599; 2 Standard Procedure, 160; id. 605; secs. 63, 65 and 66, chap. 49, laws of 1907; Archibeque v. Miera, 1 N. M. 160; Romero v. Luna, 6 N. M. 440; Sanchez v. Candelaria, 5 N. M. 400; secs. 20 and 21, chap. 49, laws of 1907; sec. 10, Organic Act of New Mexico; Speer v. Stephens, 102 Pac. 365; Bear Lake v. Budge, 75 Pac. 614; Weil on Water Rights, secs. 1192 to 1194, and 419 (1911 ed.); Turley v. Furman, 114 Pac. 278.

Judgment was based on substantial evidence. Daily v. Fitzgerald, 125 Pac. 625; Candelaria v. Miera, 13 N. M. 360; Melini v. Freig, 110 Pac. 563; Richardson v. Pierce, 14 N. M. 334; Handcock v. Beasley, 14 N. M. 239; Crabtree v. Segrist, 3 N. M. 500; Romero v. Coleman, 11 N. M. 533; Gale v. Salas, 11 N. M. 211; Bank v. McClelland, 9 N. M. 636; Torlina v. Torlish, 6 N. M. 54; Badaracco v. Badaracco, 10 N. M. 761; Bank of Commerce v. Mining Co., 13 N. M. 424; Radcliffe v. Chavez, 110 Pac. 699; Gallegos v. Sanderson, 106 Pac. 373; Daily v. Fitzgerald, 125 Pac. 625; Romero v. Desmarais, 5 N. M. 142; sec. 16, chap. 102, laws of 1905.

Appellant's alleged filings were not prior to filing made by appellee. Sec. 19, chap. 102, laws of 1905; Mays v. Bassett, 125 Pac. 609; chap. 104, laws of 1905; Taylor v. Abbott, 37 Pac. 408; Murray v. Tingley, 50 Pac. 723; Weil on Water Rights, 405 (1911 ed.); secs. 493 and 494, C. L. 1897; Hagerman Irr. Co. v. McMurray, 113 Pac. 823; Weil on Water Rights, sec. 417; Milhiser v. Long, 10 N. M. 99; Great Plains Co. v. Lamar, 71 Pac. 1119.

No merit in claiming to have acted in good faith. Lamar Co. v. Amity, 58 Pac. 600; Mold v. Lamar Canal Co.. 128 Fed. 776; Weil on Water Rights, 448; Blake v. Boze, 88 Pac. 470; Cruse v. McCauley, 96 Fed. 369; Umatilla Irrigation Co. v. Burnhart, 30 Pac. 30; sec. 10, chap. 49, laws of 1907; Weil on Water Rights, 446-7.

JULIUS C. GUNTER, HENRY L. LUTZ and H. L. BICKLEY, for appellant in reply.

Duties of the Board of Water Commissioners. Sec. 66,

chap. 19, laws of 1907; Young v. Hinderlider, 110 Pac.
1045.

JULIUS C. GUNTER, HENRY L. LUTZ and H. L. BICK-
LEY, for appellant, on motion to dismiss writ of error.

As to writ of error. Sec. 3, chap. 57, laws of 1907;
Quinebaug Bank v. Tarbox, 20 Conn. 510; Glasser v.
Hackett, 37 Fla. 358; 20 So. 532.

Dismissal of appeal does not preclude second appeal nor
writ of error if taken in due time. Harris v. Ferris, 18
Fla. 81; Johnson v. Polk Co., 24 Fla. 28; 3 So. 414;
Dailey v. Foster, 128 Pac. 71.

OPINION OF THE COURT.

ROBERTS, C. J.—On May 27, 1907, the appellee filed
its application with the territorial engineer, as authorized
by chap. 49, S. L. 1907, to appropriate the waters of the
Rayado river and certain tributary streams, for the purpose of irrigating certain lands in Colfax County, New
Mexico, in said application described. In August thereafter
the territorial engineer ordered notice to be given by appellee of a hearing on said application on October 11th following. Notice was published as required by said act, and
the appellant filed with said engineer a protest against
the approval of appellee's application. The territorial engineer, after a hearing had, declined to act upon appellee's said application, and an appeal was taken from such
refusal to act to the Board of Water Commissioners. Upon
a hearing had, the Board of Water commissioners approved the application, with the proviso "that the permit
thereunder shall not be exercised to the detriment of any
person, firm, corporation or association having prior rights
to the use of waters of said stream system." From the
decision of the Board of Water Commissioners, appellant
appealed to the District Court of Colfax County, where
the cause was heard, as required by the statute, *de novo*,
and upon such hearing the issues were found for appellee
and judgment entered in its favor, from which judgment
appellant prosecutes this appeal.

The assignments of error filed by appellant are as follows:

"1. That the court below erred in affirming the decision of the Board of Water Commissioners, directing and ordering the State Engineer to approve the application of the appellee herein for the appropriation of water of and from the Rayado river;

"2. That the court below erred in finding and adjudging that the said Board of Water Commissioners had and was possessed of the right, warrant, and authority to review the discretion of the said State Engineer in the matter of the approval of permits to appropriate;

"3. That the court below erred in rendering and entering judgment in favor of the said appellee, affirming the said decision of said Board of Water Commissioners."

Appellee contests the sufficiency of each of the above assignments of error on the ground that they are too general, indefinite and not sufficiently specific, and each error relied upon is not stated in a separate paragraph, and further, with respect to the second assignment, that it attempts to raise a question in the appellate court which was not raised nor considered in the district court, and that the assignment, even if good in form, is without merit.

The first and third assignments are in general terms and do not point out the specific error relied upon. The first assignment does not state whether the alleged error was predicated upon the failure of the court to decide in accordance with the weight of the evidence, or whether upon some point of law, the decision was erroneous. Under this general assignment the appellant might well argue many different propositions in support of a reversal of the judgment. For instance, it might contend that the district court did not have jurisdiction of the cause; that it was without power to try the cause *de novo;* that there was a failure of proof as to some material point, which appellee would be required to establish in order to secure the approval of its application, such, for instance, as that there was unappropriated water available for its application; that, as a matter of law, upon the facts proven, the court should not have approved the application, and other reasons might be urged in addition to the above. The third assignment, for the same reasons, is also insufficient. It does not point out wherein the judgment. rendered is erroneous, unless ,it be contended that the judgment affirming the decision of the Board of Water Commissioners, because of its form and language, was improper, but no such contention is urged, and no objection is made to the form or sufficiency of the judgment. This being true, this court will not examine the judgment for the purpose of passing upon its form or legal sufficiency, but will treat it, as both parties to this appeal have elected to consider it, as a final judgment, regular in form and finally disposing of the cause. This being true, the effect of the third assignment is, that the court erred in rendering judgment for the appellee. An assignment of error partakes of the nature of a pleading, and should be sufficiently specific, so that a joinder in error will present a specific issue for trial. Tested by a well established rule, adhered to in many of the decisions of the Territorial Supreme Court,

1   and followed by practically all of the states, the first and third assignments are too general to present any issue for determination.

In the case of Cevada v. Miera, 10 N. M. 62, Chief Justice Mills, speaking for the court, said:

"Five errors are assigned. The first is purely formal. '(The judgment of the court is contrary to the law)' as it does not point out in what particular such judgment is contrary to the law, and this court has held in the case of Pearce v. Strickler, 54 Pac. 748, (9 N. M. 467) and in Schofield v. Territory, 56 Pac. 303, (9 N. M. 526), that such a general assignment of error is not ground for review."

In the case of Melini v. Griego, 15 N. M. 455, the Territorial Supreme Court considered the sufficiency of the following assignments of error, viz: "That the said verdict is contrary to the law and the evidence." "That the said verdict was rendered against the weight of evidence," and "For many other manifest errors in the trial of this cause, which appear in the record and were prejudicial to the plaintiff," and said, "It has been repeatedly held by this court that an assignment of error must point out the specific error complained of," and the court refused to consider them. Similar assignments are also condemned and held insufficient in the following cases: McRae v. Cassan, 15 N. M. 495, 110 Pac. 574; Territory v. Clark, 13 N. M. 59; Candelario v. Miera, 13 N. M. 360; Maxwell v. Tufts, 8 N. M. 396.

The rule, adopted in this regard, and so consistently adhered to by the Territorial Supreme Court, finds ample and almost universal support in the other states.

An assignment of error that the trial court erred in entering judgment for one party, or against another, presents no question for review. Wales v. Graves, 72 Conn. 355; 44 Atl. 480; Clark's Invest. Co. v. Seymour, 19 App. D. C. 89; Hunter v. French, 86 Ind. 320; Wheeler, etc. v. Walker, 41 Mich. 239; City of Houston v. Potter, (Tex.) 91 S. W. 389. And see other cases collected in note 92, 2 Cyc. 997. For the reasons stated we must hold that the first and third assignments of error present no question for review.

Passing now to the consideration of the second assignment of error, which appears to be specific, we find that it predicates error upon the assumption that the lower court held that the Board of Water Commissioners had
2 and was possessed of the right, warrant and authority to review the discretion of the State Engineer in the matter of the approval of permits to appropriate water. We have searched the record, in vain, for such a holding by the trial court, and indeed, we can not conceive how any such question would, or could be involved in the case.

Sections 27 and 28, chap. 49, of the irrigation code of 1907 read as follows:

"Sec. 27. Upon the receipt of the proofs of publication, accompanied by the proper fees, the Territorial Engineer shall determine from the evidence presented by the parties interested, from such surveys of the water supply as may be available, and from the records, whether there is unappropriated water available for the benefit of the applicant. If so, he shall endorse his approval on the application, which shall thereupon become a permit to

appropriate water and shall state in such approval the
time within which the construction shall be completed,
not exceeding five years from the date of approval, and
the time within which water shall be applied to a beneficial
use, not exceeding four years in addition thereto; Provided, That the Territorial Engineer may, in his discretion ,approve any application for a less amount of water,
or may vary the periods of annual use, and the permit
to appropriate the water shall be regarded as limited accordingly.

"Sec. 28.   If, in the opinion of the Territorial Engineer,
there is no unappropriated water available, he shall reject
such application.   He shall decline to order the publication of notice of any application which does not comply
with the requirements of the law and the rules and regulations thereunder.   He may also refuse to consider or
approve an application or to order the publication of notice thereof, if, in his opinion, the approval thereof would
be contrary to the public interest."

Sec. 62 of the same act creates a Board of Water Commissioners, and provides for the appointment of the members thereof by the Governor.   Sec. 63 is in part as follows:

"It shall be the duty of said board to hear and determine appeals from the actions and decisions of the Territorial Engineer in all matters affecting the rights, priorities and interests of water users and owners of, or parties desiring to construct canals, reservoirs, or other works
for the conveyance, storage or appropriation of waters in
this territory.   Any applicant or other party dissatisfied
with any decision, act or refusal to act of the Territorial
Engineer may take an appeal to said board."

The remainder of the section provides for the procedure
required to get the cause before the board for hearing.
Sec. 65, in so far as material to the question under discussion, reads as follows:

"The decisions of said board, upon any such appeal, shall
be filed in the office of the Territorial Engineer, who shall
thereafter act in accordance with such decision.   The decision of said board shall be final, subject to appeal to the

istrict Court of the district wherein such work, or point
: desired appropriation, is situated," etc.

Section 66 provides for certifying to the District Court,
causes appealed, the record of all proceedings in the
atter by the Board of Water Commissioners, and also
rovides for a hearing *de novo* in the District Court, "ex-
ept that evidence which may have been taken in the
earing before the Territorial Engineer· and *said board*
ınd transcribed, may be considered as original evidence
n the District Court."

The act in question, as shown by the above excerpts,
learly shows that in each instance, where a hearing is
rovided for, or required, the same shall be *de novo,* or
original hearing, where the engineer, Board of Water
'ommissioners or the court hears such competent proof
s may be offered by the parties interested in the proceed-
ng and forms his or its own independent judgment rela-
ive to the issues involved. The Board of Water Commis-
ioners does not, nor is it called upon, to review the dis-
retion of the engineer. Upon appeal to it, it determines
or itself, the question as to whether the application should
approved or rejected. It is not bound, controlled or
ecessarily influenced, in any way, by the action of the
ngineer. It hears, or may hear, additional evidence, and
pon the record and such evidence as is properly before
:, it decides the question presented. Likewise in the
)istrict Court, the hearing is *de novo.* The court
ay consider such evidence as has been introduced
fore the board and engineer, and transcribed and filed
ith it, but it also hears additional evidence, and is
ot called upon to determine whether the engineer or the
oard of Water Commissioners erred in the action taken
nd order entered, but must form its own conclusion and
ter such judgment, as the proof warrants and the law
quires. It does not review the discretion of the en-
neer or the board, but determines, as in this case it
as required by the issue presented, whether appellee's
pplication to appropriate water should be granted. The
ourt, in order to form a conclusion upon the issues, was
ecessarily required to determine, for itself, whether

there was unappropriated water available; whether the approval of the application would be contrary to the public interest, and all other questions which the engineer was required, in the first instance, to determine. In such case the question recurs anew, as to whether the application shall be granted. This being true, the second assignment of error must fail, because it is not well taken.

Appellant, having presented no available error for review, the appeal will be dismissed, and, it is so ordered.

[No. 1488, May 31, 1913.]

TERRITORY OF NEW MEXICO, Appellant, v. AGOSTINO RICORDATI, Appellee.

SYLLABUS (BY THE COURT).

1. An election which is general within the meaning of the term "general election," as used in sec. 4138, C. L. 1897, is one that is held throughout the entire state or territory.

. P. 14

2. The election of September 6, 1910, was a general election within the meaning of the term "general election," as used in sec. 4138, Comp. Laws of 1897.

P. 14

Appeal from the District Court of Bernalillo County; Herbert F. Raynolds, District Judge; reversed and remanded.

FRANK W. CLANCY, Attorney General, for Appellant.

Judgment sustaining demurrer erroneous. Sec. 4138, C. L. 1897; sec. 1272, C. L. 1897.

Election in September, 1910, was a general election. Secs. 1634, 1640, 1660, 1700, 1702, C. L. 1897; Mackin v. State, 62 Md. 244; Downs v. State, 78 Mo. 128.

Indictment valid. Secs. 1272 and 4138, C. L. 1897.

MARRON & WOOD, for Appellee.

Election was special and not a general election. Sutherland on Stat. Cons., sec. 520, p. 962; Mechem on Public
Officers, secs. 173 to 176; chap. 43, C. L. 1865, secs. 2,
3, 4, 5, 33; sec. 1209, C. L. 1884; sec. 1698, C. L. 1897;
secs. 1640, 1660, 1702, C. L. 1897; chap. 113, laws of
1889; sec. 1, chap. 22, laws of 1880; sec. 1272, C. L. 1897.

Indictment cannot be sustained. Sec. 1272, C. L. 1897;
sec. 1, chap. 22, laws of 1880; sec. 17, chap. 9, laws of
1891; sec. 18, chap. 9, laws of 1891; Territory ex rel
Albuquerque v. Matson, 16 N. M. 135; chap. 9, laws of
1899.

STATEMENT OF FACTS.

The indictment, in this case, charged that the 6th day
of September, was the day of a general election in the
Territory of New Mexico, held pursuant to the provisions
of an act of Congress authorizing the people of New Mexico to form a constitution and state government; that
by the provisions of said Congressional act the Governor
of the then Territory of New Mexico, by proclamation,
dated June 29, 1910, designated the 6th day of September, 1910, as the day for said general election for delegates
to the constitutional convention, which election was duly
held on the day designated; that defendant, appellee here,
on said general election day, being then and there a liquor
dealer and having a place of business as such, did sell,
allow to be sold, give away and allow to be given away,
intoxicating liquors.

The second count of the indictment charged that upon
the same day the defendant did refuse, neglect and omit
to close his place of business between the hours provided
by statute for the closing of such places of business.

A demurrer to the indictment was interposed raising
the question that the indictment did not charge an offense because the day, upon which the alleged illegal
opening of the saloon and selling of liquor is charged to
have been done, was not a general election day within the
meaning of the statute. This demurrer was overruled, but
subsequently, by stipulation, of the District Attorney and
counsel for appellee, the order overruling the demurrer

was set aside and a pro forma judgment entered sustaining
the demurrer, from which judgment the territory appealed
to this court.

OPINION OF THE COURT.

HANNA, J.—The question presented is whether the
6th day of September, 1910, was a general election day
within the meaning of the statute under which this indictment was framed. The statute appears in the compiled laws of 1897 as sec. 4138, and is as follows:

"No license shall be issued under the provisions of the
act during a period of not less than sixty days prior
to any general election, and every liquor dealer shall close
his place of business and not sell or allow to be sold, give
away or allow to be given away, any intoxicating liquors
from his said place of business, from the hour of twelve
o'clock, midnight, last before the day of any general
election, until the hour of 12 o'clock, midnight, upon such
day of election, and shall keep his said place of business
closed between said hours, and upon conviction thereof, shall
be fined not less than twenty-five, nor more than five hundred dollars, or be imprisoned for not less than twenty
days, nor more than one year, in the discretion of the
court."

The contention of appellee is that the election of delegates to the convention, which framed New Mexico's constitution, was a special election and was not "the day of
any general election" within the meaning of the statute,
forbidding sales of intoxicating liquor on those days. It
is to be conceded that the legislative intent is controlling.
Our attention is called to the first act of the legislature,
upon the same subject, approved Feb. 6th, 1880, being
section 1 of chap. 22, laws of 1880, and appearing as sec.
1272 of the Compiled Laws of 1897, said act being as
follows:

"It shall be illegal for any person or persons in this
territory to sell, use or give, drink or dispose of any intoxicating or spirituous liquors on the day of any general or special election in this territory."

This act was entitled, "An Act prohibiting the sale

of spirituous liquors on election day," and plainly included the day of any general or special election. Sec. 4138 first quoted above, was enacted as a portion of chap. 9, laws of 1891, which act was entitled "An Act licensing the sale of intoxicating liquors and regulating the same."

The legislative intent, in connection with the act of 1880, is clearly shown to be a desire to prohibit the sale of intoxicating liquor on the day of any election in the territory, whether such election be general or special. This act has never been repealed, and the legislature has simply reaffirmed its intention to prohibit the sale of intoxicating liquor on election day by the passage of that section of the act of 1891, referred to supra as sec. 4138, C. L. 1897.

Are we to assume that because the word "special" does not appear in the second act that the legislature intended to prohibit the sale of liquor on the day of one territorial election, and to permit the sale on the day of a similar election, simply because it was a special election? On the other hand, was it not within the intention of the legislature, and the very reason for the passage of the laws in question, that on the occasion for the exercise of the highest franchise of a people, the right of suffrage, the public might be protected against the disorder that may result from the unrestrained sale and use of intoxicating liquor; that the polling places, where the public, of necessity gather on such days, might be free of rowdyism and not the resort of intoxicated or disorderly persons; that no person should exercise his high privilege while deprived of his reason, or natural intelligence.

It may be said that these reasons are good and doubtless furnish the object which inspired the legislature in the passage of the acts referred to, but that the legislature has limited the application of the second act by the use of the words "general election," because we have but one general election, viz: the biennial election of November.

The statutes and constitutions of many states have defined one particular election as the general election. This was not done in New Mexico until the adoption of our constitution, though the term, "general election," appears

in a number of our election laws.   In our opinion the
legislature was not attempting to distinguish between
different kinds of elections, or between regular or special
elections when it passed the prohibitory law respecting
the sale of liquor on the day of any general election.   It
had in mind such elections as were common to the people
of the territory, as distinguished from a local election.
It cannot be argued that the reasons pointed out for the
existence of the law are any less applicable to an election
for delegates to a constitutional convention, than to an
election for a congressman or county officer.

While fully appreciating the strict interpretation to
which the defendant is entitled in the construction of
statutes of this class, we cannot indulge in the violent
presumption that the legislature intended to classify elections which, though general in the sense that they might
be co-extensive with the boundaries of the state, or territory, yet being special, were not to be subject to the
same restriction and safeguards as are thrown about the
so-called "general election."

We find no other interpretation of the meaning of the
term "general election," as used in sec. 4138, consistent
with the intent of the legislature, as we interpret it, and
sound public policy, than that a general election, re-
1 ferred to in said section, is one that is held throughout the entire state, or territory.   See McKin v. State,
62 Mo. 244-245, and Downs v. State, 78 Mo. 128-131.

The election of September 6, 1910, for delegates to the
constitutional convention was held in every county
2 and precinct of the Territory of New Mexico, and
was as general as any November election ever will
be, or ever has been, and in our opinion, was such an election as comes within the purview of sec. 4138.

In view of our opinion, the judgment of the District
Court is reversed, and the cause remanded for further
proceedings, and it is so ordered.

[No. 1500, May 31, 1913.]

TERRITORY OF NEW MEXICO, Appellee, v. JAMES O. LYNCH, Appellant.

SYLLABUS (BY THE COURT)

1. In the superintendence of the process of empaneling the jury, a large discretion is necessarily confided to the judge, which discretion will not be revised on error or appeal, unless it appears to have been grossly abused or exercised contrary to law.

P. 29

2. Within reasonable limits, each party has a right to put pertinent questions to show, not only that there exists proper grounds for a challenge for cause, but to elicit facts to enable him to decide whether or not he will exercise his right of peremptory challenge.

P. 31

3. Where persons have authority to arrest and are resisted and killed, in the proper exercise of such authority, the homicide is murder in all who take part in such resistance.

P. 33

4. Where the arrest is illegal, the offense is reduced to manslaughter, unless the proof shows express malice toward the deceased.

P. 33

5. If the outrage of an attempted illegal arrest has not excited the passions, a killing will be murder.

P. 33

6. Nothing short of an endeavor to destroy life or inflict great bodily harm will justify the taking of life in those cases where an illegal arrest is attempted.

P. 34

7. As to the sufficiency of a warrant, it should appear

on its face to have duly proceeded from an authorized source. It need not set out the crime with the fullness of an indictment, but it should contain a reasonable indication thereof.

P. 34

8. A ministerial officer acting under process fair on its face, issued from a tribunal or person having judicial powers, with apparent jurisdiction to issue such process, is justified in obeying it against all irregularities and illegalities except his own.

P. 34

9. Where there is any evidence tending to show such a state of facts as may bring the homicide within the grade of manslaughter, defendant is entitled to an instruction on the law of manslaughter, and it is fatal error to refuse it.

P. 35

Appeal from District Court, Eddy County; Clarence J. Roberts, Associate Justice; reversed and remanded.

W. W. GATEWOOD, R. L. GRAVES, O. O. ASKREN and A. B. STOREY, for appellant.

New Mexico homicide statutes. Sec. 1060, C. L. 1897; Territory v. Montoya, 125 Pac. 622; sec. 1, chap. 36, also sec. 2, laws of 1907; Whitford v. Com., 18 Am. Dec. 774; sec. 1061, C. L. 1897; sec. 1062, C. L. 1897; sec. 1069, C. L. 1897; sec. 11, chap. 36, laws of 1907; sec. 1071, C. L. 1897; 2 Mo. Anno. Stat. 1906, sec. 1818.

As to qualification of jury. State v. Culler, 82 Mo. 623; Smith v. Moore, 74 Vt. 81; O'Mera v. Com., 75 Pa. St. 424; Gold Mining Co. v. Bank, 96 U. S. 640; Reynolds v. U. S., 98 U. S. 145; Williams v. U. S., 93 Fed. 396; Demmick v. U. S., 121 Fed. 638; Gallot v. U. S., 87 Fed. 446; State v. McDaniel, 39 Ore. 161; State v. Mott, 74 Pac. 728; Osiander v. Com., 3 Leigh. 780; State v. Simas, 25 Nev. 432; People v. O'Loughlin, 3 Utah 133; Lindsey v. State, 69 Ohio St. 215; Thomas v. People, 67 N. Y. 218; People v. Brown, 84 Pac. 204; Com. v.

Minney, 87 Pac. 1123; Walker v. State, 41 So. 878; Johnson v. State, Tex. Cr. Rep. 244; Johnson v. State, 94 S. W. 224; People v. Brown, 14 Pac. 91; Olive v. State, 34 Fla. 203; State v. McCarver, 194 Mo. 717; Kegans v. State, 16 Tex. Ct. 569; Daugherty v. State, 96 S. W. 748; Campos v. State, 76 S. W. 100; State v. Church, 98 S. W. 16; Croft v. Chicago, etc. R. Co., 109 N. W. 723; People v. Brown, 148 Cal. 743; State v. Darling, 97 S. W. 592; Leigh v. Territory, 85 Pac. 948; State v. Myers, 198 Mo. 225; Theobald v. St. Louis Transit Co., 191 Mo. 395; Shepard v. Lewiston, etc. R. Co., 65 Atl. 20; Robinson v. Com., 104 Va. 888; Hicks v. State, 54 S. E. 807; State v. Rodriguez, 115 La. 1004; Lindsey v. People, 6 Park. Crim. 244; Casey v. State, 37 Ark. 67; O'Connor v. State, 9 Fla. 215; Fahnestock v. State, 25 Ind. 231; State v. Lawrence, 38 Ia. 51; State v. Bryant, 93 Mo. 273; State v. Cockman, 60 N. C. 484; Reed v. State, 32 Tex. Cr. 25; Jones v. People, 6 Colo. 452; Stout v. State, 90 Ind. 1; State v. Field, 89 Ia. 34; Suit v. State, 17 S. W. 458; Reynolds v. U. S., 98 U. S. 145; Gallot v. U. S., 87 Fed. 446; Dammitt v. U. S., 121 Fed. 638; Williams v. U. S., 93 Fed. 396; State v. McDaniel, 39 Ore. 161; Osiander v. Com., 3 Leigh. 780; State v. Simas, 25 Nev. 432; People v. O'Laughlin, 3 Utah 133; Lindsey v. Hate, 69 Ohio St. 215; People v. Brown, 84 Pac. 204; State v. Kinney, 87 Pac. 1123; O'Mara v. Com., 75 Pa. St. 424; People v. Mather, 4 Wend. 229; People v. Edwards, 41 Cal. 640; Armistead v. Com., 11 Leigh. 657; Jackson v. Com., 23 Gratt. 919; Ortwein v. Com., 77 Pa. St. 414; State v. Beatty, 45 Kas. 492; State v. Murphy, 9 Wash. 204; Miller v. State, 29 Nev. 437; Rothschilds v. State, 7 Tex. App. 514; State v. Kingsbury, 58 Me. 238; State v. Howard, 17 N. H. 171; People v. King, 27 Colo. 507; Rogers v. Rogers, 14 Wend. 133; People v. Johnson, 46 Calif. 78; Ex parte Vermilyea, 6 Conn. 555; Holt v. People, 13 Mich. 224; State v. Hartman, 10 Ia. 589; Palmer v. State, 118 S. W. 1022; Shaftall v. Downly, 112 S. W. 176; Morgan v. Stevenson, 6 Ind. 169; McGregg v. State, 4 Black. 101; Brown v. State, 7 Ind. 576; Thiede v. Utah, 159 U. D. 510; Territory v. Emilio, 14 N. M. 147; State v.

Slater, 8 Ia. 420; Mann v. Glover, 14 N. J. L. 195; State
v. Hinkle, 6 La. 380; Holt v. People, 13 Mich. 224; Pal-
mer v. State, 118 S. W. 1022; State v. Hartman, 10 Ia.
589; Shaftall v. Downey, 112 S. W. 176; Morgan v.
Stevenson, 6 Ind. 169; State v. Weaver, 36 S. E. 499;
People v. Brotherton, 43 Calif. 530; Pointer v. U. S., 151
U. S. 396; People v. Brown, 14 Pac. 90; Watson v. Whit-
ney, 23 Calif. 375; People v. Cer Soy, 57 Calif. 102;
Ponder v. State, 27 Fla. ......; U. S. v. Alexander, 2 Idaho
354; Donovan v. People, 139 Ill. 412; Percy v. Mich.
Mut., etc., 111 Ind. 59; Hildreth v. City of Troy, 101
N. Y. 234; Mooney v. People, 7 Colo. 218; Stratton v.
People, 5 Colo. 276; DePuy v. Quinn, 61 Hunn. 237;
Monk v. State, 27 Tex. 450; Wade v. State, 12 Tex. App.
358; State v. Carries, 39 La. App. 931; Johns v. Mc-
Gonegal, 136 N. Y. 62; State v. Boner, 81 Pac. 484; State
v. Kent, 5 N. D. 516; State v. Raymond, 11 Nev. 98;
Ford v. Umatilla, 15 Ore. 313.

No ground for challenge specified. State v. Evans, 161
Mo. 95; Freeman v. People, 4 Denio 9; Territory v. Lopez,
et al., 3 N. M. 156; State v. Taylor, 134 Mo. 109; State
v. Reed, 137 Mo. 125; State v. Dyer, 139 Mo. 199; State v.
Albright, 144 Mo. 638; State v. Soper, 148 Mo. 217;
People v. Reynolds, 16 Calif. 128; People v. Hardin, 37
Calif. 258; People v. Dick, 37 Calif. 277; People v. Ren-
frow, 41 Calif. 37.

In case of doubt as to qualification of venireman, the
court should resolve the doubt in favor of the prisoner.
Holt v. People, 13 Mich. 224; People v. Brotherton, 43
Cal. 530; Coughlin v. People, 19 L. R. A. 57; Cowan v.
State, 22 Neb. 519; State v. Fourchey, 51 La. Ann. 228;
Thurman v. State, 27 Neb. 628; Keaston v. State, 40 Tex.
Cr. 139; U. S. v. Schneider, 21 D. C. 381; People v.
Weil, 40 Cal. 268; Poet v. State, 45 Ark. 165; Caldwell
v. State, 69 Ark. 322; State v. Brown, 15 Kas. 400; State
v. Stevens, 68 Kas. 576; State v. Tibbs, 48 La. Ann. 1278;
Huntley v. Territory, 7 Okl. 60; State v. Rutter, 13 Wash.
203; State v. Stentz, 30 Wash. 134; Theisen v. Johns,
72 Mich. 285; Klyce v. State, 79 Miss. 652; Rothschilds
v. State, 7 Tex. App. 519; Thompson v. State, 19 Tex.

App. 592; Hudson v. State, 28 Tex. App. 323; Blackwell v. State, 29 Tex. App. 194; State v. Kent, 5 N. D. ___; Gardner v. People, 6 Park Cr. 155; Twombly's Case, 10 Pick. 480.

In cases of veniremen, the crucial question is whether the opinion entertained would or might influence the mind of the juror. Coughlin v. People, 19 L. R. A. 57; Rozencranz v. U. S., 155 Fed. 38; Coughlin v. People, 19 L. R A. 57; Maddox v. State, 32 Ga. 581; Nelms v. State, 13 Sme. & Marsh 500; Com. v. Knapp, 20 Am. Dec. 491; sec. 3404, C. L. 1897; Lewis v. U. S., 146 U. S. 370; Schumaker v. State, 5 Wis. 324; State v. Briggs, 27 S. C. 80.

Error in overruling peremptory challenge. Hale v. State, 16 So. 389; 12 Enc. Pl. & Pr., 483; Burke v. McDonald, 3 Ida. 296; 24 Cyc. L. & Proc. 362; Stewart v. State, 13 Ark. 720; Hale v. State, 72 Miss. 140; State v. Steeves, 29 Ore. 85; State v. Mann, 83 Mo. 589; Pender v. State, 27 Fla. 370; State v. Garrington, 11 S. D. 178; People v. Car Soy, 57 Cal. 102; Patrick v. State, 45 Tex. Crim. 587; Barnes v. State, 88 S. W. 805; Bayse v. State, 45 Neb. 261; Watson v. Whitney, 23 Cal. 375; Gatzow v. Buening, 106 Wis. 1; Monaghan v. Ins. Co., 18 N. W. 800; State v. Tighe, 71 Pac. 3.

On the admission in evidence of ordinance No. 213 of the city of Roswell. Secs. 1412, 4212, 2402 and 2408, C. L. 1897; Port Huron v. McCall, 46 Mich. 565; Minton v. Larue, 23 How. 435; Lafayette v. Cox, 5 Ind. 38; Bant v. Chillicothe, 7 Ohio 31; Kirkman v. Russell, 76 Va. 956; Corvalis v. Carlib, 10 Ore. 139; Hanger v. Des Moines, 54 Ia. 193; Brenham v. Water Co., 67 Tex. 542; Tax Coll. v. Dendinger, 38 La. 261; Henke v. McCord, 55 Ia. 378; Sullivan v. Oneida, 61 Ill. 242; Phillips v. Allentown, 11 Pa. St. 481; Wilcox v. Hemming, 58 Wis. 144; Hart v. Albany, 9 Wend. 571; Kirk v. Orvell, 1 Tenn. 124; Miles v. Chamberlain, 17 Wis. 446; Hampton v. Conroy, 9 N. W. 417; Taylor v. Coronelet, 22 Mo. 105; Cutler v. Doughty, 5 Ohio 245; Rosenbaugh v. Coffin, 10 Ohio 31; Vanden v. Mount, 78 Ky. 86; Grand Rapids v. Hughes, 15 Mich. 54; State v. Ferguson, 33 N. H. 424; McQuill Munc. Ord., secs. 169-170; 1 Dill. Muc. Corp.

(4th ed.), sec. 339; 28 Cyc. 761; 1 Beach Pub. Corp.,
sec. 527; In re Cloherty, 27 Pac. 1064; Assari v. Wells, 681
Kas. 787; MacInerney v. Denver, 17 Colo. 302; Philadelphia v. Brizantine, 16 N. J. 127; State v. City of Cape
May, 63 N. J. L. 429; Kirk v. Nowell, 1 Tenn. 124; Hart
v. Albany, 9 Wend, 574; Liberty v. Brendy, 88 Pac. 1116;
In re Tuile, 71 Kas. 658; State v. Kearney, 8 N. C. 53;
State v. Walters, 97 N. C. 489; State v. May, 44 Atl. 209;
sec. 10, Organic Act of N. M.; U. S. Rev. Stats. (1878),
sec. 1926; Poindexter v. Greenhow, 114 U. S. 270; Sprague
v. Thompson, 118 U. S. 91; Pollock v. Farmer's etc.,
158 U. S. 601; Warren v. Charlestown, 2 Gray. 84; Johnson v. State, 59 N. J. L. 535; 1 Lewis Suth. Stat. Const.,
sec. 297; State v. Weed, 22 N. H. 262; Garcia v. Sanders,
35 S. W. 52; Coffin v. Carila, 8 Tex. Cr. App. 417; Sheldon v. Hill, 33 Mich. 171; Bird v. Householder, 32 Pa.
St. 168; Kramer v. Lott, 50 Pa. St. 495; Moore v. Watts,
1 Ill. 42; Fisher v. McGirr, 1 Grey 45; Rosen v. Fischel,
44 Conn. 371; Helbish v. Howe, 58 Pa. St. 93; State v.
Shackklett, 37 Mo. 280; Gruman v. Raymond, 1 Conn.
40; Savarool v. Boughton, 5 Wend. 170; Collmer v.
Drury, 16 Vt. 574; State v. Leach, 7 Com. 456; Temple
v. State, 15 Tex. App. 304; State v. Pitman, 10 Kas. 593;
Hopkins v. K. S. etc., 79 Mo. 98; Johnson v. Counsel, 16
Ind. 227; Hard v. Decorah, 43 Ia. 313; State v. Cleveland, 80 Mo. 108; Coa College v. Cedar Rapids, 120 Ia.
541; Mount Pleasant v. Beckwith, 100 U. S. 514; Minturn
v. Larne, 23 How. 435; Ottawa v. Carley, 108 U. S. 110;
Detroit v. Detroit, 56 Fed. 867; City of Roswell v. Railway Co., 16 N. M. 685; Com. Laws of 1897, sec. 2401;
Glass v. Ashbury, 49 Cal. 502; Hovey v. Mayo, 43 Me.
322; Hurford v. Omaha, 4 Neb. 336.

The court erred in admitting the warrant in evidence
over objection. U. S. v. Tureaud, 20 Fed. 621; State v.
Richardson, 34 Minn. 115; 1 Bish. New Crim. Law, sec.
204; Dougdale v. The Queen, 1 El. & B. 435; Garcia v.
Sanders, 35 S. W. 52; Coffin v. Varili, 8 Tex. Civ. App.
417; Sheldon v. Hill, 33 Mich. 171; Bird v. Householder,
32 Pa. St. 168; Cramer v. Lott, 50 Pa. St. 495; Moore
v. Walts, 1 Ill. 42; State v. Intox. Liq., 64 Ia. 300; Allen

v. Staples, 6 Grey 491; Henke v. McCord, 55 Ia. 378; Miles v. Chamberlain, 17 Wis. 446; Hampton v. Monroe, 56 Ia. 498; Taylor v. Carondelet, 22 Mo. 105; Cutler v. Doughty, 5 Ohio 245; Vanden v. Mount, etc., 78 Ky. 86; Miers v. State, 34 Tex. Cr. 161; Creighton v. State, 3 Yerg. 392.

Error as to instructions upon request. John Brown v. U. S., 159 U. S. 100; Foster's Crown Law, 319; McQuillen Municipal Ordinances, 476; Chit. Crim. Law (1819 ed.), 36 to 38; Shea v. City of Muncie, 148 Ind. 14; Lawson v. State, 55 Ala. 118; Bryant v. State, 46 Ala. 308; Haflter v. State, 51 Ala. 37; Eesspy v. State, 47 Ala. 533.

Killing reduced to manslaughter. West v. Cabell, 153 U. S. 78; Miers v. State, 34 Tex. Crim. 161; Noles v. State, 26 Ala. 31; State v. Patterson, 45 Vt. 308; Helms v. U. S., 2 Ind. Ter. 595; Jones v. State, 26 Tex. App. 1; Dyson v. State, 14 Tex. App. 454; Robertson v. State, 43 Fla. 156; Bishop Crim. Law, (6th ed.) vol. 1, 686; State v. Symes, 20 Wash. 484; Alford v. State, 8 Tex. App. 545; Johnson v. State, 5 Tex. App. 43; Ledbetter v. State, 23 Tex. App. 247; Rafferty v. State, 69 Ill. 111; Meuly v. State, 26 Tex. App. 274; Cryer v.. State, 71 Miss. 467; Com. v. Carey, 12 Cush. 246; Roberts v. State, 14 Mo. 138; Muscoe v. Com., 86 Va. 443; John Bad Elk v. U. S., 177 U. S. 529; Tacket v. State, 11 Tenn. 392; Poteete v. State, 68 Tenn. 261; Ter. v. Trapp, 16 N. M. 700; 1 Chit. Crim. L., 56; Jones v. State, 26 Tex. App. 1; 8 Am. St. Rep. 454; State v. Evans, 84 Am. St. 669; People v. Burt, 51 Mich. 199; Thomas v. State, 91 Ga. 204; Briggs v. Comm., 82 Va. 554; People v. Lewis, 117 Cal. 186; State v. Mathews, 148 Mo. 185; Powell v. State, 101 Ga. 9; State v. Thompson, 9 Ia. 188; People v. Batchelder, 27 Cal. 69; Phillips v. Com., 2 Duv. 328; C. & M. Law of Crimes, 395; 1 Bish. Crim. Law (6th ed.), sec. 853; People v. Flanagan, 60 Cal. 2; State v. Moore, 31 Comm. 479; State v. Dugan, Houst. Crim. R., 563; State v. Thompson, 9 Ia. 188; State v. Rutherford, 8 N. C. 457; Shorter v. People, 2 N. Y. 193; People v. Newcomer, 118 Cal. 263; 1 Chitty Crim. L., 35; Morgan v. Dufres, 69 Mo. ___; People v. Lewis, 117 Cal. 186; Rowe v. U. S.,

164 U. S. 546; Wilson v. State, 30 Fla. 234; Young v.
State, 2 L. R. A. (N. S.) 66; Pond v. People, 6 Mich. 150;
State v. Peacock, 40 Ohio St. 333; Mart v. State, 26 Ohio
St. 167; Brown v. People, 39 Ill. 407; State v. Dugan,
Houst. Crim. Rep., 563; Elder v. State, 69 Ark. 648;
Sparks v. Com., 89 Kas. 644; Baker v. Com., 93 Ky. 304;
3 Greenleaf on Ev., sec. 117; Powell v. State, 101 Ga.
9; Morgan v. Durfree, 69 Mo. 469; Miers v. State, 34
Tex. Crim Rep., 161; Muely v. State, 26 Tex. App. 274;
Noles v. State, 26 Ala. 31; Ross v. State, 10 Tex. App.
455; Brinkley v. State, 89 Ala. 34; Ter. v. Trapp, 16 N.
M. 700; Spearman v. State, 23 Tex. App. 224; Owens
v. State, 23 Tex. App. 224; Owens v. U. S., 130 Fed.
279; People v. Lennon, 71 Mich. 298; State v. Crawford,
71 Pac. 1031; State v. Ellis, 70 Pac. 963; People v. Fitzpatrick, 39 Pac. 605; State v. Reid, 42 Am. St. Rep. 322;
Campbell v. People, 16 Ill. 17; Richardson v. State, 7
Tex. App. 486; Logue v. Com., 38 Pa. 265; State v.
Scheele, 57 Conn. 307; Cortez v. State, 44 Tex. Cr. Rep.
169; Stockton v. State, 25 Tex. 775; Coleman v. State, 121
Ga. 594; Simmerman v. State, 14 Neb. 568; Creighton
v. Com., 83 Ky. 142; Ross v. State, 10 Tex. App. 455;
Wright v. Com., 85 Ky. 123; Territory v. Chenney, 16
N. M. 476; Morgan v. Ter., 7 Ariz. 224; Smith v. State,
59 Ark. 132; People v. Anderson, 44 Cal. 65; People v.
Harbert, 61 Cal. 544; Harris v. People, 32 Colo. 211;
State v. Rolla, 21 Mont. 582; Shorter v. People, 2 N. Y.
193; State v. Scott, 26 N. C. 409; Marts v. State, 26 Ohio
St. 162; Well v. Ter., 14 Okla. 436; Logue v. Com., 38
Pa. 265; Mahaffey v. Ter., 11 Okla. 213; State v. Shod-
well, 26 Mont. 52; Jenkins v. State, 123 Ga. 525; Greer
v. Com., 111 Ky. 93; State v. Spirly, 101 Mo. 87; State
v. Hubbard, 104 N. W. 1120; Mooney v. State, 65 S. W.
926; Gardner v. State, 40 Tex. Crim. Rep. 19; State
v. Young, 22 Wash. 273; State v. Dolan, 17 Wash. 499.

As to the duty of the trial court to instruct fully upon
the law of the case applicable to the facts. Sec. 2992
C. L. 1897; Ter. v. Nichols, 13 N. M. 23; Territory v.
Caldwell, 14 N. M. 535; Territory v. Watson, 12 N. M.
419; Territory v. Baca, 11 N. M. 559; Aguilar v. Ter.,

8 N. M. 496: Territory v. Friday, 8 N. M. 204; Territory
v. Fewel, 5 N. M. 34; Territory v. Nichols, 13 N. M. 103;
Territory v. Pino, 11 N. M. 559; Territory v. Pino, 9
N. M. 598; City etc. v. Scholton, 75 Ill. 468; Millican v.
Marlin, 66 Ill. 13; Thompson v. Duff, 119 Ill. 326; Walker
v. Camp, 69 Ia. 741; Brannum v. O'Connor, 77 Ia. 632;
McNeill v. Arnold, 22 Ark. 477; Goodell v. Lumber Co.,
57 Ark. 203; Frank v. Frank, 25 S. W. 819; McFadden
v. Farris, 6 Ind. App. 454; Union etc. Ins. Co. v. Bush-
anan, 100 Ind; Kane v. Torbit, 23 Ill. App. 311; Chicago
etc. v. Calkind, 17 Bradw. 55; Ridens v. Ridens, 29 Mo.
470; De Camp v. Packett, 42 Ill. App.; State v. Wright,
112 Ia. 436; Squires v. Gamble, etc., 86 N. W. 616.

Admission of evidence as to conversations. Greenl. Ev.
(Redf. 4th ed.) sec. 108; Com. v. Trefethen, 157 Mass.
180; State v. Hayward, 62 Minn. 474; Stewart v. State,
19 Ohio 302; Williams v. State, 4 Tex. App. 5; State v.
Winner, 17 Kas. 298; Life Ins. Co. v. Hillson, 145 U. S.
285; People v. Vernon, 49 Am. Dec. 49, note.

Error in sustaining the objection to the admission of
the testimony tendered by the defense. Dupree v. State,
33 Ala. 380; Howard v. State, 23 Tex. App. 265.

As to the remarks of the district attorney in argument.
People v. Lee Chunk, 78 Cal. 329; McDonald v. People,
126 Ill. 150; People v. Wells, 34 Pac. 1078.

H. S. CLANCY, Assistant Attorney General, for Appellee.

That the determination as to the competency of a juror
to serve must be left to the discretion of the trial judge
as to whether he should be retained or rejected. State v.
Marshall, 8 Ala. 302; U. S. v. Cornell, 2 Mason 91; Railroad Co. v. Moynahan, 5 Pac. 812; Howell v. State, 30
N. E. 716; Kumli v. Southern Pac. Co., 28 Pac. 638; State
v. Tom, 8 Ore. 177; State v. Saunders, 14 Ore. 300; Hau-
gen v. Ry. Co., 53 N. W. 771; Bayse v. State, 63 N. W.
814; Com. v. Crossmire, 27 Atl. 41; People v. McLaughlin, 37 N. Y. Suppl. 1011; 24 Cyc. 303; Smith v. Com.,
378 S. W. 586; State v. Cunningham, 12 S. W. 376; Clark

v. Com., 16 Atl. 795; Connors v. U. S., 158 U. S. 408;
Territory v. Emelio, 14 N. M. 159; U. S. v. Lewis, 2 N.
M. 459; Coleman v. Bell, 4 N. M. 21; Sanchez v. Candelaria, 5 N. M. 400; Territory v. Las Vegas Grant, 6 N. M.
87; U. S. v. De Amador, 6 N. M. 163; Buntz v. Lucero,
7 N. M. 219; Roper v. Territory, 7 N. M. 255; R. R. Co.
v. Saxton, 7 N. M. 302; Thomas v. McCormick, 1 N.
M. 369; Territory v. McFarlane, 4 N. M. 421; Territory
v. Kelly, 2 N. M. 292; Faulkner v. Territory, 6 N. M.
464; Lockhart v. Wollacott, 8 N. M. 21; Territory v.
Barnett, 8 N. M. 70; Garcia v. Candelaria, 9 N. M. 374;
Schofield v. Territory, 9 N. M. 526; Ins. Co. v. Perrin &
Co., 10 N. M. 90.

No error in refusing to instruct the jury as to manslaughter. 1 Am. & Eng. Enc. of L., 752-3; R. v. Curtis,
Fost. 135; R. v. Stockley, 1 East. P. C. 310; Roscoe's
Crim. Ev., 801; Thompson's Case, 1 R. & M. C. C. R.
80; Galvin v. State, 6 Cold. 291; Williams v. State, 44
Ala. 43; Noles v. State, 26 Ala. 31; Oliver v. State, 17
Ala. 587; Harrison v. State, 24 Ala. 67; Carroll v. State,
23 Ala. 28; Dill v. State, 25 Ala. 15; Pirtchett v. State,
22 Ala. ____; 1 Russ on Crimes, 220; 2 Bishop's Crim. L.,
secs. 641 to 643; Neeley v. Commonwealth, 93 S. W. 596;
State v. Taylor, 44 S. W. 785; Keady v. People, 74 Pac.
892; Roberson v. State, 29 So. 535; Hughes v. Commonwealth, 41 S. W. 294.

No error in denying the motion of appellant to have
the court instruct the jury to disregard remarks made
by the district attorney in argument. 1 Thomp. Tr., sec.
977; Territory v. Emelio, 14 N. M. 163.

STATEMENT OF FACTS.

The appellant was indicted by a grand jury of the County of Chaves for the murder of Roy Woofter at the City
of Roswell, in said county, and thereafter on change of
venue was tried and convicted of murder in the first degree in the District Court sitting for Eddy County. He
now brings the case into this court by appeal.

From the record, it appears that Woofter was the city
marshal of the city of Roswell, and that in the afternoon

of the 26th day of May, 1911, between the hours of four
and five o'clock, he, accompanied by Henry and Ed. Carmichael, who were city policemen encountered the defendant and one Fred Higgins in an alley of the city
of Roswell, and there informed the defendant that he had
a warrant for his arrest and for the search of defendant's
house for the purpose of seizing any intoxicating liquor
which might be found upon the premises and handed the
warrant to defendant who examined the same; that the
defendant told the deceased that he had no right to search
his house for liquor, as the same was not a place of business; that the deceased then stated that the search was
to be made, and, in company with the defendant, the two
policemen, Fred Higgins and one Red Tom, proceeded
to the house of defendant; that defendant opened the
front door of the house, and all six men entered the front
room. Shortly after entering, the defendant passed out
of the front room by a side door and into a hallway, fasten-
ing the door behind him, and the five men left in the
room immediately went out of the front door, and the
deceased, together with Henry Carmichael, went around
the house on the porch thereof to a room which was used
as a kitchen. In the meantime, according to the testimony of the defendant, having left the front room, he
went into the kitchen, slipped off his shoes and transferred
three cases of whiskey from the pantry into the dining
room, and then sat down in the kitchen, and at about
that time he saw the deceased pass the south window of
the kitchen, walking in a westerly direction and he next
saw him when he appeared at the west window, when the
deceased started to raise the screen of the window,
and at the same time Henry Carmichael appeared at the
south window "with his six shooter in his hand and tried
to look in." The defendant jumped up close to the window
at which the deceased was standing, and said "Don't you
break into this window or house or something like that;"
and the deceased "kind of stepped back and went for his
gun like this, in a stooping position," whereupon the defendant instantly shot him with a Winchester rifle, the
bullet first passing through a curtain which was on the

window and also the wire screen. The deceased, after receiving the shot, staggered away from the window in a stooping position with his hands clutching to his stomach, and was thereafter assisted by the two Carmichaels and Higgins to an adjacent house, where he was placed upon the bed and his pistol removed from a hip pocket. Subsequently, Woofter was removed to a hospital where he died the following morning, after making a dying declaration, which was introduced in evidence upon the trial of the case. In this declaration the deceased stated that he was walking along on the porch at the time he was shot and that he could not see the defendant at the time the shot was fired; that immediately preceding the firing of the fatal shot the defendant said, "Keep off my back porch," and that he knew that it was the defendant who used that language.

OPINION OF THE COURT.

HANNA, J.—The first nine errors assigned by appellant relate to the empaneling of the jury.

The first assignment predicates error, by the trial court, in sustaining a challenge for cause by the Territory, over objection of the defense, to the venireman, J. D. Merchant, on the grounds that there was sufficient proof to support the challenge, and, that the defendant was not given an opportunity to examine said venireman.

The second assignment of error is based upon the alleged failure of the territory to specify grounds for challenge, in the case of Venireman Merchant, which was sustained by the court.

The third assignment avers a lacking of proof to support the territory's challenge in the case of Venireman J. R. James.

The fourth assigns error in sustaining the territory's challenge, in the case of Venireman James, for an alleged failure to specify a ground for challenge.

The fifth error is predicated upon the trial court's action in overruling defendant's challenge for cause, to Venireman Gossett, who testified that he had a fixed and abiding opinion, predicated upon what he had read in the newspapers and conversations with different persons, which would require evidence to remove; later testifying, however, that if selected as a juror, he would decide the case solely upon the sworn testimony and not permit what he had heard to influence him in reaching a verdict.

The sixth error has to do with the trial court's action in overruling the challenge of the defendant for cause, to Venireman Schuester, who testified to an opinion arrived at through what he had heard one witness in the case say, which opinion was an abiding and fixed opinion requiring evidence to remove it. In response to questions by the court he said he would lay aside his opinion, when sworn as a juror, and would decide upon the evidence as introduced upon the witness stand.

The seventh error assigned by appellant is based upon the overruling of defendant's challenge, for cause, directed against Venireman Galton. This venireman, upon his examination, testified that he had read newspaper accounts, shortly after the occurrence, from which he formed a decided opinion concerning the guilt or innocence of the defendant, requiring evidence to remove and which was then abiding with him; later he said he thought he could try the case with the same degree of equipoise of mind and impartiality as if he had never formed an opinion.

The eighth alleged error relied upon is based upon the overruling of defendant's peremptory challenge directed against Venireman Crawford. The defendant had exhausted his quota of peremptory challenges and asserts he was wrongfully forced to use a peremptory challenge in each of the cases referred to under assignment of error, numbered 5, 6 and 7, and that it was an abuse of discretion, on the part of the trial court, to refuse to allow an additional peremptory challenge, good cause being shown.

The ninth assignment predicates error upon the refusal of the trial court to allow certain questions to be propounded to Venireman Wm. Carson, by the defense. The facts pertinent to this assignment of error can be more clearly pointed out by quoting from the record, viz:

"Q. I will ask you whether now you have any strong leaning for or against prohibition?

Mr. Fullen: We object to that method of interrogating the juror on the ground we don't believe a prohibition question enters into the trial of this case. The question is whether or not this man was justified in the killing of the man he did.

Mr. Gatewood: We would like to be heard on that.

(Jury withdrawn.)

Court: I will hear you ten minutes. Will your defense be self-defense?

Mr. Gatewood: Yes, sir.

Court: I will sustain the objection for that defense. The question of prohibition will not enter into it.

Mr. Gatewood: Exception.

(Jury returns.)

I will ask you this question: That if in the course of this trial it should be developed by the testimony that the deceased, Roy Woofter, was a strong Prohibitionist and this defendant an Anti-Prohibitionist and that the homicide grew out of those differences and issues involved therein, can you try this case under that situation of facts strictly according to the law and evidence, or would those facts that I have related be permitted to have any influence whatever over your mind in determining this case?

Mr. Fullen: We object. It is not a proper subject of inquiry, not the proper matter to qualify the juror on.

Court: Objection sustained.

Mr. Gatewood: Exception.

Mr. Carson, if it shall develop by the testimony in this case that the deceased, Roy Woofter, was a strong Prohibitionist and that this was one of the causes of differences that led up to the homicide between them, would that fact influence your mind in this case in any degree whatever against the defendant?

Mr. Fullen: We object on the same grounds.

Court: Objection sustained.

Mr. Askren: Exception."

We are of the opinion that Mr. Thompson correctly states the general rule regarding the discretion of the

1   court in respect of empaneling the jury, as follows:

"In the superintendence of the process of empaneling

the jury, a large discretion is necessarily confided to the judge, which discretion will not be revised on error or appeal, unless it appears to have been grossly abused or exercised contrary to law." 1 Thompson Trials, sec. 88.

With this principle in mind we have made a careful examination of the record pertaining to the matters referred to under the first eight assignments of error, and we find that the fifth, sixth and seventh assignments present very close questions for our consideration. For which reason we prefer to pass to the consideration of the ninth assignment which presents a more clear cut question, one at least less open to argument. Not that we would shirk our responsibility in these matters, but that our decision may rest upon less debatable ground.

What is, or is not, an abuse of judicial discretion will always remain a most difficult question for solution. In the ninth assignment we have presented a question not confined to the phase of this problem referred to as abuse of discretion, but which trenches hard upon the legal rights of the defendant. The learned Attorney General has considered the question as falling within the rule of Connors v. United States, 158 U. S. 414, where the Supreme Court said that "the court correctly rejected the question put to the juror Stewart as to his political affiliations. The law assumes that every citizen is equally interested in the enforcement of the statute enacted to guard the integrity of national elections, and that his political opinions or affiliations will not stand in the way of his duty as a juror in cases arising under the statute."

We think that the case at bar presents a materially different question from that of the Connors case, which is concerned only with the bias resulting from political affiliation. In that case, however, the trial court said that had its attention been called to the matter at the time it would have allowed the inquiry. It also appeared that the Supreme Court believed that the rejection of the question did not prejudice the substantial rights of the accused, or a new trial would have been granted.

In the case at bar we have an inquiry directed toward possible bias and prejudice resulting from a division of a

community over a great social and economic question. Political affiliations are broken down, and the community,
during the throes of the change from a wet to a dry territory, and consequent effort at enforcement of new laws,
finds itself divided in opinion and swayed by strong passions and prejudices. Those of one side may feel that
the personal liberty of the individual is encroached upon,
their property confiscated, and even their rights to continue a residence in the community challenged. The opposing view contemplates the protection of the community
from a menacing evil affecting every family and each individual. Such conflict of opinion must result in such
a condition that to refuse an inquiry into the attitude, or
bias, of an individual juror, called upon to try the accused for his life, where his alleged crime grew out of an
attempt to enforce a prohibitory liquor law, would certainly violate our American sense of justice. The least that
can be said in favor of permitting the inquiry is that
it was necessary in order that the defendant might intelligently exercise his right to peremptorily challenge.
As was well said by the Supreme Court of Missouri in
the case of State v. Mann, 83 Mo. 597:

"One may not be incompetent as a juror, and yet may
stand in such relations to the prosecutor, or the cause, as,
if known to the accused, would be deemed a good reason
for peremptorily challenging him. He is entitled to an
impartial jury, and may make such inquiries as will enable him to secure that constitutional right. Must he
exercise his right of peremptory challenge, without the
privilege of making inquiries, except such as relate to
the competency of the panel? In capital cases, the accused is imprisoned and is brought from prison and there
for the first time, possibly, meets the forty men summoned
as jurors in his case, and if blindly to make his peremptory
challenges, may strike from the panel the very men whom
he would have wished to retain, had he known their ante-
cedents. If such is the law, the right of peremptory challenge may prove a snare and, at best, is of no earthly value
to the accused." See also Lavin v. People, 69 Ill. 304;
Com. v. Egan, 4 Gray, 18.

The rule, or guiding principle, in this regard, has been correctly stated, in our opinion, by Mr. Thompson, in the following language, viz:

"Within reasonable limits, each party has a right to put pertinent questions to show, not only that there exists
2 proper grounds for a challenge for cause, but to elicit facts to enable him to decide whether or not he will exercise his right of peremptory challenge." I Thompson Trials, sec. 101. See also Faber v. C. Reiss Coal Co., 124 Wis. 562; Am. Bridge Co. v. Pereira, 79 Ill. 97; Hale v. State, (Miss) 16 So. 387; State v. Garrington, (S. D.) 76 N. W. 327; State v. Steeves, (Ore.) 43 Pac. 950; Pinder v. State, (Fla.) 26 Am. State 77; People v. Car' Soy, 57 Cal. 103; Patrick v. State, 45 Tex. Crim. Rep. 588; Basye v. State, 45 Neb. 269; Monaghan v. Agricultural Fire Ins. Co., (Mich.) 18 N. W. 800; Dunsmuir v. Port Angeles, etc., (Mont.) 71 Pac. 8.

Our consideration of the ninth assignment of error results in the conclusion that the trial court was in error in refusing to permit the inquiry into the bias or prejudice of the juror upon the question of prohibition. We are of the opinion that the case must be reversed and remanded for new trial upon this ground. Such being the case, and for the purpose of disposing of such other questions as this record indicates may arise in the new trial, we will briefly consider the remaining assignments of error.

The tenth error assigned is based upon the admission in evidence of a copy of an ordinance (No. 213) of the City of Roswell. The offer was limited first to show that the original ordinance had been passed by the city council of Roswell (and not as proof that it was a constitutional ordinance and one authorized by law); second, to show on what the complaint made by the deceased was based.

The first objection, here urged, is that the record of said ordinance was not the best evidence thereof. The record discloses that the city clerk of Roswell testified that he was clerk of said city at the time of the passage of the ordinance, and that he engrossed the same upon the official record of city ordinances, which record was produced in court and identified by him; the authenticating signatures being also proven by him. This record is the one provided for by sec. 2413, C. L. 1897, which does not provide in express terms that the record shall be received in evidence without other proof. The action referred to, however, does provide as follows, to-wit:

"But the book of ordinances herein provided for shall be taken and considered in all courts of this territory as prima facie evidence that such ordinances have been published as provided by law." This indicates an intention that these records were to be received in evidence, when conforming in all respects to said sec. 2413. It would be safer practice, nevertheless, to prove an ordinance in accordance with the terms of sec. 2412, (C. L. 1897) and avoid the necessity of proving authenticating signatures of the officers named in said section 2413.

We do not consider it necessary to further discuss the remaining objections presented under this assignment.

The eleventh assignment of error is based upon the admission in evidence, over defendant's objection, of the original affidavit, made by the deceased, upon which the warrant was based. The first objection to its admission; i. e., that no predicate therefor had been laid by proof of the enactment of any ordinance is disposed of by our opinion upon the tenth assignment of error. The appellant also urges in connection with this alleged error, that the pretended ordinance, No. 213, on which said affidavit was based expressly provides that said complaint should be made only before the police judge of said city, whereas there was and could be no such officer; that said affidavit is in the nature of a complaint for search and seizure in the enforcement of said so-called liquor ordinance, for which there is no authority of law; that a part of the supposed offense therein alleged is the keeping of liquors on hand with intent to sell or give them away, etc., whereas the statute "authorizes the municipality to provide only against the selling, giving away, etc.," of such liquors; that said affidavit on its face purports to be a complaint on information and belief, in the nature of a libel for the seizure and destruction of certain intoxicating liquors

Territory v. Lynch, 18 N. M. 15.

and is so entitled—but that there is no authority of law for such proceeding by the City of Roswell; that it was not proven that Precinct No. 1 was within or partly within the corporate limits of Roswell; that said complaint purports to be a complaint on information and belief, which is in violation of the fourth amendment of the Constitution of the United States.

The Attorney General argued that these contentions, respecting the legality, or validity of the affidavit or complaint, and warrant issued thereupon, were immaterial and irrelevant. He contended that if the complaint and warrant were illegal, and likewise the attempted search of the house, yet those facts did not justify the defendant killing the deceased.

We cannot fully agree with this conclusion of the honorable Attorney General. We are of the opinion that **3** the legality of the arrest is a material question in determining the character of the homicide. The Supreme Court of the State of Illinois in the case of Rafferty v. People, 69 Ill. 111, 18 Am. Rep. 604, on this point held:

"That where persons have authority to arrest and are resisted and killed in the proper exercise of such authority, the homicide is murder in all who take part in such resistance." See case note 66 L. R. A. 354.

And, on the other hand, it is equally well settled, that "where the arrest is illegal, the offense is reduced to **4** manslaughter, * * * unless the proof showed express malice toward the deceased." See also 2 Bishop New Crim. Law, sec. 699. Calvin v. State, 6 Gold. 283.

Mr. Bishop has given much assistance to us in our consideration of this question, and we consider his exposition of the law as laid down in said sec. 699, truly expressive of the principles controlling the subject.

We particularly approve his qualification of the rule, last laid down, that if in fact the outrage of an at**5** tempted illegal arrest has not excited the passions, a killing in cold blood will be murder.

The doctrine that nothing short of an endeavor to destroy life or inflict great bodily harm will justify the tak-

ing of life, prevails in those cases where an illegal
6 arrest is attempted.   1 Bishop New Crim. Law, sec.
868.   The reason why a man may not oppose an attempt on his liberty by the same extreme measures permissible in an attempt on his life, appears to be because
liberty can be secured by a resort to the laws.   1 Bishop
New Crim. Law, sec. 868.

In our opinion Mr. Bishop has correctly stated the law
as to the sufficiency of a warrant, when he says:

"It should appear on its face to have duly proceeded
from an authorized source.   It does not set out the
7 crime with the fulness of an indictment, but it should
contain a reasonable indication thereof."   1 Bishop
Crim. Proceed., sec. 187.

In this connection we also desire to say that we agree
with the authorities holding that a ministerial officer acting under process fair on its face, issued from a tribunal
or person having judicial powers, with apparent jurisdiction to issue such process, is justified in obeying it
8 against all irregularities and illegalities except his
own.   Appling v. State, (Ark.) 28 L. R. A. (N. S.)
548; State v. Weed, (N. H.) 53 Am. Dec. 188.

Keady v. People, 32 Colo. 57, 74 Pac. 892, 66 L. R. A.
353.   It cannot be questioned that it is a duty incumbent
upon every citizen to submit to a lawful arrest and that
resistance to an illegal arrest should be without excessive
violence.   It has been held that if a person kill a known
officer to prevent him from making an illegal arrest he
is guilty of manslaughter at least, and may be guilty of
murder if the killing was prompted by personal malice
against the officer.   Rafferty v. People, 72 Ill. 37; Toberts
v. State, 14 Mo. 138.   The law does not, and cannot,
sanction the taking of life to repel a threatened trespass
or invasion of personal rights.

A distinction is made, by the authorities, between arrests
by those who are known to be officers and by persons who
are not.   Yates v. People, 32 N. Y. 509.   In the latter
case homicide may be justified to prevent an illegal arrest
but it cannot be in the former.   The law seeks to protect
the officer in the discharge of his duty, and calls upon

the citizens to exercise patience, if illegally arrested, because he knows he will be brought before a magistrate, and will, if improperly arrested, suffer only a temporary deprivation of his liberty. Johnson v. State, 30 Ga. 426.

Under the twelfth assignment of error numerous objections are made to the warrant, which was offered in evidence in this case. A careful consideration of all would unduly lengthen this opinion. We have attempted to briefly state the general principle applicable, and must be content with that for the purposes of this opinion.

The thirteenth error assigned alleges error by the trial court in refusing a requested instruction as to manslaughter, it being urged that there were sufficient facts to require such instruction. It is needless to cite authority
9 for the proposition that where there is any evidence tending to show such a state of facts as may bring the homicide within the grade of manslaughter, defendant is entitled to an instruction on the law of manslaughter and it is a fatal error to refuse it. The facts pertaining to this question may be presented with greater certainty and detail at the next trial of this case, and it seems unnecessary to discuss the facts disclosed in the present record in connection with the present opinion.

The remaining questions having to do with matters that may not arise in the new trial, and not necessary to this opinion, will not be passed upon at this time.

For reasons given the judgment and sentence of the District Court is set aside and this cause remanded for a new trial.

[No. 1506, May 31, 1913.]

J. R. DAUGHTRY, Appellee, v. CLARA MURRY et al., Appellants.

SYLLABUS (BY THE COURT)

1. It is impracticable for the assessor to obtain the name of the real owner of a tract of land, from the official county records, as available for his inspection, and, in the absence

of fraud, an assessment against unknown owners is not invalid, because of the fact that the assessor might have ascertained the name of the real owner from the records of
conveyances in the office of the county recorder, in those
cases where the owner has failed to list his property for
taxation.

P. 41

2. It must be presumed, in the absence of a showing to
the contrary, that the assessor did his duty, and that in-as-
much as he made the assessment to unknown owners, it was
impracticable to obtain the real owner's name.

P. 42

Appeal from District Court, Quay County; David J.
Leahy, District Judge; affirmed.

C. C. Davidson, Tucumcari, N. M., for appellant.

Statutory provisions for assessment of property for
taxation. Sec. 4026, C. L. 1897; sec. 1, chap. 22, laws of
1899; sec. 4031, C. L. 1897; sec. 25, chap. 22, laws of
1899; O'Rear v. Crum, 135 Ill. 294; Young v. Joslin, 13
R. I. 675; Sweigle v. Gates, 84 N. W. 482; Clark v. Crane,
5 Mich. 151; Cromwell v. Wilson, 52 Hun. 614; Northern
Pac. R. Co. v. Galvin, 85 Fed. 811; Ferguson v. Kaboth,
73 Pac. 200; Lewis v. Blackburn, 69 Pac. 1024; Dowell
v| City of Portland, 10 Pad. 308; Black on Tax Titles
(2nd ed.), secs. 105, 111 and 208; Roberts v. National
Bank of Fargo, 79, N. W. 1049; Sutherland Statutory
Construction, sec. 489 (2nd ed.); People v. Chicago, 142
Ill. 546; Oregon, etc., Co. v. Jordan, 17 Pac. 621; Terri-
tory ex rel. Devine v. Perrin, 83 Pac. 361; Centennial
Eureka Mfg. Co. v. Juab County, 62 Pac. 1024; C. B. &
Q. R. Co. v. Cass County, 51 Neb. 369; Vicksburg Bank
v. Adams, 21 So. 401; Raton, W. W. Co. v. Raton, 9 N.
M. 70; Stewart v. Board of Co. Comrs., 11 N. M. 517;
Territory v. Perea, 10 N. M. 362; Whitney v. Thomas,
23 N. Y. 281; Sharp v. Johnson, 11 Am. Dec. 259; Baer
v. Choir, 32 Pac. 776; Zink v. McManus, 3 N. Y. Supp

487; Cooley on Taxation, (2nd ed.), 313; Blackwell on Tax Titles, 399; Crossman v. Crossman, 95 N. Y. 245.

This rule is the same notwithstanding the statute provides a method of correcting assessments. City of Wilmington v. Ricaud, 90 Fed. 214; Chicago & N. W. R. Co. v. Auditor General, 18 N. W. 586; Lewis v. Monson, 151 U. S. 544; Dougherty v. Dickey, 4 Watts & S. 146; Laird v. Hiester, 23 Pa. 452; Harbourn v. Boushey, 7 U. C. C. P. 467; Merton v. Dolphin, 28 Wis. 456; Bubb v. Thompkins, 47 Pa. 359; Price v. Mott, 52 Pa. 315; Randall v. Dailey, 66 Wis. 285; People v. Registrar of Arrears of Brookyln, 114 N. Y. 19; Milliken v. Patterson, 91 Ind. 515; Bonnell v. Roane, 20 Ark. 114; Steeple v. Downing, 60 Ind. 478; Black on Tax Titles, sec. 256; Bridge v. Bracken, 3 Cham. 75; Parker v. Smith, 4 Blackf. 70; Ward v. Montgomery, 57 Ind. 276; Hill v. Leonard, 5 Ill. 140; Latimer v. Lovett, 2 Dough. 204; Beekman v. Bigham, 5 N. Y. 366; Shackelford v. Hooker, 65 Ga. 366; Ives v. Kimball, 1 Mich. 308; Westbrook v. Willey, 47 N. Y. 457; Burke v. Burke, 170 Mass. 499; Black on Tax Titles, 255; Parker v. Overman, 59 U. S. 137; Thomas v. Lawson, 21 How. 331; Berger v. Multnomah County. 78 Pac. 224; Miller v. Cook, et al., 10 L. R. A. 292; Board v. Dill, 29 L. R. A. (N S), 1170; Deepwater Ry. Co. v. Gooch, 27 L. R. A. (N S), 388; Bushnell v. Loomis, 36 L. R. A. (N S), 1029; Luce v. Barnum, 19 Mo. App. 359; vol. 3, Cent. Dig. sec. 3367.

HARRY H. McELROY, Tucumcari, N. M., for appellant.

Tax sale void. Sec. 1, chap. 22, laws of 1899; 37 Cyc. 1378.

It is sufficient in the assessment roll to give such description as will serve to identify the property. Sec. 25, chap. 22, laws of 1899; sec. 4031, C. L. 1897.

It is lawful to assess real estate without connecting therewith any name. Williams v. Supervisors, 122 U. S. 154; 37 Cyc. 1005; James L. Witherspoon, et al., v. Benjamin S. Duncan, et al., 18 Law Ed. 339; Strauss v. Foxworth, 117 Pac. (N. M.), 831; Williams v. Supervisors,

122 U. S. 154; Lendregen v. Peppin, 24 Pac. 859; Glower
v. De Alvarez, 101 Pac. 432; Coolidge v. Pierce County,
68 Pac. 391; Keely v. Sanders, 99 U. S. 441; DeTreville
v. Smalls, 98 U. S. 517; Castillo v. McConnice, 168 U. S.
683.

Was this assessment valid in the first place? Palmer v.
Board, 42 La. Ann. 1122; C. R. I. & P. v. Wertheim, 15
N. M. 505; Fuller v. City of Grand Rapids, 40 Mich. 395.

Injunction proceedings to restrain execution of deed
upon sale. Franz v. Krebs, 21 Pac. 101; MacKinnon v.
Auditor General, 90 N. W. 329; Black on Tax Titles, 162-
3, pages 205-6; Hillinger v. Devling, 105 Pa. St., 417.

A taxpayer is liable for the consequences of mistaken
payment on another's property, if the payment is not
made through the County Treasurer's mistake. Cooley
on Taxation, vol. 2, p. 809; Browne v. Finley, 51 Neb.
465; Maxwell v. Hunter, 65 Ia. 121.

STATEMENT OF FACTS.

The plaintiff, J. R. Daughtry, brought this action in
the District Court of Quay County, to quiet title to lots
nine and ten in block one, Russell Addition to Tucumcari,
N. M., against the appellants, Clara Murry and Sarah
Jane Murry, asserting a fee simple title based upon a tax
certificate acquired by him at a tax sale of the property in
question, had on May 8, 1906, for taxes assessed against
unknown owners for the year 1905, and a tax deed subsequently procured by him after the expiration of the
period of redemption. On the 1st day of March, 1905,
the title to said property was in the Texas & New Mexico
Investment Co., which company made a sworn rendition
of its property for the year 1905, but in which return the
property was described as situate in Block seven, instead
of Block one, the evidence not being clear as to whether
the return was made by the agent of the company correctly, or whether the error was attributable to a third person, no evidence being introduced tending to show that
the error was chargeable to the assessor. The property
was not redeemed from said tax sale, and was subsequently mortgaged by T. M. Murry, who purchased from the

townsite company on May 6, 1906, and Clara Murry, his
wife, to Sarah Jane Murry. Prior to the institution of
this action and on October 23, 1909, appellee herein, J. R.
Daughtry, obtained a judgment against said T. M. Murry,
quieting in himself the title to said property as against
any claim of said Murry, the appellants in this case not
being joined as parties in said action.

Appellant, Clara Murry, filed a separate answer, denying ownership in appellee, and alleging a community interest in the proprrty, and also alleging that the property
had been returned for taxation and taxes paid thereon
before delinquency, for the period for which the property
was sold at tax sale; that her husband and herself had
made certain improvements, utilizing therefor community
funds in the sum of $1100 ($750 agreed upon by stipulation of counsel as the value of such improvements.) Sarah
Jane Murry filed a separate answer, setting up an interest
in said property as mortgagee, pleading certain irregularities in the tax title and payment of taxes before sale.
The court held that the tax title was valid, and quieted
appellee's title to the said property as against appellants.
Judgment was rendered, however, in favor of appellant,
Sarah Jane Murry, in the sum of $375, less one-half the
costs of the action, on the theory of subrogation as mortgagee to the community rights of appellant, Clara Murry,
in the improvements placed on said property subsequent
to the tax sale.

From the judgment in favor of appellee, this appeal
was granted.

OPINION OF THE COURT.

HANNA, J.—The first assignment of error relied upon
by the appellants is that the trial court erred in its conclusion that the tax sale was in all things regular and
valid. The appellants contending that the assessment to
unknown owners was an invalid assessment.

Sec. 3956 C. L. 1897, provides that it shall be the duty
of probate clerks to enter in a reception book, all instruments affecting the title to real estate, in the name of
the persons, alphabetically arranged, whose title is af-

fected thereby. Sec. 3956 was amended, by sec. 1, chap. 22, laws of 1909, by adding thereto the provision that it should also be the duty of the probate clerk "to notify the assessor, in writing, of the filing of such conveyance, the date thereof, the names of the grantor and grantee, the description by metes and bounds, if possible, of the property conveyed, and the date of recordation, which notice shall be given without charge therefor;" the said amendatory section further providing, as follows: "and the assessor shall file such notice with the papers in his office, relating to the precinct in which said property is located and be guided thereby in making his assessments against the *real owner* of the property."

By sec. 4026, C. L. 1897, it is provided that:

"All taxable property shall be listed, assessed and taxed each year, in the name of the owner thereof, on the first day of March."

By sec. 4031, C. L. 1897, it is further provided that:

"When the name of the owner of any real estate is unknown, by reason of the failure of the owner to list the same, and the assessor finds it impracticable to obtain the name, it shall be lawful to assess such real estate without connecting therewith any name, but inscribing at the head of the page the words, Owners unknown, and such property, whether lands or town lots, shall be listed as near as practicable, in the order of the numbers thereof, and in the smallest subdivision thereof possible."

The question now before us seems to turn upon the point of whether it was necessary for the assessor to turn to the records of deeds of his county and there ascertain the name of the "real owner" of the property, here involved, and failing so to do, an assessment against unknown owners is void. It may well be argued that such was the legislative intent, so far as the same may be gathered from the acts quoted above, but it also clearly appears that the Legislature intended that property should not escape taxation in those cases where "the assessor finds it impracticable to obtain the name" of the owner.

From an examination of our statute law pertaining to
the recording of conveyances, and especially with respect
to the indices thereof, it is apparent that no provision
has been made for an index, or other form of record, as
to tracts, but that an index, alphabetically arranged, as
to grantees and grantors has been deemed sufficient. See
sec. 782, C. L. 1897; sec. 23, chap. 80, S. L. 1899; chap.
87, S. L. 1903.

With this condition, as to our public records, which
the legislature is presumed to have had full knowledge of,
can it be said that it intended to require the assessor to
make a page by page examination of our record of conveyances for the purpose of ascertaining the real owner of
a given tract of land? That the Legislature well understood the impossibility of such requirement is evidenced
by the fact that it attempted to provide an independent
set of records, in the office of the assessor, by the provisions contained in sec. 1 of chap. 22, of the Session Laws
of 1899, supra.

If no transfer of a given tract of land occurred between
the date of the enactment of the statute, last referred to,
and its repeal by chap. 84 of the Sess. Laws of 1913, this
attempt to put the assessor in possession of a means of
ascertaining the name of the "real owner" would prove
futile.

From the record of the case now before us it does not
appear that the assessor had access to any record other
than the county records, and, for the reasons given, it
cannot be assumed that he could have ascertained the
name of the real owner of the lots in question, by an examination of the indices of such record which are required to be kept in the names of grantors and grantees
alphabetically arranged. In other words, the assessor
must of necessity know a present, or former owner of the
property, in order to search the records for the real owner.

We are, therefore, of the opinion that it is impracticable for the assessor to obtain the name of the real
1 owner of a tract of land, from the official county records, as available for his inspection, and, in the ab-

sence of fraud, an assessment against unknown owners is
not invalid, because of the fact that the assessor might
have ascertained the name of the real owner from the records of conveyances in the office of the county recorder, in
those cases where the owner has failed to list his property
for taxation. It must be presumed, in the absence of a
showing to the contrary, that the assessor did his
2 duty, and that inasmuch as he made the assessment
to unknown owners, it was impracticable to obtain
the real owner's name.

Our opinion concerning the validity of this assessment
makes it unnecessary for us to pass upon the curative
provisions of chap. 22, Sess. Laws, 1899, and we, therefore, hold that this assignment of error is not well taken.

The second and third assignments predicate error upon
the admission in evidence of the tax sale certificate and
deed, on the theory that these instruments did not contain the recital of pre-requisites material to the sale. The
objections are clearly disposed of by the case of Straus v.
Foxworth, 16 N. M. 442, and we, therefore, deem it unnecessary to further discuss these alleged errors.

The remaining assignments of error are not separately
treated in the brief of appellants, and are apparently
waived, except as to the seventh and eighth, the latter
assigns error in holding that the taxes assessed against the
lots in question had not been paid prior to the date of
sale.

The mistake as to the return of the property, if one
was made, and in the payment of taxes on the wrong
property subsequently, are not shown by the record in this
case to have been the fault of the taxing officer, but
rather the fault, mistake, or neglect of the agent of the
owner. The burden was upon the appellants to prove the
error, or mistake, if it existed, and they failed in this
proof.

This Court, and the Territorial Supreme Court, has
frequently held that it will not disturb the findings of the
trial court where there is substantial evidence to support

them. We think there is substantial evidence in this respect.

We note the only remaining point urged by appellants under the seventh assignment alleging error "in finding for the appellant for one-half of the value of the improvements on the lots in question." We do not understand the trial court so found in this case, but that the learned District Judge, by his 12th finding of fact, in substance. found that by a former judgment in an action instituted by appellee against T. M. Murry, (the husband of appellant, Clara Murry), the title of appellee, to the lots in question, was quieted as against T. M. Murry. To consider the merits of this assignment would be to collaterally inquire into the merits of the former suit against T. M. Murry. We understand the argument of appellants, in this connection, that Sarah Jane Murry, as mortgagee, was entitled to judgment for the full value of the improvements, the mortgage being executed after the improvements were made, she not being a party to the first suit to quiet title. We are of the opinion that she cannot now raise this point and urge its favorable consideration. Her answer and cross complaint are silent upon the question of improvements. The money judgment obtained by her, in the court below, was obtained, apparently. on the theory of her subrogation to the rights of Clara Murry's interest in the improvements.

The trial court disposed of the case upon the issues as presented by the pleadings and we cannot now consider a new issue presented here for the first time.

Finding no error in the record, the judgment is affirmed.

[No. 1506, Jan. 9, 1913.]

CLARA MURRY, et als., Appellants, v. J. R. DAUGH-
TRY, Appellee.

SYLLABUS (BY THE COURT)

A motion for dismissal not supported by brief or argument
will not be considered by this court.

OPINION OF THE COURT.

HANNA, J.—There are two motions, for our consideration, for the dismissal of the appeal, raising substantially
the same questions. The grounds assigned in support of
the motion for a dismissal as to the appellant, Clara
Murry, are all incorporated in the motion for dismissal
as to the appellant, Sarah Jane Murry, which, however, in-
corporates additional grounds. Neither of these motions
are supported by brief or argument.

We are disposed to believe that motions not deemed
worthy of argument are so lightly considered by the party
presenting same, that our time should not be consumed
by an investigation into their merits.

For the reasons stated the motions are overruled.

[No. 1545, June 16, 1913.]

THE FEDER SILBERBERG CO., Plaintiff in Error, v.
LeMAR McNEIL, et al., Defendants in Error.

SYLLABUS (BY THE COURT)

1. Proof that "demand was made by mail" implies a prepayment of postage and a deposit of the demand in a United
States postoffice, but that the letter was properly addressed
to the addressee at the place where he resides or receives
his mail is not thereby implied, and proof of that fact must
be had before the receipt of the letter by the addressee, will
be inferred.

P. 49

2. Where a surety on a fidelity bond undertakes to respond upon condition that demand be first made upon the

principal, such demand is a part of the contract and must be alleged and proved.

P. 52

Error to the District Court for the County of Santa Fe, Edmund C. Abbott, District Judge; affirmed.

WILSON, BOWMAN AND DUNLAVY, Santa Fe, N. M., for plaintiff in error.

1.   Court erred in holding that it was necessary to prove the incorporation of the plaintiff.   Clark & Marshall Corporations, sec. 83, p. 262, vol. 1, (1903) ; Id., sec. 84; Seattle Crockery Co. v. Haley, et al., 6 Wash. 302; Tragdon v. Cleveland Stone Co., 53 Ill. App. 206; Hassinger v. Ammon, et al., 160 Pa. St. 245 (suretyshop bond); City of St. Louis v. Shields, et al., 62 Mo. 247 and cases cited therein; Loaners Bank v. Jacoby, 10 Hun. (N. Y.) 143, (forthcoming bond) ; Jeff v. McCarthy, 44 Minn. 26.
2.   Court erred in holding that there was no sufficient proof of demand upon the defendant, McNeil, under the conditions of the bond.   Butchers and Drovers Bank v. De Groot, 43 N. Y. Sup. Ct. (11 Jones & S.) 341, 344; Pier v. Heinrichshoffen, 67 Mo. 163, 169, 29 Am. Rep. 501; cited in Rolla State Bank v. Pezoldt, 69 S. W. 51, (95 Mo. App. 404) ; Faulkner v. Faulkner, 73 Mo. 327, (holding notice of protest properly given by proof that the same was mailed) ; Ward v. D. A. Morr T. & S. Co., 119 No. App. 83, 95 S. W. 964; Flint, et al., v. Kennedy, 33 Fed. Rep. 820; Providence Sav. L. Assur. Soc. v. Nixon, 19 C. C. A. 414, 44 U. S. App. 316, 73 Fed. 144; Rolla State Bank v. Pezoldt, 95 Mo. App. 404, 69 S. W. 51; Oregon Steamship Co. v. Otis, 100 N. Y. 446, 3 N. E. 485; Schutz, et al., v. Jordan, 141 U. S. 213, 35 L. Ed. 705; Rosenthal v. Walker, 111 U. S. 185, 28 L. Ed. 216; Williamson v. Seeley, 48 N. Y. Supp. 195, 22 N. Y. App. Div. 289; Thompson v. Whitney, 20 Utah 1, 8; Cox v. Delmas, 99 Cal. 104; Parrott v. Byers, 40 Cal. 614; 9 Am. & Eng. Enc. Law (2nd Ed.) 111, p. 209, 211-14; Jenks v. School Dist., 18 Kans. 356; Davis v. Wells, 104 U. S.

159, 26 L. Ed. 686; Ward v. Wilson, 100 Ind. 52, 50 Am.
Rep. 763; Simons v. Steele, 36 N. H. 73.

Court erred in holding that there was no sufficient proof
of the existence, execution, loss and contents of the original bond to permit the introduction of secondary evidence
of the bond. 3 Enc. Ev., p. 344-3.

Court erred in holding that it was necessary for plaintiff to prove affirmatively that the goods were not consumed by fire. Canfield v. Tobias, 21 Cal. 349; Scottish
Nat. Ins. Co. v. Wuslerhousen, 75 Ill. App. 283, and cases
cited; Maxwell v. Bodcaw L. Co., 79 Ark. 490, 96 S. W.
152, 116 Am. St. Rep. 92; Board Co. Commrs. v. Keene,
etc., 108 Fed. 505 and 515; Birmingham Ry. v. Moore,
148 Ala. 115, 42 So. 1024; Alling v. Forbes, 68 Conn.
575, 37 Atl. 390; Kerr v. Topping, 109 Iowa 150, 80 N.
W. 321.

Court erred in holding that there was no sufficient proof
of delivery of the bond. 4 A. & E. Enc. Law (2nd Ed.)
624; Blankman v. Vallejo, 15 Cal. 645; Newlin v. Beard,
et al., 6 W. Va. 110; Ward, et al., 35 Conn. 161; Keedy
v. Moats, 72 Md. 329; Edelin v. Sanders, 8 Md. 118;
Grim v. School Directors, 51 Pa. St. 219; 2 Enc. Ev. 567-
3; 38 Cyc., 1543, note 67 and cases cited; 38 Cyc., 1544,
note 72 and cases cited; 38 Cyc., 1543, note 69 and cases
cited; 38 Cyc., 1567, note 96 and cases cited; Snydan v.
Williamson, 15 L. Ed. 981, (U. S.)

RENEHAN & WRIGHT, Santa Fe, N. M., for defendants
in error.

There was a complete failure of proof as to demand
upon LeMar McNeil. 32 Cyc. 73 and cases cited; Providence Savings Life Ass. Society v. Nixon, 73 Fed. 144;
32 Cyc. 176; Folsom v. Squire, 72 N. J. L. 430, 60 Atl.
1102; Nelson v. Bostwick, 5 Hill (N. Y.) 37; Douglass
v. Rathbone, 5 Hill (N. Y.) 143; Florsheim v. Palmer,
99 Ill. App. 559; 20 Utah 1-8.

There was no sufficient proof of loss under the bonds as
against the sureties thereon. Stearns Law of Suretyship,
sec. 153.

Fourth assignment of error is insufficient in law. Mogollon v. Stout, 14 N. M. 245, 91 Pac. 724; Territory v. Cordova, 11 N. M. 367, 68 Pac. 919.

Reply brief for defendant in error.

Loss of bond. Oil Co. v. Van Etton, 107 U. S. 333, bottom of page 2 and cases cited; Elliott on Ev., vol. 3, sec. 1608; Gillett v. Chavez, 12 N. M. 353, 78 Pac. 68.

The undertaking of a surety is accessory to that of his principal. Evans v. Kneeland, 9 Ala. 42.

Account stated cannot be questioned. White Sewing M. Co. v. Fargo, 51 Hunt. 636, 3 N. Y. S. 494; Davis v. Kingsley, 13 Conn. 285; Lasater v. Purcell M. & E. Co., 54 S. W. 425, 22 Tex. Civ. App. 33.

Secondary evidence. Burnham v. Wood, 8 N. H. 334.

OPINION OF THE COURT.

PARKER, J.—This is an action brought by plaintiff in error against defendants in error to recover the penalty of a bond executed by them to the plaintiff to secure the fidelity of LeMar McNeil as an employee of the plaintiff. The provisions of the bond in so far as they are deemed pertinent to this inquiry, are as follows:

"The condition of the above obligation is such that, whereas, the said LeMar McNeil is about to enter into the employment of the said Feder Silberberg Company, and while in such employment will be entrusted by them with merchandise to be used by him as samples in the course of his said employment as salesman for the said Feder Silberberg Company.

"Now, if the said LeMar McNeil shall account for all samples entrusted to him as aforesaid and deliver same in good condition to the said Feder Silberberg Company upon their demand, except such as may have been destroyed by fire, then this obligation shall be void and of no effect, etc."

At the conclusion of the evidence for plaintiff, defendants demurred to the evidence and moved for an instruction, and the court directed a verdict for defendants. In announcing his decision the court said:

"I do not believe that there is legal or sufficient proof in this case on the execution of the bond, the delivery of the bond, the demand upon this party, or the question of the corporate capacity, to sustain a verdict. I think this deposition fails in many respects to be as convincing and clear as it ought to be, and that being the only testimony in the case, I feel obliged to sustain the motion."

Counsel for defendants rely, in support of the judgment, principally upon the proposition that there was a failure of proof of the demand upon said LeMar McNeil for the return of the samples delivered into his custody. The evidence upon the subject is contained in a deposition, the same being the only evidence upon the subject, and is as follows:

"Interrogatory 16. If your answer to interrogatory 14 was in the negative, state whether or not demand was ever at any time made upon said LeMar McNeil by the plaintiff herein, for an accounting or return of any samples or merchandise furnished by said plaintiff to said McNeil and the result of said demands.

"Answer. A demand was made by mail upon Mr. McNeil by plaintiff herein, for an accounting and for return of the samples and merchandise furnished him by said plaintiff, but no response was made by Mr. LeMar McNeil to any such demand. No letters of the plaintiff were ever answered by the said McNeil since shortly before May 1st, 1905, when he requested that we advance him $25 on account of commission."

Objection to this evidence was interposed on the ground that the answer failed to show that the demand was securely enclosed in a postpaid envelope addressed to the last known address of McNeil. In the motion for an instruction the object of this evidence is as follows:

"That there is no sufficient or legal proof that demand was made upon the defendant, LeMar McNeil, for any accounting or return of samples, as required in the bond."

It thus appears that the objection to the evidence is not because it is not the best evidence, but because of a faulty showing as to the mailing of the demand.

Counsel for plaintiffs in error argued that from the statement "a demand was made by mail" upon said Mc-Neil for a return of the samples, there is implied the performance of all of the acts necessary to effectuate that result, including the enclosing of the demand in a properly addressed and stamped envelope and posting the same in a postoffice of the United States.

They cite a number of cases, among which are the following: Bank v. DeGroot, 43 N. Y. Sup. Ct. 341, 344; Pier v. Henrichs Hoffen, 67 Mo. 163, 169; Bank v. Pezoldt, 69 S. W. 51; Ward v. Storage Co., 119 Mo. Ap. 83; Faulkner v. Faulkner, 73 Mo. 327; Providence Savings, etc.; Society v. Nixon, 73 Fed. 144; Oregon Steamship Co. v. Otis, 100 N. Y. 446, 450; Schutz v. Jordan, 141 U. S. 213; Rosenthal v. Walker, 111 U. S. 185; Williamson v. Seeley, 48 N. Y. S. 196.

An examination of these cases will disclose that they fail to support the doctrine claimed for them by plain-

1 tiff. They hold, with a single exception, to be hereafter noticed, that the word "mailed" implies a preparation of a notice or demand for carriage by the United States mail authorities, but none of them, with the exception noted, hold that a proper address of the letter is implied from the allegation of mailing. The exception to the general rule, hereinbefore mentioned, is the case of Ward v. Storage Co., 119 Mo. Ap. 83.

In that case the doctrine announced is broader than the question involved therein. The plaintiff testified that she "sent" defendant her address, and it did not appear whether it was sent by messenger conveying words, or carrying a written communication, or whether it was by letter duly mailed. In that case the court said:

"It will be observed that the evidence of notice to defendant of plaintiff's address is not direct or positive evidence, it is rather made to depend upon a presumption that in regular course, letters are received by addressees. In order to lay a foundation for such presumption, it should be shown that the letter was duly addressed, stamped and deposited in the postoffice or place for the re-

ceipt of letters. That, however, is made to appear sufficiently by evidence that it was "mailed" to the addressee.
That a letter to be properly 'mailed' to a person, must be
addressed, stamped and deposited in a proper place for
the receipt of mail, and therefore the general statement
that a letter was mailed will be sufficient."

It thus appears that the court of Missouri was not
called upon to define what was meant by and included in
the word "mailed."

In all of the other cases cited the word "mailed" is held
to include only the proper stamping and depositing in a
United States postoffice of the letter. The true rule seems
to be stated by Mr. Chamberlayne as follows:

"That the inference of receipt from mailing should
arise it is essential that the mail matter should be properly
posted. This in turn, involves compliance with certain familiar conditions:—(a) the letter or article must be mailable matter and properly addressed; (b) the postage must
be prepaid, so far as required by the postal regulations and
(c) it must be actually deposited in the mail.

"Accordingly, no inference of receipt arises from mailing unless the letter or other article is shown to have been
properly addressed to the person for whom it was intended, at the place of his residence and at the postoffice
where he customarily receives his mail."
2 Modern Law of Evidence, Section 1058.

Mr. Wigmore states the rule as follows: "The fixed
methods and systematic operations of this government's
postal service have been long considered to be evidence of
the due delivery to the addressee of mail matter placed for
that purpose in the custody of the authorities. The conditions are that the mail matter shall appear to have conformed to the chief regulations of the service, namely, that
it shall have been sufficiently prepaid in stamps, correctly
addressed, and placed in the appropriate receptacle." 1
Wigmore on Evidence, sec. 95.

The rule is otherwise stated as follows: "Before the
presumption of delivery or receipt of a letter arises it
must appear that it was properly stampel ,directed to the

regular address of the addressee, and mailed. All of these
facts must be shown, but a statement that a letter was
mailed has been held to sufficiently show the prepayment
of postage, the latter fact being included in the former."
9 Encyc. Ev. 900.

In Henderson v. Carbondale, etc., Co. 140 U. S. 25, it
is said:

Mr. Justice Brewer speaking for the court: "This presumption, which is not a presumption of law, but one of
fact, is based on the proposition that the postoffice is a
public agency charged with the duty of transmitting letters; and on the assumption that what ordinarily results
from the transmission of a letter through the postoffice,
probably resulted in a given case. It is a probability resting on the custom of business. and the presumption that
the officers of the postal system discharged their duty. But
no such presumption arises unless it appears that the person addressed resided in the city or town to which the letter was addressed; . . . . . ."

In Equitable Life Assurance Society v. Trommhold, 75
Ill. Ap. 43, the court refused to give the following instruction asked for by the defendant:

"The jury are instructed that the placing in the mail of
an envelope properly stamped, is not even presumptive
evidence of the receipt of the same unless the same was
properly addressed, and even if the jury believe from the
evidence that a notice was placed in an envelope properly
stamped and placed in the mail, yet, unless the jury further believe from the evidence that the envelope was properly addressed to the person for whom it was intended, it
is not even constructive notice, and may be wholly disregarded."

The court in considering this request for instruction
said:

"This instruction should have been given and the refusal to give it was error."

On principle and in accordance with common experience it is perfectly apparent that the statement that a letter was mailed to a certain party necessarily includes only

such acts as are required by the postal authorities of the United States, namely, that a letter have some address and that it be properly stamped. Whether the letter is properly addressed so as to reach the addressee is a matter of no concern to the postal authorities, nor have they any information or interest in the matter. But in order to establish a set of facts from which an inference or a presumption shall arise that a given letter was received by a given addressee, it must not only appear that a letter was "mailed" but that it was properly addressed to the addressee at the place where he resides or receives his mail.

In the case at bar the record is entirely silent as to how the demand was addressed. So far as anything appears in the record the demand may have been addressed to any one of the thousands of postoffices in the United States. and McNeil, the principal in the bond sued on, may have never received the same. It therefore appears that there was no evidence of a demand upon him for a return of the samples of merchandise sufficient to support a verdict, and the court was correct in directing a verdict for the defendants in error.

Plaintiff in error argues that no demand was necessary in order to recover in this case, and cites numerous **2** cases in support of the contention. None of these cases support the doctrine for which they are cited. The cases cited by plaintiff in error are to the effect that when the principal debtor discloses by his answer that he denies his obligation, or where the principal debtor has absconded so that no demand can be made upon him, and where no damage to the surety is shown by failure to notify him of the default of his principal, the necessity of a demand or notice prior to suit is dispensed with. In most, if not all, of the cases cited, the undertaking of the surety was unconditional. But that is not this case. The defendants in error in this case are sureties upon a fidelity bond, and undertook to pay only upon condition that demand be made upon their principal and that he fail to return the samples of merchandise entrusted to him. In such case a demand is a part of the cause of action of the

plaintiff and must be pleaded and shown. 32 Cyc. 176, n.
62; Folsom v. Squire, 72 N. J. Law, 430; Nelson v. Bostwick, 5 Hill, (N. Y.) 37, 40 A. D. 310.

In Nelson v. Bostwick, supra, it is said, per Bronson. J.:

"When a party agrees to pay his own debt on request, it
is regarded as an undertaking to pay generally, and no
special request need be alleged. But it is otherwise, when
he undertakes for a collateral matter, or as a surety for a
third person. There, if the agreement be that he will pay
on request, the request is parcel of the contract, and must
be specially alleged and proved." (Citations . . . . .)
"Here there was no precedent debt or duty upon Nelson.
He was a surety and becoming so he had a right to make
his own terms. The condition of the bond is that Shumway, the principal debtor, shall pay on demand. The demand is parcel of the contract, and is in the nature of a
condition precedent to a right of action on the bond. As
no demand of the costs from Shumway was proved, there
was no breach of the condition, and no right of action had
accrued on the bond." . . . . . .

Numerous other points are argued by plaintiff in error,
but the one already discussed lies at the foundation of its
cause of action and the failure of proof in that regard is
fatal to its recovery. The other propositions advanced
will therefore not be considered.

The judgment of the court below will, accordingly, be
affirmed, and it is so ordered.

[No. 1510, June 20, 1913.]

LARKIN BECK, Appellee, v. E. R. CHAMBERS, Appellant.

SYLLABUS (BY THE COURT.)

1. A contract for the exchange of land provided "in the
event that the party of the first part shall fail to comply
with the terms thereof, within the time herein limited, the
said second party may at his option declare this contract
void, in which event all rights and liabilities hereunder shall

cease and determine." Held that the forfeiture of the contract was made optional with the second party, and if he did not see fit to exercise his option and declare the forfeiture, the contract continued in full force and effect.

P. 60

2. HELD: Further, that a declaration of the fact that the party had elected to exercise his option to cancel the contract should have been made to the first party, and until it was made, the option was not exercised and the contract continued in full force and effect.

P. 60

Appeal from District Court, San Juan County; John R. McFie, Associate Justice; reversed and remanded.

RENEHAN & WRIGHT, Santa Fe, N. M., for appellants.

Trial *de novo* in chancery appeals, in some jurisdictions. 4 Ency. L. & P. 306; Ford v. Land Association, 8 N. M. 67, 68; Torlina v. Torlitch, 6 N. M. 54; Martin v. Brown, 4 Minn. 289; Baker v. Rockabrand, 118 Ill. 370; Allen v. Logan, 96 No. 598; Miller v. Taylor, 6 Colo. 45; Durham v. Coal Co. 22 Kans. 243; Jackson v. Allen, 4 Colo. 268; Siever v. Frink, 7 Colo. 152; Bank v. Newton, 13 Colo. 250; Rittmaster v. Brisbane, 19 Colo. 375-6; Hughs v. Washington, 65 Ill. 247-8; Hegwer v. Kiff, 31 Kans. 441; Jones v. Boyd, 80 N. C. 260; Miller v. Gibbons, 34 Ark. 221; Kelly v. Carter, 55 Ark. 112, 116; 4 Ency. L. & P. 328; Trust Co. v. Seasongood, 130 U. S. 482; 4 Ency. L. & P. 679, 680 and cases cited.

Complaint does not state facts sufficient to constitute a cause of action. Powell v. Dayton S. & G. R. Co., 14 Ore. 356; Knott v. Stevens, 5 Ore. 235; Rumington v. Kelly, 7 Ohio (pt. 2), 97; Frink v. Thomas, (Ore.), 12 L. R. A. 243 and note; Gregg v. English, 39 Tex. 139; Johnson v. Jackson, 27 Miss. 498.

Court erred in finding that time was of the essence of contract. Rourke v. McLaughlin, 38 Cal. 196; Sigler v Wilk, 45 Ia. 690; Westervelt v. Huiskamp, 101 Ia. 1909;

39 Cyc. 1367; Barnard v. Lee, 97 Mass. 92; Frink v. Thomas. 12 L. R. A. 239 and note; 39 Cyc. 1369 and cases cited; 39 Cyc. 1384; Boone v. Templeman, 158 Cal. 290; 110 Pac. 947; 139 Am. St. Rep. 126 and note; Thayer v, Meeker, 86 Ill. 470; Toplitz v. Bower, 161 N. Y. 325, 333; Monson v. Bragdon, 159 Ill. 66; 42 N. E. 385; Keator v. Ferguson, 20 S. D. 473; 107 N. W. 678; 129 Am. St. Rep. 947.

Under the evidence presented to the trial court, the trial court, failing to decree specific performance in favor of the defendant, should have reopened the cause for the taking of further testimony in order to place the parties in statu quo. 39 Cyc. 1401 and cases cited. Id. pages 1399 to 1403.

In the event the Supreme Court shall hold that the contract should be rescinded, before final judgment, duty to remand case to District Court for accounting to place parties in statu quo. Secs. 38 and 40, chap. 57, laws 1907; 3 Cyc. 459, 460 and cases cited; Chicago, etc., R. Co. v. Tompkins, 176 U. S. 167.

JOHN R. McFIE, Santa Fe; J. M. PALMER, Farmington, for appellee.

Assignments not argued in the briefs will not be considered. 16 N. M. 479.

Court will not retry case and search for errors not pointed out. Pierce v. Strickler, 9 N. M. 467; Territory v. Mills, 16 N. M. 555.

Errors relied upon must be separately assigned. Bank v. Haverkampf, 16 N. M. 497.

Findings of trial court not disturbed if based on substantial evidence. Irrig. Co. v. McMurray, 16 N. M. 172; Lockhart v. Mining Co., 16 N. M. 223; Current, et al., v. Bank, 16 N. M. 642; Putney v. Schmidt, 16 N. M. 400; Richardson v. Pierce, 14 N. M. 335; Hancock v. Bearsley, 14 N. M. 239.

Appeal court will not review findings of lower court as to weight and credibility of evidence. Hamilton Min. Co. v. Hamilton, 14 N. M. 272; Rody v. Travelers Ins. Co. v.

3 N. M. 543; Ter. v. Hicks, 6 N. M. 596; Patterson v. Hewitt, 11 N. M. 1; Carpenter v. Lindaner, 12 N. M. 388.

Jurisdiction. Errors invited, waived or immaterial are not available on appeal. Gillett v. Chavez, 12 N. M. 353; A. & E. Encyc. Law (2nd Ed.) 610; Encyc. P. & P., vol. 18, 754; Paige on Contracts, 3rd vol., secs. 1360, 1627, 1640; Railroad v. Louisville Trust Co., 174 U. S. 552-567.

Time was essence of the contract. Blood v. Goodrich, 24 Am. Dec. 121; 9 Cyc. 610; Henderson, et al., v. Mc-Fadden, et al., 112 Fed, 389; 9 Cyc. 607; Wiswall v. Barbour, (N. Y. 270.)

Court will not reverse where substantial justice has been done. Pearce v. Strickler, 9 N. M. 467.

Court will examine record to ascertain whether the findings are sustained by a preponderance of evidence. Ford v. Land Association, 8 N. M. 67-68; Gallup Elec. L. Co. v. Pacific Improvement Co., 16 N. M. 86; 113 Pac. 848.

Jurisdiction. C. L. 1897, sec. 2685, sub-sections 84, 85 and 94. Stansbury v. Stansbury, 118 No. App. 427; Custy v. City of Lowell, 117 Mass. 78.

Time was not of essence of the contract. Noyes v. Schlegel, 9 Cal. App. 516; 99 Pac. 726; Peck v. Coyle, 125 Pac. 1073, (Cal.); Sherman v. Leveret, 1 Root, 169, (Conn.); Johnson v. Higgins, 108 N. W. 168, (Neb.); Van Vraken v. Cedar Rapids, etc., R. R. Co., 55 Ia. 135; Vendor and Purchaser, 20 Dec. Digest, sec. 76, sec. 187; 48 Century Digest, sccs. 121, 374, 375.

Trial court failed to find necessary ultimate facts to sustain judgment. Luna v. Cerillos Coal R. Co., 16 N. M. 71; 113 Pac. 831; C. L. 1897, sec, 2999; Burr v. R. R. and Navigation Co., 1 Wall. 102; McClure v. U. C., 116 U. S. 151; Saltonstall v. Birtwell, 150 U. S. 418.

STATEMENT OF FACTS.

This suit was instituted in the District Court of San Juan County to cancel a contract for the exchange of real estate, entered into by the parties to this action on the 12th day of February, 1909, by the terms of which appellee was to convey to appellant certain real estate, situate in San Juan County, New Mexico, in exchange for real estate owned by appellant in the state of Colorado, which was to be conveyed to appellee. By the contract it was provided:

"Abstracts of title showing title in fee, subject merely to the incumbrances aforesaid, shall be furnished the respective parties hereto to patented land within 30 days from date, and to the pasture land within 6 months from date, within which time the said exchange shall be completed, when each of the parties shall, by good and proper deeds, convey the aforesaid properties belonging to him unto the other as hereinbefore agreed.

"In the event that the party of the first part shall fail to comply with the terms thereof, within the time herein limited, the said second party may at his option declare this contract void, in which event all right and liabilities hereunder shall cease and determine."

Appellant, under the contract, was to have immediate possession of the land to be conveyed to him, and he entered thereon and expended more than $1000.00 in permanent improvements. Appellee was not to have possession of the real estate to be conveyed to him, nor to receive the rents and profits thereof, until March 1, 1910.

On August 7, thereafter, neither party having complied with the terms of the contract, relative to furnishing abstracts of title, the following agreement was indorsed upon the contract:

"Aug. 7, '09. It is hereby agreed between the parties to this contract the time is hereby extended 60 days from date of same.

(Signed)   "E. R. Chambers,
(Signed)   "Larkin Beck."

The extended time for compliance, it will be observed, expired on October 6th. On October 11th, however, appellee orally agreed that appellant should have a further extension of time to November 1st.

From the evidence it appears that on November 1st, appellant submitted to appellee an abstract of title to the

lands which he was to convey; that appellee, after examination, pointed out three or four alleged defects in the
title.   Thereupon appellant agreed that he would go to
Pagosa Springs, Colorado, at once, and have the abstract
corrected in the particulars named.   There was some conflict in the evidence as to the exact conversation between
the parties at this time, appellant testifying that appellee told him to go ahead and have the corrections made,
but to be in a hurry; while appellee testified, "I told him
I did not believe it would go through and he oughtn't to
go."   Appellant, however, went to Pagosa Springs and
had the corrections made, and on the 11th of November
deposited with the escrow holder, designated in the contract, the abstracts of title and deeds of conveyance and
other papers.   On the 29th of the same month appellee
and his attorney called at the bank where the papers were
deposited, examined them, and on the next day appellee
served upon the appellant the following notice, viz:

"Farmington, N. M., Nov. 30th, 1909.
"Earnest R. Chambers, Esq.,
      "Fruitland, N. M.
   "Sir: You are hereby notified that you have defaulted
in the terms of the contract dated February 12th, 1909,
in the matter of our exchange of lands and you are now
given written notice of my intention to declare the said
contract void.

   "You are hereby further notified to remove from my
land in Fruitland, N. M., and ·deliver possession of the
same to me or I will take immediate legal proceedings to
regain possession thereof.

   "I claim no rights under the contract over any lands of
yours therein named.

(Signed)   "Larkin Beck."
   Appellant refused to vacate the land, possession of
which he had taken under the contract, and insisted that
the contract be performed by appellee, and this suit was
instituted by appellee to cancel the contract and for a
mandatory injunction against appellant to oust him from
the land.   After hearing had, the court made findings of

fact and stated conclusions of law, and entered judgment
for appellee, cancelling said contract.   From such judgment this appeal is taken.

OPINION OF THE COURT.

ROBERTS, C. J.—This is a suit in equity to forfeit
and cancel a contract for the exchange of land, where the
defendant in the court below, appellant here, in apparent
good faith, entered into possession of the land, which he
was to obtain title to under the contract, as was his right
thereunder, and made valuable and lasting improvements.   The general rule is that a court of equity will
not enforce a forfeiture, if by any reasonable rule of construction it can avoid it.   Where, however, time of performance is of the essence of the contract, and a forfeiture
is provided for by the contract, either expressly or by
necessary implication, a default in performance within or
at the time specified entitled the party for whose benefit
the provision was inserted, to a forfeiture of the contract,
in accordance with the terms of the contract.

In this case, the trial court, by its finding of fact numbered 2, found that time was of the essence of the contract, and that, as the contract remained unperformed, on
the first day of November, 1909, it was discharged.   By
its third finding it found "That the said contract became
by operation of law and the exercise of the option of the
said Larkin Beck, fully discharged, null and void, and
that all rights and liabilities arising thereunder ceased
and determined before the commencement of this action.

It would appear that the above so-called findings are
in reality mixed findings of fact and conclusions of law,
and that there is an apparent conflict between them, because the first stated finds that time is of the essence of
the contract, and, as said contract was not performed on
the 1st day of November, 1909, it became *ipso facto* null
and void, while the third finding or conclusion is, that
the contract became null, void and discharged because of
the exercise by appellee of his option to forfeit the same.
It must be conceded, however, that if the conclusion

drawn in either finding be correct, the judgment cancelling the contract must be sustained, for on either assumption the appellee would be entitled to recover.

Conceding, without deciding that time was of the essence of the contract, as stated in the second finding,

1 does it follow that, because the contract remained unperformed on the 1st day of November, it was discharged? The contract did not provide for its nullification by the mere failure of performance on the part of appellee within the time stipulated. Its forfeiture was made optional with the appellee, and if he did not see fit to exercise his option and declare the forfeiture, the contract continued in full force and effect. Van Dyke and Drew v. Cole, 81 Vt. 379.

And a declaration of the fact that appellee had elected to exercise his option should have been made to the

2 appellant, and until it was made, the option was not exercised and the contract was not annulled, but continued in force. Coles v. Shepard, 30 Minn. 446. This being true, the contract was not terminated on the 1st day of November, by its own force, and as the appellee did not elect to declare a forfeiture until the 30th day of the month, it necessarily follows that during the intervening time the contract was valid and binding upon both parties. The undisputed evidence shows that prior to the 30th of the month the appellant deposited with the designated escrow holder the papers called for by the original contract, and having so deposited said papers, prior to the forfeiture of the contract, appellant had complied with his part of the contract. This being true, appellee could not forfeit the contract, but necessarily was required to comply on his part.

It could hardly be contended that the conversation which occurred on the 1st of the month, even if appellee's version of it be admittedly correct, would be sufficient to effect a forfeiture of the contract. He testified, "I told him I did not believe it would go through and he oughtn't to go." It would certainly require a positive and specific declaration that appellee did not intend to be further bound by the contract, and the language used could not reasonably be construed as the exercise of appellee's option to declare the contract void; nor does appellee insist, as we understand his contention, that this language amounted to the exercise of his option, for his counsel say, in their brief, "It may be, and doubtless is true, that when appellant showed appellee his abstract of title November 1st, and Beck called his attention to the defects in it, and Chambers admitted the defects and said he would have them corrected, that in some loose conversation between them, Beck may have given Chambers to understand that if he deposited in the bank perfect abstracts of title and deeds conveying a fee simple title, he would still carry out the trade."

Another principle, supported by numerous adjudicated cases, might be invoked, were it necessary, in support of appellant's insistence that the contract was valid and in full force and effect at the time he deposited his papers in escrow, viz: If the stipulation which makes the time of payment essential be not absolute that the contract shall be *ipso facto* void upon default in payment at the time, but its object and language are to give to the vendor his election and power to put an end to the agreement upon the vendee's failure in paying or performing at the appointed day, then the vendor, if he intends to avail himself of the provision, must give the purchaser a timely and reasonable notice of his intention to avoid the contract, or must do some unequivocal act which unmistakably shows that intention, for the vendor can not treat the default alone as terminating the agreement. Pomeroy on Contracts, sec. 393. The principle is supported by adjudicated cases in Iowa, Minnesota and Illinois, which will be found cited in the note to the above section.

Again, should we assume that the contract was to become *ipso facto* null and void, upon failure to perform within the time stated, it might reasonably be held that appellee had waived strict compliance as to time, by his repeated extensions and subsequent conduct. Boone v.

Templeman, 158 Cal. 290, 110 Pac. 947; 139 Am. S. R.
126. And the right may be waived by extensions of time
or indulgences granted the purchaser. Douglas v. Hanbury,
56 Wash. 63, 134, A. S. R. 1096.

Appellee, according to his own testimony, on the 29th
of November, went to the bank and examined the papers
deposited there by appellant, and further said that he
would have carried out the contract had he found the
papers correct and in proper form. This conduct, coupled
with appellant's statement, that appellee told him to go
to Pagosa Springs and secure the correction of his title
papers, clearly evidences that appellee did not intend to
rely upon the forfeiture of the contract because of appellant's failure to perform on the 1st day of November.
This being true, he could not set up the delay or default
as creating a forfeiture without giving appellant notice
of his intention and allowing him a reasonable time within which to perform. Boone v. Templeman, supra; 39
Cyc. 1384.

Therefore, upon either view it will be seen that the findings of fact and conclusions of law were erroneous. Counsel for appellee suggest in their brief that the abstract of
title presented by appellant and the deeds executed by
him were deficient; that the abstracts failed to show a
perfect title, in fee simple in appellant, and that he had
failed to prepare the deed in conformity with the contract. It is a sufficient answer to this contention to point
out that the findings do not show such facts. The facts
found were that the contract remained unperformed on
November 1st; that no further legal extension of the contract was made, and not that the abstract submitted and
deeds tendered were deficient. The findings of fact made
by the trial court "must be of the ultimate facts which
the evidence is intended to establish, sufficient in themselves, without inference or comparison, or the weighing
of evidence, to justify the application of legal principles
which must determine the case." Luna v. Coal R. R. Co.,
16 N. M. 71 and cases cited. Should this court consider
the question suggested by appellee, as to the defects in

the abstract of title and deeds of conveyance, we would be required to search the record and decide a question which was not considered by the trial court.

Other grounds for reversal are urged by appellant, but in the view we take of the case it is not necessary for us to consider them.

For the reasons stated the judgment of the lower court is reversed and the cause is remanded, with directions to set aside the judgment and to proceed in accordance with this opinion, and it is so ordered.

[No. 1537, June 20, 1913.]

TERRITORY ex rel. CECILIA BACA, et al., Appellants, v. SALVADOR BACA, et al., Appellees.

SYLLABUS (BY THE COURT)

1. A defendant, by answering over, upon demurrer over-ruled, waives all objections to the petition of the plaintiff, except to the jurisdiction of the court and the failure of the petition to state a cause of action, and, where a defendant raises by demurrer the question of a defect of parties plaintiff, and, upon such demurrer being voerruled answers to the merits, he cannot thereafter raise the same question by objecting to the introduction of evidence.

P. 67

Appeal from District Court, Bernalillo County; Ira A. Abbott, Associate Justice; reversed and remanded.

H. P. OWEN *and* GEORGE S. KLOCK, Albuquerque, for appellants.

Amended complaint stated a cause of action against appellees and sureties. No defect of parties plaintiff. No misjoinder of parties plaintiff. Dicey on Parties, 101; Hoxie v. Weston, 19 Maine 222; Sanders v. Filley, 12 Pick. (Mass.) 554; Chapin v. Vermont R. R. Co., 8 Gray (Mass.) 575; Irish v. Jonston, 11 Pa. St. 483; Wieman v.

Mainegva, 112 La. 105, 36 So. 358; Probate Court v. Potter, 52 Atl. 1085; Rossen v. Piper, 34 Me. 98; Probate Court v. Southard, 62 N. H. 228; Boile v. St. John, 28 Hun. (N. Y.) 454; Loring v. Kendall, 1 Gray 313: Glover v. Heath, 3 Mass. 252; Conant v. Stratton, 107 Mass. 474; Choate v. Arlington, 116 Mass. 252; People v. Norton, 9 N. Y. App. 179; C. L. 1897, C. 2685, subsecs. 2 and 3; Conway v. Carter, 11 N. M. 419; Williams v. Kiernan, 25 Hun. N. Y. 358; N. Y. Civ. Cod. Pro. page 449; Cridler v. Curry, 66 Barber N. Y. 337; Thayer v. Clark, 48 Barb. 243; Bramley v. Forman, 15 Hun. (N. Y.) —; People v. Struller, 16 Hun. (N. Y.) 236; McCorkle v. Williams, 20 S. E. 744; 43 S. C. 66; Pilcher v. Barratt, 62 Kans. 137, 61 Pac. 737; Southerlands Code Pleading, Practice and Forms, vol. 1, sec. 14, pages 12, 13 and 14; Marie, et al., v. Garrison, 83 N. Y. 13; Bennett v. Woodman, et als., 116 Mass. 519; Embree v. State, 85 Ind. 368; Judge of Probate v. Lane, et al., 51 N. H. 342; Cranson, Judge of Probate, v. Wilson, 71 Mich. 356; Hood v. Sood, 6 N. Y. St. Rep. 685; (Misjoinder.) Beal v. Territory, 1 N. M. 507; Butterfield Overland Dispatch Co. v. Wedeles, 1 N. M. 528; Bremen Min. Co. v. Bremen, 13 N. M. 110-18, 79 Pac. 1133; Hier v. Stapleh, 51 N. Y. 136; Encyc. P. & P., vol. 6, pages 374, 375: Perkins v. Stimmel, 114 N. Y. 359.

NEILL B. FIELD, Albuquerque, N. M., for appellees.

Parties plaintiff in suit on bond. 15 Ency. P. & Pr 491-6, and cases cited; Id. 498; People v. Pacheco, 29 Cal. 213; I Sutherland Code Pl., sec. 14; Id., sec. 18; 15 Encyc. Pl. & Pr. 710; 3 Johns Ch. Rep. 555; Davoue v Fanning, 4 Johns. Ch. 202; Dehart v. Surviving Ex'r Dehart, 3 N. J. Eq. 472-3; Brown v. Ricketts, 3 Johns. Ch. 553; Dicey, Parties to Actions, note 1, p. 119 (1040); 18 Cyc. 957; Conway v. Carter, 11 N. M. 430.

Court properly directed a verdict for defendants Steamship Co. v. Immigration Commrs. 113 U. S. 37: Oscanyan v. Arms Co., 103 U. S. 261; Butler v. National Home, etc., 144 U. S. 64.

Reply Brief for Appellants.

Answering over after demurrer waives the grounds of demurrer, except jurisdiction of court over defendant or of subject matter. C. L. 1897, sec. 2685, sub-sec. 39; Laws 1901, chap. 82, sec. 6; Wall v. McConnell, 65 Tex. 397; Clay F. & M. Ins. Co. v. Huron Salt Co., 31 Mich. 346; State v. Johnson, 52 Ind. 197; Tedrick v. Wells, 152 Ill. 217; People v. Slocum, 1 Idaho 62; Rockwood v. Brown, 1 Gray 262; Raymond v. Johnson, 11 Johns. (N. Y.) 488; Artisans Ins. Co. v. Drennan, 4 Brewst. (Pa.) 103; 15 Encyc. Pl. & Pr. 491, 492 and 493; People v. Pacheco, 29 Cal. 213; Conway v. Carter, 11 N. M. 430; Davoue v. Fanning, 4 Johns. Chan. 202; Brown v. Rickerts, 3 John. Chan. 553; Dehart v. Surviving Exec. Dehart, 3 N. J. Eq. 472, 473; Crews v. Taylor, 56 Tex. 465; E. St. Louis v. Flanigan, 26 Ill. App. 449; Hunnicutt v. Kirkpatrick, 39 Ark. 172; Haynes v. Butler, 30 Ark. 69; 15 Encyc. Pl. & Pr. 110 to 115. ·

OPINION OF THE COURT.

ROBERTS, C. J.—This action was instituted by three of five residuary legatees to recover on the bond of the administrators of the estate of Juan Baca y Garcia. The complaint set out the names of all the residuary legatees, the appointment, and qualification of the administrators, the giving of the bond and the facts showing default, and concluded with a prayer for judgment against the defendants for the penalty of the bond, and that the said sum be brought into court for distribution among the heirs at law and residuary legatees of the deceased. To this complaint the defendants interposed a demurrer upon the ground "that there is a defect of parties plaintiff in that Juana Sabedra, one of the residuary legatees, is not made a party." The demurrer was overruled by the lower court and defendants answered to the merits. Thereafter, the cause came on for trial before a jury and objection was interposed to the introduction of any evidence on the same grounds stated in the demurrer, viz: That there was a defect of parties plaintiff. The court sustained the objection and excluded all the proffered evidence, and, upon appellants' refusal to amend their complaint and bring in the additional party, directed the jury to return a verdict for the defendants, which was done and judgment entered thereon. From the judgment appellants appeal and for a reversal of the cause submit two propositions, viz. (1) There was no defect of parties plaintiff, and (2), if there was in fact a defect of parties plaintiff, such defect appeared upon the face of the complaint, and appellees having demurred to the complaint on that ground, and such demurrer having been overruled and an answer interposed to the merits, they thereby waived their right to object to the introduction of evidence on the grounds stated in their demurrer.

We will first discuss the second proposition, because, if the point made is well taken, the first ground assigned becomes of no importance.

"Defect of parties plaintiff," by sub-sec. 35 of the Code of Civil Procedure, is made a ground of demurrer, where the defect appears upon the face of the complaint, as it did in this case, if it was necessary to make all the residuary legatees parties to the suit. A demurrer on that ground having been interposed and overruled, and defendants thereafter answering to the merits, abandoned their demurrer. The case therefore stood, at the time of trial, as if no demurrer had been interposed, and the defect, if it existed, had been waived by the defendants. By sub-sec. 39 of the Code of Civil Procedure, a defendant waives all objections to the complaint, not taken advantage of by demurrer where the defect appears upon the face of the complaint, otherwise by answer, excepting only "the objection to the jurisdiction of the court over the subject matter of the action, and excepting the objection that the complaint does not state facts sufficient to constitute a cause of action." Defendants having therefore waived the objection, could not take advantage of it upon the trial of the cause by objecting to the admission of evidence. To have made the objection available, defendants should have stood upon their demurrer. The rule is thus

stated by Bliss, in his book on Code Pleading.   (3rd Ed.)
Sec. 417.

"If the demurrant wishes to take advantage of any supposed error in overruling the demurrer, he must let final
judgment be entered upon it; for if he shall answer, after
such ruling, he waives any objection to the pleading, except for two radical defects, and the question can not be
afterwards raised, either by answer or by objecting to testimony."

The question has been before the courts in a number of
cases, and it has uniformly been held that where the defect of want of a proper party to the suit is patent on the
face of the petition, if it exists at all, it can only be taken
advantage of by demurrer.   And, if after a demurrer
1   raising that point is overruled, the defendant answers
over, he thereby waives the point, and cannot raise it
anew by answer or upon the trial.

State of Missouri to the use of Saline County v. Sap-
pington, et al., 68 Mo. 454; Haughey Livery & Und. Co. v.
Joyce, 41 Mo. App. 564; Haase v. Distilling Co., 64 Mo.
App. 131; Spilane v. Mo. Pac. Ry. Co., 111 Mo. 555;
Barth v. Deuel, 9 Colo. 494; Fillmore v. Wells, et al., 10
Colo. 228; Westphal, Hinds & Co. v. Henney et ux, 49
Iowa 542; Lonkey v. Wells, 16 Nev. 271; see also the case
of Tenant v. Pfister, 45 Cal. 270, where the court say:

"It would be productive of much confusion and probable surprise to parties if a demurrer for misjoinder of
parties or the like, once passed upon may be afterwards
ir effect renewed at the trial by the mere repetition of the
same objection which has been already definitely determined in disposing of the demurrer."

This reasoning is directly applicable to this case.   Here
the demurrer had been interposed and overruled, and an
answer filed to the merits.   Appellants naturally supposed
the question was disposed of; the witnesses were all present, the jury sworn, and they were met with the objection
previously passed upon by the court.   To have amended
at that time would have necessarily resulted in confusion
and delay.

Appellees have cited the cases of Steamship Co. v. Immigration Commissioners, 113 U. S. 37, and Oscanyan v. Arms Co., 103 U. S. 261, as justifying the action of the lower court. In these cases, however, it will be found that the facts stated failed to show a cause of action. Failure of a complaint to state facts sufficient to constitute a cause of action can of course be raised at any time, and the cases therefore have no application to this case.

For the reasons stated, the judgment is reversed and the cause remanded, and it is so ordered.

[No. 1557, June 20, 1913.]

FRANK A. HUBBELL, Appellee, v. JUSTO R. ARMIJO, Appellant.

SYLLABUS (BY THE COURT)

1. The appellant has no right to dismiss his appeal in the face of a motion for affirmance well taken.

P. 69

2. The fact that appellant's attorney has been busily engaged with other matters does not constitute "good cause" for failure to file and serve assignment of error as required by Sec. 31, C. 57, S. L. 1907.

P. 70

Appeal from the District Court of Bernalillo County; H. F. Raynolds, District Judge; affirmed.

HON. FRANK W. CLANCY, Santa Fe, for appellants.

Failure to obtain approval of bond is fatal to plaintiff's right to maintain this action. Mullery v. McCann, 95 Mo. 579, 583; Richards v. McMillan, 36 Neb. 352, 357-8; McMillin v. Richards, 45 Neb. 786, 799; Holt Co. v. Scott, 73 N. W. 681; Kreitz v. Behrensmeyer, 24 L. R. A. 59, 63; Rounds v. Mansfield, 38 Me. 588; Rounds v. Bangor,

46 Me. 542; Andrews v. Covington, 69 Miss. 746-7; United States v. Eaton, 169 U. S. 331-334; United States v. LeBaron, 19 How. 78-79.

It was essential to plaintiff's title that he be commissioned by the Governor. United States v. LeBaron, 19 How. 78-9.

OPINION OF THE COURT.

ROBERTS, C. J.—Appellant failed to assign error, and serve a copy of such assignment of error on the appellee, and also failed to file a copy of such assignment of error with the clerk of the Supreme Court on or before the return day of this appeal, as required by sec. 21, chap. 57, S. L. 1907. Appellee, on the 24th of April, 1913, filed a motion to dismiss the appeal and affirm the judgment of the lower court, because of such failure. Four days thereafter, appellant filed a written dismissal of the appeal. The question presented is,—Has the appellant the right to dismiss his appeal in the face of a motion for affirmance well taken? This question was answered in the

1 negative by this court in the case of Acequia Madre v. Myers, 128 Pac. 68.

Appellant contends, however, that the motion for affirmance was not well taken, because of a showing made by his attorney excusing the default. The statute (sec. 21, chap. 57 supra) provides:

"In default of such assignment of error and filing the same the appeal or writ of error may be dismissed and the judgment affirmed, unless good cause for failure be shown."

In the case of Acequia Madre v. Myers, supra, this court said:

"Our territorial supreme court has held repeatedly that upon failure to file and serve the assignment of error, as required, and within the time limited, the appellee or defendant in error is entitled to a dismissal and affirmance, if advantage be taken of such default before it is cured, in the absence of a showing of good cause for such failure."

Here the only showing made is that appellant's attor-

Deal v. W. Co. G. Co., 18 N. M., 70.

ney is the Attorney General of the State, and has been busily engaged with other matters of importance, and

2 overlooked filing the assignment of error. The pressure other business does not constitute "good cause" within the meaning of the statute.

In the case of Hilliard v. Insurance Co., decided at the present term of this court, and not yet reported, we say,

"It has been held that the fact that an attorney had 'so much to do,' is not a sufficient excuse by his failure to file his abstract and briefs as required by the rules of the court."

In that case the rule is laid down that a showing of "good cause," excusing a default in failing to file and serve copies of briefs within the time required by rule of court, requires a showing that such default occurred by reason of facts and circumstances not within the control of the defaulting party.

The rule announced is applicable to this case, and under it the showing made is not sufficient to excuse the default.

The motion for affirmance is therefore well taken, and will be granted.

[No. 1558, June 20, 1913.]

F. M. DEAL, Appellee, v. WESTERN CLAY & GYP-
SUM PRODUCTS CO., Appellant.

SYLLABUS (BY THE COURT)

1. Where an appellant fails to file briefs within the time limited by subdivision 4 of rule XIII, the order of dismissal or affirmance goes as a matter of course, upon motion of the appellee, and no notice need be given the appellant, or his attorney.

P. 71

2. A cause affirmed, upon motion of appellee, for failure of appellant to file and serve briefs within the time required by rule of court XIII, will not be reinstated upon the docket

Deal v. W. Co. G. Co., 18 N. M. 70.

and the affirmance vacated, where the only showing made
excusing such default and failure to apply for an extension
of time within which to file briefs was, that appellant's local
attorney in this state sent the brief to its general counsel
for examination and approval. Appellant should have applied for an extension of time, within the time limit for filing
briefs, when it became apparent that it would not ·be able
to comply with the rule.

P. 72

Appeal from District Court, Lincoln County: Edward
L. Medler, District Judge; motion denied.

OPINION OF THE COURT.

ROBERTS, C. J.—The transcript in this case was filed
in the clerk's office March 1, 1913. On April 14, thereafter, appellee filed a motion to affirm the judgment of
the trial court, because of appellant's failure to file briefs
within thirty days after filing the transcript, as required
by subdivision 4 of Rule XIII of this court. It appearing from the record of the case in this court that appellant had not filed his brief ·within the time limited, and
had failed to apply for or receive an extension of time
for such purpose. The court sustained appellee's motion
and affirmed the case. Thereafter, appellant moved the
court to set aside and vacate the order of affirmance and
reinstate the cause upon the docket. The grounds upon
which it relies in the motion may be stated briefly as follows: (1) That its attorney was not served with a copy of
the motion for affirmance, and (2) that the delay in filing
the brief was occasioned by its local attorney at Carrizozo
sending to its general attorney at Des Moines, Iowa,
copies of the brief prepared in the cause, for examination,
and that the delay was caused thereby.

Neither ground stated in the motion is well taken. In
the case of Hilliard v. Insurance Co., decided at the
1 present term of this court, and not yet reported, we
held that no notice of a motion to dismiss a cause for
failure to file briefs need be given. We say:
"Where a party is in default, the order of dismissal goes

'as a matter of course, upon motion of the other party. It
is somewhat in the nature of a default judgment, and no
notice need be given to the party in default."

The case cited supra is also decisive of the insufficiency
of the second ground relied upon. The facts set forth
2 do not justify the failure on the part of appellant to
apply for an extension of time within which to file its
briefs. No such application was made.

The motion will be denied, and it is so ordered.

[No. 1512, June 30, 1913.]

A. L. MORGAN and AMERICAN SURETY COM-
PANY, of New York, Appellants, v. NATHAN SAL-
MON, Appellee.

SYLLABUS (BY THE COURT)

1. The surety on a bond for the faithful performance by the
contractor of a building contract is absolutely discharged
from liability when the obligee fails to retain not less than
fifteen (15%) per cent of the value of all work performed
and material furnished in the performance of said contract in
accordance with the terms of said bond, said surety not having consented to such alteration.

P. 80

Appeal from District Court of Santa Fe County; John
R. McFie, Associate Justice; reversed and remanded.

WILSON, BOWMAN & DUNLAVY, Santa Fe, N. M., for
appellants.

BRIEF FOR APPELLANT.

The surety was released by failure of obligee to retain
15 per cent of value of work performed and materials furnished. 2 A. & E. Ann. 766, and note; First Natl. Bank
of Montgomery v. Fidelity & Dep. Co., 40 So. 415, 5 L. R.
A. (N. S.) 418, and note; Glenn Co. v. Jones, 146 Cal.
518; Sheldon v. American Sur. Co., 131 Fed. 210; Welsh

v. Hubbschmitt Bldg. & Wdwk Co., 61 N. J. L. 507; Taylor v. Jetter, 23 Mo. 244; St. Mary's College v. Meagher, 11 Ky. L. 112; McNally v. Merc. Trust Co., 204 Pa. 596; Wehrung v. Denham, 42 Ore. 386; Coddrey v. Hahn, 105 Wis. 445; Gate v. Warrington, 37 Fla. 542; U. S. v. American Bldg. Co., 89 Fed. 925; Fidelity & D. Co. v. Robertson, 136 Ala. 379; Prairie St. Natl. Bank v. U. S., 164 U. S. 233; Calvert v. London Dock Co., 2 Keen 638; Leghorn v. Nydell, 80 Pac. 833; Hohn v. Shidler, 164 Ind. 242; Schriber v. Worm, 164 Ind. 7; Surety Co. v. Board of Co. Commrs., 79 N. W. 649; Fidelity & G. Co. v. Construction Co., 116 Fed. 145; California Sav. Bank v. American Surety Co., 87 Fed. 118; 82 Fed. 866; Foster v. Fidelity & Cas. Co., 99 Wis. 447; Star v. Milliken, 180 Ill. 458; Electric App. Co. v. U. S. Fidelity & G. Co., 110 Wis. 434; Fidelity & Cas. Co. v. Sanders, 32 Ind. App. 448; Insurance Co. v. Brim, 11 Ind. 281; Swift & Co. v. Jones, 135 Fed. 437; Sullivan v. Fraternal Society, 73 N. Y. Sup. 1094; Guaranty Co. v. Mechanics Sav. Bank, 183 U. S. 402; Knight & Gilson Co. v. Castle, 87 N. E. 976.

The limitation of time in the bond, within which suit must be brought, was not complied with, and there was no waiver of time. Marshalltown Stone Co. v. Lewis Drach Const. Co., 123 Fed. 747; Express Co. v. Caldwell, 21 Wall. 264; Holtby v. Zane, 69 Atl. 675; Ripley v. Etna Ins. Co., 30 N. Y. 136; Peoria Ins. Co. v. Whitehall, 25 Ill. 466; China Co. v. Surety Co., 152 Ill. App. 89; Granite Bldg. Co. v. Saville, 101 Va. 217; Novelty Mill Co. v. Heinzerling, 39 Wash., 244; James Riley Supply Co. v. Smith, 177 Fed. 168; Defarconnet v. Western Ins. Co., 122 Fed. 448; Taber v. Royal Ins. Co., 124 Ala. 681; Metropolitan Acc. & Ass. Co. v. Froiland, 161 Ill. 30; Williams & McNair, 98 N. C. 332; Montreal v. St. Cunegone, 32 Can. Sup. Ct. 135; Sullivan v. Cluggage, 21 Ind. App. 667; Lonergan v. San Antonio L. Co., 101 Tex. 63; Beers v. Wold, 116 Mo. 179; Killoren v. Meehan, 55 Mo. App. 427; Eldridge v. Fuhr, 59 Mo. App. 44; Fullerton Lbr. Co. v. Gates, 89 Mo. App. 201; Chapman v. Eneberg, 95 Mo. App. 128; Burns v. Fid. Co., 96 Mo. App. 467;

Truckee Lodge No. 14 v. Wood, 14 Nev. 293; Northern
Light Lodge No. 1 v .Kennedy, 7 N. D. 146; U. S. v.
Freel, 92 Fed. 299; Ryan v. Morton, 65 Tex. 262; 22 L.
R. A. 372.

There was no notice of default of the contractor within
the stipulated time. Novelty Mill. Co. v. Heinzerling, 81
Pac. 742; Knight & Gilson Co. v. Castle, 87 N. E. 976;
National Surety Co. v. Long, 125 Fed. 887.

A. B. RENEHAN, Santa Fe, N. M., for appellee.

Suit could not be commenced according to the bond.
C. L. 1897, sec. 2685, sub-sec. 17; 2 Paige on Contracts,
sec. 1121-1122; 2 L. R. A. Digest (1907), page 1703, sec.
3; Sterns' Law of Suretyship, sec. 255; Wallace v. Ins.
Co., 41 Fed. 742; Conn. Fire Ins. Co. v. Geary, 51 L. R.
A. 698; Railway Co. v. Hume Bros., 87 Tex. 218; U. S. v.
Bradley, 10 Pet. 360; 2 Paige on Contracts, sec. 1123;
O'Brien v. Miller, 168 U. S. 297.

The contractual limitation was unreasonable.   Railway
Co. v. Hume, 87 Tex. 211; Railway Co. v. Reeves, 90 Tex.
499; Railway Co. v. Harris, 67 Tex. 166; Express Co. v.
Reagan, 29 Ind. 21; Express Co. v. Carpenter, 44 Ala.
103; Railway Co. v. Stanley, 89 Tex. 466; Brown v. Ins.
Co., 24 Ga. 101; Goggin v. Railway Co., 12 Kans. 324;
1 Paige on Contracts, sec. 356.

Forfeiture discountenanced.   Palatine Ins. Co. v. Ew-
ing, 92 Fed. 114; Lamb v. Powder Riv. Live Stock Co.,
132 Fed. 443; Steele v. Phoenix Ins. Co., 51 Fed. 722;
Auspland v. Aetna Indem. Co., 81 Pac. 579; Amer. Surety
Co. v. Pauley, 170 U. S. 133; Supreme Council v. Fidelity
& Cas. Co., 63 Fed. 48; Bank v. Fidelity & Dep. Co., 128
N. C. 366.

Failure to withhold 15% does not release the so-called
surety.   Guaranty v. Construction Co., 116 Fed. 145;
Leghorn v. Nydell, 80 Pac. 833; Surety Co. v. Board, 79
N. W. 649; Madison v. Engineering Co., 118 Wis. 480;
Smith v. Molleson, 148 N. Y. 241; Grafton v. Hinkley,
111 Wis. 406.

Alterations in the contract unavailing, because not pleaded. Surety Co. v. Trust Co., 98 S. W. 403; Filbert v. Philadelphia, 37 Atl. 546; Cowles v. Guaranty Co., 72 Pac. 1033.

The nature of such contracts. Frost, Guaranty Insurance, p. 1631; Bank v. Trust Co., 80 Fed. 766; Indemnity Co. v. Woolen Mills, 92 Fed. 583; Frost, Guaranty Insurance, p. 18.

There was no person to serve. Laws 1905, p. 19.

Agents, and their power to bind. Ins. Co. v. Bostwick, 27 Ark. 539; Bank v. Ins. Co., 31 Conn. 526; Ins. Co. v. Schettler, 38 Ill. 172; Ins. Co. v. Jones, 62 Ill. 458; Ins. Co. v. Hart, 149 Ill. 513; Ins. Co. v. Karn, 39 S. W. 503; Ins. Co. v. Halloway, 72 S. W. 796; Schmidt v. Ins. Co., 2 Mo. App. 339; Williams v. U. S., 2 Pet. 102; Wilson v. Ins. Co., 16 Barb. 513; Whited v. Ins. Co., 13 Hun. 193; Sparkman v. Council, 57 S. C. 19; Ins. Co. v. Wilkinson, 13 Wall. 222; Horton v. Ins. Co., 122 N. C. 505; Geib v. Ins. Co., 10 Fed. 157; Dovey v. Ins. Co., 7 Fed. Cas. 10; Chamberlain v. Ins. Co., 80 Mo. App. 589; Gold Water v. Ins. Co., 109 N. Y. 618; Ins. Co. v. Kinneir's Admx., 29 Grat. 88; Herschel v. Ins. Co., 4 Wash. 476; Palmer v. Ins. Co., 44 Wis. 201; Robbins v. Ins. Co., 149 N. Y. 484.

The power of general agents to waive conditions and forfeitures. Ins. Co. v. Brookes, 131 Ala. 618; Ins. Co. v. Humphrey, 62 Ark. 353; Waterbury v. Ins. Co., 6 Dak. 477; Ins. Co. v. Brown, 123 Ia. 357; Ins. Co. v. Sullivan, 112 Ill. App. 500; Ins. Co. v. Duke, 84 Ind. 253; Ins. Co. v. Eagley, 71 N. E. 897; Mottocks v. Ins. Co., 74 Ia. 233; Ins. Co. v. McLanathan, 11 Kans. 533; Ins. Co. v. Allen, 77 Pac. 529; Ins. Co. v. Brown, 3 Kans. App. 225; Ins. Co. v. Earle, 33 Mich. 143; Parsons v. Ins. Co., 132 Mo. 583; Burnham v. Ins. Co., 63 Mo. App. 85; Brenner v. Ins. Co., 99 Mo. App. 718; Carroll v. Ins. Co., 40 Barb. 292; Brooks v. Ins. Co., 78 N. Y. S. 748; Benjamin v. Ins. Co., 80 N. Y. Sup. 256; Ins. Co. v. Barget, 17 Ohio Cir. Ct. R. 369; Ins. Co. v. McCrea, 8 Lea. 513; Woolpert v. Ins. Co., 42 W. Va. 647; Miner v. Ins. Co., 27 Wis. 693; Winans v. Ins. Co., 38 Wis. 342; Kahn v. Ins. Co., 4 Wyo.

419; Ins. Co. v. Allen, 128 Ala. 459; Lumber Co. v. Ins.
Co., 98 Colo. 503; Russell v. Ins. Co., 80 Mich. 407; Burdick v. L. Assn., 77 Mo. App. 633; Joy v. Ins. Co., 35 Mo.
App. 167; Forward v. Ins. Co., 25 L. R. A. 637; Thompson v. Ins. Co., 169 Mo. 13; Ins. Co. v. Caldwell, 187 Ill.
73; Ins. Co. v. McKnight, 197 Ill. 190; Life Assn. v.
Woolen Mills, 182 Fed. 508.

Estoppel to deny agency and its effect upon contractual
limitation. Mechem on Agency, secs. 86, 83; 1 Pom. Eq.
Jur. 451; Ins. Co. v. Baker, 49Ill. App. 96; Ins. Co. v.
Enslie, 78 Miss. 161; Ames v. Ins. Co., 14 N. Y. 266;
Life Assn. v. Baughman, 73 Ill. App. 549; Fritz v. Ass.
Co., 208 Pa. St. 273; Defarconnet v. Ins. Co., 110 Fed.
410; Union Central L. Ins. Co. v. Phillips, 101 Fed. 33;
102 Fed. 19.

Fidelity, Commercial and Judicial Bonds or policies, as
issued by the so-called surety companies, are contracts of
insurance. U. S. Fid. & G. Co. v. First Nat. Bank, 84
N. E. 670; Guaranty Co. v. Trust Co., 80 Fed. 766; Indemnity Co. v. Woolen Mills, 92 Fed. 584; People v. Rose,
174 Ill. 310; Peoria, etc., Co. v. Hall, 12 Mich. 202;
Mayor v. Ins. Co., 10 Bosw. 537; Hart v. Ins. Co., 12 Ia.
371; 2 May on Insurance, sec. 504; Ide v. Phoenix Ins.
Co., 2 Biss. 333; Rogers v. Aetna Ins. Co., 95 Fed. 103;
Steele v. Phoenix Ins. Co., 154 U. S. (L. ed.) 1064.

Reply brief for appellant.
Stearns on Law of Suretyship, sec. 143; Guaranty v.
Construction Co., 116 Fed. 145.

Appellee's brief on motion for rehearing.
RENEHAN & WRIGHT, Santa Fe, for appellee.
Rules overlooked by the court in its decision. American
Surety Co. v. Board, 79 N. W. 650; City of New Haven v.
National, etc., Co., 79 Conn. 482; National Bank v. Fi-
delity Co., 145 Ala. 415.

Fraud. 9 Cyc. 412, and note 73.
Value. O'Neill v. Title, Guar. & Trust Co., 191 Fed.
570.
Strictissimi Juris. U. S. v. Lynch, 192 Fed. 368; Min.

Morgan v. Salmon, 18 N. M. 72.

Co. v. Cullins, 104 U. S. 176; Guaranty Co. v. Pressed Brick Co., 191 U. S. 416; Contracting Co. v. National Surety Co., 112 Pac. 517; Cowles v. U. S. Fid. & Guar. Co., 72 Pac. 1032.

Construction. 9 Cyc. 586; Amer. Bond Co. v. Pueblo Inv. Co., 150 Fed. 24; Deposit Co. v. Laurinburg, 163 Fed. 95; U. S. F. & G. Co. v. Board, 145 Fed. 148.

Surety was not injured. U. S. F. & G. Co. v. United States, 178 Fed. 694; Baglin v. Title Co., 178 Fed. 682; McMullen v. U. S., 167 Fed. 463; Peoples Lumber Co. v. Gillard, 136 Cal. 55.

STATEMENT OF THE CASE.

This is an action brought by the appellee, Nathan Salmon, against A. L. Morgan, as principal, and the American Surety Company, as surety, on a bond for the faithful performance of a building contract by the terms of which the said Morgan was to erect a building for said Salmon in the City of Santa Fe. The bond sued upon is conditioned as follows:

"Now, therefore, the condition of this obligation is such, that if said principal shall faithfully perform said contract on his part, according to the terms, covenants, and conditions thereof (except as hereinafter provided), then this obligation shall be void; otherwise, to remain in full force and effect.

"PROVIDED, HOWEVER, AND UPON THE FOLLOWING FURTHER EXPRESS CONDITIONS:

"First: That in the event of any default on the part of the principal in the performance of any of the terms, covenants or conditions of said contract, written notice thereof, with a verified statement of the particular facts showing such default, and the date thereof shall, within fifteen (15) days after such default, be delivered to the surety at its office in the City of Santa Fe, N. M., and that in case of such default all moneys, which but for such default would be due, or would thereafter become due to the principal, shall be held by the obligee and by him applied for the indemnification of the surety.

"Second: That the liability of the surety hereunder is and shall be strictly construed as one of suretyship only; and that no suit, action or proceeding upon or by reason of any such default shall be brought or instituted against the principal or surety after the twenty-fourth day of July, 1906, and that actual service of writ or process commencing such suit, action or proceeding be made on or before such date.

"Third: That the principal shall not, nor shall the surety, be liable for any damage resulting from an act of God; or from a mob, riot, civil commotion, or a public enemy; or from employees leaving the work being done in the performance of said contract, or so-called "strikes" or labor difficulties; or from fire, lightning, tornado or cyclone; or from injury to person or adjacent property resulting from accident or negligence in the performance of such contract, and that the principal shall not, nor shall the surety, be liable for the reconstruction or repair of any work or materials damaged or destroyed by said causes or any of them.

"Fourth: That the obligee shall retain not less than fifteen (15%) per centum of the value of all work performed and materials furnished in the performance of said contract, until the complete performance by said principal of all the terms, covenants and conditions thereof, on said principal's part to be performed; and that the obligee shall faithfully perform all the terms, covenants and conditions of said contract on the part of said obligee to be performed.

SIGNED AND SEALED this 27th day of November, 1905,

(Signed)   A. L. Morgan.
(Signed)   American Surety Company of New York,
By   Robert C. Gortner,
                Resident Vice President.
Attest: Hanna & Spencer,
                Resident Assistant Secretary."

In the latter part of December, 1905, while the building was in process of erection, the contract was terminated by

the obligee discharaging the contractor because of alleged
defects in the work so far done, and on January 5th, 1906,
he entered into a new contract with another contractor
under which the building was completed January 15th,
1907.

At the time Morgan was discharged all work performed
and materials furnished in the construction of said building was paid for in full by the obligee.

After the completion of the building the appellee
brought suit for damages against the appellants on said
bond, and, a jury having been waived, the cause was tried
by the Court and judgment rendered against appellants,
from whcih judgment this appeal is prosecuted, the following, among other errors, being assigned :

"2. The Court erred in holding and finding that the
obligee complied with the requirements of the bond in the
matter of the reservation by him of fifteen per centum
(15%) of the amount due in accordance with the terms
of the bond and contract."

OPINION OF THE COURT.

LEIB, District Judge, Acting as Justice.—A number
of questions are raised by appellants in their assignment
of errors, but the findings of fact of the lower court upon
conflicting evidence are probably binding upon us as to all
these. The court concluded that the surety was not released by the failure of the obligee to retain 15% of the
value of the work performed and material furnished. as
required by the bond. Nowhere has the appellee shown
that he has complied with this condition, and it was necessary for him to do so before he could recover. On the
contrary, he admits in his evidence that payments had
been made in full. This question can, therefore, be considered by us, and, as it goes to the very heart of the matter, it will be unnecessary for us to consider any other.

The bond sued upon was given to guarantee the faithful performance of the contract to erect the building for
the appellee. This was to be constructed in accordance
with the terms of said contract, except as the same is
limited and varied by the provisions of the bond set out

in the statement of the case. The contract, amended by
the bond, then, is what we are to consider. Where the two
conflict, the terms of the latter control. In other words,
the terms of the bond which change or qualify the terms
of the contract are the limits of the surety's obligation,
and, so far as the surety is concerned, take the place of
such provisions upon the same subject as are contained in
the contract and the specifications.

"If the main contract is broader in its scope than the
limits fixed by the bond, a reference to the contract will
only incorporate so much of the same as is within the
limits of the terms of the bond." Stearns on the Law of
Suretyship, sec. 143; Asplund v. Aetna Indemnity Co.,
81 Pac. 579.

The surety had the right to specify the conditions under
which it would be held liable. The obligee was not compelled to accept these conditions, but, having done so, he
is bound by them. The provisions of the bond that 15%
of the amount due for labor performed and material furnished be retained was obviously for the benefit of the
surety, and without it therein, the bond no doubt would
never have been written. Had it been complied with by
the obligee, not only would there have been a sum remaining in his hands for the protection of the surety, but
there would also have been an additional incentive for the
contractor to carry out the terms of his contract and go
on and complete the building. By payment in full, the
temptation for dishonesty was increased, and the hope of
reward for further labor decreased, it made a different obligation that subjected the surety to risks for
which it had not contracted. We can but conclude, therefore, that the failure of the obligee to retain 15% of the
value of the labor performed and material furnished in
the construction of the building was a material variation
of the bond.

Having reached this conclusion, it logically follows that
the surety is released. There are but few rules of law
1 better settled than the one that the surety has the
right to stand upon the exact terms of his bond. If,

without his assent, the obligee departs therefrom in a material matter, it operates as a discharge. As said in Ryan
v. Morton, 65 Tex. 288,

"The liability of a surety cannot be extended beyond the
terms of the contract out of which the obligation arises. If
the contract be altered without his consent, whether he
sustain injury or the contract be to his advantage, it
ceases to be his contract, and with that ceases his obligation."

This is squarely in line with the overwhelming weight
of authority. From the leading case of Calvert v. London
Dock Company, 2 Keen 639, down to the present time,
there is a long line of authorities holding, in substance,
the doctrine just enunciated. See County of Glenn v.
Jones, 146 Cal. 518, 80 Pac. 695, and the extensive note
thereto in 2 A. & E. Annotated Cases, at page 766, where
a large number of authorities are collected. In that case
it is said:

"The liability of a surety is not to be extended by implication beyond the terms of his contract. To the extent,
and in the manner, and under the circumstances pointed
out in his obligation, he is bound, and no further. He has
a right to stand on its very terms."

Additional authorities sustaining the same doctrine are
Sheldon v. American Surety Co., 131 Fed. 210; St. Mary's
College v. Meagher, 11 Ky. L. Rep. 112, 11 S. W. 608;
Evans v. Gooden, 28 S. W. (Mo.) 439; McNally v. Mer-
cantile Trust Co., 204 Pa. 596, 54 Atl. 360; Gato v. War-
rington, 37 Fla. 542, 19 So. 883; United States v. Ameri-
can Bonding Co., 89 Fed. 925, and Prairie State National
Bank v. United States, 164 U. S. 233, 41 L. Ed. 417; in
Miller v. Stewart, 9 Wheat., 6 L. Ed. 189, the court said:

"It is not sufficient that he (the surety) may sustain
no injury by the change in the contract, or that it may
even be for his benefit. He has a right to stand upon the
very terms of his contract, and, if he does not assent to
any variation of it, and a variation is made, it is fatal."

We are not unmindful of the fact that there are some
authorities holding that a variation, such as we find in

this case, operates only *pro tanto* to discharge the surety. This, however, as we have seen, is contrary to authority and cannot be sustained by reason. Who can tell, in any given case of this character, to what extent the surety is injured? It may be that had the stipulated sums been withheld, there would have been no default. It may be that it would have made no difference. Between these two extremes of conjecture, there is a wide field for what would be, at best, very uncertain computation. Where is the Court that can approximate the damages, even after weighing, as best it can, all the complex forces that influence each individual, and are transmuted into action? Would not such an attempt lead the courts to adopt as many different rules of construction as there are contractors involved? Should not the courts enforce the contracts made by the parties, and not other and different ones? And what right have the courts to extend by implication contracts that in terms are fixed and definite? These questions answer themselves.

We think it the better rule to hold in such cases as the one before us that the surety is entirely released. For the reasons above stated, the decision of the lower Court is reversed, and this cause is remanded with instructions that the same be dismissed as to the appellant, the American Surety Company, and it is so ordered.

Hanna, J., having been of counsel in the court below, did not participate in this decision.

[No. 1533, June 30, 1913.]

J. D. LYONS, Appellant, v. B. L. KITCHELL, et al., Appellees.

SYLLABUS (BY THE COURT)

1. Any material alteration in a building contract will release non-consenting sureties upon a bond given to guarantee the faithful performance of the same; and where a contract provides for the retention by the owner of a stated percent-

age of the estimate, or stated amount, at the time of each payment to the contractor, prior to completion of the building, and the owner fails to comply therewith and pays the contractor in excess of the stipulated amount without the consent of the sureties, such overpayment is a breach of the contract by the owner, and the bond given to secure the same cannot be enforced against the sureties.

P. 88

2. It is the deviation from the terms of the contract that operates to release the surety and not the injury or damage done by such departure, and the breach of the contract ipso facto nullifies it as to the sureties.

P. 89

3. The appellate court will not weigh the evidence, but will examine it to ascertain whether or not the verdict of the jury is supporoted by substantial evidence.

P. 90

4. The admission by a party to a suit, of a material fact, which in and of itself is sufficient to defeat or authorize a recovery, affords substantial evidence, sufficient to support a verdict based thereon, in the appellate court.

P. 91

Appeal from the District Court of Curry County; John T. McClure, District Judge; affirmed.

H. D. TERRILL; H. W. WILLIAMS, Clovis, N. M., for appellant.

Court erred in overruling plaintiff's motion for judgment based on special findings 1 and 3, for the reason that there was no substantial and competent evidence to support special finding 2. Candelaria v. Miera, 13 N. M. 360.

Special finding No. 2 not supported by any substantial evidence, and was inconsistent with the general verdict; judgment should have been rendered for plaintiff. Code Civ. Pro., sec. 2993.

Payments as affecting the contract of sureties. Monroe,

et al., v. National Surety Co., 92 Pac. (Supreme Court of
Washington, 1907); Leghorn v. Nydell, 39 Wash. 17, 8
Pac. 833; Hand Mfg. Co. v. Marks, 59 Pac. 551; Com-
missioners v. Braham, 57 Fed. 179; Association v. Miller,
16 Nev. 327; Miller v. Stewart, 9 Wheat. 681; Evans v.
Graden, 28 S. W. 430; Martin v. Whites, et al., 106 S. W.
(Mo.) 610; Smith v. Molleson, 148 N. Y. 241; 42 N. E.
669; Fuller Co. v. Doyle, 87 Fed. 687; 27 Am. & Eng.
Encyc. Law 494-496 (2nd ed.); Brandt on Suretyship,
(3rd ed.) 445; Pickard v. Shantz, 70 Miss. 381; Taylor
v. Jeter, 23 Mo. 244; Watkins v. Pierce, 10 Mo. App. 595;
Brennan v. Clark, 29 Neb. 385; U. S. Fidelity Co. v.
Trustees, (Ky., 1907) 102 S. W. 325.

GEO. L. REESE, W. A. HAVENER, AND R. E. ROWELLS.
Clovis, N. M., for appellants.

Court did not err in overruling plaintiff's motion for
judgment notwithstanding the general verdict. 2 Encyc.
Pl. & Pr. 912 and cases cited: Kirk v. Salt Lake City, 32
Utah 143; 12 L. R. A. (N. S.) 1021 and note; 89 Pac.
458; Roswell v. Davenport, 14 N. M. 91; Walker v. R. R.
Co., 7 N. M. 282; 20 Am. & Eng. Encyc. of Law, 1035.

Where there is a conflict of evidence as to the facts the
verdict of the jury will not be disturbed on appeal. String-
fellow & Tannehil v. Petty, 14 N. M. 11, 89 Pac. 258;
Kitchen v. Schuster, 14 N. M. 164; Candelaria v. Miera,
13 N. M. 360; Sherman v. Hicks, 14 N. M. 439, 94 Pac.
959; Richardson v. Pierce, 14 N. M. 334, 93 Pac. 715;
Territory v. Neatherlin, 13 N. M. 491; Green v. Brown
and Manzanares, 11 N. M. 658; Cunningham v. Springer,
13 N. M. 259; 1 A. & E. Enc. L. 691, 723.

Failure to make payments as per contract alone not sufficient to relieve surety, not correct statement of law. Monroe v. National Surety Co., 92 Pac. 280; Leghorn v. Nydell, 80 Pac. 833; Philadelphia v. Fidelity and Deposit
Co., 231 Pa. St. 208; Ann. Cas. 1912B, 1085; First National Bank v. Fidelity & Dep. Co., 40 So. 415; 5 L. R. A.
(N. S.) 418; Utterson v. Elmire, (Mo.) 139 S. W. 9;

Lawhorn v. Toors, (Ark) 84 S. W. 636; O'Neal et al., v.
Kelley, (Ark) 47 S. W. 409.

Contract broken by making payments before due and
by owner taking charge of building. Bell v. Trimby,
(Tenn) 38 S. W. 100; Simonson v. Thori, (Minn) 31 N.
W. 861; Evans v. Graden, (Mo. Sup.) 28 S. W. 439; 32
Cyc. 73; County of Glenn v. Jones, et al., 146 Cal. 518;
2 Ann. Cas. 764, and note, also note in 8 Ann Cas. 241;
James Black Mas. & Con. Co. v. National Surety Co.,
(Wash.) 112 Pac. 517; Stillman v. Wickham, (Iowa) 76
N. W. 1008; Reese v. U. S., 9 Wall. 13; Taylor v. Jeter,
23 Mo. 244; Bragg v. Sham, 49 Cal. 131; Shelton v. Amer.
Surety Co., C. C. A. 94, 131 Fed. 210; Ludlow v. Simond,
(N. Y.) 2 Am. Dec. 291; Bachus v. Archer, 109 Mich.
666, 67 N. W. 913; Goto v. Warrington, (Fla.) 19 So.
883; Bell v. Paul, 35 Neb. 240, 52 N. W. 1110; Miller v.
Stewart, 9 Wheat. 681, Led. 190; Wehring, et al., v. Den-
ham, (Ore.) 71 Pac. 133; Kissing v. Allspaugh, (Cal.)
27 Pac. 655, 13 L. R. A. 418; Morgan Co. v. McRae,
(Kans.) 36 Pac. 717.

Contract altered; bondsmen released. Miller v. Stewart, 9 Wheat. 681.

Assignments of error too general for consideration.
Goode, et al., v. Colorado Invest. Co., (N. M.) 117 Pac.
856; Main v. Main, (Ariz.) 60 Pac. 888; DeMund Lumber Co. v. Stillwell, (Ariz) 68 Pac. 543; 2 Sutherland
Code Pleading and Practice, sec. 1909.

Reply brief of appellant.

Appellant sets up instructions of the court in his statement of facts. Territory v. County Commrs., 13 N. M. 89.

Overpayment of estimates. Monroe v. National Surety
Co., 92 Pac. 280; Leghorn v. Nydell, 80 Pac. 833; First
Natl. Bank v. Fidelity Co., 5 L. R. A. (N. S.) 418; Utterson v. Elmire, 139 S. W. 9; Lawhon v. Toors, 84 S. W.
636; Bell v. Trimby, 38 S. W. 100; Simonson v. Thori,
31 N. W. 861.

STATEMENT OF FACTS.

On April 30, 1909, B. L. Kitchell entered into a written contract with the appellant, to furnish all labor and

material, and build and construct for appellant a three-story, brick hotel in Clovis, for the sum of $12,350, according to certain plans and specifications attached to said contract, and made a part thereof. The contract provided, among other things, that the consideration for said building should be paid to said contractor "in lawful money of the United States, on certificates of the superintendents, payments to be made every thirty days on the estimate of the superintendent. From the estimated amount 20 per cent shall be retained until the completion of the entire work." It was further agreed in said contract that 20 per cent retained from every estimate should be held by the owner as security for the faithful completion of the work, and might be applied under the direction of the superintendent to the liquidation of any damages under the contract. On the same date, in conjunction with said contract, and supplementary thereto, the appellees as sureties for said contractor, executed to the appellant a bond in the sum of $5,000, which said bond, by reference, made the contract a part of the same, and contained the usual covenants and conditions found in building contract bonds.

This action was instituted in the District Court of Curry County to recover from the sureties on said bond, the sum of $3,804.83, with interest and attorney's fees. The appellant, in his complaint, alleged a breach of said contract and bond, in that the contractor had failed to pay for labor and material used in said building in the named amount, above the contract price, and that appellant had been compelled to pay out said sum in satisfaction of mechanic's liens filed against said building therefor. No service was had upon the contractor, B. L. Kitchell, he having left the state prior to the institution of the suit.

The sureties, to avoid liability on the bond, set up four affirmative defenses. First, changes and alterations made in the contract without the consent of the sureties. Second, a material alteration made in the contract as to the time of performance after the execution of the bond without the consent of the sureties. Third, a delay in the progress of the work upon the building upon the part of the plaintiff in installing steam heating apparatus. Fourth, a material change and alterationin the contract for the construction of said building in the manner of making payments as provided in said contract, and that the said appellant paid said contractor prematurely for his work upon said building, without retaining 20 per cent from each estimate, and without the furnishing of proper estimates, or without the knowledge or consent of the sureties. The appellant filed a reply denying the allegations in appellees' answer. Upon the issues made, the case was tried to a jury, and upon motion of the appellant, the court submitted to the jury special findings. Such scpecial findings and the answer thereto are as follows:

"1. Do you find that the change in the contract alleged by the defendants in their answer from four to five months was made prior to the execution of the bond sued upon here?

"We do.

"2. Do you find by the evidence that J. D. Lyons made payments on the construction of the Antlers Hotel building in excess of 80 per cent of the value of the work done and materials placed in the building and upon its premises?

"We do.

"3. Do you find from the evidence that the plaintiff expended $15,863.68 in payments under the contract to B. L. Kitchell and on his order and in payment of judgments and claims against said building?

"We do."

With such special findings the jury returned a verdict for the appellees. After the return of the verdict, the appellant filed a motion for judgment *non obstante veredicto*, and a motion for a new trial in the alternative, and the same having been overruled by the court, judgment for appellees was entered on the verdict, from which judgment this appeal is prosecuted.

OPINION OF THE COURT.

ROBERTS, C. J.—Appellant relies upon two propositions for a reversal of this cause, which may be stated as follows:

1.   That the trial court should have sustained his motion for judgment based upon special findings 1 and 3, for the reason there was no substantial and competent evidence to support special finding No. 2, on which the general verdict was based.

2.   Admitting that appellant in fact made payments in excess of 80 per cent of work done, and materials in the building or upon the premises, according to the estimates of the architects in charge, even then if there was no proof by appellees that the contractor never became entitled to the payments so made in excess, judgment should have been rendered by the trial court on the special findings in favor of appellant.

Discussing the two propositions in the reverse order: it may be stated as a general principle that any material alteration in the building contract will release non-consenting sureties upon a bond given to guarantee the faithful performance of the same.   And we think the courts, almost without exception, hold, that where a contract provides for the retention by the owner of a stated percentage of the estimate, or stated amount, at the time of each payment to the contractor, prior to completion of the building, and the owner fails to comply therewith, and pays the contractor in excess of the stipulated amount, without consent of the sureties, such over-payment is a breach **1** of the contract by the owner and the bond given to secure the same cannot be enforced against the sureties.   Salmon v. Morgan, et al., decided at the present term of this court; 2 Ann. Cac. 764, where all the authorities will be found collected.   See also case note to First National Bank of Montgomery v. Fidelity & Deposit Co., of Maryland, 5 L. R. A. (N. S.) 418.   Especially is this true in the case of a non-compensated surety.

Appellant insists, however, that admitting for the sake of argument there had been over-payments on some of the

estimates. the fact that he had in his hands upon completion of the building more than 20 per cent of the contract
price, appellees could not have been harmed by such over-
payments upon the estimates, and therefore would not be
discharged from liability. This contention, however, cannot be sustained, for a non-compensated surety derives no
benefit from his contract, and his object is generally to
befriend the principal. In such cases the consideration
moves to the principal, and of course he could be held
upon an implied contract, but the surety is only liable because he has agreed to become so; he is bound by his
agreement and nothing else. No implied liability exists
to charge him; he is under no normal obligation to pay the
debt of his principal. Being thus bound by his agreement
alone, and deriving no benefit from the transaction, he is
a favorite of the law and has a right to stand upon the
strict terms of his obligation. To charge him beyond its
terms, or to permit it to be altered without his consent,
would be not to enforce the contract made by him, but to
make another for him. Brandt Suretyship Guaranty, vol.
1, sec. 107. "And a discharge will be created by a departure from the terms of the contract respecting payments,
though no injury is shown." Welch v. Hubschmitt Co..
61 N. J. L. 57.

It will thus be seen that it is the deviation from the
terms of the contract that operates to release the surety,
and not the injury or damage done by such departure.
This being true, if the owner paid the contractor in excess of the payments stipulated for in the contract, it
would necessarily follow that the contract would become
null and void and unenforcible upon the departure
2   therefrom by the owner. The breach of the contract
would *ipso facto* nullify it, and from the time of its
breach it would be absolutely unenforcible against the
sureties, and no act on the part of the owner could revive
it. This being true, if the appellant paid the contractor
in excess of 80 per cent of the estimate as required by the
contract, the contract would, at the time of the over-payment ,become unenforcible against the sureties, and the

mere fact that the owner retained from subsequent estimates a sufficient amount to equalize the overpayment
so made, and held in his hands at the time of the completion of the contract the required amount, would be of no
avail to him.

By special finding No. 2, the jury found that the owner
made payments on the construction of the building in
excess of 80 per cent of the value of the work done and
materials placed in the building, and upon the premises.
Appellant contends that this finding, (and it is upon this
finding evidently that the general verdict was based) was
not supported by any substantial evidence.

It has been uniformly held in this jurisdiction that the
appellate court will not weigh the evidence and that
3 the verdict of a jury will not be disturbed on appeal
where it is supported by any substantial evidence.
Candelaria v. Miera, 13 N. M. 360. While the court will
not weigh the evidence, it will, of course, examine it to
ascertain whether or not the verdict of the jury is supported by substantial evidence. In this case all the business relative to the construction of the building in question was transacted by the appellant's son, whose authority and agency is admitted. On the trial of the case, appellant's son testified that no payment or payments had
been made to the contractor at any time in excess of 80
per cent of the estimate made by the superintendent, and
he was supported in this regard by the evidence given by
the superintendent. Opposed to this, the appellees gave
in evidence the testimony of one witness who was a sub-
contractor or workman on the building, to the effect
that some two or three months before the completion of
the building, Lyons, the agent in charge of work, admitted to him that the contractor had been paid in excess of
80 per cent authorized by the contract. The superintendent likewise admitted to another witness that payments
had been made in excess of the amount authorized by the
contract. The question, therefore, resolves itself into
whether or not the admission of a party to a suit, of a
material fact, which in and of itself is sufficient to defeat

or authorize a recovery, affords substantial evidence, sufficient to support a verdict based thereon, in the appellate court.

It may be stated in passing, that the jury might reasonably have regarded the evidence of the agent in charge of the building, as not altogether satisfactory, for the reason that he testified upon the stand that all payments made to the contractor had been made by means of checks drawn upon a bank, and yet he failed to produce and exhibit upon the trial any of the checks showing payment, but testified simply from a memorandum, without showing the loss or destruction of the checks. This evidence was admitted over objection, and of course was clearly erroneous, and would not carry the same weight with the jury that the paid checks would have done, had they been produced. It is not disputed but that the admission of the agent was properly admitted in evidence, and it has been held, apparently without conflict, that the effect of an admission, when proved, must be left to the jury and received according to its terms. 1 Ency. Ev. 615. And it has likewise been held that when a jury bases a verdict upon such an admission, and the trial judge approves the finding, the appellate court will not interfere with the trial court's discretion in refusing to grant a new trial. Burke v. Hill, 119 Ga. 38. See also Martin v. Farrell, 72 N. Y. S. 934; Stephens v. Vroman, 18 Barb. 250.

It is also stated in 1 A. & E. Ency. Law, 723, that, "Verbal admissions, deliberately made, may afford proof of the most satisfactory character."

This being true, it was the province of the jury to weigh the evidence in the case, and such admission or admis-
4 sions being competent evidence, it was the duty of the jury to give such evidence proper weight and credit, and the jury having determined that the admissions of the party were true, and the trial court refusing to disturb the findings of the jury, the appellate court will not set aside the verdict.

For the reasons stated, the judgment of the lower court will be affirmed, and it is so ordered.

State v. Byers & Buehl, 18 N. M. 92.

[No. 1508, July 8, 1913.]

THE STATE OF NEW MEXICO, Appellee, v. F. W. BYERS and C. A. BUEHL, Appellants.

SYLLABUS (BY THE COURT)

1. Sec. 24 of Chap. 124, S. L. 1905, as amended by sec. 1 of chap. 53, S. L. 1907, examined. Held: That the Board of County Commissioners, under the provisions of said section are required to divide their counties into three road districts, which shall be the same as the county commissioner districts of the county.

P. 100

2. The person subject to road tax must be notified to appear, at such time and place and with such tools as may be designated, to perform the work in lieu of road tax.

P. 101

3. The inhabitants of incorporated cities and towns are subject to the provisions of chapter 124, Session Laws of 1905, as amended by chapter 53, Laws of 1907, relative to labor upon public highways, or payment of road taxes in lieu of such labor.

P. 98

Appeal from the District Court of Bernalillo County; Herbert F. Raynolds, District Judge; reversed.

M. U. VIGIL, J. BENSON NEWELL, of Albuquerque, N. M., and FRANK W. CLANCY, Attorney General, Albuquerque, N. M., for appellants.

Inhabitants of incorporated cities and towns not required to perform labor upon the county roads. Laws 1905, chap. 124, amended by chap. 53, Laws 1907, secs. 2, 24, 25, 26, 27, 28, 31, 35, 40; C. L., sec. 2464, sec. 2411, sec. 2402, sub-div. 85; Powers v. Barney, 5 Blatch. 202 and 3; Sutherland Stat. Construction, sec. 537; C. L. 1907, sec. 660; ex parte Roberts, 11 S. W. 782; State v. Jones, 18 Tex. 874; Tavernier v. Hunt, 6 Heisk, (Tenn.) 599; Meyers v. Thacher, 8 N. E. 824; Elliott on Roads and Streets, sec. 543; Jones on Taxation by Assessment, sec. 22; Lowe v. Yolo Co. (Cal.) 96 Pac. 379; Haggett v. Hurley, 91 Me. 542, 41 L. R. A. 362; 37 Cyc. 755.

County must be divided into road districts as per statute. Tax must come clearly within the letter of the statute. 36 Cyc. 1189; Commonwealth v. Glover, 116 S. W. 769; August Bank v. Sanford, 103 Fed. 98; and cases cited.

Statute violates Constitution as to unequal taxation, and double taxation. Const., art. 8, sec. 1; Const., art. 8, sec. 2; 37 Cyc. 749, and cases cited under note 92; Hutchinson v. Ozark Land Co., (Ark.) 22 S. W. 173; County Commrs. v. Laurel, (Md.) 3 L. R. A. 528.

Road over-seer must notify all persons. 29 Cyc. 1119; and cases cited under note 57. Service must be personal.

H. S. CLANCY, Assistant Attorney General, Santa Fe, N. M., for appellee.

County Commissioners legally authorized to divide county into two road districts. Laws 1907, chap. 53, sec. 1, amending Laws 1905, chap. 124, sec. 24.

Residents of an incorporated city are not exempt from the payment of a road tax or the performance of labor in lieu thereof. C. L. 1897, sec. 1832; Laws 1901, chap. 40, sec. 23; 1 Elliott Roads and Streets, sec. 479; Creswell v. Montgomery, 13 Pa. Sup. Ct. 87; Pa. Coal Co. v. Kelly, 2 Kulp, (Pa.) 41; 37 Cyc. 332.

Payment of Road Tax and the requiring of persons to work on the highways is not double taxation. Const., art. VIII, secs. 1 and 2; I Elliott Roads and Streets, sec. 480 and cases cited; 37 Cyc. 755; State v. Wheeler, 53 S. E. 358.

STATEMENT OF THE FACTS.

This is an action brought by the State in the District Court of Bernalillo County against the appellants, to recover from each the sum of three ($3.00) dollars, as a road tax. Two causes of action are joined, the same in substance; the one against Buehl does not assert that the

notice required him to appear and work at any specified
time or place,—being merely a demand to pay the money.
No objection was raised to the joining of the two causes
of action.

Both defendants asserted the following defenses:—They
are not residents of road district No. 1, of the County of
Bernalillo, because the City of Albuquerque, where they
reside, is an incorporated city; that they are tax payers of
said city; that the city of Albuquerque has exclusive
charge of its streets and highways and is not subject to
the county highway authorities, and is not a part of road
district No. 1 of said county, and they are therefore not
subject to the jurisdiction of the road overseers of said
district.

Four grounds are assigned as the basis for the last contention, i. e.:

"First: Chapter 124 of the Laws of 1905 as amended
by chap. 53 of the laws of 1907 does not purport to include incorporated cities and towns having separate authorities in charge of their highways within the jurisdiction of the road overseers provided in said act nor their
inhabitants subject to perform labor at the demand of
such overseers but that on the contrary under the proper
construction only of the territory outside of incorporated
cities and towns.

"Second: Assuming that the act attempts to require
the inhabitants of incorporated cities and towns to perform work upon the county roads outside of their respective municipalities, though leaving them also subject to
labor upon the roads within their corporate limits, it is
inconsistent with sec. 1 of art. 8 of the Constitution, to
the effect that the rate of taxation shall be equal and uniform upon all subjects of taxation, and also inconsistent
with the provisions of section 2 of said article, that no
double taxation shall be permitted.

"Third: That in attempting to enforce the said tax
and collect the same the county commissioners of Bernalillo County have not complied with the requirements of
the statute in that instead of dividing the county into dis-

tricts, which should be the same as the county commissioner districts in the county, as required by section 24 as amended, they have attempted to divide the county into two districts, each of which includes a portion of each of the three commissioner districts in the county and then sought to compel the defendants to labor upon the roads in a section of the county on which they could not have been compelled to labor had the commissioners complied with the statute.

"The defendant Buehl presents the additional ground that he has never been given an option to perform the labor at any place or time but instead the suit is based merely on a direct demand that he pay the money provided by the statute in lieu of work and that even this notice was only served on him by mailing the same to him, while the statute makes no provision for other than personal service.

"To a joined answer of the defendants setting up the foregoing grounds of defense the plaintiff demurred and by pro forma order the District Court sustained their demurrer and the defendants electing to stand upon their answers as filed, and declining to plead over, the judgment being given for the plaintiff."

OPINION OF THE COURT.

HANNA, J.—The first point presented for our consideration by appellants' brief is that the statute does not give to the road overseers, appointed by the County Commissioners, authority to require inhabitants of cities and towns, within their respective counties, to perform labor upon the county roads. Sec. 2 of chap. 124 of the Session Laws of 1905 throws some light upon this question. The section is as follows:

"All public highways, except such as are owned and operated by private corporations, and highways within the corporate limits of any incorporated city or town, shall be maintained and kept in repair by the respective counties in which they are located."

At the time of the passage of the Act of 1905, quoted from, the supervision and control of public highways

within the limits of incorporated cities was governed by
sec. 2464, Comp. Laws of 1897, which we quote so far as
its provisions are applicable to the question under consideration.

"Sec. 2464. The city council shall have the care, supervision and control of all public highways, bridges,
streets, alleys, public squares and commons within the
city, and shall cause the same to be kept open and in repair and free from nuisances."

Sub-div. 85, of sec. 2402, Comp. Laws 1897, provides
that the city council shall have the power "to levy and collect annually from each able bodied male citizen of such
city or town, between the ages of twenty-one and sixty
years, a poll tax or require a certain amount of labor in
lieu thereof; Provided, such tax shall not exceed the sum
of one dollar per capita."

It is argued by appellants that the statutes contemplate separate systems for highway management, one for
incorporated cities and towns, and the other for the balance of the county, each with independent jurisdiction.

It is contended by the learned Attorney General that
section 1832 C. L. 1897, specially exempted an able-bodied
male person "residing within the limits of incorporated
towns and villages" from performing labor upon the public highways, or in lieu of such labor the payment of one
dollar a day for each day he was liable to labor upon the
roads. This section was repealed by section 23, chapter
40, Laws of 1901, which clearly indicates, taken in connection with the other statutes set out in appellants' brief,
the intention of the legislature to require the payment of
a road tax or the performance of labor upon the public
highways by every able bodied male citizen of New Mexico, irrespective of his place of residence.

Until the enactment of chapter 53 of the Session Laws
of 1907, it was clearly the purpose and intention of all the
legislation upon this subject to exempt persons residing
within the corporate limits of incorporated cities and
towns from labor, or road tax, in lieu thereof, upon public
highways. This intention of the legislature is shown not

only by sec. 1832, C. L. 1897, but also by sec. 26, chapter
124, S. L. 1905, which last mentioned section reads as
follows:

"Every able bodied man between the ages of twenty-one
and sixty years shall annually pay to the road overseer of
the district wherein he resides, a road tax of three dollars, or in lieu of such sum shall labor on the public roads
three days, whenever notified by the overseer as hereinafter provided, but the provisions of this act shall not apply to persons residing within the corporate limits of incorporated cities and towns."

We find, however, that sec. 26 was amended by sec. 3,
of chap. 53, Session Laws of 1907, which is as follows:

"Sec. 3. That section 26 of said act of the 36th Legislative Assembly of the Territory of New Mexico hereinbefore mentioned is hereby amended so as to read as follows:

"Sec. 26. Every able bodied man between the ages of
twenty-one and sixty years shall annually pay to the road
overseer of the district wherein he resides, a road tax of
three dollars, or in lieu of such sum shall labor on the
public roads three days, whenever notified by the road
overseer as hereinafter provided, and all moneys collected
and received by any road overseer appointed under the
provisions of this act shall be by him paid into the county
treasury to the credit of the road fund for the district
within which the said money was collected, and all moneys
paid out for work upon roads or for tools, supplies, materials or repairs, shall be paid by an order signed by the
road overseer upon the county treasurer to be paid out of
the funds set apart to the road district in which said road
overseer shall have been appointed. Any road overseer
who shall appropriate or convert to his own use any
money collected by him, or any property, tools, materials
or supplies belonging to any county, or used in any road
district provided for in this act, shall be deemed guilty of
embezzlement, and upon conviction thereof, shall be fined
not less than one hundred dollars ($100.00) nor more
than five hundred dollars ($500.00), and imprisoned in

the county jail not less than one month or more than six months."

It will be noted that the proviso of sec. 26, as it appeared in the act of 1905, has been omitted in the reenactment of section 26, as it appears in the act of 1907. Does this indicate an intention on the part of the legislature to make the act of 1905 as amended by the act of 1907, applicable to persons residing within the corporate limits of incorporated cities and towns? We are of the opinion that such was the intention of the legislature.

We are not unmindful of the fact that sec. 2 of chapter 124 of the laws of 1905 excepts highways, within the corporate limits of any incorporated city or town, from the public highways, to be maintained and kept in repair by the counties in the manner provided by said act. It may seem unreasonable that the legislature intended to tax the residents of incorporated cities and towns for the maintenance of county roads and at the same time provide that such cities and towns should depend upon their own resources to maintain the highways within their limits. We can only justify this apparent inconsistency upon the ground that the county roads are used by people of our cities and towns as well as by the country people, and that both should contribute to the maintenance of such roads. The city or town highways are more largely used by the inhabitants of such places and the burden of maintaining falls upon a larger number of people, and properly should be borne by those receiving almost all the benefit.

After careful consideration of the question, we are compelled to conclude that it was the intention of the
3 legislature in amending chapter 124 of the Session
Laws of 1095, by enacting chapter 53 of the laws of 1907, to make the inhabitants of incorporated cities and towns subject to the provisions of said act relative to labor upon public highways, or the payment of a road tax in lieu of such labor.

With respect to the contention of appellants that the liability to perform labor, or pay road tax within both a county road district and an incorporated city or town, would result in a double taxation, we have to say that the condition is analogous to that of a tax payer subject to general taxation for road purposes and at the same time called upon to perform labor or pay a road tax in lieu thereof. The question of double taxation in the latter case is disposed of in the following citation from 1 Elliott Roads and Streets, sec. 480, with which we fully agree:

"Requiring persons to work on highways, even where they are partly kept up by taxation, is not double taxation and statutes requiring such work are not unconstitutional. The theory is that requiring such labor is not taxation at all, but is the exaction of a public duty. The authorities are almost unanimous in upholding such statutes." See also 37 Cyc. 755.

The point is also made by appellants, under the second ground set forth in support of their contention, that an inequality in taxation results by virtue of the fact that the resident of an incorporated city or town must contribute to the maintenance of both city and country roads. On the theory that a public duty is to be enforced and that requiring such labor is not taxation, this question is also disposed of.

The third ground assigned is that in attempting to enforce the said road tax and collect the same the county commissioners of Bernalillo County have not complied with the requirements of the statute in that instead of dividing the county into districts, which should be the same as county commissioner districts in the county, they have divided the county into two districts, each of which includes a portion of each of the three commissioner districts in the county, and then sought to compel the defendants to labor upon the roads in a section of the county where they could not be compelled to perform labor had the county commissioners complied with the statute. We consider this objection well taken.

The statute referred to, sec. 1 of chap. 53, Session Laws of 1907, is as follows:

"Section 1.   That section 24 of chapter 124 of the laws

of the 36th Legislative Assembly of the Territory of New
Mexico, entitled, 'An act relating to public highways, approved March 16th, 1905,' be and the same hereby is
amended so as to read as follows:

'Sec. 24. The board of county commissioners shall divide their counties into not more than three road districts,
which said districts shall be the same as the county commissioner districts of the county. In each district so
formed there shall be appointed annually by the county
commissioners a road overseer of such district, who shall
hold his office for a period of one year, or until his successor is duly qualified, who shall file with the probate
clerk a sufficient bond, in the sum of not less than one
thousand $1000.00) dollars, to be approved by the board
of county commissioners, conditioned for the faithful performance of his duties as such road overseer and to secure
the payment of any money that he may receive under the
provisions of this act, and the delivery to his successor in
office of any tools or other property which he may have in
his possession at the expiration of his term of office."

Sec. 24, as thus amended. is clearly mandatory and requires that the board shall divide their counties into not
more than three road districts, which shall.be the same
as the county commissioner districts of the county.

1 By express provision of law (sec. 660 Comp. Laws of
1897) there must be three county commissioners districts. and to permit less than three road districts would
make nugatory the provision of this statute that the road
districts shall be the same as the county commissioner
districts.

There remains but one point for our consideration, i. e.,
that raised by the defendant Buehl that he was not given
an option to perform labor, at any place or time, but instead the notice served upon him was a demand for the
payment of the sum of three dollars as a road tax.

Sec. 27 of chap. 124, S. L. of 1905, provides that "the
road overseers shall notify all persons in their districts
subject to road tax between the first day of April and the
first day of September in each year, to appear at such

time and place and with such tools as he may designate, to perform the work in lieu of road tax."

Sec. 28, of the same act, provides as follows:

"Any person subject to road tax, who, after due notice has been given, refuses the same or to perform the work in lieu thereof, for a period of ten days after being so notified, according to the provisions of the preceding section, shall be considered delinquent, and it shall be the duty of the road overseer to immediately make a list of such delinquents in his district and every such delinquent shown on the said list shall be subject to the payment of such tax, which taxes shall be recovered in a separate action for each delinquent in any court of competent jurisdiction, and such penalty and taxes, or any part thereof, collected upon any such judgment shall be paid into the county treasury, to be paid out on such road where the tax was assessed and the delinquent lives, and the county treasurer shall keep a record of all such sums of money so coming into his hands."

From the foregoing it clearly appears that the person subject to road tax must be notified to appear, at such 2 time and place and with such tools as may be designated, to perform the work in lieu of road tax. The last assignment of error is, therefore, well taken.

For the reasons given the judgments of the District Court as to each defendant, are reversed, and the complaints dismissed with costs.

[No. 1549, July 31, 1913.]

FRANK L. WALRATH, Appellant, v. BOARD OF COUNTY COMMISSIONERS OF VALENCIA COUNTY, et als., Appellees.

SYLLABUS (BY THE COURT)

1. Where a county has contracted with a party to construct a court house and jail, and a tax payer seeks to enjoin the board of county commissioners from paying said

♣   ' Walrath v. Co. Com., 18 N. M. 101.

contractor for work and labor performed, and to be performed, under said contract, the contractor is an indispensable party to the suit, and where such contractor was not made a party, the court properly dismissed the petition.

P. 107

Appeal from the District Court of Valencia County; Merritt C. Mechem, District Judge; affirmed.

NEILL B. FIELD, Albuquerque, N. M., for appellant.

Act of 1909 is a local and specific law regulating county affairs. Laws of 1903, p. 134; laws 1905, p. 4; laws 1909, p. 38; 24 Stat. L. 170; ibid., sec. 7; 25 State. L. 336; Territory v. Gutierrez, 12 N. M. 272; Territory v. Beaven, 15 N. M. 361; laws 1909, p. 214; Edmunds v. Herbrandson, 14 L. R. A. 725; Henderson v. Koenig, 57 L. R. A. 659; State ex rel. Atty. Gen. v. Sayre, 4 A. & E. Ann. Cas. 656 and note 659; Harwood v. Wentworth, 162 U. S. 564.

Co. Commrs. could not, under general powers, use funds to build court house and jail. C. L. 1897, sec. 664, par. 1, 3 and 5; C. L. 1897, secs. 349-363; Session Laws 1897, chap. 42; laws 1899, p. 191; Raleigh, etc., R. R. Co. v. Reid, 13 Wal. 269; Walla Walla v. Walla Walla Water Co., 172 U. S. 22; Kepner v. U. S. 195 U. S. 125 .

Act of 1905 is inconsistent with Constitutional provisions and therefore not continued in force. Const., art. IX, sec. 9; sec. 10; art. XXI, sec. 3; art. XXII, sec. 4; sec. 12; Com. ex rel. Hamilton v. Select and Common Councils of Pittsburgh, 34 Pa. St. 311; Const., art. XXI, sec. 3; Laughlin v. County Commrs., 3 N. M. 420; Catron v. Co. Commrs., 5 N. M. 203; Crampton v. Zanriskie, 101 U. S. 601; Scipio v. Wright, 101 U. S. 665; Legal Tender Case, 110 U. S. 444; Comanche County v. Lewis, 133 U. S. 198.

H. M. DOUGHERTY, Socorro, and A. B. MCMILLEN, Albuquerque, N. M., for appellees.

Facts show over $30,000 in Court House fund and County Commrs. were proceeding lawfully. Territory v. Gutjerrez, 12 N. M. 254; Laramie County v. Albany County, et al., 92 U. S. 308; Cooley on Const., 2nd ed., 192; Windham v. Portland, 4 Mass. 389; 3 N. H. 534; Powers v. Commrs. of Wood County, 8 Ohio St. 290; Shelby County v. Railroad, 5 Bush 228; Olney v. Harvery, 50 Ill. 455; Mt. Pleasant v. Beckwith, 100 U. S. 514; Savings & Loan Association v. Alturas County, 65 Fed. 677; C. L. 1897, sec. 664, par. 1, 3 and 5.

Duty of the Court to sustain legislative action unless clearly satisfied of its invalidity. Cooley Const. Lim., 4th ed., p. 220; Baca v. Perez, 8 N. M. 187.

Duty of Court to deny relief because Campbell Bros. not made parties. Minnesota v. Northern Security Co., 184 U. S. 235.

Co. Commrs. could use fund. Session laws 1905 and 1907.

OPINION OF THE COURT.

ROBERTS, C. J.—This is an action by Frank L. Walrath against the board of county commissioners of Valencia County, and the individual members of the board, to restrain them from carrying into execution a contract for the construction of a court house and jail at the county seat of said county. The pleadings show that a contract had been entered into between the board of county commissioners and Campbell Brothers, by which the latter were to construct and complete the court house and jail, in accordance with plans and specifications, and that the contractors had begun work under said contract and had expended large sums of money thereon for labor and material. Campbell Brothers, although within the jurisdiction of the court, were not made parties to the suit. The petition was filed to test the validity of an act of the legislative assembly of the Territory, approved March 8, 1909, and being chapter 19, S. L. 1909, whereby the legislature attempted to confer upon the County of Valencia authority to use the proceeds of bonds received by it from the County of Torrance, for the purpose of constructing a court house and jail. Appellees filed an answer to the merits, upon the 'incoming of which appellant filed a motion for judgment on the pleadings. His motion was over-ruled by the court, and he elected to stand upon the motion and demanded judgment upon the pleadings. The court found that the appellant was not entitled to the relief prayed for in his complaint and dismissed the same. From such judgment this appeal was taken. For a reversal of the judgment appellant relies upon four propositions, viz:

"1. That the act in question is a local and special law in contravention of the Act of Congress commonly called the Springer Act.

"2. That the legislature havaing prescribed a method by w hich the funds for the erection of court house and pail might be raised in any county, that method is exculsive.

"3. That the act is inconsistent with certain provisions of the State Constitution, and was not continued in force by the schedule of that instrument.

"4. That the contract in question created an indebtedness of the County of Valencia which, together with the existing indebtedness of the County, exceeded four per centum upon the assessed valuation of the taxable property of the County, in violation of the restrictions of the so-called Springer Act."

But whatever may be the views of the court on the questions stated, if the court below rightfully refused the injunction, we can do nothing more than affirm the decision.

Appellees argue that the contractors, Campbell Brothers, were necessary and indispensable parties to the suit, and, if this be true, then this court would be warranted in assuming that the judgment of the trial court dismissing the complaint was rendered because no other judgment could have been rendered in the absence of a necessary and indispensable party to the suit. Jeffries-Basom v. Nation, 63 Kansas 247.

The question then to be determined is whether the contractors were necessary and indispensable parties to the suit. The rule is stated as follows, in Story's Equity Pleadings, sec. 72—

"It is the constant aim of Courts of Equity to do complete justice, by deciding upon and settling the rights of all persons interested in the subject matter of the suit, so that the performance of the decree of the court may be perfectly safe to those who are compelled to obey it, and also, that future litigation may be prevented. Hence, the common expression, that Courts of Equity delight to do justice and not by halves. And hence, also, it is a general rule in Equity, that all persons materially interested, either legally or beneficially, in the subject matter of the suit, are to be made parties to it, either as plaintiffs or defendants, however numerous they may be, so that there may be a complete decree, which shall bind them all. By this means the court is enabled to make a complete decree between the parties, to prevent future litigation by taking away the necessity of a multiplicity of suits, and to make it perfectly certain, that no injustice is done, either to the parties before it, or to others who are interested in the subject matter."

It must be apparent that Campbell Brothers, the contractors, were interested in the subject matter of the present action, for, had appellant succeeded the board of county commissioners would have been perpetually enjoined from paying them for the construction of the court house and jail. Their rights to receive compensation, under the contract, would have been determined, in a proceeding to which they were not a party. It is true they would not be bound by the judgment, and could have relitigated the very questions before the court in this case, but that fact is, under the rule stated by Story, but an additional argument in support of the necessity of making them parties to the suit. It would, indeed, present an anomalous situation, should the appellant have prevailed in the present case, and the judgment have become final, and thereafter the contractors had instituted suit and recovered against the county, and, by mandamus should attempt to force the commissioners to pay the contract price, in face of the restraining order. The very statement shows the necessity of making the contractors parties to the suit.

"One of the most essential prerequisites for a final injunction is that all persons interested in the subject matter and result should be made parties. (See Wiser v. Blackly, 1 John Ch. R. 438) Chancellor Kent observed: 'You must have before the court all whose interests the decree may touch, because they are concerned to resist the demand, prevent the fund from being exhausted by collusion.' The rule is so obviously proper that it needs no comment, nor to be supported by authority." State of Kansas v. Anderson, 5 Kansas 90.

The case cited supra was a suit to enjoin the treasurer of state from paying over the proceeds of the sale of 500,-000 acres of land granted to several railroad companies by the act of 1866, and it was there held that the railroad companies were proper and necessary parties.

In the case of Van Husan v. Heames, 96 Mich. 509, it was held that the contractor was a necessary party to a bill filed by tax payers against the president, clerk, treasurer and trustees of a village, to restrain the payment of moneys under a contract entered into by the village council for furnishing a water supply.

In the case of King v. Commissioners Court, 10 Texas Civil App. R. 114, it was held that where a county has contracted with a bridge company to issue and deliver county bonds and warrants in payment for a public bridge, and tax payers seek to enjoin the issue of the bonds, the bridge company is a necessary party to the action.

For cases of similar import, see Hutchinson v. Burr, 12 Cal. 103; Butcher v. City of Camden, 29 N. J. Eq. 478; Graham v. City of Minneapolis, 40 Minn. 436; Lussen v Sanitary District, 192 Ill. 404; Benson v. Mayor, etc., of Albany, 24 Barb. 248; City of Anthony v. State, 49 Kansas 246; Privet v. Stevens, 26 Kansas 528; Shields v. Barrow, 17 How. 130; Consolidated Water Co. v. Babcock, 76 Fed. 243; Consolidated Water Co. v. City of San Diego, 84 Fed. 369; Kircher v. Pederson, 117 Wis. 68.

In the last cited case the Court say: "Indispensable

parties, it was said, are those persons having a property interest in the controversy that will be directly affected by the decree or the enforcement thereof."

From a review of the authorities it will be seen that the contractors were indispensable parties to this action, and it is well settled, by the adjudicated cases that the Court will take notice of the absence of indispensable parties,

1 when such fact is made to appear, though not raised by the pleading or suggested by counsel, and will dismiss the plaintiff's bill, when to grant the relief prayed would injuriously affect persons materially interested in the subject matter and not made parties. Minnesota v. Northern Security Co., 184 U. S. 235; King v. Commissioners Court, supra.

It follows that the judgment must be affirmed, and it is so ordered.

[No. 1501, July 25, 1913.]

PAUBLITA CANDELARIA, et al., appellees, v. EPIMENIO A. MIERA, appellant.

SYLLABUS (BY THE COURT)

1. A defendant may not as a matter of right introduce a new cause of action by way of counter claim by means of a trial amendment.

P. 115

2. A testamentary trustee, where he is negligent or unfaithful, is responsible for the amount the property coming into his hands ought to have yielded.

P. 117

3. Where the report of an executor is so imperfect, partial and misleading as to amount to a fraud in law, items in said report may be re-examined by a court of equity notwithstanding the prior approval of the Probate Court.

P. 118

4. Monies received from the sales of possessory rights to

real estate, even if said sales were void, must be accounted
for by the Executor.

P. 119

Appeal from the District Court of Sandoval County;
Herbert F. Raynolds, District Judge; affirmed.

A. A. SEDILLO, Albuquerque, N. M., for appellant.

Court erred in excluding evidence in support of items of
counter-claim.   Amendment C. L. 1897, sec. 2685, sub-
secs. 85 and 94; Perea v. Gallegos, 5 N. M. 110; Brown
v. Gise, 14 N. M. 282; Friday v. Railway, 16 N. M. 437
and 438.

Former adjudications are not *res judicata* as to items
of counter-claim.   1 Van Fleet's Former Adjudications,
sec. 1, p. 2; 2 Black on Judgment, sec. 611; 1 Van Fleet's
Former Adjudication, sec. 2, p. 27; Belden v. State, 103
N. Y. 1, 8 N. E. 363; Lindauer v. Mercantile Co. v. Boyd,
11 N. M. 475; 21 Am. & Eng. Enc. L. (1st ed.) 227; 2
Bouv. L. Dic. 551; 37 Cyc. 342; 2 Black on Judgments,
sec. 610; Trammell v. Thorman, 17 Ark. 203; 10 Enc. of
U. S. Rep. 736; Kennedy v. Scovial, 14 Conn. 61; Eaton
& H. R. Co. v. Hunt, 20 Ind. 557; Garrot v. Johnson, 35
Am. Dec. 272, (Md.); Taylor v. Dustin, 43 N. H. 493;
Richmond v. Hayes, 3 N. J. L. (2 Penning) 84; Maybee
v. Avery, 18 Johns. 352; Same Party v. Dickerson, 85 N.
Y. 435, 39 Am. Rep. 663; Horton v. Hamilton, 20 Tex.
606; King v. Chase, 15 N. E. 9, 41 Am. Dec. 675; Metcalf v. Gillmore, 60 N. H. 174; Oglesby v. Attrill, 20 Fed.
570; Faires v. McClellan, 24 S. W. 365; Aiken v. Peak,
22 Vt. 255; Fishburne v. Engledove, 91 Va. 548, 22 S. E.
354; Hunt v. Collins, 4 Ia. (4 Coles) 56; Henry v. Davis,
13 W. V. 230; Duncan v. Holcomb, 26 Ind. 278; Height
v. City of Keokuk, 4 Iowa 199; Ferra v. Chavot, 63 Cal.
564; Van Camp v. Fowler, 133 N. Y. 600, 30 N. E. 1147;
In re Wright, 6 N. Y. Sup. 773; Crandall v. Gallup, 12
Conn. 365; In re Wilcox, 11 C. C. Rep. 115; Clark v.
Blair, 14 Fed. 812; Untereiner v. Shapard, 23 So. 219, 52

La. An. 1809; Parks v. Libby, 37 Atl. 357; Jackson v. Thompson, 64 Atl. 421, 215 Pa. St. 209; Selbie v. Graham, 100 N. W. 65, 18 S. D. 365; American Cotton Co. v. Heierman & Co., 83 S. W. 845, 37 Tex. App. 312; Hubbard Mill Co. v. Roche, 113 Ill. App. 602; Prall v. Prall, 50 So. 867, 58 Fla. 496; McKinnison v. Johnson, 52 So. 88; Kean v. Pittsburg Lead Min. Co., 105 Pac. 60, 17 Idaho 179; LeRoy v. Collins, 130 N. W. 635; Smith v. Town of Ontario, 4 Fed. 386; 23 Cyc. 1204 and cases cited; 2 Black on Judgments (2nd ed.) sec. 617 and cases cited; 23 Cyc. 1523 and cases cited; Ortiz v. Bank, 12 N. M. 519; McLean v. Baldwin, 69 Pac. 259 (Cal.); Boston & C. Smelting Co. v. Reed, (Col.) 48 Pac. 515; Sumner v. Sumner, (Ga.) 48 S. E. 727; Henderson v. Scott, 37 Hun. 412; Willis v. McKinnon, 70 N. E. 962; Interstate National Bank v. Clayton, (Tex.) 77 S. W. 44, 65 L. R. A. 820; Evans v. Woodsworth, (Ill.) 72 N. E. 1082.

Counterclaim. 18 Cyc. 563 and cases cited; Peter v. Beverly, 10 Pet. 466, 9 L. 522; Cheever v. Ellis, (Mich.) 108, N. W. 392; Roberts v. Bartlett, 26 Mo. App. 316; Martin v. Foster, 38 Ala. 688; Woods v. Ridley, 27 Mass. (5 Cush.) 119; Doty v. Cox, (Ky.) 22 S. W. 321; Clayton v. Somers, 277 N. Y. Eq. (12 C. E. Green) 230; McKenehan v. Crawford's Exec., 29 Pa. St. 390; Hill v. Buford, 9 Mo. 886; Milan v. Ragland, 19 Ala. 85; Roberts v. Bartlett, 26 Mo. App. 611; Livingston v. Newkirk, 3 Johns. Ch. 312; Appeal of Kost, 107 Pa. St. 143; Manson v. Duncanson, 166 U. S. 533; 41 L. 1105; Swift v. Harley, (Ind.) 49 N. E. 1069; In re Woolsey's Est., (N. J.) 59 Atl. 463; In re Meagley's Est., 56 N. Y. Sup. 503; Reed v. Franklin, 60 S. W. 215; In re Gill, 92 N. E. 390; Coldill v. Succession of McCullough, 20 Ann. (La.) 174; Birkholm v. Barrett, 4 Paige 148; Hart v. Bryan, 17 N. C. (Dev. Eq.) 147; Hall v. Griffith, 2 Har. & J. 143; Hearrin v. Savage, 16 Ala. 286; Billingsley v. Hendrie, 20 Md. 282.

Statute of limitations must be specially pleaded. C. L. 1897, sec. 2685, sub-sec. 66; Phillips Code Pleading ,secs. 336-337; Pomeroy Code Remedies, secs. 589-590; Laguna v. Acoma, 1 N. M. 220; 25 Cyc. 1401 and cases cited.

Rights and claims are purely equitable. Roberts v. Bartlett, 26 Mo. App. 615; Harwood v. Harper, 54 Ala. 659; Knight v. Godbolt, 7 Ala. 304; Payne v. Pusey, (Ky.) 8 Bush 564; 18 Cyc. 917; Semmes v. Magruder, 10 Md. (Ch.) 456; Brown v. Stewart, 4 Md. Ch. 368; State v. Reigart, 1 Gill (Md.) 1 ,39 Am. Dec. 628; Moore v. Bryant, (Tex.) 31, S. W. 22; Harwood v. Harper, 54 Ala, 659; Baker v. Bush, 25 Ga. 571, 71 Am. Dec. 193; Huston v. Becker, 47 Pac. 10, 15 Wash. 586.

Executor is entitled to his expenses and attorneys fees and costs sustained in any litigation. C. L. 1897, sec. 2001; Laws 1901, c. 81, secs. 32 and 34; 18 Cyc. 265, 273, 564 and 566 (D) and cases cited.

Same rule applies to a trustee. 39 Cyc. 340, 478, and 480 and cases cited; 18 Cyc. 353; 39 Cyc. 430 and cases cited; 40 Cyc. 1807 and 1809 and cases cited; 40 Cyc. 2061 and cases cited.

Real and personal estate of decedent subject to payment of debts. Laws 1907, ch. 107; C. L. 1897, sec. 2065; 18 Cyc. 182 and cases cited; 40 Cyc. 2069 and 2070 and cases cited.

Legatee entitled to nothing until debts are paid. Leake v. Leake, 75 Va. 794; 1 Story Eq. Jur., sec. 90; Bermingham v. Forsythe, 26 S. C. 358; Lewis v. Overby's Adm'r., 31 Grat. (Va.) 601, 2 S. E. 286; Succession of Willis, 33 So. 643, 107 La. 139; Horner v. Hosbrouck, 41 Pa. (5 Wright) 169.

Appellant not liable for rentals of real estate of decedent as charged by the court. Patterson v. Gaines, 6 How. 600, 12 L. 553; C. L. 1897, secs. 1995, 1996, 1997; 10 Cyc. 180 and cases cited; C. L. 1897, secs. 1995 and 2065; Laws 1907, ch. 107, art. 17; 18 Cyc. 182, 303 and cases cited; 1 Woerner Am. Law of Admin., sec. 300; 21 Cyc. 145; 18 Cyc. 826; Wood v. Ridley, 27 Mass. (5 Cush.) 149; 2 Woerner Am. L. Admin., sec. 484; New Orleans v. Christmas, 131 U. S. 191, 33 L. 99; Burney's Heirs v. Ludeling, (La.) 17 So. 877; Green v. Biddle, 8 Wheat. 75, 5 L. 547; 24 Cyc. 1176; Laws 1907, ch. 107, sub-sec. 257; Moore v.

Meat Co., 16 N. M. 107; Neher v. Armijo, 11 N. M. 67; 18 Cyc. 1136.

Claims approved by the Probate Court can only be reviewed on appeal or impeached on the ground of fraud. C. L. 1897, secs. 929 and 2015; Laws 1901, ch. 81, sec. 40; Gutierrez v. Scholle, 12 N. M. 328; Gray v. Carroll, 101 Mo. App. 110, 74 S. W. 468; Nelson v. Barnett, 123 Mo. 564, 27 S. W. 520; Bell v. Altheimer, 138 S. W. 993; Patton v. Webb, 2 Me. 257; Merrill v. Harris, 57 Am. Dec. 359; 26 N. H. 142; Dickinson v. Hayes, 31 Conn. 417; Hill v. Berger, 10 How. Bac. 264; Churchill v. Cormer, 25 Va. 479; Seawell v. Buckly, 54 Ala. 592; App v. Dreisbach, 21 Am. Dec. 447; Tate v. Norton, 94 U. S. 746, 24 L. Ed. 222; Townsend v. Townsend, 60 Mo. 246; In re Bell's Est., 75 Pac. 679; In re Marshall Est., 50 Pac. 540; Barnett v. Vanmeter, 33 N. E. 666, 7 Ind. App. 45; State v. Gray, 106 Mo. 526, 17 S. W. 500; Starr v. Willoughby, 75 N. E. 1027; 2 L. R. A. (n s) 623; State v. Stuart, 74 Mo. App. 182; Floyd v. Newton, 134 S. W. 934; Young v. Byrd, 124 Mo. 590, 46 Am. St. 461; Sever v. Russell, 58 Mass. 7, 9 Am. Dec. 528.

Real Estate means lands, tenements and hereditaments. C. L. 1897, sec. 3940.

Possessory rights in real estate are not personalty. Probst v .Presbyterian Church, 125 U. S. 182, L. Ed. 642; Gildersleeve v. N. M. Min. Co., 6 N. M. 27; Solomon v. Yrisarri, 9 N. M. 480.

Statute of Frauds in force in New Mexico. Childers v. Talbott, 4 N. M. 336; Kingston v. Walton, 14 N. M. 368.

Property still remains in specie. Beall v. New Mexico, 16 Wall. 535, 21 L. Ed. 294; Chamberlain's Appeal, 41 L. R. A. 204.

Executor is entitled to expenses of administration. C. L. 1897, sec. 2001; Laws 1901, ch. 81, secs. 32 and 34; 18 Cyc. 265, 564 and 566.

SUMMERS BURKHART, Albuquerque, N. M., for appellees.

Facts therein found (paragraph 7 of decree) were Res

Judicata. Cromwell v. Sac County, 94 U. S. 331, 24 L. Ed. 197, 198.

Refusal of court to allow amendment rested in sound discretion of the court. C. L. 1897, sec. 2685, sub-secs. 81 and 82.

Rentals from real estate proper charges against appellant. C. L. 1897, secs. 2065-2094; Dingman v. Beal, 213 Ill. 238; C. L. 1897, secs. 1445-1446; 2 Perry on Trusts, secs. 527, 608, 609; .C. L. 1897, secs. 2052, 2053; Taylor v. Culbert, 138 Ind. 67; Delavan v. German Sav. Bank, 124 N. W. 350; Landis v. Scott, 32 Pa. St. 495; Owens v. Williams, 130 N. C. 165, 41 S. E. 93; C. L. 1897, secs. 3160-3178; Laws 1907, page 285.

Equity has jurisdiction to open final report of an executor for fraud, especially where plaintiffs are infants. Perea v. Barela, 5 N. M. 458, 468, et seq.; 2 Perry on Trusts. sec. 603.

Appellant properly charged for full value of goats. 2 Perry on Trusts, sec. 266.

Trustee must keep clear, accurate and distinct accounts. 2 Perry on Trusts, sec. 841; 39 Cyc. 464 and cases cited.

OPINION OF THE COURT.

PARKER, J.—This is a suit brought to open and vacate an account of the appellant as executor of the last will and testament of Paula Garcia de Mireles, the grandmother of the appellees, and for the taking of an account under the direction of the court of all the property and moneys coming into the hands of appellant as such executor, and as trustee under the will. The action resulted in the decree against appellant for $3444.43. It appears that long prior to the institution of this suit the appellees, by Emigran Candelaria, their guardian, each brought action against appellant for money had and received to and for their use, respectively, in the sum of $1125.00, and obtained judgment, which was paid and satisfied by appellant. The record in these cases, which is in evidence in this case, discloses that the said appellees are the grandchildren of one Dionicio Mireles and said Paula Garcia de Mireles, his wife; that said Dionicio departed this life, leaving a will which was duly probated and of which said Paula and another were duly appointed executors; that the father of appellees, as guardian, demanded of said executors their share of their grandfather's estate coming to them through their mother, and were about to bring suit when a compromise was effected, whereby it was agreed that $2500.00 was the amount of their share of the personal property of said estate; that an order was afterwards made by the probate court, authorizing the loaning of said money at not less than 4% per annum; that thereafter Paula, the widow of Dionicio and grandmother of the appellees, loaned the said $2500.00 to appellant, and afterwards died. Thereupon the two actions above mentioned were brought for this money so loaned, resulting in the two judgments before mentioned. In those cases the appellant admitted the receipt of $2500.00, and accounted for the same as follows:

That by the direction of said Paula he paid $250.00 to an attorney for his services in effecting the said settlement and obtaining the said $2500.00, and paid out the balance upon the debts of the deceased Dionicio, by direction of said Paula; that he did not borrow the money and did not receive it as the money of said appellees. The court found against him upon these facts and awarded judgment.

In the present case, after denying many of the allegations of the complaint, the appellant, by way of counter claim, attempted to bring forward and obtain credit for the amount he was compelled to pay on these judgments. The court disallowed the claim on the ground that this issue was settled by the adjudication in the two former actions. The court was clearly correct. The issue in the former actions was whether the appellant had received $2250.00 of the money of the appellees, and the court found that he had. And so in this case the issue tendered is whether he had so received said money, because, if he had, he was entitled to no credit in the settlement of his accounts with the estate of said Paula on account of such payment of said judgments, and if he had not so received said money he might be so entitled to such credit. In his original answer in this case by way of counter claim, the defendant alleged the receipt of $2250.00, and alleged that he had paid out the same and more, prior to the death of said Paula as hereinbefore stated, but he did not allege that he was entitled to credit for having so paid out the said money, and, on the contrary, alleged that he was entitled to credit on account of the amount paid in satisfaction of said judgments together with expenses and disbursements in defending said former actions. During the trial appellant offered an amendment to his answer as follows:

"And the defendant further answering plaintiff's complaint herein and by way of defense and counter claim, alleges:

"That on or about June 27th, 1899, Paula Garcia de Mireles deposited the sum of $2,250.00 for the purpose of paying certain debts of the estate of Dionicio Mireles, deceased, and to pay out and disburse subject to the order of the said Paula Garcia de Mireles, to-wit, January 23rd, 1901, the said money was expended and disbursed by the defendant as directed by the said Paula Garcia de Mireles as well as other divers sums of money and that at the time of her death the said Paula Garcia de Mireles was indebted to the defendant in the sum of $2300.00, which said sum is still due and unpaid to the defendant.

"2. That the said Paula Garcia de Mireles is indebted to the defendant for money, goods, wares and merchandise turned over, sold and delivered by the defendant to the said Paula Garcia de Mireles at her request from June 14th, (27th), 1899, to January 23rd, 1901, and of the reasonable value thereof, in the sum of $2300.00, which said sum is wholly due and unpaid.

"3. That the plaintiffs, Pablita Candelaria and Andres Candelaria, infants under the age of twenty-one years, are indebted to the defendant for money, goods, wares, and merchandise turned over, sold and delivered by the defendant to Paula Garcia de Mireles, deceased, from June

14th, (27th), 1899, to January 23rd, 1901, and of the reasonable value thereof, in the sum of $2300.00, which said sum is wholly due and unpaid."

It thus appears that appellant endeavored to introduce by his amended answer an entirely new and different issue into the case. Upon the trial he evidently sought to shift his position and to accept the results of the litigation in the two former actions and to assert a claim against the estate of the said Paula, and consequently against the appellees, for the sum of $2300.00, alleged by him to have been paid, laid out and expended for the said Paula at her request, as hereinbefore stated. The court refused to allow the amendment and appellant assigns error upon the action of the court. He argues, if we understand him, that appellant was entitled as a matter of right to make this trial amendment.

We do not so understand the law. We recently have had occasion to examine the question of trial amendments, and in Loretta Literary Society v. Garcia, just decided, we held the power of the court to permit such amendment was limited by sub-section 82 of sec. 2685, C. L. 1897, so as to prevent the introduction of a new cause of action. That the cause of action sought to be introduced by the amended answer by way of counter claim, was a new and different one from that originally pleaded would seem to be plain, and, in fact, it is so argued by counsel for appellant in support of his contention that the two former judgments did not adjudicate the issue therein tendered. So, even had the court permittted the amendment, it would have been erroneous under the circumstances. The conclusion renders it unnecessary to discuss the doctrine of *res adjudicata*, to which much space is devoted in the briefs, except in one particular. Counsel for appellant argue that the doctrine of *res adjudicata* is not available to appellees because the estoppel arising out of the former adjudications is not pleaded. In this he is mistaken. It is distinctly alleged in the complaint that the $2250.00 was received by appellant to the use of appellees and that appellees were compelled to bring the suit

1

to recover the same, and that they were successful. In support of this allegation the records in the former cases were introduced and, so far as disclosed, without objection. It is true the allegation in the complaint was not in form a plea of *res adjudicata,* but more designed to characterize the conduct of appellant as antagonistic to the rights of appellees. It is likewise true that the answer of appellant is in form a counter claim, but in fact it is, in this regard, more in the nature of a denial of the allegations of the complaint, and puts them squarely in issue. Appellees in their reply simply denied the allegations of the answer by way of counter claim. They do not in terms again plead the estoppel arising out of the former judgments; but all of the facts out of which the estoppel arises were set forth in the complaint. That the estoppel was not intended to be waived, sufficiently appears throughout the case. Under such circumstances it cannot be said that the estoppel of the former judgments was not pleaded. Besides no such question was presented to the trial ocurt, so far as we can see from the record.

It appears that appellant was nominated executor, guardian and administrator by the last will and testament of said Paula, qualified and took possession of the estate. Shortly thereafter he obtained an order from the probate court authorizing him to sell all of the real estate, which he proceeded to do, and realized therefrom $1040.00, in various sums. Some of the deeds were executed as guardian, some as executor, and some as both. The court below computed interest at 4% to the date of the decree and charged the appellant with that amount. This was evidently done upon the theory that under the terms of the will of Paula, appellant was to pay 4% on all of the moneys coming into his hands as executor and guardian. That these sales were void, both sides agree. Counsel for appellant argues that this fact leaves the real estate so sold still the property of appellees and that the money so received by appellant is not their money, and he is consequently not chargeable to them for any interest thereon. He further argues that if appellant is to be charged for rentals, as such, he is chargeable only for rentals actually received by him, and in this case he received none. On the other hand counsel for appellees argues in support of the judgment that inasmuch, under the will, appellant had no power to sell, but was charged with the duty of holding the property until the infants had attained their majority, he necessarily took charge of the real estate more as guardian of the infants than as executor, and, as such, it became his duty to rent the same for their benefit. At least, he argues, he was a trustee by the terms of the will and, as such, it was his duty to preserve the estate and to realize from it the reasonable rental value for the benefit of the infants.

In this position he is correct. Appellant was not only executor of the will, but was charged with the duty of preserving the estate as trustee. He had no duty as executor **2** in regard to the real estate, but as testamentary trustee his duty extended to the whole estate, including the real estate. Under such circumstances he is chargeable with the rental value of the real estate where, as appears, he neglected to rent it, but, on the other hand, he proceeded to sell it contrary to law. That a trustee is responsible for the amount the property ought to have yielded, when he is negligent or unfaithful, see,

39 Cyc. 323, 324, note 58; Taylor v. Calvert, 138 Ind. 67; Delavan v. Bank, 124 N. W. 350; Landis v. Scott, 32 Pa. St. 495; Owens v. Williams, 130 N. C. 165.

The fact that the charge was made against appellant upon what was possibly an erroneous theory will not avail him here, as the amount of the reasonable rental value of the real estate, according to all the evidence, is greatly in excess of the amount allowed by the court against him.

Appellant complains of the disallowance of two items of $75.00 and $40.20, respectively. The argument in support of the assignment of error is that these items were included in appellant's final report, and were approved by the probate court, and that, consequently, they can be reviewed only by appeal from that judgment. The court found appellant to have been grossly negligent in the exe-

cution of his trust; that his so-called final report in no respect complied with the requirements of law, and that appellees were entitled to have the same opened and the accounts surcharged; that he kept no account of the moneys or property received by him, and that appellees were entitled to an accounting of all of appellant's doings as executor and testamentary trustee. The court found that over $1000.00 worth of property had been received by appellant which had never been inventoried or accounted for, and, on the other hand, allowed him over $800.00 for disbursements which were not included in his final report. It is true that the court did not specifically find that the judgment of approval of his so-called final
3 report was obtained by fraud, but all of the circumstances would seem to show that his said report was so imperfect, partial and misleading as to amount to a fraud in law. Whether a judgment of approval of a final report of an executor by a probate court under circumstances different from those appearing from this record could be reviewed only by appeal, it is not necessary for us to decide. But under the circumstances shown here, the case falls clearly within the doctrine laid down in Perea v. Barela, 5 N. M. 458, 472, where it is said:

"The case presented by the bill and made out by the evidence involves a trust fraudulently executed, and necessitates a discovery and an accounting. The existence of these is all that is necessary to invoke the equitable jurisdiction of the court."

It appears that the decedent had a possessory right to two ranches known as the Salada and Narajo Ranches. Appellant disposed of or sold this right, as the court found, and realized $490.00 therefrom, for which he was charged. He executed no writing for the same but simply took the money of the transferee in the case, and a ranch in exchange for the other. We are unable to understand upon just what theory appellant objects to this charge. He suggests that the right was real estate, and that a verbal sale would be void under the statute of frauds, and that

the property still remains in specie. But, even so, he
4 has received the money and certainly must account for
the same. If at some future time the appellees seek to
contest the appellant's vendees this possessory right, they
may have to settle with such vendees concerning the purchase price paid for such right. That is a matter of no
concern of appellant.

All of the other errors assigned arise upon either the
disallowance of charges by appellant, or the charging
against him of items. In each case the evidence was
conflicting and the findings can not be disturbed by
this court. No questions of law are involved.

This disposes of all of the contentions of appellant and
for the reasons stated the decree of the court below will
be affirmed, and it is so ordered.

[No. 1531, July 25, 1913.]

J. R. DAUGHTRY, appellant, v. INTERNATIONAL BANK OF COMMERCE, appellee.

SYLLABUS (BY THE COURT)

1. Where a person, as soon as he learned of an unauthorized deposit of his funds in a bank, drew drafts on the same
in order to immediately withdraw them, he will not be held
to have ratified the deposit in the absence of proof of his assent to the deposit.

P. 126

2. When trust funds have been commingled with the general funds of a bank, before a trust upon such general funds
can be imposed, as against creditors of the bank, it must appear that the trust fund in some form still exists and came
into the hands of the receiver of the insolvent bank.

P. 127

Appeal from the District Court for the County of Quay;
Thomas D. Leib, District Judge; affirmed.

REID & HERVEY and TOMLINSON FORT, Roswell, N. M.,
for appellant.

Notice to bank of trust character of the fund. Estoppel.
Rich v. Bank, 7 Neb. 201; Thomas v. Bank, 58 N. W.
943; Merchants Natl. Bank v. McAnulty, (Tex. Civ. App.)
31 S. W. 1091; Porter v. Bank, 19 Vt. 410; Rock Springs
Bank v. Luman, 42 Pac. (Wyo.) 874; Central Bank v.
Levin, 6 Mo. App. 543; First Nat. Bank v. Peisert, 2
Penn. 277; First Nat. Bank v. Blake, 60 Fed. 78; Tilden
v. Barnard, 43 Mich. 376; LeDuc v. Moore, 111 N. C.
516; Black Hills Bank v. Kellogg, 4 S. Dak. 511, (38 Am.
Rep. 197); Clerks Bank v. Thomas, 2 Mo. App. 367;
Akers v. Bank, 63 Mo. App. 316; German Nat. Bank v.
Grinstead, 52 S. W. (Ky.) 951; First National Bank v.
Dunbar, 118 Ill. 625; Atlantic Cotton Mills v. Indian Or-
chard Mills, 147 Mass. 268; New Milford Bank v. New
Milford, 36 Conn. 93; Loring v. Bodie, 134 Mass. 453;
Holden v. Bank, 72 N. Y. 286.

Estoppel. 5 Cyc. 464, note 37, and cases cited.

Who is a depositor. State v. State Bank, 42 Neb. 890;
61 N. W. 252; York, et al., v. York Market Co., 37 Atl.
1038; Marine Bank v. Fulton Bank, 2 Wall. (U. S.) 256.

If deposit at all, was one to be specially applied. 5 Cyc.,
515; Morse on Banks and Banking, (4th ed.) sec. 567;
Star Cutter Co. v. Smith, 37 Ill. App. 212.

Bank insolvent when receiving a deposit. Craige v.
Hadley, 99 N. Y. 131; St. Louis Co. v. Johnson, 133 U.
S. 566; Whitcomb v. Carpenter, 134 Iowa, 11 N. W. 825;
10 L. R. A. (n. s.) 928.

Was Buchanan's act in depositing contrary to instructions subsequently ratified by Daughtry? McLeod v.
Evans, 66 Wis. 401; In re Johnson, 61 N. W. (Mich.)
352.

Can follow trust funds if they can be identified. 3
Pomeroy Eq. Jur. (3rd ed.) sec. 1048; Taylor v. Plummer, 3 M. & S. 575.

Even though mingled they can be followed if clearly
identified. Twohy Mercantile Co. v. Melbye, 78 Minn.
357; Union Nat. Bank v. Goetz, 138 Ill. 127; Wetherill v.
O'Brien, 140 Ill. 146; Bright v. King, 20 Ky. Law 186;
Robinson v. Woodward, 20 Ky. Law 1142; Culver v.

Cuyer, 118 Ala. 602; Slater v. Oriental Mills, 18 R. I. 352;
Ober & Sons v. Cochran, 118 Ga. 396; North Dak. Co. v.
Clark, 3 N. Dak. 30; Phila. Nat. Bank v. Dowd, 38 Fed.
172.

Trust funds mingled but are still in the mass. National Bank v. Insurance Co., 104 U. S. 54; Lincoln Sav.
Bank v. Morrison, (Neb.) 57 L. R. A. 885; Bohle v. Hassenbrock, 64 N. J. Eq. 334; Roca v. Byrbe, 145 N. Y. 182;
Winstandly v. Bank, 13 Ind. App. 544; Dunham v. Seglin, 39 Ore. 291; Holmes v. Gilman, 138 N. Y. 376; State
v. Foster, 5 Wyo. 199; Shields v. Thomas, 71 Miss. 260;
Ferchen v. Arndt, 26 Ore. 121.

Where trust funds went into the estate of insolvent and
swelled it. Lincoln Sav. Bank v. Morrison, 64 Neb. 822,
57 L. R. A. 885; Knatchball v. Hallett, 13 Ch. Div. 696;
Hazeltine v. McAfee, 5 Kans. App. 119; McClure v. La
Plata Co., 19 Colo. 122; Hopkins v. Burr, 25 Colo. 502;
Kansas State Bank v. First State Bank, 62 Kans. 788;
Cushman v. Goodwin, 95 Me. 353; Shields v. Thomas, 71
Miss. 260; Tierman's Exrs. v. B. & L. Assn., 152 Mo. 135;
Midland Nat. Bank v. Brightwell, 148 Mo. 358; Metropolitan Natl. Bank v. Campbell Co., 77 Fed. 705; In re Wolf,
99 Fed. 485.

Where sufficient funds come into receiver's hands to
satisfy trust debt and funds at no time since conversion
been less than trust debt. Continental Nat. Bank v.
Weems, 69 Tex. 489; Massey v. Fisher, 62 Fed. 958;
Noone County Bank v. Latimer, 67 Fed. 27; Onotok Silk
Co. v. Flanders, 87 Wis. 237; In re Wolf, 99 Fed. 485;
Cavin v. Gleason, 105 N. Y. 256; Wulbern v. Timmons,
55 S. C. 456; Knatchbull v. Hallett, 13 Ch. Div. 696.

If trust funds went to augment estate cestui trust has a
lien on the general assets of the estate. McLeod v. Evans,
66 Wis. 401; Peak v. Elliott, 30 Kans. 156; Myers v.
Board of Education, 51 Kans. 87; Harrison v. Smith, 83
Mo. 210; People v. City Bank, 96 N. Y. 32; Hubbard v.
Alamo Co., 53 Kans. 637; Ryan v. Phillips, 3 Kans. App.
704; Independent District v. King, 80 Iowa 497; Daven
port Plow Co. v. Lamp, 80 Iowa, 722; Boyer v. King. 80

Iowa, 498; Capital Nat. Bank v. Coldwater, 49 Neb. 786; State v. Midland Bank, 52 Neb. 1; Kimmell v. Dickson, 5 S. Dak. 221; Reeves v. Pierce, 64 Kans. 502; Midland Nat. Bank v. Brightwell, 148 Mo. 358.

EDWARD R. WRIGHT, Santa Fe, N. M., and HARRY H McELROY, Tucumcari, N. M., for appellees.

If the principal ratifies the transaction of agent, who is representing two adverse interests, with full knowledge of the facts, he is bound. 31 Cyc. 1572, B. note 92; 31 Cyc. 1248, (II).

Principal must have full knowledge of all material facts at time of ratification. 31 Cyc. 1253. Unless principal chooses to act without such knowledge. 31 Cyc. 1357 (III).

Ratification may be implied. 31 Cyc. 1263, c. note 3, 1264.

Ratification with knowledge binds principal. Truslow v. Bridge Co., 57 S. E. 51; British Am. Ass. Co v. Cooper, 46 Pac. 147; 31 Cyc. 1283, 4, note 38.

Attempt to enforce contract or take advantage of it, after knowledge of facts, is ratification. 31 Cyc. 1280, (IV). note 12; Jones v. Atkinson, 68 Ala. 167; Hatch v. Taylor, 10 N. H. 538; Medomak Bank v. Curtis, 24 Me. (11 Shep.) 36; Rosenthal v. Hasberg, 84 N. Y. Sup. 290; Bank v. Brewing Co., 33 N. E. 1054; Dabney v. Bank, 3 S. C. (3 Rich.) 124; Thompson v. Mfg. Co., 53 S. E. 908; 6 L. R. A. n. s. 311; Truslow v. Bridge Co., 57 S. E. 51; 31 Cyc. 1275 (III); State v. State Bank, 42 Neb. 896.

Relation of Debtor and Creditor created by deposit of fund in bank. Bank v. Brewing Co., 33 N. E. 1054; Dabney v. Bank, 3 S. C. 124; In re Madison Bank. Fed. Cas. No. 890; Mathews v. Creditors, 10 La. Ann. 314; Baker v. Kennedy, 53 Tex. 200.

A court of equity can only decree on a case made by the pleadings. Truslow v. Bridge Co., 57 S. E. 51; Welfley v. Shenandoah, etc., Co., 3 S. E. 376.

Sufficiency of pleadings and proof to establish the trust fund. Stevens v. Williams, 91 Wis. 58; 64 N. W. 422; and cases cited; Henry v. Martin, 88 Wis. 367; 60 N. W. 263 and cases cited; In re Irish Amer. Bank, 73 N. W. 6.

Burden is upon one seeking to fix trust. In re Irish Amer. Bank, 73 N. W. 6, 70 Minn. 238; Bank v. Bank, 15 Fed. 858.

Ill. Rule. Trust funds can be followed only when they can be distinguished from other property. Moniger v. Security T. & T. Co., 90 Ill. App. 246; Union Natl. Bank v. Goetz, 138 Ill. 127; Wetherill v. O'Brien, 140 Ill. 146; Bayor v. Amer. T. & Sav. Bank, 157 Ill. 62; Lauterman v. Traveous, 73 Ill. App. 670, affirmed in 174 Ill. 459.

Not recoverable unless they can be distinguished from other money. Whitecomb v. Jacob, 1 Salk 160; Taylor v. Plummer, 3 Maule & S. 574; Ex parte Dale, 2 Ch. Div. 772; Billingsley v. Pollock, 69 Miss, 759, 13 So. 828; Bank v. Davis, 115 N. C. 226, 20 S. E. 370; Lebanon Trust & Saf. Dep., etc., 166 Pa. St. 622, 31 Atl. 334; 2 Story Eq. Jur., sec. 1258, 1259; 2 Pom. Eq. Juris., sec. 1051, 1058.

Can be recovered, though mixed, if identical money of the trust fund is in the mixture. Bank v. Dowd, 38 Fed. 172; Met. Nat. Bank v. Campbell Com. Co., 77 Fed. 705 and cases cited; Bank v. Lattimer, 67 Fed. 27; Spokane Co. v. First Nat. Bank, 68 Fed. 979 and cases cited.

Or if there has always remained on hand a balance of the mixture equal to the amount of the trust fund which originally entered into the mixture. Cavin v. Gleason, 105 N. T. 256, 11 N. E. 504; Silk Co. v. Flanders, 87 Wis. 237, 58 N. W. 383; Bank v. Weems, 69 Tex. 489, 6 S. W. 802; Knatchbull v. Hallett, 13 Ch. Div. 696.

Cestui qui trust has a lien on the general assets of that estate. Harrison v. Smith, 83 Mo. 210; Peak v. Ellicott, 30 Kan. 156, 1 Pac. 499; People v. City Bank, 96 N. Y. 32; McLeod v. Evans, 66 Wis. 401, 28 N. W. 173, 214.

Bank collecting money for another holds the same as trustee for owner. Assoc. v. Morris, 36 Neb. 31, 53 N. W. 1037.

Trust funds can be followed by cestui que trust. Italian Fruit & Imp. v. Penniman, 61 Atl. 694, 100 Md. 698, 1 L. R. A. n. s. 252, and cases cited in note; Jones v. Chesebrough, 105 Ia. 303, 75 N. W. 97; Northern Dakota Elev. Co. v. Clark, 3 N. Dak. 26, 53 N. W. 175; State v. Bank of Commerce, 54 Neb. 725, 75 N. W. 28; Woodhouse v. Crandall, 197 Ill. 104, 64 N. E. 292; 58 L. R. A. 385; Board of Fire, etc., v. Wilkinson, 44 L. R. A. 493, (Mich.); Shute v. Hinman, 56 Pac. 412, 34 Ore. 578; affirmed 58 Pac. 882, 47 L. R. A. 265; Bruner v. First Nat. Bank, 34 L. R. A. 532, (Tenn.); Crawford Co. v. Strawn, 15 L. R. A. n. s. 1100; Sayles v. Cox, 32 L. R. A. (Tenn.), see case note; Boone County Nat. Bank v. Latimer, 67 Fed. 27.

When bank fails the cestui que trust must prove his claim as a general cerditor. Dowie v. Humphrey, 91 Wis. 98, 64 N. W. 315.

Equality is equity in distributing insolvent estates. Burnham v. Barth, 89 Wis. 367-370, 62 N. W. 69; Silk Co. v. Flanders, 87 Wis. 237, 58 N. W. 383; In re Plankington Bank. 87 Wis. 378, 58 N. W. 784; Henry v. Martin, 88 Wis. 367, 60 N. W. 263; Thuemmler v. Barth, 89 Wis. 381, 62 N. W. 94.

Bank, as agent, mixing trust funds with its own. In re Johnson, 103 Mich. 109, 61 N. W. 352, and cases cited; Enright v. Earling, 134 Wis. 565, 115 N. W. 128, 27 L. R. A. n. s. 243; York v. York Market Co., 37 Atl. 1038.

Court cannot presume anything which appellee has had no opportunity to deny. Truslow v. Bridge Co., 57 S. E. 51; Welfley v. Shenandoah I. L. M. & M. Co., 3 S. E. 376.

OPINION OF THE COURT.

PARKER, J.—It appears that appellant by means of a loan which he negotiated with an insurance company, obtained a draft for $5,000.00; that he authorized one W. F. Buchanan, the president of the defendant, bank, as an individual, to endorse said draft and to pay certain debts of appellant from the proceeds thereof, and instructed him to send appellant a draft for the balance of the money

available out of said loan, to Roswell, New Mexico: that
said Buchanan endorsed said draft and paid the said
debts of appellant leaving a balance due him of $1,352.40;
that, contrary to the instructions given, said Buchanan did
not send said funds to appellant but placed the same on
deposit with the defendant bank to the credit of appellant;
that appellant never intended to become a general depositor of said defendant bank and that said deposit was contrary to his instructions and without his authority and
against his wishes; that appellant was not advised as to
the exact amount of such balance, but as soon as he ascertained that said draft had been received and that said balance had been deposited with the defendant bank, he made
a draft against said bank for the sum of $1,000.00, and
as soon as he knew the exact amount on deposit he made
an additional draft for $350.00 on such bank in order to
acquire for himself all of the available money remaining
out of said loan; that before his said drafts were honored
the defendant bank went into liquidation; that thereupon
appellant filed a claim with the receiver of said insolvent
bank for the said amount and asking that a preference be
allowed of the same over the general creditors or depositors
of said bank; that said receiver disallowed said prefer-
ences, and that thereupon appellant appealed to the District Court for the County of Quay. The receiver interposed a demurrer to the petition of appellant which was
sustained by the District Court and the preference was rejected; thereupon appellant appealed to this court.

The demurrer interposed by the receiver and sustained
by the court raised, in various forms two propositions,
viz.:—(1) Assuming that said funds were deposited in
said bank by said Buchanan without the knowledge or
consent of appellant and that said bank had knowledge of
the special character of the funds, nevertheless appellant
by his petition shows that he ratified said deposit and became a creditor of the bank, and thereby losing his right
to preference over other general creditors. (2) The fund
sought to be charged is not shown by the allegations of
the petition to have come into the hands of the receiver.

The first proposition we do not find to be well founded. It is, of course, true that the ordinary general deposit of money in a bank passes the title of the money to the bank and creates the relation of debtor and creditor between the bank and the depositor. But such relation arises only when the transaction is the ordinary business transaction and when such consequences are contemplated by the parties. In the case at bar, however, appellant never consented, in the first instance, at .least, to the creation of any such relation. His expressed instructions were to remit the balance to him. Said Buchanan accepted the agency as president of the bank and the bank necessarily had knowledge of the character of the fund. Ratifica-
1   tion of the deposit as an ordinary deposit in a bank is
sought to be established by the fact that appellant drew drafts on the deposit as soon as he learned of the violation of his instructions. We can not so interpret the facts alleged. If appellant was shown to acquiesce in the deposit a different proposition would be presented. If he had so conducted himself as to show that he was willing to allow the funds to remain on deposit and to check them out as, in the ordinary course of his business, he might require them, then he might be held to have ratified the action of his agent. But as appears, he chose one of two ways open to him to immediately withdraw the funds. He might have demanded of the bank an immediate remittance of the funds, or, as he did do, he might draw drafts on the fund and thus withdraw the same immediately. It is his assent, or non-assent, to the deposit which controls, not his method of withdrawal. The method of withdrawal may often be evidence of the depositor's assent to the deposit, but in this case no assent is shown by the mere fact of drawing drafts for the entire amount of the fund immediately upon learning of the unauthorized deposit.

The more important question is involved in the second proposition. The bare fact appears from the petition that the funds were deposited in the bank under circumstances which would make the bank a trustee. No allegation is made that the funds ever came into the hands of the receiver. Counsel for appellees argue that the receiver's report of the resources of the insolvent bank, in which it appears that assets in cash and in credits in other banks largely in excess of the claim of appellant came into his hands, was not before the court, there being no reference to the same in the petition. But they rely upon this report to show that only $81.10 in cash came into his hands. Upon this fact they base one of the grounds of the demurrer to the petition to the effect that it appears that the fund had been dissipated prior to the insolvency of the bank, and that the trust, consequently, had failed. No basis for such ground of demurrer can be found outside of the receiver's report, and we conclude that the parties and the court must have treated the same, and the facts therein contained, as before the court for consideration in passing upon the demurrer and by way of supplement to the petition.

We have then a case of a deposit of money under such circumstances as to make it a trust fund, commingled with the general funds of the bank prior to insolvency, **2** and where it appears that there comes into the hands of the receiver of the insolvent bank moneys and credits largely in excess of the claim of the said *cestui que trust*. But appellant omits to allege the essential fact necessary to enforce the trust. It appears from the petition and receiver's report that only $81.10 in money came to the receiver. Consequently, all of the appellant's money, except that amount at least, had been in some way used by the bank. Whether any of appellant's money had been deposited in the other banks where credits are shown does not appear, either from the petition or report. For all that appears these credits may have arisen from the deposit of funds long prior to the receipt of appellant's money by the bank and may bear no relation whatever to the same. The presumption, therefore, much relied upon by appellant, to the effect that if the trustee used funds out of the mass in which those of the *cestui que trust* have been commingled, the funds so used will be held to be those of the trustee and not those of the *cestui que trust*, fails. If the trustee had always had on hand from the receipt of the trust fund to the date of insolvency a sufficient amount of the commingled mass to pay the *cestui que trust*, there is room for the operation of the presumption. But where the fund has been dissipated, as in this case, allegation and proof as to what has become of it are necessary in order to trace the same. This is clearly pointed out in,

Crawford Co. Commrs. v. Strawn, 15 L. R. A. (N. S.) 1100, where, in an opinion by Judge Lurton, it is said:

"The trust fund is not traced into any of the rediscounts or collections, which in part made up the credits in these banks. That the moneys remitted were not out of the trust fund is to be presumed; for the presumption upon which equity acts in respect of the character of the funds drawn out of the commingled mass of money in the bank's vaults is that the bank drew out only its money, leaving in its vault the money which it was obligated to retain and not use for any private purpose."

See also 38 Cyc. 539-540; Lowe v. Jones, 192 Mass. 91, 7 A. E. Ann. cases, 551 and note.

No general rule on the subject following trust funds had been announced in this jurisdiction and we are not at liberty to announce one in this case owing to the condition of the pleadings. All that we can decide in this case is that, taking the most advanced and liberal position sanctioned by any of the rules in the various states as a basis of determination in favor of the *cestui que trust* under the circumstances like those in this case, still the allegations of the petition, supplemented by the facts stated in the receiver's report, are insufficient to state a cause of action.

We assume that, as against the general creditors of an insolvent bank a trust can not be impressed upon the general assets of the insolvent unless the trust fund in some form still remains in the assets and comes to the receiver. In such cases it is a right of property and not compensation for its loss that is to be enforced. We likewise assume that the burden of tracing the fund is upon the person asserting the preference and that the allegation in some form must be made showing that the fund still exists in the hands of the receiver in order to permit proof of such facts. This has not been done in this case.

We regret that this case must go off upon a question of pleading and not be determined upon its merits. But until the facts are before us under proper pleadings it will be improper for us to lay down abstract rules of law upon the subject of the right to follow trust funds and when they have or have not been sufficiently traced and identified.

For the reasons stated the judgment of the lower court will be affirmed, and it is so ordered.

[No. 1575, July 25, 1913.]

GUY H. HERBERT, Tax Assessor, Appellant, v. BOARD OF COUNTY COMMISSIONERS OF CHAVES COUNTY, Appellee.

SYLLABUS (BY THE COURT)

1. The judgment of the district court is affirmed upon the authority of State v. Romero, 124 Pac. 649, and State v. Romero, 125 Pac. 617, decided by this court on March 23, 1912.

P. 131

Appeal from the District Court of Chaves County; John T. McClure, District Judge; affirmed.

W. A. DUNN and L. O. FULLEN, Roswell, N. M., for appellant.

All laws of the Territory in force at time of admission into the Union, not inconsistent with the Constitution, remain in force. Const., art. XXII, sec. 4; People v. County Commrs. of Grand Co., 6 Colo. 202; State v. Edwards, (Mont.) 111 Pac. 734; Ex parte Schriber, (Idaho(, 114 Pac. 29; Lace v. People, (Colo.) 95 Pac. 302; State v. Dircks, (Mo.) 111 S. W. 1; Cahoon v. Commonwealth, 20

Grat. (Va.) 733; Wright v. Woods, (Ky.) 27 S. W. 979;
State v .Third Judicial District Court, (Mont.) 37 Pac.
7; Commonwealth v .Collis, 10 Phils. 430; Wattson v.
Chester & D. R. R. Co., 83 Pa. St. 254; Sheppard v. Collis,
1 Wkly Notes Cas. 494; 8 Cyc. 759; Doddridge v. Sup'rs.
v. Stout, 9 W. Va. 703; Lewis v. Lackawanna County,
(Pa.) 50 Atl. 162.

Valid and regularly enacted statutes of the Territory
for the compensation of county officers not abrogated or
repealed by Const. Doherty v. Ransom County, (N. D.)
63 N. W. 148; Norman v. Cain, (Ky.) 31 S. W. 860; State
v. Burdick, (Wyo.) 33 Pac. 131; Groves v. Slaughter, 15
Pet. 448, 10 L. Ed. 800; People v. Co. Commrs., 6 Colo.
202; Const., art. X, sec. 1.

When no compensation is fixed by law, intention of law-
makers is that the officer shall receive a reasonable compensation. Bohart v. Anderson, (Okla.) 103 Pac. 742; Ripley v. Gifford, 11 Iowa 367; Lavin v. Board of Commrs.,
151 Ill. App. 236; judgment affirmed 92 N. E. 291: 2
Lewis' Sutherlands Stat. Const. (2nd ed.) sec. 642.

Sound public policy requires that the Constitution be
construed to give county officers compensation, unless terms
absolutely prohibit it. 8 Cyc. 733; Taylor v. Taylor, 10
Minn. 107; City of Baltimore v. State, 15 Md. 376; In re
Griffin, Fed. Cas. No. 5815, (Chase 364); Const., art. X,
sec. 1.

KENNETH K. SCOTT, TOMLINSON FORT, Roswell, N. M.,
for appellee.

Salaries and fees of county officers fixed. Const., art. 10,
sec. 1.

Provision is self-executing. State v. Romero, 124 Pac.
649, 17 N. M. 81.

Territorial laws remain in force. Const., Art. 13, sec. 4.

Officers allowed no compensation where no provision
made by law. 29 Cyc. 1422; Chance v. Marion County,
64 Ill. 66; State ex rel. Delgado v. Romero, 17 N. M. 81;
Const., art. 20, sec. 9.

OPINION OF THE COURT.

ROBERTS, C. J.—This action was instituted in the court below by appellant, who is the tax assessor of Chaves County, to recover compensation for his services from the County of Chaves, as such official. The case at bar presents no features that have not been already fully considered and decided by this court. In the case of State v. Romero, 124 Pac. 649, we held that,

"The compensation of a county officer, under the provisions of section 1 of article X of the Constitution, is dependent upon the enactment by the legislature of a salary law, and he can not recover for his services until such a law is passed, and then only as provided by such act."

See also, State v. Romero, 125 Pac. 617.

No law has been enacted, fixing the compensation of tax assessors, consequently under the rule announced, in the decided case, from which we see no reason to depart, it

1 follows that the judgment of the lower court, sustaining the demurrer to appellant's complaint and dismissing the action, was proper, and will be affirmed, and it is so ordered.

[No. 1576, July 25, 1913.]

STATE OF NEW MEXICO, ex rel., THOMAS P. DELGADO, Appellee, v. W. G. SARGENT, State Auditor, Appellant.

SYLLABUS (BY THE COURT)

1. Chap. 135, Laws of 1909, interpreted and held, that the appropriations carried by that Act were limited to the insurance monies mentioned in the title.

P. 135

2. Under sec. 21, of chap. 83, Laws of 1912, only the surplus monies in the Insurance fund, over and above the amounts required to meet the appropriations under chapter 135, Laws 1909, were diverted to the State Salary fund.

P. 136

3. The last paragraph of sec. 18, chapter 83, Laws 1912, held to be void as violative of section 16 of article IV of the Constitution, which prohibits general legislation in appropriation bills.

P. 138

Appeal from the District Court of Santa Fe County; Edmund C. Abbott, District Judge; affirmed.

FRANK W. CLANCY, Attorney General, Santa Fe, N. M., for appellant.

Did the legislature of 1912 put the money, specified in chapter 135, Laws 1909, beyond the control of the auditor and treasurer so far as the continuance of payments is concerned? Laws 1905, ch. 5; Laws 1909, ch. 135; Const., art. IV, sec. 30; Session Laws 1912, ch. 83.

WILSON, BOWMAN & DUNLAVY, Santa Fe, N. M., for appellee.

Construction of statutes. Laws 1912, ch. 83; Laws 1909, ch. 135; Laws 1905, ch. 6; Laws 1887, ch. 47; Laws 1899, ch. 91; Laws 1897, ch. 37; C. L. 1897, secs. 1762-1764a; Laws 1897, ch. 38.

Repeals by implication not favored in law. McAfee v. Southern R. R. Co., 36 Miss. 669; People v. Burtleson, 14 Utah 258, 47 Pac. 87; In re Booth's will, (Ore.) 66 Pac. 710.

Title of an act cannot be resorted to in aid of its construction where the act is free from doubt or ambiguity. Cornell v. Coyne, 192 U. S. 418, 48 S. Ed. 54; Pickering v. Arrick, 9 Mackey 169.

Legislating, not appropriating, receipts of Corporation Commission into General Appropriation bill violates Constitution. Const., art. IV, sec. 16; State v. Marron, 128 Pac. 485; In the matter of Appropriation Bill, 14 Fla. 283; Commonwealth v. Gregg, 161 Pa. 586, 29 Atl. 297;

State v. Cornell, 60 Neb. 276; In re House-bill No. 168,
(Colo.) 39 Pac. 1096.

Legislature intended that all charges and appropriations
be paid, before covering surplus of Insurance fund into
Salary fund.   Laws 1912, ch. 38, sec. 21; Peoples Fire
Ins. Co. v. Lewis Parker, Rec., 35 N. J. L. (6 Vroon)
575; Laws 1909, ch. 85; People ex rel. Swigert, 107 Ill.
494; State ex rel. Bailey v. Cook, 36 Pac. 177, (Mont.);
People v. Pacheco, 29 Cal. 210; People v. Needles, 96 Ill.
577; Trustee of Fund v. Roome, 93 N. Y. 313; Cutting v.
Taylor, 3 D. 11, 51 N. W. 949, 15 L. R. A. 691.

OPINION OF THE COURT.

PARKER, J.—This is an action brought by the State
on the relation of Thomas P. Delgado, as treasurer of the
fire department of the City of Santa Fe, against William
G. Sargent, Auditor of the State, to compel the payment
of the sum of $1200.00 to relator as such treasurer.   The
respondent answered the alternative writ and alleged as
cause for his refusal to issue his warrant for said sum,
that there were no funds available for the payment of
such warrant by reason of the fact that the legislature of
1912 had diverted the fund into the state salary fund.
The District Court awarded a peremptory writ and the
State Auditor appealed to this Court.

It appears that in 1897 the legislature provided that
there should be collected from all foreign insurance companies two per cent. of the amount of all premiums collected by them within any city, town or village in the
Territory, which said sum should be paid to the fire de-
paartments of the city, town or village in which said premiums were collected.   See chapter 38, laws of 1897, compiled as section 2132, C. L. 1897.

In 1905 the legislature created the Insurance department of the Territory, provided for a Superintendent of
Insurance, and provided that all insurance companies
should pay to the Superintendent of Insurance, two per
cent. upon the gross amount of premiums received during
each year.   This act provided that these monies should be

paid into the Territorial treasury for an insurance fund and provided that the Territorial treasurer should annually, on the first day of August of each year, pay to the treasurer of the fire department of every city, town or village in the Territory a sum of money equal to the amount received by such fire department under section 2132, C. L. 1897, during the year 1904.

See chapter 5, laws of 1905.

The law remained in this form until 1909, when the legislature enacted chapter 135 of the laws of 1909, which is entitled "An act for the disposition of certain insurance money." Section 1 of that act provides for the payment of $2000.00 per annum "from the amount of money collected from the insurance companies, as defined in the act known as chapter 5, Session Laws of 1905 ,of New Mexico," to "the New Mexico Association of Firemen." Section 2 of the act omitted special reference to the insurance fund created by the act of 1905, but made an annual and continuing appropriation of specific amounts to the various fire departments of the Territory, including Santa Fe. The law remained in this condition until the session of the state legislature in 1912, when, by chapter 83 of the laws of that session, the same being the General Appropriation Bill, the legislature passed two provisions which relate to the subject in hand. The first is the last paragraph of section 18 of that chapter, and is as follows:

"All receipts of the State Corporation Commission, including all receipts of the Insurance Department of the State, shall hereafter be covered into the State Salary fund."

Section 21 of that chapter provides:

"The State Auditor is hereby directed to transfer to the State Salary fund all surplus monies in the following funds, to-wit: Insurance Fund," and ten other funds therein mentioned.

In pursuance of these two provisions the Auditor transferred all of the funds in the Insurance fund to the State Salary fund and hence answered that there were no funds available upon which he could issue his warrant.

The first proposition involved is the construction of chapter 135 of the laws of 1909. It is argued by appellant that, taking into consideration the title of this act and its provisions, the legislative intent is made to appear to limit the appropriation to the various fire departments in the Territory to monies contained in the Insurance fund. Counsel for appellee argued that by reason of the terms of section 2 of that act, which makes no reference to the Insurance fund whatever, it necessarily appears that the legislative intent was to make a general appropriation out of any public funds not otherwise appropriated. He cites authority to the effect that the title of an act can not be resorted to in aid of its construction where the act is free from doubt or ambiguity.

About the general principle relied upon there can be no controversy. But in this case an ambiguity arises out of the divergence of the literal terms of section 2 of the act from the scope of the title. If the legislative intent to make a general appropriation to the fire departments out of any money in the treasury not otherwise appropriated, had been clearly expressed in terms, the appropriation would, no doubt, control, notwithstanding the limitation in the title. To construe section 2 of the act as a general appropriation would be to ignore the title of the act, but to construe the act as limited to the insurance money is to give due effect to all of its provisions, a result always to be sought when possible. That resort to the title in aid of its interpretation is competent under circumstances like the present. See, 2 Lewis' Suth. Stat. Construction, sec. 339; 36 Cyc. 1133; Holy Trinity Church v. United States, 143 U. S. 457.

Another consideration of importance is the history of the legislation in behalf of the volunteer fire departments. No general appropriations for their support have ever been made. Their support has always been derived from monies collected from the fire insurance companies, upon the theory, we assume, that the insurance companies derive most of the real benefit from the existence and maintenance of the fire departments, and that they should, consequently, assume the cost of their maintenance. So radical a departure from a former uniform practice as to make general appropriations for the purpose would certainly be clearly and unequivocally expressed, had the legislature so intended. We conclude that the appropriation was limited to the insurance monies.

From the above conclusion it follows that the argument of appellee that section 2 of the act of 1909 was a general appropriation out of any available fund, fails.

2   The question then arises as to whether the state legislature of 1912 has disposed of the Insurance fund so that it is no longer available to meet the appropriations of the act of 1909. It is to be observed that only *surplus* monies in the Insurance fund are to be transferred under section 21, to the Salary fund. That section undertakes to deal with funds already collected and in the treasury, and directs a single act of transfer of the funds. The solution of the question turns upon a proper interpretation of the word "surplus" as used in the act. It is to be remembered that these monies had been collected from the insurance companies for the express purpose of satisfying the annual appropriations made by the act of 1909 to the fire departments. Without such use of the monies no justification for the collection of the fund can be found. While it may be true that the legislature might divert the fund, its intention so to do, in view of the circumstances, can be expressed only in clear terms. Had the legislature intended to divert the entire fund it would seem that it would have employed the plain and simple language which would direct the Auditor to transfer all the monies in the fund to the Salary fund. If only surplus monies were to be diverted, then the legislature recognized that certain charges existed by law upon the fund. If legal charges upon the fund existed, then what charges? Certainly those charges fixed by law as much as any charges authorized to be made on the fund for expenses of administration or the like. We conclude, therefore, that the legislature did not divert the monies in the fund necessary to meet the appropriations existing against the same, and that the State Auditor was in error in transferring to the Salary fund the amount necessary to pay the appropriation to the fire departments.

Very little precedent is to be found directly in point. In State v. Board of Commissioners, 94 Pac. 1004, there was a constitutional prohibition against a collection of monies by taxation for one purpose, and expenditure of the same for any other purpose, and the legislature of Kansas had authorized the expenditure of any surplus funds for the erection or repairing of court houses or county office buildings. In that case the court had occasion to define a surplus, and in so doing adopted Bouvier's definition as follows:

"That which is left from a fund which has been appropriated for a particular purpose; the remainder of a thing; the over-plus, the residue."

It is true in that case the court was not called upon to decide the question presented in this case, but the principles which we have announced were recognized by the court. The same proposition is touched upon in McConnel v. Allen, 105 N. Y. Supp. 16, but the case is of no particular value owing to the difference in the facts.

The Auditor justified his refusal to issue the warrant upon both sections of the act of 1912, above quoted. That act was approved by the Governor, June 14, 1912. Between that date and August 1st, when the appropriation of the act of 1909 became effective, monies were authorized to be collected by the Insurance department, and, presumably, were collected. The Auditor transferred both the monies already collected and on hand at the date of the passage of the act of 1912, and also the monies thereafter collected by the Insurance department. It therefore becomes necessary to pass upon the constitutionality of the last paragraph of section 18 of the act of 1912. Counsel for appellee argue that this paragraph antagonizes section 16 of article IV, of the Constiution, which prohibits general legislation in appropriation bills. That the paragraph is general legislation of a permanent character seems to be clear. It provides for a certain disposition of

Devl. Co. v. Land Co., 18 N. M. 138.

monies collected by the Insurance department which disposition of the said monies is to continue indefinitely. It
bears some relation to the appropriations made in the act
out of the Salary fund, but it goes further and provides a
permanent policy thereafter to be pursued which can bear
no relation to the appropriations made in that act. Had
the paragraph limited the transfer of the funds to that
year and to meet the appropriations made in the act, a
different proposition would be presented. In such case the
paragraph might well be held to be germane to the appropriation act and allowable, under the doctrine announced
in State v. Marron, 128 Pac. 485. But the permanent
character of the provision takes it out of the doctrine of
the Marron case and clearly renders it violative of the
Constitution. We reach this conclusion with reluc-
3 tance, it being always desirable to give effect to the
acts of a co-ordinate branch of the government when
possible.

For the reasons stated the judgment of the lower court
will be affirmed, and it is so ordered.

[No. 1588, July 25, 1913.]

FARMERS' DEVELOPMENT COMPANY, Plaintiff in
Error, v. RAYADO LAND & IRRIGATION COM-
PANY, Defendant in Error.

SYLLABUS (BY THE COURT)

1. Under section 14, chapter 57, S. L. 1907, the giving of
a bond for costs, where no supersedeas bond is given, is essential to perfect an appeal or writ of error, and where a
plaintiff in error has failed to file a cost bond, within thirty
days from the time he sues out his writ of error, and advantage is taken of such default, by defendant in error, before
it is cured, the writ of error will be dismissed.

P. 140

2. The Constitution, sec. 3, art. VI, having conferred upon

Devl. Co. v. Land Co., 18 N. M. 138.

---

the Supreme Court the power to issue writs of error and providing for the issuance of the writ by "direction of the court or by any justice thereof," such writ can only be issued in the manner therein provided.

P. 141

3. Chapter 57, S. L. 1907, should be read, as if amended by section 3, art. VI, of the Constitution.

P. 142

Error to the District Court of Colfax County; Thomas D. Leib, District Judge; writ of error dismissed.

OPINION OF THE COURT.

ROBERTS, C. J.—This cause was in the court heretofore, on appeal, which was dismissed, because of defective and insufficient assignments of error. (See former opinion, vol. 18, p. 1.) After the dismissal of the appeal, this writ of error was issued by the clerk of the Court upon a praecipe therefor, filed in his office, in accordance with the provisions of section 3, chapter 57, S. L. 1907. Defendant in Error, seeks by motion, to have the writ of error dismissed upon the following grounds, viz:—

1. That there has been no cost bond filed by Plaintiff in Error.

2. That the writ of error was not granted by the Supreme Court or a justice thereof.

3. That the said cause, having been carried to the Supreme Court by appeal in Case No. 1528, and thereafter dismissed, it could not thereafter be taken up for review by writ of error.

The questions presented will be considered in the order stated.

1. The writ of error was sued out May 30, 1913. On July 3rd, thereafter, no cost bond had been filed, and defendant in error, because of such default, moved that the writ of error be dismissed. Section 14 of chapter 57, S. L. 1907, provides as follows:

"Cost bond to be given. Whenever an appeal is taken
to the Supreme Court or writ of error sued out, by any
other party, than an executor or administrator, the Territory or other municipal corporation, and no bond for
supersedeas is given as hereinafter provided, the appellant
or plaintiff in error, shall, within thirty days from the
time of taking such appeal or suing out such writ of error,
file with the District Court, in case of appeal, and with
the clerk of the Supreme Court, in cases of writs of error,
a bond with sufficient sureties qualified as in other cases,
to the effect that the appellant or plaintiff in error shall
pay all costs that may be adjudged against him on said
appeal or writ of error, said bonds to be approved by the
respective clerks, as supersedeas bonds are approved."

By the section quoted, it will be observed, that the giving of a bond for costs, where no supersedeas bond is
given, is essential to perfect an appeal or writ of error.

1   It is one of the essential steps required by the statute,
and the general rule is that "acts required by the statute to perfect an appeal are jurisdictional and must be
strictly complied with to vest the appellate court with
power to entertain the appeal." 1 Ency. Pl. & Pr. 966.
And the rule applies to appeal bonds. While some of the
courts hold that the failure to give a bond may be waived,
no question of waiver is involved in this case, as plaintiff
in error has never tendered or offered to file the required
bond. And it would appear, on principle, that the omission could not be cured by a later compliance with the
statute after a motion to dismiss for such failure had
been filed.

Covell v. Mosely, 15 Mich. 514; Perkins v. Cooper, 25
Pac. 411, (Cal.) ; 2 Cyc. 849 and cases cited; Tedrick v.
Wells, 38 N. E. 625, (Ill.)

Plaintiff in error, having failed to file a bond within the
time required by the statute, and such requirement not
having been waived by defendant in error, the motion to
dismiss, because of such failure, is well taken.

The second ground stated in the motion should be settled for the benefit of litigants, although not essential to a

disposition of this case. Sec. 3, chap. 57, S. L. 1907, provided:

"The clerk of the Supreme Court shall issue a writ of error to bring into the Supreme Court any cause adjudged or determined in any of the Districts Courts, as provided in section 1 of this act, upon a praecipe therefor, filed in his office by any of the parties to such cause, etc."

Plaintiff in error complied with this section. Section 3 of article VI of the Constitution of New Mexico confers appellate jurisdiction upon the Supreme Court and provides, among other things, as follows:

"It shall also have power to issue writs of mandamus, *error*, prohibition, habeas corpus, certiorari, injunction, and all other writs necessary or proper for the complete exercise of its jurisdiction, and to hear and determine, the same. Such writs may issue by direction of the court or by any justice thereof."

Defendant in error contends that this provision of the Constitution renders invalid and ineffectual the authority conferred upon the clerk of the Supreme Court to issue

2   such writs, by section 3, supra. In other words, the Constitution having declared that the Supreme Court shall have the power to issue a writ of error, its issuance by the clerk, or in any other manner is impliedly prohibited. This contention appears to be sound. Cooley's Constitutional Limitations, 7th ed., p. 99, states the rule as follows:

"When the Constitution defines the circumstances under which a right may be exercised or a penalty imposed, the specification is an implied prohibition against legislative interference to add to the condition, or to extend the penalty to other cases."

The Constitution, giving, as it does to the court, the power to issue writs of error and providing the manner of their issuance, viz: "By direction of the Court or any justice thereof," impliedly inhibits the legislature from providing for the issuance of the writ in any other manner. Included in the same category with the writ of error are the writs of mandamus, prohibition, habeas corpus, etc.

The Constitution having provided for the issuance of such writs by the Court, it would hardly be contended that the legislature could authorize their issuance by the clerk.

"The affirmation of a distinct policy upon any specific point in a State Constitution implies the negative of any power in the legislature to establish a different policy. 'Every positive direction contains an implication against anything contrary to it which would frustrate or disappoint the purpose of that provision. The frame of the government, the grant of legislative power, itself, the organization of the executive authority, the erection of the principal courts of justice, create implied limitations upon the law-making authority as strong as though a negative was expressed in each instance.' People v. Draper, 15 N. Y. 544. State v. Halleck, 14 Nev. 202, 33 Am. R. 559."

Likewise, it has been held, "Where a Constitution defines the qualification of an officer, it is not within the power of the legislature to change or superadd to it, unless the power be expressly or by necessary implication, given to it." Thomas v. Owens, 4 Md. 189; see also, Lowe v. Commonwealth, 3 Metcalfe 237.

The effect of this constitutional provision is to place writs of error upon the same basis as appeals. No appeal, under the statutes, may be taken without application to the District Court entering the judgment, and an order by that court allowing the appeal. The Constitution requires that application for a writ of error be made to the Supreme Court, and the writ issues only upon order of the court, or some justice thereof.

Section 4, art. 22, of the Constitution continues in force as the laws of the State, all laws of the Territory of New Mexico, in force at the time of the admission of the 3 State into the Union, not inconsistent with the Constitution. The effect of the constitutional provision, authorizing the issuance of writs of error by the Supreme Court, and providing for the manner of their issuance, is not to repeal all the provision of said chapter 57, S. L. 1907, relative to such writs, and the procedure for per-

fecting same, time of application, etc., but only nullifies
that portion of section 3, of said act, which authorizes the
clerk of the Supreme Court to issue such writ, and said act
must be read as if amended so as to provide for the issuance of said writ by the Supreme Court, or any justice
thereof, upon application to said Court therefor. Cleveland v. Spartanburg. 54 S. C. 83. In other words, the
statute law remains in force, as modified by the provisions
of the Constitution. State v. District Court, 37 Pac. 7
(Mont.)

The third question presented in the motion need not be
considered, as the year allowed for taking an appeal or
suing out a writ of error, has expired, and the judgment
of dismissal heretofore entered leaves the judgment of the
District Court in full force and effect.

For the reasons stated, the writ of error will be dismissed, and it is so ordered.

[No. 1571, July 30, 1913.]

STATE OF NEW MEXICO, Appellee, v. RICARDO
ALVA, Appellant.

SYLLABUS (BY THE COURT)

1. It is a general rule that an indictment for a statutory
offense is sufficient when it charges the offense as the statute defines it.

P. 146

2. Corroborative evidence, whether consisting of acts or
admissions, must at least be of such a character and quality
as tends to prove the guilt of the accused by connecting him
with the crime.

P. 147

3. As a general rule, where an act is prohibited and made
punishable by statute, the statute is to be construed in the
light of the common law, and the existence of a criminal intent is essential.

P. 151

4. The legislature may forbid the doing of an act and make its commission criminal without regard to the intent of the doer, and if such legislative intent appears, the courts must give it effect although the intention of the doer may have been innocent.

P. 151

5. In a criminal prosecution the State is not required to prove a motive for the crime, if without this the evidence is sufficient to show that the act was done by the accused.

P. 151

6. It matters not how two words are spelled, what their orthography is; they are idem sonans within the meaning of the books, if the attentive ear finds difficulty in distinguishing them when pronounced, or common and long continued usage has by corruption or abbreviation made them identical in pronunciation.

P. 150

7. Pronunciation and not spelling is the test in the application of the rule.

P. 150

8. If two names spelled differently necessarily sound alike, the court may, as a matter of law, pronounce them to be idem sonans, but if they do not necessarily sound alike, the question whether they are idem sonans is a question for the jury.

P. 150

9. Exceptions to instructions must be specific.

P. 152

Appeal from the District Court of Colfax County; . Thomas D. Leib, District Judge; affirmed.

J. Leahy, Raton, N. M., for appellant.

State v. Alva, 18 N. M. 143

Indictment defective in not containing the word "ravish." Bishop Crim. Pro. (4th ed.) sec. 335 and citations; Territory v. Cortez, 15 N. M. 92.

Proof necessary to establish guilt of defendant. People v. Howard, 76 Pac. 1116, (Cal.); State v. Dalton, 17 S. W. 700; State v. Donnington, 151 S. W. 975; State v. Grubb, 41 Pac. 951; People v. Seaman, 137 N. Y. Sup. 294; People v. Kline, N. Y. Sup. 296.

Alleged confession insufficient to support verdict. 12 Cyc. 483.

H. S. CLANCY, Assistant Attorney General, Santa Fe, N. M., for appellees.

On appeal court will not consider the correctness of the instructions given by the court of its own motion. Exceptions must be specific. Beall v. Territory, 1 N. M. 507.

Omission of the word "ravish" in the indictment does not render it defective. C. L. 1897, sec. 1090; People v. Flaherty, 29 N. Y. Sup. 642; 33 Cyc. 1444; People v. McDonald, 9 Mich. 150; State v. Smith, 61 N. C. 302; State v. Hayes, 95 N. W. 296; State v. Phelps, 60 Pac. 134.

Proof of sexual intercourse. People v. Howard, 76 Pac. 1116.

Idem Sonans. Pillsby v. Pillsbury, 9 Ohio, 171; Preyer and Prior, 61 Ala. 16; Puthuff and Biddulph, 9 Ohio, 120; Samuel and Lemuel, 5 Ohio, 358; Sedbetter and Ledbetter, 7 Ind. 659; Commonwealth v. Gill, 14 Gray 400; 20 A. & E. Enc. L. 313.

OPINION OF THE COURT.

HANNA, J.—The appellant was tried and convicted in the District Court of Colfax County for carnally knowing and abusing, and having sexual intercourse with one Refugia Senega Torres, she being a female under the age of fourteen years, and brings the case into this Court by appeal.

The first objection urged in this Court is directed

against the sufficiency of the indictment because the word *"ravish"* was not contained in the indictment.

It is contended by the counsel for appellant that our statute attempts to designate or set out what constitutes rape, but yet does not do so, and, therefore, the crime must be charged pursuant to the common law, and the absence of the word "ravish" renders the indictment fatally defective.

On the other hand, it is argued by the Attorney General that rape is not charged, but the statutory offense of sexual intercourse with a female under the age of fourteen years as defined in sec. 1090, C. L. 1897, the material words of the said statute being:

"That a person perpetrating rape upon or an act of sexual intercourse with a female, when the female is under the age of fourteen years, * * * * is punishable, etc."
and that the indictment herein follows the exact language of the statute in charging that the appellant "then and there did unlawfully and feloniously carnally know and abuse, and have sexual intercourse with" the girl Refugia, she "being then and there a female under the age of fourteen years." The contention of the Attorney General being that the words in the indictment "carnally know and abuse" are mere surplusage and that the crime charged and proven is that of sexual intercourse with a female under the age of fourteen years.

We agree with this contention of the Attorney General.

1 It is a general rule that an indictment for a statutory offense is sufficient when it charges the offense as the statute defines it. People v. Flaherty, 29 N. Y. Supp. 612; Bishop on Stat. Crimes, sec. 186; 33 Cyc. 1444.

Appellant in his brief lays greatest stress upon an alleged failure of proof as to sexual intercourse and sexual penetration.

While it is true that if certain questions, addressed to the child, with their answers are alone considered, there might be some doubt as to the sufficiency of proof in the respects pointed out, but when we examine the entire record for evidence pertaining to these questions there

can be no doubt as to the sufficiency of proof, both as to
sexual intercourse and sexual penetration. While it is
true she testified that she did not know what the word intercourse meant, yet the facts testified to by her could have
left no doubt, in the minds of the jurors, that an act of
sexual intercourse had taken place between herself and the
accused.

The Supreme Court of California in the case of People
v. Howard, 76 Pac. 1116, in construing a statute somewhat
similar to ours, said:

"That sexual penetration is necessary to constitute the
crime of rape. It is therefore clear that, to sustain the
charge, the prosecution must have proved sexual intercourse, which includes and means sexual penetration. * *
* * * In some cases the facts and circumstances are such
that penetration may be inferred therefrom."

We are of the opinion that the evidence in this case
leaves nothing to be inferred, but admitting that no direct
proof appears, the fact could readily, and properly, be
inferred from the evidence introduced. We do not deem
it necessary to set out this evidence in detail, but aside
from the testimony of the child, the evidence of the witness Dudley as to the admission of the accused, at the
time of his arrest, is convincing and leaves no doubt in
our minds as to the commission of the offense charged.
We are fully convinced that the evidence is sufficient to
prove all the essential elements of the crime charged.

It is further contended that the testimony of the child
was not corroborated. We cannot agree with this. The
witness Dudley certainly corroborated the testimony
2   of the child in all essential facts and fully conforms to
the rule that corroborative evidence, whether consisting of acts or admissions, must at least be of such a character and quality as tends to prove the guilt of the accused by connecting him with the crime.

Underhill on Criminal Evidence, section 74.

The appellant claims to have been prejudiced by several
rulings by the court upon the admission or rejection of
evidence. An examination of the record as to these mat-

ters discloses no ground · supporting such claims and it
will be useless to discuss these matters in detail. With respect to the admission of the evidence of Dudley concerning the confession of the accused and the objection that it
does not appear to have been voluntary, we have only to
say that no objection was raised by appellant upon this
ground at the trial and we cannot now entertain the objection.

Counsel for appellant contends that defendant was prejudiced by the ruling of the court in not permitting the
witness, Virginia Zúnega, to answer the following question:

"Q. Was the complaining witness ever called or
known by any other name except Refugia Zúnega?"

The witness had previously testified that the complaining witness was never called by any name except Refugia
Zúnega, but had not testified that she was not known by
any other name. If she was not called by any other name
she could hardly have been known by any other name and
no error was committed in excluding the answer to the
question referred to.

It is further urged by appellant that he was prejudiced
by the ruling of the court prohibiting the complaining
witness from writing or spelling her name for the purpose of showing a variance.

We cannot find that the defendant was prejudiced in
this respect, inasmuch as the record disclosed that the defense questioned most of the witnesses upon this subject
and the responses certainly covered the subject fully. The
prosecutrix testified that her name was Refugia Zúnega;
her half brother, Sostenes Zúnega, testified that her name
was Refugia Zúnega; the mother of prosecutrix, Virginia
Zúnega, testified that prosecutrix was baptized under the
name of Narcissa Torres, but called Refugia Zúnega Torres; this witness wrote out the name Refugia Zúnega, and
testified that the father of Refugia Zúnega was Porfirio
Torres, to whom she was never married. As is pointed
out later in this opinion, the spelling of the words does
not control the application of the rule of *idem sonans*. but

the question turns entirely upon the pronunciation of the words. The matter of the name being fully brought out, there could be nothing prejudicial in excluding the evidence here complained of. There is a point referred to by appellant in this connection, however, which raises a serious question, i. e., the alleged failure and refusal of the trial court to instruct on *idem sonans*. Appellant requested such an instruction, which the trial court doubtless refused to give upon the ground that he had fully covered the ground by his instruction No. 6, which is given in the following language, viz:

"The defendant has raised the question that there is a variation between the allegations of the indictment and the proof as to the name of the prosecuting witness. The court instructs the jury that such variance is not material unless it is of such character as to mislead the defendant or to hamper him in making his defense, or to expose him to the danger of being put twice in jeopardy for the same offense. Either the true name, or the name by which the prosecuting witness was commonly known will be sufficient if alleged in the indictment and supported by the proof. Whether the name in the indictment is sufficiently supported by the proof is for you to determine from the evidence introduced in this case in the same manner as you should determine any other material allegation of the indictment."

Instruction requested by appellant was as follows:

"The court instructs the jury that the name of the complaining witness, which is charged in the indictment to be Refugia Senega Torres, is a necessary ingredient of the crime, and a necessary allegation in the indictment, and before you can find the defendant guilty of rape as charged in the indictment, you must first find from the evidence, and beyond a reasonable doubt, that the name, as charged in the indictment, is the true name of the complaining witness, or that she was known and called by such name, and answered to such name."

In a leading case, Robson v. Thomas, 55 Mo. 581, the rule is stated,

"That it matters not how·two words are spelled, what
their orthography is, they are *idem sonans* within the
6 meaning of the books, if the attentive ear finds difficulty in distinguishing them when pronounced, or
common and long continued usage has by corruption or
abbreviation made them identical in pronunciation."

We also agree that pronunciation and not spelling is
the test in the application of the rule. Faust v. Uni-
7 ted States, 163 U. S. 452. It has been well stated as
a reason for the rule, that,

"Words are intended to be spoken; and where the sound
is substantially preserved, bad spelling will not vitiate."
Pillsbury v. Dugan, 9 Ohio 118; 34 Am. Dic. 427.

The province of the court and jury in regard to the determining whether or not a name is *idem sonans* with
8 another name is determined by the following rule:—

If two names spelled differently necessarily sound
alike, the court may as a' matter of law, pronounce them
to be *idem sonans,* but if they do not necessarily sound
alike, the question whether they are *idem sonans* is a question for the jury.

State v. Williams, 68 Ark. 241, 57 S. W. 792; Spoone-
more v. State, 25 Texas Appeals 358.

In this case the trial court evidently considered that
the question was one for the jury. If the trial court could
not dispose of the question it certainly would be presumption for us to attempt to do so. We did not hear the witnesses pronounce these names, and the spelling is not such
as would necessarily point to a difference in pronunciation.
We think the court did right in submitting the question
to the jury.

Appellant also predicates error upon the refusal of the
court to give his requested instructions numbered, 2, 3.
4, 5.

We agree with the Attorney General that No. 2 had
been substantially given as the court's instruction No. 6,
so far as it could properly be given.

Instruction No. 3, requested by defendant, was to the
effect that before the jury could find the defendant guilty

upon any confession by him they must first find such confession corroborated by the other evidence, to the extent of
establishing beyond a reasonable doubt that sexual penetration had taken place.

We have already seen that sexual penetration may be
inferred from all the facts and circumstances and for this
reason, if no other existed, the instruction was properly
refused.

Instruction No. 4, asked and refused by the court, was
in substance a charge that "criminal motive or intent is
a necessary ingredient" of the crime charged in the indictment.   The offense charged is that of sexual intercourse
with a female child under the age of fourteen years.

This instruction was evidently based upon the general
rule that where an act is prohibited and made punish-
3   able by statute, the statute is to be construed in the
light of the common law and the existence of a criminal intent is essential.   12 Cyc. 148.

. In connection with the general rule, however, it must
be borne in mind that the legislature may forbid the
4 doing of an act and make its commission criminal
without regard to the intent of the doer, and if such
an intention appears the courts must give it effect although
the intention may have been innocent.

12 Cyc. 148; Wharton's Criminal Law, section 143; 1
Wigmore on Evidence, section 360.

The principal objection to this instruction, as it appears to us, is the concluding portion, which reads as
follows :—

"You must first find, from all the evidence and circumstances of the case, that defendant had a criminal motive
or intent in being in the company of the complaining witness, or sought her company with such criminal intent or
motive."

Aside from the fact that section 1090, C. L. 1897, is
clearly such an act as would pre-suppose that the legislature had not made the element of intent an indispensa-
5   ble element of the crime thereby prescribed, it is fundamental that in a criminal prosecution the State is

not required to prove a motive for the crime, if without this the evidence is sufficient to show that the act was done by the accused. 12 Cyc. 149.

There was clearly no error in refusing this instruction.

The next error assigned is the refusal to give instruction No. 5, requested by appellant, which was as follows, viz:

"The court instructs the jury that you should take into consideration all of the testimony and circumstances adduced upon the trial, together with the conduct and statements of the complaining witness, as the same has been shown to you by the evidence."

The court carefully instructed the jury in the matters covered by this instruction under his instructions numbered 9, 12 and 13. There was no necessity to further instruct as requested by appellant and no error in refusing so to do.

The only assignment remaining for our consideration is with respect to the general objection of appellant to "each and every instruction given by the court." Such objection is too general and fails to point out the specific ground for any objection. In our recent opinion, in State v. Eaker, 131 Pac. 489, this Court said:

"If an instruction be objectionable to the defendant, the court's attention should be called to it at the time it is given, so that the court could, in case it was pointed out wherein it was erroneous, have corrected the same."

In other words, the exception to the instruction must **9** be specific.

Finding no error in the record or assignments of error, the judgment of the District Court is affirmed.

[No. 1527, August 26, 1913.]

THE UNION ESPERANZA MINING COMPANY, a corporation, Appellant, v. THE SHANDON MINING COMPANY, a corporation, Appellee.

SYLLABUS (BY THE COURT)

1. A tender by a debtor to a creditor (who in good faith asserts that the amount tendered is insufficient) is not good as a tender if it be coupled with such conditions that the acceptance of the same will involve an admission by the creditor that no more is due.

P. 165

2. The right of redemption is created by statute and the beneficiary of such legislation must take the privilege burdened with all its restrictions.

P. 165

Appeal from the District Court of Sierra County; Merritt C. Mechem, District Judge; affirmed.

R. L. YOUNG and J. H. PAXTON, Las Cruces, N. M., for appellant.

Statute contemplates a tender of the purchase money paid at the execution of the sale with legal interest thereon, coupled with the demand for a release, or a reconveyance in case the land has been conveyed. Wheelock v. Tenner, 39 N. Y. 481; Storey v. Krewson, 55 Ind. 397, 23 Am. Rep. 668; Buffum v. Buffum, 11 N. H. 451; Strafford v. Welch, 59 N. H. 46; Holpin v. Phoenix Ins. Co., 118 N. Y. 165, 23 N. E. 482; Englebach v. Simpson, 12 Tex. Civ. App. 188, 33 S. W. 596-600; McKelvain v. Allen, 58 Tex. 387; Lundy v. Pierson, 67 Tex. 237, 2 S. W. 737; Hamblen v. Folts, 70 Tex. 135, 7 S. W. 834; McPherson v. Johnson, 69 Tex. 487, 6 S. W. 798; Kauffman v. Brown, 83 Tex. 45, 18 S. W. 425; Willis v. Sommerville, 3 Tex. Civ. App. 509, 22 S. W. 781; Foster v. Andrews, 4 Tex. Civ. App. 329, 23 S. W. 610; But, Halfin v.

Winkleman, 83 Tex. 165, 18 S. W. 433; Flower v. El-
wood, 66 Ill. 439; Walling v. Kinnard, 10 Tex. 509.

Equity would compel the mortgagee to remove the cloud
by executing a release, after the mortgage has been discharged.   Brown v. Stewart, 56 Md. 421; Redmond v.
Packenham, 66 Ill. 437; Frederick v. Ewrig, 82 Ill. 363;
Smith v. Van Campen, 40 Iowa 411; Kent v. Church of
St. Michael, 136 N. Y. 10, 32 N. E. 704; Allen v. Waldo,
47 Mich. 516, 11 N. W. 366; Stanley v. Valentine, 79 Ill.
544; Brewton v. Smith, 28 Ga. 442; Eckman v. Eckman,
55 Pa. St. 269; Pratt v. Pond, 5 Allen 59; Williams v.
Williams, 7 Baxt. 116; Vardeman v. Lawson, 17 Tex. 18;
Lick v. Ray, 43 Cal. 83.

Tender made upon condition that a release of the ven-
dor's lien be delivered upon final payment of the purchase
money was valid.   Johnson v. Grange, 45 Mich. 18, 7 N.
W. 188; Wheelock v. Tanner, 39 N. Y. 486; Mankel v.
Belscamper, 84 Wis. 218, 54 N. W. 500; Strafford v. Welch,
59 N. H. 46; Loughborough v. McNevin, 74 Cal. 250, 14
Pac. 369; 15 Pac. 773; Halpin v. Insurance Co., 118 N.
Y. 175, 23 N. E. 482; Bailey v. Buchanan Co. (N. Y.
App.) 22 N. E. 155; Brock v. Jones Exec'rs., 16 Tex.
467; Wood v. Hitchcock, 20 Wend. 47; Richardson v.
Jackson, 8 Mees. & W. 298; 8 Dowl. 442; Bowen v. Owen,
11 Q. B. 131; Chit. Cont. 694.

Tender stopped the subsequent interest and carried with
it the cost of suit.   Brock v. Jones, 16 Tex. 468; Fisk v.
Holden, 17 Tex. 414; Riley v. McNamora, 83 Tex. 14, 18
S. W. 141; 25 Am. & Eng. Enc. L. 926; Tasker v. Bartlett, 59 Mass. 362; Bailey v. Buchanan, (N. Y.) 6 L. R. A.
466.

Purchaser of land at an execution sale takes at his peril.
Statute controls as to demands and tender.   C. L. 1897,
sec. 2136; Milner v. Kettig, 43 Neb. 192, 47 Am. St. Rep.
748; Frost v. Atwood, 73 Mich. 67, 16 Am. St. Rep. 563-
4; Norton v. Neb. L. & T. Co., 35 Neb. 456, 37 Am. St.
R. 443; Mackenna v. Fidelity T. Co., 184 N. Y. 411, 112
St. R. 626; Sheppard v. Clark, 58 Ia. 371, 12 N. W. 316;
Pellock v. Douglas County, 39 Neb. 293, 42 Am. St. R.

582-9; Lynde v. Inhabitants of Melrose, 10 Allen 49; Harper v. Rowe, 53 Cal. 238; Harding v. Harding, 16 S. Dak. 406, 102 Am. St. R. 700; Stone v. Gardner, 20 Ill. 304, 71 Am. Dec. 270.

Purchaser of land at execution sale may recover money paid by him to raise liens and incumbrances: Annual assessment work cannot be construed to be a lien or incumbrance subject to which the land was sold. C. L. 1897, sec. 3126; 2 Lindley on Mones, sec. 624, (p. 1152); Chambers v. Harrington, 111 U. S. 353, 28 L. Ed. 453; Beals v. Cone, 27 Col. 473, 83 Am. St. R. 99; 27 A. & E. Enc. L., sec. 202 and cases cited; Frost v. Atwood, 73 Mich. 67, 16 Am. St. R. 563.

Plaintiff corporation not liable to defendant corporation for assessment work done in years 1908, 1909 and 1910. 27 Cyc. 836; 1 Snyder on Mines, sec. 489; Clark on Contracts, p. 763.

An offer to make conditional tender if refused, relieves duty of actual tender. McPherson v. Fargo, (S. Dak.), 66 Am. St. R. 723; Hoffman v. Van Dieman, 62 Wis. 362, 21 N. W. 542; Cleveland v. Rothwell, 66 N. Y. Sup. 242; Baumann v. Pinckney, 118 N. Y. 604, 23 N. E. 916; Appleton v. Donaldson, 3 Pa. St. 381; Behaly v. Hatch, Walker, 369, 12 Am. Dec. 570; Johnson v. Cranage, 45 Mich. 14; Brewer v. Fleming, 51 Pa. St. 102; Adams v. Helm, 55 Mo. 468; Thorne v. Mosher, 20 N. J. Eq. 257; Borden v. Borden, 4 Am. Dec. 32; Lambert v. Miller, 38 N. J. Eq. 117; Ashburn v. Poulter, 35 Conn. 553.

Tender was kept good. C. L. 1897, sec. 2685; Cheney v. Libby, 134 U. S. 68, 33 L. Ed. 825; 74 Fed. 52, 20 C. C. A. 291, 36 U. S. App. 720; Curtis v. Greenbanks, 24 Uah 536; Parker v. Beasley, 116 N. C., 1 L. R. A. 231; German-American Ins. Co. v. Johnson, 45 Pac. 975; Durham v. Linderman, 64 Pac. 17; Cain v. Gimon, 36 Ala. 168; Breitenbach v. Turner, 18 Wis. 140.

Redemptioner is not required to go without the jurisdiction to redeem. Southworth v. Smith, 61 Mass. 393-4; Borden v. Borden, 5 Mass. 67; Gilmore v. Holt, 4 Pick. 258; Tasker v. Bartlett, 5 Cush. 359; Putnam v. Sullivan,

4 Mass. 45; Widgery v. Monroe, 6 Mass. 449; Hale v. Burr, 12 Mass. 86; Lehman v. Collins, 69 Ala. 127; Houbie v. Colkening, 49 How. Prac. 169; Morton v. Wells, 1 Tyler, (Vt.) 381; Hale v. Patton, 60 N. Y. 233, 19 Am. R. 168.

Court erred in sustaining defendant's objection to questions on cross-examination. In re Mason, 60 Hun. 46, 14 N. Y. Sup. 434; Jackson v. Feather River & Co. Co., 14 Cal. 18; Wilson v. Dunreath Red Stone Q. Co., 77 Ia. 429, 42 N. W. 360, 14 Am. St. R. 304; Lynch v. Free, 64 Minn. 277, 66 N. W. 973.

W. H. WINTER, El Paso, Texas, for appellee.

A tender to be valid must be made in good faith. Pulsifer v. Shepard, 36 Ill. 513; Knight v. Abbott, 30 Vt. 577; Dock v. Brason, 91 Pac. 1068; McPherson v. Wiswell, 21 N. W. 391; Grace v. Means, 59 S. E. 811.

Person to whom tender is made must be given reasonable time to make calculations before accepting or making suggestions. Enc. of Ev., p. 492; Potts v. Plaisted, 30 Mich. 149; Lefferts v. Dolton, 56 Atl. 527.

Plaintiff demanded immediate release of property, which, under the circumstances, showed that tender was not made in good faith. Malone v. Wright, 34 S. W. 455; Moore v. Norman, 43 Minn. 428; Tuthill v. Morris, 81 N. Y. 94; Story v. Krewson, 55 Ind. 397; Mulder v. Seelye, 8 Barb. 408; Nelson v. Robson, 17 Minn. 284; 11 Cyc. 1337, note 78; Moore v. Norman, 18 L. R. A. 259.

Tender bad because conditioned upon a reconveyance. Tuthill v. Morris, 81 N. Y. 94; Lilienthal v. McCormick, 117 Fed. 96.

Tender must be full, clear and satisfactory—offer to pay not sufficient and not conditioned. Potts v. Plaisted, 30 Mich. 149; Knight v. Abbott, 30 Vt. 577; Lilienthal v. McCormick, 117 Fed. 89; Beardsley v. Beardsley, 86 Fed. 20; Robinson v. Cook, 6 Taunt. 336; L'Hommedieu v. Dayton, 38 Fed. 926; Coghlan v. South Car. R. Co., 32 Fed. 316; Perkins v. Beck, 4 Cranch. C. C. 68; Harden v. Dollins, 138 Ala. 399, 35 So. 357, 100 Am. St. R. 42;

Commercial Fire Ins. Co. v. Allen, 80 Ala. 571; Jones v.
Shaey, 40 Pac. 17; Perkins v. Maier & Zobelin Brewery,
134 Cal. 372, 66 Pac. 482; Barnhart v. Fulketh, 73 Cal.
526, 15 Pac. 89; People v. Harris, 9 Cal. 571; Butler v.
Hinckley, 17 Colo. 523, 30 Pac. 250; Mitchell, v. Pierson,
34 Colo. 278, 82 Pac. 446; Sands v. Lyon, 18 Conn. 18;
Sanford v. Bulkey, 30 Conn. 344; Hall v. Norwalk Fire
Ins. Co., 57 Conn. 105, 17 Atl. 356; Chandler & Wittich v.
Wright, 16 Fla. 510; Morris v. Continental Ins. Co., 116
Ga. 53, 42 So. 474; Elder v. Johnson, 115 Ga. 691, 42 S.
E. 51; DeGraffenreid v. Menard, 103 Ga. 651, 30 S. E.
560; Hess v. Peck, 111 Ill. App. 111; Conn. Mut. Life
Ins. Co. v. Stinson, 86 Ill. App. 668; Berger v. Peterson,
78 Ill. 633; Pulsifer v. Shepard, 36 Ill. 513; Martin v.
Bott, 17 Ind. App. 444, N. E. 151 Bowen v. Julius, 141
Ind. 310, 40 N. E. 700; West v. Farmers Mut. Ins. Co.,
117 Ia. 147, 90 N. W. 523; Shuch v. C. R. I. & P. R. Co.,
73 Ia. 333, 35 N. W. 429; Hopkins v. Gray, 51 Iowa 340,
1 N. W. 637; Kuhns v. Chicago, M. & St. P. R. Co., 65
Ia. 528, 22 N. W. 661; Latham v. Hartford, 27 Kans. 249;
Loeing v. Cooke, 3 Pick. 48; Thayer v. Brackett, 12 Mass.
450; Richardson v. Chemical Lab., 9 Metc. 42; Potts v.
Plaisted, 30 Mich. 149; Moore v. Norman, 43 Minn. 428,
9 L. R. A. 55; Harmon v. Magee, 57 Miss. 410; Henderson v. Cass County, 107 Mo. 50, 18 S. W. 992; McElden
v. Patton, 93 N. W. 938; Schrant v. Young, 62 Neb. 254,
86 N. W. 1085; TePoel v. Schutt, 57 Neb. 592, 78 N. W.
288; Whittaker v. Belvidere Roller-Mill Co., 55 N. J. Eq.
674, 38 Atl. 289.

If, accompanying tender, there is a demand either express or implied of a receipt in full, it will not be a sufficient tender. Sanford v. Bulkley, 30 Conn. 344; Lindsey
v. Matthews, 17 Fla. 575; Richardson v. Chemical Co.,
50 Mass. 42; Dodge v. Brewer, 31 Mich. 227.

Party making tender cannot impose condition. Noyes
v. Wykoff, 114 N. Y. 207; Beardsley v. Beardsley, 86
Fed. 22.

Statute shows that tender must be unconditional. C. L.
1897, sec. 3126.

Where there is a dispute as to the amount that is due, the debtor cannot demand a release or a receipt in full. Noyes v. Wykoff, 114 N. Y. 207; Henderson v. Cass County, 18 S. W. 992; Beardsley v. Beardsley, 86 Fed. 22; Loring v. Cooke, 3 Peck. 48; Richardson v. The Boston, etc., 50 Mass. 52; Sanders v. Bryer, 9 L. R. A. 255, 152 Mass. 141; Welch v. Adams, 9 L. R. A. 244, 152 Mass. 74 and cases cited above.

Statutes of redemption are construed strictly. Kneely v. Sanders, 99 U. S. 441, 25 L. Ed. 328; Parker v. Dacres, 130 U. S. 43; Lynch v. Burt, 132 Fed. 429; Parker v. Dacres, 130 U. S. Sup. 43; State v. O'Connor, 6 N. Dak. 285, 69 N. W. 692; Cameron v. Adams, 31 Mich. 426; Ladd v. Masòn, 10 Ore. 308; Loring v. Cook, 3 Pick. 48; Noyes v. Wykoff, 114 N. Y. 204.

Must have the money to make valid tender. Ladd v. Mason, 10 Ore. 308; Leask v. Dew, 92 N. Y. Sup. 891; Selby v. Hurd, 16 N. W. 180; Lilienthal v. McCormick, 117 Fed. 96; DeWolfe v. Taylor, 33 N. W. 154; Enc. of Evidence 12, 499.

Burden is upon the person pleading tender. Davies v. Dow, 83 N. W. 50; Pulsifer v. Shepard, 36 Ill. 513; Otis v. Boston, 10 N. H. 433; King v. Finch, 60 Ind. 420; Benson v. Howe, 47 N. W. 449; Butler v. Hannah, 15 So. 641; Engle v. Hall, 17 N. W. 239; Proctor v. Robinson, 35 Mich. 284.

To establish tender the party bearing the burden must show the production and proffer of the money. Enc. of Evidence, vol. 12, p. 482; McCally v. Otey, (Ala) 42 Am. St. R. 90; Arrowsmith v. VanHarlingen Exs., 1 N. J. L. 26; Tuthill v. Morris, 81 N. Y. 94.

Appellant could not demand that the property be fully released. 11 Cyc. 1337, note 38 and cases cited.

There being evidence to support the finding of the lower court, and when the preponderance of the evidence shows that no tender was made, the judgment of the court below will be sustained on appeal. Scheurman v. Slyninger, 90 N. W. 292; Leach v. California, 66 Pac. 786; Moyle v. Hocking, 51 Pac. 533; Com. Bank v. Liewaller, 46 Pac.

0; Randall v. Shaw, 28 Kans. 419; Natl. Mort. Co. v.
h, 47 Pac. 548; Flynn v. Wacker, 52 S. W. 342; Stamm
. Albuquerque, 62 Pac. 973; Eastman v. Gurrey, 49 Pac.
10; Sabin v. Bushe, 37 Pac. 352.

Mere written proposal of payment, unaccompanied with
roduction of the sum of money, is not good tender. Ang-
ier v. Building Assn., 35 S. E. 64; Cheilorick v. Krauss,
11 Pac. 781; Kuhns v. Ry Co., 22 N. W. 661; Court v.
Johns, 53 Pac. 601; Holt v. Brown, 19 N. W. 235; Hyams
v. Bomberger, 36 Pac. 202; Shugart v. Pattee, 37 Iowa
432.

The party making the tender must place the money in
such a position that his control over it is relinquished for
a sufficient time to enable the other party to reduce it to
possession by merely reaching out and laying hold of the
money. Sands v. Lyons, 18 Conn. 18.

Adequate and, definite sum not tendered. Knight v.
Abbott, 30 Vt. 577; State v. Spicer, 4 Houst. (Del.) 100.

Formal technical tender not dispensed with. Lowe v.
Harwood, 29 N. E. 538; Brown v. Davis, 138 Mass. 458;
Crist v. Amour, 34 Barb. 378; Frost v. Clarkson, 7 Cow.
24.

Party making tender must seek the other party and
make tender where he can be found. Leahman v. Moore,
9 So. 590; Bancroft v. Tawin, 9 N. E. 539; Leird v. Smith,
44 N. Y. 618. Debtor must make inquiry. Bigsby v.
Whitney, 5 Me. 192; White v. Perley, 15 Me. 470.

Tender on condition. Hepburn v. Auld, 1 Cranch. 321;
Perkins v. Bank, 19 Fed. Cas. 10984; Comm. Co. v. Allen,
1 So. 202; Jacoway v. Hall, 57 S. W. 12; West v. Ins. Co.,
90 N. W. 523; Sanford v. Bulkley, 30 Conn. 344; Holton
v. Brown, 46 Am. Dec. 148.

Waiver of tender cannot be established by requiring appellee to state whether, if made, he would have received it.
Bluntzer v. Dewese, 15 S. W. 29.

Tender of larger amount than is due, coupled with an
express or implied request for change, is bad. Patterson
v. Cox, 25 Ind. 261; Perkins v. Beck, 19 Fed. Cas. 10984.

No error in sustaining objection to cross-examination.

Wills v. Russell, 100 U. S. 621; Houghton v. Jones, 17 L. Ed. 503; Foster v. U. S., 178 Fed. 169; Northern Pac. v. Urlin, 158 U. S. 271.

STATEMENT OF FACTS.

This case arises out of a sale of certain mining property by the Sheriff of Sierra County, under a writ of *venditioni exponas,* who conveyed the same to the Shandon Mining Company on October 17th, 1907. On September 21st and 22nd, 1908, William Palmer, Jr., a stockholder of the plaintiff corporation, appellant here, took certain steps looking to the redemption of said mining property from the sheriff's sale referred to, which, as testified to by Palmer, were as follows:

"I presented Mr. Parker with a written proposition for redemption and took the money and told him, as president of the Union-Esperanza Mining Company, I made a tender on behalf of that Company to the Shandon Mining Company for the mining claims named, the ones that his company had bought at Sheriff's sale, October 19th, 1907. I took the money out and showed it to Mr. Parker—"

Palmer also testified that he offered the amount they were legally entitled to, which he understood to be "the amount they paid at the sheriff's sale, and interest at the rate of 6% per annum." He testified that he said he would be willing to pay for any assessment work done upon the claims in 1907 and 1908; that he had $3000.00 in actual cash; that he wanted the property released; that on the 10th day of October, 1908, he made a tender to Mr. Doran, as statutory agent of the Shandon Mining Company, at Shandon, New Mexico, but without describing the nature of such tender other than his statement that "I said to Mr. Doran what I said to Mr. Parker, using the same language."

The written proposal referred to is as follows:

"El Paso, Texas, September 21, 1908.
"Mr. Morris B. Parker,
　"Vice President Shandon Mining Company,
　　"or James H. Parker, General Manager and Treasurer,
　　　"Shandon Mining Company, El Paso, Texas.
"Dear Sir:—

"As president of the Union-Esperanza Mining Company, and on behalf of said Company, I hereby tender you the money due in order that the Union-Esperanza Mining Company may redeem from the Shandon Mining Company, the Placer Mining Claims which the said Shandon Mining Company bought at Sheriff's sale on the 19th day of October, A. D. 1907, that is to say, the San Miguel; the Union; the Esperanza and the Cayuga Chief Placer Mining Claims, situated near Apache Canon, Sierra County, New Mexico.

(Signed)　"Wm. Palmer, Jr.,
"President Union-Esperanza Mining Company."

Mr. Palmer also testified that he would not have delivered the money unless the defendant corporation had released the property or conveyed it by deed to the plaintiff corporation; that he offered $2200.00 and pay for the assessment work, that Parker demanded $3200.00.

The witness, Merrell, accompanied Palmer on two occasions when the alleged tender was made by Palmer, to Parker, but in his testimony could not state that Palmer had any definite sum of money, other than that on the first occasion he had two thousand dollars. He further testified that Palmer demanded the deed and said he was ready to pay the money on surrendering the deed. Mr. James H. Parker, an officer of the Shandon Mining Company, to whom the alleged tender was made, testified that Palmer did not offer or tender any money to him for the redemption of the property at the time of his first visit to him; and, that amounts mentioned by the witness were not acceptable to Parker; that he informed Palmer that the officers of the Company were in West Virginia and it would be necessary to consult them, which he would do by wire; that Mr. Palmer demanded a deed and it was impossible for him to give one; that Palmer returned again, the same day, after arrangements were made to have the attorney for the Shandon Mining Company present, on which occasion Palmer was repeatedly told to get his money, and stated that he did not have it with him; that on the following morning another meeting was had, when Palmer again demanded a release and deed to the property, taking what the witness supposed was some money from his right hand pocket, putting it in his left hand and then putting it into his left hand pocket. The alleged tender by Palmer, as testified to by this witness, was in this language:

"I want a deed; I want it now and will give you three days to get the deed; when you give me the deed I will give you the money, whatever is necessary."

According to this witness the entire matter hinged upon a release in full, which the witness was unwilling to give unless reimbursed for certain expenses incurred since the sheriff's sale.

Mr. W. H. Winter testified that he was attorney for the Shandon Mining Company, at the time of the alleged tender by Palmer, concerning which he testified as follows:

"Mr. Parker told me Mr. Palmer had come there and stated he wanted to redeem the property; he had refused to fix any amount he was willing to tender, and that Mr. Palmer wanted a deed for the property and also wanted a statement from the company as to all the sums that had been paid out at the execution sale, and wanted a release in full of all the amounts due. I told Mr. Palmer at that time that I was authorized to act for the company in that matter and any tender he wanted to make he should make to me. I also stated, at that time, that unless he paid the full amount to the company, the company would not give him a release in full for all that had been paid out on the property; that if he wanted he could make a tender of the amount he claimed was due and the matter of the deed would have to be taken up with the officers of the company * * * * that I had no authority to execute the

deed. Mr. Palmer talked on about a great many matters
and stated he thought he ought to be permitted to redeem
the property upon payment of the amount that was paid
out at the execution sale, with interest, and that we ought
to give him a receipt in full of all claims which we made
by reason of having paid out money on the property, or
otherwise. I told him that we could not do it; that I was
authorized to receive the tender, but not to execute a receipt in full. * * * * finally I did say, 'Mr. Palmer, I
will be here in the morning, if you are not ready to make
the tender now. I will be in my office tomorrow all day.'
He said he was going to remain over, that he could see
me there any time and then he kept on talking about
having the money and paying it out to redeem the property and finally I did say, 'Mr. Palmer, get the money;
the money looks good to the Company,' or words to that
effect. Mr. Palmer has never at any time made any tender to me. He has never asked for a deed since that even-
ing, but did at that time demand both a deed and receipt
in full for all sums that the company had paid out."

The trial court found that the plaintiff failed to redeem
the property within the time required by law, and further
that plaintiff failed to make a legal tender to the defendant
of any money necessary to redeem said property from the
sheriff's sale.

This suit was brought to redeem the property described
in the complaint and concerning which the alleged tenders
were made, and was tried by the court without a jury, the
judgment being for the defendant company, from which
said judgment this appeal was taken.

OPINION OF THE COURT.

HANNA, J.—Numerous assignments of error are made,
but this case is primarily dependent upon the sufficiency, or
insufficiency of the alleged tender, said to have been made
by Mr. Palmer for the purpose of redeeming the property
described in the complaint in this case from the Sheriff's
sale of October 17th, 1907.

It is argued by appellant that our statute governing the

redemption of land sold at execution sale contemplates a
tender of the purchase money paid at the sale with legal
interest thereon, coupled with the demand for a release, or
a conveyance in case the land has been conveyed, and, that
such conditional tender is a good tender. We quote in
full the statute referred to, as it appears in the Compilation of 1897:

"Sec. 3126. When any property shall be sold subject
to liens and encumbrances, the purchaser may pay the
liens and encumbrances and hold the property discharged
from all claims of the defendant in execution; but the defendant may redeem the property within one year after
the sale thereof, paying to the purchaser, his heirs or assigns, the purchase money with interest; when redeemed
the purchaser shall have the growing crops, and shall not
be responsible for rents and profits, but he shall account
for wastes."

The portion of the foregoing statute with which we are
now concerned is the provision for redemption within one
year upon the re-payment of purchase money with interest. Had the appellant, through its agent, made its tender of the purchase money with legal interest without at-
taching the conditions thereto concerning which there
seems to be little question, this case would present little
difficulty in its solution.

There is no dispute as to the fact that Mr. Palmer demanded a release or a conveyance and that he was informed it could not be given at the time. There is also
no doubt that the amount necessary to redeem was in dispute between the parties.

We find no convincing proof that any tender, in good
faith, of any definite sum of money was ever made. There
is clear and convincing evidence that Mr. Palmer's demand at the time of his alleged tender was that the property be released as to all claims or demands in favor of the
defendant company.

In the case of Moore v. Norman, 52 Minn. 83, 18 L.R.A.
359, it was stated as a general proposition, applicable at
least where it appears that a larger sum than that tendered

is in good faith claimed to be due, that the tender is not effectual as such if it be coupled with conditions; that an acceptance of it, as tendered, will involve an admission
1 by the party accepting it, that no more is due. The evidence of two witnesses for appellee is clear and, in our opinion, stands uncontradicted, that a release in full was demanded as a condition of the alleged tender. This condition would bring the present case within the principle quoted. It is laid down in Cyc., vol. 38, p. 152-154,

"The money or things to be delivered must be tender.d unconditionally, and a tender accompanied with some con· dition, performance of which is impossible, or which the tenderer has no right to make, as where a sum is offered as a settlement, or in full discharge, or as payment in full, is invalid." Hess v. Peck, 111 Ill. App. 111; Conn. Mut. Ins. Co. v. Stimson, 68 Ill. App. 668; Butter v. Hinckley, (Colo) 30 Pac. 250; 2 Greenl. Ev., sec. 605; Sanford v. Bulkley, 30 Conn. 344; Lindsey v. Mathews, 17 Fla. 575: Richardson v. Chemical Co., 50 Mass. 42.

Much has been said in the briefs of this case concerning the construction of the statute of redemption, quoted above as sec. 3126, C. L. 1897, and we will briefly refer to this question.

As a general rule we agree that a statutory right of redemption is to be favorably regarded, but, it is a statutory right that is not to be enlarged by judicial interpretation. We cannot extend the time allowed for redemption nor waive any condition attached by the statute.

In State v. O'Conner, (N. D.) 69 N. W. 692, it is laid down that the right of redemption is created by statute and the beneficiary of such legislation must take the privilege burdened with all its restrictions.

In the case at bar the attempt to impose conditions upon the alleged tender was an enlargement of the statu-
2 tory right of redemption and invalidated the tender.

In our opinion, there were at least two conditions attached to the tender, first the demand for a deed, second the demand that the property be released of all demands against it. It was proved that certain sums had been spent upon the property subsequent to the Sheriff's sale, and we readily see that other interests in the property other than the one growing out of the Sheriff's sale might have accrued and that a release of all demands would clearly so enlarge the redemption statute as to confer rights clearly not within the contemplation of the legislature.

Finding no error in the record, the judgment of the District Court is affirmed, and it is so ordered.

Chief Justice Roberts disqualified.

[No. 1551, August 26, 1913.]

THE STATE OF NEW MEXICO, ex rel., STANDARD HOME COMPANY, a Corporation, Relator and Appellant, v. STATE CORPORATION COMMISSION OF THE STATE OF NEW MEXICO, comprised of the individual members, H. H. Williams, M. S. Groves and O. L. Owen, Respondents and Appellees.

SYLLABUS (BY THE COURT)

1. Corporations or associations doing business by collecting monthly installments of dues for the accumulation of funds out of which to loan those contributing to such fund amounts for the purchase of homes, are subject to the provisions of chapter 72, Session Laws of 1899, entitled "An act relating to building and loan associations, as doing business in a form and character similar to that authorized to be done by building and loan associations organized under the provisions of said act."

P. 173

Appeal from the District Court of Santa Fe County; Edmund C. Abbott, District Judge; affirmed.

CATRON & CATRON, Santa Fe, N. M., for appellant.

Incorporation laws. Laws 1905, chap. 79; Laws 1899, chapter 72.

JANUARY TERM, 1913.   167

State ex rel. v. Corp. Com., 18 N. M. 166

Chapter 72, Laws of 1899, is penal. Territory v. Daven-
port, 124 Pac. 795. Must be strictly construed. U. S. v.
Lucero, 1 N. M. 422; U. S. v. Santistevan, 1 N. M. 583;
Esquibel v. Chaves, 12 N. M. 482.

Chapter 72, Laws 1899, copied from Colorado law enacted in 1897. Rev. Stat. of Colo., secs. 950-968; Bremen
Min. Co. v. Bremen, 13 N. M. 126; Romero v. Railroad,
11 N. M. 688; DeBaca v. Wilcox, 11 N. M. 352; Perea v.
Colo. Nat. Bank, 6 N. M. 4; Lutz v. A. & P. Ry. Co., 6
N. M. 500; Reymond v. Newcomb, 10 N. M. 173; Columbia B. & L. Assn. v. Lyttle, 16 Colo. App. 423.

Controlling principle of the appellant is mutuality
among its shareholders. Columbia B. & L. Assn., v. Lyttle,
16 Colo. App. 423; People's B. & L. Assn. v. Purdy, 20
Colo. App. 287.

But, the relation of appellant, Standard Home Company,
is not mutual. State v. Folk, State Treas. (Tenn.) 135
S. W. 776; People's B. & L. Assn. v. Purdy, 20 Colo. 287;
Askoy v. Fidelity, etc., Assn., 37 Colo. 432; Eversman v.
Schmitt, 53 Ohio St. 174, 41 N. E. 139, 29 L. R. A. 184;
Columbia B. & L. Assn. v. Junquist, 111 Fed. 645; King
v. Inter. B. & L. Co., 170 Ill. 135, 48 N. E. 677; Wier-
man v. Inter. B., etc., Union, 67 Ill. App. 550.

"All members must participate equally in the profits
and bear the losses, if any, in the same proportion. This
is the fundamental law of building and loan associations
organized under the different statutes throughout the Union." Bertche v. Equitable L. & Inv. Assn., 147 Mo. 343,
48 S. W. 954; Hawley v. North Side B. & L. Assn., 11
Colo. App. 93; International Imp. Co. v. Wagner, 125
Pac. 597; State of Tenn. ex Standard Trust Co., v. Folk,
135 S. W. 776; McCauley v. B. & L. Assn., 97 Tenn. 421,
31 L. R. A. 244; Setliff v. Nashville, etc., Assn., 39 S. W.
546; 20 Ann. Cas. 1253, note; 4 A. & E. Enc. of Law, (2nd
ed.) 1026; Cook v. Equitable B. & L. Assn., 104 Ga. 814;
Towle v. Am. B., L. & Inv. Co., 61 Fed. 446; Albany Mut.
B. Assn. v. City of Laramie, 65 Pac. 1911; Rhodes v. Missouri Sav. Co., 173 Ill. 629; Maroney, Jr., v. Atl. B. & L.
Assn., 116 N. C. 822.

168   SUPREME COURT OF NEW MEXICO.

State ex rel. v. Corp. Com., 18 N. M. 166

While decisions rendered after the adoption of a statute are not of the same binding effect as decisions rendered prior to such adoption, they are nevertheless of strongly persuasive effect. Harrison v. Hill, 37 Ill. App. 30; Northcut v. Eager, 132 Md. 265, 33 S. W. 1125; Myers v. McGavock, 39 Neb. 843, 58 N. W. 522; Olin v. Denver & R. G. R. Co., 25 Colo. 177, 53 Pac. 454; Attorney Gen. v. Pitcher, 183 Mass. 513.

"A contract entered into with a building and loan association organized under the laws of this state by and through which it may be enabled to evade the statute and loan its funds to a person, not a member or a shareholder of the association, is invalid and non-enforceable. National Inv. Co. v. National Sav. B. & L. Assn., 49 Minn. 517.

HON FRANK W. CLANCY, Attorney General, Santa Fe, N. M., for appellee.

Foreign building and loan associations are governed by chapter 72 of laws of 1899. Standard Home Company is a foreign association and by the "participating plan" cannot evade the statute. State v. Standard Co., 103 Pac. 1007.

"Similar" in a statute does not mean "identical." Greenleaf v. Goodrich, 101 U. S. 278, 282-3-4; Trust Co. v. Olney, 16 R. I. 185-6.

Repeal of sections 1 to 14 and section 19 of chapter 72 of the law of 1899, leaving sections 15 to 18, both inclusive, in force, and also section 20, does not destroy legislative intent as to governing foreign associations, without reference to section 1 of that act. 2 Sutherland Stat. Const., sec. 452; Ogden v. Boreman, 20 Utah 98.

STATEMENT OF FACTS.

On December 14, 1911, plaintiff, a corporation organized under the laws of the State of Delaware, made application to Secretary of the then Territory of New Mexico, for a certificate of qualification to permit it to transact business within New Mexico under the provisions of the General Incorporation Laws (chap. 79, laws 1905), making a tender of the necessary fees, etc.

On December 21, 1911, the Secretary of the then Territory of New Mexico, officially declined to issue to plaintiff a certain certificate of qualification permitting it to so transact business within New Mexico, and on January 24, 1912, the State Corporation Commission ratified and confirmed such refusal on the part of its predecessor.

Thereafter, on July 3, 1912, plaintiff, through its counsel, filed in the office of the clerk of the District Court of Santa Fe County, an information in the nature of a petition for a writ of mandamus, directed to the State Corporation Commission, to compel that body to issue to it a certificate of qualification to transact business within New Mexico under the provisions of the General Incorporation Laws.

The Attorney General voluntarily appeared in the said action and, waiving issuance of an alternative writ of mandamus, filed a demurrer to plaintiff's petition, which was sustained by the District Court of Santa Fe County, and on November 6, 1912, judgment was entered dismissing plaintiff's petition and granting an appeal to this Court.

OPINION OF THE COURT.

HANNA, J.—There is but one question in this case for our determination, i. e., is appellant subject to our statute relative to foreign building and loan associations because it is "doing business in a form and character similar to that authorized to be done" by building and loan associations organized, in New Mexico, under the provisions of chapter 72 of the laws of 1899?

The corporations, of the class referred to, which are to be considered as foreign building and loan associations, are defined, by section 15 of chapter 72, laws of 1899, as follows:

"Sec. 15. Every corporation, company or association now doing or contemplating doing business in this Terri-

tory, and having for a part of its title or name the words
"Loan and Building Association," "Building Association,"
"Building and Loan Association," "Saving and Loan Association," or "Co-operative Bank," "Saving and Investment Company," and every corporation, company or. association whose stock is payable by an accumulating fund in
regular or stated periodical installments; and every corporation, company or association doing business in a form and
character similar to that authorized by section 1 of this act,
shall, if organized or incorporated in any State or Territory other than the Territory of New Mexico, be known
in this act, as a foreign building and loan association."

Section 1, of the same act, is as follows:

"Sec. 1.   Any association of not less than three persons
hereafter incorporated under the laws of this Territory,
which shall be organized within this Territory for the purpose of raising a fund by the collection of dues or stated
payments from its members, to be loaned among its members, shall, in furtherance of such purpose, and after having complied with the requirements of this act, be authorized and empowered to levy, assess, and collect from its
members such sums of money, by rates of stated dues, fines,
interest on loans advanced, and premiums bid by members for the right of precedence in taking loans, as the
corporation may provide for in its constitution or by-laws:
also to acquire, hold and convey all such real estate and
personal property as may be legitimately pledged to it upon
said loans, or may otherwise be transferred to it in the due
course of its business."

Appellant has, at considerable length, pointed out the
characteristics of building and loan associations, attempting to demonstrate that it differs from such associations
so much that its business cannot be said to be similar.
It is to be conceded that the prevailing characteristic of
building and loan associations is mutuality among stock-
holders.   In other words, an equal participation of members in profits and losses.   This element, it is urged, is entirely lacking in the case of appellant corporation, and it
is pointed out that appellant, under its articles of incor-

JANUARY TERM, 1913. 171

State ex rel. v. Corp. Com., 18 N. M. 166

poration, has the power to guarantee to its contract holders that the contracts purchased by them will mature at a definite time and guarantee them a definite amount.

On the other hand, the Attorney General contends that if the business, of appellant, is similar to that of building and loan associations, it comes within the provisions of our law as to such associations.

It is to be noted that sec. 1 of our statute, authorizes the incorporation of associations for the purpose of raising funds by the collection of dues or stated payments from its members, to be loaned among its members, from which premise appellant urges that because it sells its contracts to persons who are not members, but to any and all persons, which contracts are not stock in the company but only a so-called investment contract, the holders of which have no voice in the management of the company, and do not share in its profits or losses, therefore, the essential element of mutuality is lacking so far as the affairs of this company is concerned, and there can be no similarity between its business and that of an association as described in sec. 1 of the act. We are not prepared to agree with this contention of appellant.

An examination of the "investment home purchasing contract," a part of the record in this case, discloses that "the prompt payment of a monthly installment of dues of $6.00 * * * * until eighty monthly installments of dues have been paid" is the consideration expressed in the contract.

The second paragraph of the contract provides for the return of dues paid, "with its pro rata share of profits," not exceeding a maximum sum of $720.00, or a minimum sum of $528.00.

The third paragraph is designated as "Loan provisions" and provides that after the prompt payment of six monthly installments the owner of the contract "is eligible to receive a loan or funds to purchase a home in the sum of $1000.00 * * * * out of the loan or reserve fund" of the particular series to which the contract belongs. If this method of doing business is not clearly a raising of a

172   SUPREME COURT OF NEW MEXICO,

State ex rel. v. Corp. Com., 18 N. M. 166

fund by the collection of dues or stated payments from its members to be loaned among its members, we are at a loss to classify the method. In our opinion, the method is so "similar" to that customarily adopted by building and loan associations as to fall within the intent and purposes of sec. 15 of the act of 1899. While the contributing party may be called a stock holder in the one case and a contract "owner" in the other, nevertheless, in either case the parties are seeking the same end in substantially the same manner.

In the case of the State of Kansas v. The Standard Real Estate Loan Company, 80 Kans. 695' 103 Pac. 1007, which was a proceeding in the nature of quo warranto against the corporation, resulting in a judgment of ouster, the Supreme Court say:

"The legislature has prescribed a scheme for domestic concerns of this character; but it is not necessary that the plan of a foreign association be identical with that provided for in the statute to subject such an association to the law requiring a license. Neither is it necessary that the scheme of the foreign association should conform to that of any other already in use, provided in essence and effect such association performs the functions and accomplishes the purpose for which building and loan associations are usually organized. That the defendant organization clearly does. Its charter is studiously blind as to the object of its creation. The plan does appear, however, in an "investment contract," which the defendant issues and sells in the place of shares and stock. It is not necessary to incumber the reports with a copy of this instrument or a feature by feature analysis and discussion of its provisions. It is unique, presents a system differing in many formal respects from that of building and loan associations generally, and eliminates altogether some of the incidents of ordinary plans; but the vital and essential features of even the type prescribed for Kansas associations appear, and the court finds that the defendant is a foreign building and loan association, has procured no certificate of authority to do business in this state from the bank commissioner, is therefore doing business in our state contrary to law, and ought to be ousted."

We quote this opinion with approval, believing it particularly applicable to the facts of the present case. Having had access to an abstract of the records in the Kansas case, we have compared the so-called contract of that case with the contract in the present case, and in their principal provisions they are almost identical, so much so, in fact, as to point to a common authorship.

The Kansas statute upon the subject of the admission of foreign building and loan associations into that state is not as definite as ours and does not use the term "similar," therefore, there are more substantial reasons for our conclusions than could exist in the Kansas case.

We are clearly of the opinion that corporations or associations doing business by collecting monthly installments of dues for the accumulation of funds out of which to

1 loan those contributing to such fund amounts for the purchase of homes are subject to the provisions of chapter 72, Session Laws of 1899, entitled "An act relating to building and loan associations, etc.," as doing business in a form and character similar to that authorized to be done by building and loan associations organized under the provisions of said act.

Finding no error in the record, the judgment of the District Court is affirmed.

[No. 1544, August 27, 1913.]

CHARLES C. BRADEN, Appellant, v. WATER SUPPLY COMPANY of Albuquerque, New Mexico, a corporation, Appellee.

SYLLABUS (BY THE COURT)

1. A tax payer has no such direct interest in an agreement between a municipality and a corporation for supplying water as will allow him to sue ex contractu for breach, or ex delicto for violation of the public duty thereby assumed.

P. 179

Appeal from the District Court of Bernalillo County; Herbert F. Raynolds, District Judge; affirmed.

B. F. ADAMS and JOHN W. WILSON, Albuquerque, N. M., for appellant.

A. B. McMILLEN, Albuquerque, N. M., for appellee.

Contract of Water Company was with the City of Albuquerque and not with individuals, to supply water for extinguishing fires. Guardian Trust Co. v. Fisher, 200 U. S. 57; Judiciary Act 1789, chap. 20, sec. 34, (U. S.); Revised Statutes (U. S.) section 721; Vol. 4, Enc. of U. S. Sup. Ct. Rep. 1049, and cases cited in note 86; Water Co. v. Freeport, 180 U. S. 595; Burges v. Seligman, 107 U. S. 20.

A city owning its own water works cannot be held liable for failure to furnish sufficient water supply to extinguish fires. 2 Dillon on Municipal Corporations, 975; Wheeler v. Cincinnati, 19 O. St. 19; Fowler v. Water Works Co., 83 Ga. 222, 9 S. E. 673; Wainwright v. Water Co., 78 Hun. 146; Tainter v. City of Worcester, 123 Mass. 311; VanHorn v. City of Des Moines, 63 Ia. 447, 19 N. W. 293; Hayes v. City of Oshkosh, 33 Wis. 314; Stone v. Water Co., 4 Pa. Dist. Rep. 431; House v. Water Works Co., (Tex.) 31 S. W. 179; Boston Safe D. & T. Co. v. Salem Water Co., 94 Fed. 241; Metropolitan Trust Co. v. Topeka Water Co., 132 Fed. 704.

If city, owning its own water company, would not be bound, then there is no privity of contract to bind this appellee to individuals. Boston Safe D. & T. Co. v. Salem Water Co., 94 Fed. 241; Metropolitan Trust Co. v. Topeka Water Co., 132 Fed. 704.

Contract is between the city of Albuquerque and the Water Supply Company and there is no privity of contract with the citizens who happen to live in Albuquerque. Nickerson v. Bridgeport Hydraulic Co., 46 Conn. 24, 33 Am. Rep. 1; Fowler v. Athens City Water Works Co.. 83 Ga. 219, 20 Am. St. Rep. 313; Bush. v. Artesian Hot &

Cold Water Co., 43 Pac. 69; Fitch v. Seymour Water Co., 139 Ind. 214, 47 A. S. R. 158; Davis v. Clinton Water Works Co., 54 Ia. 59, 37 A. R. 185; Ferris v. Carson Water Co., 16 Nev. 44, 40 Am. Rep. 485; Akron Water Works Co. v. Brown, 10 O. Cir. Ct. Rep. 620; Beck v. Kittaning Water Co., 11 Atl. 300; Stone v. Union Water Co., 4 Pa. Dist. R. 431; Foster v. Lookout Water Co., 71 Tenn. 42; Houston v. Houston Water Works Co., (Tex) 22, S. W. 277, 31 S. W. 179; Becker v. Keokuk Water Works, 79 Ia. 419, 18 Am. St. R. 377; Phoenix Ins. Co. v. Renton Water Co., 42 Mo. App. 118; Howsmon v. Renton Water Co., 119 Mo. 304, 41 Am. St. R. 654; Eaton v. Fairbury Water Works Co., 37 Neb. 546, 40 A. S. R. 510; Britton v. Green Bay & Ft. H. Water Works Co., 81 Wis. 48, 51 N. W. 84; Boston Safe D. & T. Co. v. Salem water Co., 94 Fed. 238; Metropolitan Trust Co. v. Topeka Wat. Co., 132 Fed. 702; Atkinson v. Newcastle, etc., Water Co., L. R. 2 Exch. Div. 441; Vrooman v. Turner, 69 N. Y. 280; 25 Am. Rep. 195, 197; Mott v. Mfg. Co., (Kans.) 28 Pac. 289; Anderson v. Fitzgerald, 21 Fed. 294; Davis v. Water Works Co., 6 N. W. 126, (Iowa.)

"The petitioner does not allege or show any privity of contract between plaintiff and defendant. The plaintiff is a stranger, and the mere fact that she may find benefits therefrom by the protection of her property in common with all other persons whose property is similarly situated, does not make her a party to the contract or create a privity between her and the defendant." Davis v. Water Works Co., 6 N. W. 126; Becker v. Water Works, 44 N. W. 694; Clark v. City of Des Moines, 19 Ia. 212; McPherson v. Foster, 43 Ia. 57; Jones Neg. Mun. Corp., sec. 31; Beck v. Water Co., 11 Atl. 300; House v. Water Works Co., 22 S. W. 377; Fitch v. Water Co., 37 N. E. 982; Ferhis v. Water Co., 16 Nev. 44; Nickerson v. Hydraulic Co., 46 Conn. 24; Bush v. Artesian Water Co., 43 Pac. 69; Ferris v. Crescent Water Co., 16 Nev. 44, 40 Am. Rep. 485-7.

Contract must have been made for his benefit as its object. Howsmon v. Trenton Water Co., 41 Am. St. Rep.

654; Heller v. Sedalia, 53 Mo. 159, 14 Am. Rep. 444; City
of Kansas v. O'Connell, 99 Mo. 357.

City had no authority to make a contract to indemnify
the plaintiff that would be binding on another.   Howsmon
v. Trenton Water Co., 41 Am. St. Rep. 654-660; Foster
v. Lookout Water Co., 3 Lea. 49; Eaton v. Fairbury Water
Works Co., 37 Neb. 546, 40 Am. St. R. 510-18; Boston
Safe D. & T. Co. v. Salem Water Co., 94 Fed. 238; Metropolitan T. Co. v. Topeka Water Co., 132 Fed. 702, 3, 4;
German Alliance Ins. Co. v. Home Water Co., 226 U. S.
220.

STATEMENT OF FACTS.

The plaintiff brings this action as a citizen and tax
payer of Albuquerque, alleging that the defendant company was granted a franchise April 7, 1894, to furnish
water for public and domestic use, to the residents of said
city, and all water necessary for the extinguishing of fires
during the continuance of the franchise, which was for a
period of twenty-five years.   Plaintiff further alleges, in
his complaint, that the contract between the city and
Water Company was for the use and benefit of all the
property owners and inhabitants of the City of Albuquerque, among them the plaintiff, a property owner whose
property was taxed to raise money to pay hydrant rentals
to the defendant company; that on July 9, 1909, his property was destroyed by fire; that a fire alarm was turned
in and the fire department arrived with hose, fire engine
and other appurtenances in less than ten minutes; that
the fire company attached its hose, which was in every respect adequate, to two fire hydrants sufficiently near to afford water adequate for the ready extinguishment of said
fire if there had been proper water pressure; that defendant carelessly and negligently refused to furnish the hydrants with sufficient water pressure to extinguish said
fire, and by reason of such tortious and negligent conduct,
on the part of the defendant, the plaintiff's property was
destroyed; that the failure of defendant to provide sufficient water with proper pressure, as provided by ordin-

ance and contract, was not prevented by accident, but was a result of a wanton, careless and willful disregard of the duties and obligations to the several inhabitants of the City of Albuquerque.

Defendant's demurrer to the complaint assigned the following grounds:

"(1). Because there is no privity of contract between the plaintiff and defendant in this cause;

"(2). Because the alleged contract set forth in plaintiff's complaint does not contemplate the liability sued for;

"(3). Because in and by said contract set forth in said complaint said defendant company is not an insurer against loss by fire and does not contract to extinguish fires;

"(4). Because said complaint otherwise and in other respects fails to state facts sufficient to constitute a cause of action."

The demurrer was sustained and plaintiff prosecutes this appeal.

OPINION OF THE COURT.

HANNA, J.—The question presented for our consideration is whether the defendant under its ordinance, contract and franchise is liable to a private citizen, and tax payer, for loss by fire at a time when it is alleged there was insufficient water pressure to extinguish the fire, and not the water pressure required to be maintained under the contract, which condition was the result of the negligence and wrong doing of the water company, and a violation of a duty and obligation owed to the plaintiff.

The section of this franchise necessary for our consideration is section 8, and is as follows:

"Sec. 8. The said company or its assigns shall furnish to the City of Albuquerque, in consideration of the granting of this franchise, all water necessary for the extinguishment of fires and for fire purposes free of charge.

The first ground of demurrer was the alleged lack of privity between the plaintiff and defendant. It is contended by appellant that the contract between the company and the city was for the use and benefit of the several inhabitants of the city, he being one. In the first case we can find dealing with the question now under consideration, (Nickerson v. Bridgeport Hydraulic Co., 46 Conn. 24, 33 Am. Rep. 1) it was held that the property owner was a stranger to the agreement with the municipality, and therefore could not maintain an action against the company for a breach of contract with the city. This view has been quite generally adopted in the later decisions upon the subject. In the recent case of German Alliance Ins Co. v. Home Water Co., 226 U. S. 220, it was held by the Supreme Court of the United States that a tax payer has no claim against a water supply company for damages resulting from a failure of the company to perform the contract with the municipality.

We fully appreciate the fact that this opinion is not necessarily controlling upon us and that the case is one of first impression so far as this court is concerned, but this able opinion by Mr. Justice Lamar, in the case last referred to, throws much light upon the question before us, and finding that it correctly sets forth the trend of the authorities to be found upon this subject, we desire to quote, at length and with approval, from the opinion. Speaking of the many decisions upon the question of the right of a taxpayer to look to the water company for damages arising out of an alleged breach of contract by the company, Justice Lamar says:

"From them it appears that the majority of American courts hold that the taxpayer has no direct interest in such agreements, and, therefore, cannot sue *ex contractu*. Neither can he sue in tort, because, in the absence of a contract obligation to him, the water company owes him no duty for the breach of which he can maintain an action *ex delicto*. A different conclusion is reached by the Supreme Courts of three States, in cases cited and discussed in Mugge v. Tampa Water Works, 52 Fla. 371. They hold that such a contract is for the benefit of taxpayers, who may sue either for its breach, or for a violation of the public duty which was thereby assumed."

In the same connection Mr. Dillon observes (Dillon's Municipal Corporations, p. 2303 et seq.) that:

"The question of the *liability of a water company furnishing water to a municipality and its inhabitants under* an ordinance or contract, to respond in damages to a resident owner of property destroyed by fire, on account of the failure of the water company to fulfill its contract with the city to furnish an adequate supply of water at a stipulated price for the extinguishment of fires, has many times received the consideration of the courts, and the weight of authority is that the *contracting company is not chargeable with any greater liability than the city itself*; that the contract is between the city and the water company only; that there is no privity of contract between the individual citizen, though a taxpayer who contributes to the fund disbursed by the city in the payment of hydrant rentals for fire protection, and the water company, which will enable the property owner to recover damages so sustained. But in Kentucky, North Carolina and Florida, the courts have reached a different conclusion, and have held that an *inhabitant of a city* who has suffered loss by fire by reason of the water company's breach of its contract with the city to furnish water for fire protection *may,* as a party for are collected in the case note to Home, et al., v. Presque Isle Water Co., 104 Me. 217, 71 Atl. 769, 21 L. R. A. (N. S.) 1021.

We therefore find that the weight of authority is against
   the rights of a property owner to maintain an action
1 against the water company for loss of his property
   proximately resulting from its failure to provide sufficient water for fire purposes, as required by its contract with the municipality. The cases supporting this conclusion are collected in the case note to Home, al., v. Presque Isle Water Co., 21 L. R. A. (N. S.) 1021.

The courts following the weight of authority, upon this question, do so upon the principle that there is lacking of that privity essential to the conferring of a right of action upon a third person not a party to the contract upon which his rights are necessarily predicated.

It may be conceded to be the general rule that a contract is only intended for the benefit of those who made it and we agree with Mr. Justice Lamar (Ger. All. Ins. Co. v. Water Sup. Co., supra), that "Before a stranger can avail himself of the exceptional privilege of suing for a breach of an agreement to which he is not a party, he must, at least, show that it was intended for his direct benefit."

The views of those courts constituting the majority view upon this question may to some seem inconsistent with justice and reason, and may seem to create a condition abhorrent to the law in that a right seemingly exists for the violation of which there is no remedy, it being generally conceded that the property owner has no right of action against the municipality. To any fair mind there is apparent injustice in the condition resulting from a failure of the water supply company to furnish water for fire purposes in apparent violation of its contract obligation to do so, notwithstanding its customary readiness to promptly collect the usually large compensation for hydrant rentals.

In the case under consideration the compensation to be paid and which presumably was paid, was a large and fair compensation, yet it is here charged that the company failed to give that which it contracted to give for this consideration. We might desire to find a method for the correction of this form of abuse of privilege by a public utility company, but can we do so by a violation of long established legal principles, or by remaking the contract between the parties? It seems to us that it is incumbent upon the public to exercise greater care in granting public franchise for long terms of years, that our legislatures might well consider the legislation of other states designed to protect the public against the reckless granting of one-sided franchises under which the public has but little recognition.

The authorities following the minority line of decisions upon this question, lay stress upon the fact that the defendant is a public service corporation. While that is true, they have the right to stand upon their contract, though improvidently made, and it is not for us to impose a liability not contemplated by it.

It is to be noted, in the present case, that the question of water pressure is confined to the requirement that the company furnish sufficient supply of good water for domestic and manufacturing purposes, at a maximum pressure of sixty pounds to the square inch, under section 5 of the franchise. The section quoted, supra, (sec. 8) referring to water for fire purposes, is an undertaking to *furnish to the City of Albuquerque* all water necessary for the extinguishing of fires and for fire purposes. We are not overlooking appellant's contention that this undertaking is for the benefit of the several inhabitants of the, city, including himself, but we cannot agree that the indirect interest of plaintiff below constitutes that privity necessary to confer a right of action. As said by Mr. Justice Lamar in the case of German Alliance Ins. Co. v. Water Sup. Co., 226 U. S. 220,

"The interest which each taxpayer has therein was indirect,—that incidental benefit only which every citizen has in the performance of every other contract made by and with the government under which he lives, but for the breach of which he has no private right of action. He is interested in the faithful performance of contracts, of service by policemen, firemen and mail contractors, as well as in holding to their warranties the vendors of fire engines. All of these employes, contractors, or vendors are paid out of taxes. But for the breaches of their contracts the citizen cannot sue though he suffer loss, * * * *

"Each of these promisors of the city, like the Water Company here, would be liable for any tort done by him to third persons. But for acts of omission and breaches of contract, he would be responsible to the municipality alone. To hold to the contrary would unduly extend the contract liability, would introduce new parties with new rights, and would subject those contracting with municipalities to suits by a multitude of persons for damages which were not, and, in the nature of things, could not have been, in contemplation of the parties.

"The result is that plaintiff cannot maintain this action, and though based upon the general principle that the parties to a contract are those who are entitled to the rights, is in accordance with the particular intent of those who made this agreement."

The reasoning of this opinion is, in our opinion, controlling upon us in the case under consideration.

The Water Supply Co., of Albuquerque, did not contemplate the liability of an insurer when it entered into its contract with the city and it would be only by a strained construction of such contract that we could hold the company liable, in this case, under the authority of the decisions from Kentucky, North Carolina and Florida.

In this case, as in the South Carolina case, (German Alliance v. Water Co., supra) the plaintiff largely relied upon the decision of the Supreme Court in Guardian Trust & D. Co. v. Fisher, 200 U. S. 57, 50 L. Ed. 367, 26 Sup. Ct. Rep. 186, which latter decision is fully discussed in the German Alliance Ins. Co. case, by Mr. Justice Lamar, who points out that the Fisher case could not have decided the primary question as to the right of the taxpayer to sue, as that issue had been finally settled by the state court and that the Fisher case did not overrule the principle announced in Second National Bank v. Grand Lodge, F. & A. M., 98 U. S. 124, 25 L. Ed. 76, that a third person cannot sue for the breach of a contract to which he is a stranger unless he is in privity with the parties and is therein given a direct interest.

For the reasons given, we conclude that there was no right of action in this appellant as against the Water Supply Co., which conclusion disposes of the case and makes it unnecessary to inquire into the remaining grounds of demurrer. The judgment of the District Court is, therefore, affirmed.

[No. 1493, August 28, 1913.]

STATE OF NEW MEXICO, on the relation of Stella Sittler, Appellant, v. THE BOARD OF EDUCATION of the Town of Gallup. New Mexico, Appellee.

SYLLABUS (BY THE COURT)

1. Mandamus cannot be maintained to compel reinstatement of a school teacher who has been removed by the school officers and whose relation to the school authorities rests wholly in contract. It is only where the teacher, by positive provision of law, has a fixed tenure of office, or can be removed only in some prescribed manner, and where, consequently, it is the plain ministerial duty of the school board to retain him, that mandamus can be maintained.

P. 187

2. A school teacher has no fixed tenure of office by provision of law in this jurisdiction and his rights are measured by the terms of his contract with the school officers.

P. 190

Appeal from the District Court of McKinley County; Herbert F. Raynolds, District Judge; affirmed.

A. T. HANNETT, Gallup, N. M.; VIGIL & JAMISON, Albuquerque, N. M., for appellant.

Relator was entitled to a peremptory writ of mandamus, under the pleadings, when the court found that she was discharged. Merrill on Mandamus, vol. 1, pages 293-294 and 353; Marshman v. Conklin, et al., 21 N. J. Eq. 548; Bachman v. Sepulveda, 39 Cal. 689.

A judgment not supported by the pleadings is as fatally defective as if not sustained by verdict or findings. Munday v. Vail, 34 N. J. L. 418; Reynolds v. Stockton, 43 N. J. Eq. 211 ;Black on Judgments, vol. 1, sec. 183; Hoover v. Binkley, 51 S. W. 73; Stearns Ranchos Co. v. McDowell, 134 Cal. 562, 66 Pac. 724; Breckenridge Merc. Co. v. Bailif, 16 Colo. App. 554; Burns, etc., L. Co. v. Doyle, 71

Conn. 742, 43 Atl. 483; 71 Am. St. R. 235; Jackson v. Miles, 94 Ga. 484, 19 S. W. 708; American Fur. Co. v. Batesville, 35 N. E. 682; W. W. Kendall Boot Co. v. Davenport, 65 Pac. 688; State v. St. Paul, 52 La. Ann. 1039, 27 So. 571; McGregor v. J. C. Ware Constr. Co., 188 Mo. 611, 87 S. W. 981; State v. Haverly, 62 Neb. 767, 87 N. W. 959; Badaracco v. Badaracco, 10 N. M. 761, 65 Pac. 153; Husted v. VanNess, 158 N. Y. 104, 52 N. E. 645; Wilson v. Taylor, 98 N. C. 275, 3 S. W. 492; Seiberling v. Mortinson, 10 S. D. 644, 65 N. W. 202; Thompson v. Keck Mfg. Co., 107 Tenn. 451, 64 S. W. 709; Paris 1st Baptist Church v. Fort, 93 Tex. 215, 54 S. W. 892, 49 L. R. A. 617; Seamster v. Blackstock, 83 Va. 232, 2 S. E. 36, 5 Am. St. R. 262; Magnuson v. Clithero, 101 Wis. 551, 77 N. W. 882; Reynolds v. Stockton, 140 U. S. 254, 35 L. Ed. 464.

Relator was entitled to a writ of mandaums as she was discharged and did not resign. High on Extra. Remedies, page 263; Merrill on Mandamus. 140; 35 Cyc. 1094; Gilman v. Bassett, 33 Conn. 298; Morley v. Power, 73 Tenn. 691; Brown v. Owen, 23 So. 35; Whitman v. Owen, 25 So. 669; People v. Van Sicklen, 43 Hun. 540.

Defendant had no right to discharge relator upon the findings of this case if the pleadings were sufficient to raise the question of the right to discharge. C. L. 1884. secs. 1108 and 1110; C. L. 1897, secs. 1534-35; Laws of 1907, chap. 97; Arnold v. School District, 78 Mo. 276; Kings Lake D. & L. District v. Jamison, 75 So. 679, 176 Mo. 557; Biggs v. School City, etc., 90 N. E. 105; Carver v. School District, 113 Mich. 524; 2 How. Stat., par. 5155; Thompson v. Gibbs, 34 L. R. A. 548; Laws 1901, ch. 43, sec. 5; Wallace v. School District, 69 N. W. 772; School City of Lafayette v. Bloom, 46 N. E. 1016.

Relator could not be discharged without a competent and sufficient hearing, which was not given her. Thompson v. Gibbs, 34 L. R. A. 548; Wheatley v. Division Bd. of Education, 139 S. W. 969; Freemont County v. Shuck., 113 Pac. 511.

ALFRED RUIZ, Gallup, N. M.; GEO. S. KLOCK, Albuquerque, N. M., for appellee.

The relator was properly discharged and in accordance with the terms of the contract. C. L. 1897, page 830; Armstrong v. School District, 28 Kans. 345; School District v. Colvin, 10 Kans. 284; Scott v. School District, 8 N. W. 399; Am. & Eng. Enc., vol. 25, 19, (2 Ed.); Tripp v. School District, 50 Wis. 651; Loehr v. Board of Education, 108 Pac. 327; Harby v. Board of Education, 83 Pac. 1082; State, ex rel. Lewellen, v. Smith, et al., 69 N. W. 115; School District v. Maury, 53 Ark. 471; Steinson v. Board of Education, 165 N. Y. App. 431.

After appellant had tendered her resignation and the same had been accepted by the Board, she could not withdraw it. Mimack v. U. S., 97 U. S. 426; A. & E. Enc. Law, (2 Ed.) vol. 21, 848-9.

Appellant cannot resort to mandamus in this case. Kennedy v. Board of Education, 82 Cal. 483, 22 Pac. 49; Miller v. Harvey, 215 Pa. St. 104; Burton v. Fulton, 49 Pa. St. 154; C. L. 1897, sec. 2760.

The appeal in this case should be dismissed. Englehart, 17 N. M. 299; C. R. & P. Ry. Co. v. Dey, 76 Iowa 281, 41 N. W. 18.

OPINION OF THE COURT.

PARKER, J.—This is a proceeding in mandamus on the relation of appellant, who was a school teacher employed to teach in the public schools of Gallup, in McKinley County. There was a written contract of employment in the usual form, and which also contained the following provision:

"It is further understood that the Board may remove you at any time, upon thirty days' written notice, should your work or conduct be unsatisfactory to said Board, and you shall then be entitled to such installments as are due up to the date on which such removal takes effect."

Relator entered upon her duties as such teacher on September 4th, 1911, and continued therein until the 12th day of January ,1912. Between September 4th, 1911, and December 12, 1911, friction and difficulty arose between relator and the principal of the schools. On December 12, 1911, the relator was requested to meet with the Board for the purpose of discussing the situation then present in the school. The relator met with the Board, and a complaint in writing, filed against her by the principal of the school, was read to her, and the matters therein contained were discussed at length by the parties. At said meeting the Board decided, after due consideration had upon the complaint and the answer of relator, to request relator's resignation, which was done in writing. On the following day relator tendered her resignation in writing, to become effective January 12, 1912. The District Court found that under the circumstances the resignation was not a voluntary resignation, and that the transaction between the Board and the relator amounted to a discharge of her. The court found that the relator was removed as such teacher pursuant to the provision of the contract heretofore quoted, and that the Board had the right, under said contract, to request the relator's resignation or to discharge her.

The basis for the action of the Board in removing the relator is disclosed by its letter requesting her resignation, which is as follows:

"After due consideration of all the evidence before the Board, both pro and con, it was decided that it would not be to the best interests of the school for you to retain your present position. The lack of harmony on the corps, and the feeling that exists between you and Mr. Twining, (the principal), would be a prevailing feature that would menace the good government of the school."

It appears that the Board had no complaint of relator as a teacher, or as a most worthy woman. The difficulty all arose out of the strained relations between relator and the principal, to whose orders she was subject, and which were of such a character and extent as to endanger the discipline, good order and welfare of the school. Under these circumstances the Board removed the relator, and

she brought mandamus to be reinstated.   The District
Court denied the relief and dismissed the proceeding, and
the relator appealed.

A fundamental error lurks in the argument of counsel for appellant, to the effect that mandamus can be maintained under the circumstances in this case.   It is a general principle of universal application that mandamus is
not an available remedy for enforcement of contract rights,
because there is another adequate remedy in the ordinary
course of law, in the form of an action for damages.   High
Ex. Leg. Rem. (3rd ed.), sec. 25; 25 A. & E. Ency. of
Law, (2nd ed.) 20; 26 Cyc. 163, 164.

Even under the Common Law Procedure Act of Great
Britain, of 1854, which greatly broadened the scope of the
remedy ,mandamus is still not there available for the enforcement of contractual rights.   The reasons for the construction of the act are clearly pointed out by Lord Campbell, C. J., in Benson v. Paull, 6 El. & Bl., 273, 119 Eng.
Rep. 865.

The principle mentioned is specifically applied to a case
of this kind in State v. Smith, 49 Neb. 755, and in Board
of Education v. State, 100 Wis. 455.

It is only where the teacher, by positive provision of
law, has a fixed tenure of office, or can be removed
1   only in a certain prescribed manner, and where, consequently, it is the plain ministerial duty of a school
board to retain him, that mandamus can be maintained.
This was the condition of affairs in all of the cases relied
upon by counsel for appellant.   Thus in Gilman v. Bassette,
33 Conn. 298, the teacher was restored to her position by
mandamus because the governing body of the school had
so ordered and the order was disobeyed by an inferior committee.   So in Morley v. Power, 73 Tenn. (5 Lea.) 691,
the court held that by reason of the terms of the statute
a teacher could be removed only for certain causes named,
and that none of these causes existed, the defense being in
the case, that the teacher had never been elected.   In People v. Van Sicklen, 43 Hun. 537, the teacher had not been
removed, but was excluded from the school by reason of a

rule of the school officers to the effect that only two teachers could be employed, and there were already two teachers who were senior in rank to her. Her rights to hold the place were expressly provided for by statute, and no removal had been attempted. The court, consequently, held that mandamus was a proper remedy. In Brown v. Owen, 23 So. 35, the holder of a first grade state license was selected by a school district to teach for the ensuing year, which selection was certified to the county superintendent. The superintendent refused to enter into a contract with him, as required by the statute, and he brought mandamus. The court held that the superintendent had no discretion and was compelled by mandamus to enter into the contract with the teacher.

A leading case on this subject is Kennedy v. Board of Education, 22 Pac. 1042. It appears that in California, by reason of the terms of their statute, the holders of city certificates, when elected, can be dismissed only for violation of the rules of the Board of Education, or for incompetency, unprofessional or immoral conduct. As construed by the courts there, after having been once elected to teach in a city in California, in case the term for which the teacher is not specified in the contract, a right to hold the place indefinitely, unless removed for the causes men· tioned in the statute. The plaintiff in the case cited had not been removed for any of the causes mentioned in the statute, but was transferred to a school of lower grade and had a lower compensation. The court held that the transfer to a lower grade of school was a removal within the meaning of the statute, and that mandamus would lie to reinstate her in a school of the proper grade. By reason of the terms of the statute, the court held that a teacher once elected acquired a right of continuing and permanent character in the nature of an office, and that, consequently, there was a lack of power in the school officers to remove her. The court clearly points out that it is only by reason of the terms of the statute that they hold mandamus to be an available remedy. In discussing another section than the one under which the right to hold the place is held to exist, the court says:

"Therefore, if this section stood alone, we might consistently hold that the teacher became, by such employment, an employe, in the ordinary sense of the term; that her right to the position must depend upon her contract, and that alone; and that the only restraint upon the right of the board to dismiss her or remove her would rest in the contract, and a violation of such contract would only entitle her to an action for damages, and not to mandamus, to be restored to her place. This section contains no limitation as to the time for which a board of education in a city may employ a teacher. There is such a limitation, but it is confined in terms to boards of trustees. Therefore, such board of education may, under this section, employ a teacher for 1 year or 10, or for an indefinite time, as, for example, during the competency or good behavior of the teacher employed. But we have another section, forming a part of the same statute, bearing directly upon the question; and the two must be construed together."

Then follows a quotation and discussion of the section under which the holding in the case is made. The court further says:

"The writ of mandamus may issue in this state 'to compei the admission of a party to the use and enjoyment of a right or office to which he is entitled, and from which he is unlawfully precluded.' Code Civil Procedure, section 1085. It may be conceded that a right to hold the position of teacher in the public schools would not be a 'right' within the meaning of this section, if such right depended solely upon a contract with the board of education and the term for which such position should be held were not fixed by the statute. But such is not the case. As we have seen, the term for which the respondent was entitled to hold her position was not fixed by any contract with appellant. The duration of her term of service is fixed by the statute; and her removal from it was not merely a violation of a contract, but of an express provision of law forbidding such removal. Although her right to take the position depended upon the act of appellant, the right to continue in it was preserved to her by the statute; and to take it from her was to deprive her of a right given her by law, and to which she has a right to be restored by mandamus."

The distinction above pointed out between cases where the relation between the teacher and the school officers rests in contract and those where the relation rests in positive law, is thus clearly pointed out in the California case, and furnishes a ground for the refusal of mandamus in the one case and the granting of it in the other.

Counsel for appellant seek to draw from our statutes a conclusion which we cannot adopt. No provision in our statutes has been pointed out which would authorize the holding that a teacher in the public schools of this state has any tenure of office otherwise than as provided by the contract which he makes with the school officers. In the absence of some controlling provision of law, we know of no reason to build up around school officers any restrictions as to the form of contracts which they may make with the school teachers, or any restrictions upon their powers of removal.

2

That in the absence of some controlling provision of law, the authority to employ includes the power to dismiss, see,

> 25 A. & E. Ency. of Law, (2nd ed.) 19;
> People v. Hyde, 89 N. Y. 11;
> Wallace v. School District, 50 Neb. 171;
> Loehr v. Board of Education, 108 Pac. 327;
> Harby v. Board of Education, 83 Pac. 1082.

This is especially so where the right is specifically reserved in the contract as in this case.

The cases relied upon by counsel for appellant for the contrary doctrine, are all cases discussing the rightfulness or wrongfulness of the dismissal of the teacher, and arose upon actions for damages for breach of the contract or injunctions, and turned upon the statutory provisions of the particular jurisdiction. That is not the question in this case. The question here is whether the Board had the power which it attempted to exercise, and we hold that it had.

The suggestion that section 5 of chapter 43, laws 1901, providing for the dismissal of teachers affected with tuberculosis is exclusive, and prevents dismissal for other reasons, is without merit, as is the suggestion that the relator had no hearing.

It follows, from what has been said, that the judgment of the District Court was correct, and should be affirmed, and it is so ordered.

[No. 1518, August 28, 1913.]

BENJAMIN B. SPENCER, Appellant, v. GROSS-KELLY COMPANY, Richard Dunn & Edward B. Wheeler, co-partners trading under the name, MORA TIMBER COMPANY, Appellees.

SYLLABUS (BY THE COURT)

1. A judgment will be reversed where there is no evidence to support the verdict upon which it is based.

P. 194

Appeal from the District Court of Bernalillo County; Herbert F. Raynolds, District Judge; reversed and remanded.

MARRON & WOOD, Albuquerque, N. M., for appellant.

The cutting of the timber on sections 1 and 2 was never enjoined by legal process, as provided in the contract. Rodgers Locomotive Works v. Erie Ry. Co., 20 N. J. Eq. 379; 20 Enc. Pl. & Pr., 664, and cases cited; Perea v. Harrison, 7 N. M. 666.

No evidence to authorize submission to the jury of the question of plaintiff's acquiescence or waiver of rights under the contract. Hoxie v. Home Ins. Co., 32 Conn. 21; Kent v. Warner, 11 Allen 563; Bishop on Contracts,

sec. 792, (ed. 1887); Shaw v. Spencer, 100 Mass. 395;
Bennecke v. Conn. Mut. Life Ins. Co., 105 U. S. 355;
Ripley v. Etna Ins. Co., 30 N. Y. 164; Merchants Ins.
Co. v. La Croix, 45 Tex. 168; Article on Waiver, 28 Enc.
Pl. & Pr., 1st ed., 526.

E. W. DOBSON, MANN & VENABLE, Albuquerque, N. M.,
for appellees.

It is a well established rule of construction of contracts,
that the intent of the parties governs. 9 Cyc. 577; Chesa-
peake & Ohio Canal Co. v. Hill, 15 Wall. 94; Mauran v.
Bullus, 16 Pet. 528.

Courts in construing contracts will adopt the construction which the parties themselves give to certain terms
used. Dist. of Columbia v. Gallagher, 124 U. S. 505;
Clark v. Carlisle Gold Min. Co., 5 N. M. 323, 21 Pac. 356.

The matter in dispute, under the issues in this case, was
a question for the jury to determine, and was fairly submitted. Clark v. Carlisle Gold Min. Co., 5 N. M. 323.

Upon the question of waiver the issue was properly submitted to the jury and its finding is sustained by the evidence. Pence v. Langdon, 99 U. S. 578; Territory v.
Clark, 13 N. M. 59; Territory v. Hicks, 6 N. M. 596;
Territory v. Barrett, 8 N. M. 70; Schofield v. Territory,
9 N. M. 526; District of Columbia v. Camden Iron Works,
181 U. S. 454; Williams v. Bank of United States, 2 Pet.
102; Nickerson v. Nickerson, 80 Me. 100; Robinson v.
Penn. F. & Ins. Co., 90 Me. 389.

Plaintiff, by acquiescence, was estopped from denying
that he had not waived his right to claim damages under
the contract. Holliday v. Stewart, 151 U. S. 229; Speake
v. U. S., Cranch 28, 3 L. Ed. 645; Deen v. Milne, 113 N.
Y. 303; Hempy, et al., v. Griess, 51 N. Y. Sup. 1072; In
re Pierson's Estate, 46 N. Y. Sup. 557.

Authority of an attorney at law to represent his client
Moulton v. Bowker, 115 Mass. 40; Hirsch v. Fleming, 77
Ga. 594; McClosky v. Sutro, 64 Cal. 485; Thompson v.

Pershing, 86 Ind. 303; Benson v. Carr, 73 Me. 76; Ohl-
quest v. Farwell, 71 Iowa 231.

Where the defendant is present in court when an order
is made authorizing a writ of injunction he is bound to
observe it. Danville Banking & Tr. Co. v. Parks, 88 Ill.
170; Murphy v. Harker, 41 S. E. 585; Haws v. Fellows,
78 N. W. 812; Ex parte Lennon, 166 U. S. 548; Ex parte
Richards, 117 Fed. 658; Seattle Brew. & Malt. Co. v.
Hansen, 114 Fed. 1011.

OPINION OF THE COURT.

PARKER, J.—Appellants sued appellees for damages
for alleged breach of a contract for the cutting of certain
timber on certain lands of appellees. The contract contained a provision as follows:

"It is further agreed and understood, by and between
said parties that should the cutting of the said timber on
said west half of section 1 and on said section 2, be enjoined by legal process the said party of the first part will
not claim damages on account of such suspension of said
work from the said party of the second part."

Appellees answered that the United States had brought
suit to enjoin them from cutting timber on said lands;
that they had been served with an order to show cause
why said injunction should not issue; that thereupon H.
W. Kelly, one of the appellees, had agreed, for all of appellees, with the United States Attorney for the District
of New Mexico, that they would refrain from cutting said
timber during the pendency of said suit; and that appellant was thereupon, on December 26, 1907, notified by
Richard Dunn, one of the appellees, of said agreement, in
which he acquiesced and made no claim whatever to any
right to cut the said timber, and never demanded of defendants the right to cut timber, thereupon, after said
date. On December 26, 1907, the said Richard Dunn
wrote appellant as follows:

"On account of a law suit instituted against us by the
U. S. Government, to dispossess us of the lands we bought
in this township, among which are a part of section one

and all of section two, you will please discontinue the cutting of timber on those sections at once, and not resume
cutting until this litigation is ended.

"Kindly acknowledge receipt of this and greatly oblige."

To this letter the appellant replied as follows:

"I am in receipt of your letter regarding the cutting of
timber—will try to get up in two or three days."

Shortly after the date of this letter the appellant and
the said Richard Dunn had various conversations concerning this matter and they both give their versions of what
was said. The appellant testified that he was never notified of any such agreement between Kelly and the United
States Attorney, but that he was told by Dunn that the
appellees had been enjoined from cutting the timber.
Dunn testified to several conversations with appellant, but
in none of those conversations does he state that he ever
informed the appellant of the agreement between Kelly
and the United States Attorney. He states that he informed appellant that there was a suit brought by the
Government in consequence of which appellees had to
withhold from cutting the timber and as a consequence
they could not consent to appellant cutting on the lands
in question; that he supposed, from his information, that
there was some kind of an order restraining the cutting
of the timber. The court submitted this question to the
jury upon the theory that it was incumbent upon the appellees to satisfy them by preponderance of the evidence
that the appellant knew of the arrangement between the
United States and appellee, Kelly, and knew or believed
that the cutting of the timber had not been actually enjoined by legal process, and that, with knowledge of these
facts, he consented and agreed that his right to cut said
timber would not be insisted upon by him.

This was evidently a correct theory had it been supported by any evidence in the case. The trouble with
1   the case is that a certain set of facts is pleaded and
there is no evidence whatever in the record to support
that theory. Had the appellees pleaded that the appellant acquiesced in their request to refrain from cutting

the timber, as contained in their letter of December 26, 1907, there is ample evidence in the record to support such acquiescence. They pleaded, however, an entirely different set of facts, viz:—that the appellant was informed of the agreement between the United States Attorney and the appellees, of which there is absolutely no evidence in the record.

It is impossible for this court to amend the pleadings for the reason that at every step throughout the trial, counsel for appellant objected to any departure from the allegations of the answer.

For the reasons stated, the judgment of the court below will be reversed and the cause remanded with instructions to award a new trial, and it is so ordered.

[No. 1532, August 28, 1913.]

TERRITORY OF NEW MEXICO, Appellee, v. COMMIE E. PRATHER, Appellant.

SYLLABUS (BY THE COURT)

1. The jury must be selected, empaneled and sworn in the manner required by the statute, and a material departure from the statutory method, by which a party is deprived of a substantial right, is ground for reversal.

P. 199

2. Where the statute requires the jury to be selected by lot, all other methods are impliedly prohibited, and the right to have the jury so selected is a substantial right, the deprivation of which must be presumed to be prejudicial to a party.

P. 201

3. Sections 995, 997, 1001 and 1002, R. S. 1897, construed, and held to require the selection of jurors, summoned upon a special venire, by lot.

P. 204

Appeal from the District Court of Chaves County; John T. McClure, District Judge; reversed and remanded.

K. K. Scott; O. O. Askren, for appellant.

Court erred in not selecting a jury as required by law. C. L. 1897, secs. 995, 997, 1001 and 1002; 7 How. Pr. 441.

Jurymen must be obtained from ballots, folded and placed in a box by the clerk, and not by calling the names as they appear, in order, on the list of the special venire. Territory v. Carmody, 8 N. M. 376.

Hearsay testimony is not admissible. Mitchell v. State, 114 Ala. 1, 22 So. —; Baldwin v. St. L. K. & N. R Co., 68 Iowa 37, 25 N. W. 918.

It was imperative for the prosecution to show by competent testimony that the said Satterwhite was without the state, as a predicate precedent to the proof of Satterwhite's testimony, given on a former trial. Kitchner v. Laughlin, (N. M.) 23 Pac. 175.

Mr. Young testified from hearsay only, therefore court erred. Drigger v. U. S. (Okla.) 95 Pac. 612.

"Before any proof whatever of the former testimony of an absent witness is admissible, it must be proved that such witness is absent from the state, either permanently or for such an indefinite time that his return is merely contingent or conjectural, or that said witness cannot with due diligence be found within the state." Reynolds v. U. S. 98 U. S. 115; Harris v. State, 73 Ala. 495; Thompson v. State, 106 Ala. 67, 17 So. 512; Louisville & N. R. Co. v. Whitely Co., 100 Ky. 413, 38 S. W. 678; State v. Able, 65 Mo. 357; Reynolds v. Fitzpatrick, 28 Mont. 170, 72 Pac. 510; Young v. Sage, 42 Neb. 37, 60 N. W. 313; Jackson D. Potter v. Bailey, 2 Johns. 17; Powell v. Waters, 17 Johns. 176; Crary v. Sprague, 12 Wend. 41, 27 Am. Dec. 110; Draper v. Stanley, 1 Heisk 432; Piano Mfg. Co. v. Parmenter, 56 Ill. App 258; Edwards v. Edwards, 93 Iowa 127, 61 N. W. 413; Lesassier v. Dashiell, 14 La. S. 467.

It is prerequisite to the admission of a transcript of testimony, taken on a former trial of the case, that such transcript be proved to be a correct statement of the former testimony. Wollen v. Wire, 110 Ind. 251, 11 N. E. 236; Morris v. Hamerle, 40 Mo. 489; Coughlin v. Hauessler, 50 Mo. 126; Mattox v. U. S., 156 U. S. 237; Burnett v. State, 87 Ga. 622, 13 S. E. 552; Luetgert v. Volker, 153 Ill. 385, 39 N. W. 113; Smith y. Scully, 66 Kans. 139, 71 Pac. 249; People v. Sligh, 48 Mich. 54, 11 N. W. 782; Reynolds v. Fitspatrick, 28 Mont. 170, 72 Pac. 510.

Earl Iden should have been sworn as a witness and testified in the presence of defendants of what the former testimony of Satterwhite was, refreshing his memory from his notes taken at the former trial. Reid v Reid, 73 Cal. 206, 14 Pac. 781; People v. Carty, 77 Cal. 213, 19 Pac. 490; Cerrusite Min. Co. v. Steele, 70 Pac. 1090; Stayner v. Joyce, 120 Ind. 99, 22 N. E. 89; Herrick v. Swomley, 56 Md. 462; Byrd v. Hartman, 70 Mo. App. 57; State v. Ambrose, 47 Neb. 233, N. W. 306; Jordon v. Howe, 95 N. W. 853; People v. Lee Fat, 54 Cal. 527; Kean v. Com., 10 Ky. 190, 19 Am. Rep. 63.

An oath is essential before any testimony whatever may be introduced against the accused, except dying declaration. State v. Williams, 49 W. Va. 220, 38 S. E. 495; Coleman v. State, 43 Tex. Crim. 15, 63 S. W. 322; Chappell v. State, 71 Ala. 322.

Statute does not declare the legal value of such stenographic notes as evidence. Kirchner v. Laughlin, (N. M.) 23 Pac. 175.

Court erred in telling the jury to consider the paper as read to them to be the testimony of the said Satterwhite in this trial, the same as if he were present in person and testifying. Jackson v. Bailey, 2 Johns 17; Ballenger v. Barnes 14 N. C. 460; State v. Hooker, 17 Vt. 658; Quinn v. Halbert, 57 Vt. 178; State v. Fetterly, (Wash) 74 Pac. 810.

Supreme Court shall examine the record and on the facts therein contained alone shall award a new trial, re-

verse or affirm the judgment of the district court   Laws
1907, ch. 57, sec. 38.

FRANK W. CLANCY, Attorney General; HARRY S.
CLANCY, Assistant Attorney General, Santa Fe, N. M., for
appellee.

The jury was properly entpaneled. C. L. 1897, sec. 1002.
No error in the special instruction given by the court.
Territory v. Donahue, 16 N. M. 17.
Where an instruction given is identical in principle
with one which is refused the refusal is not error. City of
Chicago v. Moore, 28 N. E. 1071; Chicago Trans. Co. v.
Kinnare, 115 Ill. App. 115; Chicago U. T. Co. v. Leach,
117 Ill. App. 167-74; Franks v. Matson, 71 N. E. 1011;
Glove Co. v. Trans. Co., 106 N. E. 749; Hirte v. Railway
Co., 106 N. E. 1068; R. R. Co. v. Anderson, 56 N. E. 331;
Coal Co. v. Haenni, 35 N. E. 162; Chicago U. T. Co. v.
Jacobson, 75 N. E. 508; Kyle v. People, 74 N. E. 146;
Chicago v. Moore, 28 N. E. 1071; Railway v. Matthewson,
72 N. E. 443; State v. Stockhammer, 75 Pac. 810.
"When the substance of requested charges has been fully
given in instructions, it is not error to refuse to repeat the
instructions, though expressed in different language."
Kennard v. State, 28 So. 858.
Error assigned upon the admission of the transcript in
the present case is a mere technicality. Under all the circumstances and in the absence of any reason to believe that
defendant was in any way prejudiced, we submit that the
ends of justice will be better served by disregarding this
objection. 1 Thompson Trials, sec. 200; People v. Clem-
inson, 250 Ill. 163; Wallace v. People, 159 Ill. 446; Jennings v. People, 189 Ill. 320; Barbor v. People, 203 Ill.
543; Wistrand v. People, 218 Ill. 323.

OPINION BY THE COURT.

ROBERTS, C. J.—This is an appeal from a conviction
of murder in the second degree. The regular panel of
jurors having been exhausted, before completion of the

trial jury, a special venire was issued, for twenty additional talesmen. The return of the sheriff showed service
upon seventeen of the said talesmen, all of whom were
placed in the box and examined as to their general qualifications to serve as jurors; four were excused for various
reasons, leaving thirteen names upon the list, qualified to
serve as jurors. The names of the thirteen jurors, so
found to possess the general qualifications required, were
not written on separate slips of paper and placed in a box
and withdrawn therefrom, but were called from the list
returned by the sheriff, in the order in which their names
appeared upon the list. When the first name was called,
appellant objected, and asked that the thirteen names be
written on separate slips, placed in a box and drawn by
lot. His objection was overruled and the request refused,
the trial court holding that only the names of jurors upon
the regular panel were required to be written upon separate slips and drawn by lot, and that the jurors upon the
special venire, under the statute were required to be called
from the list returned by the sheriff, in the order in which
their names appeared upon the list. Appellant renewed
his objection as each juror was called, and exhausted all
of his peremptory challenges, and there yet remained upon
the list the names of four jurors who had not been called
into the jury box. Thus it will be seen that appellant is
without the rule announced by the Supreme Court of
Louisiana, in the case of State v. Dorsey, 40 La. Ann. 739,
which is stated in the syllabus as follows:

"An objection to the effect that the names of persons
who are summoned as tales jurors were not written on
ballots and placed in the venire box and drawn therefrom,
but that the same were called from a list that was made
out and furnished to the counsel by the sheriff, will not
prevail in case it appears that the entire list was exhausted before the panel was completed."

The jury must be selected, empaneled and sworn in the
    manner required by the statute, and a material depar-
1 ture from the statutory method, by which a party is
    deprived of a substantial right is ground for reversal.

24 Cyc. 255. Where the statute requires the jury to be selected by lot, all other methods are impliedly prohibited; Territory v. Carmody, 8 N. M. 376, and the right to have the jury so selected is a substantial right, the deprivation of which must be presumed to be prejudicial to a party. A statute of Alabama required the name of each juror to be written upon a separate slip of paper, folded, placed in a box and drawn therefrom by lot. The provision was disregarded by the trial court, and the names were called from the list returned. The Supreme Court in discussing the question say:

"On the trial, in such a case, the statute directs how the jury shall be drawn. This statute confers certain rights upon the accused, which enable him to obtain a fair and impartial trial, * * * * * The directions thus given are peremptory. They cannot be disregarded by the Courts. Ex Parte Chase, 43 Ala. 303; 3 Chitty's Gen. Pr., 53, 54, 56. The names of the jurors must be written on separate slips of paper, and each name by itself, folded or rolled up, placed in a box or some substitute therefor, and shaken together, and then the slips drawn out, one by one, until the jury is completed, as prescribed in the statute. Brazier v. State, 44 Ala. 387."

The object of statutes requiring the drawing of jurors by lot, is to secure for the trial of a cause, fair and impartial jurors. By leaving the selection of jurors to chance, the parties are never able to know in advance that any particular person will be called into the jury box, hence the temptation to tamper with jurors is to some extent removed. Again, such statutes remove from the court or sheriff the power to place any particular juror in the box for the trial of a case. "In the United States, the usual mode for presenting jurors for acceptance or rejection is by drawing from a box or receptacle, ballots, slips, or substitutes therefor containing the names of persons summoned or directed to attend, which have been placed therein in accordance with the requirements of law." 12 Encl. Pl. & Pr., 375.

In the case of State v. Holmes, 54 Mo. 153, the Supreme

Court of Missouri construed a statute of that state, with
reference to the empaneling of juries, which provided that
the sheriff or other officer summoning a jury, should deliver to the clerk a list of all jurors summoned, who should
strike from the list the names of all persons excused by
the court or challenged for cause, or peremptorily challenged by the parties; and that the clerk should record in
his minute book the first twelve names remaining on the
list; and that the jurors whose names were thus recorded,
should be the jurors to try the cause for which they were
selected. In the case decided, two of the persons, whose
names were among the first twelve on the list, were omitted to be called, and were thereby excluded from the jury.
The Court say:

"The law is peremptory, that the first twelve names remaining on the list shall be recorded, and that the names
thus recorded shall be the jury to try the cause for which
they are selected. The first twelve constitute the properly
selected jurors, and neither party can be deprived of this
selection without his consent. * * * * If the court may
refuse to have two called among the first twelve, it may refuse a half dozen, and if it is not bound to take the first
twelve it may take the last twelve. Such a practice would
not only set at defiance the plain mandates of the statute,
but it would lead to a confusion and uncertainty utterly
destructive of the rights of the parties."

Where the statute requires that the jurors must be selected by lot the statutory form must be followed. Thompson on Trials, 2nd ed., sec. 96. It will thus be seen

2 that if the statute requires the jurors to be so selected,
and jurors are selected in some other manner, over a
party's objection, it is reversible error. It therefore remains to be determined whether the statute of New Mexico
requires the selection of jurors, summoned to complete
the panel, where the regular panel has been exhausted, to
be by lot. The sections of the statute relating to this subject are contained in C. L. 1897, and read as follows:

"Sec. 995. At the opening of the court the clerk must
prepare separate ballots, containing the names of the per-

sons returned as jurors, which must be folded as nearly alike as possible, and so that the name cannot be seen, and must deposit them in a sufficient box."

"Sec. 997. Before the name of any juror is drawn, the box must be closed and shaken, so as to intermingle the ballots therein; the clerks must then, without looking at the ballots, draw them from the box, through a hole in the lid, so large only as conveniently to admit the hand."

"Sec. 1001. The jury consists of twelve men, chosen by lot, as prescribed in this chapter, and sworn to try and determine the issue by a unanimous verdict."

"Sec. 1002. If a sufficient number cannot be obtained from the box to form a jury, the court may, as often as is necessary, order the sheriff to summon so many persons qualified to serve as jurors as it deems sufficient to form a jury; the jurors so summoned must be called from the list returned by the sheriff, and so many of them, not excused or discharged, as may be necessary to complete the jury, must be empaneled and sworn."

It is contended by the State that sec. 1002, supra, requires the names to be called from the list of special venire returned by the sheriff, and that the provisions of section 995 and 997 apply only to the regular panel. It is hardly to be presumed that the legislature intended to adopt one method for calling the names on the regular panel and another distinct and different method for those on the special venire. The reasons for the selection of trial jurors by lot would appear to be the same in either case. But it is contended that the legislature, by the language employed in section 1002, viz:—"the jurors so summoned must be called from the list returned by the sheriff." meant that the juror must be called from such list into the trial jury box to be examined on his voir dire in the order in which his name appeared upon such list, without such name being placed in a box by the clerk and drawn by lot The practice, universally followed in New Mexico, has been to call the jurors, from the list returned by the sheriff, into the jury box, to be examined as to their general qualifications as jurors, and so many, as are found to possess such general qualifications, and as are not excused by the court, are retained as jurors and their names are placed in a box, in the same manner as are the names on the regular panel, and drawn therefrom by lot, as required, until the panel is complete or the names exhausted. And such we believe to be the correct interpretation of the statute. "The jurors so summoned must be called from the list" refers simply to the preliminary examination of the proposed jurors, as to their general qualification, and the making up by the clerk of the list of names which he places in the box, upon separate slips of paper. It was intended, evidently, that all the names upon the list returned by the sheriff should be called, and the persons summoned should be examined as to their general qualification for jury duty, and from the list of those found eligible for jury duty the jury in the particular case should be selected, but by lot, as in the case of the regular panel, for section 1001 says, "the jury consists of twelve men, chosen by lot, as prescribed in this chapter," etc. If we should hold that the names of jurors summoned to complete the panel need not be drawn by lot, then section 1001 would necessarily be limited in its meaning and application to a jury selected from the regular panel. But it is contended that the language used in section 995, supra, indicates that its provisions only apply to the regular panel, viz:—"At the opening of the court the clerk must prepare separate ballots," and it would be impossible for the clerks to prepare separate ballots, containing the names of jurors upon the special venire in the manner prescribed. But if we consider the entire statute, the object in view, the purpose to be accomplished, the evident intent of the legislature, it will be seen that the various sections can be brought into accord and a sensible and intelligent effect given to each in furtherance of the general design of the legislature. All the sections of the statute under consideration were enact- ed at the same time as a part of one act. It was the evident purpose to provide for the selection of jurors by lot. To give to section 995 the narrow construction contended for by the State would preclude the selection of jurors by lot, where it was necessary to issue a special venire to complete the panel· because it would be impossible to place their names in the box at "the opening of court."

"In the exposition of a statute the intention of the law maker will prevail over the literal sense of the terms; and its reason and intention will prevail over the strict letter.

"When the words are not explicit the intention is to be ·collected from the context; from the occasion and necessity of the law; from the mischief felt and the remedy in view; and the intention is to be taken or presumed according to what is consonant with reason and good discretion." 1 Kent's Com., 461.

In enacting this statute it is apparent that the prime object in view was the selection of trial jurors by lot, **3** and to give to section 995, supra,· the construction suggested would practically destroy the entire act, and defeat the evident purpose. The provision in question, requiring the clerk, "at the opening of the court," to perform the named duties, at most is only directory, Lewis· Sutherland Stat. Cons., sec. 612, and is satisfied by the performance of the duties imposed at any time prior to the drawing of the names of the jurors from the box.

The trial court erred in calling the jurors for their voir dire examination from the list returned by the sheriff, instead of having such names drawn by lot, as required by the statute, over appellant's objection. For the error thus ·committed, this cause is reversed and remanded, and a new trial is ordered.

[No. 1538, August 28, 1913.]

J. S. and M. E. WILLIAMSON, Appellants, v. CHAS A. STEVENS, Sheriff Lincoln County· New Mexico, Appellee.

SYLLABUS (BY THE COURT)

1.· The form of execution and authentication of bills of sale for the transfer of title to live stock, except sheep, is

prescribed by section 119, C. L. 1897, which requires such
bills of sale to be acknowledged by some officer authorized to
take acknowledgments of conveyance of real estate, and which
section, in that regard, repeals, by necessary implication, the
provisions of section 75, C. L. 1897.

P. 206

Appeal from the District Court of Lincoln County;
Edward L. Medler, District Judge; reversed and remanded.

GEORGE B. BARBER, Lincoln, N. M., for appellants.

Valid sale of cattle in this state is accomplished by delivery of animals, accompanied by a written bill of sale
signed by vendor and acknowledged by him. C. L. 1897,
sec. 119; section 75 of the C. L. 1884 repealed by laws
1895 (C. L. 1897, sec. 119.)

Husband and wife may enter into contracts with each
other. Laws 1907, chap. 37, sec. 15.

Bill of sale, Exhibit "D," complies with statute. C. L.
1897, s. 119.

Court erred in ruling out Exhibit "B," which is an ex-
emplified copy of a judicial record. 17 Cyc. 326, and
cases cited.

Exhibit "C" was a certified copy of a deed, certified to
by the clerk of a court of record, and the same is admissible in evidence as an office copy. 17 Cyc. 326.

Possession of personal property is good evidence of title
against all persons except the owner. Rogers v. Bates, 1
Mich. N. P. 93-94; Tolerton & Stetson Co. v. Petrie, 82
N. W. 199-201, 12 S. D. 595; Words & Phrases, vol. 6,
5467.

H. B. HAMILTON, Carrizozo, N. M., for appellee.

OPINION OF THE COURT.

PARKER, J.—This is an action of replevin brought by
the appellants in the Court below against the appellee. It

was tried before the court, without a jury, and resulted in
a judgment for the appellee.

It appears that the appellee was Sheriff of Lincoln
County, and, as such, levied execution upon some cattle
as the property of one R. J. Wood. The defence was that
the cattle were not the property of R. J. Wood, but were
the property of Mattie M. Wood, the appellant's vendor.
To show the ownership of Mattie M. Wood, appellants offered in evidence a bill of sale which the court excluded
for the reasons set out in his findings, as follows:

"The plaintiff attempted to prove that Mattie M. Wood
was the owner of these cattle by virtue of a bill of sale
which the court ruled out on the ground that the same
does not comply with the statute of New Mexico. The
statute requires that bills of sale of cattle must be in writing and signed before two witnesses. The plaintiff in
this case, having failed to show that Mattie M. Wood was
the owner of these cattle in the manner required by law,
at the time she executed the bill of sale to the plaintiff,
judgment must go for the defendant. The law only provides one manner of transfer of range cattle, that is, by
bill of sale conforming to the statute."

It thus appears that the court held it was necessary, in
order to transfer the title to range cattle in this state, that
the bill of sale must be executed and witnessed by two
witnesses. In this the court was in error. The section of
the statute under which the District Court held that the
bill of sale must be witnessed by two witnesses, is section
75, C. L. 1897. This section was enacted as section 11 of
chapter 47 of the laws of 1884. The error into which the
court fell, no doubt, arose out of an error in the annotations, of the compilers of the Compiled Laws of 1897, in
which they cite this section as coming from section 7 of
chapter 52, laws of 1897.

The law upon the subject of bills of sale of live stock, is
section 119, C. L. 1897, which comes from section 15 of
chapter 6 of the laws of 1895, and provides an entirely
1   different form in which bills of sale shall be authenticated. It provides that bills of sale of animals shall,

instead of being witnessed by two witnesses, be acknowledged by the vendor before some officer authorized to take
acknowledgments to deeds of conveyance. The act of 1895,
being inconsistent with that of 1884, in this regard, operates, of necessity, as a repeal by implication of the earlier
provisions. Bills of sale of sheep must be witnessed. Sec.
166, C. L. 1897.

It follows that the District Court committed error in
excluding the bill of sale, and for the reasons stated the
judgment of the court below will be reversed, and the
cause remanded with instructions to award a new trial, and
it is so ordered.

[No. 1550, August 29, 1913.]

MARY MARGARET YOUNG, et al., Appellants, v.
IṢAAC N. WOODMAN, et al., Appellees.

SYLLABUS (BY THE COURT)

1. Neither the rule to the effect that where the facts required to be shown are of a negative character, the burden
of evidence may sometimes be sustained by proof rendering
probable the existence of the negative facts, nor the rule to
the effect that where knowledge or means of knowledge are
almost wholly with the party not having the burden of proof,
when all the evidence within the power of the moving party
has been produced, the burden of evidence may some times
shift to the party having the knowledge or means of knowledge, excuses the party having the burden of evidence from
showing, no matter with what difficulty, sufficient facts, necessarily inconsistent with the position of the adverse party,
to cause the court to say that a prima facie case has been
made out requiring explanation, in which event, such showing, in connection with silence of the adverse party, may be
sufficient to produce positive conviction in the mind of the
court or jury.

P. 211

Appeal from the District Court of Taos County;
Thomas D. Leib, District Judge; affirmed.

A. C. VOORHEES, Raton, N. M., for appellees.

"The burden is upon the party, plaintiff or defendant,
who asserts that a contract or conveyance was obtained by
fraudulent representations, or that a will was obtained by
fraud or undue influence."

Jones on Evidence, sec. 190;
Bank v. Lampierre, 4 P. C. 572;
Wallace v. Mattice, 118 Ind. 59;
Bowden v. Bowden, 75 Ill. 143;
Betty v. Fishel, 100 Mass. 448;
Smith v. Ogilvie, 127 N. Y. 143;
Wellborn v. Tiller, 10 Ala. 305;
Baldwin v. Parker, 99 Mass. 79.

OPINION OF THE COURT.

PARKER, J.—This is an action to cancel and set aside
a certain contract for the use of water, and to quiet title
of appellants in and to certain water rights involved in
the said contract. The contract which is the subject of
dispute is dated October 6, 1909, and recites that for and
in consideration of the sum of $150.00 paid, and $25.00
additional to be paid the first day of each and every year
thereafter, the appellants' testator agreed with I. W. Woodman, one of the appellees, that he would permit the said
Woodman to use the water from three of his water rights
in the Latir Creek, from six o'clock P. M. to six o'clock
A. M. and on each and every Friday and Saturday from
April 15th to September 15th of each year.

The bill of plaintiff is based upon three propositions,
viz., that the signature of plaintiffs' testator, attached to
the contract, is not, in fact, his signature; second, that if
the same is his signature, it was procured at a time
when he was not in a condition, by reason of ill health and
sickness, or temporary intoxication, to realize and understand what kind of an instrument he was signing; and

third, that there was no consideration of any kind for said alleged transfer or contract.

At the conclusion of the testimony the chancellor·· upon motion of appellees, awarded judgment for them, upon the ground that the allegations of the complaint had not been sustained.

An examination of the testimony discloses that the. appellant, Mary Margaret Young, was the widow and executrix of the last Will and Testament of Henry J. Young, deceased, who executed the contract, and that the other appellants are the daughters of the deceased. The widow and one of the daughters testified in the case, and neither of them attempted to say that the signature to the contract of the husband and father, was not genuine, nor was any evidence of any character to that effect offered by the plaintiffs. There was, therefore, an entire failure of proof upon this point.

Not a word of testimony was offered to show that the deceased was in such a condition of ill health, or in such a state of intoxication, as not to be able to understand what he was doing. There was, therefore, an absolute failure of proof in support of the second proposition.

In support of the third proposition advanced in the bill· the widow testified that she was familiar with the business transactions of her deceased husband, and that no trace of the receipt by him of the $150 was to be found in any of his books or papers, or in the banks where he deposited his funds. This proof was clearly insufficient to establish want of consideration for the contract, the provision for the annual payment of $25,00, standing alone, furnishing sufficient consideration.

The answer alleges that prior to the date of the contract. the deceased offered to act as the agent of Isaac N. Woodman, one of the appellees, to secure a water right for him. and a certain verbal agreement was thereupon entered into; that said Woodman afterwards learned that the particular water right which was to be purchased for him by the deceased, had been purchased by the deceased for himself; that thereupon, in order to avoid a law suit, the de-

fendant and said deceased compromised their differences
by entering into the contract hereinbefore mentioned.

The testimony for appellants was almost wholly devoted
to the proof of the fact that the deceased and Woodman
did not meet together on the day of the date of the contract, and that, consequently, the deceased could have
signed no such contract, and could have received no such
consideration. In the absence of some evidence tending
to show that the deceased had not in fact executed the contract, that is to say, that his signature thereto was not
genuine, this proof was immaterial. The evidence shows
that the appellee, Woodman, and the deceased saw each
other at the store and residence of the deceased on the 7th
and 8th of October, at one of which times it was entirely
possible for the contract to have been executed. If the
contract was in fact executed, and there is no evidence to
the contrary, it was immaterial that it was dated the 6th,
if it was in fact executed on the 7th or 8th. The widow
testified that Woodman showed her the contract and she
had opportunity to say whether the signature was genuine,
which she failed to do.

The appellees, therefore, neglected an opportunity to
show the truth, if, indeed, it was true that the deceased had
not executed the contract. The widow, on cross examination, was shown a check of the appellee, Woodman, to the
deceased, which was endorsed to the bank in which the
Youngs did their banking business. The amount and date
of the check is not shown by the record, and hence, the
evidence is of no particular value; but the appellant made
no effort whatever to show that the check, by reason of its
date, or amount, was inapplicable to the payment of the
consideration of $150.00 mentioned in the contract.

The case as it stands, then, furnishes no basis for the
application of the rule, relied upon by appellants, to the
effect that where the facts required to be shown are of a
negative character, the burden of evidence may sometimes
be sustained by proof rendering probable the existence of
the negative fact, or the rule to the effect that where
knowledge or means of knowledge are almost wholly with

the party not having the burden of proof, when all the evidence within the power of the moving party has been produced, the burden of evidence may sometimes shift **1** to the party having such knowledge or means of knowledge. Neither of those rules excuses the party having the burden of evidence from showing, no matter with what difficulty, sufficient facts, necessarily inconsistent with the position of the adverse party, to cause the court to say that a prima facie case has been made out requiring explanation, in which event, such showing, in connection with silence on the part of the adverse party, may be sufficient to produce positive conviction in the mind of the court or jury. See, 16 Cyc. 936, 937; 1 Elliott on Ev. 141; 2 Chamberlayne's Modern Law of Ev., section 996; 2 Wigmore Ev., sec. 2483, et seq. Col. Coal Co. v. U. S., 123 U. S. 307; Denver, etc., R. Co. v. U. S., 191 U. S. 84.

In this case no fact was produced necessarily inconsistent with the entire validity of the contract, and hence, the appellants failed to make out a prima facie case.

It follows that the judgment of the court below was correct, and should be affirmed, and it is so ordered.

[No. 1526, October 4, 1913.]

STATE OF NEW MEXICO, Appellant, v. H. A. INGALLS, Appellee.

SYLLABUS (BY THE COURT)

1. The true test of the validity of a statute, alleged to contain two subjects, one of which is not clearly expressed in the title, in conformity with sec. 16 of art. IV of the Constitution, is whether the title fairly gives reasonable notice of the subject matter of the statute itself.

P. 219

2. The generality of a title to an act of the legislature is no objection to it so long as it is not made a cover to legislation incongruous in itself, and which by no fair intendment

can be construed as having a necessary or proper connection.

P. 220

3. If there be more than one subject mentioned in the act, if they be germane or subsidiary to the main subject, or if relative directly or indirectly to the main subject, having a mutual connection, and are not foreign to the main subject, or so long as the provisions are of the same nature and come legitimately under one general denomination or subject the act is not unconstitutional.

P. 220

4. The law regulating the use of automobiles alone, of all the vehicles which use the highway, is not invalid special legislation.

P. 221

5. Sec. 3 of chapter 28, Session Laws of 1912, imposing license fees for automobiles, in excess of the expense of administering the act, is a revenue measure, and as such is a valid exercise of power by the legislature.

P. 222

6. Double taxation in the objectionable and prohibited sense exists only where the same property is taxed twice when it ought to be taxed but once, and to consider such double taxation the second tax must be imposed upon the same property by the same state or government during the same taxing period.

P. 223

7. There is no constitutional objection to the levy of a license tax for the privilege of carrying on a particular business and at the same time a tax on the property employed in the business.

P. 223

8. The requirement of equality and uniformity in taxation applies only to taxes in the proper sense of the word levied

with the object of raising revenue for general purposes, and not to such as are an extraordinary and exceptional kind, and is, under a constitutional provision providing for equality in taxation, to be restricted to taxes on property, as distinguished from such as are levied on occupations, business or franchises, and as distinguished also from exactions imposed in the exercise of the police power rather than that of taxation.

P. 224

9. Chapter 28, Session Laws of 1912, fixing an annual fee of $10 for a license fee for operating an automobile, is not unconstitutional, as a property tax imposed without regard to the value of the property on which it is made, but is a license tax, since the character of the tax is not determined by the mode adopted in fixing its amount.

P. 224

Appeal from the District Court of Chaves County; John T. McClure, District Judge; reversed and remanded with instructions to overrule the demurrer.

HARRY S. CLANCY, Assistant Attorney General, for appellant.

The subject of the act, "An Act to Provide for State License on Automobiles," is clearly expressed in its title. Session Laws 1912, chap. 28; Commonwealth v. Gregg, 161 Pa. 586.

The act in question is constitutional, viewed from any point. Cleary v. Johnston, 74 Atl. 538; Berry, Laws of Automobiles, par. 86; State ex rel. v. Hudson, 78 Mo. 302; State v. Hipp, 38 Ohio 225; State v. Unwin, 64 Atl. 163; 68 Atl. 110; Kane v. Titus, 80 Atl. 453.

Imposition of license fees for revenue purposes was clearly within the sovereign power of the state. City of Buffalo v. Lewis, 84 N. E. 809; People v. Schneider, 103 N. W. 172; Commonwealth v. Boyd, 74 N. E. 225; Mark v. District of Columbia, 37 L. R. A. (N. S.) 440, and note

on page 440; Constitution of N. M., art. VIII, secs. 1 and
2; Bill of Rights, sec. 18, Const. of N. M.; 4th and 5th
Amendments to the Const. of the United States.

R. D. Bowers, Roswell, N. M., for appellee.

Chapter 28, Laws 1912, is unconstitutional because it
embraces more than one subject, and the subject of the act
is not clearly expressed in the title. Sec. 16, art. IV, Const.
N. M.; Cooley, Const. Lim. 97-99 and 171-83; Davis v.
State, 7 Md. 151, 61 A. D. 331, and note; State v. Nom-
land, 3 N. D. 427, 44 A. S. R. 572; Ritchie v. People, 155
Ill, 98, 46 A. D. 315.

Contended that the amount is a tax and not a license
fee imposed for regulation. Bailey v. People, 190 Ill. 28,
60 N. E. 98; Chaddock v. Day, (Mich.), 4 L. R. A. 809.

License is a permission to do something which, without
the license, would not be allowable. Youngblood v. Sexton, 32 Mich. 419, 20 L. R. A. 654; Sinot v. Davenport,
63 U. S. (22 How.) 227, 16 L. Ed. 203; Sonora v. Curtin,
137 Cal. 535, 70 Pac. 674; Conklin Co. v. Chicago, 127
Ill. App. 103; Schmidt v. Indianapolis, 168 Ind. 637, 80
N. E. 632.

Under the police power the act must tend to the preservation of the lives, the health, the morals and the welfare
of the community. Health Com. v. Rector, 145 N. Y. 32,
45 A. S. R. 579; Lawton v. Steele, 152 U. S. 133; N. O.
Gas Co. v. La. Co., 115 U. S. 650; People v. Gillson, 109
N. Y. 389, 4 A. S. R. 465; Young v. Com., 101 Va. 853,
45 S. E. 327; State v. Cary, 126 Wis. 141, 105 N. W. 327.

Power to license is an essential part of the police power
and, therefore, of the power to regulate. In re Guerrero,
69 Cal. 88, 101 Pac. 261; Vamsamt v. Harlem Co., 59 Md.
335; State v. Forcier, 65 N. H. 42, 17 Atl. 577; Com. v.
Newhall, 164 Mass. 338, 41 N. E. 647; Hubman v. State,
61 Ark. 482, 33 S. W. 843; Cache County v. Jensen, 21
Utah 207, 61 Pac. 303.

The act does not attempt to regulate the business. Com.

v. Kingsbury, 85 N. E. 848, (Mass.); Nuller v. Jones, 80 Ala. 89; Fisher v. Brower, 159 Ind. 139, 64 N. E. 614.

Property rights cannot be invaded under the guise of a police regulation for the preservation of the health, safety or welfare of society when such is clearly not the purpose sought. Bailey v. People, 190 Ill. 28, 60 N. E. 98; The Slaughter House Cases, 16 Wall. 36-37; State v. Moore, 22 L. R. A. 472 (9 N. Car.); St. Paul v. Traeger, 25 Minn. 248, 33 A. R. 462; Ex parte Braun, 74 Pac. 780.

The exaction in this act is a tax. Tiedman, Federal Control of Persons and Property, vol. 1, page 495.

A license is made for regulation, but not a tax for revenue. Cooley, Taxation, 396; Ellis v. Frazier, 38 Ore. 4621, 63 Pac. 642; Cooley Const. Lim. 245.

A tax is a charge upon persons or property to raise money for public purposes. 1 Cooley, Taxation, 1; Perry v. Washburn, 20 Cal. 350; Hanson v. Vernon, 27 Ia. 47.

A license is imposed to compensate for the expense of issuing certificates and probable expense of regulating and controlling the operation of the automobile licensed. 1 Cooley Taxation, 1141, and cases cited; Banta v. Chicago, 172 Ill. 204, 50 N. E. 233; Price v. People, 193 Ill. 114, 61, N. E. 844; 86 A. S. R. 306; Van Hook v. Selma, 70 Ala. 361, 45 A. R. 85; State v. Neineman, 80 Wis. 253, 27 A. S. R. 34.

Any excess over such expense becomes revenue and, consequently, is taxation. Kans. City v. Grush, 151 Mo. 128, 52 S. W. 286; In re Guerrero, 69 Cal. 88, 10 Pac. 261; North H. Co. v. Hoboken, 41 N. J. L. 71.

Fee will be presumed reasonable unless the contrary appears upon the face of the law itself. Atkins v. Phillips, 26 Fla. 281, 8 So. 429; Seattle v. Barto, 31 Wash. 141, 71, Pac. 735; Gamble v. Montgomery, 147 Ala. 682, 39 So. 353; The Laundry License Case, 22 Fed. 703.

Nature of the subject regulated determines the amount to be exacted and if the amount is out of proportion to the expense involved it will be declared a tax. Ex parte Braun, 141 Cal. 204, 74 Pac. 780; Berry, Law of Automobiles, secs. 84 to 88.

"There is nothing in the business or proposed regulations for which the city is likely to incur any special expense." Laundry License Case, 22 Fed. 703; State v. Bean, N. Car. 554; Jacksonville v. Ledwith, 26 Fla. 163, 23 A. S. R. 574; P. C. & Ry. Co. v. State, 16 L. R. A. 380; Chicago v. Collins, 175 Ill. 445; Ellis v. Frazier, 53 L. R. A. 454; Johnston v. Macon, 62 Ga. 645; Livingston v. Paducah, 80 Ky. 656; Davis v. Petrinovich, 112 Ala. 654, 36 L. R. A. 615; Brooklyn v. Nodine, 26 Hun. 512; Ex parte Gregory, 20 Tex. App. 210; Joyce v. E. St. Louis, 77 Ill. 156.

The tax is not uniform upon the whole of the class. Livingston v. Paducah, 80 Ky. 656; Danville v. Shelton, 76 Va. 325; Worth v. Ry. Co., 89 M. Car. 291, 45 A. R. 679; St. Louis v. Spiegel, 75 Mo. 145; Ellis v. Frazier, 53 L. R. A. 454 (Ore.); Sims v. Jackson Parish, 22 La. Ann. 440; Woodbridge v. Detroit, 8 Mich. 301; Pittsburg, etc., v. State, 16 L. R. A. 380, (Ohio.)

Chapter 28 is void insofar as it imposes a tax of $10 in that said imposition is double taxation. Const. N. M., art. VIII, sec. 2; 1 Cooley Taxation, (3rd ed.) 394, et seq.; Ellis v. Frazier, 53 L. R. A. 454; Chicago v. Collins, 174 Ill. 445.

Act is void for indefiniteness, there being no provision made for regulation. Cooley Taxation, 1149; Mathews v. Jensen, 21 Utah, 207; Christy v. Elliott, 216 Ill. 31, 108 A. S. R. 196; Pittsburg Ry. v. State, 16 L. R. A. 380.

Act is violative of provisions of Federal Constitution and the Constitution of N. M., providing that no person shall be deprived of life, liberty or property without due process of law. Unwen v. State, 73 N. J. 529; Powell v. Penna., 127 U. S. 678; Meffert v. Medical Board, 1 L. R. A. (N. S.) 811; Quimby v. Hazen, 54 Vt. 139.

The act in question is unconstitutional in that it denies to automobile owners the equal protection of the laws. Berry, Law of Automobiles, sec. 41 and cases cited.

STATEMENT OF FACTS.

This case was instituted in the District Court of Chaves

County by the filing of an information against the appellee, charging him with unlawfully operating and maintaining an automobile contrary to the form of the statute. (Chapter 28, Session Laws 1912.)

To this information the appellee filed a demurrer, which being sustained, the cause was brought to this Court upon appeal by the State.

OPINION OF THE COURT.

HANNA, J.—The first ground of the demurrer is in substance that the act of the legislature upon which the information is based, chap. 28, Session Laws 1912, is unconstitutional for the reason that the act embraces more than one subject and the subject is not clearly expressed in the title. The title of the act is, "An Act to Provide for State License on Automobiles."

It is argued by appellee that the object of the act is two-fold: (a) To license automobiles, and (b) to raise revenue for road purposes. The statute in question, sec. 3, chap. 28, Session Laws of 1912, provides that,

"The fee for a license under this act shall be ten (10) dollars annually * * * * and such license fee shall be in addition to the ordinary property tax. * * * ** shall be paid to the Secretary of State * * * * and the said Secretary of State shall pay same over to the State Treasurer, who shall credit the amount thereof to the State Road Fund. Provided: That an additional fee of one (1) dollar for the issuance of any such license and of fifty (50) cents for the annual renewal thereof shall be collected from each owner by the said Secretary of State. Provided further: The said fee of one (1) dollar and the said renewal fee of fifty (50) cents, together with all fees hereinbefore provided for and required to be paid for duplicates of tags or plates issued by the Secretary of State, and collected by him, shall be used for the purpose of defraying the expenses incident to the administration of this act in the office of said Secretary of State, and any surplus at the end of the fiscal year shall be turned over to the State Treasurer and credited to said road fund."

The question for our present consideration, then, is, has the legislature by providing for a ten dollar license fee to be covered into the State Road Fund rendered the act void and unconstitutional by violating sec. 16 of art. IV of the State Constitution, which provides that the subject of every bill shall be clearly expressed in its title, and no bill embracing more than one subject shall be passed except general appropriation bills, etc.?

The aim and necessity of this constitutional provision is apparent. The reason for its existence is a matter of history in nearly all our States. Its purposes as outlined by Mr. Cooley, are:

First, to prevent hodge-podge or "log-rolling" legislation; *second,* to prevent surprise or fraud upon the legislature by means of provisions in bills of which the titles give no intimation, and which might therefore be overlooked and carelessly and unintentionally adopted; and *third,* to fairly apprise the people of the subjects of legislation in order that they may have opportunity of being heard thereon.

Cooley's Const. Lim. (7th Ed.) 205.

Concerning the particularity required in stating the object of the bill, Mr. Cooley says that the general purpose of such constitutional provisions is accomplished when a law has but one general object, which is fairly indicated by its title; that to require every end and means necessary or convenient for the accomplishment of this general object to be provided for by a separate act relating to that alone, would be unreasonable and render legislation impossible.

Cooley's Const. Lim. 205.

Bearing in mind that there is a general disposition to construe this constitutional provision liberally, rather than to embarrass legislation by a construction whose strictness is unnecessary to the accomplishment of the beneficial purposes for which it has been adopted, (Cooley's Const. Lim. 209) we will pass to the consideration of whether this act of the legislature of 1912, (chap. 28) is objectionable because it contains more than one subject not clearly expressed in the title.

The great variance as to facts involved in the numerous cases we have examined leave us without many precedents to which we can point for the purpose of illustrating the principle which we have concluded is controlling as to this phase of the case.

We have found that a number of the State Constitutions contain the word *object* in the sections similar to the one here under consideration, while others contain the word *subject*. The Constitution of the State of Texas formerly contained the word *object* in its section upon this subject, and a later convention substituted the word *subject* therefor, which corresponds with our provision.

Judge Bonner, in Stone v. Brown, 54 Texas 341, observes that,

"It may be presumed that the convention has some reason for substituting a different word from that which had been so long in use in this connection and that in the light of judicial expressions the word 'subject' may have been substituted as less restrictive than 'object.' "

While appellee is not clear in his contention upon this first ground of the demurrer, we assume that the dual subjects referred to by him are to be classified as an attempted exercise of the police power by the general provision with respect to licensing automobiles, which clearly come within the title of the act, and an attempt at taxation for general revenue which it may be contended could not be included within the purview of the subject as expressed in the title of this act.

In our opinion, the true test of the validity of a statute under this constitutional provision is: Does the title fairly give such reasonable notice of the subject matter of

1 the statute itself as to prevent the mischief intended to be guarded against? If so, the act should be sustained. The reason of the rule not applying to such cases the rule itself does not apply.

Mr. Cooley says:

"The generality of a title is therefore no objection to it

so long as it is not made a cover to legislation incon-
2 gruous in itself, and which by no fair intendment can
be construed as having a necessary or proper connection."

Cooley's Constitutional Lim. 206.

The subject of the act of 1912 was "to provide for State
license on automobiles." The disposition of the funds resulting from the collection of the license was perhaps even
a necessary part of the act and certainly is not incongruous to the subject expressed in the title.

In the case of Fahey v. State, 27 Tex. App. 159, it was
conceded that the object of the acts was to regulate the
sale of intoxicating liquors, to collect revenue, and divers
other purposes and objects, but it was held that unless
3 there was more than one subject in the act it was
constitutional. It was further held in the same case
that if there be more than one subject mentioned in the
act, if they be germane or subsidiary to the main subject,
or if relative directly, or indirectly, to the main subject,
having a mutual connection, and not foreign to the main
subject, or so long as the provisions are of the some nature
and come legitimately under one general denomination or
subject, the act cannot be held unconstitutional.

We fully agree with the views quoted, and are of the
opinion that the act of 1912, chap. 28, did not contain
more than one general subject, or at least that the subject
was germane to that expressed in the title, if we concede,
for the purpose of argument, that two subjects were included in the act. See,

Com. ex rel. Appellant v. Gregg, 161 Pa. 586;
Black's Const. Law, pp. 382 and 384;
David's Law of Automobiles, sec. 31.

(2) The second ground of the demurrer was that the
act in question, chap. 28, Session Laws 1912, is void as imposing a tax that is not equal and uniform, and is violative
of sec. 1 of art. VIII of the Constitution, in that the rate
of taxation is not equal and uniform as to all vehicles, but
is an arbitrary exaction levied upon all automobiles regardless of value.

The third ground of the demurrer raises the question of double taxation. These objections falling under a general classification, will be considered together.

In the case of State v. Swagerty, 203 Mo. 517, 10 L. R. A. (N. S.) 601, the principal objection urged against the act was that it was a special law, because it legislated only upon automobiles and did not attempt to legislate upon all vehicles using the public highways. The court held that the act applied to and affected alike all members of the same class and was, therefore, a general and not a special law. A similar holding was had in the case of Christy v. Elliott, 216 Ills. 31, 1 L. R. A. (N. S.) 215.

See, David's Law of Motor Vehicles, secs. 30 and 42;

Huddy's Law of Automobiles, p. 42.

In the matter of double taxation, we believe that the case of Cleary v. Johnson, (N. J.) 74 Atl. 538, comes nearest to meeting conditions similar to those of the case now before us. In that case it was held that a legislative enactment providing for the payment of an annual fee for the registration of an automobile could not be regarded as double taxation, and therefore unconstiutional. We desire to quote, with approval, somewhat extensively from this opinion; the Court said, in this connection:

"Now the ground of differentiation, insisted upon by the counsel for the plaintiff in certiorari, between the former and the present act, is that, while the former act provides for a $1 license fee imposed by force of the police power residing in the state, the present fees are imposed as a tax for the purpose of revenue. Regarding this point, it is to be remarked that there is nothing in the record brought up which exhibits the legitimate expenses to which the state is put in its course of registering, regulating, and licensing automobiles. The evidence upon which the writ was allowed is not evidential upon this hearing. If it could be resorted to, the facts stated do not show that the charges are so unreasonably in excess of the cost of regulating and supervising automobiles as to compel us to say that the charges are not regulative. The state furnishes a central office, official assistance, clerical force, and legal ad-

vice by the Attorney General's office, for which no sep-
5 arate charges are made, but which indirectly are an expense to the state. It does not follow that the amounts
paid for certain specific services by certain officers represent all the cost and expense to which the state is subjected. Therefore the fact that receipts from fees for
registration and for licenses largely exceed the sum specifically charged for the maintenance of the automobile
department does not prove that the fees are extortionate
for regulative purposes. Nor would the fact that the
public treasury is incidentally augmented by the fees paid
for automobile registration and licenses have the effect of
making such registration and license fees a tax. Berry,
Laws of Automobiles, par. 86, and cases cited. Nor do the
provisions of paragraph 37, already exhibited, demonstrate
that the fees imposed are beyond the limits of regulative
charges. It does not follow that, because all the receipts
from the automobile department are paid over to the commissioner of public roads, the cost to the state for the regulation of automobiles may not proximate the sum so paid.
The cost of maintaining the automobile department, as
already remarked, is in a degree entangled with the cost
of maintaining other departments, and such cost may be
paid out of any state fund, while the specific receipts from
the automobile department may be paid into the general
state fund. For an instance, the fact that all license fees
are paid into the school fund for the amount for which
they are assessed and the cost of the regulation is paid out
of a general revenue raised by tax, is of no consequence in
determining the character of the fee. State ex rel v. Hudson, 78 Mo. 302; State v. Hipp, 38 Ohio 199. So it does
not appear that the fees fixed are taxes for revenue. Regarding them as fees for the purpose of regulating, they
fall within the rule laid down in the case of Enwen v.
State, supra; but, *if the imposition is to be regarded as
license fees imposed for revenue, it does not follow that
the imposition of such fees is beyond the power of the
Legislature."*

It will be noted from the foregoing that the facts in

evidence were not deemed sufficient to indicate that the statute was a revenue measure; in a later New Jersey case, however, this issue was squarely before the court. The case being Kane v. State, 80 Atl. 453, and from the opinion we quote the following:

"The first contention made in his behalf is that the automobile law of 1908 is invalid, because the license fees exacted by it are not limited to the cost of registration and inspection, and the act is therefore intended as a revenue measure. In Cleary v. Johnston, supra, the proofs submitted were not considered by the Court to be demonstrative that the statute was a revenue measure; the Court, however, pointed out that if such was conceded to be its object the law was nevertheless not invalid on that account, for the reason that the imposition of license fees for revenue purposes was clearly within the sovereign power of the state. We agree with counsel of the plaintiff in error that the proofs taken in the present case satisfactorily show that the present automobile law is a revenue measure, but hold, in accordance with the view expressed by the Supreme Court and above adverted to, that in passing it the legislature was fully within the powers conferred upon it by the Constitution."

It is also laid down in 37 Cyc. 753, 754, that,

"Double taxation in the objectionable and prohibited sense exists only where the same property is taxed twice
6 when it ought to be taxed but once, and to consider such double taxation the second tax must be imposed upon the same property by the same state or government during the same taxing period."

We fully agree with the enunciation of general principles just quoted, and with the further rule that there
7 is no constitutional objection to the levy of a license tax for the privilege of carrying on a particular business and at the same time a tax on the property employed in the business.

37 Cyc. 754;

State v. Jones, 9 Idaho 693, 75 Pac. 819;

St. Louis v. Bircher, 7 Mo. App. 169;

Morgan v. Com., 98 Virginia 812, 35 S. E. 448.

In the case of. Kane v. State, supra, (80 Atl. 453), it was contended, as is also contended in the case now under consideration, that the imposition of a license tax is a property tax, and invalid because it is imposed without regard to the value of the property upon which it is laid. We fully concur in the holding there made that the character of the imposition is not to be determined by the mode adopted in fixing its amount, but that the imposition is a license or privilege tax charged in the nature of compensation for the damage done to the roads of the state by the driving of these machines over them, and is properly based, not upon the value of the machine, but upon the amount of the destruction caused by it.

With respect to the contention of the appellee that the act in question is unconstitutional in that it denies to automobile owners the equal·protection of the law, we find that the controlling principle in this connection is that the requirement of equality and uniformity in taxation applies

8   only to taxes in the proper sense of the word, levied with the object of raising revenue for general purposes, and not to such as are an extraordinary and exceptional kind, and is, under a constitutional provision providing for equality in taxation, to be restricted to taxes on property, as distinguished from such as are levied on occupations, business or franchises, and as distinguished also from exactions imposed in the exercise of the police power rather than that of taxation.

37 Cyc. 731.

It has been held that a license is not a tax on property. and, therefore, is not affected by statutory provisions for ascertaining the value for purposes of taxation.

Fla. Cen. & P. Railway Co. v. Columbia, 54 S. C. 266.

Clearly our statute (chapter 28, S. L. 1912) could not be held to conflict with our constitutional provision

9   with respect to equality and uniformity under the authorities holding that the constitutional provision is restricted to a property tax, with which conclusion we agree.

We have fully considered the remaining grounds of the demurrer, but do not consider it necessary to discuss these questions.

We conclude that the demurrer should have been overruled, and that the judgment of the District Court must be reversed, and the cause remanded with instructions to overrule the demurrer, and it is so ordered.

[No. 1539, October 14, 1913.]

AMINDA LOHMAN, as Executrix, etc., Plaintiff; GEORGE LYNCH and EDWARD C. WADE, Cross-Complainants, Appellees, v. NUMA REYMOND, Appellant.

SYLLABUS.

1. Where, in a suit to compel an accounting by trustees, cross-complainant, at the time of filing his cross-complaint for appointment of a receiver, was justified from the record in believing that he would only be required to present and prove his title to claims transferred to him in the receivership proceeding, and for that reason only set up the assignment of such claims to his capacity to join in the suit to compel the trustees to account, his cross-complaint was not based on the instrument of assignment; and hence the assignment, when offered in evidence, was not objectionable because such instrument, or a copy thereof, was not filed in compliance with Code Civ. Proc., sub-sec. 307, (Laws 1907, c. 107), providing that, when any instrument of writing on which the action or defense is found is referred to in the pleadings, the original or a copy shall be filed with the pleading, if within the power or control of the party wishing to use the same, and if the original or a copy be not filed or a sufficient reason given for the failure to file it, the instrument may not be admitted in evidence.

P. 231

2. Where, in a suit to compel trustees to account, the trial court did not hear all of the witnesses testify, an assignment that the court erred in finding that certain claims has been assigned to cross-appellant L. required a review on appeal of all the evidence in the case.

P. 234

3. An instrument in the form of a release of claims of three creditors of an insolvent against the insolvent's trust estate to L., together with the oral testimony explaining the same, might be properly held to amount to an assignment of such claims to L.

P. 234

4. Alteration of an instrument by interlineation by one who was acting as a friend of both parties, and who drew the original instrument at a time prior to his becoming interested in behalf of either party, was not a fatal alteration.

P. 235

5. Where cross-complainant alleged that a certain release of claims against an insolvent's estate was made only on one condition, while defendant charged that the release was made on the same and also on another condition, such allegations presented a complete issue, and no reply was necessary.

P. 235

6. By going to trial on the merits and not objecting to evidence, defendant waived any right he may have had consequent on cross-complainant's failure to reply to defendant's answer.

P. 236

Error to the District Court of Dona Ana County; Frank W. Parker, Associate Justice; affirmed.

N. C. FRENGER, Las Cruces, N. M., for appellant.

The writing, Exhibit "A," was not entitled to be admitted in evidence because not filed with cross-complaint. Session Laws 1907, chapter 107; 3 Wigmore on Evidence, secs. 1845 to 1860; 31 Cyc. 556; Code Civ. Pro. (N. M.)

Ordinarily neither the verdict of a jury nor the findings of fact of a trial court will be disturbed in the appellate court when they are supported by any substantial evidence. Candelaria v. Miera, 13 N. M. 360; Territory v. Hicks, 6 N. M. 596..

But, in this case, this Court should review the entire record and try this cause de novo, following the rule in appeals in equity. Puritan Co. v. Toti and Gradi, 14 N. M. 425.

It is the practice to examine the record to ascertain if substantial evidence exists. Hancock v. Beasley, 14 N. M. 239; Mining Co. v. Hamilton, 14 N. M. 271.

There could have been no ossignment because the assignee gave no consideration. 4 Cyc. 31.

Exhibit "A" was a release, and being without consideration, it is void. 34 Cyc. 1048-1054; 24 A. & E. Enc. L. 287, (2nd Ed.)

J. H. PAXTON, Las Cruces, N. M., for appellee.

Not necessary to file the original or a copy of the instrument held to be evidence, with the cross-complaint. Laws 1907, sub-sec. 307; Latterett v. Cook, 1 Ia. 1, 63 Am. Dec. 428; Fisher v. Patton, 134 Mo. 32, 33 S. W. 451, 34 S. W. 1096.

The instrument was not the foundation of the action Horne v. Mullis, 46 S. E. 663, 119 Ga. 534; Diggs v. Way, 51 N. E. 429, 54 N. E. 412, 22 Ind. App. 617; Vannice v. Green, 14 Ia. 262; Bryson v. Kelly, 53 Ind. 486; Duffy v. Carman, 3 Ind. App. 207, 29 N. E. 454; Williams v. Frybarger, 9 Ind. App. 558, 37 N. E. 302; Lester v. People, 150 Ill. 408, 41 Am. St. 375; State v. Wenzel, 77 Ind. 428: Worley v. Moore, 77 Ind. 567; Shetterly v. Axt., 76 N. E. 901, 77 N. E. 865, 37 Ind. App. 687; Conn v. State, 25 N. E. 443, 125 Ind. 514.

Established by the evidence of the written instrument, and by evidence aliunde, that Numa Reymond assigned to George Lynch all his claim against the estate of the Lynch Brothers. Moore v. Lowery, 25 Ia. 336, 95 Am. Dec. 790.

No particular form is necessary to constitute an assignment. Metcalf v. Kincaid, 87 Ia. 443, 43 Am. St. 391; Drake on Attachments, sec. 562; McDaniel v. Maxwell, 21 Ore. 202, 28 Am. St. 740; Hull v. Smith, 8 How. Prac. 281.

An assignment for valuable consideration will not be set aside for technical error. Noble v. Hunter, 2 Kans. App. 538, 43 Pac. 994.

Intent governs, though inappropriate terms have been used. Ellis v. Secor, 31 Mich. 185, 18 Am. Rep. 178; Crone v. Braun, 23 Minn. 239; People v. Tioga Com. Pleas, 19 Wend. 73; Buchanan v. Taylor, (Pa.) Add. 154; Gulf, C. & S. F. Ry. Co. v. Cusenberry, 5 Tex. Civ. App. 114, 23 S. W. 851; Hinkle v. Wanzer, 17 How. 353, 15 L. Ed. 173; Hooker v. Eagle Bank, 30 N. Y. 83, 86 Am. Dec. 351; Macklin v. Kinealy, 141 Mo. 113, 41 S. W. 893; Tatum v. Ballard, 94 Va. 370, 26 S. E. 871.

Alterations appearing in the instrument held to evidence an assignment from Numa Reymond to Lynch, are not such as to affect the validity or admissibility in evidence. Ames v. Brown, 22 Minn. 257; 1 Greenl. Ev., sec. 189; Yeager v. Musgrave, 28 W. Va. 90; White Sewing Machine Co. v. Dakin, 86 Mich. 581, 49 N. W. 583, 13 L. R. A. 315; Barlow v. Buckingham, 68 Ia. 169, 26 N. W. 58; Sharpe v. Orme, 61 Ala. 263; Sill v. Reese, 47 Cal. 294; Andrews v. Burdick, 62 Ia. 714, 16 N. W. 275; Hervey v. Harvey, 15 Me. (3 Shep.) 357; Ames v. Colburn, 77 Mass. (11 Gray) 490, 71 Am. Dec. 723; McRaven v. Crisler, 53 Miss. 542; Foote v. Hambrick, 70 Miss. 157, 35 Am. St. 631; Lee v. Butler, 167 Mass. 426, 57 Am. St. 466 Equitable Mfg. Co. v. Allen, 76 Vt. 22, 56 Atl. 87, 104 Am. St. 915; Lee v. Alexander, 9 B. Monroe 25, 48 Am. Dec. 412; Pierson v. Grimes, 30 Ind. 129, 95 Am. Dec. 673; Wallace v. Tice, 51 Pac. 733, 32 Ore. 283; Brooks v. Allen, 62 Ind. 401; Murray v. Peterson, 6

Wash. 418, 33 Pac. 969; Goodfellow v. Inslee, 12 N. J.
Eq. (1 Beasl.) 355; Condict v. Flower, 106 Ill. 105; Deer-
ing Harvester Co. v. White, 72 S. W. 962; 110 Tenn. 132;
Mathias v. Leathers, 68 N. W. 449, 99 Ia..18; Forbes v.
Taylor, 35 So. 855, 139 Ala. 286.

There was no tacit admission, by Lynch's failure to reply to Reymond's answer, of Reymond's allegation that his
agreement was conditioned upon the joinder of all other
creditors.

The allegation of the cross-complaint and the denial in
the answer, when taken together, make a definite and
clear cut issue. Stephen on Pleading, 154; Hill v. Smith,
27 Cal. 476; Watkinds v. So. Pac. R. Co., 38 Fed. 711, 4
L. R. A. 241; Wahl v. Murphy, (Ky.) 9 S. W. 375;
Smith v. L. & N. R. Co., 95 Ky. 11, 23 S. W. 652, 22 L.
R. A. 72; Union Ins. Co. v. Murphy, (Pa.) 4·Atl. 352.

Where a special plea amounts to no more than the general issue, which has also been pleaded, no replication is
necessary. King v. Burnham, 101 N. W. 302, 93 Minn.
288; Johnson v. Andrews, 68 N. Y. Sup. 764, 34 Misc.
Rep. 89; Luther v. Brown, 66 Mo. App. 227; Jordan v.
Buschmeyer, 97 Mo. 94, 10 S. W. 616; Goddard v. Fulton,
21 Cal. 430; Arthur v. Brooks, 14 Barb. 533.

By going on trial on the merits and not objecting to
evidence, Reymond waived any right he may have had,
consequent upon Lynch's failure to reply to his answer.
Coler v. Boar dof Co. Commrs., 6 N. M. 117; Faucette v.
Ludden, 117 N. C. 170, 23 S. E. 173; Looney v. Linney,
(Tex. Civ. App.) 21 S. W. 409; Sawtelle v. Muncy, 48
Pac. 387, 116 Cal. 435; Sigafus v. Porter, 179 U. S. 116,
21 Spu. Ct. R. 34, 45 L. Ed. 113; Union P. R. Co. v. Snyder, 152 U. S. 684, 14 Sup. Ct. R. 756; 38 L. Ed. 597.

STATEMENT OF FACTS.

On December 6, 1892, the cross-complainant, George
Lynch, and his two brothers, since deceased, executed their
deed of trust for the benefit of creditors to the plaintiff,
Martin Lohman, and to the defendant, Numa Reymond, as
trustees. Numa Reymond having left the country, Mar-

tin Lohman, trustee, had instituted this suit against Numa
Reymond, trustee, and the creditors as defendants, including George Lynch and William Lynch, surviving members of the firm of Lynch Brothers, to remove Numa Reymond as such trustee. Numa C. Frenger was appointed
by order of the court trustee in place of Numa Reymond.
Thereafter, and during the year 1909, George Lynch
filed his cross-complaint in the nature of a bill in equity
praying for an accounting by the trustees and the appointment of a receiver for the trust estate to take poossession
and dispose of the same under the provisions of said trust
deed and under the direction and order of the Court.

George Lynch alleged in his cross-complaint that he is
also interested as a creditor of the estate by assignments
from other creditors, in addition to his interest as a residuary beneficiary. Martin Lohman and Numa Reymond, being in court only as trustees, undertook, nevertheless, to
answer the cross-complainant in their individual and personal capacity, and to litigate their individual controversies with Lynch in this suit. The suit was tried upon
the issues made by the cross-complaint of George Lynch,
the answer of plaintiff Martin Lohman, the reply of defendant George Lynch, and the answer of defendant Numa
Reymond. It is also stipulated in the case that the reply
of George Lynch to the answer of Martin Lohman shall
be treated as a reply of Edward C. Wade as co-cross-com-
plainant with George Lynch, to the answer of Numa Reymond. The vital question upon the appeal is whether
Numa Reymond assigned to George Lynch his claim as a
creditor against the estate in question.

On or about December 13, 1906, Numa Reymond, John
H. Riley and Martin Lohman, for the consideration of
their mutual promises and for the express consideration
of one dollar in hand paid, agreed together orally to release (or assign) and did release (or assign) to George
Lynch their claims against the trust estate of Lynch
Brothers. In pursuance of this oral agreement (or assignment) they executed and delivered to George Lynch a
written instrument appearing on its face to be a release

to George Lynch, of all their claims against George Lynch. The trial court found as a fact that the said Lohman, Riley and Reymond did in fact assign to George Lynch their claims against Lynch Brothers and upon conflicting evidence the trial court found that this assignment was made conditionally. The typewritten instrument in evidence contained a condition written with a pen below, after the signatures of the parties.

OPINION OF THE COURT.

ABBOTT, D. J.—The vital question for decision in this case is raised by the first assignment of error, which is "That the District Court erred in admitting in evidence the release submitted by appellees George Lynch and Edward C. Wade and marked exihibt "A" under their evidence, upon the ground that the same was referred to in appellee's cross-complaint, and the same, or a copy thereof, was not filed with said cross-complaint, the same having been within their power and control, and no sufficient reason having been given for failure so to do,—and which said cross-complaint and their action thereby was founded, as to their rights claimed against appellant, upon said release, it being an instrument in writing."

The argument of appellant is that in so far as appellee George Lynch claims to be the owner of the credits of appellant under said estate of Lynch Brothers, this action was founded upon the writing appearing in evidence as exhibit "A." It is referred to in the cross-complaint, the same, or a copy thereof, was not filed with said cross-

1 complaint, though within the power and control of said George Lynch, and no sufficient reason was given for failure to do so. The said writing was therefore not entitled to be admitted in evidence, under sub-section 307 of the Code of Civil Procedure, which is as follows:

"When any instrument of writing upon which the action or defense is founded is referred to in the pleadings, the original or a copy thereof shall be filed with the pleading, if within the power or control of the party wishing to use the same, and if such original or copy thereof be not filed

as herein required, or a sufficient reason given for failure
to do so, such instrument of writing shall not be admitted
in evidence upon the trial."

It is evident upon the face of the record that George
Lynch filed his cross-complaint against Numa· Reymond
only in Reymond's capacity as trustee. He prayed for an
accounting by the trustees and the appointment of a receiver for the trust estate. Unless George Lynch had
something more than a mere interest as residuary beneficiary of the trust estate, it is questionable whether he would
have an interest sufficient to entitle him to maintain his
action, and it was therefore proper to allege that certain
creditors had assigned their claims against the trust estate
to Lynch so as to show Lynch's interest and right to sue.
The written instrument from Reymond, Riley and Lohman
to Lynch was not pleaded as a basis of the action, nor was
any recovery sought upon it. Lynch did not sue as assignor individually or personally; there was no occasion
to do so; nor could he know that there ever would be such
action. He was justified in taking the position that he
would only have to present his title in the receivership proceedings. In his cross-complaint he was not seeking to
confirm his title to the claims of Lohman, Reymond and
Riley against the trust estate.

The record shows that up to the time of the filing of
the answer of Lohman and Reymond to the cross-complaint,
that Lohman and Reymond were only sued in the action
in their capacity as trustees. So far as the record shows,
Lynch could not then know that there would be any occasion for personal suit against any of the creditors who had
released (or assigned) their claims to him. The trustees,
Lohman and Reymond, however, being in court only as
trustees, undertook to answer the cross-complaint in their
individual and personal capacity and to litigate their individual controversies with Lynch in this suit under his
cross-complaint. At the time of filing his cross-complaint
he was, from the record, justified in thinking he would
only have to present his title in the receivership proceedings. To question his right and title to the claims of

Lohman, Reymond and Riley against the trust estate in
his cross-complaint, in which he was suing for an accounting and receivership, would have been improper pleading.
It is a copy of the instrument on which the suit is founded
which is to be attached to plaintiffs' complaint, and not
the evidence required to sustain his case. In this case the
release from Reymond, Lohman and Riley was not the instrument upon which the action of appellee was founded,
but nothing more than a part of the evidence upon which
he had a right to rely in case his title to the claims of
Lohman, Reymond and Riley was questioned. It was
proper for appellee to set forth all of his interest in the
trust estate so that his right to maintin his action might
be unquestioned. Suppose it was shown upon the face of
his cross-complaint that the claim of creditors were in so
large amount that appellee would certainly have no interest as residuary beneficiary. The record shows in this case
that the appellee did not base his title wholly upon the so-
called release, but that an oral agreement previous to the
written instrument was also relied upon. He had no reason to believe that his title to the claims of Reymond.
Lohman and Riley would be questioned in this action and
his cross-complaint was not based upon such instrument
and it therefore becomes not only unnecessary but improper for the same to have been set forth in his cross-
complaint, and his action not being founded thereon, the
same was not inadmissible in evidence. Lattourett v. Cook,
1 Cole's 1. (Ia.), 63 Am. Dec. 428; Fisher v. Patton, 134
Mo. 32, 33 S. W. 451, 34 S. W. 1096; Horne v. Mullis, 46
S. E. 663. 119 Ga. 534; Diggs v. Way, 51 N. E. 429, 54 N.
E. 412, 22 Ind. App. 417; Vannice v. Green, 14 Ia. 262;
Bryson v. Kelly, 53 Ind. 486; Duffy v. Carman, 3 Ind. App.
207, 29 N. E. 454; Williams v. Frybarger, 9 Ind. App.
558, 37 N. E. 302; Lester v. People, 150 Ill. 408, 41 Am.
St. Rep. 375; State v. Wenzel, 77 Ind. 428; Worley v.
Moore, 77 Ind. 567; Shetterly v. Axt., 76 N. E. 901, 77
N. E. 865, 37 Ind. App. 687; Conn. v. State, 25 N. E.
443, 125 Ind. 514.

The written instrument having been properly admitted

in evidence, it remains to be determined what is the legal
effect of said instrument, and this question is directly raised
by the 8th assignment of error, which is,

"That said Court erred in finding that in law the appellant has assigned over to the appellee, George Lynch, his
claim in and to the Lynch Brothers estate."

Appellee claims that it is established by the evidence of
the written instrument held to have been an assignment
from Numa Reymond to George Lynch, and by evidence
aliunde, that Numa Reymond assigned to George Lynch
all his claims against the estate of Lynch Brothers. Appellant argues that there is no evidence that a verbal contract or agreement to assign to George Lynch was made.
The decision of this question brings us to an examination
of the whole of the evidence in the case, under the
2   rule announced in the case of Gallup Electric Light
Co. v. Pacific Improvement Co., 16 N. M. 86, as the
trial judge did not hear all of the witnesses testify. The
finding of the trial court that an assignment of the claims
of appellants Reymond, Lohman and Riley against the
trust estate to George Lynch was made, was based not only
upon the written instrument heretofore referred to, but
upon the oral testimony as well.

We have carefully examined the entire record in this
case, and are of the opinion that the finding of the trial
court in this regard is sustained by a fair preponderance
of the evidence. The instrument admitted in evidence in
this case in the form of a release of the claims of Rey-
3   mond, Lohman and Riley against the trust estate to
George Lynch, together with the oral testimony explaining the same, was properly held by the trial court to
be in legal effect an assignment of such claims to George
Lynch. Moore v. Lowrey, 25 Ia. 336, 95 Am. Dec. 790;
Metcalf v. Kincaid, 87 Ia. 443, 43 Am. St. Rep. 391;
Drake on Attachments, sec. 562; McDaniel v. Maxwell,
21 Or. 202, 28 Am. St. Rep. 740; Hull v. Smith, 8 How.
Prac. 281; Noble v. Hunter, 2 Kan. App. 538, 43 Pac.
994; Ellis v. Secor, 31 Mich. 185, 18 Am. Rep. 178;
Crone v. Braun, 23 Minn. 239; People v. Tioga Common

Pleas, 18 Wend. 73; Buchanan v. Taylor, (Pa.) Add. 154; G. C. & S. F. Ry. Co. v. Cusenberry, 5 Tex. Civ. App. 114, 23 S. W. 851; Hinkle v. Wanzer, 17 How. 353, 15 L. Ed. 173; Hooker v. Eagle Bank, 30 N. Y. 83; Macklin v. Kinealy, 141 Mo. 113, 41 S. W. 893; Tatum v. Ballard, 94 Va. 370, 26 N. E. 871.

The alterations appearing in the instrument held to evidence an assignment from Numa Reymond to George Lynch are not such as to affect its validity or admissibility in evidence, the same not having been done by the parties to alter its meaning, but only by interlineation by the person who was acting as the friend of both parties and who drew the original instrument at a time prior to his becoming interested in behalf of either party. Ames v. Brown, 22 Minn. 257; Yeager v. Musgrave, 28 W. Va. 90; White Sewing Machine Co. v. Dakin, 86 Mich. 581, 49 N. W. 583, 13 L. R. A. 315; Barlow v. Buckingham, 68 Ia. 169, 26 N. W. 58; Charpe v. Orme, 61 Ala. 263; Sill v. Reese, 47 Cal. 294; Andrews v. Burdick, 62 Ia. 714, 16 N. W. 275; Hervey v. Harvey, 15 Me. 357; Ames v. Colburn, 77 Mass. 390, 71 Am. Dec. 723; McRaven v. .Crisler, 53 Miss. 542; Foote v. Hambrick, 70 Miss. 157, 35 Am. St. Rep. 631; Lee v. Butler, 167 Mass. 426, 57 Am. St. Rep. 466; Equitable Mfg. Co. v. Allen, 76 Vt. 22; Lee v. Alexander, 9 B. Monroe, 25, 48 Am. Dec. 412; Piersol v. Grimes, 30 Ind. 129, 95 Am. Dec. 673; Wallace v. Tice, 51 Pac. 733, 32 Or. 283; Brooks v. Allen, 62 Ind. 401; Murry v. Peterson, 6 Wash. 418, 33 Pac. 969; Goodfellow v. Inslee, 12 N. J. Eq. 355; Condict v. Flower, 106 Ill. 105; Deering Harvester Co. v. White, 72 S. E. 962, 110 Tenn. 132; Mathias v. Leathers, 68 N. W. 449, 99 Ia. 18; Forbes v. Taylor, 35 So. 855, 139 Ala. 286.

There was no admission, by Lynch's failure to reply to Reymond's answer, of Reymond's allegation that his **5** agreement was conditioned upon the joinder of all other creditors.

The allegation of the cross-complaint was to the effect that Reymond (together with other creditors) by his writing released directly to Lynch his claim against the trust estate.

"Subject *only* that the claim so released should not inure to the use and benefit of any other creditors of said Lynch Brothers."

The denial in Reymond's answer is as follows:

"Said Reymond denies all of the allegations of paragraphs five and six of said cross-complaint, but on the contrary avers that he agreed to release all his rights as creditor in and to the said Lynch estate in favor of the said George Lynch (upon the condition, however, that all the other creditors of the said estate likewise relinquish their claims, and upon the further condition that the said relinquishments should inure to the sole benefit of the said George Lynch."

The issue is therefore formed by contrary averments, Lynch averring that the release was made only upon one condition, and Reymond averring that the release was made upon the same condition and an additional condition. The allegation of the cross-complaint and the denial in the answer, when taken together, make a definite and clear-cut issue. Watkins v. So. Pac. R. Co., 38 Fed. 711, 4 L. R. A. 241. Affirmative allegations in an answer are not necessarily new matter, so that a replication becomes necessary. If they in fact only show that some essential allegation of the complaint is not true, then they are only a traverse. Goddard v. Fulton, 21 Cal. 430; Luther v. Brown, 66 Mo. App. 227; Jordan v. Buschmeyer, 97 Mo. 94, 10 S. W. 616; King v. Burnham, 101 N. W. 302, 93 Minn. 288; Johnson v. Andrews, 68 N. Y. S. 764, 34 Misc. Rep. 89; Union Ins. Co. v. Murphy, 4 Atl. 352; Smith v. L. & M. N. Ry Co., 95 Ky. 11, 23 S. W. 652, 32 L. R. A. 72.

By going to trial on the merits and not objecting to evidence, Reymond waived any right he may have had,
6   consequent upon Lynch's failure to reply to his answer. Coler v. Board of Co. Commrs., 6 N. M. 117; Faucette v. Ludden, 117 N. C. 170, 23 S. E. 173; Looney v. Linney, 21 S. W. 409; Sawtelle v. Muncy, 48 Pac. 387,

117 Cal. 435; Sigafus v. Porter, 179 U. S. 116, 21 Sup. Ct. Rep. 34, 45 L. Ed. 113; Union P. R. Co. v. Snyder, 152 U. S. 684, 14 Sup. Ct. Rep. 756, 38 L. Ed. 597.

All of the assignments of error being disposed of, the judgment of the lower court will be affirmed for the reasons given.

Parker, J., being disqualified, did not participate in this opinion.

[No. 1569, October 14, 1913.]

J. M. PALMER, Appellant, v. FRANK B. ALLEN, Appellee.

SYLLABUS (BY THE COURT)

1. A bill of exceptions will be stricken from the transcript on appeal, upon motion therefor, when no notice has been given the adverse party of the time and place of its proposed settlement and signing, as required by sec. 26, chap. 57, S. L. 1907.

P. 239

2. A bill of exceptions, in a case tried to a jury, must be settled and signed by the judge of the court in which the case was tried, and where the record fails to show that such bill of exceptions was signed by the judge it will be stricken from the files, upon motion.

P. 239

3. Where the assignment of errors is copied into appellant's brief, and the brief is served upon appellee's counsel, service of a separate copy of the said assignment of errors is not necessary.

P. 239

Appeal from the District Court of San Juan County; Edmund C. Abbott, District Judge; motion denied in part and sustained in part.

PERKINS & MAIN, Durango, Colorado, for appellant.

The valuation placed upon services of an attorney in this case is preposterous,and wholly unsupported by the evidence, and directly contrary to the law governing such cases. Thompson v. Burtis, 70 Pac. 603.

The true rule, as to value, succinctly stated. Head v. Hargrave, 105 U. S. 45.

EDWARDS & MARTIN, Farmington, New Mexico, for appellee.

In all cases tried by a jury the bill of exceptions must be signed, sealed and settled by the trial judge, or his successor. Sec. 25-6, page 112, Laws 1907; Territory v. Rudabaugh, 2 N. M. 222; Wheeler v. Fick, 4 N. M. 16; Evans v. Baggs, 4 N. M. 68; Hays v. U. S., 9 N. M. 524; Street v. Smith, 15 N. M. 97; Ross v. Berry, 16 N. M. 778.

Assignments of error should be written on separate paper and filed in the cause, and shall also be copied into the brief. Sec. 21, page 112, Laws 1907; Puritan Co. v. Toti, 16 N. M. 1; Gonzales v. A. T. & S. F. Co., 3 N. M. 518.

Necessity for taking and saving exceptions. U. S. v. Sena, 15 N. M. 202; State v. Eaker, 131 Pac., 17 N. M. 379; U. S. v. Cook, 15 N. M. 124; State v. Lucero, 131 Pac. 491.

OPINION OF THE COURT.

ROBERTS, C. J.—Appellee has filed a motion to strike the bill of exceptions from the files in this case on two grounds, (1) Because appellant failed to give appellee five days' notice of his intention of applying to the judge of the court in which the cause was tried to sign and settle the bill of exceptions, and, (2) that the said bill of exceptions was not signed and sealed by the judge of the court in which said cause was tried.

Both grounds of the motion are seemingly well
1 taken. Sec. 26, chap. 57, S. L. 1907, in so far as material, reads as follows:

"After such trial any party to the action may require the court stenographer to transcribe the whole or
any part of his stenographic notes, and when the stenographer shall have transcribed his notes he shall file the same
in the office of the clerk of the court in which the action
in which they were taken was tried, and thereupon, either
party to said cause desiring to have the same or other matters under section 25 of this act embodied in a bill of
exceptions may give five (5) days' notice to the opposite
party of his intention of applying to the judge of the
court in which said cause was tried, to have the judge of
said court sign and seal the same in proper form, as a bill
of exceptions. Upon such notice, unless said transcript or
other matters tendered shall be shown to be incorrect, and
in that case after its correction, the judge or his successors, shall settle, sign and deliver the said transcript as a
bill of exceptions, adding thereto such additional matters
properly sought to be added."

The record fails to show, as it should, that the required
notice was given. Further, appellee, by the affidavit of his
attorney, shows that no notice of any kind or character
was served upon him by appellant. This case was tried
to a jury, and the testimony, rulings of the court, objections made and exceptions taken, on the trial, could only
be brought into the record by being incorporated into a
bill of exceptions, and such bill of exceptions, under the
statute, (sec. 26, chap. 57, S. L. 1907, supra) must be
signed by the "Judge of the court in which the cause
2 was tried." The record filed in this court fails to
show that the said bill of exceptions was signed by any
judge. Therefore, for the reasons stated, the motion of
appellee to strike the said bill of exceptions from the file
will be sustained.

Appellee's motion to strike the assignment of errors
3 from the files, because of appellant's failure to serve
the same upon his counsel, as required by sec. 21,

Lorenzino v. James, 18 N. M. 240.

chap. 57, S. L. 1907, will be denied, because appellee admits service upon his counsel of a copy of the brief filed by appellant, which said brief contained a copy of said assignment of errors, and it is so ordered.

[No. 1583, October 14, 1913.]

O. LORENZINO, Appellant, v. STATE OF NEW MEXICO ex rel., JOHN JAMES, Appellee.

SYLLABUS (BY THE COURT)

1. Under section 4, chapter 115, S. L. 1905, where liquor is being sold "outside of the locality for which such license was granted," it is the duty of the board of county commissioners to cancel the license, and such board has no discretion in the matter, where the facts exist, which authorize the cancellation.

P. 244

2. The word "may," as used in the statute, is employed in the sense of "shall."

P. 244

3. The board of county commissioners, in determining the fact as to whether liquor is being sold outside of the locality for which the license was granted, acts only in a ministerial capacity; and, where the facts upon which it acts are not disputed, mandamus is the proper remedy to compel the cancellation of a liquor license, where liquor is being sold thereunder outside of the locality for which such license was granted.

P. 244

4. Section 4129, C. L. 1897, construed, and held not to authorize the cancellation of a liquor license.

P. 245

Appeal from the District Court of McKinley County: Herbert F. Raynolds, District Judge; affirmed.

Lorenzino v. James, 18 N. M. 240.

A. T. HANNETT, Gallup, New Mexico, for appellant.

Decision of the county commissioners, in view of the discretionary power vested in the board, is not reviewable on mandamus. Laws 1905, chap. 115, sec. 4; Dillon on Municipal Corporations, sec. 1489; Kimberlin v. Commission, 104 Fed. 563; Friel v. McAdoo, 181 N. Y. 588; Spelling, Extraordinary Remedies, sec. 1368; 19 A. & E. Enc. L. (2nd Ed.)

The existence or non-existence of an adequate remedy at law is a test to which the alternative writ must be put before the peremptory writ will issue. State v. Mayor, 4 Neb. 260; C. L. 1897, sec. 4129; Laws 1905, chap 115. sec. 4; People v. Green, 64 N. Y. 499; Bailey v. Lawrence, 51 N. W. 331.

Mandamus is a harsh remedy and is to be substituted for the ordinary proceedings only in extraordinary cases. Blair v. Maryle, 80 Va. 485; State v. New Orleans R. R. Co., 42 La. Ann. 138.

M. E. HICKEY, Albuquerque, N. M., for appellee.

The Court did not err in overruling the respondent's motion to quash the alternative writ of mandamus. The words "at" and "in" are often used as synonymns. Graham v. State, 1 Ark. 171; Kaler v. Tufts, 81 Mo. 63, 16 Atl. 367; Rogers v. Galloway Female College, 64 Ark. 637, 44 S. W. 454-55.

If license was used outside of the Diamond Mine the board had authority to revoke it. Laws 1905, chap. 115, sec. 4.

Court did not err in finding that the relator had no plain, speedy, and adequate remedy at law. Chap. 115. Laws 1905, amends section 2124, C. Laws 1897, and repeals section 1129, C. L. 1897.

Injunction, to abate a public nuisance, cannot be maintained by an individual unless he can show conclusively that he has received special injury or loss from such public nuisance. N. P. Ry. Co. v. Whalen, et al., 149 U. S. 457, 37 L. Ed. 689.

Court did not err in finding that it had a right and power to review the action of the Board of County Commissioners. Ex parte Crane, 5 Pet. 190; Ex parte Bradley, 19 L. Ed. 218; Wood v. Strothers, 18 Pac. 768.

Each aggregation of individuals living in close proximity, as is customary in village life, must be treated as a village. State v. Meek, 67 Pac. 77, (Wash.); Territory v. Stewart, 23 Pac. 408, (Wash.); In re Edgewood Borough, 18 Atl. 646, (Penn.)

The word "may," although permissive in form, is in reality mandatory and should be read as though it were "shall," instead of "may." People v. Commissioner of Highways, 130 Ill. 482, 82 N. E. 596; Supervisors of Rock Island Co. v. U. S., 71 U. S. (4 Wall) 435, 18 L. Ed. 419.

Reply brief for appellant.

Appellant had a right to appeal from the decision of the District Court. Laws 1907, chap. 57, sec. 1; In re Meade's Estate, 49 Pac. 5; Wier v. Gland, 88 Ill. 490; Pierce v. Gould, 143 Mass. 234; Noland v. Johns, 108 Mo. 431; Henry v. Jeans, 47 Ohio St. 116.

Appellant had sufficient interest in the subject matter of the suit to entitle him to become a party to said suit or to appeal. McFarland v. Pierce, 151 Ind. 546; Tillinghast v. Brown University, 24 R. I. 179.

An amendatory statute repeals only in so far as it conflicts with the statute amended. There is no conflict between these two statutes. C. L. 1897, sec. 4129, and sec. 4, chap. 115, Laws 1905.

Even though this statute were not in effect, running a saloon under a void license or in defiance of the statutes is a public nuisance, which was a crime at common law and indictable as such, and could be abated. Bishop New Crim. Pro., vol. 2, sec. 871; 60 Pa. 367; 1 Bishop New Crim. Pro., sec. 275, sub-div. 3.

OPINION OF THE COURT.

ROBERTS, C. J.—The principal question involved in

this appeal is, whether mandamus is an available remedy,
to compel the revocation by the board of county commissioners of a liquor license where liquor is being sold thereunder, "outside of the locality for which such license was
granted." The lower Court granted the writ, upon an
agreed statement of facts. By the statement it was stipulated that the facts stated in the petition filed with the
board of commissioners, were to be taken as true by the
District Court. In the petition it was averred that the
building where liquor was being sold under the license
sought to be cancelled, was not "within the limits of said
village," of Diamond Camp, where the licensee was authorized to sell intoxicating liquor. The holder of the license
prosecutes this appeal, and for a reversal of the cause presents three propositions, which may be stated as follows:

(1) In determining whether the license should be cancelled, the board of county commissioners act judicially,
and, therefore, mandamus will not lie. (2) Relator had
an adequate remedy under section 4129, C. L. 1897, and
could not, therefore, maintain this action, and (3) that
the building where liquor was being sold under the license,
was not within the limits of the village. In view of the
stipulation, however, appellant is concluded as to the third
proposition.

The first question is based upon the construction of sec.
4, chap. 115, S. L. 1905, which reads as follows:

"Any retail liquor license granted as provided for by
law may be revoked by the board of county commissioners
of the county wherein the same was or is issued, for the
purpose of conducting a saloon outside of any incorporated village, town or city, when any saloon is conducted
therein, and the license money paid shall be forfeited, for
the following reasons, to-wit: *Provided,* That the authorities mentioned herein, upon a hearing given any person so
licensed, shall be satisfied that such person has violated
any of the provisions specified in said license, or by selling or attempting to sell retail liquor aforesaid outside of
the locality for which such license was granted, or if such
person is conducting a disorderly or ill-governed saloon

house or place, or a place of resort for idle or dissolute persons, or conducts any gambling therein without having a license therefor, or by permitting women to frequent such saloon."

Appellant argues, first, that the legislature, by the use of the word "may," in conferring upon the board the power to revoke the license, intended to invest the

1   board with the discretion to revoke the license, at its pleasure, even though the license was being used in violation of the terms of the act. Such construction, however, is erroneous, and it is plainly apparent that the word "may" was used in the sense of "shall." While the word "may," as used in the statute, is permissive in form, in reality it is mandatory and must be read in the sense of "shall," in order to give effect to the legislative intention. If the word is permissive, then boards of county commissioners could permit intoxicating liquors to be sold at any place, within their jurisdiction, without regard to population. Such was never the legislative intent.

"The word "may" in a statute will be construed to mean 'shall' whenever the rights of the public or third persons depend upon the exercise of the power or the performance of the duty to which it refers. And such is its mean-

2   ing in all cases where the public interests and rights are concerned or a public duty is imposed upon public officers, and the public or third persons have a claim *De Jure* that the power shall be exercised." People v. Commissioner of Highways, 130 Ill. 182, 22 N. E. 596; Supervisors of Rock Island Co. v. U. S., 71 U. S. 435.

It, therefore, follows that the board of commissioners had no discretion in the matter of the cancellation of the license, if, in fact, it was being used outside of the locality for which such license was granted. It is true the board was required to determine whether the facts existed, which

3   required the cancellation of the license, but in so satisfying itself that the state of facts existed, which required the cancellation of the license, it acted only in a ministerial capacity.

A duty to be performed is none the less ministerial be-

cause the person who is required to perform it may have
to satisfy himself of the existence of the state of facts
under which he is given his right or warrant to perform
the required duty. Board of Commrs. v. State ex rel.
Brown, 147 Ind. 476; 'Flournoy v. City of Jeffersonville,
17 Ind. 169; Wilkins v. State, 113 Ind. 514; State v.
Johnson, 105 Ind. 463; Mayor, etc., v. Dean et al., 62 Ill.
App. 41. The board, in informing itself, therefore, as to
facts, upon which it was required to act, did not act judicially, but only in a ministerial capacity, and where the
facts are admitted, as in this case, mandamus is the
proper remedy to compel the cancellation of the license
by the board, if the relator had no other adequate or specific remedy to secure the enforcement of the right and
the performance of the duty which he sought to coerce.
Harleson v. South San Joaquin Irr. Dist., 128 Pac. 1010
(Calif.)

    This brings us, therefore, to a consideration of the
4 question as to whether relator could have resorted to
    some other legal remedy and thereby have secured the
cancellation or revocation of the license. It will be noted
that the statute above quoted does not provide for any appeal, or review by any court of the action of the board of
commissioners. Appellant contends, however, that relator
had an adequate and effective legal remedy, under section
4129, C. L. 1897, which reads as follows:

"Any place where liquor is sold, or in any way disposed
of, in violation of this act, is hereby declared to be a public nuisance, and shall be abated as such, upon information or complaint filed before any court of competent jurisdiction."

but it will be noted that the above section of the statutes does not provide for the cancellation of the license,
but only for the abatement of the "place." Under this
section the court could prohibit the selling of liquor at the
place, where it was sold in violation of the act, but would
have no power to cancel the license under which it was
sold. In the present case the relator might properly have
proceeded under this section to abate the selling of liquor

at the place complained of, but the license held by respondent would have continued in full force and effect and might have been used properly in the place for which it had originally been issued. The statute in question did not, therefore, afford an adequate 'remedy, to accomplish the purpose sought in this proceeding.

Finding no error in the record, the judgment is affirmed, and it is so ordered.

[No. 1597, October 14, 1913.]

Ex Parte

H. C. DeVORE.

Habeas Corpus.

SYLLABUS (BY THE COURT)

1. Common law crimes are recognized and punished in New Mexico, by virtue of sec. 3422, C. L. 1897, which provides, "In criminal cases, the common law as recognized by the United States and the several states of the Union shall be the rule of practice and decision."

P. 258

2. The word "recognize," used in the above section, is given various significations by the lexicographers. Webster, among other definitions, defines its meaning to be "to avow knowledge of." Century Dictionary, "to know again." Webster defines the meaning of the verb "know" to be, among others given, "to recognize." In the above section the word "recognized" was used in the sense of "known," and as used was intended to adopt the common law of crimes, as known in the United States and the several states of the Union, which was the common law, or lex non scripta of England, as it existed at the time of the Independence of the United States, supplemented and modified by such British statutes as were of a general nature and not local to that kingdom.

P. 256

3. Penal statutes are to be strictly construed, but are not

Ex Parte DeVore, 18 N. M. 246.

to be subjected to a strained or unnatural construction in order to work exemptions from their penalties. Such statutes are to be interpreted by the aid of the ordinary rules for the construction of statutes, and with the cardinal object of ascertaining the legislative intention.

P. 254

4. Where a statute does not specifically repeal or cover the whole ground occupied by the common law, it repeals it only when, and so far as directly and irreconciliably opposed in terms.

P. 259

5. Where a party is confined in prison, the legality of the imprisonment does not rest upon the mittimus, but upon the judgment, and a prisoner who has been legally and properly sentenced to prison can not obtain his discharge simply because there is an imperfection, or error, in the mittimus.

P 259

6. While common law crimes are recognized and punished in this state, common law penalties are not inflicted, but the punishment therefor is prescribed by sec. 1054, C. L. 1897.

P. 261

7. Where petitioner, in his application for the writ of habeas corpus, sets forth certain grounds for his discharge, which his counsel fail to discuss in their brief, or upon the argument of the case, the court assume that such points are waived and will not consider the same.

P. 262

Original proceedings in the Supreme Court before Roberts, C. J., Parker and Hanna, Justices; writ of habeas corpus discharged.

RENEHAN & WRIGHT, Santa Fe, New Mexico, for petitioner.

Statutes involved herein. C. L. 1897, secs, 1054, 1055, 2871.

In all the courts in this Territory the common law as recognized in the United States of America, shall be the rule of practice and decision. Leitsendorfer v. Webb, 1 N. M. 34; Montoya v. Donahoe, 2 N. M. 214; Terr. v. Maxwell, 2 N. M. 250; C. L. 1897, sec. 3422.

Statutes adopting the common law. 8 Cyc. 373;

    Kansas, C. L. 1879, sec. 6190;

    Colorado, Mills Ann. Stats., sec. 4184;

      Chilcott v. Hart, 45 Pac. 391; Herr v. Johnson, 11
      Colo. 393;

    Alabama, Ordinances of 1787, art. 2;

      State v. Caywood, 2 Stew. 360;

      Barlow v. Lambert, 28 Ala. 704, 65 Am. Dec. 374;

      Ferguson v. Selma, 43 Ala. 400;

    Nevada, General Statutes, sec. 3021;

      Reno Smelt. Works v. Stevenson, 20 Nev. 269; 19
      Am. St. 19;

      Van Sickle v. Haines, 7 Nev. 249;

    South Carolina, General Statutes, sec. 2738;

      Edwards v. Charlotte Ry. Co., 39 S. C. 472, 39 Am.
      St. 746;

    Nebraska, Cobbey's Ann. Stat. 1903, sec. 6950;

      Kinkead v. Turgeoon, 109 N. W. 744, 7 L. R. A.
      (N. S.) 316;

    Indiana, Rev. Stat. 1881, sec. 2356;

      Sopher v. State, 169 Ind. 177, 14 Ann. Cas. 27;

    Texas, Revised Statutes, art. 3258;

      Swayne v. Oil Co., 98 Tex. 597, 8 Ann. Cas. 1117.

Excess of jurisdiction; review by habeas corpus. 1 Bailey on Habeas Corpus, ch. 5.

There are no common law crimes of the United States. Benson v. McMahon, 127 U. S. 466; 8 Cyc. 385; 6 A. & E. Enc. L., 289, and cases cited; McKennon v. Winn, 1 Okla. 327, 22 L. R. A. 501 and case notes.

In the United States courts the common law is merely a source of definition. 8 Cyc. 386; U. S. v. Palmer, 3 Wheat. 610; In re Green, 52 Fed. 104; U. S. v. Hudson,

7 Cranch. 32; U. S. v. Coolidge, 1 Wheat. 415; U. S. v. Brittain, 108 U. S. 199-206.

There is absolutely no uniformity as between the states of this Union in their recognition of what constitutes the common law. Herr v. Johnson, 11 Colo. 393; Watson v. State, 116 Ga. 607, 21 L. R. A. (N. S.) 1, and case note.

There are only two decisions of our own court construing sec. 3422: Borrego v. Territory, 8 N. M. 460; Territory v. Herrera, 11 N. M. 143.

All other prison breaches were misdemeanors. Randall v. State, 22 Atl. 46, 43 N. J. L. 488; New Jersey Gen. Stat., sec. 12, Crimes.

Statutes defining crimes in this State. C. L. 1897, secs. 1041, 1042, 1043, 1044 and 3422.

Burglary not being punishable by death, prison breach, (if the common law crime is in force in New Mexico), is merely a misdemeanor, and as such punishable under the provisions of sec. 1055, C. L. 1897. Randall v. State, 22 Atl. 46; Weaver v. Commonwealth, 29 Pa. St. 445.

General discussion of the crimes of prison breach, rescue and escape. 2 Bishop New Crim. Law, chap. 35.

Sentence imposed is in violation of the State Constitution. Const., art. II, sec. 13; 12 Cyc. 963; Southern Express Co. v. Commonwealth, 41 L. R. A. 436; Bailey on Habeas Corpus, vol. 1, sec. 54, et seq.

Section 1054, C. L. 1897, is of doubtful validity.

(Additional Authorities.)

What constitutes cruel and unusual punishment. Terr. v. Ketchum, 10 N. M. 721; Weems v. U. S., 217 U. S. 349, 19 Ann. Cas. 705, and note.

Cases construing statutes similar to sec. 1054, C. L. 1897. Frese v. State, 23 Fla. 267, 2 So. 1; In re Yell, 107 Mich. 228, 65 N. W. 97; Martin v. Johnson, 11 Tex. Civ. App. 628, 33 S. W. 306; Latshaw v. State, 156 Ind. 194, 59 N. E. 471; State v. Williams, 77 Mo. 310.

Argument on Behalf of State.

FRANK W. CLANCY, Attorney General, Santa Fe, N. M.

Construction of statutes. C. L. (1897) 2871 and 3422, 1054.

Common law in force. Browning v. Browning, 3 N. M. 659-675.

No conflict between section 1043, C. L. 1897, and other sections under consideration.

Chapter 6, Laws 1880, held to refer to criminal, as well as civil cases, the same as sections 2985 to 2989, also section 2990, and 2994 to 2998.

Prison breach is either a felony or a misdemeanor, according as the imprisonment was for a crime of the one grade or the other. 2 Bishop Crim. Law, sec. 1070.

No argument in the brief has presented any doubt upon the validity of sec. 1054, C. L. 1897. Johnson v. People, 22 Ill. 314-316.

Memorandum Brief in Reply.

RENEHAN & WRIGHT, Santa Fe, N. M., for petitioner.

Sec. 1054, C. L. 1897, passed in February, 1872, cannot be construed as fixing penalties for common law crimes because passed four years before sec. 2871, C. L. 1897, which adopted common law crimes in New Mexico. Therefore, common law crimes did not exist prior to the passage of sec. 2871.

Section 2871, C. L. 1897, fixes the measure of recognition, that the common law as recognized in the United States of America, shall be the rule of practice and decision.

Section 2871, C. L. 1897, is no more effective to adopt the common law crimes as part of the criminal law of New Mexico, than is sec. 3422 of the Compiled Laws.

When sec. 2871, C. L. 1897, is construed in the light of the definitions contained in sec. 1041 to 1044, there can be but one conclusion; and that is that common law crimes are not adopted as part of the criminal law of New Mexico by either secs. 1054 or 2871.

OPINION OF THE COURT.

ROBERTS, C. J.—This is an original application for the writ of habeas corpus by H. C. DeVore, who pleaded guilty to an indictment returned against him by the grand jury of Otero County, on the 29th day of October, 1912, charging him with the offense of "prison breach," upon which plea of guilty he was sentenced by the District Court to serve a term in the state penitentiary of not less than ten, nor more than twelve years. He bases his right to the writ upon the following grounds.

(1) Prison breach is not a statutory offense in New Mexico and the common law of crimes is not in force in this state. (2) Admitting the common law of crimes to be in force in New Mexico, the punishment inflicted was not authorized under such law. (3) The sentence imposed is violative of section 13, art. XI, of the State Constitution.

It is admitted by the Attorney General that there is no statute in New Mexico, defining the crime of prison breach and providing punishment therefor. Counsel for petitioner and the State agree that petitioner was indicted and sentenced for a common law offense and it necessarily follows that if the common law of crimes is not in force in this State the petitioner is unlawfully restrained of his liberty, as the District Court would have no jurisdiction of such an offense. The initial question, therefore, to be determined is whether or not the common law of crimes is in force in this state. It is conceded, that if such law was in force prior to the adoption of the Constitution, it was carried forward by the Constitution as the law of the State.

New Mexico was acquired by the United States from Mexico by the Treaty of Guadalupe Hidalgo, February 2, 1848. The common law was not recognized by Mexico, and had no place in the jurisprudence of New Mexico prior to its cession to the United States. Consequently, it would require a specific enactment, by Congress, or the Territorial legislature, to adopt the common law. It is not claimed that Congress so legislated, but the Attorney

General does contend that the Territorial legislature, in 1851, by sec. 18 of an act entitled "An act, regulating the practice in the District and Supreme Courts of the Territory of New Mexico," made the common law of England the rule of practice and decision in criminal cases. The section, which is incorporated into C. L. 1897, as section 3422, reads as follows:

"In criminal cases, the common law as recognized by the United States and the several States of the Union, shall be the rule of practice and decision."

On behalf of the petitioner it is urged that this statute was ineffectual to adopt the common law, as a part of our criminal jurisprudence, because, in the United States courts, common law crimes are, and were, not punishable, and such law is, in such courts, merely a source of definition; and further, that at the time of the enactment of the above section, the common law of crimes was not universally recognized by the several States of the Union. As remarkable as it may appear, the effect of the statute has never before been presented squarely to the Supreme Court of the Territory or State.

In the case of Territory v. Waller, 2 N. M. 470, the section was referred to by Chief Justice Axtell, but its scope was not discussed. In the case of Borrego v. Territory. 8 N. M. 446, the Court quoted the section, and said:

"By providing that the common law, as recognized by the United States and the several States of the Union, should be the rule of practice and decision in the Territory, the legislature has vested the Supreme Court with jurisdiction to review judgments in criminal cases, by writ of error."

And later, in the case of Territory v. Herera, 11 N. M. 129. the Territorial Supreme Court again referred to this section and held that under its provisions, the common law rule. which it evidently considered to have been adopted thereby, required the Court, in a capital case, before pronouncing sentence upon the defendant to ask him "if he had anything to say why sentence should not be pronounced" in the absence of a statute dispensing there-

with. In the case of Territory v. Montoya, decided by
the State Supreme Court, and reported in 125 Pac. 622,
Mr. Justice Hanna, speaking for the Court, says:

"The common law of crimes is in force in New Mexico,
except where it may have been repealed or modified by
statute." ·

But it will be noted that the question was not directly
involved in the case, and, therefore, the language may be
considered *obiter dictum.*

It is interesting to note that in each of the above cases
the Court seemingly treated the above statute as having
adopted the common law of crimes in New Mexico, without question. The cases cannot be considered controlling
authority, however, because the question was not directly
involved, as, in none of the cases was the defendant being
prosecuted for a common law crime. It is, therefore, the
duty of this Court to determine, as an original proposition, the question of the effect of the statute.

Counsel for petitioner admits that it was the intention
of the legislature, by the adoption of the section in question, to incorporate into the Territorial law common law
crimes, but insists that the language employed will not
permit the Court to give effect to such intention. If it
be true, that the legislature so intended, and certainly no
other purpose is apparent, then it is the duty of the Court
to give effect to such intention, if it can be done without
unreasonably perverting the language employed. The difficulty is occasioned by the words used, viz., "recognized
by," for the United States has never recognized the common law of England, if by that term is meant "adopted"
or "applied" as a rule of decision. As stated, there is no
common law of the United States; the common law is
merely a source of definition. (8 Cyc. 386; U. S. v. Palmer, 3 Wheat. 610; U. S. v. Hudson, 7 Cranch 32; U. S.
v. Britton, 108 U. S. 199.)

Prior to 1848, New Mexico, as heretofore observed, was
a part of the Republic of Mexico, and subject to the laws
of that country, and such laws were of course retained in
the Territory, except insofar as modified by the laws of the

United States or the Territory. In Mexico the common law
was unknown and it is hardly to be presumed that the legislature of New Mexico would intend to make the common
law the source of definition for a system of laws, in no
wise related to the common law. Having become a part
of an Anglo-Saxon nation, it is evident the law-making
power was attempting to conform the criminal laws of the
Territory to the customs and institutions of that race of
  people, and so attempted to adopt the common law,
3 insofar as it applied to public wrongs. Penal statutes
  are of course to be strictly construed, but they are not
to be subjected to any strained or unnatural construction
in order to work exemptions from their penalties. Such
statutes must be interpreted by the aid of the ordinary
rules for the construction of statutes, and with the cardinal object of ascertaining the intention of the legislature
36 Cyc. 1183. In the case of U. S. v. Winn, Fed. Cas.
No. 16, 740, Mr. Justice Story says:
"And where a word is used in a statute, which has various known significations, I know of no rule, that requires
the Court to adopt one in preference to another, simply
because it is more restrained, if the objects of the statutes equally apply to the largest and broadest sense of the
word. In short, it appears to me, that the proper course
in all these cases, is to search out and follow the true intent of the legislature, and to adopt that sense of the
words which harmonizes best with the context, and pro-
motes in the fullest manner the apparent policy and objects
of the legislature."
And the rule, relative to construction of criminal statutes, is thus stated by the Supreme Court of Massachusetts,
in the case of Commonwealth v. Loring, 8 Pick. 370:
"But it is said that penal statutes admit of no latitude
of construction; that they are to be taken strictly, word
for word, let the consequences be what they may. It is
true, it is so laid down as a general rule, and the reason
is, that the Court shall not be allowed to make that an of-
fence which is not so made by the legislative enactment.
But the rule does not exclude the application of common

sense to the terms made use of in an act, in order to avoid an absurdity which the legislature ought not to be presumed to have intended. There are cases which show this, although precedents should not be required to sustain so reasonable a doctrine."

The fundamental rule in the construction of a statute is to ascertain and give effect to the intention of the legislature. The intention, of course, must be the intention expressed in the statute, and where the meaning of the language employed is plain, it must be given effect. But where the language of a statute is of doubtful meaning, or where an adherence to the strict letter would lead to injustice, absurdity or contradictions, the duty devolves upon the Court of ascertaining the true meaning. 36 Cyc. 1106. And it is a well settled rule, in the construction of a statute, that the spirit or reason of the law will prevail over its letter, especially where the literal meaning is absurd, 36 Cyc. 1108, and words may be rejected and others substituted. James v. United States Fidelity and Guarantee Co., (Ky.) 117 S. W. 411. In dealing with this subject, Mr. Endlich, in his work on interpretation of statutes, page 400, sec. 295, says:

"Where the language of a statute, in its ordinary meaning and grammatical construction, leads to a manifest contradiction of the apparent purpose of the enactment, or to some inconvenience or absurdity, hardship, or injustice presumably not intended, a construction may be put upon it which modifies the meaning of the words and even the structure of the sentence. This is done sometimes by giving an unusual meaning to particular words, sometimes by altering their collocation, or by interpolating other words, under the influence, no doubt, of an irresistible conviction that the legislature could not possibly have intended what its words signify, and that the modifications thus made are mere corrections of careless language, and really give true intention."

The word "recognize" is given various significations by the lexicographers. Webster, among other definitions, defines its meaning to be, "to avow knowledge of." One

definition, found in Century Dictionary, is "to know again," a definition, given the verb "know," by Webster, is "to recognize." The word could not have been
2 used in the sense of "adopted" or "practiced," for, as already shown, the United States did not adopt the common law. The United States courts "recognized" it only in the sense that it was "known" to such courts. The common law was known in the "United States and the various States of the Union," but was not adopted as the rule of practice and decision in the United States, nor all of the States. The common law of crimes, as known in the United States and the various States of the Union, was of course the *lex non scripta* of England, as it existed at the time of the Independence of the United States, supplemented and modified by such British statutes as were of a general nature and not local to that kingdom. And where adopted by any State, only such parts were carried into the body of the law as were applicable to the conditions of the adopting State, and not in conflict with its Constitution and laws. While the common law of crimes was not the rule of practice and decision in many of the States, in 1851, when this statute was enacted, still it was recognized by the United States and all the States, if the term be used in the sense of "known," for all the Courts, both National and State, were necessarily familiar with the common law. If we ascribe to the word "recognized" the meaning of "known," the question of the proper construction of the statute and its effect is easy of solution. This, we think, may properly be done, without going to the extreme sanctioned by many of the courts in the construction of statutes, in order to give effect to the legislative intent.

That this is the proper construction of the section we think is made more manifest by a resort to the history of the time when this law was enacted and its passage through the legislature. At the time of the acquisition of New Mexico, its people used the Spanish language exclusively, and very little English was spoken. Three years thereafter, when this section was enacted, the house of repre-

sentatives was composed of nineteen native citizens of the
Territory, and but six English-speaking representatives,
while the council was máde up of ten native citizens and
two Anglo-Americans.   Every act introduced was necessarily translated into either English or Spanish, according
to the language in which it was originally drawn.   The
act, of which this section was a part, was originally introduced in the English language, in its present form.   It
was translated into the Spanish prior to its enactment as
follows :
"En causas criminales la ley comun conocida en los Estados, y los varios Estados de la Union, sera la regla para
la practica y la decision."
The word used in the Spanish translation, to express
the meaning of the word "recognized," in the original
English bill, it will be noted was "conocida," which means
"known."   The correct word, which should have been
employed to express the same meaning in Spanish would
more properly have been "reconocida," nevertheless, the
word used, "conocida," meaning "known," shows clearly
the legislative intent to adopt the common law as known
in the United States and the various States of the Union,
and would warrant the construction which we have placed
upon the act.
In the case of Douglas v. Lewis, 3 N. M. 596, Justice
Henderson, speaking for the Territorial Supreme Court,
says :
"This statute was enacted in 1853.   We are warranted
in looking back at that period to ascertain the surround-
ings of the legislature, the language in which the act was
passed, the difficulty and improbability of a verbally correct translation into English, and determine by these and
other considerations what was meant by the use of words
and somewhat obscure phrases employed in the section as
it now appears in the statutes of the Territory."   See also
36 Cyc. 1117.
If the above statement of the rule is correct, we may
properly consult the Spanish translation of the act, and
profit by such light as it may shed upon the meaning of

the language used, where ambiguous and uncertain words have been employed to express the legislative intent, where it appears that such translation was made before the enactment of the statute and was before the legislature during the consideration of the measure. Of course the Court must necessarily be governed by the language of the original act, and is not authorized to look to the language employed in the translated bill or act and base its decision thereon, (sec. 3800, C. L. 1897), but certainly it is warranted in resorting to all legitimate facts and circumstances which will aid it in arriving at the true meaning of words of doubtful import found therein.

If we have correctly interpreted the section, it necessarily follows that the Territorial legislature adopted the common law as the rule of practice and decision in criminal cases, thereby incorporating into the body of our law the common law, *lex non scripta* of England, and such British statutes of a general nature not local to that kingdom, nor in conflict with the Constitution or laws of the United States, nor of this Territory, which were applicable to our condition and circumstances, and which were in force at the time of our separation from the mother
1   country. That this was the effect of the statute is settled by repeated decisions of the Territorial Supreme Court and the State Court, in construing section 2871, C. L. 1897, which provides:

"In all the courts in this Territory the common law as recognized in the United States of America, shall be the rule of practice and decision."

It was urged in this case by the Attorney General, that, even admitting that sec. 3422 was invalid and ineffectual, the common law of crimes was adopted by the section just quoted, as the language therein employed was sufficiently broad and comprehensive to effectuate such result. The point is seemingly well taken, (State v. Pulle et al., 12 Minn. 164.) But we need not discuss it, in view of our conclusion that the prior section did so.

It was suggested, by counsel for the petitioner, upon the argument of this case, that as the legislature of 1854 en- ·

acted a somewhat comprehensive code of criminal laws, it must be presumed that it intended to abrogate common law crimes. It is not contended that the code, so enacted, specifically repealed sec. 3422, supra, or that it covered

4 the whole ground occupied by the common law, and it is well settled that where a statute does not specifically repeal or cover the whole ground occupied by the common law, it repeals it only when, and so far as directly and irreconciliably opposed in terms. State v. Pulle, et al., supra.

Petitioner contends that he is imprisoned for "escape" and not for "prison breach;" that "escape" at common law was a misdemeanor, and that the Court must look to the common law and be guided by it in determining the sentence to be imposed.

It is true the mittimus delivered to the warden of the penitentiary recites that petitioner was convicted of the crime of "Escape from jail," but the legality of the imprisonment does not rest upon the mittimus, but upon the judgment, (Sennott's case, 146 Mass. 489) and a prisoner who has been legally and properly sentenced to

5 prison can not obtain his discharge simply because there is an imperfection, or error, in the mittimus. (People ex rel. Trainor v. Baker, 89 N. Y. 461.) Upon an examination of the indictment in this case, we find the charging part, (omitting unimportant portions of the indictment), as follows:—

"Did then and there, the time and place aforesaid, wilfully and feloniously, from and out of said common jail, as aforesaid of Otero County, New Mexico, aforesaid, located at Alamogordo, Otero County, New Mexico, as aforesaid, *break out,* escape and go at large, etc."

It will thus be seen that the atttempt was made to charge petitioner with prison breach, rather than escape, for, an essential element of prison breach, lacking in escape, is, that there must be a breaking, and petitioner is charged with the breaking. The judgment recites that the defendant entered a plea of guilty to the charge contained in the indictment, which is followed by the sentence of the court, all showing clearly and unmistakably

that petitioner was sentenced for the offense charged
against him in the indictment.

At the time of the breach, petitioner was in jail under a
charge of burglary, as shown in the indictment. Burglary,
under our statutes, is a felony. Bishop's New Criminal
Law, 8th Ed., sec. 1076, in discussing the common law
crime of prison breach, quotes with approval the following
excerpt from Gabbett's Criminal Law:

"Breach of prison, or even the conspiracy to break it,
was felony at the common law for whatever cause, criminal or civil, the party was lawfully imprisoned; but the
severity of the common law was mitigated by the statute
De Frangentibus Prisonam, 1 Edw. 2, st. 2. So that to
break prison and escape, when lawfully committed for
any treason or felony, remains still felony at common
law; and to break prison when lawfully confined on any
inferior charge was, by this statute, punishable only as a
high misdemeanor, by fine and imprisonment."

From the known eminence and ability of the author, we
conclude, without further research that the above statement of the law is correct. When petitioner broke and
escaped from jail, he was confined therein on a felony
charge and the breach was, therefore, a felony, and punishable as such. The common law punishment for the
crime need not be looked to further than to determine the
grade of the offense, for by sec. 1042, C. L. 1897, "Crimes
and public offenses are divided into: First, Felonies; and
second, Misdemeanors," and the next succeeding section
defines a felony to be: "A felony is a public offense punishable with death, or which is, or in the discretion of the
court, may be punishable by imprisonment in the penitentiary or Territorial prison; or any other public offense
which is, or may be, expressly declared by law to be a
felony."

This statute was enacted in 1854 and under its terms
the crime for which petitioner was convicted would be a
felony, because at the time of the breach he was lawfully

imprisoned on a felony charge, punishable by impris-
6 onment in the state penitentiary. But it is contended
that the Court had no power or authority to impose a
sentence of from ten to twelve years upon petitioner, because at common law all felonies were punishable by
death. It is not necessary to review or determine the
question suggested, because in this State the common law
penalties are not recognized or imposed. Section 1054, C.
L. 1897, reads as follows:

"When a criminal is found guilty in the District Courts
of this Territory of any felony, for which no punishment
has been prescribed by law, the said criminal shall be punished by a fine of not less than fifty dollars, or by imprisonment in the Territorial prison for not less than
three months, or both at the discretion of the court."

Petitioner contends, First, that this statute does not
apply to common law offenses, but only to statutory crimes,
for which no punishment has been prescribed, and, Second,
that the section is of doubtful validity. Relative to the
first proposition, it may be stated that counsel for petitioner has failed to point out any statute of the Territory
or State which denominates an act a crime and fails to fix
the punishment therefor. After a careful search, we have
failed to find such a statute. It is to be presumed that
the legislature had some object in view when it enacted
the section, and, as we view it, the manifest purpose was
to provide for the punishment of common law crimes.
That the punishment imposed by the common law, for
crimes and misdemeanors, in many instances, was excessive and not suited to our conditions and circumstances can
not be doubted. Felonies under the common law of England, occasioned the forfeiture of lands and goods, but
not so in the United States. The statute used the term
"for which no punishment has been prescribed by law,"
and as employed in the section, refers to statutory law.
Thus, where no statute of the State fixes the punishment
for any crime, the Court is directed to impose the penalties provided by the act in question.

As used in this statute, the term "prescribed by law"

must be construed to mean prescribed by the statute law.

The validity of the section is so well settled by the adjudication of the courts, that the question need not be discussed. See, Frese v. State, 23 Fla. 267, 2 South 1; In re Yell, 107 Mich. 228, 65 N. W. 97; Martin v. Johnson, 11 Tex. Civ. App. 628, 33 S. W. 306; State v. Williams, 77 Mo. 310.

The third ground stated in the application for the writ is not discussed in the brief filed on behalf of the petitioner, nor was it upon the argument of the case, and it will not, therefore, be considered by the Court.

7

For the reasons stated the petitioner will be remanded to the custody of the warden of the State penitentiary, to be dealt with according to law, the writ of habeas corpus will be discharged, and it is so ordered.

[No. 1509, July 30, 1913.]

STATE OF NEW MEXICO, Appellee, v. JOSE SANCHEZ y ARMIJO, Appellant.

SYLLABUS (BY THE COURT)

1. The admission in evidence of a confession by the accused is to be determined by the fact of whether the same was made freely and without hope of benefit to his cause.

P. 267

2. The judge, and as a preliminary without which no confession can go to a jury, determines, on testimony laid before him, both for and against, whether or not to admit the confession; the burden being on the prosecuting power that tenders it. His decision covers, besides the law, the fact, as to which it is not ordinarily to be disturbed or reviewed; and the jury can pass merely on the effect of the confession in evidence.

P. 268

3. The court may, even after it has admitted a confession

in evidence, rule it out if satisfied that the confession was not free and voluntary, by subsequent evidence.

P. 268

4. If there be a conflict of evidence and the court is not satisfied that the confession was voluntary, the confession may be submitted to the jury, under instructions to disregard it if upon all the evidence they believe it was involuntary.

P. 268

5. This Court will not review the discretion of the trial court in the matter of permitting a child of tender years to be sworn, as a witness, under the provisions of sec. 3016, Comp. Laws of 1897, except in a clear case of abuse of such discretion.

P. 270

6. Exceptions to the decisions of the court upon any matter of law arising during the progress of a cause must be taken at the time of such decision and no exceptions shall be taken in any appeal to any proceeding in a District Court except such as shall have been expressly decided in that court.

P. 271

Appeal from the District Court of Socorro County; Merritt C. Mechem, District Judge; affirmed.

ELFEGO BACA, MANN & VENABLE, Albuquerque, N. M., for appellant.

Court erred in permitting the alleged statements of appellant before the coroner's jury to be used in evidence against him in the trial for murder. Const., Bill of Rights, sec. 15; Hendrickson v. People, 10 N. Y. 13, 61 Am. Dec. 721; People v. McMahon, 15 N. Y. 384; People v. Mondon, 103 N. Y. 211, 57 Am. Rep. 709; Adams v. State, 129 Ga. 248, 58 S. E. 822, 17 L. R. A. (N. S.)

468; Tuttle v. People, 33 Colo. 243, 70 L. R. A. 33; Counselman v. Hitchcock, 142 U. S. 547, 35 L. Ed. 1110;
Emery's case, 107 Mass. 172, 9 Am. Rep. 22; State v.
Simmons Hardw. Co., 109 Mo. 118, 15 L. R. A. 676, 18
S. W. 1125; State v. Speis, 86 N. C. 600; State v. O'Brien,
43 Pac. 1091; State v. Clifford, 86 Ia. 550, 41 Am. St. R.
518; 3 Am. & E. Enc. L. 488; Wharton's Crim. Ex., sec.
668-9; State v. Mathews, 66 N. C. 106; State v. Rorie, 74
N. C. 148; 1 Greenl. on Ev., secs. 225-6 and notes; Wood
v. State, 22 Tex. App. 431, 3 S. W. 336; 2 Best on Ev.,
sec. 557; State v. Young, 60 N. C. 126; Clough v. State,
7 Neb. 320; Schoeffler v. State, 3 Wis. 823; Farkas v.
State, 60 Miss. 847; State v. Young, 119 Mo. 495, 24 S.
W. 1038; Com. v. Rockwell, 19 Pa. Co. Court, 631; Twiggs
v. State, 75 S. W. 531; Bram v. U. S. 168, U. S. 533, 42
L. Ed. 568; 1 Wigmore on Ev., extensive note to sec. 852.

Tests by which such evidence is to be judged as to its admissibility. Territory v. Emilio, 14 N. M. 147; Wigmore
on Ev., sec. 822; 3 Enc. Ev. 328.

Rule not restricted to actual cases or trials before a
petit jury. Counselman v. Hitchcock, 142 U. S. 547, 35
L. E. 1110.

Coroner's inquest was in fact a preliminary examination. C. L. 1897, secs. 3373 to 3377.

Threats vitiate a confession. 1 Wigmore on Ev., sec.
833.

Court erred in admitting the testimony of Miguel Castillo because he was incapable of understanding the sanc-
tity of an oath. 1 Greenleaf on Ev. (16 Ed.). sec. 367.

Court erred in refusing instructions as to the right of a
traveler to carry arms even in a settlement through which
he was passing. 32 Cyc. 1249; 6 Words & Phrases, 5813,
and cases cited.

HARRY S. CLANCY, Assistant Attorney General. Santa
Fe, N. M., for appellee.

Court did not err in admitting the statement made by
appellant. Bram v. United States, 168 U. S. 432; Wilson
v. United States, 162 U. S. 624.

Question should be left to the jury whether the confession was voluntary or involuntary. Commonwealth v. Preece, 140 Mass. 267; People v. Howes, 81 Mich. 396; Thomas v. State, 84 Ga. 613; Hardy v. United States, 3 Dist. Col. App. 35.

Court did not err in admitting the testimony of Miguel Castillo. C. L. 1897, sec. 3016.

No reversible error in court's failure to give requested instructions because no exception taken upon court's refusal. State v. Lucero, 17 N. M. 484; State v. Eaker, 17 N. M. 379; Laws 1907, ch. 57, sec. 37.

STATEMENT OF FACTS.

The appellant was indicted, tried and convicted at the March, 1912, term of the District Court of Socorro County, of the crime of murder in the second degree, and sentenced to a term of fifty years in the penitentiary at hard labor.

Immediately after the homicide the appellant surrendered himself to a Justice of the Peace, stating that he had killed the deceased in self-defense. He was shortly, thereafter, taken before a coroner's jury, where he responded to certain questions addressed to him concerning the homicide, the admission in evidence of these statements by him presenting the principal question raised upon this appeal. There is no denial of the homicide, but the defense urged was solely one of self defense.

OPINION OF THE COURT.

HANNA, J.—The first error assigned by appellant, is that the trial court erred in permitting the alleged statements of appellant before a coroner's jury to be used in evidence against him in the trial for murder.

The statements were made before the coroner and jury at an official investigation of the cause of the homicide; the appellant was under arrest at the time, and taken to the inquest by an officer who had him in custody; he was questioned by the coroner and members of the jury as to his connection with the homicide; it does not appear that he was permitted to consult counsel, or that he was warned

that his statements might be used against him; appellant
knew that he was under arrest charged with the murder
of deceased, and testified at the trial that the officer having him in custody had threatened his life if he did not
make the statements; and, that the officer, his father-in-
law, remained in the room and in hearing when the statements were made. Appellant further testified, upon his
cross-examination, that neither the Justice of the Peace
nor any member of the jury threatened him, but that
"They were all very mad" and that he thought it would
allay their anger to make the statements he did.

The appellant had surrendered, after the homicide, to
the Justice of the Peace and was shortly taken before the
coroner's jury. The answers of the accused were more in
the nature of an attempted justification of his act, on the
ground of self defense, than a confession of the crime
charged.

His testimony as to the alleged threat of his father-in-
law was flatly contradicted by the witness Aragon, the
father-in-law, as was also his testimony concerning the
attitude of the jury toward him, which was contradicted
by several members of the coroner's jury.

A careful examination of the entire record fails to disclose any inducement, offered by anyone, for the making
of the alleged confession and the only element of fear that
may enter into the question is the disputed fact of the alleged threat by the father-in-law. The Justice of the
Peace, acting as coroner, testified that the statements made
by appellant at the time of the inquest were voluntary.

While the witness, Gregorio Garcia, was testifying, he
being the person who reduced to writing the statement
made by appellant, objection was made to his testifying,
concerning such statement, upon the ground that the coroner had no right to question the appellant, and upon the
further ground that it had not been shown that the coroner's jury had been duly impaneled. This objection, in
our opinion, was not sufficient to raise the point that this
confession was an involuntary one.

The fundamental principle of exclusion of confessions,

as laid down in the Emilio case, 14 N. M. 156, is that
1 they are to be excluded when induced by threats or
promises, hope or fear, because, under the circumstances, the temptation to speak falsely is so great as to
render the statement entirely untrustworthy.

We do not consider that the present case falls within
this rule. The only inducement hinted at in the present
case is the alleged threat of the father-in-law, which was
contradicted and quite evidently not believed by the jury.
It was purely a question of fact and disposed of by the
jury.

The second principle of exclusion of confessions, as set
forth in the opinion of Mr. Justice Parker, in the Emilio
case, is:

"That that portion of the fifth amendment to the Constitution of the United States which provides that no person 'shall be compelled in any criminal case to be a witness against himself,' excludes involuntary confessions."

The present case differs from the Emilio case in that
the accused was questioned by the coroner, while in the
Emilio case he began to talk of his own volition. Was the
appellant compelled to bear witness against himself?

We are not unmindful of the fact that when the witness, Matta, the Justice of the Peace, was asked what the
appellant said before the coroner's jury, objection was
made, by counsel for appellant, that it should first be determined by the court whether the statement was voluntary. The witness had previously testified that he had
offered no inducement or promise in connection with the
statement and that the same was voluntary.

The District Court ruled that the statement, up to that
time, appeared to be voluntary, and permitted the witness
to testify concerning the statement. The appellant, at
this time, made no offer to show that the statement was
involuntary, and we think it was incumbent upon him to
do so before he can predicate error upon the action of the
trial judge in admitting the testimony in the light of his
information at that time.

The rule, in this regard, as enunciated by Mr. Bishop,

in vol. 1, New Crim. Proc., sec. 1220, meets with our full approval and we believe it to be decisive upon the question. It is as follows:

"Sec. 1220. The Judge * * * * , and as a preliminary without which no confession can go to a jury, determines, on testimony laid before him, both for and against, whether or not to admit the particular one; the burden being on the prosecuting power that tenders the confession. His decision covers, besides the law, the fact, as to which it is not ordinarily to be disturbed or reviewed, and the jury can pass merely on the effect of the confession in evidence."

We agree with this rule as laid down by Mr. Bishop and while counsel for appellant was correct in stating that it was the duty of the trial court to pass upon the volun-

2 tary character of the confession before submitting it to the jury, yet, as stated by the trial court, up to that point the statement appeared to be voluntary, positive evidence to that effect had been introduced and the appellant offered no evidence tending to challenge the voluntary character of the alleged confession. Therefore, we think the court committed no error in admitting the confession in view of the evidence then before the court.

Subsequently in the course of the trial the defendant testified concerning the alleged threat of his father-in-law, and for the first time, by way of evidence, the defendant

3 challenged the voluntary character of his alleged confession. It is sufficient to meet this condition, thus developed, to say that the Court may, even after it has admitted a confession in evidence, rule it out if satisfied by subsequent evidence that the confession was not free and voluntary.

Metzger v. State, 18 Fla. 481; Briscoe v. State, 67 Md. 6; Ellis v. State, 65 Miss. 44, 7 Am. State Rep. 634.

We are also of the opinion that if there be a conflict of evidence and the Court is not satisfied that the con-

4 fession was voluntary, the confession may be submitted to the jury, under instructions to disregard it if, upon all the evidence, they believe it was involuntary.

12 Cyc. 482, and cases there cited; also Wilson v. United States, 162 U. S. 613-624.

There was a conflict of evidence in this respect, in the present case now under consideration, and the trial judge submitted the question to the jury in his instructions No. 25, which we quote in full:

"In order that the statements made by the defendant before the coroner's jury can be taken as evidence against him, the jury must believe such statements to have been voluntarily made. If the defendant made such statements by reason of the slightest hope of benefit or the remotest fear of injury, then such statements were not voluntarily made, and if you shall believe that the defendant did not make such statements, voluntarily, you will not, in arriving at your verdict, take into consideration such statements as evidence against him; but on the other hand, if you believe such statements were voluntarily made, then you will give them such weight as evidence as you may believe them entitled to."

By this submission of the question to the jury, the trial court was within its rights and the right of the defendant was fully preserved. It might well be questioned that the alleged confession was voluntary, but it was a question, as it finally developed, for the jury and was properly left to the jury in view of the conflict in the evidence as to its character.

We therefore conclude that the first assignment of error is not well taken.

The next alleged error complained of is that the Court erred in admitting the testimony of Miguel Castillo, upon the ground that he did not understand the nature of an oath. The witness was a boy, fifteen years of age, apparently ignorant and illiterate. It is argued by counsel for appellant that his answer to the following question, viz:

"Q. Do you understand that God will punish you if you do not tell the truth? A. Probably, yes."
was a slender thread upon which to predicate the competency of this witness' testimony. We agree with the At-

torney General that sec. 3016, C. L. 1897, is controlling upon this question; this section is as follows:

"Sec. 3016. Hereafter in the courts of this Territory no person offered as a witness shall be disqualified to give evidence on account of any disqualifications known to the common law, but all such common law disqualifications may be shown for the purpose of affecting the credibility of any such witness and for no other purpose: *Provided,* however, that the presiding judge, in his discretion, may refuse to permit a child of tender years to be sworn, if, in the opinion of the judge, such child has not sufficient mental capacity to understand the nature and obligation of an oath."

The trial court had an opportunity to examine this witness and observe his demeanor, and could judge his mental capacity from his manner of testifying. This Court
5 could not intelligently review the discretion of the
trial judge in the matter of question as to whether a child of tender years possesses sufficient mental capacity to understand the nature and obligation of an oath.

The legislature, in its wisdom, has vested the trial court with a discretion in such matters, which will not be reviewed, by this Court, except for a gross abuse of such discretion. This assignment is, therefore, not well taken.

The only remaining error complained of is based upon the refusal of the Court to give instructions numbered 18, 26, and 27, asked for by defendant.

While we are of the opinion that the refusal to give these instructions worked no injury to the defendant, the question of error is disposed of by the fact that no exception was taken by the defendant, to the refusal of the Court to give either of said instructions.

In the recent cases of State v. Lucero, 131 Pac. 491, and State v. Eaker, 131 Pac. 489, we held that the correctness of and instructions given by the trial court will not be reviewed by this Court unless objection is interposed to the giving of such an instruction, and the same principle

applied to both cases. This assignment of error is
6 fully disposed of by sec. 37, chap. 57, Session Laws of
1907, which provides that exceptions to the decisions
of the Court upon any matter of law arising during the
progress of a cause, must be taken at the time of such decision and no exceptions shall be taken in any appeal to
any proceeding in a District Court except such as shall
have been expressly decided in that Court.

Finding no reversible error in the record, the judgment
of the District Court is affirmed.

OPINION OF THE COURT ON REHEARING.

HANNA, J.—A rehearing of this cause was granted,
upon the question as to whether or not appellant had been
deprived of his constitutional right, not to be "compelled
to testify against himself in a criminal proceeding." The
Court, upon a reconsideration of the case upon the motion
for rehearing, entertained grave doubt as to the admissibility of the statements of the defendant, because of his
having been called upon by the Justice of the Peace and
ex-officio coroner to make a statement of the facts under
which he took the life of the deceased, the defendant at
the time being under arrest, charged with the crime, notwithstanding the fact that the Justice of the Peace testified that the statement had been voluntarily made, because such official qualified his statement by saying, "because I asked him the questions." In the argument, on
rehearing, the question has been ably presented by the
learned counsel for appellee, but upon a re-examination of
the record in the case, we find that the question is not
before the Court for consideration, and need not be determined, because the alleged error was not pointed out by
appellant in his motion for new trial. The only specification of error in his motion for new trial, which could be
considered as in any manner attempting to raise the question is the following:

"Because the Court erred in overruling each and every
objection made by the defendant's counsel in the progress

of the trial when the witnesses were examined, to which counsel for defendant duly excepted."

This was not sufficient to call to the attention of the trial court, its alleged error in admitting in evidence the statement or confession of defendant, and under the rule announced in the case of State v. Eaker, 131 Pac. 489, decided at the present term of this Court, the question will not be considered by the Court.

For the reasons stated the former opinion will be adhered to, and it is so ordered.

[No. 1623, October 16, 1913.]

STATE OF NEW MEXICO ex rel. FRED FORNOFF, Appellee, v. WILLIAM G. SARGENT, Auditor of the State of New Mexico, Appellant.

SYLLABUS (BY THE COURT)

1. Where the Constitution of a State creates an office and prescribes the salary for such office, the necessity for legislative appropriation for such office is dispensed with on the ground that such provision in a State Constitution is proprio vigore an appropriation.

P. 278

2. This rule has been extended to a general law fixing the salary of a public officer, and prescribing its payment at particular periods.

P. 279

3. Held, That the Act of 1905 (chap. 9) creating a force of Mounted Police, fixing salaries of its members, and providing for payment thereof, was repealed by the Act of the legislature of 1909, (chap. 127, sec. IV) insofar as it provided for salaries and membership of the force, and that, therefore, a writ of mandate directed to the State Auditor requiring him to make a levy to pay such salaries is not issuable, because the appropriation by the Act of 1905 has ceased

to be a continuing appropriation, and the legislature has failed to make appropriation for the present fiscal year.

P. 280

4. When a statute professes to repeal absolutely a prior law, and substitutes other provisions on the same subject, which are limited only till a certain time, the prior law does not revive after the repealing statute is spent, unless the intention of the legislature to that effect be expressed.

P. 280

Appeal from the District Court of Santa Fe County; Edmund C. Abbott, District Judge; reversed, with instructions to dismiss.

Brief for Respondent and Appellant.   .

IRA L. GRIMSHAW, Assistant Attorney General, Santa Fe, N. M.

Mounted Police Department created. Laws 1905, ch. 9. Amended by Laws 1909 ch, 127.

Chap. 108, sec. 12, Laws 1903; sec. 28, ch. 89, Laws 1907, and sec. 11, chap. 127, Laws 1909, not applicable because every legislature has passed a general appropriation bill.

Appropriation made by legislature for the Mounted Police in 1912, ending December 1, 1913. No provision made since that time.

Brief for Petitioner and Appellee.

FRANCIS C. WILSON, Santa Fe, N. M., for petitioner.

Chap. 9, Laws 1905, as amended by sec. 4, ch. 127, Laws 1909, constitute a continuing appropriation and it is immaterial whether the legislature of 1913 appropriated for the Mounted Police or not.

Where the Constitution of a State creates an office and

prescribes the salary the necessity for legislative appropriation for such office is dispensed with on the ground that such provision in a State Constitution is proprio vigore an appropriation. Thomas v. Owen, 4 Md. 189; State v. Hickman, 9 Mont. 370, 23 Pac. 740, 8 L. R. A. 403; State ex rel. Buck v. Hickman, 10 Mont. 497, 26 Pac. 386; State v. Weston, 4 Neb. 216; Weston v. Herdman, 64 Neb. 29, 89 N. W. 384.

Rule extended to a general law fixing the salary of a public officer. Nichols v. Comptroller, 4 Stew. & P. (Ala.) 154; Reynolds v. Taylor, 43 Ala. 420; Goodykoontz v. Acker, 19 Colo. 360, 35 Pac. 911; People v. Goodykoontz, 22 Colo. 509, 45 Pac. 415; Ristine v. State, 20 Ind. 328; State v. King, 67 S. W. 812, (Tenn.); State v. Burdick, 4 Wyo. 281, 33 Pac. 125; State v. Grimes, 7 Wash. 191, 34 Pac. 833; State v. Kennedy, 10 Mont. 485, 26 Pac. 197; Terrill v. Sparks, 135 S. W. 519; State v. Eggers, 91 Pac. 819, (Nev.); State v. Eggers, 128 Pac. 987; Menefie v. Askew, 107 Pac. 159; State v. Bordelon, 6 La. Ann. 68; Humbert v. Dunn, 84 Cal. 57, 24 Pac. 111; McCauley v. Brooks, 16 Cal. 28.

Cases apparently contrary to this contention are not in point or have been overruled. Meyers v. English, 9 Cal. 341; Proll v. Dunn, 80 Cal. 220; Pickle v. Finley, Comptroller, 91 Tex. 484; Shattucks v. Kincaid, 31 Ore. 379; Kingsbury v. Anderson, 5 Idaho, 771; Laddy, Aud., v. Cornell, 120 Pac. 153; Campbell v. State, S. & S. Mon. Commissioner, 115 Ind. 591; Henderson v. Board, etc., Monument, 28 N. E. 127.

If the State Auditor's contention, that a specific appropriation is necessary for each year, then the appropriations made in 1909 and 1912 having expired, the original act of 1905, is in full force and effect and a levy is necessary under the terms of said act as amended in 1909. Laws 1907, chap. 89, sec. 20; Rose v. Lampley, 146 Ala. 445; Crosby v. Patch, 18 Ga. 438; Home for Inebriates v. Reis, 95 Cal. 148; People v. Henwood, 123 Mich. 317; Great N. R. R. Co. v. U. S., 155 Fed. 945; Laws 1909, chap. 127, sec. 4; Laws 1912, ch. 83, sec. 13; Holcombe v. Burdick, 33 Pac. 131; 36 Cyc. 1099; 36 Cyc. 1100.

Brief on Motion for Rehearing.

FRANCIS C. WILSON, for appellee.

Holding of the Court, that the Law of 1909 absolutely repealed the law of 1905, is obviously erroneous. Sutherland on Stat. Constr. (2 ed.) 237.

Legislature never intended a total repeal. Crosby v. Patch, 18 Cal. 441.

Act of 1909 did not assume to cover the entire ground of the law of 1905; the changes being for the most part mere modifications.

Where there is no express repeal, but a repeal by implication only, if the statute containing the implied repeal is allowed to expire, it was the intention of the legislature to revive the first. U. S. v. Twenty-five cases of Cloth.; 28 Fed. Cases No. 16,563; Collins v. Smith, 6 Whart. (Pa.) 294, 36 Am. Dec. 228; Dykstr v. Holden, 151 Mich. 289, 11 N. W. 74; 36 Cyc. 1101 .

Reply Brief of Appellant on Motion for Rehearing.

IRA L. GRIMSHAW, Assistant Attorney General, Santa Fe, N. M., for appellant.

Law of 1909 repealed the law of 1905 and substituted a new system, plan and arrangement of the Mounted Police Department. Upon the repeal of the act of 1909, the act of 1905 was not re-enacted because no such intention was therein expressed. 36 Cyc. 1101.

STATEMENT OF FACTS.

This is an action in mandamus to compel the State Auditor, William G. Sargent, to make a tax levy, sufficient to raise twelve thousand dollars for the support and maintenance of the Mounted Police of the State, upon the theory that by the legislative act, (chap. 9, Laws of 1905) creating such force, a continuing appropriation was made for the salaries and expenses of said force and the failure of the legislature, at the session held this .year, to appropriate for the salaries and expenses of said force does not justify a failure, upon the part of the State Auditor, to make a levy for the purpose aforesaid.

To the petition for the writ an answer was filed by respondent, setting up, among other things, that sec. 4, chap. 127, of the laws of 1909 repealed the provisions of chap. 9 of the laws of 1905, under which it was claimed by relator that a continuing appropriation had existed, and that he was only under the duty of making tax levies to meet the appropriation made by the legislative session of the year 1913.

A demurrer to this answer was filed and sustained by the lower Court, from which judgment the respondent appealed.

OPINION OF THE COURT.

HANNA, J.—The first error assigned is predicated upon the action of the District Judge in sustaining the demurrer to the answer.

By the act of 1905, (chap. 9) providing for the organization and equipment of the Mounted Police, it was provided that the Governor be authorized to muster into service one company of police, to consist of one Captain, who should receive $2000.00 per annum as salary; one Lieutenant at $1500.00 per annum; one Sergeant at $1200.00 per annum, and not more than eight privates at $900.00 per annum.

After providing for the equipment and duties of the officers and men, the act provided (sec. 12) that "it shall be the duty of the Auditor of this Territory to draw his warrant on the Territorial Treasurer at the end of each month for the pay of each officer and man in said company," and by sec. 13 of the same act, it was further provided that there should be annually levied and collected a tax of one-half mill, to constitute a fund known as the New Mexico Mounted Police Fund, upon which warrants should be drawn.

By sec. 14, of the act of 1905, the total cost and expense of the organization, equipment and support of said company was limited to $13,000.00 for any one year.

The act of 1905 continued in force unamended until the legislature of 1907, as a part of the appropriation bill passed at that session, increased the salary of members of the force by twenty-five dollars monthly, in lieu of expenses and railroad fare, for each member, and making appropriation for the 58th, 59th and 60th fiscal years to cover such increase of salary.

This act of the legislature recognized the continuing character of the appropriation provided by the act of 1905 except so far as it impliedly repealed the appropriation for expenses of members of the force, which was covered by sec. 14 of the 1905 act, thus leaving that act providing only for the salaries as increased by the act of 1907, and a contingent fund of not to exceed $1,200.00 per annum provided for by section 15 of the act.

In 1909 the legislature made provision for the Mounted Police in the appropriation bill of that session, by appropriating for the support and maintenance of the force, $12,000.00, or so much thereof as might be necessary. It being further provided by this act that the force should consist of one Captain, one Sergeant and four Privates, and the salaries of each were fixed at $2000.00, $1500.00 and $1200.00 per annum, respectively. It is to be noted that this was a departure from the terms of the act of 1905, providing for the organization of the force, in that the force was reduced by the elimination of the Lieutenant and four Privates.

The act of 1909 also provided for the payment of actual and necessary expenses of members when necessarily absent from their stations, and for authority in the Governor to appoint additional members, temporarily, when necessity therefor existed, to be paid at the same rate as privates of the regular force. The provisions thus contained in the appropriation bill of 1909 for the Mounted Police concluded with the proviso: "that chapter 9, laws of 1905, in so far as the same is in conflict with the provisions, is hereby repealed, and sec. 13, of said act, directing the Territorial Auditor to make a levy for the support of the Mounted Police of one-half mill is hereby specifically re-pealed, and the Territorial Auditor is hereby directed, when making levies for other purposes, to include a levy sufficient to cover the appropriation above named for the support of the Mounted Police herein."

This last mentioned act of the legislature continued in full force and effect until the session of the first State leg-islature, which met in 1912, when the same provisions of the appropriation bill, as passed by the legislature of 1909, with reference to the Mounted Police, were re-enacted as a part of the appropriation bill of 1912, except that the provision of the 1909 act directing the Auditor to make a levy sufficient to cover the appropriation was omitted from the act of 1912. The appropriation bill thus passed by the legislature of 1912 (chap. 83, laws of 1912) was limited to the first fiscal year under Statehood, and in 1913 the legislature failed to make any provision or appro-priation for the support and maintenance of the Mounted Police. The question of whether resort can not be had to the act of 1905 and whether that act created a continuing appropriation such as will justify a writ of mandate di-rected to the State Auditor requiring him to make a levy of $12,000.00 for the support and maintenance of the Mounted Police is therefore presented.

It is contended by appellee in support of this proposi-tion that it has been held that where the Constitution of a State creates an office and prescribes the salary for such office, that the necessity for legislative appropriation

1 for such office is dispensed with on the ground that such provision in a State Constitution is *proprio vigore* an appropriation. Thomas v. Owen, 4 Md. 189; State ex rel. Rothwell v. Hickman, 9 Mont. 370, 23 Pac. 740, 8 L. R. A. 403; State ex rel. Buck v. Hickman, 10 Mont. 497, 26 Pac. 386; State ex rel. Roberts v. Weston, 4 Neb. 216; Weston v. Hirdman, 64 Neb. 29, 89 N. W. 384.

And that this rule has been extended to a general law
fixing the amount of the salary of a public officer, and
2 prescribing its payment at particular periods.   Reynolds v. Taylor, 43 Ala. 420; Goody Koontz v. Acker,
35 Pac. 911; State v. Louis Bordelon, et al., 6 La. Ann.
68; McCauley v. Brooks, 16 Cal. 11; Terrell v. Sparks,
(Tex.) 135, S. W. 519; State v. King, (Tenn.) 67 S. W.
812; Ristine v. Indiana, 20 Ind. 328; Faulk v. Strother,
24 Pac. 110; Menefee v. Askew, 107 Pac. 159; State ex
rel. Norcross v. Eggers, 128 Pac. 986; State ex rel. Wade
v. Kenney, 26 Pac. 197; State ex rel. Brainerd v. Grimes,
34 Pac. 833; State ex rel. Henderson v. Burdick, 33 Pac.
125.

It has been generally conceded and frequently held that
the rule, last referred to, is not violative of a constitutional provision similar to that of ours (sec. 30 of art.
IV) that "except interest or other payments on the public debt, money shall be paid out of the treasury only upon
appropriations made by the legislature."

In re continuing appropriations, (Col.) 32 Pac. 272.

With the principles, or rules, enunciated we fully agree
and believe them to be fully supported by the great weight
of authority.

The question remains, however, as to whether they are
applicable to the state of facts here presented for our consideration.   There can be no doubt that the rule would be
applicable if we were considering the act of 1905 standing
alone, and unaffected by subsequent legislation.   We find,
however, that the compensation or salary of each officer
and member of the force was changed by the act of 1907,
which provision clearly operates as a modification of the
provisions of the act of 1905 relative to salary and substitutes the larger amounts provided by the act of 1907.
We do not lose sight of the contention of appellee that
the act of 1907 recognized the continuing character of the
appropriation contained in the act of 1905 and by amendment increased the salary of each man, and were we to
adopt this view of the matter, and disregard the fact that
the appropriation bill of 1907 was limited in its effect to

the 59th and 60th fiscal years, we would still be confronted with the fact that in 1909 the legislature again changed the salaries of the officers of the force and abolished one officer, as well as reduced the number of privates from eight to four, by the terms of this act repealing all provisions of the act of 1905 in conflict with its provisions and specifically repealing sec. 13 of the act of 1905 relative to a levy of one-half mill.

We, therefore, find that the act of 1905, while unrepealed as to many of its provisions respecting the duties of the force and etc., is silent as to the matter of the salaries of officers and men, and a clear intention shown on the part of the legislature to make changes in salaries and organization of the force, by the provisions contained

3   in the appropriation acts of the legislatures of 1907 and 1909. We believe it is indisputable that the life of the acts of 1907 and 1909 is to be limited to the fiscal years for which their enacting clauses purport to make appropriations, at least so far as the appropriations in question are concerned, and that with the expiration of those years these acts ceased to have any force or effect.

In this connection we find that in an early case in the Supreme Court of the United States, Minis v. United States, 15 Peters, 445, it was said by Justice Story, that:

"It would be somewhat unusual to find engrafted upon an act making special and temporary appropriations, any provision which was to have a general and permanent application to all future appropriations."

With this view we fully agree. The act of 1905 having been repealed so far as the salaries of the officers were concerned and the number of the force changed by an act of the legislature which was subsequently lapsed, can

4   it be said that the former act, i. e., that of 1905, was only suspended and therefore subsequently restored to life, as to those provisions which had been repealed, when the repealing acts expired by limitation.

We think not, in the absence of any evidence of intention on the part of the legislature to revive the former provisions, of the act of 1905, as to the salary and membership of the force. To hold otherwise would be to construe an intention, on the part of the legislature of 1913, which failed, or refused, to appropriate for the Mounted Police, to revive the act of 1905 in all its terms, increase the force from four privates, to which it had been limited by later acts, to eight, to provide for an additional officer, and further that all salaries should be as first fixed by the act of 1905.

Such would be a violent presumption as to the intention of the legislature. By the act of 1905 a continuing appropriation was clearly created and was so recognized by the legislature of 1907, but in 1909 the legislature in effect created a new force and definitely fixed salaries for the fiscal year covered by the act, repealing all parts of the act of 1905 in conflict with said act of 1909. Had the legislature of 1909 simply amended the act of 1905, the principle would be different, but the positive repeal of these essential provisions of the act of 1905, with only temporary provision substituted, which has since lapsed, cannot be held to suspend the repealed provisions, or revive them upon the expiration of the repealing provisions. To construe the intention of the legislature otherwise, would do violence to the rule that when a statute professes to re peal absolutely a prior law, and substitutes other provisions on the same subject, which are limited only until a certain time, the prior law does not revive after the repealing statute is spent, unless the intention of the legislature to that effect be expressed. 36 Cyc. 1101.

Believing that the provisions of the act of 1905 with respect to salaries and officers and men constituting the force, had been repealed by the act of 1909, we do not think that the principles of law, referred to, are applicable to this case, and we hold that the District Court was in error in sustaining the demurrer.

We, therefore, reverse the judgment of the District Court and remand the case with instructions to dismiss the petition.

Bass v. Insurance Co., 18 N. M. 282.

[No. 1593, October 21, 1913.]

EDWARD BASS, Administrator of the Estate of C. Gordon Bass, Deceased, Appellant, v. THE OCCIDENTAL LIFE INSURANCE COMPANY, Appellee.

SYLLABUS (BY THE COURT)

1. Section 1, chap. 57, S. L. 1907, gives to "Any person aggrieved by any final judgment," etc., the right of appeal. Under this statute the right of appeal is not confined to a party to the suit, but any person directly interested and injuriously affected by the judgment may appeal.

P. 284

2. All the facts, entitling the person, not a party to the record, to appeal should be stated in the application for appeal.

P. 285

Appeal from the District Court of McKinley County; Herbert F. Raynolds, District Judge; motion to dismiss denied.

Brief on Motion to Dismiss Appeal.
ALONZO B. McMILLEN, Albuquerque, N. M., for appellee.

Statutes governing proceedings taken to revive causes. C. L. 1897, secs. 3091, 3092, 3093, 3094, 3100.
One who is not a party to the record cannot appeal any more than can a judgment be rendered against one who is not a party. Cyc. p. 84-6; Judson v. Love, et al., 35 Cal. 464.

Brief of Appellant on Motion to Dismiss.
A. T. HANNETT, VIGIL & JAMISON, Albuquerque, N. M., for appellants.

Statutes cited are entirely immaterial because not applicable to the case at bar. C. L. 1897, sec. 3091.

Case of Judson v. Love, 35 Cal. 464, not in point. Question here presented is: Who may take an appeal? Laws 1907, ch. 57, sec. 1.

An administratrix de-bonis-non of an estate was a party. 2 Cyc. 627, and note on same page; Adams v. Woods, 8 Cal. 306; Weer v. Gand, 88 Ill. 490; Henkleman v. Peterson, 40 Ill. App. 540; Nolan v. Jones, 108 Mo. 431, 18 S. W. 1107; Clark's Code Civ. Pro. N. C. (1900), article 547; Mutual Life Ins. Co. v. Houchins, 27 So. 657; Zinc Co. v. Hesselmeyer, 50 Mo. 180; Striklin v. Galloway, 137 S. W. 804.

OPINION OF THE COURT.

ROBERTS, C. J.—Edward Bass, administrator of the estate of C. Gordon Bass, deceased, instituted suit in the District Court of McKinley County against the appellee on a policy of insurance issued, as alleged in the complaint, on the life of the deceased. Upon the trial of the cause, the jury, under instructions of the Court, returned a verdict for the defendant, upon which judgment was entered December 9, 1912. Thereafter, the record recites, that on the 12th day of May, 1913, application for appeal was filed, which reads as follows:—

"Comes now Susie Bass, heretofore appointed administratrix de bonis non of the estate of C. Gordon Bass, deceased, by order of the Probate Court of McKinley County, dated March 4, 1913, and says that as such administratrix de bonis non she is aggrieved by the final judgment and decision of the District Court of McKinley County in the above entitled cause, and therefore prays an appeal to the Supreme Court of the State of New Mexico."

It is next recited in the record:—

"This cause coming on to be heard upon the application for appeal of Susie Bass, administratrix de bonis non of the estate of C. Gordon Bass, deceased, and it appearing to this court that Susie Bass, as such administratrix de bonis non, has been aggrieved by the final judgment of this Court in the above entitled cause, and this Court being sufficiently advised in the premises, it is herewith ordered and adjudged that said appeal be and the same is hereby allowed, etc."

Appellee has filed a motion to dismiss the appeal upon two grounds, viz:—(1) "That the appellant, Susie Bass, as administratrix de bonis non of the estate of C. Gordon Bass, deceased, was not a party to said cause in the District Court, and had no right of appeal; (2) For the reason that if Susie Bass was the successor to the plaintiff Edward Bass, as administrator of the estate of C. Gordon Bass, deceased, there was no proper action, rule, notice or judgment of revivor by which to make her a party or give her a right of appeal."

The motion thus interposed raises the question as to who may appeal, or sue out a writ of error, under section 1, chapter 57, S. L. 1907, by which section, "Any person aggrieved by any final judgment or decision of any District Court," etc., "in any civil cause" may take an appeal or sue out a writ of error. If, under this section, the right of appeal is confined to a party to the cause in the District Court, it is evident that appellee's motion to dismiss is well taken, for it can not be contended, in the absence of a judgment or order of revivor, that the administratrix de bonis non herein, was a "party to the suit," the record disclosing that the suit was instituted by the administrator, and conducted by him and in his name until after the entry of the judgment. It is true similar statutes have been construed to give a right of appeal only to a "person" who was a party to the suit in the Court below (Gannon v. Doyle, 16 R. I. 726; Southern Railroad Co. v. Glenn, 102 Va. 536; Parker v. Reynolds, 32 N. J. Eq. 290), but

1 the greater weight of authority supports the construction that such a statute gives to one directly interested, though not a party to the action, the right of appeal. (Dickerson's Appeal, 55 Conn. 223; Labor v. Nichols, 23 Mich. 311; Henry v. Heanes, et al., 47 Ohio St. 116; Nolan v. Johns, 108 Mo. 431, and see authorities collected in note 3, 2 Ency. Ply. & Pr. 169.) The rights of the person appealing must, however, be injuriously affected by the judgment from which he seeks to appeal, and this fact it

appears may be shown *de hors* the record, (Ency. Pl.
2 & Pr. 169), and should be made plainly to appear in
the application for the appeal and, unless the showing
made satisfies the judge of the District Court of such facts,
the appeal should be denied.

In this case the application for the appeal was made by
the administratrix de bonis non, and it is to be presumed
that the trial judge satisfied himself that the applicant
was duly and regularly appointed and qualified as such,
otherwise he would not have entertained the application.

This fact being established, it would necessarily follow
that she was, as such administratrix de bonis non, aggrieved by the final judgment against her predecessor, the
plaintiff in the case, for, had the plaintiff prevailed, the
estates would have profited by the judgment recovered.

For the reasons stated, the motion to dismiss the appeal
will be denied, and it is so sordered.

[No. 1613, October 30, 1913.]

A. B. M'MILLEN, Appellee, v. FIRST NATIONAL
BANK OF CLOVIS, Appellant.

SYLLABUS (BY THE COURT)

1. Where a party who is in default, having failed to file
briefs within the time limited by the rules of the court, tenders such briefs for filing at the same time that a motion to
affirm the judgment because of such default is tendered, the
motion to affirm will be denied.

P. 286

Appeal from District Court of Bernalillo County; Herbert F. Raynolds, District Judge; motion denied.

A. B. McMillen, Albuquerque, N. M., for appellee.

H. L. Patton, Clovis, N. M., for appellant.

OPINION OF THE COURT.

ROBERTS, C. J.—The question now before the Court arises upon a motion filed by appellee to affirm the judgment of the trial court, because of appellant's failure to file briefs within the time prescribed by the rules of the Court. Appellants' time expired on the 15th day of October. The motion was filed on the 29th day of the same month. However, the clerk of the Court received appellant's briefs by the same mail, and at the same time appellee's motion was received. Consequently, at the time the motion was filed, appellant was not in default, as his briefs were in the hands of the clerk, and he had cured the default before advantage had been taken of the same. The motion to affirm the judgment will, therefore, be denied, and it is so ordered.

Justice Hanna being absent from the State, did not participate.

[No. 1493, November 7, 1913.]

STATE OF NEW MEXICO on relation of STELLA SITTLER, Appellant, v. THE BOARD OF EDUCATION OF THE TOWN OF GALLUP, State of New Mexico, Appellee.

SYLLABUS.

1. Where assignments of error questioned the correctness of findings of fact, appellant having brought up the record proper only, the appellee was justified in bringing up the transcript by certiorari, and the cost thereof could be taxed by the clerk of the Supreme Court as provided by laws 1907, c. 57, sec. 34.

P. 288

2. Costs in the District Court can not be taxed on appeal, where no cost bill is filed in the Supreme Court showing the taxation of such costs.

P. 289

3. In order to recover on appeal costs incurred in the District Court, they must be taxed prior to the filing of the transcript on appeal or writ of error, and the transcript must include a certificate of the clerk of the District Court as to such costs.

P. 289

4. After the filing of the supplemental transcript, and the argument and submission of the case, it is too late for appellee to suggest a dimunition of the record, to include in the transcript a certificate of the taxation of costs in the District Court.

P. 289

Appeal from the District Court of McKinley County; Herbert F. Raynolds, District Judge; motion sustained.

Brief on Motion to Strike Certificate of Costs.
A. T. HANNETT, Gallup, N. M.; VIGIL & JAMISON, Albuquerque, N. M.

Practice in this state requires the costs to be taxed prior to the filing of the transcript in the Supreme Court. Daily v. Fitzgerald, 130 Pac. 247-248.

Evidence introduced on a trial is not, ordinarily, a part of the record. 2 Cyc. 1062; Laws 1907, ch. 57, sec. 24.

Two requisites: 1, the stenographer's notes must be transcribed; and, 2, they must be properly certified by the court or referee. Oliver Co. v. Burtner, et al., 128 Pac. 62 (N. M.)

Brief of Appellee in Opposition to Motion to Strike Costs.
Taxation of costs is, ordinarily, a ministerial duty. querque, N. M.

Taxation of costs is, ordinarily, a ministerial duty. Abbott v. Mathews, 26 Mich. 176; C. L. 1897, secs. 3155-3156-3157 and 3158; Mathews v. Matson, 3 N. Y. Civ. Pro. R. 157.

Appellant did not prepare record as required by statute. Laws 1907, ch. 57, sec. 31.

Statute governing cases bringing up more of the record than is called for in the praecipe. Laws 1907, ch. 57, secs. 24, 31.

Costs had been taxed by the clerk of the District Court, upon notice to the attorneys for the appellant. Daily v. Fitzgerald, 130 Pac. 247, not in point.

Costs of only four witnesses were taxed. C. L. 1897, sec. 3155.

Compensation for transcript of stenographer. Laws 1907, ch. 57, sec. 27.

Costs of clerk. C. L. 1897, sec. 1019.

OPINION OF THE COURT.

PARKER, J.—The relator brought up a record which consisted of the record proper, only. She assigned error which questioned the correctness of findings of facts, and
1   which could only be considered by examining the evidence taken in the court below. The appellee was, therefore, justified in bringing up the transcript of evidence by certiorari, the cost whereof may be taxed by the clerk of this Court. Chapter 57, laws 1907, sec. 34.

The transcript was filed by the relator and appellant on June 14, 1912. On August 26, 1912, the appellee moved for certiorari and suggested diminution of the record in the following particulars, viz., that the evidence and exhibits in the case, and the findings of fact and conclusions of law by the Court had been omitted from the transcript. In response to the writ of certiorari, the clerk sent up, and there was filed in this Court, on November 1, 1912, a supplemental transcript, together with a cost bill showing the costs of both parties to be $23.70. The case was argued and submitted March 4, 1913. On April 12, 1913, appellee again moved against the clerk for the order requiring him to have portions of the supplemental transcript properly certified by the District Judge, and to certify up a cost bill, including witness fees not theretofore taxed. On April 14, 1913, appellee served notice of application to tax costs before the clerk of the District Court, which attorneys for appellant ignored and the clerk taxed $79.20 as costs of witnesses of appellee. The clerk thereupon certified up a copy of the notice to tax costs before him, but has not sent up any cost bill.

It thus appears that the appellee is not entitled to tax in this Court the $79.20 for witness fees in the Court
2 below, for two reasons. (1) There is no cost bill filed in this Court showing the taxation of such costs. (2) Under the doctrine held by this Court in Dailey et al. v. Fitzgerald et al., 130 Pac. 247, all costs accruing in the District Court must be taxed prior to the filing of the transcript in this Court, on appeal or writ of error and a certificate of the clerk of the District Court as to such
3 costs must be included in the transcript of record, and no recovery can be had in this Court for costs not so taxed and certified.

It is true that these costs were not properly certified with the original transcript in this case, as they had not, at that time, been taxed. Had they been taxed it would
4 have been competent for the appellee to suggest a diminution of the record and have them certified up as a part of the same. The appellee has never suggested any diminution of the record in this regard, until after the filing in this Court of its supplemental transcript, and the argument and submission of the case. The suggestion, therefore, comes too late.

It follows, therefore, that the motion to strike out the alleged cost bill will be sustained and the clerk of this Court will tax the costs of the supplemental transcript as costs in this Court, as provided by law, and it is so ordered.

Justice Hanna being absent from the state, did not participate.

[No. 1577, November 29, 1913.]

J. B. WOOD and J. A. DAVIS, co-partners, doing business under the firm name and style of Wood-Davis Hdw. Company, Plaintiffs in Error, v. J. H. SLOAN, Defendant in Error.

SYLLABUS.

1. Const., art. VI, sec. 3, providing that the Supreme Court shall have jurisdiction to issue writs of error which may be issued by the direction of the Court or any justice thereof, repealed Laws 1907, c. 57, sec. 3, providing for the issuance of writs of error by the clerk of the Court.

P. 292

2. Where the Supreme Court, upon statehood appointed the clerk of the former Territorial Court to be clerk of the Supreme Court and allowed him to continue to issue writs of error, as had been the practice before statehood, writs of error, so issued, with the knowledge and acquiescence of the Supreme Court and the justices thereof, must be taken to be issued at their direction within Const., art. VI, sec. 3, providing for that manner of issuing writs of error.

P. 293

Error to the District Court of Santa Fe County; Edmund C. Abbott, District Judge; writ of error allowed.

Brief on Motion for Order Nunc pro Tunc.
FRANCIS C. WILSON, Santa Fe, N. M., for plaintiff in error.

The Court having taken jurisdiction since its organization of writs issued by the clerk, it will be presumed that such procedure was allowed by direction of this Court. Rev. Stat. U. S., sec. 999.

A writ of error is a writ of right and issues as of course, in the absence of statutory provisions or rule of the Court to the contrary. Van Antwerp v. Newman, 4 Cowen 82; 15 Am. Dec. 340; Drowne v. Stimpson, 2 Mass. 441-45;

Singer v. Talcott Store Co., 51 N. E. 622, 176 Ill. 48; McIntyre v. Sholtz, 29 N. E. 43-44, 139 Ill. 171; Yates v. People, 6 Johns. 338; Anonymous, 16 N. J. L. 271.

Under the English practice the writ was one of right and granted ex debito justitiae. Tidd's Pr., 1134; Reg. v. Paty, 2 Salk 503; Jaques v. Cesar, 2 Saund. 100, note 1.

"Direction" construed in the sense of authority to direct as circumstances may require, and not as requiring "direction" in order to confer authority on the clerk to act. In re Durand, 12 Atl. 650-52, 60 Vt. 176; First Natl. Bank v. Prager, 91 Fed. 689, 34 C. C. A. 51; Mathias v. Mathias, 104 Ill. App. 344, 66 N. E. 1042; Pearce v. Bowker, 115 Mass. 129; Hagar v. Ward, 115 Mass. 130, (note); Ladd v. Forsee, 163 Mo. 506, 63 S. W. 831.

Such result is unnecessary since this Court being a court of last resort is the exclusive judge of its own jurisdiction. State v. Wanpaca County Bank, 20 Wis. 640; Bridge Co. v. Stewart, 3 How. 413; First Natl. Bank v. Lewis, et al., 45 Pac. 890, 13 Utah, 507.

Cannot be questioned by the lower court whose judgment was under review. People v. Clark, 1 Parker Cr. R. 360; Dowdy v. Wamble, 110 Mo. 280, 19 S. W. 489; Farmers Dev. Co. v. Rayado L. & I. Co., 18 N. M. 1; Manier v. Trumbo, Fed. Cas. 18,309; Lincoln v. Bishop, 13 Ohio 249; Ohio R. R. Co. v. Ohio, 10 Ohio 360.

In order that the record of the Court may conform with its decision in the Farmers Development case, the Court may enter a Nunc pro Tunc order approving the writ as of the date when it was issued. Farmers Development Co. v. Rayado Land & Irrigation Co. 18 N. M. 1.

Brief on Motion to Quash.

RENEHAN & WRIGHT, Santa Fe, N. M., for defendant in error.

The statute gives any person aggrieved by judgment or decision the right to sue out a writ of error within one year from the date of the entry of the judgment. Laws 1907, ch. 57, sec. 1; sec. 3 and sec. 21; Art. VI, sec. 3,

Const. of N. M.; A. & E. Enc. L., vol. 21, p. 741, (2 ed.) ;
Order nunc pro tunc. Gray v. Brignardello, 1 Wall.
627; In re McQuown, Okla., 1907; 91 Pac. 689; A. & E.
Enc. L., vol. 21, p. 741; Perkins v. Hayward, 132 Ind.
95; Secou v. Leroux, 1 N. M. 388; Wilmerding v. Cor-
bin Banking Co., 128 Ala. 268; Secou v. Leroux and Ortiz,
1 N. M. 388; Wilson v. Vance, 55 Ind. 394; Hyde v. Curl-
ing, 10 Mo. 389; Turner v. Christy, 50 Mo. 145; Priest v.
McMaster, 52 Mo. 60; State v. Jeffors, 64 Mo. 376; Hans-
borough v. Fudge, 80 Mo. 387; Briant v. Jackson, 80 Mo.
318; 29 Cyc. 1516, and cases cited; Gibson v. Chouteau.
45 Mo. 171; In re Skerretts Est., (Cal) 22 Pac. 85; State
ex rel. v. Langley, 43 Pac. 845; Lombard v. Wade, et al.,
61 Pac. 856; Black on Judgments, sec. 132.

It may be stated as a general rule that, where a court
has omitted to make an order which it might or ought to
have made, such order can not be entered nunc pro tunc
at a subsequent term. In re Skerrett, 80 Cal. 62; Hegeler
v. Henckell, 27 Cal. 492; Gibson v. Chouteau, 45 Mo. 171;
Wilson v. Vance, Admx., 55 Ind. 394; 72 Fed. 14.

OPINION OF THE COURT.

PARKER, J.—This cause is here on writ of error. A
motion was filed by defendant in error to dismiss the writ
on the ground that the same had been issued by the clerk
of this Court without the direction of this Court or a
Justice thereof. Thereupon plaintiff in error filed a motion to enter *nunc pro tunc* as of the date of the issuance
of the writ of error an order approving, allowing and con-
firming its issuance.

In Farmers Development Co. v. Rayado Land & Irrigation Co., 134 Pac. 216, we had this matter before us. A discussion and decision of it was entirely unnecessary to a
decision of that case, the plaintiff in error having failed
for want of a cost bond, as pointed out in the opinion.

1   For the purpose of settling the practice, however,
we did discuss this matter in that case, and held that
section 3, of article VI, of the Constitution, repealed, *pro
tanto*, section 3 of chapter 57, Laws of 1907, regulating

the issuance of writs of error. This holding was correct, and we do not desire, now, to depart from it in any particular. The holding was that such writs must be issued by "direction of the Court or any Justice thereof."

The further question is presented in this case, not mentioned or argued in that case, viz: What amounts to a "direction" by the Court or any Justice thereof?"

It is to be remembered that for years, under the Territorial regime, it had been the uniform practice provided by law, for the clerk to issue these writs upon the filing of a praecipe for the same by the interested parties. Upon the advent of Statehood and the formation of this Court, we appointed the clerk of the former Territorial Court to be the clerk of this Court. It then and there become our duty to instruct the clerk that writs of error hereafter could be issued only by "direction" of the Court, or a Justice thereof. This we failed, formally, to do. In accordance with his former custom and practice, he proceeded to issue these writs, when applied for and we have proceeded to hear and determine causes in large numbers brought before us in this manner. While no former orders had been made allowing the writs, each member of the Court has had personal knowledge of this course of conduct. Each member has, from time to time, been actually present and known personally of the issuance of some of these writs, and has acquiesced in and consented to the act, as 2 well as the general course of practice. Under such circumstances, we hold that such writs have been issued by "direction" of the Court, or some Justice thereof, within the meaning of the Constitution. To hold otherwise is to put form above substance, to convert the failure of duty on the part of the Court itself into a trap for the unwary litigant, and to unsettle large and important interests heretofore determined by the Court.

Of course, a Court speaks only in one way, viz: through its orders and judgments. For the sake of formality and regularity, therefore, an order will be entered, allowing the writ of error in this case, *nunc pro tunc,* as to the date

of the issuance of the same, and the motion to dismiss the
writ of error will be denied, and it is so ordered.

Three other cases, viz: Rio Puerco Irrigation Co. v. H.
A. Jastro, Nos. 1546 and 1547, and Stephen Canavan v.
Kate Canavan, No. 1562, are in the same condition, and
the same order will be entered in each of them.

[No. 1568, October 14, 1913.]

STATE OF NEW MEXICO, Appellee, v. PEDRO
ANALLA, Appellant.

SYLLABUS (BY THE COURT)

1. Where appellant relies upon a failure of proof as to
ownership of an alleged stolen animal, it is incumbent upon
him to present a complete transcript of all the evidence adduced in the trial court. Failing to do so, the appellate
court will presume that the facts necessary to support the
verdict were disclosed by evidence not incorporated in the
bill of exception.

P. 296

2. Nothing is to be presumed in aid of an affidavit in support of a motion for a continuance, and it is incumbent upon
the party applying for a continuance to show the materiality
of the facts which he claims the absent witness will substantiate.

P. 298

3. In the absence of a showing of abuse of discretion
vested in the trial judge by sec. 12, chapter 116, Session
Laws 1905, the appellate court will not review the action of
the court in returning to the jury box the names of veniremen, drawn to complete the panel.

P. 298

4. Appellant can not avail himself of alleged errors by
the trial court in giving, or refusing to give, instructions,

State v. Analla, 18 N. M. 294.

where he interposed no objection to the action of the court and failed to save exceptions.

P. 299

Appeal from the District Court of Lincoln County; Edward L. Medler, District Judge; affirmed.

PRICHARD & HOWARD, Santa Fe, N. M., for appellant.

Court erred in not granting a continuance of this cause on the motion and affidavit of the defendant. Territory v. Leary, ... N. M. 186; Territory v. McFarlane, 7 N. M. 423; Territory v. Yee Dan, 7 N. M. 443; Texas, S. F. & N. Ry. Co. v. Saxon, 7 N. M. 304.

Appellant was entitled to a jury from the vicinage, or the body of the County in which he was tried. Session Laws 1905, ch. 116, sec. 12; Hewitt v. Saginaw, 71 Mich. 287; Houghton Comm. Council v. Huron Copper Co., 57 Mich. 547; Zanone v. State, 97 Tenn. 101.

No proof of ownership of the animal, under the statute, alleged to have been stolen. C. L. 1897, secs. 67 and 107; Territory v. Smith, 12 N. M. 235; Pryor v. Portsmouth Cattle Co., 6 N. M. 52; Territory v. Caldwell, 14 N. M. 535.

Court erred in calling the jury and giving them the instruction as shown on page 15 of the transcript. Territory v. Donahue, 113 Pac. 601, not controlling now and announces a dangerous rule. Dunsmore v. State, 67 Ind. 306.

HARRY S. CLANCY, Assistant Attorney General, Santa Fe, N. M., for appellee.

No error in denying the motion for continuance. 9 Cyc. 202; State v. Cochran, 49 S. W. 562; Hubbard v. State, 7 Ind. 160; Moody v. People, 20 Ill. 315; Steele v. People, 45 Ill. 152; State v. Pagels, 92 Mo. 308, 4 S. W. 931; State v. Mitchell, 98 Mo. 657, 12 S. W. 379; McLean v. State, 28 Kans. 372; State v. Clark, 37 La. Ann. 128;

Adams v. People, 109 Ill. 444; State v. Kindred, 49 S. W. 845.

No error in empanelling the jury. Laws 1905, ch. 116, sec. 12; Clinton v. Englebrecht, 13 Wall. 434.

No error in the special instruction given by the Court. Territory v. Donahue, 16 N. M. 17.

OPINION OF THE COURT.

ROBERTS, C. J.—Appellant was indicted, tried and convicted in the District Court of Lincoln County of the larceny of a horse. The indictment contained two counts, the first of which alleged ownership of the horse by Esequiel Sandoval, while the second count states the owner of the horse to be "Pablo Fresquez, the legally appointed, qualified and acting guardian of Esequiel Sandoval, a minor, and as such guardian has the care, custody, control and possession of the property of the said Esequiel Sandoval." The first ground urged for a reversal by appellant is, that there was no proof of ownership of the animal alleged to have been stolen, as charged in the indictment. In support of his contention appellant sets out in his brief, portions of the transcript of the evidence which seemingly support his contention. We have gone over the transcript carefully and find that the District Attorney failed to ask the various witnesses who testified in the case the Christian name of the boy who was alleged to be the owner of the horse. He, as did the witnesses, always referred to him as "Mr. Sandoval," or "the Sandoval boy," but while this is true, the evidence clearly shows that the Sandoval referred to was the ward of Pablo Fresquez, and said Fresquez, who testified as a witness, clearly identified the stolen property as belonging to his ward, and the State caused the witness to produce a certified copy of his letters of guardianship of the boy, which were admitted in evidence. It is true the letters do not
1 appear in the transcript of the evidence, but it was incumbent upon the appellant, relying as he does upon a failure of proof, to present a complete and full transcript of all the evidence. Not having done so, the Appellate

Court will presume that the facts necessary to support the verdict were disclosed by the evidence not incorporated in the bill of exceptions.

Appellant moved the Court to grant him a continuance of this cause upon the ground of the absence of a witness, and in support of such motion filed his affidavit, the material portion of which reads as follows:

"That said witness is an important witness for the defendant in this: That if said witness were present he would testify that on the 30th day of November, 1911, he was at the camp of this defendant some few miles north of Tinnie and remained there the whole of said day, that he saw this defendant leave said camp about the hour of 12 M., on said day, and when he left said camp he was riding a sorrel horse and leading a gray horse that belonged to Santiago Lucero, that the witness was familiar with both the horse that this defendant was riding, and the gray horse that the defendant was leading, and knows that the sorrel horse belonged to the defendant and that the gray horse was owned by the said Santiago and has been owned by him for some time heretofore. That said witness, if he were present, would identify said horse which the defendant at this time has in his possession in the town of Carrizozo and is ready and willing to exhibit the same to this Court and could prove by said witness, if he were here, that it is the same identical horse that the defendant led away from said camp on the said 30th day of November, 1911. The witness would further testify, if he were present, that said gray horse was to be delivered by the said defendant at the house of one Felipe Vigil near Tinnie under direction of the said Santiago Lucero as the witness had been advised. Defendant further states that he knows of no other witnesses by whom he can prove the facts above stated, viz., the fact that the defendant left defendant's camp riding said sorrel horse and leading said gray horse, and the further fact that he returned to the said camp on the said day without said gray horse."

Appellant failed to show, in his affidavit, how the above

facts were material, or might become material upon the
trial of the case. The witness might have testified to
all the facts alleged, and still such testimony would have
had no bearing upon the guilt or innocence of the defendant. In the indictment appellant was charged with the
larceny of a horse, but no description of the horse was set
forth, and it was incumbent upon him, in his affidavit
2   for a continuance, to show in what manner such facts
were material to his defense. Nothing is to be presumed in aid of an affidavit in support of a motion for a
continuance. The presumption is, that where a party applies for a continuance he makes as strong a case as the
facts will warrant. Another fatal objection to the sufficiency of the affidavit was, the failure of appellant to aver
therein the truth of the facts, which he claimed the absent
witness would substantiate, or his belief that such facts
were true. 9 Cyc. 203. From the above it is apparent
that the trial court did not err in overruling the motion
for a continuance.

Appellant assigns as error the action of the Court below in refusing the names of a number of persons drawn
from the jury box to complete the panel, who resided at
points distant from the place where Court was in session.
The Court acted under the provisions of section 12, chapter 116, of the Session Laws of 1905, which authorizes a
judge in his discretion to return to the box the name of
any person drawn to fill a vacancy, or as a talesman, who,
in the opinion of the judge, resides so far from the place
where the court is held as to render it inexpedient to
3   summons such person. No showing has been made of
any abuse by the judge of the discretion vested in him
by the statute, and in the absence of such a showing the
Appellate Court will not review the question.

Appellant complains of the refusal of the Court to give
a requested instruction, and of the action of the Court in
sending for the jury and further instructing the jurors as
to their duty to arrive at a verdict if possible. Appellant
cannot avail himself of these alleged errors, however, because he interposed no objection to the action of the court

and saved no exceptions. In the brief filed on his behalf
the contention is made that exceptions were saved, but
4   that such exceptions are not shown by the record. The
Appellate Court is bound by the record, however, and
will not, therefore, review the action of the Court in giving and refusing instructions.

Finding no reversible error in the record, the judgment
of the lower Court will be affirmed, and it is so ordered.

ON MOTION FOR REHEARING.
OPINION OF THE COURT.

ROBERTS, C. J.—Appellant has filed a motion for rehearing, wherein he contends that the Court overlooked a
point raised in his brief, upon the former hearing of the
case, viz:—that there was no proof of brand as required
by sections 67 and 107, C. L. 1897, and, therefore, no
sufficient proof of ownership of the animal alleged to have
been stolen. We have re-examined the record, and find
that the witness, Romualdo Fresquez, testified that he saw
the appellant leading or driving the horse away, and that
he recognized the horse as the property of Sandoval. Other
witnesses testified to the same effect, and so far as we have
been able to find, no one of the witnesses for the State
predicated his knowledge of the ownership of the animal
upon the brand. It is only necessary to introduce a certified copy of the recorded brand in evidence, where the evidence of ownership depends upon the brand on the animal.
Gale & Farr v. Salas, 11 N. M. 211.

For the reasons stated, the motion for rehearing will be
denied, and it is so ordered.

Rogers v. Lumber Co., 18 N. M. 300.

[No. 1580, December 2, 1913.]

W. E. ROGERS, Appellee, v. KEMP LUMBER COMPANY, Appellant.

SYLLABUS (BY THE COURT)

1. On appeal to the District Court from a Justice of the Peace a cause is triable de novo.

P. 302

2. In the absence of a contract, express or implied, between attorney and client, fixing the stipulated percentage which the payee is entitled to recover from the payor, in case of default and the placing of the note in the hands of an attorney for collection as the compensation which the attorney is to receive, the attorney is only entitled to recover from his client the reasonable value of his services.

P. 303

Appeal from the District Court of Chaves County; John T. McClure, District Judge; reversed ,with directions to enter judgment for $25 in appellee's favor.

REID & HERVEY, Roswell, N. M., for appellant.

Appellee contends that he is entitled to be paid for legal services the amount of attorney's fees provided for in the note. 17 Idaho 364, 106 Pac. 299, 27 L. N. S. 111; Peacock, Hunt & West Co. v. Thaggard, 128 Fed. 1005; Camp v. Peacock, Hunt & West Co., 129 Fed. 1005, (affirmed) ; Watson v. Jones, 101 Ill. App. 572; Weston v. Wiley, 78 Ind. 54; Burns v. Scroggins, 16 Fed. 734; Jones on Mortgages, (6th ed.) vol. II, sec. 1606; Reed v. Catlin, 49 Wis. 686, 6 N. W. 326; Bank v. Treadwell, 55 Cal. 379; Matheson v. Rogers, 84 S. Car. 459; 19 A. & E. Ann. Cas. 1066.

Where an attorney is employed to foreclose a mortgage, he is entitled to a reasonable fee for the services rendered, and that the fee is based not upon a stipulation in the note or mortgage, but upon the actual value of the ser-

vices rendered. Elkin v. Rives, 35 So. 200, 82 Miss. 744;
27 Cyc. 1501; Jones on Mortgages, (6th ed.) vol. II, sec.
1925; Varnum v. Maserve, 8 Allen 158; Thompson v.
Drennen, 95 Ala. 463, 10 So. 638; 3 A. & E. Enc. L.
(2nd ed.) 419; People v. Delaware Co., 45 N. Y. 202.

Court below erred in holding in effect that there was
fraud, mistake or error, by allowing appellee to recover
more than the amount of the account stated. Words &
Phrases, vol. 1, p. 93, and cases cited; 1 A. & E. Enc. L.
(2nd ed.) 442, 456; Harrison v. Henderson, (Kan.) 72
Pac. 878; Auzerais v. Naglee, 74 Cal. 60, 15 Pac. 371; 1
A. & E. Enc. L. (2nd ed.) p. 460; 1 Cyc. 454, 455; Brown
v. Gise, 14 N. M. 282, 91 Pac. 719.

W. E. ROGERS, Roswell, N. M., for appellee.

A stipulation for attorney's fees in a note such as in
this case is as much a contract as if it were written on a
separate piece of paper. Wilson Sew. Mach. Co. v. Mo-
reno, et al., 7 Fed. Rep. 806.

Appellee's employment was a general one and not limited to the drawing of the foreclosure notice; therefore.
he was entitled to the fee provided for in the note. Bosley
v. Pease, 32 S. W. 148; 3 Am. Enc. L. (2nd ed.) 431;
Tinsley v. Moore, 25 S. W. 148; Marrel v. Hoyt, 18 S. W.
424; Neese v. Riley, 14 S. W. 65; Montgomery v. Crass-
thwait, 24 Am. St. 832; Bank of Comomerce v. Fuqua,
28 Am. St. R. 461; Wingley v. Matson, 24 Am. St. Rep.
335; Bowie v. Hall, 9 Am. St. R. 433.

OPINION OF THE COURT.

ROBERTS, C. J.—Appellee instituted suit before a
Justice of the Peace in Chaves County to recover the sum
of $85.00, alleged to be due him from the appellant as
attorney's fees. In the Justice Court appellant interposed a plea to the jurisdiction of the Justice of the
Peace, which was overruled, and thereupon it declined to
plead further and judgment was rendered in favor of appellee for the sum prayed in his complaint. Appel-

lant appealed to the District Court, and there conceded
the jurisdiction of the Justice of the Peace, whereupon
appellee moved for judgment of the District Court affirming the judgment of the Justice of the Peace, which
motion was overruled, and which ruling of the Court is
    assigned as error by appellee upon a cross appeal. The
1 assignment is wholly without merit, as the case, in
    the District Court, is triable *de novo,* upon the merits
under our statute.

The facts necessary to be stated to understand the question raised by appellant, by his assignment of errors, may
be briefly stated as follows:—Appellant held a power of
sale mortgage, securing a note which provided, upon default, for ten per cent. additional upon the amount of
principal and interest unpaid "for attorney's fees, if placed
in the hands of an attorney for collection." The mortgagor
being in default, appellant consulted appellee, as an attorney, relative to the procedure to be taken by it to foreclose the mortgage and its rights under the mortgage and
had him draw a pencil memorandum of a notice of sale
which appellant caused to be published as required by
law. Appellant sold the property under the notice of sale
for $850.00, which was sufficient to cover the principal, in-
terest and costs of sale, not including any charge, however, for attorney's fees. Appellee claims that he is entitled to 10% of the amount due on the note, at the time
of sale as attorney's fees, by reason of the stipulation in
the note above set out. Appellant, on the other hand, insists that he is only entitled to reasonable compensation,
and as the evidence introduced upon the trial in the District Court, without dispute, shows that $25.00 is the rea-
sonable value of the services performed by appellee, his
recovery should .be limited to that amount. There was
some claim made by appellant to the effect that there was
an account stated between the parties for $10.00 as com-
pensation, but as appellee testified that this sum was for
only a part of the work done by him, viz: drawing the notice of sale, and did not include advice and consultation,

we will not consider the question, but will treat it as not being involved in the case.

It will thus be observed that the question in the case is as to whether or not the stipulation in a note of a fixed percentage as attorney's fees, is the measure of compensation between attorney and client, where a dispute arises between them as to the attorney's compensation, in the absence of a contract, express or implied, fixing such amount as compensation. Upon the question no authorities have been cited by either party, but on principle it would seem that the question must be answered in the negative. The stipulated amount in the note is the limit of the payee's right to recover from the payor, and is inserted solely for his benefit, and to compensate him for damages and expense entailed upon him by reason of the payor's default. As between payee and his attorney, in the absence of a contract, express or implied, the attorney is not limited to the percentage stated in the note, nor does it measure his

2 compensation. He is entitled to recover only the reasonable value of his services. As the undisputed facts in this case show that the reasonable value of appellee's services, based upon the *quantum meruit* are $25.00, this cause is reversed and the District Court is directed to enter judgment in appellee's favor for said sum, and it is so ordered.

[No. 1587, December 2, 1913.]

W. B. HARRIS, Appellee, v. E. F. HARDWICK, Appellant.

SYLLABUS (BY THE COURT)

1. A agreed with B that he would procure a mortgage on land owned by A to be foreclosed and sold on execution. B agreed to become a purchaser of the land at such sale, and to pay to A the difference between the price he was required to pay for the land less than $3500.00. The contract was fully performed, and B was placed in possession of the land.

under a deed executed to him under such foreclosure proceedings. He refused to pay A the agreed difference of
$925.00. Held, that the vendor could recover the stipulated
price.

P. 310

2. The statute of frauds is no bar to an action for the
price of land actually conveyed, where the deed has been accepted or title has otherwise passed, although the grantor
could not have been compelled to convey, or the grantor to
accept a deed, because the contract was oral.

P. 309

Appeal from the District Court of Eddy County; John
T. McClure, District Judge; affirmed.

ED. S. GIBBANY; G. T. BLACK, Roswell, N. M., for appellant.

No action shall be brought upon any contract for the
sale of lands, tenements or hereditaments, or any interest
in or concerning them, unless the agreement shall be in
writing, etc. Stat. Frauds, sec. 4.

Statute of Frauds in force in New Mexico. Childers v.
Talbot, 16 Pac. 275.

Evidence of a parol modification, in a material particular, of a written contract required by the Statute of Frauds
to be in writing, is inadmissible and such a contract is
not enforceable in any court. Jones on Evidence (2nd
ed.) 444; note, 4 L. R. A. (N. S.) 980-1; Warvelle on
Vendors, 2nd ed., 1-169; 20 Cyc. 287; 29 A. & E. End.,
824, par. 8; 100 Amer. Dec. 169-172; 1 Addison on Contracts, Abbott's Ed., 201; 1 Chitty on Contracts, 11 Am.
Ed., sec. 154; Bishop on Contracts, sec. 771; Fry on Specific Performance, 3d Am. Ed., sec. 777; Brown on Statute of Frauds, secs. 441, et seq.; 2 2Reed on Stat. Frauds,
secs. 454, et seq.; McConathy v. Lanham, 76 S. W. 536;
Heths Exec. v. Woolridges Exec., 18 Am. Dec. 751; Abell
v. Munson, 100 Am. Dec. 165; Blood v. Goodrich, 24 Am.

Dec. 121; Emerson v. Slater, 22 How. 28, 16 L. Ed. 360;
Kingston v. Walters, 93 Pac. 700; Swain v. Seamens, 9
Wall. 254; Adler v. Freeman, 16 Cal. 140; Mitchell v.
Universal Life Ins. Co., 54 Ga. 290; Rigsbee v. Bowler,
17 Ind. 169; McEwan v. Ortman, 34 Mich. 325; Brown
v. Sanborn, 21 Minn. 402; Long v. Hartwell, 34 N. J. L.
124; Shultz v .Bradley, 57 N. Y. 646; Espy v. Anderson,
14 Pa. 311.

When it is shown that a party has pursued a certain
course of action, he is bound by estoppel in pais from setting up or alleging other facts inconsistent with his former action. 8 Eng. Pl. & Pr. 10; 11 Am. & Eng. Enc
422; Machine Co. v. Wood, 43 L. R. A. 449.

Where a contract is partly in writing and partly in
parol, the legal effect thereof is to reduce the whole to the
plane of a parol contract. Snow v. Nelson, 113 Fed. 353.

OSBORN & ROBINSON, Roswell, N. M., for appellee.

The Statute of Frauds will not avail the pleader thereof
where such would result in the commission of a fraud.
Kingston v. Walters, 93 Pac. 700; Kofka v. Rosicky, 25
L. R. A. 207.

The Statute of Frauds is no bar to an action for the
price of lands actually conveyed where the deed has been
accepted or title has otherwise passed, although the grantor could not have been compelled to convey, nor the
grantee to accept a deed. 20 Cyc. 294, 299; Kingston v.
Walters, 93 Pac. 700; Swain v. Seamens, 76 U. S. (9
Wall.) 254; note to Frame v. Frame, 5 L. R. A. 323;
McKenzie v. Harrison, 120 N. Y. 260, 8 L. R. A. 257;
McCreery v. Day, 119 N. Y. 1, 6 L. R. A. 257.

Any act done by the promisee at the request of the
promisor is a sufficient consideration for the promise made
to him. Ballard v. Burton, 16 L. R. A. 664; Anson on
Contracts, 62; Judy v. Louderman, 48 Ohio St. 562; 1
Parsons on Contracts, 444; Burr v. Wilcox, 13 Allen
272; Doyle v. Doxin,, 97 Mass. 213, 93 Am. Dec. 80;
Phoenx Mut. Ins. Co. v. Raddin, 120 U. S. 183.

Evidence of a parol modification of a written contract is admissible and such contract will be enforced in any court. Cummings v. Arnold, 37 Am. Dec. 155; Marsh v. Bellew, 45 Wis. 38; Bryan v. Hunt, 70 Am. Dec. 262; Toledo, St. L. & K. C. R. Co. v. Levy, 127 Ind. 168; Oiler v. Gard, 23 Ind. 212; Cincinnati, U. & Ft. W. R. Co. v. Pearce, 28 Ind. 502.

A parol contract may be added to a written one and the two may stand together. Greenwalt v. Kohne, 85 Pa. 369; Ewaldt v. Farlow, 62 Ia. 212; Reynolds v. Hassan, 56 Vt. 449; Collingwood v. Merchants Bank, 15 Neb. 118; Kingston v. Walters, 93 Pac. 700.

The parol contract established a subsequent arrangement between the parties. Wood v. Russell, 1 Cent. Rep. 336; Lynch v. Henry, 75 Wis. 631.

A party seeking to enforce an alleged contract must first show performance of all conditions precedent by him to be performed, or a sufficient waiver of the same by the adverse party.

Hitchins v. Pettingale, 58 N. H. 386.

The Statute of Frauds cannot be set up as a protection, to fraud. Kinard v. Hiers, 44 Am. Dec. 643; Teague v. Fowler, 56 Ind. 569; Rogers v. Rogers, 87 Mo. 257; Green v. Green, 55 Am. Rep. 256; Barnard v. Flinn, 8 Ind. 204; Leahey v. Leahey, 11 Mo. App. 413; Turner v. Johnson, 95 Mo. 431.

Appellant's Brief on Motion for Rehearing.

This case does not come within the rule laid down in the case of Kingston v. Walters, 93 Pac. 700.

STATEMENT OF FACTS.

On the 3rd day of April, 1908, appellee and appellant entered into a written contract whereby the appellee agreed to convey by good and sufficient warranty deed to appellant certain real estate in Eddy County, New Mexico. By the terms of the contract, appellant was to pay appellee, as consideration for the real estate, the sum of $3500.00, and appellee was to furnish to appellant an abstract of title, showing fee simple title in appellee, with the exception of a certain mortgage in the sum of $1703.15, and interest thereon from the 28th day of October, 1907, at the rate of 10% per annum, and taxes for the last half of the year 1908, which sums were to be paid out of the purchase price or assumed by appellant. On the day of making and executing said contract, appellant paid to appellee the sum of $300.00, which sum, however, under the contract, was only required to be deposited in escrow. The amount of the mortgage, interest and taxes named in said written contract amounted to $2,225.00, which sum, together with the $300.00 paid to appellee, deducted from the stipulated purchase price of $3500.00, left remaining the sum of $925.00, for which sum appellee recovered judgment in the lower Court.

About two weeks after the signing of the written contract, and while said contract was in full force and effect, appellant requested appellee to have said mortgage foreclosed, stating to appellee, as his reasons therefor, that by means of the foreclosure, he, the appellant, could and would acquire a more perfect title, or a title that he would prefer to the said land, and appellant agreed orally with appellee and bound himself unto appellee, not only to carry out his contract of purchase for the land aforesaid, but further agreed that he, appellant, would purchase the land at the foreclosure sale, or would cause the same to be purchased for his use and benefit and would thereby protect appellee fully in the transaction, to the end that appellee would receive, and appellant would pay appellee the amount of the balance due under said written contract.

Pursuant to the understanding and agreement aforesaid, appellee requested the holder of said mortgage to foreclose the same, which was done, because of such request by the holder thereof, in September, 1908, and at the sale had thereunder, the land was purchased by appellant, through his attorney and agent, for the amount of the judgment, plus $7.94. At the sale there was one other bidder, the mortgagee, who bid the amount of the judgment. Appellant entered into possession of the land, and still retains such possession.

From the evidence it appears that there was a judgment lien on said real estate, inferior, however, to the mortgage lien, and it was because of this lien, and in order to free the land therefrom, that appellant requested that the mortgage be foreclosed.

Appellant, upon the trial, disputed the above facts and denied the making of the parol agreement, but as the Court rendered judgment for appellee and found the issues in his favor, the above must be accepted as the facts in the case, for there was sufficient evidence to support appellee's theory of the case.

From judgment rendered, appellant prosecutes this appeal.

OPINION OF THE COURT.

ROBERTS, C. J.—There are several assignments of error in this case by appellant, all presenting ,however, but one proposition worthy of consideration, which may be stated as follows:—Under the Statute of Frauds, which is in force in this State, "no action shall be brought upon any contract or sale of lands, tenements or hereditaments, or any interest in or concerning them, or upon any agreement that is not to be performed within the space of one year from the making thereof, unless the agreement upon which such action shall be brought, or some memorandum or note thereof, shall be in writing, signed by the party to be charged therewith, or by some person thereunto by him lawfully authorized." Appellant here urges that a recovery in this case is precluded by the above provision of the statute, because the subsequent modification of the written contract was in parol, and was, therefore, not enforcible. If appellee was seeking to compel appellant to carry out the terms of the parol agreement to become a purchaser at the foreclosure sale, the Statutes of Frauds could probably be successfully invoked as a defense to the action. In this case, however, the contract was fully performed by appellee, and likewise, by appellant, except the payment of the consideration. Appellee caused the mortgage to be foreclosed and the property to be sold as he agreed to do. Appellant purchased the property at the sale, and took possession of the same, which he still retains, all under parol contract.

"The statute is no bar to an action for the price of land actually conveyed where the deed has been accepted or
2 title has otherwise passed, although the grantor could not have been compelled to convey, or the grantor to accept a deed, because the contract was oral." 20 Cyc. 294, and case cited.

The case of Arnold v. Stephenson, 79 Ind. 126, was almost identical with the case at bar. There a judgment has been recovered against A and an execution levied upon his land. Prior to the sale under the execution, B agreed verbally with A to buy in the land at the sale and to pay off a mortgage upon the land and certain other charges and to pay to A the difference between the amounts so paid and the stipulated price of $6,000.00. B purchased the land at the sale, paid only a portion of the debts which he agreed to assume, and refused to pay A any further money under the agreement. B took possession under the sheriff's deed, and was in possession at the time of the institution of the suit. To a complaint reciting the above facts, a demurrer was interposed and sustained. Judge Elliott, speaking for the Court, says:—

"We think that in cases of the class to which the one under consideration and that cited belong, it should be held that, where the purchaser receives a sheriff's deed, and acquires full title and complete possession of the land, he cannot escape liability upon the ground that the statute of frauds prohibits the enforcement of verbal contracts for the sale of an interest in land. We accordingly hold that where the agreement is so far performed that the purchaser acquires a perfect title and full possession of the property, the vendor may recover the stipulated price. This is in accordance with the rule stated by Mr. Browne, 'when so much of a contract as would bring it within the Statute of Frauds has been executed, all the remaining

stipulations become valid and enforcible, and the parties to the contract regain all the rights of action they would have had at common law.' Browne Statute of Frauds, sec. 117. This rule secures justice. Appellee obtained a title by the sheriff's sale, and the most rigid adherence to the requirements of the statute could have given him nothing more. The execution of the contract is really none the less complete because the land passed by the sheriff's deed instead of by the conveyance of appellant.
1 Schenck v. Sithoff, 75 Ind. 485. Appellee has secured all he bargained for, and he ought to pay what he promised. It is so well settled, that the Statute of Frauds cannot be made the means of perpetrating a fraud, that authorities need not be cited. Appellee, under the facts, parted with a substantial interest in his property, upon the faith of appellant's promise. Appellant received all that he asked or required under the contract, for his promise and the statute cannot be interposed to enable him to receive the benefit without yielding the agreed consideration.

Finding no available error in the record, the judgment of the trial court is affirmed, and it is so ordered.

* ———————————

[No. 1602, December 2, 1913.]
In re JUAN LUJAN,
   HABEAS CORPUS.

SYLLABUS (BY THE COURT)

1. Where a District Court is without power to suspend the execution of the judgment in a criminal cause, or to withhold the commitment, an order so made, attempting to do so, is null and void and without force and effect, and amounts to surplusage.

P. 313

2. Where a defendant, duly sentenced by a District Court to serve a definite term in the State penitentiary, is permit-

ted to go and remain at large, under a void order of the Court, he may be taken into custody and compelled to serve the term fixed in the judgment, even though a longer period of time than that for which he was sentenced has elapsed since the sentence was imposed.

P. 314

Original proceeding in the Supreme Court. Habeas Corpus.

IRA L. GRIMSHAW, Assistant Attorney General, Santa Fe, N. M., for respondent.

The court had power to provide that the commitment should not issue so long as the defendant remained out- side of New Mexico. Gibson v. State, 68 Miss. 841; 12 Cyc. 773; State v. Whitt, 117 N. C. 804; Weaver v. People, 33 Mich. 296; Weber v. State, Ohio, 41 L. R. A. (N. S.) 427; People v. Forsyth, 23 L. R. A. (N. S.) 856; People v. Patrick, 118 Cal. 332; State v. Hatley, 110 N. C. 552; 12 Cyc. 774; Ex parte Bugg, 145 S. W. 831; Spencer v. State, 140 S. W. 688; Roberts v. Wansley, 137 Ga. 439; State v. White, 140 S. W. 1059.

Arrest of petitioner, after the expiration of the term of imprisonment named in the sentence, is legal and valid. State v. Kitchens, 27 Am. Dec. 412; State v. Chancellor, 47 Am. Dec. 558; Muller v. Evans, 115 Ia. 102, et seq.; State v. Cockersham, 23 N. C. 204; In re Collins, 8 Cal. App. 370; Fuller v. Miss., 39 L. R. A. (N. S.) 242; Gibson v. State, 68 Miss. 241; State v. Spencer, 38 L. R. A. (N. S.) 680; In re Leo Hinson, 36 L. R. A. (N. S.) 343; People v. Pateick, 118 Cal. 332; Neal v. State, 69 Am. St. R. 176; In re Webb, 89 Wis. 354; Ex parte Vance, 13 L. R. A. 574; Dolan's Case, 101 Mass. 219; State v. Abbott, 33 L. R. A. (N. S.) 112; O'Dwyer v. Kelly, 133 Ga. 824; Ex parte Clara Moore, 12 Cal. App. 161; In re Herbert L. Collins, 8 Cal. App. 367.

STATEMENT OF FACTS.

On September 25, 1908, Juan Lujan, the petitioner herein upon a plea of guilty to an indictment charging him with the crime of assault with a deadly weapon, was, by the District Court of Eddy County, sentenced to serve a term of imprisonment of two years in the Territorial penitentiary at Santa Fe, New Mexico. The judgment of the Court was in the following words, viz:——

"Now comes the Territory by her District Attorney and comes the defendant in his own proper person in custody of the sheriff and the defendant being asked if he has anything to say why the sentence of the Court should not be passed against him, nothing says and the Court, pursuant to a plea of guilty heretofore entered herein, assessed his punishment at imprisonment in the Territorial penitentiary at hard labor for the full period of two years and that he pay the cost of this prosecution.

"It is therefore considered and adjudged by the Court that the defendant, Juan Lujan, be imprisoned in the Territorial penitentiary, situate at Santa Fe, New Mexico, for the full term of two years, and that he pay the costs of this prosecution to be taxed and that execution issue therefor and the sheriff of Eddy County is hereby ordered to deliver the said Juan Lujan to the Superintendent or Warden of the said penitentiary and that the said Superintendent or Warden of the said penitentiary confine the said Juan Lujan in said penitentiary for the full term of two years from the date of the confinement hereunder, and until said costs are discharged by operation of law and that commitment issue therefore.

"And it is further ordered that if the defendant shall forthwith remove himself from the Territory of New Mexico the commitment hereunder shall not issue so long as he shall remain absent from the said Territory"

No commitment was issued in said cause until July 17, 1913, when an order was made by the District Court of said County, directing the issuance of a commitment because of a violation of the terms of the order upon which commitment was withheld, and thereafter petitioner was taken into custody and confined in the State penitentiary at Santa Fe. Thereupon petitioner applied to this Court for his release upon a writ of habeas corpus.

OPINION OF THE COURT.

ROBERTS, C. J.—The power to suspend the execution of a sentence in a felony case is conferred upon the District Courts of the State by sec. 1, chap. 32, S. L. 1909. The order of suspension in this case, however, was made prior to the enactment of the statute, and petitioner's application for his release from the custody of the warden of the State penitentiary is predicated upon the assumption that the District Court, when it sentenced petitioner, upon his plea of guilty, in the absence of a statute so authorizing, had not the power to provide "that if the defendant shall forthwith remove himself from the Territory of New Mexico, the commitment hereunder shall not issue so long as he shall remain absent from the Territory of New Mexico." If it be conceded that the Court had the power to make the order, suspending the execution of the judgment, it would follow necessarily that, upon violation of the order, the Court would have the right to revoke the order, and commit the defendant. On the

1 other hand, if the Court was without power to suspend the execution of the judgment, or withhold the commitment, then the order so made attempting to do so, would be null and void and without force and effect, and would amount to surplusage. Spencer v. State, (Tenn.) 140 S. W. 597, and cases cited; Fuller v. Miss., 39 L. R. A. (N. S.) 242. This being true the only question involved in this case is whether the Court has lost its power to enforce the execution of its judgment providing for the imprisonment of petitioner in the State penitentiary for a period of two years, by reason of the fact that more than said period of time has elapsed since the imposition of the sentence. In other words, can a sentence be satisfied until it has been actually served, in the absence of a pardon? While there is a conflict of authority upon the proposition, we believe the correct rule was laid down by the Mississippi Supreme Court in the case of Fuller v. Miss., 57 Southern 6; 39 L. R. A. (N. S.) 242.

"It is immaterial that a longer period of time than that for which appellant was sentenced has elapsed since the sentence was imposed. While at large under this void **2** order, to which he did not object, appellant was in the same situation that he would have been had, he simply escaped from custody. In such case the sentence is not satisfied until it has been actually served. Ex parte Bell, 56 Miss. 282; 1 Bishop's Crim. Proc., 4th ed., 1384; Spencer v. State, (Tenn.) 38 L. R. A. (N. S.) 680, 140 S. W. 597; State v. Abbott,. 87 S. C. 466, 33 L. R. A. (N. S.) 112, 70 S. E. 6; Ann. Cas. 1912 B. 1189; Miller v. Evans, 115 Iowa 101, 56 L. R. A. 101, 91 Am. St. 143; 88 N. W. 198; Neal v. State, 104 Ga. 509, 42 L. R. A. 190, 69 Am. State Rep. 175, 30 S. E. 858; Tanner v. Wiggins, 54 Fla. 203, 45 So. 459, 14 Ann. Cas. 718."

See also, In re Leo Hinson, (N. C.) 36 L. R. A. (N. S.) 343; People v. Patrick, 118 Calif. 332; Ex parte Vance, 13 L. R. A. 574; Dolan's Case, 101 Mass. 219; O'Dwyer v. Kelley, 133 Ga. 824; In re Herbert L. Collins, 8 Cal. App. 367.

For the reasons stated, petitioner will be remanded to the custody of John B. McManus, superintendent of the State penitentiary, to be dealt with according to law and the writ of habeas corpus will be discharged, and it is so ordered.

[No. 1606, December 2, 1913.]

THE STATE OF NEW MEXICO, Appellant, v. JOHN COATS, et al., Appellees.

SYLLABUS (BY THE COURT)

1. Where a Justice of the Peace, under sec. 3, chap. 57, S. L. 1907, finds that a criminal prosecution has been instituted "maliciously, or without probable cause," and taxes the

costs against the prosecuting witness, and the prosecuting witness appeals from such judgment, the case should be docketed as the State v. The Prosecuting Witness, and not as originally entitled.

P. 316

2. In such a case, where the prosecuting witness appeals from a judgment of the Justice of the Peace taxing him with the costs, the District Court is required to try the question as to whether the prosecution was instituted maliciously, or without probable cause de novo and must enter its own independent judgment in the case. In such case the discretion conferred by the statute upon the Justice of the Peace is necessarily transferred to the District Court.

P. 317

3. Upon such appeal the burden is upon the State to show that the prosecution was instituted maliciously, or without probable cause.

P. 318

Appeal from the District Court of Sierra County; Merritt C. Mechem, District Judge; affirmed.

EDWARD D. TITTMAN, Hillsboro, N. M., for appellant.

Statute under which the Justice of the Peace taxed costs against the prosecuting witness. Laws 1907, ch. 61, sec. 3.

The person on whose oath of information any criminal prosecution shall have been instituted shall be considered the prosecutor. C. L. 1897, sec. 3441; Ill. Central R. R. v. Herr, 54 Ill. 356, 359; State v. Millian, 3 Nev. 409; Philips v. Bevans, 23 N. J. L. (3 Zab) 373; U. S. v. Sandford, 27 Fed Cas. 952.

Appellate Courts will not review matters that are entirely in the discretion of the Court below unless such discretion has been abused. 3 Cyc. 342, k, and cases in note 57; 11 Cyc. 153, d, and cases in note 64.

Court's finding as to costs is conclusive. 11 Cyc. 272, note 64.

There is no absolute right of appeal. 24 Cyc. 655, 3;
2 Cyc. 520, note 88; C. L. 1897, secs. 3305, 3307, 3317,

OPINION OF THE COURT.

ROBERTS, C. J.—G. W. Bledsoe was the prosecuting
witness in an information filed by the District Attorney,
before a Justice of the Peace, against John Coats and his
wife, wherein they were charged with conducting a disorderly house within three hundred yards of a school house.
Upon trial the defendants were acquitted, and the Justice
of the Peace found that the prosecution was instituted
"maliciously and without probable cause," and taxed the
costs against Bledsoe and ordered him committed until
the costs should be paid. From the judgment taxing him
with the costs, Bledsoe appealed to the District Court. In
the District Court the State filed a motion to dismiss the
appeal, on the ground that the District Court was without
jurisdiction to try the case, because no appeal could be
taken from the judgment of the Justice of the Peace. The
Court overruled the motion and called the case for trial,
and the State offering no evidence, a judgment was entered discharging Bledsoe from the payment of the costs
of the case. From such judgment the State appeals, and
predicates error upon two grounds, viz: (1) The imposition of costs, upon the prosecuting witness, resting solely
within the discretion of the Justice of the Peace, no appeal lies to review such discretion, and (2) upon appeal, in
such a case, the burden was upon the appellant, and in the
absence of any evidence it was the duty of the Court to
enter judgment for the State.

Before considering the question stated, it is probably
advisable to notice a question of practice, presented by
the record in this case, but not discussed by counsel. The
case is docketed in this Court, and was apparently so docketed in the District Court, as the "State of New Mexico v.

1   John Coats, et al.," the defendants in the original
case. This is improper. The case against John Coats
was disposed of by the judgment of the Justice of the
Peace, and when he taxed the costs against Bledsoe, the

judgment therein became a judgment on behalf of the State against said Bledsoe, and so it should appear in subsequent proceedings, involving such judgment.

Appellant's brief is devoted chiefly to a discussion of the first ground upon which error is predicated. The section of the statute, under which the Justice of the Peace imposed the costs of the case upon the prosecuting witness, reads as follows:—

Section 3, chap. 61, S. L. 1907.) "Upon the trial of any criminal case, whenever the Court or Justice of the Peace shall be satisfied that any such case has been instituted maliciously, or without probable cause, the Court may in its discretion tax the costs therein against the prosecuting witness, in which event such witness shall stand committed until such costs be fully paid."

The argument is advanced, that the imposition of costs upon the prosecuting witness, resting in the discretion of the Justice of the Peace, such discretion will not be reviewed by an Appellate Court. This would be true, if the Appellate Court simply reviewed the judgment of the **2** Justice of the Peace and reversed or affirmed the same, but under our statute, (sec. 3317, C. L. 1897), the case, in the District Court, must be tried *de novo*, and the District Court necessarily is required to enter its own independent judgment. This being true, the discretion conferred upon the Justice of the Peace by the section of the statute first quoted, is necessarily transferred to the District Court by the appeal. To establish the contrary rule, the State relies upon the following quotation from 11 Cyc. 272:

"In North Carolina, where the Court decides whether grounds exist for imposing costs on the prosecutor, its finding that the facts warrant the imposition, is conclusive."

But that this rule applies only to appeals from the District Court to the Supreme Court, is clearly shown by the North Carolina Supreme Court in the case of State v. Hamilton, 106 N. C. 660:

"Section 738 empowers the Court to imprison the prose-

cutor for nonpayment of costs, if it shall adjudge that the
prosecution was frivolous and malicious. This is held constitutional. State v. Cannady, 78 N. C. 539. These findings of fact by the Court below have been repeatedly held
conclusive and not reviewable by this Court on appeal.
State v. Adams, 85 N. C. 560; State v. Owen, 87 N. C.
565; State v. Dunn, 95 N. C. 697. Though such findings
of fact by a Justice of the Peace are reviewable by the Superior Court on appeal. State v. Murdock, 85 N. C. 598;
State v. Powell, 86 N. C. 640."   .

By sec. 3305, C. L. 1897, Bledsoe had the right to appeal to the District Court from the judgment against him.
This being true, the District Court properly overruled the
motion to dismiss the appeal.

As the case was triable *de novo* on appeal, the burden
was upon the State to show that the prosecution was
3 instituted "maliciously or without probable cause,"
and the State failing to offer any evidence upon the
trial, the District Court properly dismissed the case and
discharged the prosecuting witness.

Finding no errors in the record, the judgment of the
District Court is affirmed, and it is so ordered.

[No. 1507, June 7, 1913.]

LORETTO LITERARY SOCIETY, Appellee, v. MELI-
TON GARCIA et al., Appellants.

SYLLABUS (BY THE COURT)

1. In permitting amendments, upon the trial, the Court is
limited by sub-sec. 82 of the Civil Code to such amendments
as do not change "substantially the claim or defense." Held
that the trial court was without authority, in an action in
ejectment, to permit the filing of a trial amendment for specific performance of a contract to convey real estate, as
such amendment introduced a new cause of action.

P. 324

Appeal from the District Court of Sandoval County;
Herbert F. Raynolds, District Judge.

FELIX H. LESTER (deceased); N. B. FIELD, Albuquerque, N. M., for appellants.

Court erred in failing to grant defendant's motion for judgment, when plaintiff rested, having failed to prove its title to the property. C. L. 1897, sec. 3950; not repealed until 1901; Laws 1901, ch. 62, secs. 5, 6, and 32.

It was an abuse of discretion by the Court to permit plaintiff to file its amended complaint. C. L. 1897, sec. 2685, sub-sec. 82; Louisville & N. R. Co. v. Pointer's Admr., 69 S. W. 1108, 1110; Shields, et al., v. Barrow, 17 How. 130; Bird v. Stout, 40 W. Va. 43, 20 S. E. 852; Edgell v. Smith, 40 S. E .402; Maynard v. Green, 30 Fed. 643; 31 Cyc. 409, 412; Snead v. McCoual, et al., 12 How. 407; Walden v. Boadley, et al., 14 Peters 156; Carter v. Dilley, 167 Mo. 564, 67 S. W. 232; Enc. Pl. & Pr., vol. 1, p. 548, et seq.; Daw v. Jewel, 45 Am. Dec. 371; Carmichael v. Argard, 52 Wis. 607, 9 N. W. 470; Lawe v. Hyde, 39 Wis. 345; Johnson v. Filkington, 62 Wis. 67; Lane v. Cameron, 38 Wis. 603; Supervisors v. Decker, 34 Wis. 378; Lackner v. Turnbull, 7 Wis. 205; Newton v. Allis, 12 Wis. 378; 31 Cyc. 411, 414; City of Columbus v. Anglin, 48 S. E. 318, 321; Maxwell v. Harrison, 52 Am. Dec. 385; Fletcher's Equity Pl. & Pr., 416, and note.

Payment of the purchase price is not sufficient part performance to take an oral contract for the sale of real estate out of the statute o ffrauds. Forrester v. Flores, 28 Pac. 107; Purcell v. Minor, 4 Wall. 513; Williams v. Morris, 95 U. S. 444; Duff v. Hopkins, 33 Fed. 599-607.

Mere holding over by a tenant after the expiration of his lease is not part performance to take the case out of the statute. Koch v. National B. & E. Ass., 107 Ill. 497, 27 N. E. 530; Green v. Groves, 109 Ind. 519, 10 N. E. 401; Emmel v. Hayes, 102 Mo. 186; Brady v. Brady, 7 Pa. St. 157; Cristy v. Barnhart, 14 Pa. St. 260; Swale v. Jackson, 126 Ind. 282.

Court erred in refusing to sustain plaintiff's motion to strike out a portion of paragraph 3 of the amended complaint. Lynch v. Grayson, 5 N. M. 488.

Court erred in refusing to allow defendants to withdraw

their answer and to be permitted to file their demurrer to
the amended complaint. 31 Cyc. 276; Rothwell v. Denver
U. Stockyard Co., 90 Pac. 1127; Marion v. Clise, 21 Pac.
909; Foothaker v. City of Boulder, 22 Pac. 469; Bijou Co.
v. Lehmann, 43 So. 632; Kelly v. Strouse, 43 S. E. 280;
Harvey v. Hackney, 14 S. E. 822.

FRANK W. CLANCY, MARCOS C. DE BACA, for appellee.

No valid objection can be found as to the amended
complaint. C. L. 1897, 2685, sub-sec. 33; Ffister v. Dascey, 65 Cal. 403, 405; Bidwell v. Insurance Co., 16 N. Y.
263, 267; Water Co. v. Flume Co., 108 Cal. 549; Tootle
v. Kent., 12 Okla., 674, 681, et seq. and cases cited.

Motion and Argument for Rehearing (Appellees.)

Defendants waived their objections to the amended
complaint by filing an answer to it. Hudson v. Cahoon,
193 Mo. 547, 556-7-8-; Hendricks v. Calloway, 211 Mo.
536, 557; Hubbard v. Slavens, 218 Mo. 598, 616-7; White
v. Railroad, 202 Mo. 539, 561-2; Campbell v. Wilcox, 10
Wall. 421; Beattie Mfg. Co. v. Gerardi, 65 S. W. 1035-
1037; Scovill v. Glasner, 79 Mo. 449, 454-5; Curtis v.
Bachman, 84 Ga. 218.

Amendment to the complaint was a proper one. Steele
v. Brazier, 123 S. W. 477-482; Courtney v. Blackwell, 150
Mo. 245, 271-2; Erskine v. Markham, 66 S. E. 286; Booth
v. Langley Co., 51 S. C. 412, 417-8; Birt v. Southern
Railway Co., 69 S. E. 233; Gannon v. Moore, 104 S. W.
139; Duckwall v. Brooke, 65 S. W. 357; Ins. Co. v. Strain,
70 S. W. 274; Adams Oil Co. v. Christmas, 101 Ky. 564;
Young v. McIllhenny, 116 S. W. 728; Stone v. Trust Co.,
130 S. W. 825; Lottman v. Barnett, 62 Mo. 159; Newman v. Insurance Association, 76 Ia. 56; Cox Shoe Co. v.
Adams, 105 Ia. 402; Henson v. Cline, 118 N. W. 754;
Barnes v. Hekla Ins. Co., 75 Ia. 11; Snider v. Windsor,
93 Pac. 600; Hopkinson v. Conley, 88 Pac. 550; Railway
Co. v. Ludlum, 63 Kans. 719; Craven v. Russell, 118 N.
C. 564; Russell v. Denson, 54 So. 439; Rochester Borough
v. Kennedy, 78 Atl. 133; Hoboken v. Gear, 27 N. J. L.
265; Miller v. Railroad Co., 70 Atl. 175; McCandless v.

Inland Acid Co., 42 S. E. 449; Pavloski v Klassing, 68 S. E. 511; Craven v. Walker, 101 Ga. 845.

The code, taken as a whole, makes such an amendment as the one in the present case admissible and proper. Code Civ. Pro. N. M. (1897), secs. 33, 44, 63, 68, 28, 82, 85, 86, 94; Erskine v. Markhama, 66 S. E. 286; Hoboken v. Gear, 27 N. J. L. 265; Hopkinson v. Conley. 88 Pac. 550; Courtney v. Blackwell, 150 Mo. 245; Young v. McIllhenny, 116 S. W. 728.

OPINION OF THE COURT.

ROBERTS, C. J.—The original complaint in this case contained the ordinary allegations of a suit in ejectment; plaintiff alleging, among other things, that it was the owner and seized in fee of the property therein described. After the evidence was all adduced, appellee filed a trial amendment, by leave of Court, over appellant's objection, retaining all the original complaint and adding thereto paragraphs 3, 4 and 5, in which it alleged in substance that the deed from Barbara Leal de Garcia to Barbara Aragon de Montoya, upon which it relied to prove its title, was void because the husband failed to sign it, but claiming that plaintiff was entitled to a deed for the premises in question from the appellants, by virtue of a contract made between them and Mrs. Montoya, by which they agreed to deed her the property for six hundred dollars, which she had paid them, and praying that appellants be compelled to execute a deed to appellant for the premises, and that it be given a judgment for the possession of the same. By the trial amendment filed, it appears that appellee sought to set up facts entitling it to specific performance of an oral contract to convey real estate, and to secure such relief, by trial amendment to a complaint in an ejectment suit. The question presented is as to the power of the trial Court to permit such an amendment upon the trial of the case, over objection timely interposed. The solution of the question depends upon the proper construction of sub-sec. 82 of sec. 2685, C. L. 1897, which reads as follows:

"The Court may, at any time before final judgment, in
furtherance of justice, and on such terms as may be
proper, amend any record, pleading, process, entry, return,
or other proceeding, by adding or striking out the name of
any party, or by correcting a mistake in the name of a
party, or a mistake in any other respect, or by inserting
other allegations, material to the case, or, when the amendment does not change substantially the claim or defense,
by conforming the pleading or proceeding to the facts
proved."

It will be observed that the section quoted limits the
power of the Court to permit a trial amendment, to such
an amendment as "does not change substantially the claim
or defense." In the case of Ellis v. Flaherty, 70 Pac. 586,
the Supreme Court of Kansas construed the word "claim"
in a code provision, apparently identical with sub-sec. 82,
supra, and held that, "The word 'claim,' as therein used,
was synonymous with 'cause of action.'" This being accepted as a correct interpretation of the meaning of the
word, it necessarily follows that the trial Court is only
authorized to permit such an amendment upon the trial
of the cause "by conforming the pleadings or proceedings
to the facts proved," as does not introduce a new cause of
action or substantially change the cause of action upon
trial. This being true, it would follow that if the facts
herein alleged, in the amendment offered, constituted
a new cause of action, the Court erred in permitting it to
be filed, for it is uniformly held that no amendment of a
complaint can be allowed upon the trial, which introduces
into the case a new cause of action. Patrick v. Whitley,
75 Ark. 465, and see note to case in 5 A. & E. Ann. Cas.
672, where the authorities are collected.

In support of the right to file the trial amendment, the
appellee relies upon the case of Pfister v. Dascey, 65 Cal.
403, and similar cases holding that,

"All the matters complained of related to the same
property, were parts of one design to defraud, and affected all the parties who defended the action. Under
these circumstances, we see no reason why an action to set

aside the conveyances averred to be fraudulent, and to recover possession of the land to which such conveyances related, should not be prosecuted in the same motion. This
is certainly permissible under our system. Resort has
been frequently had to such procedure in cases of mines
where an action to enjoin the working of the mines, and
to recover possession of them, have been joined." Other
cases upon which it relies are, Bidwell v. Insurance Co.,
16 N. Y. 263; Water Co. v. Flume Co., 108 Cal. 549;
Tottle v. Kent, 12 Okla. 674. We have examined all these
cases, and find that they deal with joinder of causes of
action in the same complaint, and not with the power of
the Court to permit the introduction of a new and different cause of action upon the trial by amendment. They
are all based upon code provisions, similar to sub-sec. 33
of the New Mexico Code of Civil Procedure, which is as
follows:

"The plaintiff may unite in the same complaint several
causes of action, whether they be such as have been heretofore denominated legal or equitable, or both, where they
all arise out of:

"First, the same transaction or transactions connected
with the same subject of action."

By this provision it will be observed that the law-making power recognized that several causes of action might
arise out of the "same transaction or transactions connected with the same subject of action," and that such
causes of action could all be joined in the same complaint.
Under this provision of the code, undoubtedly the facts
set forth in the amendment in this case could have been
joined with the possessory action originally, for, the subject of the action in the possessory action was the land and
the plaintiff's title taken together, and any transaction
connected with either the land or the title would be connected with the subject of action.

McArthur v. Moffett, 146 Wis. 564; 33 L. R. A. (N. S.)
264. In the case last cited, which is perhaps the best
reasoned case that can be found on the proper construction
of the code provision last quoted, the Court held that a

statutory action to quiet title and a common law action to recover damages for trespass upon the property involved, could be joined under the statute permitting the joinder of causes of action which arose out of transactions connected with the same cause of action. In that case, however, the Court recognizes that two causes of action exist, for it says:

"We have before us two causes of action,—one by the owner of certain lands to prevent the assertion of a wrongful claim of title to those lands, and another to recover for a wrongful entry on the same lands by the same persons."

Under the same reasoning, in the case now under consideration, the amended complaint would present two causes of action,—one to recover possession of lands, with damages, and the other to secure specific performance
1   of an oral contract to convey, by warranty deed, the same lands. This being true, the amended complaint would neccessarily introduce into the cause, upon the trial, a "new cause of action," not permissible as a trial amendment.

As was said in the case of Louisville & N. R. Co. v. Pointer's Admr., 69 S. W. 1108, "A plaintiff will not be allowed to amend his cause of action by changing it. The office of the amendment is to perfect or complete that which is begun, but is incomplete."

In the case of Bird v. Stout, 40 W. Va. 43, 20 S. E. 852, the Court say:

"An amended bill must not introduce another and different cause of suit from that of the original bill, but an amended bill is no departure from the original if it tends to promote a fair hearing of the matter of controversy on which the suit was originally really based, provided it do not introduce a new substantive cause of suit different from that stated, and different from that intended to be stated, in the original bill. An amended bill can not be allowed containing statements inconsistent with the nature of the original bill or changing the cause of suit. By it allegations may be changed and modified, and others added, provided the identity of the cause of action be preserved."

See, also, Edgell v. Smith, 40 S. E. 402; Snead v. Mc-
Coual, et al., 12 Howard 407; 31 Cyc. 409; 1 Ency. Pl. &
Pr. 548; Zeller v. Kellogg, 66 Hin. 194; Ellis v. Flaherty,
supra.

Various tests have been applied by the courts for the
purpose of determining whether a new cause of action is
presented by way of amendment. The following will be
found stated in 31 Cyc. 417:

"(1) If the cause of action in the suit is regarded as
the act or thing done or omitted to be done, whether the
amendment sets out a new act or thing as the cause of
action, or whether it states in a different form the original
act or thing as the cause; (2) whether the intention of
the plaintiff at the time of instituting the suit and filing
the amendment is the same; (3) whether a recovery on
the original pleading would be a bar to a recovery on the
amended one, or vice versa; (4) whether both the original
and amended pleadings are subject to the same plea; (5)
whether the same measure of damages is applicable to
both pleadings; and (6) whether it would require substantially the same evidence to support the action after the
amendment as before."

Tested by these rules it would be manifest that the
amendment herein permitted introduced a new cause of action; for the reason stated the trial court erred in permitting the filing of the trial amendment, and the cause will
therefore be reversed, with instructions to the District
Court to sustain the appellant's motion to strike the trial
amendment from the files, and it is so ordered.

[No. 1507, December 3, 1913.]

LORETTO LITERARY & BENEVOLENT SOCIETY,
Appellee, v. MELITON GARCIA et al., Appellants.

NEILL B. FIELD, Esq., Albuquerque, N. M., for appellants.

F. W. CLANCY, Esq., Santa Fe, N. M., for appellee.

OPINION ON REHEARING, ADHERING TO FORMER
OPINION.

ROBERTS, C. J.—A rehearing was granted in this

cause, because of appellee's insistence, supported by a well
prepared brief, that the Court had erred in its former
opinion, in holding that the amendment was not permissible, as a trial amendment, because it · introduced a new
cause of action, and a desire on the part of the Court to
reinvestigate the question. By sub-section 96 of section
2685, C. L. 1897, the Court is enjoined "so to construe
the provisions of law relating to pleading and amending
the same, and so to adapt the practice thereunder * * * *
and to afford known, fixed and certain requirements in
place of the discretion of the Court or the Judge thereof,"
and mindful of this injunction, in the construction of
sub-sec. 82, it is apparent we should not adopt appellee's
construction, unless clearly, warranted by the adjudications
of other Courts, or upon reason such construction appeared
to be warranted by the language of the section. If the
construction contended for were adopted, the only limitation upon the power of the trial Court to permit the
amendment to be made would be, that it must not introduce a new cause of action, not related or connected with
the subject of action. In other words, a party by
amendment might introduce any cause of action, which he
might have originally united in the same complaint with
that upon which the trial was proceeding, where they arose
out of the same transaction or transactions connected with
the subject of action, subject, of course, to the discretion
of the trial Court to permit the amendment. In support
of his contention, counsel for appellee has cited many authorities, which he contends support his contention, but a
review of the cases will, we think, show that in the main
they do not conflict with the former opinion in this case,
but many of them tend rather to support the reasoning of
the Court.

The first case relied upon is Steele v. Brazier, decided
by the Springfield Circuit Court of Appeals, and reported
in 123 S. W. 477. In that case, however, the amendment
was not made during the trial, but prior to the trial, and
the statute there discussed was sec. 593, Rev. St. 1899
(Ann. St. 1906, p. 619), which is substantially the same

as sub-sec. 33 of our Code of Civil Procedure, and relates
solely to causes of action that may be united in the same
petition. The Court uses the following language, which
is quoted by appellee:

"The plaintiff cannot be allowed to introduce an entirely new cause of action, but may, by amendment, introduce such additional causes of action as under the provision of the statute could be united in the same petition.
Such is the general rule in those states that have adopted
the modern codes of pleading and practice." The language
of the Court is not entirely clear, but what it evidently intended to hold was that the plaintiff could not introduce
an entirely new subject of action, but so long as the causes
of action arose out of "the same transaction or transactions
connected with the same subject of action" there was no
objection to their being brought in by amendment; necessarily, prior to trial, for that was the question under consideration, and not a trial amendment. The distinction between amendments made prior to trial and those made
upon the trial and after the evidence has been heard, or a
portion of the evidence, is clearly pointed out by the St.
Louis Court of Appeals, in the case of Robertson v. Springfield Ry. Co., 21 Mo. App. 633. There an amendment had
been filed after a reversal of the cause on appeal and remand, which the trial Court, upon motion, struck from
the files, for the reason that the plaintiff thereby sought to
change the cause of action. The action of the lower Court
was based upon a code provision identical, apparently,
with sub-sec. 82 of our code, which the Court of Appeals
held had no application to an amendment made prior to
trial. The Court say:

"It is easily perceived that the limitation, 'when the
amendment does not change substantially the claim or
defense' applies exclusively to a case of 'conforming the
pleading or proceeding to the facts proved.' Such a case
can only exist after the evidence has been heard. * * * *
The cases cited for the defendant have no application to
an amendment made upon leave, before or pending the
trial. In Parker v. Rodes, (79 Mo. 88), the evidence had

been submitted and closed, when the amendment introduced a new and different cause of action. This of course was improper under the statute, and was so held."

The case of Courtney v. Blackwell, 150 Mo. 245, is also cited and relied upon, but that was an amendment made prior to trial and the distinction pointed out by the Circuit Court of Appeals in the last case applies.

The case of Erskine v. Markham, 66 S. E. 286, supports appellee's contention. There the amendment was made after considerable testimony had been taken and while the cause was still under reference, and complaint was made that the amendment entirely changed the original cause of action and substituted a new one. The Court say:

"As we cannot say the amendments were not in furtherance of justice, we must affirm the judgment of the Circuit Court. Since the case of Taylor v. Railroad Co., 81 S. C. 574, 62 S. E. 1113, it must be regarded as settled that even a new cause of action may be inserted by way of amendment, if it be done in furtherance of justice." .

The above quoted excerpt contains all that is said in the case on the subject, and it is evident that the Court based its decision entirely on the case cited. A study of the case referred to will disclose that no such doctrine was announced, but on the contrary, it was distinctly stated, "The limitation of the power of amendment to conform the pleadings to the facts proved that the amendment shall not change substantially the claim or defense is by its terms applicable only to amendments proposed while the Court is hearing the evidence, or after it has heard it, and not before the trial." The amendment there was made after the cause had been reversed on appeal and remanded for a new trial, and prior to the trial, and was not a trial amendment.

Another South Carolina case is also relied upon, (Booth v. Langley Co., 51 S. C. 412), but the Court in that case upheld the amendment upon the ground that it did not substantially change the claim of plaintiff. The Court say:

Literary Soc. v. Garcia, 18 N. M. 318.

"The only question is, did the Circuit Judge have the power to grant the amendment during the progress of the trial? He seems to have supposed that the amendment would substantially change the claim of plaintiff, or, to use his own language, would make 'an entirely new case and a new answer.' If that were so then he would have been right, as he could not, during the progress of the trial, grant an amendment which would substantially change plaintiff's claim."

The Court then reviews the South Carolina cases, citing many which support the views of this Court in the former opinion, all of which it approves.

In another South Carolina case, (Birt v. Southern Railway Co., 69 S. E. 233), an action was brought against a railroad company for damage to property caused by fire communicated from a railroad engine with an allegation of negligence, and it was held that it would be proper to amend the complaint during trial, after evidence had been taken, by striking out the allegation of negligence so as to make the action one under section 2135 of the Code of 1902, which made railroad corporations liable for damage by fire communicated by its engines without regard to the question of negligence. The decision is based entirely upon Brown v. Railroad, 83 S. C. 557, 65 S. E. 1102. In Brown v. Railway, the opinion was written by Justice Woods, who held that the amendment could not be made, under the code, as it "substantially changed the claim," and many cases are cited supporting his conclusions. Two justices dissented, which made the dissenting opinion the law of the case, holding that the amendment was properly permitted, but no reason is given, further than a statement that "such amendments are within the discretion of the Circuit Judge, and where, as here, there has been no abuse of discretion, this Court should not interfere," and no authority is cited in support of the holding. Indeed, many decisions of South Carolina are to the contrary.

The case of Gannon v. Moore, 104 S. W. 139, (Ark.) is not in point, as the question there involved was not the power of the Court to permit a trial amendment. There is nothing to show when the amendment was made, and the only question considered was the "tolling of the statute of limitations till the filing of the amendment."

Four Kentucky cases are cited, (Insurance Co. v. Strain, 70 S. W. 274; Duckwall v. Brooke, 65 S. W. 357; Adams Oil Co. v. Christmas, 101 Ky. 564; Young v. McIllhenny, 116 S. W. 728), but in each of these cases the amendment was made before the trial. In the first case cited, the amendment was upheld on the ground "that it did not state a new cause of action, as the relief sought by both involves the same question, depends upon the same evidence, and to which the same defense would generally arise." And the Kentucky Code contains a provision not found in our Code, which would seemingly imply that it was not the intention to limit amendments to the same cause of action. The provision reads as follows:—

"Courts may permit amendments authorized by this chapter to be made without being verified, as prescribed in section 142, unless a new and distinct cause of action or defense is thereby introduced."

The following Iowa cases are cited and relied upon by appellee: Newman v. Insurance Association, 76 Iowa 56; Cox Shoe Co. v. Adams, 105 Iowa 402; Hanses v. Cline, 118 N. W. 754; Barnes v. Hekla Ins. Co., 75 Ia. 11. In these cases, however, the amendments were made prior to trial. It is true, however, that the Court, in passing upon the question, uses language which might reasonably be held to apply to amendments offered during trial. That Court has given a very liberal construction to the statute, but our attention has been called to no case, where upon the trial, it has permitted an amendment to be made which "substantially changed the claim or defense." The distinction between amendments before trial, and during or after trial, is clearly pointed out by that Court in the case of Taylor v. Taylor, 110 Iowa 207, and with this distinction in view it can hardly be said that the cases relied upon by appellee apply to the question involved in this case. The Court, after setting out the Code provision, which is apparently identical with sub-section 82, say:

"The clause 'when amendment does not change substantially the claim or defense,' has reference solely to 'conforming the pleadings or proceedings to the facts proved,' and does not limit the portion of the action preceding."

From this it will be seen that the Court draws a distinction between amendments which may be made prior to trial, and those which may be introduced upon the trial.

Some few states hold that an amendment introductive of a new cause of action is allowable at any stage of the trial, but such holding is in direct conflict with the decisions of a great majority of the states. 31 Cyc. 411.

Appellee further contends, that no new cause of action was introduced, and cites several cases which, it is claimed, supports this theory. The one most directly in point is the cause of Pavloski v. Klassing, 68 S. E. 511, (Georgia.) It must be admitted that there is a great deal of confusion, in the decided cases, as to what is a "new cause of action," due largely, we think, to a failure to differentiate between "subject of action" and "cause of action." The distinction is clearly pointed out in the case of McArthur v. Moffett, (cited in the former opinion) by the Wisconsin Court, and, in our opinion, disposed of this contention.

Appellee next urges that appellants waived their objection to the amended complaint by filing an answer to it. This point, however, not having been raised upon the first hearing of the case, will not be considered upon rehearing.

For reasons stated, we adhere to our former opinion.

[No. 1553-4, December 3, 1913.]

CITY OF TUCUMCARI, Appellee, v. D. A. BELMORE, Jr., Appellant.

SYLLABUS (BY THE COURT)

1. The addition or omission of the suffix "Jr." is immaterial in either a civil or criminal proceeding. The person so styled is presumed, in the absence of some proof to the

contrary, to be the same person referred to whenever his name appears with, or without, the suffix.

P. 337

2. Where, in a judgment covering several cases, by inadvertence or otherwise, one or more cases are included over which the Court had no jurisdiction to render judgment, this Court has jurisdiction, under section 38 of chapter 57 of the Laws of 1907, to modify the judgment by eliminating such case, or cases, from the judgment.

P. 338

3. Where a city ordinance is not before the Court, and where a judgment for violation of the same is an ordinary judgment for money in the amount of a fine, and where no imprisonment is imposed, and where the nature of the act charged against the defendant is not criminal in character and is not punishable by any general law of the State, but relates solely to a local regulation of the city for the safety and welfare of its inhabitants, the proceeding will be treated by this Court as a civil and not a criminal proceeding.

P. 339

4. Where the certificate of the trial judge to an alleged bill of exceptions is not certified to by the clerk of the Court, and is not shown to have been filed in the clerk's office, neither the alleged bill of exceptions to which it relates, nor the said certificate will be considered by this Court.

P. 340

Appeal from the District Court of Quay County; Thomas D. Leib, District Judge; modified and affirmed.

C. II. HITTSON, Tucumcari N. M.; F. C. WILSON, Santa Fe, N. M., for appellant.

Court erred in assuming jurisdiction of this cause and forcing the defendant to go to trial over his objection without a full panel; only twelve qualified jurors remained on the panel when case was called, when there should have been twenty-four. Laws 1905, ch. 116, sec. 25.

Twelve jurors of the regular panel were disqualified by the trial of the case the day before, which case involved same issues and between same parties. Gartwaite v. Tatum, 76 Am. Dec. 402; Swarnes v. Sitton, 58 Ill. 155.

Motion for new trial does not have to be filed within five days after verdict. Laws 1907, ch. 57, sec. 60.

A judgment relating to matters not before the Court is extrajudicial and of no effect. Sache v. Gillette, 112 N. W. 386, 11 L. R. A. (N. S.) 803.

Judgment is void because it is without legal authority and in excess of the amount allowed by law in such cases. C. L. 1897, sec. 2403.

Section 18 of the City Ordinance 47 does not name or define a crime or offense and is a mere blanket section. Alwin v. Morley, 108 Pac. 778; Evans v. Willis, 19 L. R. A. (N. S.) 1050; Maclay Co. v. Meads, et al., 112 Pac. 195; Dicta in State v. Medler, 131 Pac. 976.

F. C. WILSON, Santa Fe, N. M., for appellant.

Judgment is void for lack of jurisdiction of the Court to enter a judgment against this defendant. 12 Enc. Pl. & Pr. 188; 1 Black on Judgments, 241-242; McFadden v. Ross, 108 Ind. 512, 8 N. E. 151; Ritchie v. Sayres, 100 Fed. 520; Spoors v. Coen, 44 Ohio St. 497, 9 N. E. 132; Louis v. Smith, 9 N. Y. 502; 61 Am. Dec. 706; Boogher v. Frasier, 99 Mo. 325, 12 S. W. 885; Sandoval v. Rosser, 26 S. W. 932; 23 Cyc. 684; Freeman on Judgments, (4th ed.) 116.

Judgment is void for lack of legal authority in the Court to enter judgment for costs. Dillon on Municipal Corporations, (5th ed.) vol. 2, p. 962, and cases cited.

C. C. DAVIDSON, Tucumcari, N. M., for appellee.

There was no proper record or bill of exceptions filed in the District Court. 3 Cyc. 97, 106; Judkins v. Wilson, 40 N. E. 39; Board of Commrs. v. Huffman, 31 N. E.

570; Guirl v. Gillette, 24 N. E. 1036; Board of Commrs. v. Hemphill, 41 N. E. 965; Riverside Rubber Co. v. Midland Mfg. Co., 57 N. E. 958; DeHart v. Board of Commrs.. 41 N. E. 825; German Nat. Bank v. Terry, et al., 67 N. W. 856; Pearce v. State, 12 S. E. 926; Helsel v. Seiger, 34 Pac. 237; Rock Island v. Riley, 26 Ill. App. 171; Huber Mfg. Co. v .Busey, 43 N. E. 967; 21 Cent. Dig. 94-97; Laws 1907, ch. 57, sec. 26.

Errors assigned but not considered in appellant'e brief are deemed abandoned or waived and will not be considered by the Court. Gregory v. Cassan, 15 N. M. 496; A. & C. R. R. Co. v. D. & R. G., 16 N. M. 281; Riverside Co. v. Hardwicke, et al., 16 N. M. 479; Aetna Ins. Co. v. Lipsitz, 14 A. & E. Enc. Cas., vol. 14, p. 1070.

Assignments must specifically point out the error complained of. Terr. v. Cordova, 11 N. M. 367, 68 Pac. 919; Chaves v. Lucero, 13 N. M. 368, 85 Pac. 392, 6 L. R. A. (N. S.) 793.

No motion for a new trial was ever made before the lower Court. C. L. 1897, sec. 2685, sub-sec. 133, is in no manner amended or repealed by sec. 60, ch. 57, of the laws of 1907.

New trial. Motion not having been considered is the same as stricken and leaves nothing before the Court for review. Cunningham v. Springer, 13 N. M. 259, 82 Pac. 232; L. & L. & G. Ins. Co. v. Perrin, 10 N. M. 90, 61 Pac. 124; Schofield v. Terr., 9 N. M. 526, 56 Pac. 306; Schofield v. Slaughter, 9 N. M. 422, 54 Pac. 757; Henry v. Cartwright, 13 N. M. 384, 85 Pac. 1043.

Omission of "Jr." is only a formal defect that can be corrected by this Court. Romero v. Silva, 1 N. M. 157.

Where there is substantial evidence to support the verdict, it will not be disturbed by the Appellate Court. Sherman v. Hicks, 14 N. M. 439, 94 Pac. 959; Richardson v. Pierce, 14 N. M. 334, 93 Pac. 715; Territory v. Neatherlin, 13 N. M. 499, 85 Pac. 1044.

A prosecution under a city ordinance is a civil and not a criminal proceeding and the Court may direct a verdict under the circumstances disclosed in the case at bar.

Armijo v. N. M. Town. Co., 3 N. M. 427; Herrera v. Chaves, 2 N. M. 86.

(Case No. 1554.) Brief for Appellee.

Errors not referred to in the argument or authorities cited will not be considered. Riverside Co. v. Hardwick, et al., 16 N. M. 479; A. & C. R. R. v. D. & R. G., 16 N. M. 281; Gregory v. Cassan, 15 N. M. 496; Aetna Ins. Co. v. Lipsitz, 14 A. & E. Ann. Cas. 1070.

"A bill of exceptions must be authenticated or certified or it will not be considered by the Appellate Court." 5 Cyc. 108.

"A transcript of the evidence which has no formal commencement as a bill of exceptions, and was not filed in the clerk's office, is insufficient to bring the evidence into the record, although it concluded as a bill of exceptions, and was signed by the trial judge as such." Jenkins v. Wilson, 40 N. E. 39.

Record must show that the bill of exceptions was filed in the Court below. Board of Commrs. 31 N. E. 570; Loy v. Loy, 90 Ind. 404; Hessian v. State, 17 N. E. 614; Guirl v. Gillett, 24 N. E. 1036; Riverside Rubber Co. v. Midland Mfg. Co., 57 N. E. 958; Board of Commrs. v: Hemphill, 41 N. E. 565.

A so-called bill of exceptions must be certified to be a bill of exceptions by the clerk of the trial Court, or it is not entitled to be considered as a part of the record. De-Hart v. Board of Commrs., 41 N. E. 825; German Nat. Bank v. Terry, et al., 67 N. W. 856; Pearce v. State, 12 S. E. 926; Helzel v. Seiger, 34 Pac. 237; Rock Island v. Riley, 26 Ill. App. 171; Huber Mfg. Co. v. Busey, 43 N. E. 967; 3 Cyc. 97; Richmond & D. R. Co. v. McGee, 50 Fed. 906.

Last paragraph of the certificate of the trial Court contains a statement that certain parts of the so-called record are untrue. This statement constitutes sufficient grounds for dismissing the appeal. Hatcher v. Smith, 84 Ga. 451, 11 S. E. 1064; 21 Cent. Dig., secs. 94-97.

City v. Belmore, 18 N. M. 331.

Preparation of a bill of exceptions. Laws 1907, ch. 57, secs. 25, 26.

Assignments of error must specifically point out errors complained of. Territory v. Cordova, 11 N. M. 367; Ruiz v. Territory, 10 N. M. 120; Ceveda v. Miera, 10 N. M. 62; Schofield v. Territory, 11 N. M. 526; Pearce v. Strickler, 9 N. M. 467; Friday v. Railway Co., 16 N. M. 434.

. Procedure pertaining to new trials. C. L. 1897, sec. 2685, sub-sec. 133; not repealed or amended by ch. 57, laws of 1907.

No abuse of discretion is shown that would in the least degree justify this Court in reversing the case. Cunningham v. Springer, 13 N. M. 259, 82 Pac. 232; L. & L. & G. Ins. Co. v. Perrin, 10 N. M. 90, 61 Pac. 124; Schofield v. Territory, 9 N. M. 526, 66 Pac. 306; Schofield v. Slaughter, 9 N. M. 422, 54 Pac. 757; Archboques v. Miera, 1 N. M. 160; Henry v. Cartwright, 13 N. M. 384, 85 Pac. 1043; Bushness v. Coggshall, 10 N. M. 561, 62 Pac. 1101; Territory v. Christman, 9 N. M. 652, 58 Pac. 343; L. L. Min. Co. v. Henry, 9 N. M. 149, 30 Pac. 330.

Suit upon a city ordinance is a civil, or at least only quasi-criminal, proceeding and the degree of exactness in stating the charge is not required as in indictments. Dillon on Municipal Corporations, vol. 2, sec. 639, (5th ed.); Nichols v. Salem, Oregon, 89 Pac. 804; C. L. 1897, sec. 2617.

Record discloses a most palpable violation of the ordinance and the judgment of the lower Court should be affirmed. Putney v. Schmidt, 16 N. M. 400; N. M. Ry. Co. v. Hendricks, 6 N. M. 80, 27 Pac. 416.

Errors in giving or refusing instructions cannot be considered where the instructions were not brought up in the transcript. Reagan v. E. P. & N. E. Ry. Co., 106 Pac. 375.

Formal defects can be cured in the Supreme Court. Romero v. Silva, 1 N. M. 157.

OPINION OF THE COURT.

PARKER, J.—These cases both arise out of judgments

for violations of an ordinance of the City of Tucumcari. The first case is a judgment for violation of section 6 of Ordinance No. 47, which prohibits wooden buildings within certain prescribed fire limits of the city, and the second case is a judgment for the violation of section 18 of the ordinance, which prohibits the keeping and maintaining of such buildings within such fire limits, each day they are so kept or maintained constituting a separate offense.

Appellant assigned numerous errors in each case, but the record not having been properly preserved, they are not here for review. An additional brief was filed which presents some questions arising upon the record proper, which will be considered.

In both cases the appellant is styled D. A. Belmore Jr., · in the complaint. In No. 1553, the verdict follows the complaint in this regard, but the judgment omits the suffix "Jr." from the name. In No. 1554, both the verdict and the judgment omit the suffix.

Appellant argues that the judgments are void for want of jurisdiction of the person of the defendant, by reason of this variance in the name. In No. 1553, this variance in the name was never called to the attention of the Court, and in No. 1554 it was not called to the attention of the Court until January 4, 1913, the appeal having been taken to this Court on October 10, 1912. The defendant on that date filed a motion to vacate the judgment, based partly on this ground, which was denied by the Court. A sufficient reason for the action taken would seem to be that, at the time the application to vacate the judgment was made, the appeal had been taken and perfected by filing a supercedeas bond. Even had the District Court then had jurisdiction to vacate the judgment, the action taken was nevertheless, correct. The addition or omission of the suffix "Jr." is immaterial in either a civil or a criminal proceeding. The person so styled is presumed, in the absence

1 of some proof to the contrary, to be the same person referred to whenever his name appears with, or without, the suffix. 29 Cyc. 267, 268; People v. Collins, 7 Johns. 549; Teague v. State, 40 So. 312; State v. Cafiero,

36 So. 492; Com. v. Beckley, 44 Mass. 331; City of San
Francisco v. Randall, 54 Cal. 408; State v. Grant, 22 Me.
171; Windom v. State, 72 S. W. 193; 36 Cen. Dig., Title
Name, sec. 3.

The appellant complains, not that he was not charged,
tried and adjudged to pay a fine, but he complains that
the judgment in one case, and the verdict and judgment in
the other, failed to follow the complaint, and to style him
as "Jr." There is no intimation in the record that there is
another Belmore' to whom the judgment could apply.

It appears that counsel for the City, in No. 1554, moved
to consolidate all causes pending against the defendant,
giving their docket numbers. It appears from a recital in
one of the orders made in the case, that the parties in
open court stipulated that the verdict and decision in No.
527, which was the case actually tried, should apply to
and govern causes Nos. 527 to 529, inclusive, and Nos.
532 to 552, inclusive, between the same parties, the issues
therein being identical. The final judgment, however, ad-
judges a fine of $25 in each case, numbered 527 to 553,
inclusive. This leaves cases Nos. 530, 531 and 553 without the terms of the stipulations, and renders the judgment, it is argued, void on its face, for want of jurisdiction. Counsel for appellee, in his brief, asserts that No.
527 was tried and that there were only twenty-two other
cases covered by the stipulation. This would seem to show
that in so far as the judgment purports to cover cases
2 numbered 530, 531 and 553, it was without jurisdiction
and void. But this does not render the whole judgment void. The part of the judgment which was rendered
without jurisdiction is severable from that which was
within the jurisdiction of the Court. It is perfectly apparent that the discrepancy arises out of a mere clerical error,
but, if it did not, and was intentional on the part of the
Court, we have the power to render the proper judgment
here, by eliminating the three cases numbered 530, 531 and
553. Chapter 57, section 38, laws of 1907; Tagliaferri v.
Grande, 16 N. M. 486.

The conclusion reached in the preceding paragraph is

based upon the theory that the proceedings against the
defendant are civil and not criminal proceedings. Whether
we might not modify the judgments, even were the proceedings criminal, we do not decide as it is not involved.

The assumption that the proceedings are civil and not
criminal is based upon the form of the judgment, it being an ordinary judgment for money in the amount of a
fine, which the Court assessed. No imprisonment is imposed, nor is any provided for as a means of collection of
the judgment. The nature of the act charged against the
defendant is such as to show that it is not a crime in any
sense, is not punishable by any general law of the State,
but relates solely to a local regulation of the city, for the
safety and welfare of its inhabitants. Under all of
3 the authorities, at least the great weight of authorities,
such proceedings under such circumstances are civil
and not criminal. 2 Dillon Munic. Corp. (5th ed.), secs.
749, 750; 3 McQuillan Munic. Corp., sec. 1030; section
2407, C. L. 1897, provides for two forms of proceedings
for the violation of city ordinances, viz:—one civil in
form and providing that the first process shall be a summons; the other a warrant for the arrest of the offender,
based upon affidavit. The section provides for a fine or
penalty, and for imprisonment as a means of collection of
the same. Whether the ordinance in this case authorizes
imprisonment, we are not at liberty to ascertain, the ordinance not being before us for consideration, as will be
presently pointed out. The record is in such condition as
to preclude a careful consideration of the nature of such
proceedings as these, and we reserve the proposition for
discussion in some future case where it may be clearly
raised.

For the same reason we cannot consider the question
raised by appellant to the effect that the ordinance does
not provide for the collection of costs and that, therefore,
the judgment must be unwarranted in so far as the costs
are concerned.

The certificate of the trial Judge, settling the bill of
exceptions, appears on the last page of the transcript, and

is the last entry therein. Preceding it is the clerk's certificate to the transcript. The fact that the Judge's
4 order settling the bill of exceptions was ever. filed in the
clerk's office, or that the Judge, in fact, ever made the
under such circumstances, there is no bill of exceptions be-
no argument nor authority to support the conclusion that,
under the circumstances, there is no bill of exceptions before us, and we are precluded from examining the same as
to the contents of the ordinance or any other matters therein contained.

For the reasons stated, the judgment below will be
modified so as to exclude therefrom numbers 530, 531
and 553, and as modified they will be affirmed, and it is
so ordered.

[No. 1556, December 4, 1913.]
WILLIAM FRASER, Appellant, v. STATE SAVINGS
BANK et al., Appellees.

SYLLABUS (BY THE COURT)

1. The Court is only required to find the ultimate facts in
controversy, raised by the issues in the case, and is not
required, nor is it proper, to set out the evidence upon which
it relies in determining such ultimate facts.

P. 350

2. Findings are not to be construed with the strictness of
special pleadings. It is sufficient if from them all, taken together with the pleadings, the Court can see enough upon a
fair construction to justify the judgment of the trial Court,
notwithstanding their want of precision and the occasional
intermixture of matters of fact and conclusions of law.

P. 351

3. Where the trial Court hears all the witnesses testify
and is thus able to observe their manner and demeanor while
testifying, the Appellate Court will not review the evidence

further than to determine whether or not the findings are supported by substantial evidence; in the absence of such an overwhelming weight of evidence against such findings as would clearly show that the trial Court erred in its conclusions drawn therefrom, and, in an equity case, where the Court hears the witnesses ore tenus, there is no reason for a departure from the rule.

P. 352

4. Mere inadequacy of consideration is not sufficient, in and of itself, to avoid a contract.

P. 356

5. Where parties to a contract, construe it as having created a partnership relation, and act upon such construction, the Court will not, after rights have accrued thereunder, by reason of such construction, give to the contract a different construction, which would be at variance with the understanding of the parties to it.

P. 357

Appeal from the District Court of Taos County; Thomas D. Leib, District Judge; affirmed.

RENEHAN & WRIGHT, Santa Fe, N. M., for appellant.

There are no findings of facts; hence, the decree is inoperative. Luna v. Coal R. R. Co., 16 N. M. 71; Miles v. McCallan, 3 Pac. 610; Elder v. Frevert, 3 Pac. 237; Trustees v. Retsch, 151 N. Y. 321, 37 L. R. A. 305; Brock v. R. R. Co., 114 Ala. 431; Rhodes v. Bank, 66 Fed. 512, 34 L. R. A. 742; Searcy County v. Thompson, 66 Fed. 92.

Mere conclusions of law, though called findings of fact, are not so. Murphy v. Bennett, 68 Cal. 528.

So-called findings, if findings at all, are not founded on sufficient evidence. Millheiser v. Long, 10 N. M. 99; Potters v. Hewitt, 11 N. M. 1; Land Co. v. Gutierrez, 10 N. M. 177; Torlina v. Trorlicht, 6 N. M. 54; Light Co. v.

Improvement Co., 16 N. M. 94; Richards v. Pierce, 14 N.
M. 334; Hancock v. Beasley, 14 N. M. 239; Robero v.
Coleman, 11 N. M. 537; Rush v. Fletcher, 11 N. M. 555;
Carpenter v. Lincoln, 12 N. M. 388; Gale & Farr v. Salas,
11 N. M. 211; Ortiz v. Bank, 12 N. M. 519; Marquez v.
Land Grant, 12 N. M. 445.

Duty of this Court to consider all of the facts in this
case and enter such a decree as "may be agreeable to law."
Laws 1907, sec. 38, p. 116; Armijo v. Electric Co., 11 N.
M. 250.

Sufficient and substantial evidence. Jones on Ev. (2d
ed.), p. 6; 37 Cyc. 506; Jenkins v. Alpena Cement Co.,
147 Fed. 643.

Admission by conduct. 1 Greenl. Ev. (16th ed.) sec.
195, and cases cited.

Court should follow the principle that in equity the
whole record will be considered without regard to findings
of fact. 4 A. & E. Enc. L., p. 572; 13 A. & E. Enc. L.,
570, 571, notes 7 and 8.

A contract partly written and partly parol is not a
written contract. Cunningham v. Fiske, 13 N. M. 331.

Partnership agreement is within the Statute of Frauds.
22 Enc. L. (2d ed.) 67; Wilson v. Ray, 13 Ind. 1; Wahl v.
Barnum, 116 N. Y. 87, 5 L. R. A. 623; Packet Co. v.
Sickles, 5 Wall. 594.

Such a partnership could be dissolved by either party at
any time. Wahl v. Barnum, 5 L. R. A. 594.

Even where a partnership is for a fixed term, one partner can dissolve it subject to liability for damages for
breach of contract, unless circumstances are such as would
entitle him to a decree of dissolution, but the remedy is at
law. 30 Cyc. 651; Karrick v. Hannaman, 168 U. S. (L.
Ed.) 484; C. L. 1897, sec. 2647; Benton v. Roberts, 4
La. Ann. 216; Murrell, v. Murrell, 33 La. Ann. 1233;
Gillett v. Chaves, 12 N. M. 353.

The word "should" is imperative. 36 Cyc. 434; Smith
v. State, 142 Ind. 288; Lynch v. Bates, 139 Ind. 206.

Fraser had a right to dissolve the partnership, if one,

being accountable for damages only. 22 Enc. L. 205; 30 Cyc. 651, n. 8.

Fraser was within his rights when he modified the contract with Martin. 30 Cyc. 663, 688.

In no event did the minds of Fraser, Bidwell and Probert meet upon a copartnership agreement which did not exclude from its operation the Manly deal. 1 Page on Contracts, sec. 28, et seq., secs. 55, 62, 74, 77, et seq.

Duress, undue influence, gross inadequacy of consideration, etc., would render the deeds and copartnership agreement void. 1 Page on Contracts, secs. 221 to 235, inc.

The deed and the partnership agreement construed together at most created a lien in favor of Bidwell and Probert. 2 Page on Contracts, sec. 1123 and 1752.

A. C. VOORHEES, Raton, N. M.; FRANK T. CHEETHAM, Taos, N. M., for appellees.

The law recognizes the right of a man to dispose of his property as he sees fit. Eyre v. Potter, 15 How. 59-60; French v. Shoemaker, 11 Wall. 333.

Mere inadequacy of price is in itself no ground for setting aside a contract. Wharton on Contracts, sec. 165; Eyre v. Potter, 15 How. (U. S.) 42; Wharton on Contracts, sec. 518; Lee v. Kirby, 104 Mass. 420; Harrison v. Town, 17 Mo. 237; Davidson v. Little, 22 Penn. St. 245.

All the contested facts material to the issue in this case have been found by the trial court and there is substantial and sufficient evidence to sustain the same. Miles v. McCallan, 1 Ariz. 491, 3 Pac. 810; Runkle v. Burnham, 153 U. S. 216; St. Louis v. Rutz, 138 U. S. 226; Zang v. Stover, 2 N. M. 29; Crolot v. Maloy, 2 N. M. 198; Vasquez v. Ppielgelburg, 1 N. M. 464; Romero v. Desmarais, 5 N. M. 142, 20 Pac. 787.

This rule has been generally followed by the courts in New Mexico. Moore v. Western Meat Co., 16 N. M. 107, 115 Pac. 787, 78 Fed. 776.

Findings cannot be examined in this Court, even if against the preponderance of the evidence. Romero v.

Desmarais, 5 N. M. 142, 20 Pac. 787; Waldo v. Beckwith, 1 N. M. 97; Archibeque v. Miera, 1 N. M. 188; Rube v. Abreu, 1 N. M. 247.

Court is limited, in reversing, to the consideration of the correctness of the findings of the law and must affirm if there be any evidence in support thereof. Beuttel v. Magone, 157 U. S. 154; Lehnen v. Dickson, 148 U. S. 71, 70 Fed. 776; Moore v. Meat Co., 16 N. M. 107, 113 Pac. 827.

Cannot reverse where there is "sufficient" or "substantial" evidence to sustain the findings. Torlina v. Trorlicht, 5 N. M. 148, 21 Pac. 68; Field v. Romero, 7 N. M. 630, 41 Pac. 517; Givens v. Veeder, 9 N. M. 256, 30 Pac. 316; De Baca v. Pueblo, 10 N. M. 38, 60 Pac. 73; Romero v. Coleman, 11 N. M. 553, 70 Pac. 559; Rush v. Fletcher, 11 N. M. 335, 70 Pac. 559; Ortiz v. Bank, 12 N. M. 519, 78 Pac. 529; Candelaria v. Bank, 13 N. M. 360, 84 Pac. 1020; Moore v. Meat Co., 16 N. M. 107, 113 Pac. 827; Baker v. Trujillo de Armijo, 128 Pac. 73.

Co., 121 U. S. 325; Undue Influence, Old Age, etc. Curtis v. Kirkpatrick, 75 Pac. 760; Chrisman v. Chrisman, 18 Pac. 6; Eddy's Appeal, 109 Pa. St. 406, 1 Atl. 425; President, etc., et al., v. Merritt, 75 Fed. 480; Buckney v. Buckney, 38 W. Va. 168, 18 S. E. 383; Parsons on Contracts, 383; Beach Modern Law of Contracts, pp. 1818-1819, and cases cited; Wharton & Stille Med. Juris., pp. 4, 5; Devlin on Deeds, par. 68; Drefahl v. Security Sav. Bank, 107 N. W. 179; Harlan v. Harlan, 102 Ia. 701, 72 N. W. —; Eyre v. Potter, 15 How. 59.

Fraud. Maxwell Land Grant S. v. Maxwell Land Grant

Has a partner the right to dissolve a partnership for a stipulated time? Karrick v. Hannaman, 168 U. S. 335, 42 L. Ed. 489; Rutland Marble Co. v. Ripley, 77 U. S., 10 Wall. 339; Batten, Specific Performance, 165-167; 3 Lindley, Partnerships, ch. 10, par. 4; Pomeroy, Specific Perf., par. 290; Scott v. Rayment, L. R. 7 Eq. 112; Satterthwait, v. Marshall, 4 Del. Ch. 337; Reed v. Vidal, 5 Rich. Eq. 289; Somerby v. Buntin, 118 Mass, 279, 19 Am. Rep. 459; Story, Partnerships, par. 275; Gerard v.

Gateau, 84 Ill. 121, 25 Am. Rep. 438; Henn v. Walsh, 2 Edw. Ch. 129.

Mere dissatisfaction by one partner will not justify him in filing a bill for a dissolution. Story, Partn., pars. 275-6; Story, Eq. Jur., par. 673; Lindley Partn., p. 575, par. 2; Ferrero v. Buhlmeyer, 34 How. Pr. 33; Pearpoint v. Graham, 4 Wash. C. C. 232; Peacock v. Peacock, 16 Ves. Jr. 49; Cash v. Warnshaw, 66 Ill. 402; Van Kuren v. Trenton Loco. & Mach Mfg. Co., 13 N. J. Eq. 302.

RENEHAN & WRIGHT, for appellant on rehearing.

Probert's failure to testify raises a presumption that his testimony would be damaging. Young v. Corrigan, 208 Fed. 436.

Court should have considered every phase of the testimony and awarded appropriate relief. Rexford v. Woodland Co., 208 Fed. 296; Saunders v. Paper Co., 208 Fed. 442.

There were no findings of facts. Luna v. Railroad Co., 16 N. M. 71.

The minds of the parties must meet as to all the terms of the contract. 9 Cyc. 245, 398, 408; Hearne v. Marine Ins. Co., 20 Wall. 488; Sells v. Sells, 1 Drewry & Shales, 42; Mortimer v. Shortall, 2 Drewry & Warren, 372; Smith v. Mackin, 4 Lans. 46; Page v. Higgins, 5 L. R. A. 152, note and cases cited; Rowland v. Railroad Co., 29 Am. St. 175; Hartford & New Haven Railroad v. Jackson, 63 Am. Dec. 177; Green v. Stone, 55 Am. St. Rr. 577, (N. J. Eq.); Rogers v. Collier, 23 Am. Dec. 153; Burkhalter v. Jones, 3 Pac. 559; 1 Page Contr., secs. 74 and 77; Chitty on Contracts, (6 Eng. Ed.) p. 13; Sawyer v. Hovey, 3 Allen 331; 2 Pom. Eq. Jur. (3d ed.) sec. 870; 1 Parsons on Contracts, 483; Benjamin on Sales, sec. 398; Henry School Twt. v. Meredith, 32 Ind. App. 607; Calhoun v. Teal, 30 So. 288; Fifer v. Clearleld Co., 62 Atl. 1122; Kelly v. Ward, 60 S. W. 311; Crispill v. Cain, 19 W. Va. 438; Boehm v. Yanquell, 15 Ohio C. C. 454; Moore v. Cox, 51 Pac. 630.

One of the most satisfactory evidences of fraudulent intent on the part of the grantee will be found in his activity in procuring the conveyance. Booth v. Turtle, L. R. 16 Eq. 183; Catalini v. Catalini, 19 Am. St. R. 73; Goodwin v. McMinn, 74 Am. St. R. —; Diwee v. Thompson, 90 S. W. 193; Clark v. Haney, 50 Am. R. 536; Danzeisen's App., 73 Pa. 65; Barton v. McMillan, 20 Can. S. C. 404; Barnard v. Flinn, 8 Ind. 204; Seichrist's Appeal, 66 Pa. 237; 9 Cyc. 245, and citations; 9 Cyc. 394, and citations; Moffett, et al., v. City of Rochester, 91 Fed. 28; Champion v. McCarthy, 228 Ill. 87; Shedd v. Seefeld, 230 Ill. 118.

The effect of inconsistent allegations and denials in the answer of defendants. 31 Cyc. 92; Schlesinger v. McDonald, 106 N. Y. App. 570; Losch v. Pickett, 12 Pac. 822; Butler v. Kaulback, 8 Kans. 668; Wright v. Bacheller, 16 Kans. 259; Wiley v. Keokuk, 6 Kans. 94; Schenk v. Schency, 10 N. J. L. 276; 39 Cent. Dig., sec. 81; 31 Cyc. 87 and cases cited.

STATEMENT OF FACTS.

On December 16, 1910, the appellant and the appellees, John B. Bidwell, and A. Clarence Probert, made and executed the following agreement, viz:—

"THIS AGREEMENT, made and entered into this 16th day of December, 1910, by and between WILLIAM FRASER as party of the first part, and JOHN B. BIDWELL and A. CLARENCE PROBERT, as parties of the second part, that for and in consideration of the sum of Two Thousand dollars and other more valuable consideration we hereby form ourselves into a joint and co-partnership under the firm name and style of FRASER, BIDWELL & PROBERT for the purposes of developing, improving, selling and disposing of the mineral properties of the said William Fraser within a period of two (2) years' time from this date, or as long thereafter as the said William Fraser may agree to and with said parties of the second part, and in further consideration for the time and monies expended by the said John B. Bidwell and A.

Clarence Probert a Warranty Deed has been executed and
given to each one of the said parties of the second part,
conveying an undivided one-third interest in and to all of
said mining properties belonging to the said William
Fraser and if said mining properties are not sold or disposed of within the said period of time mentioned above
then said warranty deeds are to be void and of no effect
and the said mining properties mentioned in said warranty deeds are to revert back to the said William Fraser.

"It is further hereby mutually understood and agreed
that in the event of an expiration or forfeiture of this
agreement or contract that all monies expended by the
said John B. Bidwell and A. Clarence Probert, parties of
the second part, that the said William Fraser hereby
agrees to reimburse and pay back the whole amount of
said monies in the form of a lien against all of said properties mentioned in said Warranty Deeds, so that the said
John B. Bidwell and A. Clarence Probert shall not be out
any moneys that were expended in this copartnership or
transaction by them.

"IN WITNESS WHEREOF, the said parties have
hereunto set their hands and seals the day and year first
above written.

(Signed)   "William Fraser   (Seal)
(Signed)   "John B. Bidwell   (Seal)
(Signed)   "A. Clarence Probert (Seal)
"Signed, Sealed and delivered in presence of
(Signed)   "J. Wright Giddings
(Signed)   "Fidel Cordoba, Jr.
(Signed)   "Enrique Gonzales."

On the same day, and as part of the same transaction,
appellant made, executed and delivered to each of the
above named appellees a warranty deed, signed by appellant and his wife, by which he conveyed to each, respectively, an undivided one-third interest in and to all his mining
properties, therein named, and also a like interest in and
to a toll road owned by him in the Rio Hondo Canon leading to said mining properties and the grantor's rights in

the Laroux Grant.   On the same day, or shortly thereafter, Bidwell placed to Fraser's credit in the Taos Savings Bank .or applied on Fraser's debts, approximately
$2,000.00.

Thereafter, on February 18, 1911, Fraser, Bidwell and
Probert made and entered into a written contract with
Charles T. Martin, by which they agreed to convey to him
for the sum of $77,500, all the property above mentioned.
The contract was signed by Fraser, Bidwell and Probert,
a co-partnership, by each of the individuals, composing the
alleged partnership, and by Martin.   By the terms of the
contract $20,000 was to be paid in cash and the balance
was to be paid in two installments, at stated times.   Pursuant to the contract, the $20,000 was paid, which was
turned over to Probert, and by him deposited in the Taos
Savings Bank, out of which sum all of Fraser's debts were
paid, amounting to approximately the sum of $10,000,
and some cash was distributed to each of the parties to the
so-called partnership agreement by Probert.   Deeds to
the property were executed by the three parties, as required by the contract, which were placed, under the contract, in escrow with the Hanover National Bank of New
York City, for delivery to Martin upon compliance by him
with the terms of the contract.   Subsequently, Martin paid
to the Hanover National Bank the first installment of $18,-
500, as required by the contract, which payment was made
in September, 1911.   Immediately prior to such payment,
Fraser instituted this suit in the lower Court for the dissolution of the alleged co-partnership between Fraser, Bidwell and Probert; the recision of the two deeds for one-
third interest each in Fraser's property to Probert and
Bidwell; the accounting for $20,000, part of which had
been taken by Bidwell and Probert, with proper commission allowances to Probert and Bidwell for their services
quantum meruit, and their reimbursement for their expenditures under the co-partnership agreement; the appointment of a receiver to carry out the undertaking with
Charles T. Martin; the injunction of Probert and Bidwell
and the State Savings Bank from interfering with Fraser

in carrying out the contract with Martin and certain modifications thereof to which Fraser alone had agreed, and to restrain Probert and Bidwell from directing the Hanover National Bank not to receive the payment of $18,500 about to fall due as modified by certain agreements made by Fraser, individually, and the authorization of the receiver to take and hold, under proper bond, the money Martin should pay under said contract. The basis of the complaint was fraud, in that advantage had been taken by Bidwell and Probert of Fraser's weakened mental condition, in the transaction.

The appellees answered, denying all the allegations of fraud and overreaching and the weakened condition of Fraser, and alleged full performance of the contract on their part. They also set up fraud on Fraser's part in his attempted dissolution of the partnership agreement.

Charles T. Martin intervened, for the purpose of securing advantage of certain modifications in the original contract of purchase, made by Fraser just prior to the institution of this suit.

B. G. Randall, receiver of the Taos Savings Bank, also intervened for the purpose of subjecting Probert's interest in the funds, should he ultimately be adjudged entitled thereto, to certain indebtedness owing by him to the bank.

Trial was had to the Court in equity, which found the issues in the main case in favor of Bidwell and Probert, and against Fraser, and in favor of Randall, receiver, upon his claims against Probert. The intervention of Martin was determined against him. The plaintiff, Fraser, appealed to this Court, as likewise did the intervener, Martin. Subsequently, the appeal as to Martin was dismissed, at his request.

Additional facts appear in the opinion.

OPINION OF THE COURT.

ROBERTS, C. J.—While many claimed errors are assigned, we will confine our consideration to those only which appellant has discussed in his brief, and upon the hearing of the cause in this Court.

Complaint is first made that the findings of fact made by the trial court are mere conclusions of law, and therefore, the decree made is inoperative, because not supported by findings, such findings having been requested by appellant. It would require unnecessary space to incorporate all the findings of fact and conclusions of law made by the trial court. It is perhaps sufficient, to state that the Court found: that the parties entered into the so-called partnership agreement set out in the statement of facts, on the date herein named; that pursuant to such partnership agreement, Fraser and wife made, executed and delivered to Bidwell and Probert, deeds to one-third interest each, in and to the property described in the complaint; that Bidwell and Probert performed all the conditions of said agreement, on their part to be performed; that there was a good and sufficient consideration for the said deeds; that said deeds were executed and delivered by plaintiff as his free and voluntary act, and without any undue influence or duress of Bidwell and Probert; that at the time of making such partnership agreement and executing said deeds, said Fraser was of sound mind and had the mental capacity to make said contract and execute said deeds; that the attempted dissolution of the co-partnership by Fraser, was an attempt to defraud Bidwell and Probert. Certain other facts were found not involved in this appeal, however, as such facts affected only the intervenors, Martin, and Randall, the receiver of the Taos Savings Bank.

The Court is only required to find the ultimate facts in controversy, raised by the issues in the case. Here

1 the questions to be determined were, (1) the mental condition of Fraser at the time he entered into the contract with, and executed the deeds, to Probert and Bidwell, and, (2) were said deeds executed and delivered by Fraser to Bidwell and Probert freely and voluntarily and without any undue influence or duress on the part of either Bidwell or Probert? These were the main issues in the case, the ultimate facts which the Court was re-

quired to determine in order to render a judgment. In
38 Cyc. 1980, it is stated:

"The setting out of matters of evidence and subordinate
facts in the findings is neither necessary, nor proper, as a
finding of ultimate facts necessarily includes all the probative facts, together with the inferences therefrom, and
it is the province and duty of the Court to state ultimate,
rather than evidentiary or probative, facts in its findings."

The Court was not required, nor would it have been
proper, to set out the evidence upon which it relied in determining the ultimate facts found. Nor does the fact
that conclusions of law may have been intermixed with
the findings of fact, render such findings so objectionable
as to require a reversal of the case. In the case of Baker
v. De Armijo, decided at the last term of this Court, and
reported in 128 Pac. 73, we quoted, with approval, the
following excerpt from the case of O'Reilly v. Campbell,
116 U. S. 420, 6 Sup. Ct. 422, 29 La. Ed. 669:

"Findings are not to be construed with the strictness of
special pleadings. It is sufficient if from them all, taken
    together with the pleadings, we can see enough upon
2 a fair construction to justify the judgment of the
    Court notwithstanding their want of precision and the
occasional intermixture of matters of fact and conclusions
of law."

Tested by this rule, we think the findings are sufficient
to support the judgment.

Appellant next contends that the findings of fact are not
supported by sufficient evidence, and further that it is
the duty of this Court, this being an equity case, to
review all the evidence in the record, and, regardless
of the findings of the trial Court, enter such a decree as
"may be agreeable to law." In other words, notwithstanding the rule adopted and always adhered to by the Territorial Supreme Court, that it would not, where the trial
Court heard all the evidence ore tenus, and thus had the
opportunity of observing the witnesses while testifying,
and was thereby enabled to judge from their manner and
demeanor while testifying, the weight to which their testi-

mony was entitled, disturb the findings of fact made by
the trial Court, if such findings were supported by substantial evidence, or, as sometimes stated, "by sufficient
evidence." Of course, where the testimony is taken by an
examiner, or by deposition, or is in the main, so taken,
and this Court has the same opportunity as the trial Court
possessed of determining the facts, the reason for the rule
does not exist, and the Appellate Court will review the
evidence and arrive at its own conclusion as to the facts
established thereby. But, where, as in this case, the
3   Court heard all the witnesses testify, and observed
     their manner, demeanor and appearance while on the
stand, this Court will not review the evidence further than
to determine whether or not the findings are supported
by substantial evidence, in the absence of such an overwhelming weight of evidence against such findings as
would clearly show that the trial Court erred in its conclusions drawn therefrom. In an equity case, where the
Court hears all the witnesses testify, there is no reason
for a departure from the rule. Under the old equity practice such cases were heard entirely upon written evidence,
which doubtless, and correctly so, established the practice
that the Appellate Court would review and weigh the
evidence, but under modern practice the reason for the
rule no longer exists.

Upon the trial of the case, a great deal of testimony was
introduced for the purpose of showing that appellant was
mentally inefficient at the time he entered into the contract of December 16, 1910. On his behalf, it was established that about six months prior thereto, he was thrown
from a buggy and received a severe blow on the head, from
which he was unconscious for from ten days to three
weeks. Witnesses, for appellant, detailed various circumstances and conduct on his part thereafter, upon which
they based the opinion that he was of unsound mind. Two
physicians testified as experts, that from a review of the
facts detailed by other witnesses, and examinations which
they had made of appellant, he was of unsound mind at
the time of making the contract. On the other hand, the

physicians who attended him during his illness, testified that there was a complete recovery from the injury and that he was restored to a normal condition mentally, about two weeks after the injury. Upon the trial, there was introduced in evidence, a great many letters written by appellant, dating from about four weeks after his injury to some months after the signing of the contract in question, all of which, without exception, appeared to have been written by a man in possession of all his mental faculties. Indeed, such letters were remarkably clear, explicit and concise, and would hardly be reconciliable with mental deficiency or unsoundness of mind on the part of the writer. Again, the experts for appellant testified that the condition of his mind would naturally become worse, his intellect would become gradually impaired, and that the disease with which he was suffering was "progressive." That in no event could there be hope of improvement in his mental condition; that at the time of the trial he was in a worse condition mentally, or at least was no better than he was at the time he executed the contract December 16, 1911. Appellant testified as a witness upon the trial, and was subjected to a rigid cross examination. From his testimony it appears that he knew all the details of his business, even to the minutest details, and there is nothing whatever to suggest an impaired intellect. It is probable that the trial Court gave considerable weight to his testimony, and his maner and conduct upon the stand, in arriving at the conclusion that he was of sound mind, as also the letters written by him, before and after the contract was executed. From a review of the evidence, it appears that the findings in this respect are supported by substantial evidence, and are not subject to attack here.

Nor was there any evidence of duress, fraud or overreaching. It is true, Fraser was, at the time he entered into the contract with Bidwell and Probert, in straightened circumstances, but neither of the appellees had anything to do with bringing about such condition. The evidence discloses that Fraser owed about $10,000, some of which was past due; that his property had been sold for taxes, and interest on some of his other debts was past due and pressing. He required for his immediate necessities, approximately $2,000, which Bidwell agreed to, and did advance under the contract. The written contract, set out in the statement of facts, it is admitted by all parties, did not express the entire agreement between the parties. All agree that Bidwell was to, and did, advance the sum of $2,000, and that he was further to drive a tunnel and develop the property and put it in shape for examination by purchasers. Immediately upon signing the contract, he repaired to the property and began work agreed to be done. Probert, on the other hand, was to find a purchaser for the property, and to pay all expenses connected therewith. Fraser contended, upon the trial, that the agreement which he made with Bidwell and Probert, did not include the deal which was consummated. That it was expressly excepted from the contract, and he was to have the right to proceed with the sale, which was being promoted by Mr. Manley, of Denver. This was denied by Bidwell, Probert not testifying. But the letters which Fraser wrote to Probert, while the Manley deal was pending and about to be consummated, furnish strong evidence that no such exception was made from the contract. He advised Probert of every detail of the proposed deal, and asked his advice. Spoke of the three acting in concert in the matter, and, we think, justified the trial Court in concluding that no exception whatever was intended by Fraser or the parties.

From the transcript of the evidence, it appears, without dispute, that Fraser sent for Bidwell to come to his house two or three days prior to December 16, the date when the contract and deeds were signed. His object was to induce Bidwell to engage with him in the tie and lumber business. Bidwell declined to go into the business, because of the uncertainty of the title to the land upon which it was proposed to operate. During the conversation, Bidwell told Fraser that he had about $2,000 in cash which he was not using at the time. That Fraser asked him to loan the money, to enable him to pay his

pressing debts and taxes; Fraser claims Bidwell agreed
to do so, but this is denied by Bidwell. The next day, at
Fraser's suggestion, they went into Taos and called to see
Mr. Probert, who was unknown to Bidwell. The next day
Bidwell and Probert had a talk, in the absence of Fraser,
but at Fraser's suggestion, relative to some plan to as-
sist Fraser. Bidwell says they agreed upon the plan which
was consummated in the contract. The next day Bidwell
submitted the details of the proposition to Fraser, which
he accepted, he claiming, however, that the Manley deal
was excluded therefrom, and that Probert was to find a
purchaser for the property at a price of not less than
$300,000. It will be seen that there is no suggestion of
fraud or duress, or overreaching, in the above recital of
the facts leading up to the making of the contract and
executing the deeds. Fraser had ample time to consider
the proposition, having taken the deeds out over night for
his wife's signature. Mere inadequacy of consideration is
not sufficient, in and of itself, to avoid a contract.

4. In the case of Eyre v. Potter, 15 How. 59, the Supreme Court of the United States say:

"Against an array of evidence like this, the question of
equivalents or of the exact adequacy of consideration cannot well be raised. The parties, if competent to contract,
and willing to contract, were the only proper judges of
the motive or considerations operating upon them; and it
would be productive of the worst consequences if under
pretexts however specious, interests or dispositions subsequently arising could be made to bear upon acts deliberately performed, and which have become the foundation of important rights in others. Mere inadequacy of
price, or any other inequality in a bargain, we are told, is
not to be understood as constituting per se a ground to
avoid a bargain in equity. For courts of equity, as well
as courts of law, act upon the ground that every person
who is not, from his peculiar condition or circumstances,
under disability, is entitled to dispose of his property in
such manner and upon such terms as he chooses; and
whether his bargain be wise and discreet or otherwise, or

profitable or unprofiitable, are considerations not for the courts of justice, but for the party himself to deliberate upon."

"Again, it is ruled that inadequacy of consideration is not of itself a distinct principle of equity. The common law knows no such principle. The consideration, be it **4** more or less, supports the contract. Common sense knows no such principle. The value of a thing is what it will produce, and it admits no precise standard. One man, in the disposal of his property may sell it for less than another would. If courts of equity were to unravel all these transactions, they would throw everything into confusión, and set afloat the contracts of mankind. Such a consequence would of itself be sufficient to show the injustice and impracticability of adopting the doctrine that mere inadequacy should form a distinct ground for relief. Still there may be such an unconscionableness or inadequacy of consideration in a bargain, as to demonstrate some gross imposition or some undue influence; and in such case, courts of equity ought to interfere, upon satisfactory ground of fraud; but then, such unconscionableness or such inadequacy should be made out as would, to use an expressive phrase, shock the conscience, and amount in itself to conclusive and decisive evidence of fraud."

Again in another case the same Court used the following language which fits the circumstances of the case at bar:—

"Enough appears in the record to convince the Court that the respondent was in straightened circumstances, that his business affairs had become complicated, that he was greatly embarrassed with litigations, that he was in pressing want of pecuniary means, but the Court is wholly unable to see that the complaint is responsible for these circumstances, or that he did any unlawful act to deprive the respondent of his property, or to create those necessities or embarrassments, or to compel him to do what he acknowledges he did do, which was to yield to the pressure of the circumstances surrounding him, and as a choice of evils accepted the advance of five thousand dollars and the shares assigned to him, in the new organization as proposed, and voluntarily signed both the agreement and the assignment. Such an act as that of signing those instruments, under circumstances disclosed in the record, must be regarded, both in equity and at law, as a voluntary act, as it was not attended by any act of violence, or threat of any kind, calculated in any degree to intimidate the party or to force the result, or to compel that consent which is the essence of every valid contract. Suppose he consented reluctantly, as he avers, still the fact is he did consent when he might have refused to affix his signature to the instrument, as he had repeatedly done for the year preceding, and having consented to the arrangement and signed the instruments he is bound by their terms, and must abide the consequences of his own voluntary act, and unless some other of his defenses set up in the answer have a better foundation." French v. Shoemaker, 14 Wall. 333.

Counsel for appellant next insists that the agreement, entered into by the parties, did not constitute a partnership contract, but was at most a brokerage agreement. Had the parties to the contract not treated it as constituting a partnership agreement, we would be inclined to agree with counsel, but all the acts of the parties, and circumstances in evidence, from the time of making the contract in December, until the conclusion of the sale to Martin, plainly show that Fraser, and Bidwell and Probert, recognized that a partnership existed between them, by virtue of said contract, and treated each other accordingly. Having placed a construction upon the contract, and acted thereunder, the Court will not, at this time, and after all the rights have accrued, give to the contract a different construction, which would plainly be at variance with the understanding of the parties to it. 30 Cyc. 360.

Appellant contends that, as the written agreement did not embrace the entire contract between the parties, and a part of it rested in parol, that it was a parol contract, and that the partnership agreement was within the Statute of Frauds, first, because it was not to be performed within a year, and, second, because it concerned land.

This question is not involved in the case, however, as it was not raised by the pleadings.

What we have already said in the case disposes of appellant's contention that the Court erred in not decreeing the dissolution of the partnership. The only basis in the complaint for the dissolution of the relations between the parties was the unsoundness of appellant's mind at the time of the execution of the contract by which the partnership was formed, and the alleged fraud, duress and overreaching of appellant at that time. On these issues the Court found for the appellees; consequently, there was no ground for a decree of dissolution.

For the reasons stated, the judgment of the lower Court will be affirmed, and it is so ordered.

[No. 1590, December 5, 1913.]

KEINATH, SCHUSTER and HUDSON, a partnership composed of A. C. Keinath, Neal M. Schuster and E. A. Hudson, Appellee, v. J. D. H. REED, Appellant.

SYLLABUS (BY THE COURT)

1. In an action for commissions earned by a broker in effecting an exchange of property of his principal, where the complaint pleaded a written contract of employment of the broker by the principal to make an exchange and a written contract of exchange between the principal and a customer procured by the broker; an answer which alleged (a) that the principal had not accepted the property of the customer; (b) that the principal had not accepted the customer as a proper party with whom to make an exchange other than on the terms of the written contracts entered into by them; (c) that the written contracts of exchange were intended by the parties to be merely stipulations by which an exchange of property might be effected and not a valid, binding and enforceable contract of exchange; (d) that the broker had not done all

he was required to do in order to earn his commissions; (e) that the customer had failed to perform his part of the contract; tendered issues of law and not of fact.

P. 367

2. Where the answer raises issues of law only, the case is ripe for judgment on the issues of law involved and a motion for judgment on the pleadings is properly entertained.

P. 367

3. Under an employment to sell or exchange the property of his principal, a broker has fully performed his undertaking when he procures a customer, with whom the principal makes a valid contract of sale or exchange.

P. 367

4. In an action by a broker for commissions earned by him in effecting an exchange of the property of his principal, where the complaint pleads a valid and enforceable written contract between the principal and a customer procured by the broker, to exchange property, it was not necessary for the complaint to allege that the customer was "in a position and able to convey a perfect title to the property which he proposed to exchange."

P. 368

5. In such a case the principal by entering into a contract of exchange with the customer produced by the broker, accepted the customer as able, ready and willing to make the exchange.

P. 368

6. A stipulation that "both parties hereunto have this day deposited in escrow with K., S. & H. this contract and a copy of the original contract, his demand note for $1000.00 as evidence of good faith and as a forfeit in event either party hereto fails or refuses to comply with the terms of the contract as therein provided" held to be a penalty.

P. 369

7. In an action for a broker's commissions for effecting an exchange of real estate where the complaint states the making of a valid written contract of exchange between the principal and the customer procured by the broker, the complaint need not further state that the customer was able, ready and willing to complete the exchange on the terms of the contract; or that he made any effort to that end; or the refusal of the principal to complete it.

P. 370

8. In an action based upon a written contract which is admitted by the answer, the intentions of the parties as to what should be the effect of the contract is to be decided by the Court upon an inspection of the contract.

P. 370

9. An allegation in the answer of what the parties intended or did not intend the contract should effectuate, raises a question of law to be decided by the Court.

P. 370

Appeal from the District Court of Eddy County; John T. McClure, District Judge; affirmed.

J. B. ATKESON, Artesia, N. M., for appellant.

The Court erred in sustaining plaintiff's motion for judgment on the pleadings. Thomas v. Ray, 110 Pac. 48; Idaho Pac. Min. Co. v. Green, 94 Pac. 161; Pac. Mill Co. v. Inman Poulson & Co., 90 Pac. 1099; Town of Mapleton v. Kelly, 117 Pac. 52; Miles v. McCallan, 3 Pac. 610; Johnson v. Manning, 29 Pac. 101.

,Court erred in his judgment because the complaint filed herein fails to state facts sufficient to constitute a cause of action. Estee's Pleadings, 177-332; McGavock v. Woodlief, 20 How. 221, 15 L. Ed. 884; Ayers v. Thomas, 47 Pac. 1013; Colburn v. Seymore, 76 Pac. 1058; Howe v. Bratrude, 86 N. W. 747; Moore v. Snow, 23 N. W. 401; Crockett v. Grayson, 36 S. E. 477; Czarnowski v. Holland,

78 Pac. 890; Hildenbrand v. Lillis, 51 Pac. 1008; Gunn v. Bank of California, 33 Pac. 1105; Knock v. Emmerling, 22 How. 69, 16 L. Ed. 292; Plant v. Thompson, 22 Pac. 726; Kyle v. Rippy, 26 Pac. 308; Zittle v. Schleisinger, 65 N. W. 892; Freedman v. Gordon, 35 Pac. 879; Emens v. St. John, 29 N. Y. Sup. 655; Folsom v. Hesse, 53 N. Y. Sup. 783; Grausel v. Dean, 67 N. W. 275.

Court erred in holding that the contract was a valid binding and enforceable contract. Sheperd-Teague Co. v. Hermann, 107 Pac. 622; 31 Cyc. 1509, and foot note authorities; Creussel v. Dean, 67 N. W. 275; Barber and Hilderbrand, 60 N. W. 594; Condict v. Crowdry, 34 N. E. 781.

Where parties enter into an alternative contract, wherein they provide for the measure of damages for the breach thereof, they are bound thereby to the exclusion of any other remedy. Barrett v. Geesinger, 53 N. E. 576; Barker v. Critzer, 11 Pac. 382; Klemschmidt v. Klemschmidt, 24 Pac. 266; Bodine v. Glading, 59 Am. Dec. 749; Smith v. Washington, 154 U, S. 559, 19 L. E. 187; Mallory v. Globe-Boston Cop. Min. Co., 94 Pac. 1116.

Courts make a distinction between classes of contracts. Barnes v. Roberts, 5 Bosw. 73; Kalley v. Baker, 132 N. Y. 1; Lunney v. Healey, 44 L. R. A. 612; 31 Cyc. 1507.

The broker must strictly perform the services required of him, according to the authority conferred upon him. Wilson v. Sturgis, 71 Cal. 226; Neilson v. Lee, 60 Cal. 565; Nesbitt v. Helsor, 49 Mo. 383; Hoyt v. Shepherd, 70 Ill. 309; Hayden v. Grillo, 26 Mo. App. 289.

G. U. McCRARY, Artesia, N. M., for appellee.

Court erred in sustaining the plaintiff's motion for judgment on the pleadings. Moses T. Yoder v. Randol, et al., 83 Pac. 537, 3 L. R. A. (N. S.) 576; Felch v. Deaudry, 40 Cal. 439; McMurray v. Gilford, 5 How. Pr. 14; Fargo v. Vincent, 60 N. W. 858; Hemme v. Hayes, 55 Cal. 337; McDonald v. Pincus, 13 Mont. 83; Bowles v. Double, 5 Pac. 918; Wallace v. Beasley, 22 Ore. 572; American Co. v. Bradford, 27 Cal. 367.

Allegations in a pleading denying the legal import of a

written contract, will not be considered by the Court. 12 Enc. Pl. & Pr., 1038, 1039, and cases cited; Board of Education v. Shaw, 15 Kan. 33.

A pleading which merely denies that the defendant is indebted to the plaintiff is the statement of a mere legal conclusion. Enc. Pl. & Pr., vol. 12, p. 1043, and cases cited; Knox County Bank v. Lloyd, 18 Ohio St. 353; 12 Enc. Pl. & Pr., p. 1024, and cases cited; Estee's Plead-Levinson v. Schwartz, 22 Cal. —; Van Schaack v. Winne, ings, vol. 2, sec. 3172; Hensley v. Tartar, 14 Cal. 508; 16 Barb. 85; Armstrong v. Heide, 94 N. Y. S. 434, 47 Misc. Rep. 609, 9 Cyc. 732, and cases cited; Fox v. Ryan, 88 N. E. 974, 240 Ill. 391; Watkins Land Mfg. Co. v. Thetford, 966 S. W. 72; Friestedt v. Dietrich, 84 Ill. App. 604; Jenkins v. Hollingsworth, 83 Ill. App. 139; Luning v. Healey, 76 N. W. 558, 44 L. R. A. 593; Ault v. Dosher, 92 N. Y. S. 439, 79 N. E. 1100; Pollatschek v. Goodwin, N. Y. S. 682; Charles v. Phillips, 84 N. Y. S. 867; Hipple v. Lair, 82 Atl. 46; Francis Roche Appt. v. Nellie A. Smith, 51 L. R. A. 510; Gilder v. Davis, et al., 20 L. R. A. 398.

Complaint failed to state facts sufficient to constitute a cause of action. Yoder v. Randol, et al., 83 Pac. 537, 3 L. R. A. (N. S.) 576.

A person undertaking to find a purchaser is required to do no more than to find a purchaser. McFarland v. Lillard, 28 N. E. 229, 50 Am. St. R. 234.

Where the seller accepts a proposed purchaser and enters into a valid contract with him, the broker's commissions are earned whether the purchaser subsequently fails to perform his contract. Friestedt v. Deitrich, 84 Ill. App. 604; Parker v. Estabrook, 44 Atl. 484; Luning v. Healey, 76 N. W. 558; Stauffer v. Linenthal, 64 N. E. 643; Ault v. Doscher, 79 N. E. 1100; Springer v. Orr, 82 Ill. App. 558; Charles v. Cook, 84 N. Y. S. 867; Hipple v. Lair, 82 Atl. 46; Seabury v. Fidelity Ins. Co., 54 Atl. 498; Gilder v. Davis, et al., 20 L. R. A. 398; Roche, Appt., v. Smith, 51 L. R. A. 510; Warde v. Cobb, 148 Mass. 518, 54 N. E. 873; McFarland v. Lillard, 50 Am. St. R. 234; Coleman's

Ex'r v. Meade, 76 Ky. 358; Brackenridge v. Claridge, 42
S. W. 1005; Odell v. Dozier, 30 S. E. 811; Mattes v. Engel,
89 N. W. 651; Flinn v. Jordan, 100 N. W. 326; Watkins
Land Mtg. Co. v. Theford, 96 S. W. 72; Fox v. Ryan, 88
N. E. 974; Hamberger & Dreyling v. Thomas, 118 S. W.
770.

Whether the contract was enforceable was a question for
the construction of the Court. Friestedt v. Deitrich, 84
Ill. App. 604; Jenkins v. Hollingsworth, 83 Ill. App. 139.

Appellant pleaded conclusions of law and not statements of fact. Armstrong v. Heide, 94 N. Y. S. 434, 9
Cyc. 732.

There is no averment in the pleading to show that the
contract has not been consummated. Mattes v. Engel, 89
N. W. 651.

Broker is entitled to his commission if the purchaser
presented by him entered into a valid contract. Friestedt
v. Deitrich, 84 Ill. App. 604; Jenkins v. Hollingsworth,
83 Ill. App. 139; Parker v. Estabrooke, 44 Atl. 481.

Vendor may enforce specifically a contract for the pur-
chase of land though it stipulates for a sum as liquidated
damages or a penalty on its breach. Moss & Raley v.
Wren, 118 S. W. 149; Newton v. Dixon, Moore v. Smith,
116 S. W. 143; Dailey v. Litchfield, 10 Mich. 29; Gordon
v. Brown, 39 N. C. 399; Lyman v. Gidney, 114 Ill. 388;
Hull v. Sturdivant, 46 Me. 34; Hubbard v. Johnson, 77
Me. 139; Hooker v. Pynehan, 74 Mass. 550; Dike v.
Green, 4 R. I. 285; Shuman v. Willetts, 23 N. W. 358;
Hunter v. Bales, 24 Ind. 299.

Agreement to deposit demand notes for $1,000 in es-
crow was a stipulation for liquidated damages and not a
penalty. Moyses v. Schendorf, 87 N. E. 401; Gobble v.
Linder, 76 Ill. 157; Morse v. Rathburn, 42 Mo. 594, 97
Am. Dec. 359; Harper v. Estabrooke, 44 Atl. 484.

Appellant's Reply Brief.

Mallory v. Globe-Boston Cop. Min. Co., 94 Pac. 1156;
Yoder v. Randol, 3 L. R. A. (N. S.) 576; Roche v. Smith,
51 L. R. A. 510.

STATEMENT OF THE CASE.

The appellee, plaintiff below, brought this action to re-cover the sum of $500.00 as a commission for the sale of certain real estate belonging to the appellant.

The complaint alleges (a) that on or about the 13th day of June, 1912, the defendant was the owner of certain real estate, and that defendant listed said real estate with plaintiff for sale or exchange, by executing a written list contract, a true copy of which is attached to the complaint marked Exhibit "A;" the listing contract recites: "I, J. D. H. Reed, hereby authorize and appoint Keinath, Schuster & Hudson of Artesia, N. M., as my agent to sell or exchange the within described real estate, now owned by me, to-wit: (describing the real estate and prices fixed) for services rendered by said agent in making the sale of said land, or being instrumental in any manner, whatsoever, in selling or transferring said property, I agree to pay to said agent a commission of Five Hundred Dollars." (b) that acting by authority of and in pursuance to the agency so created the plaintiff did procure one G. E. Shackleton, who was an acceptable party to defendant and with whom defendant entered into a valid binding written contract, providing for the exchange of said defendant's real estate, for certain real estate of the said Shackleton, a copy of which written contract is attached to the complaint as Exhibit "B;" by the contract mentioned the defendant and Shackleton agree to exchange properties, each assuming certain encumbrances existing on the other's property, each to have full and peaceable possession of the property of the other on or about Oct. 1, 1912, or as mutually agreed otherwise, with the further provision that Shackleton was to have until July 10, 1912, to investigate and approve the property he was trading for; (c) that on the 6th day of July, 1912, the defendant and Shackleton entered into another written contract, designed and intended to be a continuation of contract herein referred to as Exhibit "B," which supplemental contract is attached to and made a part of the complaint and marked Exhibit "C," and at the same time the defendant and

Shackleton executed their promissory notes each for the sum of $1000.00, payable on demand, copies of which notes are attached to the complaint as parts of Exhibit "C;" the contract marked Exhibit "C" is as follows: "Continuation of contract of sale made between G. E. Shackleton, party of the first part, and J. D. H. Reed, party of the second part, in the exchange of the several properties as provided for, in the original contract made and executed in Palisade, Colorado, on June 28th, 1912, Witnesseth:—Party of the first part has this day accepted the property of party of the second part, and agrees to accept the trade and deed his property to said second party as provided for in the original contract above mentioned and of which this is a part. Both parties hereunto have this day deposited in escrow with Keinath, Schuster & Hudson, this contract and a copy of the original contract, his demand note for $1000.00 as evidence of good faith and as a forfeit in event either party hereto fails or refuses to comply with the terms of the contract as therein provided." The note of Shackleton was payable to Reed and vice versa; (d) that at the time defendant entered into said contract, the defendant accepted said Shackleton as a proper and suitable person with whom to make such contract and that plaintiff, "acting in good faith, did all it was requested or required to do by defendant in the way of effecting a valid and binding contract aforesaid and did by its efforts become the procuring cause in producing for said defendant the said G. E. Shackleton for the purposes aforesaid."

The defendant's answer admits (a) the execution of Exhibit "A;" (b) admits that appellee procured Shackleton to exchange property with him, but denies that he entered into a valid and binding contract with said Shackleton, but admits he did enter into a stipulation, setting out the terms upon which he and Shackleton were to exchange properties and that Exhibit "B" attached to the complaint is a copy thereof; (c) admits the execution of contract Exhibit "C" attached to the complaint and the notes therein mentioned, but denies that the notes were to be a payment on the properties, or for any other purpose, except to be a forfeiture and for the special purpose of indemnifying each, respectively, against the loss which they might sustain in case the other failed to perform his part of the stipulation by which the sale was made to be effected, or to perfect the sale; and further denies that defendant accepted the property of G. E. Shackleton, except upon the condition of the original stipulations by which the exchange was to be made between defendant and G. E. Shackleton; (d) denies that he accepted Shackleton as a proper and suitable party with whom to make such contract as was made, except on the condition and with the understanding that the said Shackleton would perform his part of the stipulation in the contract; and denies further that the plaintiff did all that was required of it in the way of effecting a valid and binding contract between defendant and Shackleton. By way of new matter the defendant in his answer alleged: (a) that he employed the plaintiff to sell or exchange his property, as is stated in the copy of listing contract Exhibit "A" of plaintiff's complaint and that plaintiff was not to have any commission on the exchange of the property unless the exchange was perfected or completed; that the contract Exhibit "B" was intended to be a stipulation upon which he and Shackleton were to exchange properties and was not a valid, binding and enforceable contract of sale; (c) that the notes set out in Exhibit "C" were executed for the purpose of indemnifying himself and Shackleton, in damages, in case the other party failed to perform his part of the stipulations in the contract Exhibit "B" and for no other reason; (d) that the said Shackleton failed to perform the stipulations in his contract Exhibit "B" and for that reason the exchange of property was never effected between defendant and Shackleton. Plaintiff moved for judgment in its favor upon the pleadings. Motion granted and judgment rendered as prayed in the complaint.

OPINION OF THE COURT.

MECHEM, D. J.—Appellant insists that by his answer he raised the following issues of fact: (1) Whether or not appellant accepted the property of Shackleton; (2) Whether or not appellant accepted Shackleton as a proper party with whom to make an exchange other than upon the conditions in the contract or stipulations Exhibit "B;" (3) Whether or not appellee had done all it was required to do in order to earn its commission; (4) Whether or not the contract, or stipulations Exhibit "B" between appellant and Shackleton, was intended to be a stipulation by which an exchange of property was to be effected or whether it was intended to be a valid, binding and enforceable contract; (5) Whether or not the contracting party, Shackleton, failed to perform the contract, or stipulation, Exhibit "B," and if that was the reason why the exchange was never effected between appellant and said Shackleton.

1 Argument is not required to demonstrate that the issues raised on these points were issues of law and not of fact. The question whether Shackleton's failure to comply with his agreement, was a good defense will be discussed hereafter, but the allegation of that fact presented no issue because admitted by the motion for judgment.

2 As the pleadings stood, the case was ripe for judgment on the issues of law involved and the motion for judgment was properly entertained.

It is contended by appellant that the appellee does not plead a performance of the terms of its employment, because the exchange of properties was not consummated The law is well settled, that under an employment to sell or exchange the property of his principal, a broker has **3** fully performed his undertaking when he procures a customer, with whom the principal makes a valid contract of sale or exchange. Shepherd-Teague Co. v. Herman, 107 Pac. 622; Ward v. Cobb, 148 Mass. 518, 12 Am. St. 587; Wilson v. Mason, 158 Ill. 304, 42 N. E. 134, 136, 49 Am. St. 152; Odell v. Dozier, 30 S. E. 813; Scully v. Williamson, 26 Okla. 19, 108 Pac. 395; Ann. Cases 1912 A 1265; Kalley v. Baker, 132 N. Y. 1, 28 Am. St. 542.

Nor as claimed by counsel was it necessary for appellee to aver that Shackleton was "in a position and able to con-

vey a perfect title to the property which he proposed
4 to exchange to defendant." By entering into the contract of exchange the appellant accepted Shackleton as
able, ready and willing to make the exchange. In Roche
v. Smith, 176 Mass, 595, 58 N. E. 152, 79 Am. St. 345,
the Court said:

"It was held in Knapp v. Wallace, 41 N. Y. 477, where
the broker was employed to find a person to convey land
to be paid for in money, and in Kalley v. Baker, 132 N. Y.
1, 28 Am. St. 542, 29 N. E. 1901, where the broker was
employed to find a person to convey land to be paid for by
conveyance of other land, that is to say, to effect an exchange, that where the principal makes a valid agreement
with the customer produced by a broker, the broker has
earned his commission, even if it turns out that the customer cannot make a good title and the land is not conveyed, providing the broker acted in good faith in the
matter. In the opinion of a majority of the Court those
cases were rightly decided. The question is the same in
the two cases; the only difference is that in one case payment is to be made in money, in the other, by a conveyance of other land. The ground on which this is set-
5 tled is that by entering into a valid contract with the
customer produced by the broker the principal accepts
the customer as able, ready and willing to buy land and
pay for it."

In Fox v. Ryan, 240 Ill. 391, 88 N. E. 974, the reason
for this doctrine is well stated:

"The vendor of property is not required to accept a purchaser without opportunity for investigation as to his ability to comply with the terms of the contract, but where he
does accept such purchaser, uninfluenced by fraud or mis-
representation, it is a determination by him of the purchaser's ability to perform his contract, and, if the purchaser afterwards fails to perform it, the seller cannot
defeat the broker's commission on the ground that the
purchaser was not able to buy the property."

Appellant insists that the contract is not enforceable because of the provision in regard to the notes de-

posited by the parties in escrow "as evidence of good faith
and as a forfeit" for non-performance. In his answer
the appellant alleged that these notes were given for the
purpose of indemnifying the party not in default in damages. The contract, however, speaks for itself, as its language is plain. It appears conclusively that the notes
were given simply for the purpose of securing the performance of the contract. The word "forfeit" in its ordinary
use in cases of contract is synonymous with "mulct, fine
or penalty." State v. Baltimore & O. R. Co., (Md.) 12
Gill & J. 399, 38 Am. Dec. 319, and see other cases cited
in Words & Phrases, vol. 3, p. 2893. In the case of Van
Buren v. Digges, 52 U. S. (11 How.) 461, 467, the Court
said:

"The second exception by the defendant states, that in
addition to the evidence previously tendered by him he
offered proof tending to show that the amount of ten per
centum on the contract price stipulated' to be forfeited if
the house was not entirely finished and ready for occupation, as therein provided, on the 25th of December, 1844,
was intended by the parties as and for liquidated damages,
that would result and fairly belong to the said defendant
by reason of said failure to finish the said house on the 25th
of December, 1844; and that the Court refused to hear
the evidence thus tendered. In the refusal of the Court
to admit the evidence thus tendered we think they decided
correctly. It would have been irregular in the Court to
go out of the terms of the contract, and into the consideration of matters wholly extraneous, and with nothing upon
the face of the writing pointing to such matters as proper
or necessary to obtain its construction or meaning. The
clause of the contract providing for the forfeiture of ten
per centum on the amount of the contract price, upon a
failure to complete the work on a given day, cannot properly be regarded as an agreement or settlement of liquidated damages. The term forfeiture imports a penalty;
6 it has no necessary or natural connection with the
measure or degree of injury which may result from a
breach of contract, or from an imperfect performance. It

implies an absolute infliction, regardless of the nature and extent of the causes by which it is superinduced. Unless, therefore, it shall have been expressly adopted and declared by the parties to be a measure of injury or compensation, it is never taken as such by courts of justice, who leave it to be enforced where this can be done in its real character, viz., that of penalty."

We do not decide that a provision for liquidated damages in a contract such as this renders it unenforceable, but that in this case the provision considered is plainly in the nature of a penalty to secure the performance of the contract, which of itself is no bar to specific performance.

From the law announced on the question above discussed it follows that the further objections of the appellant, viz: that the complaint failed to state a cause of action because it is not alleged that Shackleton was able, ready and willing to complete the exchange on the terms of contract "B," or that he made any effort to complete the exchange or that the defendant refused to complete the exchange of properties, and that the Court erred in

7   holding that by entering into the contract, the appellant accepted Shackleton as able, ready and willing to make the exchange, are not well taken.

Appellant insists that by his answer he raises as an issue of fact the question of whether the contracts "B" and "C" were mere stipulations of the terms of a pro-

9   posed exchange and not intended by the parties to be enforceable contracts or to be enforced. Appellant does not plead any other contract which would vary the terms of contracts "B" and "C" and what the parties

8   intended by those contracts was for the Court to decide by an inspection of the contracts unaided by proof aliunde.

There is no error disclosed by the record and the judgment is therefore affirmed.

[No. 1591, December 5, 1913.]

S. S. EVANTS, Appellee, v. A. L. TAYLOR, Appellant.

SYLLABUS (BY THE COURT)

1. The surety on the note·of a minor, given in payment for real estate, is discharged from liability thereon, where the minor on becoming of age, disaffirms the contract and restores the property purchased.

P. 375

2. Where an infant purchased real estate, and upon coming of age ,disaffirms the sale, he must in order to make the disaffirmance· effectual restore the property, if he has title to it, to his vendor, and in such case the duty to restore becomes a right to restore, which the vendor may not defeat by refusing to take back the property.

P. 376

3. A defective allegation in a pleading can only be raised by a demurrer distinctly specifying the defect as a ground of objection. Sub-sec. 36, sec. 2685, C. L. 1897.

P. 377

Appeal from the District Court of Eddy County; John T. McClure, District Judge; reversed and remanded.

J. B. ATKESON, Artesia, N. M., for appellant.

Court erred in sustaining plaintiff's motion for judgment on the pleadings. Laws 1907, ch. 107, sec. 3 of sub-sec. 308; amending sub-sec. 62 of sec. 2685, C. L. 1897.

Amendments to pleadings should be liberally allowed in the furtherance of justice. Snider v. Winslow, 93 Pac. 600; Kindall v. Lincoln Hardware & Implement Co., 76 Pac. 992.

Where the pleadings raise a material question of fact which must be determined before a judgment can be rendered, a motion for judgment on the pleadings should be denied. Thomas v. Ray, 110 Pac. 48; Idaho Pac. Min. Co. v. Green, 94 Pac. 161; Pac. Mill. Co. v. Inman Paulson & Co., 90 Pac. 1099; Town of Mapleton v. Kelley,

117 Pac. 52; Miles v. McCallan, 3 Pac. 610; Johnson v. Manning, 29 Pac. 101.

The acceptor of any bill of exchange or any other principal obligor in any contract, may be sued either alone or jointly with any other party who may be liable thereon. Rev. Stats. of Texas, (1911) art. 1842, p. 413.

When an amended answer is filed, after having leave of the court to do so, a motion to strike it out should be denied. Sears v. Dunbar, 91 Pac. 145; Clemens v. Hanley, 41 Pac. 658.

It is error to strike out an amended answer which constitutes a good defense. Hozey v. Buchanan, 16 Pet. 215, 10 L. Ed. 941; Mandelbaum v, Nevada, 8 Wall. 314, 19 L. E. 480; Pastene v. Pardini, 67 Pac. 681; Brainard v. Buck, 184 U. S. 104, 45 L. Ed. 453; Hardin v. Boyd, 113 U. S. 756, 28 L. Ed. 1141; Jones v. Van Doren, 130 U. S. 684, 32 L. Ed. 1077; Kirby v. Muench, 82 N. W. 93; Berry v. Hull, 30 Pac. 936; Ratliff v. Summers, 46 S. E. 712; Gregg v. Groebeck, 40 Pac. 202; Idaho Pac. Min. Co. v. Green, 94 Pac. 161; Tom Boy Min. Co. v. Green, 53 Pac. 845.

The court should liberally exercise its discretion in allowing amendments, so that the cause may be decided on its merits. Green v. Gavin, 105 Pac. 761; Rude v. Levy, 96 Pac. 560; Richner v. Plateau Live Stock Co., 98 Pac. 178; Trover v. City of San Francisco, 109 Pac. 617; Dunbar v. Griffiths, 93 Pac. 654; Brown v. Lutin, 64 Pac. 674.

Court erred in rendering judgment against this defendant because it appeared from the pleadings in the case that defendant was only a surety for the minor defendant. Benjamin on Contracts, sec. 32, p. 133; Ogden Neg. Instruments, sec. 132; Joyce's Defenses to Com. Paper, sec. 63; Armijo v. Neher, 11 N. M. 643.

Defenses of a minor, who executed a contract, will avail sureties where the undertaking of the sureties goes to the whole consideration. Joyce's Defenses to Com. Paper, sec. 68, p. 83; Baker v. Kennett, 54 Mo. 82; Patterson v. Cave, 61 Mo. 439.

General rule is that the law of the place where the contract is entered into governs, unless intent of the parties is evident from the instrument. 9 Cyc., sec. 3, p. 582.

If one of the defendant parties is a surety upon the contract he may have the question of suretyship determined by setting up such fact in his answer. Rev. Stats. of Texas, 1911, art. 6331, p. 1354; Cruger v. Moore, 8 Tex. 69; Wiley v. Pinson, 23 Tex. 488; Mitchell v. DeWitt, 25 Tex. Sup. 180; Stroop v. McKenzie, 38 Tex. 133.

Where an infant maker of a note disaffirms the contract upon reaching majority and surrenders the consideration therefor, the surety is discharged. Childs on Suretyship, p. 236; Keokuk Co. St. Bank v. Hall, 76 N. W. 832; Baker v. Kennett, 54 Mo. 82; Joyce's Defenses to Com. Paper, sec. 68, p. 83; Patterson v. Cave, 61 Mo. 439; Stearns on Suretyship, sec. 104, p. 149.

J. H. JACKSON, Artesia, N. M., for appellee.

Court did not render judgment on the pleadings, but entered a default judgment. No abuse of discretion. Laws 1907, ch. 107, sec. 3, sub-sec. 308.

Art. 1842, Rev. Stats. of Texas, has never been pleaded.

Must set out a statute in haec verba or set out the substance of it with such distinctness as to enable the Court to judge of its effect. 20 E. & E. Enc. Pl. & Pr., 598; Hemstead v. Reed, 6 Conn. 490; Brackett v. Norton, 4 Conn. 517; Swank v. Hufnagle, 111 Ind. 453; Mendenhall v. Gately, 18 Ind. 149; Tyler v. Kent, 52 Ind. 583; Milligan v. State, 86 Ind. 553; Wilson v. Clark, 11 Ind. 385; 36 Cyc. 1242.

Question of suretyship not material to the issues of this case. Presumption is that the law of Texas is identical with our own, and that presumption continues until a different substantive law of Texas is pleaded and proven. 9 Enc. Pl. & Pr., 542; Peck v. Noee, 97 Pac. 865; Brackett v. Sonnemann, 106 Pac. 715; Long v. Dufor, 113 Pac. 58; H. S. Banking Co. v. Veale, 114 Pac. 229; M. K. T. Ry. Co. v. McLaughlin, 116 Pac. 811; State v. Collins, 124

Pac. 903; 35 Cyc. 1240; Sayles Texas Stats., art. 3813, 3815; Laws 1907, sec. 119, p. 181, (N. M.)

Law of 1907 went into effect before the execution of the notes, in this case. Negotiable Instrument law of New Mexico, laws 1907, ch. 83; Cellers v. Meachem, 89 Pac. 426; Wolstenholme v. Smith, 97 Pac. 329; Vanderford v. Farmers & Mechanics Nat. Bank, 10 L. R. A. (N. S.) 129; Richards v. Market Exchange Bank Co., (Ohio) —, N. E. 1000.

Obligation of this surety not annulled even though minor maker did avoid the contract. Am. & E. Enc. L., vol. 27, p. 467; St. Albans Bank v. Dillon, 73 Am. Dec. 295, and note on Infancy; Smyley v. Head, 2 Rich. 591; Maledon v. Lefore, 36 S. W. 1102; Conn v. Coburn, 7 N. H. 386; Hicks v. Randolph, 59 Tenn. 352; Winn v. Sanford, 145 Mass. 302.

STATEMENT OF FACTS.

This action was brought by S. S. Evants on two promissory notes, dated October 26, 1908, executed at Hereford, Texas, payable to the order of Evants and signed by W. O. and A. L. Taylor, in the order named. Each note recites that it is given as part payment on a certain described property in the Town of Hereford, Texas, a vendor's lien being retained to secure the notes. W. O. Taylor, appeared by his guardian, ad litem, J. C. Davis, and answered that at the time he signed the notes he was a minor about the age of eighteen years and that the notes were given in consideration of a deed from plaintiff to him for the real estate described in the notes, which deed is attached to and made a part of his answer, and further says "this defendant specially tenders back to plaintiff a deed to said property which this defendant is filing in this case as a tender to plaintiff, tendering back to plaintiff all that was received on account of signing said notes. And this defendant offers to do all things which the Court may find to be proper and just for him to do in order to effect a disaffirmance of the notes and seeming obligation aforesaid with justice and fairness to the plaintiff in conformity with law." The plaintiff filed a reply denying the matters alleged in the answer except as to the statement that defendant had signed the notes. Thereafter, on Sept. 3, 1912, W. O. Taylor filed an amended answer containing substantially the same allegations with the addition that he alleges he arrived at the age of 21 years on July 5, 1912, and "that he now disaffirms and revokes the said contract and refuses to perform the conditions in the contracts or notes." To which answer plaintiff replied denying all the facts so alleged except the execution of the notes. A. L. Taylor, by his answer admitted the execution of the notes, that he signed said notes as surety for W. O. Taylor, and that the consideration of the notes was the conveyance of the property described in them to W. O. Taylor, who was at the time an infant; that since attaining his majority he "disaffirms and revokes" said notes, and "has tendered back and surrendered back to plaintiff in this cause the lots and real estate for the payment of which the two notes in question were given." This allegation appears in A. L. Taylor's second and third amended answers. The appellee demurred to the second amended answer on the ground that it stated no defense in law; which demurrer was sustained and appellee on Jan. 17, 1913, filed his third amended answer, which was stricken from the files on the motion of appellee because it contained no facts not formerly pleaded and held insufficient to which ruling of the Court appellant excepted and refused further to plead and judgment was entered against him as prayed in the complaint.

OPINION OF THE COURT.

MECHEM, District Judge—The question presented is:

1 Will a surety on a note sued on by the original payee, given by an infant for the purchase price of real estate conveyed by the payee of the note to the infant, be discharged from liability, where the principal on coming of age, disaffirms the deed conveying the real estate and tenders back a deed to the payee? If the late infant on arriving at his majority may disaffirm the deed and if such disaffirmance renders it void ab initio, propositions not questioned, and if the deed tendered vests the payee in all that he ever parted with, in consideration of the note, which it does as far as the record in this case discloses, then the consideration of the note is wiped out or extinguished. The defense is failure of consideration, which is good as between the original parties to the note. Sec. 28, chapter 83, laws 1907. We are of the opinion that the question stated must be answered in the affirmative. Baker v. Kennett, 54 Mo. 82; Keokuk County State Bank v. Hall, 106 Iowa 540, 76 N. W. 832; Kyger v. Sipe, 89 Va. 507, 16 S. E. 627.

It is true that the plea of infancy is a personal defense and as such cannot avail the surety, but this only applies to the contract itself upon which the surety is bound, in this case, the note, and does not extend to the consideration for the note. Where the principal is discharged because of incapacity. to contract the surety stands in the position of principal promisor. His promise in this case was based upon a consideration moving to his principal, which has failed, through no fault of his. His obligation cannot be extended beyond the note. He cannot be held to have promised that W. O. Taylor, on attaining his majority would not avoid the deed. He did not guarantee both the note and the consideration for the note.

The cases cited by counsel for appellee support the rule that a discharge of the principal by reason of infancy does not discharge the surety, but in all the cases so cited the contract was supported by valuable consideration.

Appellee states that by his amended reply to the second amended answer of W. O. Taylor, he alleges that he **2** refuses to take back the property or a deed for the same. The pleading mentioned is not in the record, but as this cause must be reversed we will treat the point as raised. It may be disposed of very easily upon principle. Where an infant receives anything by reason of a contract, which he disaffirms upon coming of age, he must restore what he received under the contract in order to make the disaffirmance effective. He cannot avoid the

contract and still retain the fruits of it. 22 Cyc. 614.
Now if the right of the infant to disaffirm is absolute, of
which there can be no doubt, and in order to exercise that
right he must restore the thing received, if he still has it,
then the duty to restore becomes a right to restore, otherwise the right to disaffirm would depend upon the will of
the opposite party.

    The allegation of tender is attacked because it is not
    shown how the tender was made. This defect was
3 apparent on the face of the answer and should have
    been taken advantage of by a demurrer, distinctly
specifying this ground of objection. Sub-section 36, sec.
2685, C. L. 1897. For aught that the record shows the
Court below ruled on the effect of a tender and not
whether a tender was well pleaded.

    The judgment of the lower Court is reversed and the
cause remanded for further proceedings not inconsistent
with this opinion.

[No. 1605, December 11, 1913.]

HAROLD L. CRANE, Trustee, Appellee, v. WILLIAM
W. COX, Treasurer and Ex-officio Collector of Dona
Ana County, Appellant.

SYLLABUS (BY THE COURT)

1. Section 34, chapter 84, Laws 1913, directs the collector
to offer for sale "each parcel of property upon which any
taxes are delinquent as shown by the tax rolls." Held to
authorize the sale of property for taxes which had become
delinquent prior to the year 1913.

P. 381

2. Chapter 84, Laws of 1913, as construed to authorize the
sale of property for taxes delinquent previous to the time the
act became effective. Held not to operate retrospectively in
respect to such taxes.

P. 386

3. A preliminary injunction will not be granted to restrain the sale of property for taxes, unless the tax payer first pays so much of the tax as he admits is just.

P. 386

Appeal from the District Court of Dona Ana County; Edward L. Medler, District Judge; reversed and remanded.

FRANK W. CLANCY, Attorney General, Santa Fe, N. M., for appellant.

Defendant was proceeding in exact conformity with the act of 1913. Laws 1913, ch. 84, sec. 34-40.

Laws of 1913 is a valid exercise of legislative power. Sec. 1, ch. 84, laws 1913, repeled ch. 22, laws of 1899.

Judgment of the lower Court could not have been founded on sec. 34, ch. 84, laws 1913.

HOLT & SUTHERLAOD, Las Cruces, N. M., for appellee.

No formal assignment of errors appears to have been filed or set forth in appellant's brief. Laws 1907, ch. 57, sec. 21.

Is the language of sec. 34, ch. 84, laws 1913, retroactive? Laws 1912, ch. 84, sec. 34; Id. sec. 22, 23.

Authority to sell real estate for delinquent taxes must be expressly conferred by statute, and this authority will not apply to taxes already delinquent unless it is expressly made retroactive. 36 Cyc. 1206; 37 Cyc. 1280; Hall v. Perry, 72 Mich. 202, 40 N. W. 325; McNaughton v. Martin, 72 Mich. —, 40 N. W. 327; Nowlen v. Hall, 128 Mich. 274; Norris v. Hall, 124 Mich. 170, 82 N. W. 832.

The general rule of law requires courts to always construe statutes as prospective, and not retroactive, unless constrained to the contrary course by the rigor of the phraseology. Cooley on Taxation, p. 292; 36 Cyc. 1206; Price v. Law, 52 Penn. St. 315-16; Leete v. St. L. State Bank, 21 S. W. 788; 36 Cyc. 1208, note; Williamson v.

N. J. S. R. R. Co., 29 N. J. Eq. 334; U. S. v. Hteh, 3 Cranch. 399; Citizens Gas Light Co. v. Alden, 44 N. J. Law 654.

It is not enough that words used in an act *may* be given a retrospective, without doing violence to their meaning, or that such course may coincide with their common understanding. Garrett v. Doe, 30 Am. Dec. 643; Halpin v. Prosperity Loan, etc., Association, 102 Ill. App. 316; Aultman, etc., Mfg. Co. v. Fish, 120 Ill. App. 314; Baltimore City App. Tax Court v. Western Md. R. R. Co., 50 Md. 274; Gaston v. Miriam, 33 Minn. 271, 22 N. W. 614; Reynolds v. McArthur, 7 L. Ed. 470; 36 Cyc. 1206, note; Ukiah Bank v. Gibson, 39 Pac. 1069; Sohn v. Waterson, 17 Wall. 596; 21 L. Ed. 738; Harvey v. Tyler, 2 Wall. 347, 17 L. Ed. 875.

In every case of doubt, the doubt must be resolved against the retrospective effect. 37 Cyc. 1208.

The statute must be strictly construed. 36 Cyc. 1173, 1189; Maysville v. Maysville Str., etc., Co., 126 Ky. 673, 108 S. W. 960; McNally v. Field, 119 Fed. 445; U. S. v. Wigglesworth, 28 Fed. Cas. 16,699.

The title of the act should be considered in order to arrive at the legislative intent. Thomas v. Collins, 24 N. W. 553.

Reply Brief for Appellant.

IRA L. GRIMSHAW, Assistant Attorney General, Santa Fe, N. M.

Laws 1913, ch. 84, sec. 34; 37 Cyc. 1257; City of Oakland v. Whipple, 44 Cal. 304; Treece v. American Association, 122 Fed. 598, 55 Tenn. (8 Heith) 440; In re George R. Powell, 55 Tenn. (8 Heith) 444; Holthaus v. Adams County, 74 Neb. 862; Hosmer v. Peojle, 96 Ill. 61.

STATEMENT OF FACTS.

The complaint contains substantially the following allegations: That the plaintiff is the holder of the legal title to certain mining claims in Dona Ana County, upon which there are due delinquent taxes for the years of 1904 to

1912, inclusive; that the defendant, the Treasurer and ex-officio Collector of Dona Ana County, had on the 14th day of June, 1913, and for four consecutive weeks thereafter, published a notice that he would, on August 4, 11913, sell all property upon which any taxes were delinquent in said county, as shown by the tax rolls, to satisfy the taxes, penalties and costs due thereon and that unless restrained, plaintiff is informed and believes said officer will make such sale; and plaintiff further alleged that the valuation of his property for purposes of taxation for the several years mentioned, was erroneous and grossly in excess of the real taxable value thereof; that the attention of the District Attorney and defendant had been called to said erroneous and excessive assessments and a request made upon them for a correction and change of the same, to avoid injustice to the plaintiff; a letter from plaintiff's counsel to the officers was attached to the complaint as showing such deman;d that unless defendant be restrained, as aforesaid, plaintiff will suffer great and irreparable injury and that he is without adequate remedy at law; plaintiff prayed the issuance of a temporary writ of injunction restraining the defendant from selling or attempting to sell any of the plaintiff's property for delinquent taxes, penalties or costs; that defendant be required to show cause why such injunction should not be made perpetual and further in the event the Court should hold the defendant authorized by law to make the threatened sale, that a hearing be had upon the validity of the various assessments, whether or not the valuations upon which said assessments were based were not grossly in excess of the real taxable value of said property and whether or not defendant is entitled to charge against the said property the several items of interest, costs and penalties and that the levies and assessments be adjusted and changed so as to avoid injustice to plaintiff. The defendant demurred on the ground that the complaint on its face failed to state a cause of action, because it showed that defendant was proceeding to sell the plaintiff's property in accordance with section 34, chapter 84, laws of 1913. The demurrer was overruled and the de-

fendant electing to stand on his demurrer and refusing to
further plead, final judgment was entered granting the
permanent injunction as prayed for in the complaint.

OPINION OF THE COURT.

MECHEM, D. J.—Chapter 84, laws of 1913, went into
effect immediately upon its approval, March 18, 1913,
1   and as it expressly repealed chapter 22, laws of 1899,
it provides the only procedure for the sale of property
for delinquent taxes.

Section 34 of the act reads as follows:

"Within forty-five days after the first day of June in
each year the collector shall prepare, and cause to be published for not less than once in each week, for four consecutive weeks, in some newspaper published in his County,
or if there be no newspaper published in the County, then
in some newspaper published in the State and of general
circulation in the County, notice that he will, on the day
specified in said notice, at the hour of 10 o'clock in the
forenoon, at the court house of the County, offer for sale,
separately and in consecutive order, each parcel of property upon which any taxes are delinquent, as shown by the
tax rolls, or so much thereof as may be necessary to realize
the respective amounts due, which sale shall continue until not later than four o'clock in the afternoon, and from
day to day at the same hours, until all of said property
shall be sold, or until the amounts due shall be paid or
realized; but such sales shall not continue for more than
thirty days, and the collector shall make record of his acts
and doings as hereinafter provided."

It is admitted that the words "each parcel of property
upon which any taxes are delinquent, as shown. by the tax
rolls" is broad enough to include taxes delinquent both
before and after the time the law becomes effective. But
it is said, first, that to hold that the act does apply to
taxes delinquent before it became effective is to give it a
retrospective operation; and second, in view of the well
known rule of statutory construction that "Words in a
statute ought not to have a retrospective operation, unless

they are so clear, strong, and imperative, that no other meaning can be annexed to them, or unless the intention of the legislature cannot be otherwise satisfied," (U. S. v. Heth, 3 Cranch. 399-413; Sohn v. Patterson, 17 Wall. 598), this act should be limited to a prospective operation that is applicable to taxes becoming delinquent subsequent to the passage of the act only.

In the first position assumed, viz: that if the act applies to taxes delinquent before its passage it is retrospective law, correct? If it is not, then no opinion need be given on the second.

"A retrospective or retroactive law, in the legal sense, is one which takes away or impairs vested rights acquired under existing laws, or creates a new obligation, imposes a new duty, or attaches a new disability in respect to transactions or considerations already past." 36 Cyc. 1201; Society for Propagating the Gospel v. Wheeler, 2 Gall. 139; Sturges v. Carter, 114 U. S. 511; Gladney v. Snyder, 172 Mo. 318, 72 S. W. 554, 60 L. R. A. 880, 95 Am. St. Rep. 517; Gage v. Steward, 127 Ill. 207, 19 N. E. 702, 11 Am. St. 116; Rich v. Flanders, 39 N. H. 304; Chicago, etc., R. R. Co. v. State, 47 Neb. 549, 66 N. W. 624, 41 L. R. A. 481, 53 Am. St. Rep. 557; Black on Interpretation of Laws, sec. 114.

A law is not retrospective or a law does not operate retrospectively simply because it applies to transactions which originated before the law took effect, but it is the nature of the application that is determinative. This view was well put by the Supreme Court of Nebraska in Chicago, etc., R. R. Co. v. State, supra, in the following words:

"A statute does not operate retroactively from the mere fact that it relates to antecedent events. A retrospective law has been defined as one intended to affect transactions which occurred or rights which accrued, before it became operative as such, and which ascribes to them affects not inherent in their nature in view of the law in force at the time of their occurrence. Bishop on Written Laws, sec. 83; Black on Interpretation of Laws, sec. 114."

Crane v. Cox, 18 N. M. 377.

In Smith v. Auditor General, 20 Mich., 398, the Court, speaking through Justice Cooley, said:

"We do not understand it to be questioned that it was competent for the legislature to make the general provisions of the act of 1869 apply to the taxes previously assessed and returned, so far as subsequent proceedings to be taken by the State were concerned, if they had seen fit to do so. The question is whether they have expressed an intention to that effect. Unless that intention distinctly appears, the familiar rule of construction which presumes that legislation is designed to have prospective operation only will require the Court to hold that the legislative purpose was that this act should apply only to the taxes subsequently assessed. For although to apply it to taxes previously levied would not, so far as the course of official proceeding for the enforcement thereof is concerned, be strictly retrospective, in the proper sense of the term, yet so far as it increased penalties, or in any manner affected the tax payer's rights or interest as they depended upon previous acts of delinquencies, it would be plainly so, and the purpose of the legislation to give it that operation is not to be presumed where the words are ambiguous, or reasonably susceptible of a different construction."

In the case of In re Taxes in Hennepin County v. Baldwin, 62 Minn. 518, 65 N. W. 80, where a statute provided that "if any tax is prevented from being collected, the auditor should add the amount to the tax for the current year," the Court said, construing the act with respect to its operations:

"The argument of counsel for the landowner upon the fourth question is wholly based on the proposition that laws 1885, c. 2, sec. 23, Gen. St. 1894, sec. 1631) is prospective in the sense that it only authorizes the auditor to add to the tax for the current year taxes for other years, which shall, after the passage of the act, be prevented from being collected.

"In support of this contention he relies on the phrase 'if any tax is prevented from being collected.'

"The statute in question does not impair any vested

right, or create any new right, or impose any new obligation. It is purely remedial and merely gives a remedy for
enforcing existing rights and obligations. Such statutes
are to be liberally construed in order to accomplish the
beneficent purpose for which they were enacted; and, unless a different legislative intent is expressed or clearly implied, they will generally be construed to apply to rights
and obligations that accrued before enactment as well as
to those to accrue after. Such, we think is the construction which should be given to the statute under consideration."

In Gage v. Stewart, 127 Ill. 207, 11 Am. St. 116, a
statute declaring that hereafter no purchaser at a tax sale
shall be entitled a deed unless he has complied with certain
conditions designated in said statute, was held to apply to
sales previously made for which no deed had issued and
for which the landowner yet retained the rights of redemption. In answer to the argument that so applied, the statute was retrospective, the Court said:—

"It is insisted that the sale occurring October 21, 1878,
the law then in force will control in the subsequent proceedings necessary to maturing the tax title, and therefore
no notice to the owner was required to be shown as a prerequisite to the making of the deed. We are of the opinion
that the section of the act of 1879 was intended to take effect *in praesenti* as to all notices served thereafter, and to
apply to all purchasers at tax sales and their assignees, irr-
spective of when the sale for taxes was made. This, we think.
the clear import of the language employed. The provision is
not in respect of sales hereafter to be made, but is that 'hereafter no purchaser or assignee of any such purchaser, of
any land or lot, for taxes, etc., at any sale, etc., shall be entitled to a deed until he shall have complied with the conditions prescribed in that section of the statute.' The amended act applied to all steps to be taken after it went into effect and which could be performed according to its requirements. Nor does this construction give the act a
retrospective operation, as seems to be supposed. The-

rule undoubtedly is, that a retrospective effect will not be given to a statute unless the legislative intent that it shall so operate is clearly manifested. But no such effect is sought to be given this statute. The legislature, for the better protection of those having the right of redemption, required that notice be served upon the owner, if found to be in the county, at least three months before the expiration of redemption. No other change affecting the right of the purchaser or holder of the certificate of purchase is wrought by this amendment. It in no way affects or applies to the sales, or any of the precedent steps in the proceeding, lawful under the former statute, but relates exclusively to acts to be performed by the purchaser, or his assigns, subsequent to its taking effect and by the performance of which, his inchoate right to the land under his certificate, might ripen into a title. These requirements—of giving notice of the sale, when redemption will expire, and making proof thereof to the clerk—are in the nature of remedies to be pursued by the purchaser or holder of the certificates of purchase to mature and perfect the title of his land under the sale. As to all these acts which could be performed by the purchaser or his assignee after the statute became in force, it would necessarily operate prospectively. Bac. Abr. Statute 9."

In Sturges v. Carter, 114 U. S. 511, a statute of Ohio which authorized an auditor to go back four years to correct false returns where formerly by statute he could not for that purpose go behind his annual settlements with the treasurer, was attacked as being a retroactive law and as such in conflict with the Constitution of Ohio. The Court said:

"In our opinion, no right of the taxpayer has been invaded by the act of 1878. His investments in stocks and bonds were subject to taxation; the taxes upon such investments were due to the State and the act of 1878 merely provided a method by which the taxes might be assessed and collected in spite of the annual settlements made by the auditor. It gave a new remedy to the State for enforcing a right which it had all the time possessed, namely, the right to the taxes upon property liable to taxation. Such an act is not a retroactive law within the meaning of the Constiution of Ohio.

"In the case of Society for Propagating the Gospel v. Wheeler, 2 Gall. 139, Mr. Justice Story thus defines a retroactive, or, as he calls it, a retrospective law: 'Upon principle, every statute which takes away or impairs vested rights acquired under existing laws, or creates a new obligation, imposes a new duty, or attaches a new disability in respect to transactions or considerations already past, must be deemed retrospective.' The act of 1878 took away no vested right of the taxpayer, it imposed upon him no duty or obligation, and subjected him to no disability in reference to past transactions."

The point is not made, that the operation of the statute of 1913, complained of by the appellant, would, in
2 any manner, affect any right he possessed under the previous law or in any wise change his status; nor, do we, from a careful reading of the statute, see that such a consequence is to be reasonably anticipated. The statute does not interfere with any act done under—or any condition that exists by reason of—the former law. It merely provides for the sale of property upon which a lien for taxes has been ascertained, fixed, and declared, giving to the lien no force or effect which it did not possess under the law by which it was created. It is, therefore, held that, upon the question as here presented, the act of 1913, in providing for the sale of property for taxes delinquent for years previous to 1913, does not operate retrospectively.

Counsel for appellee contend that the complaint states a cause of action by the allegation of excessive assess-
3 ments, which they say entitles the appellee to relief under the provisions of section 23 of the act. This phase of the case was not passed upon by the lower Court. We do not express any opinion on the question. However, it is very clear that appellee is not entitled to an injunction preliminary to a hearing upon the alleged excessive assessments. By a letter attached to the complaint

written by appellee's attorneys to the District Attorney, it is said that the valuations, if reduced 50%, would represent the reasonable value of the properties. He must pay on that basis before he is entitled to a preliminary injunction in any event. Albuquerque Bank v. Perea, 147 U. S. 87; Cooley on Taxation, vol. 11, page 142.

The proper procedure in such case is announced in Albuquerque Bank v. Perea, supra, as follows:—

"It is a profitable thing for corporations or individuals whose taxes are very large to obtain a preliminary injunction as to all their taxes, contest the case through several years' litigation, and when, in the end, it is found that but a small part of the tax should be permanently enjoined, submit to pay the balance. This is not equity. It is in direct violation of the first principles of equity jurisdiction. It is not sufficient to say in the bill that they are ready and willing to pay whatever may be found to be due. They must first pay what is conceded to be due, or what can be seen to be due on the face of the bill, or be shown by affidavits, whether conceded or not, before the preliminary injunction hsould be granted. The State is not to be thus tied up as to that of which there is no contest, by lumping it with that which is really contested. If the proper officer refuses to receive a part of the tax, it must be tendered, and tendered without the condition annexed of a receipt in full for all taxes assessed."

The judgment of the lower Court is reversed and remanded for further proceedings not inconsistent with this opinion.

[No. 1395, September 1, 1913.]

PUEBLO OF ISLETA, Plaintiff in Error, v. FRED-
ERICK TONDRE et al., Defendants in Error.

]No. 1408, September 1, 1913.[

PUEBLO OF ISLETA ,Appellant, v. J. A. PICARD et
al., Appellees.

SYLLABUS (BY THE COURT)

1. Chapter 49, laws of 1907, does not regulate community
acequias construted prior to the passage of the act as to
the right to change the point of diversion from the stream
into such acequias.

P. 391

2. Said chapter authorizes the enlarging of an old community acequia by condemnation proceedings.

P. 395

(1395). Error to the District Court of Bernalillo
County; Ira A. Abbott, Associate Justice; affirmed.

FRANCIS C. WILSON, Santa Fe, N. M., for plaintiff in
error.

Petitioners failed to allege and prove that they had
complied with the laws of the Territory of New Mexico as
to the appropriation and diversion of public waters, which
is a necessary jurisdictional allegation. Laws 1907, ch.
49, secs. 3, 12, 45, 25, 44, and 61.

The right of eminent domain is the right to take private
property for public use. Wheeling, etc., R. R. Co. v. Toledo, etc., R. R. Co., 72 Ohio St. 368, 74 N. E. 209, 106
Am. St. 622.

The petition should show a clear right to condemn the
property described. Lewis on Eminent Domain, vol. 2,
p. 988; Richland School Twp. v. Overmeyer, 164 Ind.
382, 73 N. E. 811; Laws 1907, ch. 49, sec. 3; Laws 1905,
ch. 97; United States v. Hogg, 112 Fed. 909, 111 Fed.

292; New Cache la Poudre Irr. Co. v. Water Supply & Stor. Co., 68 Pac. 781.

In interpreting the irrigation code the Court may consider, not only the entire statute in order to give effect to all its provisions, but may take into consideration the ends to be accomplished. Dunlap v. United States, 173 U. S. 65, 43 L. Ed. 616.

(No. 1408.)

FRANCIS C. WILSON, Santa Fe, N. M., for appellant.

The right of plaintiff to enjoin the defendants from the use of ditch and headgate of the Los Charcos ditch is not *Res Adjudicata,* because District Court was without jurisdiction. 1 Freeman, Judgments, sec. 120; Brown, Jurisdiction of Courts, sec. 1.

A void judgment is, in legal effect, no judgment. 1 Freeman, Judgments, secs. 117-120; Zalesky v. Iowa State Ins. Co., 70 N. E. 187, 102 Iowa 512; Babbitt v. Field, 52 Pac. 775, 6 Ariz. 6.

Defendants have not complied with the law governing changes in the point of diversion of ditch. Chicago, etc., R. Co. v. Porter, 78 Ia. 426.

Not necessary to allege damages and the complaint would have been sufficient without such an allegation. Walker v. Emerson et al., 26 Pac. 968; Moore v. Water Works, 68 Cal. 146, 8 Pac. 816; Conkling v. Pacific Ind. Co., 25 Pac. 399.

Injunction should be allowed. Parker v. Griswold, 17 Conn. 288; Starford v. Felt, et al., 16 Pac. 900.

Where a statute prescribes the method by which the right to change the point of diversion can be acquired, the statute must be followed. New Cache la Poudre Irrig. Co. v. Water Sup. & Stor. Co., 68 Pac. 781.

FRANK W. CLANCY, Attorney General, Santa Fe, N. M., for defendants in error and appellees.

Plaintiff in error should have obtained a decision setting out findings of fact and conclusions of law, in the District Court. C. L. 1897, sec. 2999; Radcliffe v. Chaves, 15 N. M. 262.

The statute of 1907 has no application to the proceedings of the commissioners of old community acequias. Laws 1907, ch. 49.

The right to condemn does not necessarily depend upon the act of 1907. Laws 1907, ch. 49, sec. 3; C. L. 1897, sec. 23, et seq.

Reply Brief for Plaintiffs in Error and Appellants.

Laws 1907, ch. 49, sec. 35; C. L. 1897, sec. 2999; Radcliffe v. Chaves, 15 N. M. 262; Suffolk Gold Min. & Mill. Co. v. Miguel Co. Min. & Mill. Co., 48 Pac. 828; New Cache la Poudre Irr. Co. v. Water Supp. & Stor. Co., 68 Pac. 781; Weil Water Rights, (3d ed.), vol. 2, pp. 544, 547.

OPINION OF THE COURT.

PARKER, J.—Both of the above cases involve the same questions, and will be considered together, as was done by counsel for the respective parties in their briefs. The first of the above cases involves the validity of a proceeding for the condemnation of a right-of-way for an irrigation ditch through the lands of the plaintiff in error. The condemnation proceedings were instituted by the defendants in error for the purpose of securing a right-of-way and a headgate, taking the water from the Rio Grande River at a point of diversion different from that which had formerly been employed for that purpose. The proceedings resulted in the condemnation of the land and the payment into court of the amount awarded in that proceeding. The second of the above cases was an equity proceeding for an injunction to restrain alleged trespass by reason of the operation of the new ditch constructed over the right-of-way awarded in the condemnation proceedings above referred to. The claims of the plaintiff in error in the first action, and the appellant in the second action, are based in each instance upon a single proposition, which may be

stated as follows: That by reason of the provisions of
chap. 49, of the laws of 1907, it became necessary to apply
for, and obtain, a permit from the then Territorial, now
State Engineer, to change the point of diversion of water
from any natural stream in the State into any irrigating
ditch, and the defendants in error, and appellees, having
obtained no such permit, were not authorized to maintain
condemnation proceedings, or change the point of diversion of water from the Rio Grande, and were consequently
trespassers in all of their acts.

It appears that both the plaintiff in error and appellant,
and the defendants in error and appellees are, and have
been, for many years past, appropriators of water for the
purpose of irrigation from the Rio Grande River.   The
head-gate of the ditch of defendants in error had been
washed away by a change in the banks of the Rio Grande,
and it became necessary for them to seek a new head-gate,
together with a considerable length of ditch from the new
point of diversion, in order to be able to use the water for
the purposes required.

It is contended by counsel for plaintiff in error that the
legislature had not only the power to regulate the
1 right to the use of the waters of the State by persons
who had acquired water rights long prior to the passage of the act above mentioned, but that it did in
said act, in terms, provide for such regulation. It is argued by counsel for appellee that a fair construction of
the terms of the act shows that it speaks prospectively
from the date of its passage, and was never intended to,
and does not apply to, water rights acquired prior to the
passage of the act, or to the means of enjoying the same.
It becomes necessary, therefore, to examine the act as a
whole and to determine the legislative intent therefrom,
there being some little obscurity in the same.   The title
of the act is as follows: "An Act to Conserve and Regulate the Use and Distribution of the Waters of New Mexico; to Create the Office of Territorial Engineer; to Create a Board of Water Commissioners, and for other purposes." Sec. 12 of the act provides that the Territorial

Engineer shall have the supervision of the apportionment
of water in this Territory according to the licenses issued
by him and his predecessors, and the adjudications of the
courts.   This section would seem to limit the jurisdiction
of the Territorial Engineer to such water rights as had
been acquired under licenses issued by him or his predecessors.   Sec. 13, provides for the division of the State
into water districts and Sec. 14, provides that after such
division, after the application of a majority of the water-
users of any district, the State Engineer may appoint a
water master for such district, who shall have charge of
apportionment of waters in his district.   These two sections would seem in no way to refer to old established
water rights or community acequias, but to speak to the
future and to provide for a condition of affairs to be
brought about by the districting of the State under the
supervision of the Territorial Engineer.   Until the same
had been done it would seem to confer no power and require no duty of the State Engineer in regard to the use
of any water right.   Sec. 19 provides for a hydrographic
survey of each stream system in the State, and sec. 20
provides for the filing with the Attorney General of the
data so accumulated and, at the request of the State Engineer, to require the Attorney General to bring' a suit
on behalf of the State for the determination of all
rights to the use of water in such system.   These two sections also speak to the future, and have no application to
water rights acquired prior to the passage of the act and
the means of enjoying the same.   Sec. 24 of the act requires every applicant intending to acquire the right to
the beneficial use of any of the public waters of the State
to make application to the State Engineer for a permit
to appropriate the same, and the works to be employed
for such purpose are to be subject to the approval of the
State Engineer.   This section requires the applicant or
proposed appropriator of water to furnish the State Engineer with plans and specifications of the proposed works.
Sec. 25 further deals with the detail of the data required
to be furnished to the State Engineer by the proposed ap-

propriator, and provides that the plans of construction
may be amended with the approval of the State Engineer,
and contains the following proviso:

"Provided further that a change in the proposed point
of diversion of water from a stream shall be subject to the
approval of the Territorial Engineer under the provisions
of sec. 45, hereof, and shall not be allowed to the detriment of the rights of others having valid claims to the
use of water from said stream."

Counsel for plaintiffs in error rely much on this proviso and argue that it was intended to apply to all ditches
regardless of when the same were constructed, or the right
to appropriate the water was acquired. We do not so
understand the provisions of sections 24 and 25. They
speak entirely of water rights to be acquired by means of
filing a petition with the State Engineer, and do not in
terms, nor do we think in intent, attempt to deal with any
ditches or water rights acquired before the passage of the
act. Sec. 45, referred to in the proviso, does not purport
to modify the terms of sec. 25 of the act.

The only direct application of the chapter to prior existing rights occurs in sec. 59, which is as follows:

"Nothing contained in this act shall be construed to impair existing, vested rights or the rights and priorities of
any person, firm, corporation or association, who may have
commenced the construction of reservoirs, canals, pipe
lines or other works, or who have filed affidavits, applications or notices thereof for the purpose of appropriating
for beneficial use, any waters as defined in section 1 of
this act, in accordance with the laws of the Territory of
New Mexico, prior to the passage of this act; Provided,
however, That all such reservoirs, canals, pipe lines or
other works and the rights of the owners thereof shall be
subject to regulation, adjudication and forfeiture for
abandonment, as provided in this act."

At first glance it might seem that this section expressly
subjects all prior rights to regulation in accordance with
the terms of the chapter, but a more careful examination
of the section leads, we think, to the opposite conclusion.

It is seen that two classes of rights are mentioned in the section, viz: "existing, vested rights," or "the rights and priorities of any person, firm, corporation or association, who may have commenced the construction of reservoirs, canals, pipe lines or other works, or who have filed affidavits, applications or notices thereof." Then follows the proviso which applies the feature of regulation to these "reservoirs, canals, pipe lines, or other works and the rights of the owners thereof," only, and omits to mention the first class of rights above pointed out. In determining the meaning of this section, and the scope of the application of the regulation feature, resort should be had to the then existing legislation. We had at the date of the passage of the act in question, chap. 102, laws of 1905. Sec. 19 of that act required notice or application to be made to the Territorial Engineer, which office was first created by that act, by "all persons, associations, or corporations who shall desire to construct any dam or dyke for the purpose of storing, appropriating or diverting any public waters," and required them to submit plans and specifications of the proposed works. The section contains two provisos. The first is to the effect that if the proposed works are, in the opinion of the Territorial Engineer, not of sufficient importance to have the provisions of the section applied to it, he might suspend the operation of the section, and in case of works of great importance, where life or property would be in danger by the failure of such works, the Territorial Engineer might require certain precautions therein mentioned to be taken by the persons proposing to construct the works. The second proviso excludes from the operation of the section all works requiring the expenditure of less than Two Thousand Dollars. It thus appears that the class or kind of works referred to in sec. 59, of chap. 49, under discussion, must refer to the class of works, concerning which, under the act of 1905, application was not required to be made to the Territorial Engineer, and not to small community ditches or acequias, which involve no danger to life or property, and which are of comparatively insignificant cost.

Counsel for appellants argue that sections 3 and 61 of
the act provide the only means whereby an acequia al-
2 ready constructed can be enlarged by condemnation
proceedings, as was done in these cases, and that therefore the defendants in error and the appellees must necessarily have been acting under the said chap. 49 in the proceedings which were taken; that therefore their rights are
controlled by the terms of that chapter.

We think the conclusion is faulty in the foregoing argument. Assuming that no other provision of law exists
authorizing the condemnation proceedings taken in these
cases, than sections 3 and 61 of chap. 49, still it does not
follow that the proceeding cannot be maintained. The
question is whether old, prior existing rights of the kind
presented by plaintiff, are subject to regulations by the
State Engineer. If they are not, as we conclude, it does
not follow that the owner of such a right cannot pursue
condemnation proceedings under sections 3 and 61 of the
chapter. The terms of the sections are broad, and include
every person having a water right, and there is nothing
in the terms of either section restricting the class of persons entitled to enjoy the right of condemnation, to those
persons who are seeking either to initiate a right, or whose
rights are regulated by the terms of the act. It therefore
follows that the proceedings in condemnation were regular and properly maintained.

Further contention is made by counsel for plaintiff in
error and appellant, to the effect that there was a defect
of parties, but this error, if error it was, was cured by the
bringing in of the absent party, who adopted the pleadings of the plaintiff in each case and the judgment was in
each case rendered in its favor.

In this connection it may be stated, that the question involved in these cases is no longer of any importance except to the immediate parties, insofar as it relates to public community acequias, established and in operation prior
to March 19, 1907, for by chap. 26 of the Session Laws of
1912, it is provided that no application to or permit from

the State Engineer is necessary to change the point of diversion of such an acequia.

For the reasons stated, the judgment of the lower Court in each of the cases will be affirmed, and it is so ordered.

We Concur: David J. Leahy, District Judge.

I Dissent: Clarence J. Roberts, C. J.

DISSENTING OPINION.

ROBERTS, C. J.—The facts are stated in the majority opinion, and need not be here repeated. / The sole question presented by these cases, is as to whether or not it was necessary for the appellees and defendants in error to allege and prove that they had applied to the Territorial Engineer for permission to change the point of diversion of their intake ditch, and had secured a· permit from such official so to do, prior to the institution of their proceedings in condemnation./ If such application and permit were required, by reason of existing statutes, then it is conceded that the lower Court committed an error and a reversal is necessary. A consideration of the question involves two propositions, which may be stated as follows: First, did the legislature have the power to regulate the manner and method of changing the point of diversion of a pre-existing water right, and, second, do the provisions of the act of 1907 apply, in this regard, to an appropriator of water, who had perfected and completed his appropriation prior to the passage of the act?

Discussing the two propositions in the order stated, it is but fair to counsel for appellees and defendants in error to state, that but seeming little reliance is placed upon the first proposition, although the question is stated in his brief. I do not regard the question as an open one, and believe it has been answered in the affirmative, as often as presented. Water, in the natural stream, in all those States where the common law with respect to the use of water and the right thereto is altogether ignored, is held to be the property of the public, or the State as the representative of the public. Wiley v. Decker, 11 Wyo. 496, 73 Pac. 210. Water in the natural stream, thus being the property of the public, or State, and its economical use, beneficial application and full duty contributing so materially to the prosperity of the people, as a whole, and to the general welfare of the State, the State has the right to provide reasonable regulations for its distribution and application, in order to advance such objects and protect the rights of all persons enjoying or participating in the right. The waters of the State, being thus impressed with a public interest, the State, under its police power, clearly has the right to regulate the distribution and use thereof. Under the power of regulation, which of course must be reasonably exercised, no one would contend that the legislature would be authorized to impose regulations which would be confiscatory. In this case the regulations are not claimed to be confiscatory, or unreasonable ,but the statement is made, unsupported by argument, however, that the legislature could not provide for the regulation of a pre-existing right to the use of water.

A review of a few of the authorities will, I think, clearly and unmistakably demonstrate the right to regulate, old as well as new rights to the use of water.

In the case of C. B. & Q. Ry. Co. v. People ex rel. Drainage Commisisoners, 200 U. S. 561, Mr. Justice Harlan, speaking for the Court, says,

"We hold that the police power of a State embraces regulations designed to promote the public convenience or the general prosperity, as well as regulations designed to promote public health, the public morals or the public safety."

It must be recognized by every one, familiar to any extent with conditions in the arid region, that the general prosperity of a State, situated therein, is dependent upon the economical distribution and use of water, and regulations designed to secure and promote such economical use and distribution, and secure the full duty of water, come clearly within the police power of the State. Again, the legislature of New Mexico, as I view the effect of the sections of the act of 1907, hereinafter set out, determined that it was necessary in order to protect the rights of other water users, that an appropriator, desiring to change the

point of diversion of his water, should, by an orderly procedure upon notice to all other water users who might be
affected by such change have his right to make such change
determined in advance, thereby preventing injury to
others and long and protracted litigation. The right of
an appropriator of water, to change the point of diversion
thereof, has always been recognized by the courts in the
arid States, but such right is universally denied where
such change will be detrimental to the rights of other appropriators, whether subsequent or prior to the right of
the party desiring the change.

If it be admitted that the legislature has the right to
regulate the use and distribution of water, under its police power, such right to regulate must be held to extend
to rights in existence at the time of the attempted regulation. As said by Mr. Justice Waite, in the case of Munn
v. Illinois, 94 U. S. 113,

"It matters not in this case that these plaintiffs in error
had built their warehouse and established their business
before the regulations complained of were adopted. What
they did was from the beginning subject to the power of
the body politic to require them to conform to such regulations as might be established by the proper authorities
for the common good."

The power, exercised by the legislature in this case, as I
construe the statute, comes clearly within the police power
of the State, as defined by Judge Cooley, and quoted with
approval by a number of the courts of last resort.

"Police power, in a comprehensive sense embraces the
whole system of internal regulation by which the State
seeks not only to preserve the public order and to prevent
offenses against the State, but to establish for the intercourse of citizens with citizens those rules of good man-
ners and good neighborhood which are inculcated to prevent a conflict of rights and insure to each the uninterrupted enjoyment of his own, so far as is reasonably consistent with the like enjoyment of rights by others. State
ex rel. Star Pub. Co. v. Associated Press, 159 Mo. 410, 60
S. W. 91; Commonwealth v. Bearse, 132 Mass. 542."

A proceeding, for an orderly determination in advance, of the right of an appropriator of water to change the point of diversion thereof, certainly is calculated to, "prevent a conflict of rights" between citizens, and to insure to each the "uninterrupted enjoyment of his own, so far as it is reasonably consistent with the like enjoyment of the rights of others," and the interests of the State are involved, and its rights should be protected. Irrigation Co. v. Wayer Supply Co., 29 Colo. 469.

Statutory proceedings, similar to the provisions now under consideration, have been upheld in many of the States, and have likewise been held to apply to rights existing at the date of the passage of the act. See Weil on Water Rights in the Western States, (3rd ed.) sec. 506; New Cache la Poudre Co. v. Water Supply Co., 29 Colo., 469, 68 Pac. 781; Farmers', etc., Co. v. Gothenberg, etc., Co., 73 Neb. 223, 102 N. W. 487. Weil says, (3rd ed., sec. 507): "Under the recent water codes, the appropriator is usually required by statute to apply to the State Engineer for a permit before changing the point of diversion."

To deny to the State the power to regulate the exercise of a right to use water, where such right was acquired and perfected antecedent to the attempted regulation, would, in my opinion, be inimical to water users and detrimental to the prosperity of the State. If the legislature could not make provisions for the manner of changing the point of diversion, the existence of power in the legislature to make any regulations whatever, applicable to such old rights, must likewise be denied. It could not provide for the maintenance, as to such rights, of suitable headgates, diversion wiers, dams, measuring devices, or other appliances for the economical use and distribution of water. In fact, it could provide no regulations whatever, be they ever so essential for the protection of the rights of others or the public generally. I do not believe further argument is necessary; in fact, it appears to me so concededly within the police power of the State, as to require no argument whatever, to establish the affirmative of the proposition.

The principal contention of appellees, however, is, that a fair construction of the terms of the act shows that it speaks prospectively from the date of its passage, and was never intended to, and does not apply to water rights acquired prior to the passage of the act, or the means of enjoying the same. The act in question is remedial, and should therefore be liberally construed, so as to make it effectual against the evil which it was intended to abate, if such construction will not deprive any individual of his just rights. See Irrigation Co. v. Water Supply Co., supra, holding such a statute to be remedial, and sec. 686 (2d ed) Lewis' Sutherland Statutory Construction, as to construction of remedial statutes. And the intention of a remedial statute will always prevail over the literal sense of its terms, and, therefore, when the expression is special or particular, but the reason is general, the expression should be deemed general. Lewis' Sutherland Statutory Construction, section 687. And likewise, in construing a statute, consideration must also be given to the result which will follow such a construction, and if it be evident, that such proposed construction will lead to an absurdity, or will render the statute impotent, it is not to be presumed that the legislature intended it to have such meaning. The same author on statutory construction, quoted above, says:

"A result which will follow from one construction or another of a statute is always a potent factor and is sometimes in and of itself conclusive as to the correct solution of the question of its meaning." Sec. 487, and

"Statutes will be construed in the most beneficent way which their language will permit to prevent absurdity, hardship or injustice; to favor public convenience and to oppose all prejudice to public interests." Sec. 490, Lewis' Sutherland Stat. Cons., and again, in the same section, the author says:

"In construing an act of the general assembly, such a construction will be placed upon it as will tend to advance the beneficial purposes manifestly within the contemplation of the general assembly at the time of its passage; and courts will hesitate to place such a construction upon its terms as will lead to manifest absurd consequence, and impute to the general assembly total ignorance of the subject with which it undertook to deal."

In view of these general rules, for the construction of statutes, let us consider the act of 1907, in so far as it is involved in this proceeding, and determine from the act, the intent of the legislature and the meaning properly attributable to the language used. The act in question is comprised of 73 sections, and was intended, I believe, to constitute a complete code of the law of irrigation. By this act the legislature of the Territory attempted to place New Mexico in the forefront of the arid States, in securing proper State control and regulation of irrigation enterprises. It is a matter of history, which I apprehend cannot be controverted, that those States which have provided for a complete system of State control of irrigation have developed and prospered most amazingly. Colorado and Wyoming may be cited among the States early to adopt such a system, and the result has been that millions of dollars have been expended in the construction of irrigation works, which has resulted in unbounded prosperity to the States. New Mexico, prior to 1905, did not attempt to provide for such control, and the result was that no outside capital came into the Territory for investment in such enterprises. True, under the old system there was more or less development done, but almost exclusively by local capital. In 1905 the Territorial legislature enacted chapter 102, "An act creating the office of Territorial Irrigation Engineer, to promote irrigation development and conserve the waters of New Mexico for the irrigation of lands and other purposes," by which it attempted, in a way, to provide for State control, but experience demonstrated that the act was not sufficiently comprehensive and modern to place New Mexico abreast of her sister States, and in 1907, the act was repealed and the present comprehensive, modern and efficient code was enacted. Under the latter act millions of dollars have been expended in irrigation enterprises in New Mexico, and the resources of the State have amazingly increased. Therefore, I do not believe the Court should, unless the language of the act expressly requires, so interpret it as to undermine its foundation or impair its efficacy.

It appears to me, that the construction contended for by appellees, that "the act speaks prospectively from the date of its passage," if adopted, would place New Mexico in the anomalous situation of having a complete, modern irrigation code, with State supervision and control, applicable to all rights acquired thereunder, but such rights impaired and hampered by the lack of any supervision or control of rights theretofore acquired. Why, I would ask, is there any more reason for State regulation of a water right perfected in 1907, than there is of a right acquired by appropriation in 1906? In many instances, some of which will be enumerated later, the State has provided for the control and supervision of water rights, and the instrumentalities through which such rights are made available, but to illustrate the absurdity of the suggested construction we need only consider those sections of the act which provide for the change of the point of diversion. Granted that the claimed construction is sound, we then have a class of water users who may change their point of diversion, so far as the statute is concerned, at their own pleasure, regardless of the injury other appropriators may suffer, without let or hindrance. I say, in so far as the statute is concerned, and do not desire to be understood as asserting that they may exercise the right to the injury of others, because such would not be correct, for it has always, so far as I know, been uniformly held by the courts, that an appropriator of water may not change his point of diversion to the injury of other appropriators. Now this being true, A, an appropriator of water under rights perfected in 1906, from a stream system, might move his point of diversion up or down the stream, without regard to the act in question, while B, an appropriator under rights initiated and perfected under the act of 1907, taking his water from a stream directly opposite A's point of diversion, would be required to follow the statutory procedure. What reason or argument can be advanced in support of the reason for such a distinction by the legislature? I believe none, and the Court should not make the distinction unless compelled to do so by clear and explicit language in the act.

As I read the act, however, its language is plain and the meaning clear. Section 45 reads as follows:

"An appropriator of water may use the same for other than the purpose for which it was appropriated, or may change the place of diversion, storage, or use, in the manner and under the conditions prescribed in sections 25 and 44 of this act."

It will be noted that this language is as plain and explicit as it could well be expressed. It says that an appropriator of water may change the place of diversion in the manner and under the conditions prescribed in the sections referred to. The maxim, *"expressio unius est exclusio alterius,"* applies, and it follows that an appropriator of water has no right to change the point of diversion in any other way or manner.

"Where authority is given to do a particular thing, and the mode of doing it is prescribed, it is limited to be done in that mode; all other modes are excluded." Lewis' Sutherland Stat. Cons., section 492.

The section does not say, "an appropriator under this act," but says, "an appropriator," clearly, I think, referring to any appropriator, however or whenever his right might have been acquired. "Appropriators are diverters of the waters of a stream" (Lux v. Haggin, 69 Cal. 255), and the article "an" is equivalent to "any," (Kauffman v. Superior Court, 115 Cal. 152, 46 Pac. 904), so that the section may fairly be held to mean "any appropriator." This being true, it must be held to apply to any appropriator, whether his rights were perfected precedent or subsequent to the act of 1907, unless the meaning is changed by the sections 25 or 44 of the act. Section 25 makes provision for the correction of an original application for the appropriation of water and the amendment of the plans of ·construction, and concludes with the following proviso:

"Provided, further, that a change in the proposed point of diversion of water from a stream shall be subject to the approval of the Territorial Engineer, under the provisions of section 45 hereof, and shall not be allowed to the detriment of the rights of others having valid claims to the use of water from said stream."

Now the mere fact that this proviso is in connection with an original application under the act of 1907, can have no bearing upon the construction of section 45, because the later section only refers to section 25 for the conditions under which the change may be made, viz: Such right shall be subject to the approval of the Territorial Engineer, and shall not be allowed to the detriment of the rights of others having valid claims to the use of water from said stream.

Section 44 is as follows:

"All water used in this Territory for irrigation purposes, except as otherwise provided in this act, shall be considered appurtenant to the land upon which it is used, and the right to use the same upon said land shall never be severed from the land without the consent of the owner of the land; but by and with the consent of the owner of the land, all or any part of said right may be severed from said land, and simultaneously transferred, and become appurtenant to other land, or may be transferred for other purposes, without losing priority of right theretofore established, if such changes can be made without detriment to existing rights, on the approval of an application of the owner to the Territorial Engineer. Before the approval of such application, the applicant must give notice thereof by publication, in the form required by the Territorial Engineer, once a week for four consecutive weeks in a newspaper of general circulation in the stream system in which the tract or tracts of land may be situated."

It will be seen that this section, in so far as applicable, simply prescribed the procedure to be followed.

If the language of the sections quoted was so indefinite and uncertain as to require judicial construction, which it does not, recourse to the title of the act would remove the ambiguity or supply the omission. It is well settled, that where the meaning of the body of the act is doubtful, reference may be had to the title to remove the ambiguity or to supply an omission. 36 Cyc. 1133, and authorities stated. The title of the act in question reads as follows:

"An act to conserve and regulate the use and distribution of the waters of New Mexico, and to create the office of Territorial Engineer, to create a Board of Water Commissioners, and for other purposes."

If the claimed construction be sound, it will be seen that the title of the act does not correctly express the real intention of the law-making body, for, by such title the legislature declared that it was enacting a law "to conserve and regulate the use and distribution of the waters of New Mexico," whereas, in fact, it was only intending to conserve and regulate the unappropriated waters of the Territory. It is too elementary to require the citation of authorities, that water flowing in a natural stream is the property of the public or the State, and does not become the property of the appropriator until he has diverted it into his ditch or canal. While the appropriator, under the law prevailing in this State, has the right to divert and use such water, nevertheless, so long as it is in the natural channel, he has no claim to any specific water. Certainly the legislature recognized that all the waters of the State, flowing in the natural channels, were the property of the State, and declared that it would regulate and conserve such waters. Not a portion of such waters, but all.

Counsel for appellees cites certain sections of the act, which he claims shows that the legislature was speaking prospectively. True it is, many sections may be found which do speak prospectively, for, it would have been impossible for the legislature to provide a complete code, applicable to both old and new rights, without making some provisions for the acquiring, in the first instance, of a new right to appropriate and use water, or the determination of the rights of old appropriators. Section 12 of the act may be cited as an example. It provides that the Territorial Engineer shall have the supervision of the apportionment of water in this Territory according to the licenses issued by him and his predecessors, and the adjudication of the courts. No one will contend, I apprehend, that this section undertakes to prescribe and limit the powers of the engineer, under the act. It simply defines his power in that particular regard. It necessarily speaks prospectively, for the legislature well knew that under the former laws, in force in the Territory, many water users had old rights to the use of water, with no evidence thereof in any public office. Certainly the Engineer could not supervise the apportionment of water to such rights, without an adjudication by some tribunal, and necessarily a judicial tribunal, of the rights of the old appropriators. The act therefore provided for the determination of such questions, by the courts, and thereafter gave the Engineer supervision of the apportionment of water to all water users of a stream system. But said section 12 did not attempt to curtail any of the other powers or duties conferred upon such official by other sections of the act. The same reasoning applies to sections 13 and 14. While these sections and many others might be cited which do speak prospectively, still a number of other sections might be quoted, which show clearly that it was the intention of the legislature to provide regulations and make provisions for the enjoyment and protection of old rights as well as new. I will refer to a few.

Section 4, after providing for the appointment of a Territorial Engineer, says, "He shall have general supervision of the waters of the Territory, and of the measurement, appropriation and distribution thereof, *and such other duties as are required by this act.*"

Section 32, in part, is as follows:

"If the Territorial Engineer, shall, in the course of his duties, find that *any* works used for storage, diversion or carriage of water are unsafe and a menace to life or property, he shall at once notify the owner or agent, specifying the changes necessary and allowing a reasonable time for putting the works in safe condition."

Section 33 makes it a misdemeanor to use works for the storage, diversion or carriage of water contrary to the instructions of the Engineer, after inspection by him and notice that the same are unsafe. And such works may not be used until the Engineer gives notice that the same are safe. Now can it be claimed that these sections only apply to works constructed under the act? Section 32 says "any works," and the evident purpose is to protect life and property. Is there any more reason for protecting life and property from unsafe dams and canals, constructed under the act of 1907 than those constructed under any previous act? If the act was intended only to apply to future appropriators, then an old appropriator might continue to use a dam that was a menace to life and property without authority in any official to compel the owner to make such works safe. Clearly such was not the intention, but the Engineer was given jurisdiction over old as well as new works in this regard.

Section 37 is as follows:

"In any suit concerning water rights, or in any suit or appeal provided for in this act, the Court may in its discretion submit any question of fact arising therein to a jury, or may appoint a referee or referees to take testimony and report upon the rights of the parties."

If the act speaks only of new rights, then the Court would have no power, under the act, to submit a question of fact to a jury, if old rights were involved in the litigation.

Section 42 provides that where a party entitled to use water, fails, for the period of four years, to apply the same to beneficial use, such unused water shall revert to the public. If the act only applies to new rights, then an old appropriator might fail to beneficially use water for any number of years, and still would not forfeit his right thereto.

Section 44 makes all water appurtenant to the land,

where used for irrigation, and provides for the transfer of a water right separate and apart from the land, by following a prescribed procedure. Following out the argument contended for, an old appropriator could not sever his water right from the land and transfer it. And likewise, under section 45, supra, an old appropriator would have no authority to use the water for any other purpose than that for which it was appropriated.

The next section provides that every ditch owner shall, when requested by the Territorial Engineer, construct and maintain a substantial head-gate at the point where the water is diverted, and construct a measuring device. Now there is as much reason to require an old appropriator to maintain a substantial head-gate as a new appropriator. Such requirements were evidently intended to protect the public against damage by reason of a ditch taking too much water and breaking through banks, and also to conserve the waters.

Section 47 makes it a misdemeanor for any person to interfere with, injure or destroy any dam, head-gate, weir, bench mark or other appliance for the diversion, carriage, apportionment or measurement of water. If this section only applies to new rights, then an old appropriator would have no protection, under the statute, in this respect   Section 48 makes the unauthorized use of water, to which another person is entitled, a misdemeanor. Does it mean, a person only entitled to the use of water under the act?

Section 50 reads as follows:

· "Whenever any appropriator of water has the right-of-way for the storage, diversion, or carriage of water, it shall be unlawful to place or maintain any obstruction that shall interfrere with the use of the works, or prevent convenient access thereto. Any violations of this section shall be a misdemeanor."

Section 57 provides for the adoption of rules and regulations by water users, and clearly applies to old as well as new works, and likewise, I think, sections 63, 71 and 72 clearly were intended to apply to all water users.

It is contended, however, that by the peculiar wording

of section 59, that it is evident the act in question was
only intended to apply to certain water rights and irrigation works. The section is as follows:

"Nothing contained in this act shall be construed to
impair existing, vested rights or the rights and priorities
of any person, firm, corporation or association, who may
have commenced the construction of reservoirs, canals,
pipe-lines or other works, or who have filed affidavits, applications or notices thereof for the purpose of appropriating for beneficial use, any waters as defined in section 1
of this act, in accordance with the laws of the Territory
of New Mexico, prior to the passage of this act; Provided,
however, that all such reservoirs, canals, pipe-lines or other
works and the rights of the owners thereof shall be subject to regulation, adjudication and forfeiture for abandonment, as provided in this act."

As I read the section it does not justify such a construction. It specifically says that the act in question
shall not impair existing vested rights. Without this
declaration, the act could not have done so, but this was
inserted, in my judgment, by the legislature, because of
the fact that it had provided for the regulation of such
rights, and disclaimed any intention, in so doing, of im-
pairing any existing vested rights. But it is argued that
the proviso shows that it was not the intention to regulate
such old rights. An examination of the proviso will show
that this argument is faulty, because, if it be admitted to
be sound, then we have only regulation for such reservoirs,
canals, pipe-lines or other works, of those owners "who
may have commenced the construction of reservoirs, canals,
pipe-lines or other works, or who have filed affidavits, applications or notices thereof for the purpose of apportioning
for beneficial use, any waters as defined in section 1 of
this act, in accordance with the laws of the Territory of
New Mexico, prior to the passage of this act," and have
no regulations whatever for rights perfected at that time,
or those acquired under the act of 1907. Such, of course,
was never the intention of the law-makers, for there is no
reason whatever for the regulation of such rights to the

exclusion of all others. The legislature, in my judgment, by the terms of the act in question had provided clearly for the regulation of all rights, but in section 59, it had said that the act should not impair existing vested rights, or the rights of any person who had commenced the construction of their works, etc., and not desiring to remove such unperfected rights from the regulations provided for all other rights, as a matter of precaution inserted the proviso, so as to remove all doubts, and to bring such rights again within the operation of the statute, if perchance they had been taken out by the wording of the first part of the section.

It is also suggested that the works referred to in the section 59 are those, which, under the act of 1905, application must be made to the Territorial Engineer for a permit to construct, and that it does not refer to small community acequias. I would ask what evidence there is in the record in this case to show that the ditch in question, and the works connected with it, cost less than $2000. As I read it, I have not been able to find a word or syllable tending to make any such showing. Nor is there any proof showing the character of the proposed ditch, or the fact that it will involve no danger to life or property. Such claimed construction must be erroneous, for section 59 refers to applications, initiated by affidavit, thus clearly bringing rights initiated under both chapters of the Session Laws of 1905 within the purview of the section.

It is further suggested that the question involved in this case is no longer of practical importance, except to the immediate parties, in so far as it relates to community acequias, established and in operation prior to March 19, 1907, because by chapter 26 of the Session Laws of 1912, it is provided that no application to or permit from the State Engineer is necessary to change the point of diversion of such an acequia. The act of 1912 reads as follows:

"Section 1. That it shall not be necessary for the officers of public community acequias established and in operation prior to March 19, 1907, to make any application to, or obtain any permit from, the Territorial Engineer or the Board of Water Commissioners in order to change the place of diversion; provided, that by such change no increase in the amount of water appropriated shall be made beyond the amount to which the acequia was formerly entitled.

"Section 2. That it is necessary for the preservation of the public peace and safety of the inhabitants of the State of New Mexico, that the provisions of this act shall become effective at the earliest possible time, and therefore an emergency is hereby declared to exist, and this act shall take effect and be in full force and effect from and after its passage."

To the casual observer, it would appear that the act of 1912 was passed, because of the issues involved in this very case, for such act is applicable only to community ditches; and that the authors of the act realized that under the act of 1907 all appropriators of water were placed upon an equal footing in the matter of regulations therein provided for. If the act has any effect or influence on the present case, it must be only to clearly demonstrate that the construction for which I contend is sound, and was so recognized by the legislative branch of the government, else why the necessity for the act. Under well established rules of construction, the act of 1912 amounts to a legislative construction of the former act, and such legislative declaration of the meaning of the former act should govern the construction thereof.

"If it can be gathered from a subsequent statute *in pari materia* what meaning the legislature attached to the words of a former statute, they will amount to a legislative declaration of its meaning, and will govern the construction of the first statute. Morris v. Mellin, 6 Barn. & Cress. 454, 7 Barn. & Cress. 99; The United States v. Freeman, 3 Howard 556."

And Cyc., vol. 36, p. 1142, lays down the rule thus, "A construction of a statute by the legislature, as indicated by the language of subsequent enactments, is entitled to great weight."

In this case. in addition to the plain language of the act

of 1907, we have as a further guide the construction of the act by a subsequent legislature, in full accord with the views herein announced, and it seems to me there is no escape from the conclusion that sections 44, 45 and 25 of the act of 1907 apply to old as well as new rights, and include community acequias, as well as all others, and that these causes should be reversed.

For the reasons stated, I am compelled to dissent.

CLARENCE J. ROBERTS, C. J.

OPINION OF THE COURT ON MOTION FOR REHEARING.

PARKER, J.—The motion for rehearing is founded upon the proposition that the construction placed upon the irrigation act by this Court makes it class legislation, and renders it obnoxious to section 18 of article II of the Constitution, which has the usual guarantee of "equal protection of the laws." It would seem to require neither argument nor citation of authority for the proposition that, given a reasonable classification of subjects, "equal protection of the laws" is had, if all within any given class are treated alike. That all such classification must be based upon some reasonable distinction, is to be conceded. Counsel for appellants argues, in support of this motion for rehearing, that the classification which results from the construction of the Irrigation Act by the Court, is arbitrary and capricious, and has no reasonable basis upon which to rest. We cannot agree to the contention.

In the first place, regulation of any given business, occupation or right, should be provided for only when there is some reason or necessity for the same. Any given right of the citizen ought to be enjoyable without any supervision or restraint, unless the nature of the right, or of its exercise, is of such a character as to require the same in justice to the rest of the public. Applied to the old public community acequias, as is the case here, there seems to us to be no reason or necessity for any such regulation or restraint as is contended for by plaintiff in error. While perhaps without the field of judicial notice, it is nevertheless a matter of common knowledge that these acequias were constructed by the joint efforts of the settlers, whose lands were to be irrigated, without the aid of engineers or without head-gates of anything like a permanent character. There is no storage system in connection with them. They simply are ditches running out into a stream from which the water is taken. The bank of the stream, except at especially favored locations, is constantly subject to erosion in times of high water, and the head-gates, such as they are, must each year be renewed or replaced at points either above or below the original point of diversion as the exigencies of the situation arise. The same situation often arises several times during the irrigation season. It, therefore, becomes a necessity to warn out the people and to reconstruct the head-gates at once, or the crops for that season will perish. The situation of such public community acequias appears, therefore, to be unsuited to the regulation contended for which involves advertisement and delay for at least four weeks. The legislature is to be presumed, when it passed the act of 1907, to have examined the whole field, and to have determined that there was, by reason of the character of the appropriations and diversions of water for irrigation theretofore made, no reason for regulation or supervision of the means of diverting and carrying of such water. A singular fact in this connection appears. An examination of the records of the State Engineer's office discloses the fact that not a single permit has been granted by him to a public community acequia to appropriate water since the passage of the act of 1907, from which we infer that the legislature correctly determined, when it passed the act, that the whole field suitable to the assertion of such rights as those in this case, had been covered, and that in the future, waters for irrigation were to be stored in large volumes, conducted over large areas, under one system, and, therefore, that supervision and control of such operations was desirable and necessary in behalf of the public welfare, health and safety. There was reason, therefore, for the classification made.

The act in terms applies only to such rights as have been initiated but not perfected, and to the rights which might be initiated and perfected thereunder. It does not apply in terms to perfected rights.

Assuming that under section 24 of the act, public community acequias, as well as all other appropriators, must now apply to the State Engineer for a permit to make an appropriation of water, and must submit to the regulation imposed by the act, if, at some future time, a public community acequia shall have applied to the State Engineer for a permit to appropriate water, and shall have obtained the same, and shall thereupon object to. the regulation feature of the act, the question then may arise as to whether the classification, by the act, of prior appropriators into one class, and subsequent · appropriators into the other class, is capricious and discriminatory. Until such a contingency, the question is not before us for determination. The denial of equal rights or the imposition of unequal burdens can be pleaded only by those who show that they belonged to the class discriminated against. 8 Cyc. 791; Cooley's Const. Lim. (7th ed.)̓ 232; Kansas City and Union Pac. R. Co., 59 Kan. 427, 53 Pac. 468, 52 L. R. A. 321; State v. Currens, 111 Wis. 431, 87 N. W. 561, 56 L. R. A. 252; Brown v. Ohio Valley R. Co., 79 Fed. 176.

To this class, if the act is indeed discriminatory, the plaintiffs in error in this case do not belong.

Whether a new appropriator who initiates a right, under the act, could ever question its constitutionality. as construed, is not before us for decision, and we do not decide the same, but it would seem to be doubtful if a person who accepts the benefit of a State could, under any circumstances, be heard to complain of its unconstitutionality. See Cooley's Const. Lim. (7th ed.) 554; Ferguson v. Landram, 5 Bush 230, 96 A. D. 350; Moore v. Napier, 42 S. E. 997; Motz v. Detroit, 18 Mich. 495; Dewhurst v. Alleghany, 95 Pa. St. 437; Andrus v. Board of Police, 6 So. 603; Dodd v. Thomas, 69 Mo. 364; Ralston v. Oursler, 12 O. St. 105; State v. Mitchell, 31 O. St. 592, 610.

It is to be said in this connection, that coounsel do not present the alleged unconstitutionality of the act, as construed by us, as directly available to plaintiffs in error, but it is presented more by way of argument against the construction adopted by us.

We fully appreciate the force of the argument, and fully realize the duty of the Court to so construe an act as to make it constitutional, rather than otherwise. But even assuming, but not admitting, that our construction does render the act open to objection of this kind, the terms of the act, as we read them, preclude us from departing from the construction heretofore adopted.

Strength is added to the argument in support of our construction of the act, by reference to some other section not alluded to in the opinion. Section 57 provides that all rules and customs of water users from a "common canal, lateral or irrigation system" shall remain undisturbed by the act, "but, nothing in this section shall be taken to impair the authority of the Territorial Engineer and water master to regulate the distribution of water from the various stream systems of the Territory to the ditches and irrigation systems entitled to water therefrom, under the provisions of this act." Section 58 provides that no water master shall be appointed under this act until the prior rights to the use of water have been determined in one or more stream systems in this Territory, under the provisions of the act. Sec. 12 of the act gives supervisory control over the apportionment of water "according to the licenses issued by him or his predecessors and *the adjudications of the courts.*"

These three sections would seem to provide that when adjudication has been had, under the provisions of the act, of priorities of water rights, and when a water master has been duly appointed for any given water district, then, and not before, does the State Engineer acquire jurisdiction to regulate the distribution of water to the various ditches and irrigation systems, both old and new, in said

water district. After adjudication, old rights would seem
to be subjected to the regulation and control by the State
Engineer, and the power to regulate the distribution of
water to any given irrigation system, would seem to include the power to regulate the point and means of diversion. After adjudication, old rights would seem, by the
terms of the act, to come into the same general class with
new rights initiated and perfected under the terms of the
act, at least so far as the regulation feature is concerned.

The wisdom of postponing the jurisdiction of the State
Engineer until after adjudication of the priorities, is at
once apparent. Without adjudication, there is no evidence
before the State Engineer, except such as he may gather
ex-parte in his investigations of the various stream systems, upon which to base his action as to the rights and
priorities of water right owners who acquired their rights
prior to the passage of the act. As to all rights initiated
under the provisions of the act, he has in his office evidence, complete and satisfactory, as to the relative rights
of all of the water right owners in that class. And after
all, the only reason for supervision of the point of diversion, except when large storage or diversion, or both, might
endanger life or property, is to prevent the encroachment
of one right upon another. If these rights have not been
determined, there is no basis for the exercise of the supervisory power.

The only other section of the act which might be construed to militate against the conclusion reached by the
Court, is section 46, which provides that every ditch owner
is required, when requested so to do by the State Engineer,
to construct and maintain a substantial head-gate at a
point where the water is diverted, and a measuring device,
of a design approved by the State Engineer, at some practicable point for measuring and apportioning the water,
as determined by the State Engineer. At first glance,
this section might seem to authorize the State Engineer
to require head-gates and measuring devices for the distribution of waters in all cases. But, as we have heretofore seen, the power to apportion and distribute waters as

between old and new water right owner, arises only after adjudication of their respective priorities, and hence has no application to old water rights, at least so far as the distribution of water is concerned, until such adjudication is had. It may be that under this section, the State Engineer has the power to compel the installation of headgates and measuring devices in all ditches in the State, for the purpose of determining the amount of water flowing in such ditches, and thus gather valuable data for future use in his office, or in the courts. But for the purpose of apportionment of water, as before seen, he has no jurisdiction over any old ditch system, until the rights and priorities of the owners of such system have been adjudicated in accordance with the terms of the act.

For the reasons stated, the motion for rehearing will be denied.

Roberts, C. J., dissents.

[No. 1581, December 17, 1913.]

ROSWELL NURSERY COMPANY, Appellee, v. FRED MIELENZ, Appellant.

SYLLABUS (BY THE COURT)

1. An abstract question, disconnected with the granting of relief in a case, and the determination of which would not affect the result, becomes an academic question which this Court will not consider.

P. 422

2. In the case of a breach of an executory contract for the sale of goods, by vendee before title has passed the vendor, as a general rule, cannot recover on the contract price, but his right is limited to an action for damages .

P. 422

3. Where an executory contract provides for the manufacture of an article after a particular pattern or style, so that

it would be useless, or practically useless, to anyone except the person for whom made, or in the case of trees prepared for planting, upon breach by the vendee before delivery, the measure of damages is the whole contract price.

P. 422

Appeal from the District Court of Chaves County; John T. McClure, District Judge; affirmed.

H. M. D.ow, Roswell, N. M.; R. C. Dow, Roswell, N. M., for appellant.

In case of the breach of an executory contract for the sale of goods, the seller cannot recover on the contract price but his right is limited to an action for damages. Acme Food Co. v. Older, 17 L. R. A. (N. S.) 807, et seq. and note; John Deere Plow Co. v. Gorman, 59 Pac. 177; American Hide & Leather Co. v. Chalkley, 44 S. E. 705; McCormick Harvesting Mach. Co. v. Balfney, 81 N. W. 10; Stewart v. Scott, 15 S. W. 463.

R. D. Bowers, Roswell, N. M., for appellee.

The findings of fact made by a court under section 2999, C. L. 1897, must be the same as, and take the place of the "special findings" of a jury as provided in section 2993, C. L. 1897. Lynch v. Grayson, 5 N. M. 487, 25 Pac. 992.

Findings of fact must be in writing. Know v. Trafalet, 94 Ind. 348; Conner v. Marion, 112 Ind. 517; May v. Cavender, 29 S. Car. 598, 7 S. E. 489; McGray v. Humes, 116 Ind. 103; Monroe v. Frenchtown, 98 Mich. 431; Rogers v. Bonnet, 2 Okla. 553; Williams v. Stevens Co., 72 Wis. 487; 2 Cyc. 1037.

Findings of fact must be filed with the clerk. Lloyd v. McWilliams, 137 U. S. 576; Blumenthal v. Asay, 3 Utah 507; Swanstrom v. Marvin, 38 Minn. 359; McCrady v. Jones, 36 S. Car. 136; 2 Cyc. 1037.

For only by being in writing, signed by the judge and

filed with the clerk, do they become a part of the record. Graham v. Bayne, 18 How. (U. S.) 60; 15 L. Ed. 265; Maverick v. Burnly, 30 S. W. 566; Taylor v. Keeler, 51 Conn. 399; Jones v. Block, 30 Cal. 227; Seibert v. Minn. R. Co., 58 Minn. 72.

Findings of fact must be of the ultimate facts. Powers v. U. S., 119 Fed. 562, 56 C. C. A. 128; Campbell v. Campbell, 16 N. Y. Supp. 165; Steele v. Matteson, 50 Mich. 313, 15 S. W. 488; Pearce v. Burns, 22 Mo. 577; U. .S v. Pugh, 99 U. S. 265, 25 L. Ed. 322; Singer Co. v. Stephens, 169 Mo. 1, 68 S. W. 903; Norris v. Jackson, 9 Wall. (U. S.) 127.

A general finding for the plaintiff is a finding that every fact necessary to a recovery by him has been proved. Knaggs v. Mastin, 9 Kans. 532; Early v. Hamilton, 75 Ind. 276; Castner v. Richardson, 18 Colo. 496; Blanc v. Paymaster Co., 95 Cal. 524; Stewart v. Sprott, 37 S. Car. 605; Kehoe v. Burns, 84 Wis. 372.

Conclusion of the trial court will not be disturbed on appeal unless clearly against the weight of the evidence. Eagle Min. Co. v. Hamilton, 14 N. M. 271, 94 Pac. 949.

The plaintiff had separated the defendant's trees from all others and set them apart as the defendant's property. Benjamin, Sales, 6th ed., p. 298, et seq.; Mechem, Sales, 721, et seq.

STATEMENT OF FACTS.

The plaintiff in the District Court obtained a judgment against the appellant for $119.25, being the contract price of certain trees ordered by appellant on February 29, 1912, for delivery in the Spring of that year, which order, in part, defendant attempted to countermand, before delivery had been made, by a letter dated March 20, 1912, wherein he said, "have been trying hard to get around to the tree planting; hard luck seems to be hitting our work all the way through; just won't be able to put in the one ten-acre block; had to build a terraplane; too much salt grass in it; and couldn't get enough dirt, so it won't work, Consequently would like to cancel that part of the order. Think will be able to get at the other ten-acre block next week." A few days later, i. e., March 26th, defendant again wrote as follows:

"Friend Johnson:—

"Your letter received regarding trees. What I want is to be relieved of the order for the 10 acres, as just can't get the water there to put them in; as to healing them in, wouldn't think of that for one minute; nor would I haul water. Taking this order over as I did, and what have done for your here, seems as if you ought to be able to reciprocate since am up against it.

"Would also like to know about the cottonwoods, as if I get in the 10 acres, will want cottonwoods around them, even if real late I believe; seems as if they ought to do well if set out as late as April 15; would want the mountain cotton-wood only. Let me know about your experience in setting them out that late. It will cramp me to get out the 10 acres by that time, but believe the apples are all right that late; if we can get together, would want the trees for the 10 acres at once, and will heal them in here; that ought to set them back a little, and believe by time have ground in shape and water on it, that they will do good.   "Yours truly,
                                          "Fred Mielenz."

Plaintiff's uncontradicted testimony is that upon the receipt of the first of these letters he had the trees in the healing ground ready for shipment. That 170 trees, included in the order, he had purchased from another nurseryman, having grown the rest himself, and that the trees were a total loss if he didn't deliver them.

The shipment was made on the 3rd or 4th of April, and was rejected by defendant and after remaining in the depot, at point of delivery, for two or three months, was burned by the railroad company.

At the conclusion of the trial, the Court announced that he would find for the plaintiff. Whereupon counsel for defendant made oral request for certain findings relative to which the transcript reads as follows:—

"Finding of fact requested by the defendant: Mr. H.
M. Dow. 1. Did Mr. Johnson as agent of the Roswell
Nursery Company in this case have notice or receive notice prior to the shipment of the trees in question that the
defendant didn't wish to carry out his order? 2. Prior to
the shipment in question did Mr. Johnson as agent of the
Roswell-Nursery Company regard Mr. Mielenz as having
countermanded his order?

"The Court: I will give you the first finding of fact.
Now the second finding of fact, did this man regard Mr.
Mielenz as having countermanded the order, his position
was, he had no right to countermand it. I find the fact
that this man notified him he didn't want the trees prior
to the shipment. Answer to first finding, Yes.

"Mr. H. M. Dow: I will ask for another finding to
make it more specific: Did Mr. Johnson have notice from
the defendant prior to the shipment of the trees that the
defendant didn't want the trees that he had ordered?

"The Court: I will say yes to that."

OPINION OF THE COURT.

HANNA, J.—The first question presented for our consideration is that the judgment is contrary to the findings
of fact. In this connection appellee urges that the so-
called findings of fact are not the findings of fact contemplated by sec. 2999 of the Compiled Laws of 1897, because not in writing, or requested in writing, or signed
by the judge and filed with the clerk.

In view of our conclusion in this case that the findings
of fact are not contrary to the judgment rendered for reasons that will appear in this opinion, the contention of
appellee becomes an abstract question, disconnected with
the granting of relief in this case, and the determination
of which would not affect the result arrived at. 2 Cyc.
533.

The appellant asserts that the judgment is contrary to
the findings.

Our view being that the order in question could not be

countermanded, as an abstract proposition of law, for
1 which reason the objection of appellant fails and our
opinion upon the subject of appellee's contention with
respect to the findings becomes purely an academic question which we decline to pass upon.

A careful examination of the record discloses that the
trial court proceeded upon the theory that the order, upon
which the contract involved in this case was based, could
not be countermanded under the circumstances of the case.
Such properly considered to be contrary to the judgment
rendered in the case.

The correctness of the view of the trial court will be
considered under the next proposition for consideration,
viz: that the judgment is contrary to law, because the
order sued on had been countermanded before plaintiff
had done everything required by the contract.

We cannot see that there had been a revoking of the
order previously given, though there was an expressed
desire to avoid responsibility for half the order. It, also,
appears that before defendant attempted a partial countermand of his order, he had been advised by plaintiff in a
letter, dated March 13, 1912, that the trees were ready for
shipment, having been placed in the healing ground.

The appellant contends that in the case of a breach of
an executory contract for the sale of goods, before de-
2 livery, the seller cannot recover on the contract price,
but his right is limited to an action for damages.

We do not disagree with appellant's contention in this
respect and that the principle is supported by the great
weight of authority is clear, (see authorities collected in
case note to Acme Food Co. v. Older, 17 L. R. A., N. S.
808), but the principle, like so many others, is not
3 without exception. We find that the principle in question has no application to a case where one has contracted to manufacture articles upon order according to
specifications to be designated, and had purchased all the
necessary material and parts, but had not assembled the
same. Gardner v. Deeds & Hirsigg, 4 L. R. A. (N. S.)
740.

The necessity and reason for the exception to the principle, admitted to be controlling in the case of executory contracts generally, is well stated in an editorial note to the case last cited, in the following language:

"And the general rule can have no application, unless it appears that, upon breach by the vendee, the vendor could have placed the commodity on the market, and, by thus disposing of it, have relieved himself from the consequences of the vendee's default. If the article manufactured is made after a particular pattern or style, so that it would be useless, or practically useless, to anyone except the person for whom made, it would seem as if the vendor should be entitled to recover the whole contract price."

The reasoning of this editorial note is peculiarly applicable to the present case. The defendant had received an order for certain fruit trees one and two years old, and before the desire of plaintiff to change or modify his order was received, had ordered a part of the trees from another nurseryman, and had dug up other trees from his own nursery, cutting the same back and putting them in the healing ground ready for shipment.

It also appears that undisputed testimony, to the effect that inability to deliver the trees would result in their total loss, was introduced. Under such circumstances, we do not think the general principle should apply, but on the other hand, that the case falls more fairly within the exception generally invoked in the case of manufactured articles.

Finding no error in the record, the judgment of the District Court is affirmed.

[No. 1603, December 17, 1913.]

J. S. EDWARDS et al., Plaintiffs; THE CLOVIS NA-
TIONAL BANK, Appellees, v. J. S. FITZHUGH,
Defendant, Appellant.

SYLLABUS (BY THE COURT)

1. A's property was sold under foreclosure judgment, to
satisfy the mortgages of B Senior and C Junior mortgages;
C at the sale bid in the property for the sum of the mortgage
debts, interest, and costs as shown by the judgment. After
the sale B discovered that he had been overpaid. Such overpayment was caused by an erroneous calculation of interest.
B paid the excess into court. Held that as long as the judgment remained in force, the sum paid by B into court is not
a surplus of the foreclosure sale, remaining after the mortgage debts were satisfied, and as such the property of A as
mortgagor and owner of the equity of redemption.

P. 426

2. Where the appellant has no interest in a sum of
money, an assignment of error that the trial court erred in
its disposition of such sum, will not be considered on appeal.

P. 426

Appeal from the District Court of Curry County; G. A.
Richardson, District Judge; affirmed.

HARRY L. PATTON; H. D. TERRELL, Clovis, N. M, for
appellant.

The doctrine of caveat emptor applies. Hord's Admrs.
v. Colbert, 28 Gratt. (Va.) 49.

The client cannot plead negligence of his attorney as
grounds for relief. Williams v. Jones, (N. M.) 85 Pac.
399; 3 A. & E. Enc., 2d ed., 324; Putnam v. Day, 22
Wall. 64; Terry v. Commercial Bank, 92 U. S. 454; 24
Cyc. 42; Reed v. Dyer, 83 Va. 275; Long v. Weller's Estate, 29 Gratt. 347.

Relief will not be granted where the surprise or mistake

was due to the parties' own negligence, or could have been prevented by the exercise of ordinary prudence. 27 Cyc. 1714; Parkhurst v. Cory, 11 N. J. Eq. 233; Houseman v. Wright, 50 N. Y. App. Div. 606.

A bidder who was not a party to the action would be entitled to no relief under allegations such as are contained in appellee's motion, and appellee, by becoming a bidder at the sale, assumes a like position. Hord's Admrs. v. Colbert, 28 Gratt. 49; Gregory v. Peoples, 80 Va. 355.

A. W. HOCKENHULL, Clovis, N. M., for appellees.

Reply brief for appellant:
Counsel fails to cite in full the general rule as to payment of surplus. 27 Cyc. 1767.

Questions raised for the first time on appeal will not be considered by the appellate court. Romero v. Coleman, 11 N. M. 533; Chaves v. Myers, 11 N. M. 333.

A party cannot plead the negligence of his attorney as grounds for relief. Williams v. Jones, 85 Pac. (N. M.) 399.

STATEMENT OF FACTS.

In this action, the appellant Fitzhugh, had been sued on two mortgages, of which one Brickey was the senior and the Clovis National Bank the junior mortgagee. Judgment was confessed by Fitzhugh and a sale of the property conveyed by the two mortgages was ordered and made. The Clovis National Bank became the purchaser at the sale, bidding what appeared by the judgment the total of the two mortgage debts, interest, costs and attorney fees. The Bank paid Brickey the amount due him as appeared from the judgment. After being paid Brickey discovered he had been overpaid in the sum of $772.78, the mistake being due to an erroneous calculation of interest. Being willing to refund what did not belong to him, but in a manner that would not expose him to any liability, he asked to be permitted to pay the sum into court. The Clovis National Bank then filed its motion to re-open the case, set aside and correct Brickey's judg ment, correct its bid and if necessary order a resale of the property and order the sum in court paid to it. Fitzhugh opposed this motion, claiming the fund. Upon hearing . the court found that the Bank was entitled to the money, ordered the sum paid into court and held for the further order of the court. Fitzhugh appeals.

OPINION OF THE COURT.

MECHEM, D. J.—The appellant's claim to the fund is put upon one ground, viz: that it is a surplus, of **1** the foreclosure sale remaining after the satisfaction of the mortgagedebts, and as such belongs to him as mortgagor and owner of the equity of redemption.

Although the appellee asked that the judgment be set aside and corrected, this was not done and the judgment remains in full force and effect. The judgment is con- clusive as to the amount of the mortgage debts. As far as the record shows, the property was sold for less than the amount of the mortgage debts, interest, attorney's fees and costs. Therefore there is no surplus. Such being the foundation of appellant's claim to the fund in· contro- versy, the court did not err in denying it.

As the appellant has no right to the fund, he is not **2** interested in its disposal and for that reason the as- signment of error to the finding of the court that the appellee is entitled to the fund, is not considered.

The judgment of the lower court is affirmed.

[No. 1618, December 17, 1913.]
STATE OF NEW MEXICO, Relator, v. OWEN N. MARRON, State Treasurer, Respondent.

SYLLABUS (BY THE COURT)

1. The deposit of the Permanent School Fund of the State in interest-bearing deposits in banks, under the provisions of Joint Resolution No. 14, Laws of 1913, is an investment of the same.

2.   Whether the word "securities" as used in the enabling
act and the Constitution is not limited to public obligations
for the payment of which the taxing power is available, is
not decided because its decision is not necessary to a determination of this case, and is not discussed by counsel.

P. 439

3.   Said Joint Resolution No. 14, insofar as it requires the
deposit of these funds in banks, is beyond legislative power
and void.

P. 440

4.   The Governor, Secretary of State and Attorney General
have power to eliminate by means of disapproval any given
form or forms of investment, and thereby bring the State
Treasurer to one single form of investment, and in such
event, he is subject to mandamus to perform all acts necessary to accomplish the same.   Whether he does not possess
discretion, as to the safety of the investment, which he may
exercise independent of control by mandamus, not decided,
because not involved.

P. 441

5.   The alternative writ of mandamus in this case examined, and found to be inadequate to justify the issuance of a
peremptory writ.

P. 443

ORIGINAL IN THE SUPREME COURT.
MANDAMUS.   DENIED.

FRANK W. CLANCY, Attorney General, for state.

Brief of Respondent resisting application for peremptory mandamus.

FRANCIS E. WOOD, Albuquerque, N. M., for respondent.

If the investment of school monies by the State Treas-

urer requires the exercise of any discretion or judgment
on the part of the respondent mandamus will not lie.
Goodrich v. Guthrie, 58 U. S. 284; U. S. v. Seaman, 58
U. S. 225; Regents, etc., v. Vaughn, 12 N. M. 333; United
States v. Black, 128 U. S. 40.

Duty was upon the State Treasurer to seek safe inter
est-bearing securities in which to invest the school funds.
The power of the Governor, Secretary of State, and Attorney General is only to approve or disapprove proposed
investments. Laws 1907, ch. 104, sec. 36; Const. N. M.
art. XXII, sec. 6, 7; C. L. 1897, sec. 225; Enabling Act.
sec. 9, 10; Const., art. XXI, sec. 9; Const., art. XII, sec.
2, 7.

The act of the State Treasurer in retaining and depositing these funds at interest in banks, pending more profitable investment, is in strict compliance with his legal duty.
Laws 1907, ch. 104; art. XXII, secs. 6, 7, Const. of N.
M.; Joint Resolution No. 14, 1913; Const., art. VIII,
sec. 10.

OPINION OF THE COURT.

PARKER, J.—This is a proceeding in mandamus to
compel the investment of the Permanent School Funds of
the State in the State Highway Bonds.

It appears that respondent, as State Treasurer, received
from the Territorial Treasurer, at the inception of the
State government, the sum of $110,453.52, the result of
the sales of public lands of the United States in the Territory, under the terms of the Act of Congress of June
21, 1898, 30 Stat. L. 484, 6 Fed. Stat. Ann. 482. These
funds, at the time respondent took office, were deposited
in banks, in pursuance to the provisions of sec. 36 of chapter 104, laws of 1907, where they still remain. Since
Statehood, respondent has received funds of the same
class and from the same source in the amount of $10,-
587.31 and $3,825.86 as proceeds of the sale of school
lands in the State. All of these funds constitute the Permanent School Funds of the State.

Chapter 104, laws of 1907, was repealed by section 79

of chapter 82 of the laws of 1907, leaving no statutory
authority for the deposit of these funds in banks, until the
session of the State legislature of 1913.

By section 10 of the enabling act, 36 Stat. L. 557, 1
Sup. 1912, Fed Stat. Ann. 357, it was provided as follows:
"Sec. 10.   That it is hereby declared that all lands
hereby granted, including those which, havaing been heretofore granted to the said Territory, are hereby expressly
transferred and confirmed to the said State, shall be by
the said State held in trust, to be disposed of in whole or
in part only in manner as herein provided and for the
several objects specified in the respective granting and
confirmatory provisions, and that the natural products and
money proceeds of any of said lands shall be subject to the
same trusts as the lands producing the same." * * * * *
"A separate fund shall be established for each of the
several objects for which the said grants are hereby made
or confirmed, and whenever any moneys shall be in any
manner derived from any of said land the same shall be
deposited by the State Treasurer in the fund corresponding to the grant under which the particular land producing such moneys were (sic) by this act conveyed or confirmed.   The State Treasurer shall keep all such moneys
invested in safe interest-bearing securities, which securities shall be approved by the Governor and Secretary of
State of said proposed State, and shall at all times be
under a good and sufficient bond or bonds conditioned for
the faithful performance of his duties in regard thereto
as defined by this act and the laws of the State not in
conflict herewith."

By section 7 of article XII of the Constitution of the
State, it was provided as follows:—
"Sec. 7.   The principal of the permanent school fund
shall be invested in the bonds of the State or Territory
of New Mexico, or of any county, city, town, board of
education or school district therein.   The legislature may
by three-fourths vote of the members elected to each house
provide that said funds may be invested in other interest-
bearing securities.   All bonds or other securities in which

any portion of the school fund shall be invested must be first approved by the governor, attorney general and secretary of state. All losses from such funds, however occurring, shall be reimbursed by the state."

In pursuance of the provisions of this section of the Constitution, the State legislature of 1913, (by a required three-fourths vote of each house, it is assumed by counsel on both sides), passed Joint Resolution No. 14, which is as follows:

"Section 1. That the principal of the permanent school fund may be invested in an interest-paying deposit in any bank or banks in this state, in the manner hereinafter provided.

"Sec. 2. It is hereby made the duty of the Governor, State Treasurer, Attorney General and Secretary of State, to ascertain which bank or banks in the State will pay the highest rate of interest for the deposit of the said permanent school fund and deposit the same therein upon said bank or banks giving a bond as hereinafter required.

"Sec. 3. Before the making of the deposit of the said permanent school fund in any bank or banks applying therefor, the said bank or banks shall make, execute and deliver a bond to the State of New Mexico in a penalty which shall not be less than one and one-fourth the amount of the deposit applied for and which it is to receive, conditioned that such bank will promptly pay out to, the parties entitled thereto, all such public monies in its hands upon lawful demand made therefor and will whenever thereunto required by law, pay over to the State Treasurer such monies. The surety on such bond shall be a surety company authorized to do business under the laws of the State and such bond shall be approved as to form by the Attorney General, and as to the sufficiency by the Governor, State Treasurer and Secretary of State."

In pursuance of said joint resolution No. 14, the Governor, Secretary of State, Attorney General and State Treasurer, met on June 16, 1913, and decided to request bids from banks for the deposit of the entire Permanent

School Fund, amounting to $121,040.78, and accordingly the State Treasurer requested bids for the deposit of the same from the banks of the State, to be received up to July 1, 1913. Many of the banks responded, and offered to pay interest at rates ranging from three and one-half per cent to seven and five-eighths per cent per annum.

At a meeting of said officers, held on July 1, 1913, for the purpose of opening and passing on said bids, the following resolution was adopted, the respondent, as said Treasurer, voting in the negative, viz:

"RESOLVED, That all of the bids received from the various banks for deposits of the Permanent School Fund be rejected for the purpose of investing said funds in the State Highway Bonds, the difference in the rate of interest received, which would be about four cents per annum per capita of school children as shown by the last enrollment, being so small as to be more than offset by the benefits to be derived from the construction of highways to the schools themselves as well as to all other interests."

On July 7, 1913, the respondent addressed a letter to the Governor, Secretary of State and Attorney General, which is as follows:—

"Dear Sir:

"I am firmly of the conviction that the investment of the Permanent School Fund of the State in the securities offered under House Joint Resolution No. 14, by the banks offering the highest rate of interest in the bids opened on Tuesday last, the first of July, is the best and safest investment that could be made of these funds.

"In the resolution rejecting these bids, which is as follows, (the preceding resolution) you do not base your disapproval of these securities upon the ground that they are not safe nor that they would not bring the largest returns to the Permanent School Fund, but solely upon the ground that it was for the purpose of investing these funds in the Highway Bonds.

"I deem it to be my duty, under the law, to most respectfully decline to invest these funds in the Highway Bonds for the reason that the Highway Bonds yield only

4%, while the bank securities offered will average more than 6% and for the further reason that the value of the Highway Bonds, measured by the best bids obtained therefor, is only 77, while we would be required to pay par or 100.

"I respectfully request, therefore, that you indicate to me whether or not you deem these bank securities offered to be unsafe. In the event that you approve the same as to their safety, I will make the investment in the proper bank securities.

"Yours very truly,"

On July 10, 1913, the Governor, Secretary of State and Attorney General addressed to the respondent a letter, in reply to his letter of July 7, as follows:—

"We decline to pass upon the question as to whether the bank securities are unsafe or not, as it is no part of our duty to do so, nor have you any right to demand of us that we should pass on that question, especially after we have united in rejecting the bids of the banks for the avowed purpose of investing the funds in the State Highway Bonds.

"We cannot find any provision of law giving you any authority to make any investment of this fund except as directed by us, nor are you in any way charged with any responsibility as to such investment. No investment of the fund can be made in any securities unless they are first approved by the Governor, Secretary of State and Attorney General, and if there should be any resulting losses from such investment the State must reimburse them, but there is nothing to make you officially or personally liable for what is done.

"Therefore, we now say to you that, under existing circumstances, we approve of the investment of this fund in the State Highway Bonds, and that we will not approve of its investment in any other securities at this time."

The State Treasurer, still persisting in his refusal to withdraw these funds from the bank and invest them in the State Highway Bonds, this proceeding was instituted by the Attorney General, ex-officio, in behalf of the State.

It is to be. observed that the enabling act imposes
no restrictions, in terms, as to the class of interest-bearing securities in which the funds may be invested, the only
restriction in this regard being that they be "safe." The
supervising control over the investment, conferred upon
the Governor, and Secretary of State by that act, however, would seem to vest in them power to exclude any given
class of securities which might, in their judgment, be
deemed unsafe. On the other hand, the Constitution expressly limits, in terms, the class of securities in which
these funds may be invested, until the legislature shall
otherwise provide. The supervising body is enlarged by
the addition of the Attorney General. Otherwise the enabling act and the Constitution are the same in substance
and effect, except that, by the Constitution, the Treasurer
is not, in terms, charged with the duty of investing the
funds. This latter divergence we deem of no importance,
as it would seem clear in the light of both provisions, that
it is still the duty of the State Treasurer to invest the
funds in interest-bearing securities, subject to the restrictions and the supervision and control provided for in the
Constitution. As before stated, the legislature of 1913,
by said joint resolution No. 14, attempted to pursue the
power conferred by the constitutional provision and provided that these funds should be "invested in an interest-
bearing deposit in any bank or banks in this State," in
the manner in the resolution provided. The deposit,
when made, is not for any definite period of time, but is
"conditioned that such bank will promptly pay out to the
parties entitled thereto, all such public moneys in its hands
upon lawful demand made therefor, and will whenever
thereunto required by law pay over to the State Treasurer
such moneys." It thus appears that, by the terms of the
resolution, these funds are always subject to the immediate call of the State Treasurer and the bank makes no
contract to retain them and may at any time, we assume,
surrender them to him. The funds are subject to the
check of the State Treasurer at any time in favor of any
person entitled to receive the same by reason of some in-

vestment thereof, or the State Treasurer may at any time
recall the funds from any given bank or banks. The words
"required by law," in this connection, must evidently mean
that whenever, by reason of demand of the State Treasurer, the legal duty to return the funds arises, the bank or
banks are "required by law" to return the same. Otherwise, if it be required to have a new act of legislation before the banks can be held to be "required by law" to return the moneys, then, when the State Treasurer has once
deposited them in a bank, they must remain there until
the legislature recalls them, regardless of the solvency or
insolvency of the bank and the consequent danger of loss
of the funds and vexatious litigation with the sureties on
the bank's bonds. Such could not have been the legislative intent as expressed in the joint resolution. The State
Treasurer must be held to have at all times the right to
immediately call for the funds, either for the purpose of
investing them in interest-bearing securities. or of re-
calling them from any bank in which, for any reason satisfactory to him, or for no reason, he no longer desires the
deposit to remain.

We have, then, a case where the enabling act and the
Constitution require the investment of the Permanent
School Fund of the State in interest-bearing securities,
and where the legislature has authorized and required the
deposit of these funds in banks subject to the call of the
State Treasurer, and the question is. whether this is an
investment of the funds within the meaning of the provisions of the enabling act and the Constitution.

Various cases are reported in which the question as to
what amounts to an investment of public and private
funds has arisen. In State v. McFetridge, 54 N. W. 1, 84
Wis. 473, 20 L. R. A. 223, the State Treasurer of Wisconsin was sued on his official bond for interest received
by him on deposits in banks of the public funds, and his
liability was made to turn upon whether his act in making the deposit was lawful or unlawful, which, in turn,
depended upon whether or not the deposit was an investment of the funds. If it was an investment of the funds

it was unlawful, because the concurrence of the Governor and Commissioners of public Lands was necessary, and had not been obtained. The Court said :—

"If those deposits were 'investments' within the meaning of the above statutes, they were unlawfully made. Were they investments? The distinction between a general deposit of money in a bank, payable at any time on demand, and an investment of such money, is plain and substantial. By such a deposit the depositor does not lose control of the money, but may reclaim it at any time. True, he loses control of the specific coin or currency deposited, but not of an equal amount of coin or currency having the same qualities and value, which, as we have seen, is all that is required of him. But if the funds in the treasury are invested in United States or State bonds, or in loans on time to counties, cities, etc., the treasurer loses control thereof, and the same cannot be replaced in the treasury until such bonds are paid or sold, or such loans become due, and are collected by the due course of law. The retention by the treasurer of substantial control over the funds in the one case, and his loss of such control in the other, mark the leading distinction between a mere deposit of the funds and an 'investment' thereof, as those terms are used in statutes."

In State v. Barclay, 58 N. W. 172, 39 Neb. 353, 23 L. R. A. 67, a different definition was given to the word. The Constitution of that State required the investment of the Permanent School Fund in the United States, or State, securities, or registered county bonds, and the legislature provided that all public funds should be deposited in banks which should pay interest and give security for the safety of the funds, and hold the funds subject to check by the State Treasurer. Mandamus was brought to compel the deposit of some of these funds in a bank, and it was held that in-so-far as the act authorized or required the deposit of the educational funds, it provided for an "investment" of the same in a manner not authorized by the Constitution, and was, therefore, invalid. The Court defined the word "investment" as including bank deposits, notwithstanding they are subject to immediate withdrawal.

As applied to private funds, the word "investment" has been frequently defined. Thus in Law's Estate, 144 Pa. St. 499, 14 L. R. A. 103, a guardian had deposited funds of his ward in a bank awaiting investment. The bank was to pay three per cent interest, and he was to give two weeks' notice before withdrawing the funds. The bank failed and the guardian was sought to be charged with the loss, on the theory that he had invested the moneys and was, consequently, liable. The Court said:

"Was this transaction with the Bank of America a deposit of the money, or was it a loan or investment of it? A deposit is where a sum of money is left with a banker for safekeeping subject to order, and payable, not in the specific money deposited, but in an equal sum. It may or may not bear interest, according to the agreement. While the relation between the depositor and his banker is that of debtor and creditor simply, the transaction cannot in any proper sense be regarded as a loan, unless the money is left, not for safe-keeping, but for a fixed period at interest, in which case the transaction assumes all the characteristics of a loan."

In Jennings v. Davis, 31 Conn. 134, 143, it is said:—

"It is not stated whether the money was deposited in the bank for safe-keeping merely, or in the character of a loan to the bank for which a stipulated rate of interest was to be paid during its continuance there; nor is is material to inquire, because, in either case, the deposit (being a general, as contradistinguished from a special one) created a debt in favor of the depositor and against the bank, and then the money became "invested" in that debt, and being thus invested in the name of Mrs. Morehouse, was protected by the statute against her husband's claims upon it." See also 4 Words and Phrases, title Investment, where many cases are collected.

The Wisconsin and Pennsylvania cases draw a distinction between deposits for a definite period of time and those which are subject to call by check or order, holding that the former would constitute an investment, and that the latter would not. The Nebraska-Connecticut cases recognize no such distinction, and rely upon the well-known principle that upon the deposit of funds in a bank, the title to the money passes to the bank, and the relation of debtor and creditor arises between the bank and the depositor. This is so whether the money is subject to call, or whether the debt of the bank to the depositor matures at some specified future time. The law applies to a transaction, in either form mentioned above, an obligation to pay its debt to the depositor according to the terms of the deposit.

We assume that had the legislature, in its joint resolution No. 14, provided for the deposit of these funds for stated periods of time, no one would question that their deposit in that form would be an investment for the same. If this is so, then the legislature might have provided for annual, or semi-annual, or quarterly, periods of time, or even a shorter period, so that the transaction of depositing these funds would be, in substance and effect, as a practical matter, the same as it now is provided for in said joint resolution. It may be that the definition of the word "investment" by the Wisconsin and Pennsylvania courts is more scientifically correct, but we can see no good reason to unduly hamper the legislative branch of the government by adopting a construction of the enabling act and the Constitution which would subserve no useful purpose. The legislature has, to all intents and purposes, accomplished by the joint resolution all that it could accomplish by a more scientifically drawn act, if, indeed, it has not added to the security and safety of these funds by providing that they may be withdrawn at any time, from any bank in which they may have been deposited.

1   We, therefore, hold that the deposit of the Permanent School Funds of the State in banks, in pursuance of provisions of said joint resolution, is an investment of the same, unless prohibited by the considerations mentioned in the next paragraph.

The Attorney General argues that the words "other

interest-bearing securities" are to be construed *ejusdem generis* with the class of securities specifically mentioned in the section of the Constitution, and that, therefore, bank deposits are prohibited as a form of investment of these funds.

The argument has great force. Taking into consideration the character of the fund provided by the Federal government for the education of the youth of the State, its permanency and ever-increasing volume, the evident care with which the donor has safeguarded the same by the terms of its grant, and the character of the investments enumerated in the Constitution, there is presented to the mind, at once, the question whether it was not the intent of both congress and the constitutional convention, by the use of the word "securities," to limit the investment of these funds to some form of obligation for the payment of which the taxing power is available. It may be said, however, that the taxing power of the State is available to reimburse the fund in case of loss for any reason. But loss of the fund is exactly what is not to be desired and every consideration, consistent with the circumstances and language used, should be indulged to avoid the possibility of the same. On the other hand, the rule of construction mentioned may not be employed unless the same is consonant with the intent of congress and the constitutional convention as expressed in the enabling act and the Constitution.

In this connection, it may be said that while the Permanent School Fund, at present, is comparatively small, it is to be borne in mind that this fund is a permanent fund for all time, and must, necessarily, constantly and rapidly increase. The proceeds from the sales of the lands so bountifully granted by the United States for educational purposes, will swell this fund so that within a comparatively short time it may reach such proportions as that it may become difficult to find in the class of securities enumerated in the Constitution a place for the profitable investment of the same. The legislature, it may be said, should be left free, if possible, to meet such condi-

tions when they arise, and for that reason, the restricted
interpretation, before mentioned, ought not to be applied.

We expressly decline to decide this proposition at this
time, and what has been said is for the purpose, merely,
of calling attention to the question, so that its import-
2   ance may be more fully appreciated. We decline to decide the question because its decision is not necessary
to a decision of this case, and because the same was not
fully treated by counsel ·in argument or in the briefs.
When, if it shall be, in some case in future, the question is
clearly presented to the Court, and fully argued, we shall
then feel that it is proper to dispose of it.

The legislature, in said joint resolution No. 14, has
·attempted to control the discretion of the Governor, Secretary of State·and Attorney General in the exercise of
their supervisory control over the investment of these
funds. The act is mandatory in terms, and requires them,
absolutely, to deposit the funds in banks. In this the leg·
islature has evidently exceeded its constitutional power.
The Constitution has conferred upon the Governor, Secretary of State and Attorney General the power to approve or disapprove any proposed investment of these
funds. This discretion is in no way limited, but is absolute. It is not confined to the question as to whether the
investment is safe or not. If for any reason, lack of safety, length or shortness of time for which the loan can be
obtained, rate of interest obtainable, or any other consideration of public policy, any given investment of these
funds is deemed inadvisable, the Governor, Secretary of
State and Attorney General clearly have the power to
withhold their approval, and we know of no authority,
neither legislative nor judicial, to control this discretion.
The grant of legislative power in the section of the Constitution is not a grant of power to direct the investment
in any particular form of security. The selection of the
investment is not a legislative function under the provisions of the Constitution.

We, therefore, hold that said joint resolution, insofar

3   as it requires the deposit of these funds in banks, is beyond the legislative power and void.

This conclusion leaves the respondent without any authority to make these deposits, the approval thereof having been expressly refused by the Governor, Secretary of
State and Attorney General.

The real, practical, controversy between the State
Treasurer on the one hand, and the Governor, Secretary of
State and Attorney General on the other, is as to who
has the right to select the securities for the investment of
these funds.   The State Treasurer, believing in the validity of the joint resolution, and being desirous of obtaining
the largest possible return in the way of income on the
money, insists upon the deposit of the funds in banks.
In his right to do so, over the objection of the Governor,
Secretary of State and Attorney General, as we have seen,
he is mistaken.   On the other hand, the Governor, Secretary of State and Attorney General, notwithstanding the
income will be slightly less, insist upon the investment in
the State Highway Bonds.   It is argued by the Attorney
General that the greater permanency of the investment in
these bonds, the direct benefit of good public highways to
the schools themselves, and the subserving of the general
welfare of the people of the State, more than counter-
balance the temporary slight loss in income.   It is argued
for the State Treasurer that, as he is charged by the enabling act with the duty of keeping the funds constantly
invested and is required to give bond for the faithful
performance of his duty, he must secure the highest possible income from these bonds consistent with safety.   On
the other hand, the Attorney General argues that there is
no liability of the State Treasurer on his bond so long as
he, in good faith, invests the funds within the constitutional restrictions, and with the approval of the Governor, Secretary of State and Attorney General.   In this
position he is correct.   It is to be observed, in this connection, that no absolute duty is imposed upon the State
Treasurer to invest these funds.   The duty of doing so is
conditioned upon his obtaining the approval of the Gov-

ernor and Secretary of State, by the enabling act, and of
the same officers, together with the Attorney General, by
the Constitution. If he endeavors to obtain this approval
and exhausts all available sources, and fails to obtain it,
his duty and, consequently, his liability, necessarily ceases.

We have then, simply, a question as to who, the State
Treasurer on the one hand, or the Governor, Secretary of
State and Attorney General on the other, has the right to
determine the particular form of investment in which
these funds may be placed. It is argued that this supervisory power of the Governor, Secretary of State and Attorney General is in the nature of a veto power.   This
may be admitted.

The usual and orderly course of procedure, we assume,
would be for the State Treasurer to submit to the Governor, Secretary of State and Attorney General, a list of
available and safe investments for approval. He is, no
doubt, primarily chargeable with the duty of ascertaining
these available channels of investment, and is entitled to
present the same for approval, and to urge upon the Governor, Secretary of State and Attorney General the advisability and expediency of making such investments. It
4 nevertheless remains true that the Governor, Secretary
of State and Attorney General have the power to eliminate any given form of investment and by that process of
elimination they may reduce the State Treasurer to one single form of investment, that being the one form left to him
which will receive the necessary approval. Thereupon,
there arises, except under circumstances to be hereafter
mentioned, a ministerial duty on the part of the State
Treasurer to invest the funds. This duty does not arise
by reason of any order or direction of the Governor, Secretary of State and Attorney General. The State Treasurer
occupies as important a position, and is charged with even
greater responsibility than they are, in regard to the investment of these funds. His ministerial duty arises out
of the law provided by Congress in the enabling act, for
the administration of this fund, and which act requires
the fund to be kept invested in safe, interest-bearing se-

curities. The duty is ever-present, and is never discharged
until the whole field has been explored, and exhausted without avail. It is the law of the administration of the trust.
not any. order or direction of the Governor, Secretary of
State and Attorney General, which furnishes the basis for
any remedy against. the State Treasurer by mandamus. If
a given investment, under such circumstances, is safe,
there is no discretion left in the State Treasurer under the
terms of the rule for the administration of his trust prescribed by the enabling act. He must invest the funds in
safe, interest-bearing securities, and he may be compelled
to do so by mandamus.

At this point a consideration presents itself which is not
directly nivolved in this case. It is this. By the terms of
the enabling act, which, together with the Constitution, is
the law for the administration of this trust, the State
Treasurer is charged with the duty of safely investing these
funds, and must give bond for the faithful performance of
this duty. It, therefore, becomes his duty to inquire into
and pass upon the safety of any given investment before
it is made, and he may have a discretion in that regard,
not subject to control by mandamus. This discretion, if
possessed by the State Treasurer, is of no importance
where the proposed security is one of those specifically
enumerated in the Constitution, as in this case. But if the
proposed investment were bank deposits, as now authorized
or were in some other form, as might be provided by the
legislature in the future, then this discretion of the State
Treasurer, if he possesses the same, might become of vast
importance in safe-guarding the fund. Whether important, or unimportant, in any given case, is not the question. If it is possessed by him, he is entitled to exercise
it, and it cannot be controlled by mandamus. As before
stated, this question is not directly involved in this case,
and is not relied upon in argument, and, for that reason,
we expressly refrain from deciding whether the State
Treasurer has this discretion, or, if he has, just what its
nature and extent is, reserving the question for future determination when it arises.

State v. Marron, 18 N. M. 426.

If the State Treasurer has the discretion hereinbefore mentioned, he is not, of course, subject absolutely to mandamus to make any particular form of investment of these funds. But when, by the process of elimination, heretofore mentioned, he is left with but one form of available investment, he may be proceeded against and put in motion, and compelled to do all of such acts, including the exercise of such discretion as he may possess, as are required of him by the law of his trust, all to the end that it shall be determined whether the given investment shall be made or not.

A practical difficulty is presented by the record in this case. Chapter 58, laws of 1912, authorizes the issuance of these bonds, section 4 requires the bonds to be sold at not less than par and accrued interest from the next preceding interest date, and requires four weeks' publication of notice of the time and place of sale. No such notice has been given, and the proposed sale under the

5 former notice was not continued by the State Treasurer.

The proceeding, in its present form, is not broad enough to compel the State Treasurer to re-advertise a sale of these bonds, nor to bid at such sale the amount required by the act. As we understand the rule, relief may be granted for less than what is prayed for, but not more, and the acts sought to be enforced must be specifically pointed out in the alternative writ. High Ex. Leg. Rem., sec. 450; 26 Cyc. 466; State v. Cavanao, 30 La. Ann. 237; People v. Dulaney, 96 Ill. 503; State v. Einstein, 46 N. J. L. 479. This has not been done in this case, and the relief sought, for this reason alone, must be denied.

The peremptory writ is denied.

CONCURRING OPINION.

ROBERTS, C. J.—I do not believe that any duty rests upon the Governor, Secretary of State and Attorney General to seek out the mode or avenue of investment of the school fund. It was never the intention to place upon these officials this duty. Their power, as stated by Justice Parker, is simply a veto power. This being true, the

power cannot be exercised in advance of its lawful requirement. It might be argued with as much consistency,
that the governor of a state could say in advance of the
legislature that he vetoed a pending bill, prior to its passage by that body.

The construction sought to be placed upon the Constitution and enabling act by the Governor, Secretary of
State and Attorney General would strip the Treasurer of
all discretion in the matter of investing the school fund
and relieve him from all responsibility in this regard, cast-
ing this duty upon three men, no one of whom is required
by law to execute a bond for the faithful performance of
his duties in this respect. Such I do not believe was ever
the intention of Congress or the constitutional convention.
In the enabling act we find this language:

"The State Treasurer shall keep all such moneys invested in safe interest-bearing securities, which securities
shall be approved by the Governor and Secretary of State
of said proposed State, and shall at all times be under a
good and sufficient bond or bonds conditioned for the
faithful performance of his duties in regard thereto as defined by this act and the laws of the State not in conflict
therewith."

Thus placing upon the State Treasurer the duty of keep·
ing these funds invested in safe interest-bearing securities,
but the securities in which the funds are invested must
be approved by the Governor and Secretary of State.

The constitutional convention adopted sec. 7 of art.
XII, which reads as follows:—

"The principal of the Permanent School Fund shall be
invested in the bonds of the State or Territory of New
Mexico, or of any county, city, town, board of education
or school district therein. The legislature may by three-
fourths vote of the members elected to each house provide
that said funds may be invested in other interest-bearing
securities. All bonds or other securities in which any portion of the school fund shall be invested must be first approved by the Governor, Attorney General and Secretary

of State. All losses from such funds, however occurring, shall be reimbursed by the State."

It will be observed that the clause quoted, does not in specific terms require the Treasurer to invest the funds, but it says the "funds shall be invested," and in view of the enabling act requiring the Treasurer to perform this duty, it must be presumed that the Constitution likewise requires the same duties of this official. It was the purpose of Congress and the constitutional convention to throw every possible safeguard around this trust fund, so that it might forever remain intact for the benefit of the schools of the State. With this end in view, they placed the duty of keeping this fund invested upon the fiscal officer of the State, supposedly because the Treasurer would be in close touch with financial affairs, the issuance and sale of bonds and securities by the State and its subdivisions, and he thereby be enabled to propose the best investment for the fund, from time to time. He was, by the enabling act, required "at all times to be under a good and sufficient bond or bonds conditioned for the faithful performance of his duties in regard thereto." As an additional safeguard to the fund, the enabling act provided that the securities in which the Treasurer proposed to invest the fund should be "approved by the Governor and Secretary of State." This provision was carried forward in the State Constitution, but the further approval of the Attorney General, the law officer of the State, was also required, as an additional safeguard. Thereby, requiring the affirmative sanction of four separate individuals before the money could be invested; first, the proposition by the Treasurer to invest, and second, the approval of each of the officials named. But it is argued, that the Treasurer, by failing to propose any investment of the fund, might retain the same in his hands and derive a profit therefrom. This argument is based upon the assumption that the Treasurer would be remiss in his duties. The law always presumes that an official will do his duty, and, it might be further said, that no Treasurer would dare assume the risk which such action would entail. If he should be so remiss in his sworn duty, he would, of course, be liable on his bond, at the suit of the State for the interest which could have been procured by an investment of the fund, and would further be liable for all loss that might accrue to the fund. Again, it might be said, that the investment of the fund could likewise be prevented by either the Governor, Secretary of State or Attorney General, by the failure to approve of proposed investments. These officials are not required to give bond for the faithful performance of the duties imposed upon them in this regard. The securities in which the Treasurer is authorized to invest the funds are specified in the Constitution. In the named, or authorized, securities only can he propose investments. While mandamus would not lie to compel him to propose to the three named officials an investment of the fund in any particular security, it would issue to compel him to propose the investment in some of the named securities, leaving it to his discretion to propose the avenue of investment, within the limits fixed. The writ would set him in motion. High's Extraordinary Legal Remedies, sec. 34.

I do not understand by what rule of grammatical construction the word "approve" can be given the meaning of "direct." The words are not synonymous, and the meaning is in no wise related. The word "approve" is defined by Webster to mean "to sanction officially; to ratify; to confirm; to regard as good; to commend; to think well of." It will be seen that the word relates, for its object, to something already done, made or said by another. How could the named officials approve, unless something was proposed by the Treasurer? In the case now under consideration the Treasurer proposed to invest the funds, by depositing them in banks, upon certificates of deposit. This was the proposition before the officials for their approval. They did not approve, consequently the Treasurer had no right to invest the funds in that manner. This was the only question before them, or that was proposed for their consideration and approval. The three officials went further, however, and directed the Treasurer to invest the funds in the State Highway Bonds. True, it is argued that they did not "direct," but by a process of elimination and disapproval, confined the Treasurer to this one avenue of investment, but it amounts to the same thing as "directing," and it would hardly be argued that these officials could do indirectly what they could not do directly.

In the case of Thaw v. Ritchie, 5 Mackay 200, the Supreme Court of the District of Columbia discussed the word "approve" as used in a statute which authorized the Orphan's Court to order a sale of real estate, but provided that the realty should not thereby be diminished without the approbation of the general court of Chancellor. The Court says:—

"The action of the Orphan's Court must precede that of the Chancellor, and it is this action which he is to approve. He is not to order or decree a sale, which would be the appropriate terms for an original proceeding before him, but is to APPROVE, which term is only appropriate to a revisory proceeding. And as the statute clearly contemplates a previous decree by the Orphan's Court, it must be this which is to receive his approbation,"

The term "approve," only being appropriate to a revisory proceeding, the enabling act and our Constitution therefore must have contemplated a proposed action by the State Treasurer, which would be revised by the officials named.

In the case of Long v. Commissioners, 75 Ohio State 539, the Supreme Court of Ohio say "The word 'approve' seems to relate for its object to some thing made, done or said by another."

In the case of Old Colony Trust Co. v. City of Atlanta, 83 Fed. 39, it was contended ,on behalf of the city, that it had the power to fix the rates of fare and freight, by reason of a provision in the ordinance which read, "provided that the rates of fare and freight upon said railroad shall be subject to the approval of the mayor and city council of the city of Atlanta." The power was denied, the Court holding that the power to approve rates did not grant the right to fix the rates originally.

It seems to me that the construction contended for by the Attorney General would destroy, in the main, the purpose of the carefully worded provision in the enabling act and Constitution, and relax the safeguards which Congress and the framers of the Constitution sought to place over the administration of this sacred fund. Our government is a government by the people, through chosen representatives. Some of the officers, it is true, are required to execute a bond for the faithful performance of their duties, but acts, within their discretion, and within the limits of their power to act, and not corruptly or wilfully done, are without the terms of the bond. Many officials are not required to execute any bond. All, however, are answerable before the bar of public opinion for their stewardship. It has always been the policy of the law to require public records to be kept of the actions and doings of public officials, so that the public might have full information, at all times, relative to such matters, and be able to judge of the conduct and doings of their representatives. This, I judge, is largely the purpose of the carefully framed provisions relating to the investment of this fund. The State Treasurer is required to propose to the three officials named, an investment of the school fund in certain bonds specified. By his proposition, he goes on record as being willing to invest this fund in the named security, at the rate of interest specified and for the price stated in his proposition. If the three men, each approve, he can proceed to make such investment; if they disapprove, he must look further. Now, if the Treasurer should propose a poor investment for the fund, he is answerable to the people. If, on the other hand, the three officials named, or any one of them, should refuse to approve a good investment for the fund and force the Treasurer, by elimination, to propose a poor investment, such official, or officials, would be held accountable by the people, and by them only, for they are not under bond. Suppose, for instance, that the State Treasurer should propose to pay 125 for bonds selling in

the market for but par, would he not be severely criti-
cised for so doing and never afterwards entrusted with
place or power? Or, on the other hand, suppose the State
Treasurer should propose to the three officials the purchase of solvent securities, within the class named, which
would pay the fund 6% interest, and the proposition should
be rejected and the Treasurer forced to invest in securities
returning only 3% or 4%. For a breach of duty in either
of the supposed cases, it is probable that the official would
only be answerable before the bar of public opinion. It
was the design, however, of the framers of the provision,
that the public should have full information, and so important was it considered that the people should be able
to fix the responsibility, that each official was required
to assume the whole of the same. No investment could be
made without being proposed by the State Treasurer, and
hence he was not to be permitted to escape responsibility
by shouldering it upon the other three officials. On the
other hand, the proposed investment could not be made
without the affirmative approval of each of the state officials named, so that no one man could say that the act
was done without his concurrence. All were answerable
alike to the people for the management of the fund. The
construction contended for would absolutely absolve the
State Treasurer from his accountability to the people for
the management of the fund, and so long as he followed
the directions of the three officials named, he would be
held blameless. All opportunity for the people knowing
how profitable an investment might be made of the fund
can be cut off at once by the Governor, Attorney General
and Secretary of State, adopting a resolution, as was done
in this case, that they will approve only the one named
investment. This being true, and the Treasurer being
bound thereby, how is he to present to them more advan-
tageous sources of investment? Again, no one of the three
is under bond, and this construction relieves the only
bonded official from liability, so long as he follows the
directions given him.

Before mandamus will lie, it must be determined that

the investment of school moneys by the State Treasurer requires the exercise of no judgment or discretion on his part.

"The only acts to which the power of the courts by mandamus extends are such as are purely ministerial and with regard to which nothing like judgment or discretion in the performance of his duties is left to the officer but that wherever the right of judgment or decision exists in him it is he and not the courts who can regulate its exercise." Goodrich v. Guthrie, 58 U. S. 284.

An added reason might be given for the above conclusion that the Governor, Secretary of State and Attorney General have not the right to direct in advance, the action of the State Treasurer relative to the investment of the school fund. The fund is by law committed to the care and custody of the Treasurer. While now, the money in his hands, is only slightly in excess of one hundred thousand dollars, eventually it will amount to millions. He is the only official who keeps a daily check on this money and knows the amount of the same. When received, it is by him, and he is not required by law to account to either of the three officials. Suppose, for instance, that the resolution adopted by the board be treated as sufficient authority for him to invest the school funds in the State . Highway Bonds. The other officials are occupied with a multiplicity of duties, which necessarily occupy much of their time. They do not keep in touch with the amount of money on hand, belonging to this fund, and might assume that a small amount is being invested by the Treasurer in the channel authorized. In the meantime, millions of dollars come into the Treasurer's hands, which he, acting under the authority conferred by the three officials, and as required by their resolution, invests in the named securities, when it might never have been the intention of the three officials to authorize such an amount to be invested. Such was never the intention. Upon the Treasurer was placed the responsibility of keeping the fund invested and for so doing he would be held responsible under his bond, which he is required to execute as a guaranty of

his conduct in that regard. He is the custodian of the
fund and at all times is fully informed as to the daily receipts. He dare not permit it to lie idle without investment, and must present to the officials named a proposition
to invest it, so often and as soon as he has on hands an
amount justifying investment. The board should have at
the time each investment is proposed, an opportunity of
passing upon the advisability of the proposed investment.
The bond market, as is well known, is subject to fluctua-
tion. Each proposed purchase of bonds, were an individual buying, would be governed as to price, by the market
value of such a security. Should we, by a strained construction, hold that the three officials, by a resolution, may
authorize the Treasurer to act for an indefinite time in the
purchase of securities, regardless of changing conditions
of the market, such, I believe to be foreign to the purpose
of Congress and the constitutional convention.

Again, the resolution adopted by the three officials, and
upon which this action of mandamus is predicated, reads
as follows:

"Resolved, that all of the bids received from the various
banks for deposits of the Permanent School Fund be rejected for the purpose of investing said funds in the State
Highway Bonds, the difference in the rate of interest received, which would be about four cents per annum per
capita of school children as shown by the last enrollment,
being so small as to be more than offset by the benefits to
be derived from the construction of highways to the
schools themselves as well as to all other interests."

Which may be considered as supplemental by the following extract from a letter sent by the three officials to
the State Treasurer:

"Therefore, we now say to you that, under existing circumstances, we approve of the investment of this fund in
the State Highway Bonds, and that we will not approve
of its investment in any other securities at this time."

If mandamus will lie, it must be that the Treasurer
has no discretion in the matter of the investment, and
must blindly follow the direction contained in the above

resolution. That is, he must invest these funds in the
State Highway Bonds, regardless of the price which he
might be compelled to pay for the same. Suppose, for
instance, that he should purchase these bonds at a pre-
mium of twenty-five cents on the dollar, could he justify
under the above resolution or direction? Again, is the
above direction sufficient warrant for his action, should
he buy the bonds, and would he not be required to report
to the three officials the price which he paid for the bonds?
If it is not sufficient warrant for his so acting, clearly
mandamus would not lie to compel him to act.

The question is as to who, the State Treasurer on the
one hand, or the Governor, Secretary of State and Attorney General on the other, has the right to determine the
particular form of investment in which these funds shall
be placed. It seems to me that the answer is plain, that
neither has the right, but the form of investment must be
concurred in by the four officials named, and any one of
the four has the power to prevent any particular form of
investment.

I concur in the denial of the writ.

[No. 1648, December 23, 1913.]
IN THE MATTER OF THE APPLICATION OF JOE
CICA AND SAVA MARIJANOVIC FOR A WRIT
OF HABEAS CORPUS.

SYLLABUS (BY THE COURT)

1. The writ of habeas corpus is not a writ of error, nor
does it, except when perverted, discharge the functions of a
writ of error.

P. 456.

2. Error or irregularities in the course of the proceedings
at or anterior to the trial, which, if presented to an appellate
court by way of appeal or writ of error, must necessarily result in the reversal of the judgment, are not sufficient, for

that reason, as grounds for the release of a prisoner upon application for a writ of habeas corpus.

P. 456

3. As to jurisdictional questions, a judgment under which the prisoner is held is aided by the same presumptions as in other cases of collateral assault. If the record is silent as to jurisdictional facts, jurisdiction is presumed.

P. 457

4. A sentence is legal so far as it is within the provisions of law and the jurisdiction of the court over the person and the offense, and only void as to the excess, when such excess is separable and may be dealt with without disturbing the valid portion of the sentence.

P. 460

Habeas Corpus.

A. C. VOORHEES, ELMER E. STUDLEY, Raton, N. M.. for petitioners.

Courts will not take judicial notice of the ordinances of cities; they should be pleaded and proven as special laws. 28 Cyc. 393, 394, 395, note 41; Garlanad, et al., v. City of Denver, 19 Pac. 460; Williams v. Augusta, 4 Ga. 509; Davenport v. Bird, 34 Iowa, 524; Cooper v. People, 41 Mich. 403; C. L. 1897, sec. 2407.

Justice courts under the laws of this state are courts of limited jurisdiction and their records must show affirmatively their power to act. 24 Cyc. 497; C. L. 1897, sec. 2408.

Record does not disclose the arraignment of the petitioners. Arraignment and plea will not be presumed from recitals in the record that the defendant appeared, and that a jury was selected, empanelled and sworn. 12 Cyc. 889; Crain v. U. S. 162, U. S. 625; State v. Wood, 71 S. W. 724; Ex Parte Walton, 101 Pac. 1034.

The Court, sitting in habeas corpus proceedings, acts

upon the body of the defendant, and inquires into the single question, whether he is legally in custody.   State v. Gray, 37 N. J. L. 368, 1 Am. Crim. R. 556.

The judgment would be void and illegal if rendered by a court of general jurisdiction, and, therefore, it must be void when rendered by a Justice of the Peace.   15 A. & E. Enc. L. (2d ed.) 172; People v. Riseley, 38 Hun. (N. Y.) 280, 4 N. Y. Crim. 109; People v. Carter, 48 Hun. 165; In re Fury, 19 N. J. L. 14; Foy v. Taiburt, 9 Fed. Cas. No. 5020, 5 Cranch, C. C. 124.

Our statute was taken from the State of Missouri, and the interpretation by the courts of that State, prior to our adoption are binding upon our courts.   Armijo v. Armijo, 4 N. M. 133; Bremen Min. Co. v. Bremen, 13 N. M. 126, 79 Pac. 1133.

In habeas corpus proceedings the court will examine the record solely for the purpose of ascertaining the fact of the jurisdiction of the court, whose judgment is being questioned in the said proceeding, and will be limited in such examination to what the record discloses.   C. L. 1897, sec. 2781, 2797, sub-secs. 1 and 6; Ex Parte Page, 49 Mo. 291; In re Craig, 32 S. W. 1122.

The court must not only have jurisdiction over the person and the subject matter, but authority to render the particular judgment.   Ex Parte Cox, 32 Pac. 197; Ex Parte Gudenoge, 100 Pac. 39; People v. Liscomb, 60 N. Y. 559.

The judgment of the Justice of the Peace was an entirety.   Ex Parte Kelly, 65 Cal. 154; Ex Parte Sylvester, 81 Cal. 199; Ex Parte Yarborough, 110 U. S. 651; In re Graham, 138 U. S. 461, 34 L. Ed. 1051; State v. Gray, 37 N. J. 368; Freeman on Judgments, vol. 2 (4th ed.), sec. 625.

Unless the court rendering the judgment had jurisdiction to render the particular judgment, it is a nullity. Black on Judgments, sec. 258; 21 Cyc. 296, and citations; Ex Parte Gudenage, 100 Pac. 39; Ex Parte Webb, 51 Pac. 1027; In re Graham, 138 U. S. 461; In re Stewart, 16 Neb. 193; Brown, Jurisdiction of Courts, sec. 101;

Church, Habeas Corpus, sec. 368; Ex Parte Page, 49 Mo. 291; In re Craig, 32 S. W. 1122; Ex Parte Cox, 32 Pac. 197; Com. Davis v. Licky, 26 Am. Dec. 40; People, Stokes, v. Riseley, 38 Hun. 280; A. & E. Enc. L. (2d ed.) vol. 7, p. 37; Geyger v. Stoy, 1 Dallas 135.

ORIE L. PHILLIPS, Assistant District Attorney, Raton, N. M., for State.

STATEMENT OF FACTS.

This was a petition for a writ of habeas corpus. The petitioners allege that:

On the 18th day of November, 1913, a complaint was filed before J. M. Gauna, a Justice of the Peace in precinct No. 20, of Colfax County, attempting to charge an offense against the petitioners under a city ordinance of the city of Raton, said ordinance being designated as Ordinance No. 133 in said complaint, but charged to have been Ordinance No. 135 in the return and answer of the Sheriff to the writ of habeas corpus. On the day the complaint was filed, the petitioners were sentenced to sixty days in the common jail of Colfax County and to pay a fine of twenty-five dollars, and to pay costs amounting to seven dollars and fifty cents each, and a commitment was issued accordingly. The petitioners were, in accordance with the mandate of the so-called commitment, taken into custody by Abe Hixenbaugh, Sheriff of Colfax County, and by him imprisoned in the county jail on the 18th day of November, 1913, and there they remain.

The Sheriff, by way of response to the writ, filed his return thereto. Thereupon the petitioners moved to quash the return and discharge the prisoners upon the petition and return of the officer. The return, which was designated "return and answer," admitted all the material allegations of the petition, except the averments with respect to the ordinance upon which the prosecution was based in the Justice Court.

OPINION OF THE COURT.

HANNA, J.—The petitioners contend that the judgment rendered by the Justice of the Peace, upon which the commitment is based, was void for the following reasons:—First, because there was no arraignment of the defendants; second, because the judgment sentencing each of the defendants to sixty days in the county jail and to pay a fine of twenty-five dollars and costs was excessive, and beyond the power of the court to impose.

In considering the first ground of objection to the judgment it is necessary to admit the well-settled principle
1 that: the writ of habeas corpus is not a writ of error, nor does it, except when perverted, discharge the functions of a writ of error. 2 Freeman on Judgments, sec. 620; Hurd Habeas Corpus (2d ed.), 328.

Pursuant to this principle it has been quite universally held that errors or irregularities in the course of the
2 proceedings at or anterior to the trial, which, if presented to an appellate court by way of appeal or writ of error, must necessarily result in the reversal of the judgment, are not sufficient, for that reason, as grounds for the release of a prisoner upon application for a writ of habeas corpus. Freeman on Judgments (4th ed.) sec. 620; Ex Parte Siebold, 100 U. S. 371. .

The particular phase of the question here raised, i. e., that there was no arraignment of the defendants, does not seem to have been passed upon by any court of last resort, save that of the Supreme Court of Indiana, which Court held, in the case of Winslow v. Green, 155 Ind. 368, 58 N. E. 259, that: Where one had been tried and convicted in the superior court, he will not be released by habeas corpus because he was not arraigned and did not plead in such court, since, as such errors do not go to the jurisdiction of the court, its judgment is not subject to collateral attack. In that case, as in the case now under consideration, it was not denied that the court had jurisdiction both of the subject matter and the person of the defendant.

Our Territorial Supreme Court, in the case of In re

Peraltareavis, 8 N. M. 27, 41 Pac. 538, following Ex Parte
Seibold, 100 U. S. 371, said:—

"That the only ground on which that Court, (United
States Supreme Court) or any court, without special statute authority, will give relief on habeas corpus, is where
there is want of jurisdiction over the person or the cause
or some other matter rendering the proceedings void, as
distinguished from what is merely erroneous and reversible."

Our habeas corpus statute was adopted prior to the rendition of the opinion on the Peraltareavis case, and was
doubtless carefully considered by the Court at that time.
We do not concede that the failure of the record, in this
case, to show affirmatively an arraignment of the defendants is a jurisdictional defect that would render void the
judgment in the case, and subject it to collateral attack.

It has been held that as to jurisdictional questions, a
judgment under which the prisoner is held is aided
3 by the same presumptions as in other cases of collateral assault. If the record is silent as to jurisdictional facts, jurisdiction is presumed. Freeman on Judgments, sec. 619; Ex Parte Ah Men, 77 Cal. 198.

In concluding our discussion upon this subject, we desire to say that it is not contended by the petitioners that
no arraignment was had, but their contention is entirely
based upon the failure of the record to disclose the fact of
arraignment.

The further contention of petitioners respecting defects
in the complaint and impropriety of holding that the
prosecution was had under Ordinance No. 135, of the
City· of Raton, when the complaint was originally made
under Ordinance No. 133, are likewise collateral attacks
upon the judgment of the justice court which cannot now
be entertained in this proceeding for the reason given.

This leaves for our consideration the question that the
judgment sentencing each of the defendants to sixty days
in the county jail and to pay a fine of twenty-five dollars
and costs was excessive, and beyond the power of the

court to impose. The ordinance upon which the judgment was based provides:

"Sec. 3. Any person violating any provisions of this ordinance shall be deemed guilty of a misdemeanor, and upon conviction, shall be fined in a sum of not exceeding twenty-five dollars, or by imprisonment in the county jail for a period not exceeding sixty days."

It is urged by the petitioners that our statute is substantially the same as the statutes of Idaho and Missouri, and that our statute was adopted from the Missouri statute after it had been construed by the Supreme Court of that State, in the case Ex Parte Page, 49 Mo. 291. We are not convinced of the correctness of this contention, though there is great similarity between the statutes.

The facts involved in the Missouri case, however, are not the same as those with which we are now concerned. This case being similar to that of Ex Parte Mooney, 26 W. Va. 36, 53 Am. Rep. 59, from the opinion in which we desire to quote at length with approval:

"It is insisted, however, that as the Court had no legal right under the statute to sentence the petitioner both to confinement in the penitentiary and to pay a fine, it exceeded its jurisdiction, and thereby the whole proceeding became illegal and void. In support of this view the cases of Ex Parte Page, 49 Mo. 291; Rex v. Ellis, 5 Barn. & Cress. 395, and Rex v. Bonne, 7 Ad. & Ellis, 58, are relied on by counsel for petitioner. The two latter cases were decided upon writs of error by the Court of King's bench, and by reason of the peculiar constitution of that court, the determination of such cases by it have no analogy to the proceeding by habeas corpus in our courts. I do not, therefore, regard those cases as authority in this case. The other case, from Missouri, was in some respects different from the one before us. In that case the extreme limit which the court could inflict as a punishment for grand larceny was fixed by statute at seven years' confinement in the penitentiary; but the court sentenced the prisoner to such confinement for that crime for ten years. The court on habeas corpus held that the trial court by that sentence had exceeded its jurisdiction and therefore, under the provisions of the statute of that State, the petitioner was discharged. The statute referred to declared that when a prisoner is brought up on habeas corpus, if it appear that he is in custody by virtue of process from any court or judicial officer, he can be discharged only in one of the following cases, 'First, where the jurisdiction of such court or officer has been exceeded, either as to matter, place, sum or person. * * * * Sixth, where the process is not authorized by any judgment, order or decree, nor by any provision of law.' Wagn. Stat. 690, sec. 35.

"The judge who delivered the opinion of the court after quoting said statute, says: 'It seems to me that the court in passing the sentence exceeded its jurisdiction in the matter and that it did not act by authority of any provision of law. This application, therefore, I think comes within the meaning of the statute.' 49 Mo. 292.

"It seems clear from the opinion that the court decided that case under the influence of the statute, and consequently it can be no precedent and can have no application in a State like ours, where no such statute exists.

"But if the case could be regarded as decided upon principle it must be disapproved, since it is not only contrary to the general rules hereinbefore stated, but it is in positive conflict with numerous other and seemingly better considered decisions of courts of other States. In re Petty, 22 Kans. 277; Ex Parte Parks, 93 U. S. 18; People v. Jacobs, 66 N. Y. 9; People v. Liscomb, 60 N. Y. 559; s. c. 19 Am. Rep. 211; People v. Baker, 89 N. Y. 460."

As pointed out in this opinion (Ex Parte Mooney) the sentence under consideration by the Missouri case was not severable, while in the Mooney case, fine and imprisonment having been imposed and one or the other being in excess of the statutory provision, it was held that the sentence was void as to the excess only, the sentence being severable.

In the Idaho case, Ex Parte Cox, 32 Pac. 197, a judgment imposed a sentence of five years for violation of an Idaho statute, when the statute in question authorized a

maximum penalty of two years. This case is similar to
the Missouri case of Ex Parte Page, which was cited by
the Idaho Supreme Court with approval.

In a later case, Ex Parte Crenshaw, 80 Mo. 447, where
the court exceeded the limit of punishment in imposing a
fine of $500, the Supreme Court held:

"Notwithstanding these errors in the proceeding of the
court, we cannot discharge the prisoner, since the order
for his commitment, until he shall have obeyed the order
to restore the goods, was a legitimate exercise of the
power of the court. Neither this nor any other court can,
on a petition for habeas corpus, discharge the prisoner for
a mere irregularity in the proceedings. It must be for an
illegality which renders the commitment void. Hurd on
Habeas Corpus, 327. Here the court had jurisdiction,
and the imprisonment of the petitioner until he should
comply with the order of the court, was warranted by law.
After he shall have restored the goods the prisoner will
be entitled to his discharge, the other requirements of the
judgment being nullities. Feely's Case, 12 Cush. 598;
People v. Markham, 7 Cal. 208."

The great weight of authority is that where a court has
jurisdiction of the person and the offense, the imposi-
4   tion of a sentence in excess of what the law permits
does not render the legal or authorized portion of the
sentence void, but only leaves such portion in excess open
to question and attack. In re Taylor, 45 L. R. A. 136.
See also authorities collected in note.

Counsel for petitioners contends that this rule is not
applicable to the present case because the judgment is not
separable. In this he is mistaken, as the judgment here
is separable. The principle is better stated, in its entirety, in the following language: A sentence is legal so
far as it is within the provisions of law and the jurisdiction of the court over the person and the offense, and
only void as to the excess, when such excess is separable
and may be dealt with without disturbing the valid portion of the sentence. United States v. Pridgeon, 153 U. S.

48; State v. Klock, 18 So. 957, 48 La. Ann. 67; Ex Parte Mooney, 26 W. Va. 36, 53 Am. Rep. 59.

It is our conclusion that the sentence in this case is separable and that had petitioners paid the fine or suffered the imprisonment they would be entitled to the writ, but having done neither, they are not entitled to release. In Ex Parte Lange, 18 Wall 163 (21 L. Ed. 872) it was held that:

"The error of the court in imposing the two punishments mentioned in the statutes when it had only the alternative of one of them, did not make the judgment wholly void."

In that case the petitioner before applying for a writ of habeas corpus had paid the fine imposed. He was discharged.

For the reasons given, the writ is denied.

REPORT OF CASES

DETERMINED IN THE

SUPREME COURT

OF THE STATE OF NEW MEXICO

JANUARY TERM, 1914

[No. 1559, January 10, 1914.]

CHARLES NOTESTINE, Appellee, v. W. B. ROGERS,
Appellant.

SYLLABUS (BY THE COURT)

An order in habeas corpus proceedings discharging petitioner is not appealable, in the absence of a statute granting
such right.

P. 466

Appeal from the District Court of Chaves County; John
T. McClure, District Judge; appeal dismissed.

O. O. ASKREN; J. C. GILBERT, Roswell, N. M., for appellee, on motion to dismiss.

The decision of the trial court in the habeas corpus case
attempted to be appealed from is not of that final and
conclusive character necessary to support a review by writ
of error or appeal; and, that no right of appeal exists. 21
Cyc. 338, (11) and notes; Mead v. Metcalf, 25 Pac.
729; Ex parte White, 84 Pac. 242; State v. Ray, 105
Pac. 46; State v. Brownell, 50 N. W. 413; 9 Enc. Pl. &
Pr. 1072, par. XVII and notes.

This court cannot pass upon the validity of the proceedings had in the trial court. Standard Enc. Pro., vol. 2, p.
138, par. 2 and notes 73-74; Enc. Pl. & Pr. 341, par. 4
and note.

Record fails to disclose that the said Rogers had, at the time of his attempted appeal, such an interest over the subject matter, or as a party to the habeas corpus proceeding which would entitle him to appeal from the decision of the trial court. 2 Standard Enc. Pro. 198-99 and 200, pars. 7 and 8 and notes; 2 Enc. Pl. & Pr. 341, par. 4.

D. W. ELLIOTT, Roswell, N. M., for appellant on motion to dismiss.

Right of appellant to appeal. Constitution of N. M., art. VI, sec. 2; Laws 1907, ch. 57, sec. 1; Sutherland Code Pleading, vol. 2, sec. 2396, and cases; In re Borrego, 8 N. M. 657; Winnovich v. Emery, 93 Pac. 988; Garfinkle v. Sullivan, 80 Pac. 188; Ex parte Tom Tong, 108 U. S. 556; Ex rel. Durner v. Huegin, 85 N. W. 1046, et seq.

A proceeding in habeas corpus is a civil and not a criminal proceeding. Farnsworth v. Montana, 129 U. S. 104; Ex parte Tom Tong, 108 U. S. 556; Kurtz v. Moffitt, 115 U. S. 487; In re Foye, 21 Wash. 250, 57 Pac. 825; In re Baker, 21 Wash. 259, 57 Pac. 827; In re Sylvester, 21 Wash. 263, 57 Pac. 829; Meade v. Metcalf, 7 Utah 103, 25 Pac. 729; In re Plasby, 3 Utah, 183, 1 Pac. 252.

Finality of the judgment of the lower court. Honerine M. & M. Co. v. Tellerday Steel P. & T. Co., 30 Utah 449, 85 Pac. 626.

An appeal does not, of its own force, suspend the judgment in a habeas corpus proceeding. 21 Cyc. 338-41; State v. Kirkpatrick, 54 Ia. 373, 6 N. W. 588.

Many courts, where the right of appeal is expressly given by statute, deny the right of appeal from a mere refusal to grant the writ. But upon this question the courts differ. 21 Cyc. 340, notes 31, 32.

The assessment of costs against any person establishes the status of such person as a party to the action, and establishes his right to prosecute an appeal. 2 Cyc. 629, and cases cited; Ex rel. Durner v. Huegin, 85 N. W. 1046; Hayward v. Lombard, 9 How. 230, 13 L. Ed. 245;

464   SUPREME COURT OF NEW MEXICO,

Notestine v. Rogers, 18 N. M. 462.

7 Enc. Pl. & Pr. 856; Holmes v. Jennison, 14 Pet. 540, 10 L. Ed. 501.

Who is "party to a suit?" C. L. 1897, sec. 2685, subsec. 5; 5 Enc. Pl. & Pr. 463.

Any person aggrieved by any final judgment or decision of any district court may, at his election, take an appeal or sue out a writ of error to the Supreme Court, etc." Const. (N. M.), art. VI, sec. 2; Laws 1907, ch. 57, sec. 1; In re Foye, 57 Pac. 826.

Judgment in habeas corpus proceeding is a final judgment and therefore subject to review upon appeal. State v. Hill, 10 Minn. 63; Dirks p. State, f3 Tex. 227; Atwood v. Atwater, 51 N. W. 1073; Yudkin v. Gates, 22 Atl. 776; Henderson v. James, 39 N. E. 805; Ornilaus v. Ruis, 161 U. S. 502.

D. W. ELLIOTT, for appellant.

Repeals by implication are not favored, and where the last statute does not specifically repeal the old law, they will, if possible, be construed together. Hagerman v. Meeks, 13 N. M. 576; Cortsey v. Terr, 7 N. M. 99; U. S. v. Greathouse, 166 U. S. 601; Wilmot v. Mudge, 103 U. S. 217; State v. Prouty, 84 N. W. 670; Laws of N. M., 1884, ch. 39, sec. 13; Laws of 1891; Laws 1909, ch. 117; Frost v. Weine, 157 U. S. 16; U. S. v. Healey, 160 U. S. 36; Railway Co. v. U. S., 127 U. S. 406; Bartlet v. King, 12 Mass. 537.

Power given to boards of trustees. Laws 1891, ch. 32; Laws 1893, ch. 46; C. L. 1897, sec. 2470; Laws 1907, ch. 59; C. L. 1897, sec. 2402.

Court erred in holding that section 2470, of the Compiled Laws, was, by necessary implication, repealed and nullified by chapter 117 of the laws of 1909. Ex parte Crow Dog, 109 U. S. 156; Murdock v. City of Memphis, 20 Wall. 590; Laws 1907, ch. 59; C. L. 1897, sec. 2402; Wood v. U. S., 16 Pet. 342; Daviess v. Fairborne, 3 How. 36; U. S. v. Tynen, 11 Wall. 88; State v. Stoll, 17 Wall. 427.

Court erred in holding that chapter 117, laws of 1909,

limited and restricted the exercise of the powers granted
to municipalities. Laws 1909, ch. 117; Laws 1891, ch.
32; C. L. 1897, secs. 2476-2492; Laws 1912, ch. 67.

Court erred in holding that the Town of Dexter did not
have the power and authority to enact said Ordinance No.
18. Const. N. M.; New Orleans v. Louisiana, 115 U. S.
650; Lake View v. Rosehill Cem. Co., 70 Ill. 191; In re
Jacobs, 98 N. Y. 98; Town of Selma v. Brewer, 98 Pac.
61; Crowley v. Christensen, 137 U. S. 86; Edgar v. Mc-
Donald, 106 S. W. 1135; Murphy v. California, 32 Sup.
Ct. 697; Words & Phrases, vol. 6, par. 5429; Wice v. Chicago & N. W. Ry. Co., 56 L. R. A. 268; St. Paul v. Haugh-
bro, 2 A. & E. 580; Burlingame v. Thompson, 11 A. & E.
64; Booth v. Illinois, 184 U. S. 425; Johnson v. City of
Great Falls, 16 A. & E. Ann. Cas. 974.

OPINION OF THE COURT.

ROBERTS, C. J.—Appellee was arrested and held in
custody by appellant, who was the Marshal of the village
of Dexter, in Chaves County, New Mexico, under and by
virtue of a warrant issued by a Justice of the Peace, filed
with him against appellee, charging him with a violation
of an ordinance of said village of Dexter. Application
was made to the Judge of the Fifth Judicial District for
a writ of habeas corpus by appellee and, upon the hearing, he was discharged from the custody of the Marshal.
From the order made the town Marshal prosecutes this
appeal, which appellee has moved to dismiss, upon the
ground that no appeal can be taken from an order made
in habeas corpus proceeding, either discharging or remand-
ing a petitioner.

The prevailing doctrine in the State courts of this
country is thus stated in 9 Am. & Eng. Ency. Pl. & Pr.
1072:

"Independent of statutory provisions, the best doctrine
appears to be that a decision in a habeas corpus case is
not of that final and conclusive character necessary to
support a review by writ of error, and that no right of
appeal exists."

The text is supported by the great weight of authority as will be seen from an examination of the case notes appended to the following cases, reported in Am. & Eng. Ann. Cases, viz: Wisner v. Burrell, Ann. Cas. 1912 D, 356, Bleakley v. Smart, 11 Am. & Eng. Ann. Cas. 125, Cormack v. Marshall, 1 Am. & Eng. Ann. Cas. 256.

And see also an extensive case note to the case of Wisner v. Burrell, 34 L. R. A. (N. S.) 755. While the great weight of authority supports the text above quoted, some courts hold otherwise. The best reasoned case to the contrary which has been called to our attention is 'that of Winnovich v. Emery, 93 Pac. 988, but an examination of the cases cited by the Utah court in support of its holding will show that some, but not all, of the cases upon which it relies for support were based upon statutes granting the right of appeal. •

In this State, the right of appeal in such cases, is not granted by statute, unless it is conferred by sec. 1, chapter 57, S. L. 1907, which reads as follows:

‚"Any person aggrieved by any final judgment or decision of any District Court in any civil cause may, at his election take an appeal or sue out a writ of error to the Supreme Court of the Territory at any time within one year from the date of the entry of the same."

Did the legislature intend that habeas corpus proceedings should be governed by the provisions of said chapter 57, supra? If so, then the speedy remedy which this great writ was designed to afford to a party unlawfully deprived of his liberty would not be available in this State. By section 16 of said chapter 57, the appellant may file a supersedeas bond, the amount of which in a case like this would be fixed by the Judge of the District Court, which would stay the execution of the judgment and prevent the discharge of the petitioner. By section 21 of said act, as amended by sec. 2, chap. 120, S. L. 1909, the appellant would have 130 days in which to perfect the appeal, and if the case followed the ordinary course it would probably be six months before the appeal could be heard, should appellant desire to delay the same. It will thus be seen that the Appellate Procedure Act makes no appropriate provision for the review of habeas corpus proceedings. Elaborate and specific provisions governing the exercise of the right to the writ of habeas corpus are found in the Compiled Laws of 1897, (sections 2781 to 2817, inclusive) but no right of appeal is expressly or impliedly granted by the act from which said sections were taken. (Chap. 1, S. L. 1884.) Under sec. 2783, the petitioner was authorized to apply for the writ to the Supreme or District Court, or to any Judge thereof, who was in the district where the prisoner was detained, or, if the Judge in such district had refused to grant the writ, then petitioner might apply to any Judge of any other district. In other words, he could exhaust the whole judicial power of the Territory, by repeated applications, until he secured his release. And, although he might be discharged, he could be again arrested and imprisoned upon the same charge, if "indicted therefor, convicted thereof, or committed for want of bail by some court of record having jurisdiction of the cause," etc. (Sec. 2808, C. L. 1897.) As was well said by the Criminal Court of Appeals of Oklahoma, in the case of Ex Parte Johnson, 98 Pac. 461:—

"Had it been intended to provide for appeals in HABEAS CORPUS, some appropriate provision would have been made. Its omission affords the best evidence to the contrary, and, if anything is wanting to remove all doubt, it will be found in the nature and object of this great writ as a constitutional right; its purpose being to afford a speedy remedy to a party unjustly accused of the commission of a crime without obstructing or delaying public justice, both of which objects would be defeated by the delays consequent upon an appeal. Any other rule would operate practically to subvert the constitutional safeguards and the fundamental rights of the citizen."

That the legislature could provide for appeals in such cases is not doubted, but until it does so, in clear and unequivocal language, and under suitable regulations which do not impair the constitutional provisions governing the right to the writ, the courts will deny such right.

For the reasons stated, the appeal will be dismissed, and it is so ordered.

Canavan v. Canavan, 18 N. M. 468.

[No. 1562, January 10, 1914.]

STEPHEN CANAVAN, et al., Plaintiffs in Error, v. KATE CANAVAN, Defendant in Error.

SYLLABUS (BY THE COURT)

1. Under section 14, chapter 57, S. L. 1907, a cost bond is required, on appeal or writ of error, only for the protection of the appellee or defendant in error, and is not essential in order to confer jurisdiction upon this Court.

P. 470

2. Where a cost bond is required by statute, on appeal or writ of error, only for the protection of the adverse party, failure to give the same may be waived.

P. 471

3. A general appearance, without objecting to the failure to file a cost bond, operates as a waiver.

P. 472

Error to the District Court of Bernalillo County; Herbert F. Raynolds, District Judge; motion to dismiss writ of error denied.

CHARLES A. SPIESS, Las Vegas, N. M.; EDWARD A. MANN, BURKHART AND COORS, Albuquerque, N. M., for plaintiffs in error.

A. T. HANNETT, Gallup, N. M., and VIGIL & JAMISON, Albuquerque, N. M., for defendants in error.

OPINION OF THE COURT.

ROBERTS, C. J.—The writ of error herein was sued out on the 11th day of March, 1913. On the 18th day of April, 1913, the attorneys for the defendant in error joined the attorneys for plaintiff in error in a stipulation, which was filed in this Court. The terms of the stipulation are not material to a decision of the question now before the Court. The fact that it was entered into and filed, however, is important, because thereby defendant in error necessarily entered a general appearance in the cause, in this Court; such stipulation not being limited in this regard. On July 15, 1913, defendant in error moved to dismiss the cause, because of the failure of plaintiff in error to file a cost bond, as required by section 14, chapter 57, S. L. 1907, within the time specified. On Dec. 22, 1913, plaintiff in error filed an application for leave to file a cost bond, which was tendered with such application.

The question for determination is, whether the giving of a bond for costs was waived by the general appearance of defendant in error, after the default. If the giving of a bond for costs, within the time specified, is essentiaal in order to confer jurisdiction upon this Court to issue a writ of error, of course there would be no question but that such requirement could not be waived by the adverse party. On the other hand, if such a bond is merely for the protection of appellee or defendant in error, it could be waived. (By section 2, chapter 57, S. L. 1907, appeals are allowed by the District Court in which the judgment or decree was rendered.) Writs of error are issued by direction of the Supreme Court or any Justice thereof (Farmer's Development Co. v. Rayado Land & Irrigation Co., 134 Pac. 216, 18 N. M. 1.) Sec. 14, of said chap. 57, reads as follows:

"Whenever an appeal is taken to the Supreme Court or writ of error sued out, by any other party, than an executor or administrator, the Territory, county or other municipal corporation, and no bond for supersedeas is given as hereinafter provided, the appellant, or plaintiff in error, shall, within thirty days from the time of taking such appeal or suing out such writ of error, file with the district clerk, in cases of appeal, and with the clerk of the Supreme Court, in cases of writs of error, a bond with sufficient sureties qualified as in other cases, to the effect that the appellant or plaintiff in error shall pay all costs that may be adjudged against him on said appeal or writ of error, said bonds to be approved by the respective clerks, as supersedeas bonds are approved."

This section does not require the filing of the bond prior to the granting of the appeal by the District Court, or the issuance of the writ of error by this Court, but such bond is to be filed within thirty days after taking such appeal or suing out the writ of error. The power of the District Court to grant the appeal is not dependent upon the filing of the bond, nor is the power of this Court to issue a writ of error withheld until the bond is filed. Many States have statutes, which require the filing of an appeal bond as a condition precedent to the allowance of an appeal. Under such statutes the trial court would not have power to grant an appeal, until the precedent steps had been taken. The court thus being without authority to act, could not by its order granting the appeal confer upon the appellate courts jurisdiction of the cause. One case will sufficiently illustrate the principle. The statutes of Missouri authorized appeals from the Probate to the Circuit Court. After providing for the filing of an appeal bond and an affidavit of merit, a section of the statute reads as follows: "After such affidavit and bond have been filed and approved, the appeal shall be granted," etc. In the case of Greene v. Castello, 35 Mo. App. 127, the Court held that the Circuit Court had no jurisdiction of a cause on appeal from the Probate Court, where the appeal had been granted without compliance with the requirements of the statute.

Under our statute, however, the filing of the bond within the specified time is not necessary to our jurisdiction.

1   It attaches upon the allowance of the appeal or the issuance of the writ of error. Other statutory requirements of course must be complied with in order to give the Court jurisdiction over the parties, but it acquires jurisdiction of the cause by the allowance of the appeal or issuance of the writ of error. Many steps are required of the appellant or plaintiff in error before he can bring the case to a hearing on the merits, and a failure on his part to comply with the statutory requirements, advantage being taken thereof by his adversary, may preclude a hearing on the merits and result in a dismissal of the appeal. For instance, he must file his assignments of error within a specified time, and if he fails to do so, and the appellee moves to dismiss before the default has been cured, the

motion will be granted. The failure to file such assignments of error, however, does not affect the jurisdiction of
the Court. The statute also requires the issuance and service of citation upon the adverse party where a writ of
error is sued out, but this requirement it has been held is
waived by the voluntary appearance of the defendant
2 in error. Dailey v. Foster, 128 Pac. 71. Under the
provisions of our statute, an appeal bond is given
solely for the protection of the appellee or defendant in
error. It is not required for the protection of the officers
of the District Court, as they are authorized by law to require the payment of their fees in advance in all civil
cases, (sec. 1801, C. L. 1897; sec. 13, chap. 112, S. L.
1905) and in this Court the appellant or plaintiff in error
is required to deposit the sum of $20.00 as advance costs,
and such further sums as may from time to time be required. (Sec. 3, rule IV.) This being true, there would
seem to be no good reason why the appellee or defendant
in error could not waive the bond. And he does waive the
default when he appears and interposes no objection to the
irregularity. This holding, is, we think, consonant with
the decisions of other Courts under similar statutes.

In the case of Thompson v. Lee, 28 Ala. 454, Justice
Stone in discussing the question says:—

"The bond, or security for costs, required by section
3041 of the Code, was obviously intended to protect parties and the officers of the Court, against insolvent litigants. This legislative regulation is binding on us; and
whenever the appeal bond or certificate is substantially
defective, or entirely wanting, and the fact is in due time
brought to our notice, we are bound to respond to the motion, and to repudiate the cause. While adjusting the
rights of appellants, we must observe and guard the legal
rights of all others interested in the record. But I hold
that these mere property rights may be waived, without
at all affecting the binding efficacy of our judgments. I
hold, further, that when there has been joinder in error,
arguments on the merits, or other act done which admits
the case rightfully in this Court, the motion to dismiss
for insufficient or defective appeal, comes too late."

And in the case of L. & N. R. R. Co. v. Lile, 154 Ala.
556, the same Court say:

"But if this be not true (speaking of a defective bond)
in the absence of any appeal bond, the jurisdiction of this
Court to review the judgment is clear and beyond controversy; and the failure of the appealing party to give such
a bond is a mere irregularity, which the appellee may
waive." To the same effect, see also Wilson v. Dean, 10
Ark. 308; Jester v. Hopper, 13 Ark. 43; Ross v. Tedder,
10 Ga. 426; March v. Griffith, 53 N. C. 264; Jones v. Henderson, 149 Ind. 458; Kehler v. Walls, 94 S. W. 760.
(Mo. App.)

"The failure to file a bond may, of course, be waived by
a joinder in error, by filing a brief, or by any similar act,
but if the objection that no bond was filed is duly made,
the conclusion must be that the appeal as in terms is ineffective." Elliott's Appellate Procedure, sec. 249.

And the same author, sec. 376, says:

"In the very great majority of cases an appearance without objecting to the failure to file a bond operates as a
waiver."

When defendant in error signed the stipulation before
mentioned, she recognized the case as pending in this
3 Court, and thereby elected to waive the statutory requirement that a cost bond should be filed, for her
benefit and protection. She had the right to move for
the dismissal of the cause for such failure, but elected not
to do so, and recognized the efficiency of the proceedings
by which the appeal had been effected. After doing so it
was too late for her to attempt to raise the question.

In the case of Farmers Development Co. v. Rayado Land
& Irrigation Co., 134 Pac. 216, an excerpt is quoted from
1 Ency. Pl. & Pr. 966, which would imply that the giving
of an appeal bond was essential to confer jurisdiction
upon the appellate court. No such question, however, was
involved in that case, as there was a failure to give the
bond, which was taken advantage of promptly by a special appearance and a motion to dismiss. The question of
waiver was not involved. The authorities cited in support
of the proposition laid down in 1 Ency. Pl. & Pr., supra,

however, do not sustain the text, and only hold that acts required by law, to confer upon the District Court power to grant an appeal, are jurisdictional and must be strictly complied with, to vest the appellate court with power to entertain the appeal.

Many states have statutes which provide that, in order to render an appeal effectual for any purpose, undertaking on appeal shall be executed. In such states the courts uniformly hold that the giving of the bond cannot be waived by the parties. See, Marx v. Lewis, 24 Nev. 306; Hoffman v. Owens, 103 Pac. 414 (Nev.); Brown v. Chicago, Milwaukee & St. Paul Ry. Co., 10 S. D. 633.

As defendant in error does not question the right of plaintiff in error to file the tendered bond, in the event that she waived the failure to file the same within the time limited, by her appearance; nor the power of the Court to permit the filing of the bond after the expiration of the thirty days, plaintiff in error will be permitted to file the same.

For the reasons stated, the motion to dismiss the writ of error will be denied, and plaintiff in error will be given permission to file the tendered bond, and it is so ordered.

[No. 1582, Janary 10, 1914.]

D. H. PICKERING and LAURA PICKERING, his wife, Appellants, v. J. M. PALMER, Administrator of the Estate of M. B. Scott, Deceased, and W. T. DUFUR, as Sheriff of San Juan County, New Mexico, Appellees.

SYLLABUS (BY THE COURT)

1. A judgment rendered by a Justice of the Peace, before the return day of the summons, is void, as being without jurisdiction.

p. 477

2. A person against whom a Justice of the Peace has rendered a judgment void for want of jurisdiction, is not

bound to appeal or remove the same by writ of certiorari, even though he have actual notice of the existence of the judgment.

P. 478.

3. In this State, where a Justice of the Peace has no power to set aside his judgments or grant a new trial, and where upon appeal or certiorari to the District Court the cause is triable de novo only, one against whom a void judgment has been rendered by a Justice of the Peace, is not, though with actual notice thereof, guilty of laches and negligence sufficient to bar his right to an equitable remedy against such judgment, because he fails to appeal or sue out a writ of certiorari.

P. 479

4. An action for damages for trespass under a void judgment and execution issued thereunder, is not such a plain, speedy and adequate remedy at law, as will bar an action to enjoin the enforcement of the judgment.

P. 480

Appeal from the District Court of San Juan County; Edmund C. Abbott, District Judge; reversed and remanded.

EDWARDS & MARTIN, and F. A. BURDICK, Farmington, N. M., for appellants.

A demurrer admits all facts well pleaded. Railroad Co. v. Railroad Co., 13 N. M. 345; Dame v. Cochite, 13 N. M. 10; Minor v. Marshall, 6 N. M. 194.

Facts show the rendition of a void judgment and the issuance of a void execution, and the wrongful seizure of property thereunder. Lohman v. Cox, 9 N. M. 509; Pickering v. Current, 16 N. M. 37; Holzman v. Martinez, 2 N. M. 288; 3 A. & E. Enc. of Law, 715; C. L. 1897, sec 2685, sub-sec. 109; C. L. 1897, sec. 3267; 12 A. & E. Enc. 402; 24 Cyc. 497; Brown v. Keene, 8 Peters 115; Earle v. McVeigh, 91 U. S. 503; Bank v. Lewinson, 12 N. M.

147; Davis v. Tilleston Co., 6 How. 114; Lockhart v.
Leeds, 12 N. M. 168; Meister v. Moore, 96 U. S. 78.

The District Courts of this State possess a superin-
tending control over inferior tribunals. Territory v. Valdez, 1 N. M. 537; Muniz v. Herrera, 1 N. M. 365.

The statement that "plaintiffs had a plain, speedy and
adequate remedy at law," is a mere conclusion of law.
Streator v. Linscott, 95 Pac. 42.

Power of equity is not to be limited by statute, or other-
wise, where such limitations would work injustice and
wrong. Territory v. Valdez, 1 N. M. 533; Muniz v.
Herrera, 1 N. M. 365; Gutierrez v. Pino, 1 N. M. 392;
In re Henriquez, 5 N. M. 177; Lockhart v. Woollacot, 8
N. M. 24; El Capitan Co. v. Lees, 13 N. M. 413; C. L.
1897, sec. 3367; Smith v. Merrill, 55 Pac. 824; Dial v.
Olsen, 36 Pac. 175; Bassett v. Mitchell, 19 Pac. 671;
Olson v. Nunally, 28 Pac. 149; Merriman v. Walton, 30
L. R. A. 876, and note; Elliott v. Lessee of Piersol, 7 L.
Ed. 170; Kimball v. Short, 43 Pac. 321; Chester v. Mil-
ler, 13 Cal. 558; Chicago, M. & St. P. Ry. Co. v. Third
National Bank, 134 U. S. 276; Sheldon v. Motter, 53
Pac. 90; Gregory v. Diggs, 45 Pac. 261.

J. M. PALMER, Farmington ,N. M., for appellees.

An appeal will lie from a judgment of the Justice of
the Peace, whether void or voidable. Douthitt v. Bailey,
14 N. M. 530; 24 Cyc. 423; De Baca v. Wilcox, 11 N. M.
352; Livermore v. Campbell, 52 Cal. 75; White v. Crow,
28 L. Ed. 113; Lohman v. Cox, 9 N. M. 509; Gutierrez
v. Pino, 1 N. M. 392; Kerr v. Murphy, et al., 8 A. & E.
Ann. Cas. 1138, 69 L. R. A. 499.

Plaintiffs must exhaust their legal remedies before com-
ing to a court of equity for relief. Kerr v. Murphy, 8 A.
& E. Ann. Cas. 1141; Grand Chute v. Winegar, 15 Wall.
373, 21 U. S. (L. Ed.) 174; Carney v. Hadley, 22 L. R.
A. (N. S.) 233; 22 Cyc. 769, and cases cited; Mastick v.
Thorp, 29 Cal. 444.

Equity will not afford relief to a party who has been
negligent in obtaining a legal remedy. Vantilburg v.

Black, 3 Mont. 459; McCormick v. Hubbell, et al., 5 Pac.
314; Texas M. R. Co. v. Wright, 88 Tex. 346, 31 S. W.
613; Houston E. & W. T. R. Co. v. Ellisor, 37 S. W. 972;
4 Standard Enc. of Procedure, 478; 16 N. M. 37; 14 N.
M. 530.

Reply Brief for Appellants.

Mastick v. Thorp, 29 Cal. 444; In re Debs, 39 L. Ed.
1102; Davis v. Tileston Co., 6 How. 114; C. L. 1897, sec.
2685, sub-sec. 96; 23 Cyc. 1089; Levy v. Ortega, 9 N. M.
392; Hagerman v. Meeks, 13 N. M. 571; Oliver v. Enri-
quez, 16 N. M. 326; People ex rel. Carrilla v. De La
Guerra, 24 Cal. 78; 12 A. & E. Enc. 206, note; Orleans
v. Ripley, 25 Am. Dec. 175; Pickens v. Coal Riv. B. &
T. Co., 24 L. R. A. (N. S.) 356; Bank v. Bryan, 13 Bush.
419; Enix v. Miller, 54 Ia. 551; Bank v. Burnam, 61 Mo.
76; U. S. v. Bliss, 172 U. S. 322, 43 L. Ed. 463.

STATEMENT OF THE CASE.

The complaint states that the deceased Scott sued them
in the Justice of the Peace court for precinct No. 2, San
Juan County, for debt in the sum of $100.00. That the
summons in the action was served on them on the 19th day
of November; 1910, commanding them to appear on the
24th of the same month. That on the 23rd of November,
1910, the said Scott wrongfully and unlawfully induced
the Justice of the Peace to hear the evidence in the case
and to render judgment therein in the sum of $100.00
and costs of suit against the appellants. That on the
25th day of July, 1911, an execution was issued, based
on the said judgment, and placed in the hands of the
Sheriff of San Juan County, and that the Sheriff on the
1st day of August, 1911, took and levied upon several
head of cattle of appellants and unless restrained will sell
said cattle. An injunction was prayed.

Appellees demurred, on the ground that the complaint
failed to state a cause of action because on its face it appears that the plaintiffs had in the action therein referred
to, a plain, speedy and adequate remedy at law, by ap-

peal from said judgment or by writ of certiorari. The demurrer being sustained by the court, the plaintiffs elected to stand on their complaint, and refused to further plead, and judgment was rendered dismissing the action.

OPINION OF THE COURT.

MECHEM, D. J.—The judgment was void because there was no service of appellants to appear on the day it

1 was rendered. The Justice had no jurisdiction to render the judgment. It is not a question, whether the appellants had proper notice, as in the case cited by counsel, (Kerr v. Murphy, 19 S. Dak. 184, 8 A. & E. Ann. Cases), but whether they had any notice at all. In the case cited the defendant was given but two days' notice when the statute required three days' notice. The court held that "the police justice considered the return before him and erroneously decided that the plaintiff in the action had had proper notice."

It was an irregularity in a preliminary proceeding, not an entire want of the preliminary proceeding. The distinction is drawn between "a want of jurisdiction and a defect in obtaining jurisdiction" (1 Freeman on Judgments, sec. 126), between "a case where there is no service whatever and one which is simply defective or irregular" (id.) As was said in Leonard v. Sparks, 117 Mo. 103, 22 S. W. 899, the defendant in the latter case has his day in court to object to the process. The test is in such cases whether the court had a right to decide or whether having the right to decide its judgment was merely erroneous. In this case the Justice of the Peace had no right to decide.

While the complaint was demurred to because it showed on its face that the appellants had a remedy at law by appeal or certiorari, yet at the time of the bringing of this action their time for availing themselves of those remedies had long since passed. Before they will be denied the relief they ask, they must have lost the right to those legal remedies by their laches or negligence. Assuming that the appellants had actual knowledge that the judgment had been given against them, were they legally bound to appeal from it or remove it to the District Court by writ of certiorari? In a very similar case, National Metal Company v. Greene Consolidated Copper Companay, — Ariz.—, 89 Pac. 535, 9 L. R. A. N. S. 1062, the Court said:—"If the allegations in this complaint are true, there was no service whatsoever, and the judgment, though not void on its face, is void in fact; and plaintiff's only adequate protection lies in this action. That it did not act upon the information acquired from Pellegrin, was not neglect, was not 'sleeping in its rights,' it was inaction in reliance upon its legal rights, in reliance upon the constitutional guaranty of due process of law. Such is not the inaction which bars relief in equity. To accomplish such a bar, it is said that the inaction must be such as amounts to a violation of a positive legal duty.' Pom. Eq. Jur., 2nd ed., 856, p. 1187."

And in Cooley v. Barker, 122 Iowa 440, 98 N. W. 289; 101 Am. St. 276, being an action to enjoin the enforcement of a judgment of a Justice of the Peace, it was said:—

"Appellees contend that the plaintiff is not entitled to relief because of laches, and for the further reason that he does not show that he was not in fact indebted to the plaintiff in the judgment. There is no foundation either in fact or in law for the first proposition. Plaintiff had no occasion to act until some attempt was made to enforce the void judgment. When that was done, he brought this action. It was timely, and defendants were in no manner prejudiced by the delay."

If one having actual notice of a judgment given against him by a court having no jurisdiction, must act, then the judgment is not void to all intents and purposes, an impossible conclusion. If the judgment is void, and no
     rights can be acquired under it, can any correspond-
2 ing burdens or obligations be put on others by reason
     of it? If the judgment was void as to appellants, why would they be compelled to take notice of it any more than any other person in the whole world? Nor can it reasonably be said because of notice, because there being no

legal notice there is nothing of which one is bound to take cognizance. If this is so, then a court may render judgment upon the sole showing that the defendant knew that a suit had been brought against him or even that a suit was going to be brought against him. Siling v. Hendrickson, 193 Mo. 365, 92 S. W. 105.

These considerations would appear to be conclusive against the proposition that the appellants were bound to act, though they knew the judgment had been given against them.

Nor would the remedies by appeal or certiorari seem adequate, as those remedies are given and controlled **3** by our statutes. By availing themselves of those remedies, the appellants would have waived the violation of their rights of which they now complain. On both appeal and writ of certiorari, the case is tried in the District Court de novo, and no advantage can be taken of an error in the Justice of the Peace court as to process. If the Justice had jurisdiction of the subject matter of the action and could have obtained jurisdiction of the persons of the defendants, on appeal or certiorari the District Court has complete jurisdiction, because to pursue either course, the appellants must have entered their general appearance. Crolot v. Maloy, 2 N. M. 198.

In addition to waiving their rights, the appellants would have been compelled to give bond, pay a docket fee in the District Court and perhaps employ an attorney. The amount involved does not effect the principle involved. In a case involving a few dollars, a poor man might be compelled to abide an invasion of his rights.

If the statutes permitted the Justice of the Peace upon a special appearance to set such a judgment aside, or if, on removal, the District Court might reverse for such an error and cast the party at fault in the costs, the case would be different. Such legal remedies would be as complete, practical, and as efficient to the ends of justice and its prompt administration, as the remedy in equity.

Nor do appellants have a plain, speedy and adequate remedy at law in an action against the Justice of the

Peace or the officer acting by virtue of the execution,
4 as announced in Gutierrez v. Pino, 1 N. M. 392,
where it was said that the fact that the legal remedy
for a wrong is expensive and inconvenient, will not give
a court of chancery jurisdiction, but that decision must be
treated as overruled by the Supreme Court of the United
States. In the case of Walla Walla v. Walla Walla Water
Co., 172 U. S. 1, where it was said:

"This Court has repeatedly declared in affirmance of the
generally accepted proposition that the remedy at law, in
order to exclude a concurrent remedy at equity, must be
as complete, as practical, and as efficient to the ends of
justice and its prompt administration, as the remedy in
equity."

The remedy appellants now seek is beyond any doubt far
more complete, practical and efficient to the ends of justice and its prompt administration than any known action at law.

For the reasons above stated, the judgment of the lower
court is reversed, and this cause remanded.

[No. 1585, January 10, 1914.]

STATE OF NEW MEXICO, Appellee, v. LOUIS ROB-
ERTS and JOHN LUMPKIN, Appellants.

SYLLABUS (BY THE COURT)

1. Where, in a prosecution instituted for a violation of
sec. 79, C. L. 1897, the indictment charges that the defendants "then and there, unlawfully and feloniously did take,
steal and knowingly drive away, etc.," the animal in question, it is not necessary to further allege that the owner was
thereby deprived of the immediate possession of the animal.
                                                    P. 483

2. The verdict of a jury will not be set aside on appeal
when it is supported by substantial evidence.
                                                    P. 485

3. Upon cross examination the State has the right to expose to the jury the relations existing between the witnesses testifying and the defendant, and the fact that the witnesses have been frequently used by the defendant to establish an alibi was proper to go to the jury for the purpose of weakening the evidence given by the witnesses on their direct examination.

P. 485

4. Evidence that a witness for the State expects to receive a reward upon conviction of the accused can properly be elicited upon cross examination of such witness for the purpose of showing his interest in the result of the prosecution.

P. 486

5. Such witness, however, cannot be interrogated as to a reward offered for the arrest and conviction of parties other than the defendants, or in which the witness had no prospective interest.

P. 486

6. Where, on cross examination, a witness is asked a question the answer to which calls for an explanation, the adverse party has the right, on redirect examination, to ask the witness to explain the same.

P. 487

Appeal from the District Court of San Miguel County; David J. Leahy, District Judge; affirmed.

C. H. HITTSON, Tucumcari, N. M., for appellants.

Indictment is defective for the reason that it does not allege that the owner was deprived of the possession of the animal in question. Alwin v. Morley, 108 Pac. 778; Territory v. Cortez, 103 Pac. 264.

Proof of ownership must be positive. 25 Cyc. 125; Schaubert v. State, 12 S. W. 732; Crockett v. State, 14 Tex. App. 226.

Identification of the parties accused should be positive and complete. People v. Ong Git, 111 Pac. 630; People v. Williams, et al., 242 Ill. 197; Moore on Facts, vol. II, page 1367, articles 1222-23-27.

An attempt to gain possession of the property, however persistent or continued, will not constitute larceny; there must be such a taking away of the property that the accused acquires complete dominion over it and supersedes the possession of the owner. Molton v. State, 53 Am. St. 97; State v. Rozeboom, 29 L. R. A. (N. S.) 37; Clark v. State, 128 S. W. 131; Hicks v. State, 28 S. E. 917; Edmonds v. State, 70 Ala. 8; Wolf v. State, 41 Ala. 412; Williams v. State, 63 Miss. 58; People v. Meyer, 17 Pac. 431.

Error in allowing the State to ask witness Bell about his having testified in behalf of the defendant Roberts at other times and in other cases, wherein Roberts was accused of the larceny of cattle. 6 Enc. of Ev. 145; Insurance Co. v. Mercantile Co., 13 N. M. 254; 3 Enc. of Ev. 13.

E. P. DAVIES, Assistant Attorney General, Santa Fe, N. M., for appellee.

The sufficiency of an indictment will not be considered, where the objection was not raised by demurrer or by motion to quash or in arrest. Sec. 79, C. L. 1897; Territory v. Church, 14 N. M. 226.

Formal defects in indictments are cured by plea and trial. Haynes v. U. S., 9 N. M. 519.

Exceptions to the decisions of the Court upon any matter of law arising during the progress of the trial must be made at the time of the decision. Sec. 37, ch. 57, Laws 1907; Territory v. Leslie, 106 Pac. 378; Territory v. O'Donnell, 4 N. M. 196; Territory v. Alarid, 106 Pac. 371; Territory v. Gonzales, 15 N. M. 30.

The Supreme Court will not attempt to usurp the province of the trial jury by weighing the evidence where the verdict is supported by substantial evidence. Territory v.

O'Donnell, 4 N. M. 196; Territory v. Maxwell, 2 N. M.
250; Cunningham v. Springer, 13 N. M. 259.

Obtaining possession of the animal in question did not
constitute larceny. Terr. v. Wilburn, 10 N. M. 402; State
v. Jackson, 65 N. C. 305; Garris v. State, 35 Ga. 247;
Harrison v. People, 50 N. Y. 518; Eckels v. State, 20 O.
St. 508.

The extent to which cross-examination of a witness may
be carried is largely a matter of discretion with the trial
judge. Zane v. De Onativia, 73 Pac. 856; Sandell v.
Sherman, 40 Pac. 493; Grimbly v. Harold, 57 Pac. 558;
Insurance Co. v. Mercantile Co., 13 N. M. 256.

OPINION OF THE COURT.

ROBERTS, C. J.—Omitting the formal parts, the indictment to which defendants pleaded not guilty, and
upon which they were tried and convicted, reads as follows:

"That Louis Roberts, and John Lumpkin, late of the
County of San Miguel, State of New Mexico, on the 28th
day of July, in the year of Our Lord One Thousand Nine
Hundred and Twelve, at the County of San Miguel aforesaid; one head of neat cattle of the value of fifteen dollars of the property of the Red River Valley Company, then
and there being, unlawfully and feloniously did take, steal
and knowingly drive away; contrary to the form of
1 the statute, etc." Appellants contend that the indictment is defective and insufficient because of its failure to allege that the owner was deprived of the possession of the animals in question. The indictment was
predicated upon sec. 79, C. L. 1897, which, in so far as
pertinent, reads as follows:—

"Any person who shall steal, embezzle or knowingly kill,
sell, drive, lead or ride away, or in any manner deprive the
owner of the immediate possession of any neat cattle, etc.,
'shall be punished by imprisonment, etc.'"

The form of indictment herein was approved by the
Territorial Supreme Court in the case of Territory v.
Garcia, 12 N. M. 87, and has been generally employed in
prosecutions under this section since that case was de-

cided. The point here raised, however, was not called to
the attention of the Court in that case. The section
quoted was enacted for the protection of stock upon the
range and is much broader in its scope than the ordinary
larceny statute.

"It enumerates three distinct crimes, viz:—1st, stealing of animals; 2nd, embezzlement of animals; and 3rd,
knowingly killing or otherwise depriving the owners of
animals of their immediate possession." Territory v. Cortez, 15 N. M. 92.

Under the third class it will be seen that it is a violation of the statute to knowingly kill, sell, drive, lead or
ride away, or in any maner deprive the owner of the immediate possession of any neat cattle, etc. The last clause
was inserted merely to cover any method or means which
might be employed to deprive the owner of the immediate
possession of an animal, not enumerated by the previous
words employed, and in charging the offense it is not necessary to allege that the owner was deprived of the immediate possession of the animal, where one of the enumerated statutory words are employed, as in this indictment.
Here it is alleged that the defendants unlawfully and
feloniously did steal, take and drive away the animal in
question. If they did this, necessarily the owner was deprived of the immediate possession of the animal, and
such an allegation would have been merely a conclusion
drawn from the facts previously stated.

"Facts and not conclusions must be averred in an indictment, but matters of necessary inference or conclusion
from the facts averred need not be alleged." 22 Cyc. 303.
The indictment was sufficient.

The appellants, in the third, fourth and fifth points of
their brief contend (a) that the evidence as to the ownership of the animal in question was insufficient; (b) that
there was not sufficient evidence as to the identity of the
defendants, and, (c) the evidence was insufficient to prove
the asportation of the animal. Upon each of these questions, however, there was substantial evidence, which, if

believed by the jury, warranted the verdict. It has
2 been uniformly held in this jurisdiction that a verdict will not be set aside when it is supported by substantial evidence. Territory v. Trapp, 16 N. M. 700.

The defense interposed by appellants was an alibi, to
substantiate which James Bell and J. W. Dickey were
called as witnesses. Upon cross-examination the State
asked Bell if he had not testified on behalf of Louis Roberts before, and if he was not surety on his bond, and if
he had not theretofore been surety for him in criminal
cases, all of which questions were answered in the affirmative. Dickey was asked how many times he had been used
as a witness by defendant, Louis Roberts, to establish an
alibi, in cases where Roberts was accused of stealing cattle, to which he answered "three times." The purpose of
these questions was of course to show the friendly relations
which existed between the witnesses and the accused, and
to discredit their testimony, and for such purpose was
3 clearly admissible. The State had the right to expose
to the jury the relations existing between the witnesses and the defendants, and the fact that the witnesses
had been frequently used by one of the defendants to establish an alibi, was proper to go to the jury for the purpose of weakening the evidence given by the witnesses on
their direct examination.

"As a general rule any matter which tends either to
elucidate or to discredit the testimony given by the witness is a proper subject of cross-examination. Accordjng-
ly a party has a right upon cross-examination to draw out
anything which would tend to contradict, weaken, modify,
or explain the evidence given by the witness on his direct
examination, or any inference that may result from it
tending to support in any degree the opposite side of the
case." 40 Cyc. 2481; State v. McGahey, 3 N. D. 293.

Upon the trial one of the witnesses for the State was
asked and answered the following questions, upon cross-
examination:

"Q. Is it not a fact that you have personal knowledge
that the Red River Cattle Company were at that time
having a standing reward of a large amount of money for

the arrest and detection of these particular defendants for cattle stealing?

"A. No, I did not know it.

"Q. You had no knowledge of any reward that was offered as to these boys? .

"A. No, sir.

"Q. Had you any knowledge of a general reward at that time for the detection, and arrest and punishment of any persons charged with cattle stealing from the Bell Ranch?"

To the last question an objection was interposed, which was sustained by the Court. This the appellants claim was prejudicial error.

Evidence that a witness for the State expected to receive a reward upon the conviction of the accused could

4 properly be elicited on cross-examination of such witness, for the purpose of showing his interest in the result of the prosecution. The witness had stated that he had no knowledge of any reward offered as to these defendants. Let us suppose, that in answer to the excluded inquiry the witness had stated that the Company had a standing reward offered for the arrest and conviction of

5 John Doe for cattle stealing. Would such fact have any bearing upon the issues being tried? Assuredly not. Again, from the evidence it appears that the witness was in the employ of the Company, and that he was acting under directions and in the line of his duty when he surprised the defendants in the act of driving away the animal in question. The fact that a reward might have been offered for the arrest and conviction of the defendants could not have influenced the witness to color or manufacture evidence, unless he came within the terms of the reward and expected to profit thereby. The excluded question, it will be seen, did not bring either the defendants or the witness within its terms, and was, therefore, properly excluded. Error cannot be predicated upon the exclusion of a question upon cross-examination, which does not appear to be material or relevant, and where no statement is made by counsel to the Court showing the materiality or relevancy of such question.

Error is also assigned because the Court permitted the State, upon re-direct examination, to ask a witness why he expected the defendants to appear, while he and another witness were watching for cattle thieves. The inquiry, however, was opened by the defendants in their cross-examination, when they asked the witness if he expected these defendants to appear while they were watching for thieves. The witness answered that he did.
6 This fact having been brought out by the defendants, it was proper for the State to go further and show why the witness expected the defendants to appear.

Finding no error in the record, the judgment of the District Court is affirmed, and it is so ordered.

[No. 1612, January 10, 1914.]

CARRIE M. CHILDERS, Individually and as Executrix of the Estate of William B. Childers, Appellant, v. ADOLPH J. LAHANN, Appellee.

SYLLABUS (BY THE COURT)

1. An appearance, in practice, is a coming into court as a party to a suit, whether as plaintiff or defendant, and is a formal proceeding by which a defendant submits himself to the jurisdiction of the court.

P. 490

2. The question as to whether a party has appeared and submitted himself voluntarily to the jurisdiction of the court should be tried by the record and not by other evidence.

P. 491

3. When a party takes an appeal in open court he must see that the record affirmatively shows that it was taken in open court, and where the record is silent upon the question the presumption is that the appeal was not so taken, and in such case it is incumbent upon the appellant to cause citation to be issued and served upon appellee.

P. 491

4. Where good cause is shown for the failure to cause citation to be issued and served upon appellee as, and within the time, required by statute, the appellate court can extend the time for serving the citation and will permit a citation to be issued and served at any time before the end of the term of the appellate court to which the appeal was properly returnable.

P. 493

Appeal from the District Court of Lincoln County; Edward L. Medler, District Judge; motion to dismiss appeal denied.

E. W. Dobson, Albuquerque, N. M., for appellant.

John Y. Hewitt, White Oaks, and E. C. Wade, Jr.. Santa Fe, N. M., for appellee.

No briefs.

OPINION OF THE COURT.

ROBERTS, C. J.—The order granting an appeal in this case was signed by the District Judge on the 16th day of June, 1913. No extension of time to perfect the appeal was asked for or granted, hence the return day was 130 days thereafter (sec. 2, chap. 120, S. L. 1909.) The transcript of the record and assignments of error were filed in due season, but citation was not issued and served upon the appellee as required by sec. 2, chap. 57, S. L. 1907. Because of appellant's failure so to do, appellee, by special appearance, moves the dismissal of the appeal. Sec. 2, chap .57, supra, in so far as material, reads as follows :—

"When an appeal is taken, unless the same is taken in open court, which fact shall be shown by the record, citation shall be issued by the clerk of the District Court directed to and citing the opposite party to appear in the Supreme Court and answer such appeal on the return day thereof."

The section further provides how such citation shall be served.

Appellant admits that no citation was issued or served upon appellee; that the return day was October 25, 1913. But she resists the motion to dismiss the appeal, on the ground that appellee has entered a general appearance in the case in this Court. The issuance and service of citation is waived by the voluntary appearance of the appellee or defendant in error. Daily v. Foster, 128 Pac. 71. The claim of appellant is not based upon any formal entry, plea, motion, or act of the appellee shown by the records of this Court, but is founded solely upon a letter received by her attorney from one of appellee's attorneys, and the reply of her said attorney thereto. The letters are as follows:

"El Paso, Texas, Nov. 2, 1913.
"E. W. Dobson,
    "Albuquerque, N. M.
"Dear Mr. Dobson:
    "Your letter of the 28th ult. was forwarded to me here, and I wish to thank you for the offer to extend courtesies in case of Childers v. Lahann.

"If it is not asking too much, I would like to have the case continued to the January Term, when I hope to be able to attend to it. I am here under treatment and improving slowly, but am unfit for work. By extending the time for hearing of the case as indicated, you will greatly oblige. Mr. Hudspeth will sign a stipulation if one is necessary.   "Yours truly,
                            "John Y. Hewitt."

To which appellant's attorney replied as follows:—
"John Y. Hewitt,
    "El Paso, Texas,
"My Dear Judge:—
    "Yours of the 2nd inst, received. I told Mr. Hudspeth that I would grant any reasonable time for you to file briefs in the case of Childers v. Lahann and so far as I am concerned the case can be taken up at the January term. After your reply brief is filed it may be that I will

want to answer the same, although at the present time I
think I have covered all points that I could.

"I will sign any stipulation that you or Mr. Hudspeth
may desire, although this letter is sufficient and I assure
you no advantage will be taken and you will be granted
the time that you desire.   "Yours truly,
                                   "E. W. Dobson."

No application for a continuance was made to the Court
by appellee, and no entry of any kind was made by the
Court in the case in this regard.   On November 26, the
motion to dismiss was filed.

The solution of the question depends upon the effect of
the letters quoted, for, if they constituted an appearance
by appellee in this Court, the motion to dismiss is not well
taken.

Bouvier's Law Dictionary defines appearance, in practice, as follows:—

"A coming into court as a party to a suit, whether as
plaintiff or defendant.

"The formal proceeding by which a defendant submits
himself to the jurisdiction of the court."

It could hardly be contended that the letters which
passed between the attorneys would constitute an appearance, within the definition of the term above quoted.

1   There was no "coming into court," for no action by
the court was asked by appellee.   No paper, motion or
pleading of any kind was filed by appellee, nor was any
relief asked of the Court.   Had appellee applied to the
Court for a continuance, such act would have constituted
an appearance and the Court would have jurisdiction over
his person.   And the question, as to whether a party has
appeared and submitted himself voluntarily to the jurisdiction of the court, should be tried by the record and not
by other evidence.   Were this not true the door might be
opened to fraud and imposition.   As to the acts necessary
to constitute an appearance and how established, the Supreme Court of Indiana say:—

"To constitute an appearance so as to give jurisdiction
over the person of a defendant in this State, there must
be some formal entry, plea, motion, or act, or word spoken

in said cause in court which should be shown by the record." Kirkpatrick, etc., Co. v. Central Electric Co., 159 Ind. 639.

In the case of Scott, et al., v. Hull, et al., 14 Ind. 136, the defendants sought to remove the cause to the Federal Court, and the question arose as to whether they had not voluntarily appeared in the case in the State Court, by appearing before an officer upon the taking of depositions by plaintiffs, and also by defendants taking depositions, to be used upon the trial of said cause. The Court say:—

"By bill of exceptions, it appears that these facts were established by evidence other than the record, * * * * * There should be some formal entry, or plea, or motion, or official act (3 Blackf. 226) to constitute an appearance; and this should be of record, and tried by the record. 6 Com. Dig. 8; Kanouse v. Martin, 15 How. (U. S.) 198."

The Supreme Court of West Virginia, in the case of Groves v. County Court, 42 W. Va. 587, say:

"Appearance is the first act of the defendant in court (1 Tidd, Prac. 262; 6 Com. Dig. tit. 'Pleader,' B 1, p. 6) and the appearance of the defendant is triable by the record which is a verity (1 Co. Litt. 260; 1 Chit. Pl. 512.)" See also Colby v. Knapp, 13 N. H. 175.

In vol. 2, Standard Ency. Proc. 491, the rule is stated as follows:

"There should be some formal entry of record, 'or plea, motion, or official act, to constitute an appearance,' and this should be tried by the record and not by other evidence."

In this case, the fact that the court would be required
2 to resort to evidence outside of the record, in order to
   ascertain that appellee had appeared, renders appellant's contention untenable.

Appellant contends, however, that as the record in this case does not show affirmatively that the appeal was not taken in open court, the Court will not presume such
   fact, unless it is made to appear by evidence or sworn
3 statement. When an appeal is taken in open court,
   the fact must be shown by the record, and when the record fails to so show, citation should issue and service

be had on the appellee prior to the return day. (Sec. 2,
chap. 57, S. L. 1907.) Appellant does not contend that
the appeal was in fact taken in open court, but only that
the record does not show that it was not so taken. Where
a party takes an appeal in open court, it is incumbent upon
him to see that the record affirmatively shows that it was
taken in open court, and where the record is silent upon
the question, the presumption is, that the appeal was not
so taken.

Appellant asks, in the event the Court should hold that
appellee has not entered a general appearance herein, that
he be permitted to have citation issued and served. While
under the statute, (sec. 20, chap. 57, S. L. 1907, as
amended by sec. 1, chap. 120, S. L. 1909), all appeals,
writs of error, bonds, summons, citations and other process, in the Supreme Court are returnable one hundred
and thirty days after the appeal is taken, or such writs
are issued, the Territorial Supreme Court, in construing
similar language used, in sec. 2, chap. 114, S. L. 1905,
held that the Supreme Court could extend the time for
serving the citation, and could permit a citation to be issued and served at any time before the end of the next
ensuing term. Baca v. Anaya, 14 N. M. 20.

"In the interpretation of reenacted statutes the Court
will follow the construction which they received when previously in force. The legislature will be presumed to
know the effect which such statutes originally had, and by
re-enactment to intend that they should again have the
same effect. * * * * * It is not necessary that a statute
should be re-enacted in identical words in order that the
rule may apply. It is sufficient if it is re-enacted in substantially the same words." Lewis Sutherland Statutory
Construction, (2d ed.) sec. 403, and authorities cited.

The "next ensuing term" was defined by the Territorial
Supreme Court, in the case of Paden, et al., v. Placer Co.,
15 N. M. 345, to be "the term of the Appellate Court to
which it was properly returnable." The Court say, "But
no case has been called to our attention in which it has
been permitted later than that or unless for good cause
shown."

Following the construction given the statute by the Territorial Supreme Court, we conclude that it is within the power of this Court to permit appellant to procure citation to be issued by the clerk of the District Court of Lincoln County, returnable 130 days after its issu-
4 ance, to be served upon appellee as required by law, if good cause has been shown for the failure to issue and serve the same. The question, therefore, remains as to whether appellant has shown such "good cause" as will excuse the default. The reason stated for the failure to have citation issued and served, briefly summarized, are as follows:

After the appeal was taken, appellant's attorneys had a great deal of correspondence with appellee's attorneys with reference to locating the papers and testimony which were lost. Said attorneys agreed to and did stipulate in writing as shown by the record, that certain exhibits need not be copied in full in the record, but that abstracts of the same, which were set forth in the stipulation, could be incorporated into the record to be "used upon appeal;" that appellant's attorney applied to appellee's attorneys for an extension of time within which to file his brief, which was granted, but no written stipulation was entered into in this regard; that frequent conversations were had between said attorneys concerning said appeal; that by reason of the above appellant's attorney was led to believe that appellee's attorneys had waived citation and intended voluntarily to appear in this Court, in said cause.

In addition to the above the record of this cause, in this Court, discloses that appellant has acted in the utmost good faith in prosecuting her appeal. Within the time limited by statute she filed with the clerk a printed transcript of the record; filed her assignment of errors and served a copy thereof on appellee's attorneys and likewise filed and served printed copies of her brief. The Court has jurisdiction of the cause, but not of the appellee, because of the failure to serve citation. All that remains to give the Court jurisdiction over both the cause and the parties, is the issuance and service of citation. We are of the opinion that the above facts, all of which are admitted, furnish good cause for a denial of the motion to dismiss the appeal, and warrant the Court in permitting appellant to sue out and serve citation on appellee. The Court is always reluctant to dispose of any cause except upon the merits of the questions involved, unless required to do so by plain and explicit provisions of the statute, rule of court, or established procedure.

For the reasons stated, the motion to dismiss the appeal will be denied, at this time, and appellant will be given the right to sue out and serve citation, and it is so ordered.

[No. 1613, January 10, 1914.]

ALONZO B. M'MILLEN, Appellee, v. FIRST NATIONAL BANK OF CLOVIS, Appellant.

SYLLABUS (BY THE COURT)

1. Under the decisions of the Supreme Court of Texas, a failure to indorse upon an alias or pluries execution the number of previous executions which have been issued on the judgment, as required by sec. 7, art. 3729, Rev. Civ. Stat. Tex. 1911, is merely an irregularity, which does not render the execution and sale thereunder void.

P. 500

2. Statutory provisions as to the order of sale and the manner of making it are for the benefit of the defendant alone and can be waived by him, and, where there are irregularities in this regard, and he does not move promptly, he is considered to have waived them.

P. 501

3. Where a court renders final judgment in a cause, it has no jurisdiction to proceed further except in carrying out the terms of the judgment, and where that is left to nonjudicial officers, their power is fixed by the terms of the judgment, and, when once executed, the power is ended.

P. 502

4. Every person may disregard judicial proceedings which are nullities and without jurisdiction.

P. 502

5. Appellee was not estopped to deny the invalidity of the proceedings had under the third execution, where it is not shown that he caused such execution to issue, or had knowledge of its issuance, or acquiesced therein.

P. 502

Appeal from the District Court of Bernalillo ·County; Herbert F. Raynolds, District Judge; affirmed.

HARRY L. PATTON, Clovis, N. M., for appellant.

Provisions for sale under Texas statute, sec. 3, art. 3729, Rev. Stats. of Texas; Pierson v. Hammond, 22 Tex. 585; Young v. Smith, 23 Tex. 598; Borden v. Tillman, 39 Tex. 262.

· Which was the regular sale? Sec. 7, art. 3729, Rev. Stat. of Texas; art. 2281, Rev. Stat. Texas; Driscoll v. Norris, 2 Tex. Civ. App. 602; 21 S. W. 629; Freeman on Executions, sec. 54; Frankfort Bank v. Markley, 1 Dana 373.

Is plaintiff estopped? 16 Cyc. 795; 16 Cyc. 799; Prudential Real Estate Co. v. Hall, 116 N. W. 40; Kennedy v. Afdal, 82 N. E. 291; Loeb v. Struck, 42 S. W. 401; 16 Cyc. 809.

Can this issue be determined upon collateral attack? Smith v. Perkins, 16 S. W. 805; Moore v. Johnson, 34 S. W. 771; Smith v. Olson, 56 S. W. 568; Taylor v. Snow, 47 Tex. 462; Boggess v. Howard, 40 Tex. 153.

A. B. McMILLEN, Albuquerque, N. M., for appellee.

The alleged omission in the second order of sale was, at most, an irregularity; did not invalidate the sale and the objection could not be raised by appellant. Morris v.

McMillen v. Bank, 18 N. M. 494.

Hastings, et al., 7 S. W. 649; Freeman on Executions, 339; Howard v. North, 5 Tex. 308.

This suit is not a collateral attack upon the Texas case, but is in support of it so far as there was jurisdiction and authority to act. Freeman on Executions, sec. 74; Voorhees v. Bank of U. S., 10 Pet. 477; Blaine v. Charles Carter, 4 Cranch. 328; Wheaton v. Saxton, 4 Wheat. 456; Thompson v. Tolmie, 2 Pet. 157; U. S. v. Arredondo, 6 Pet. 729.

There was no estoppel as to plaintiff, but only as to appellee. 5 Enc. of U. S. Rep. 918; Bein v. Heath, 6 How. 228; Morgan v. Railroad Co., 96 U. S. 716; Merchants Bank v. State Bank, 10 Wall. 604; Leather Manufacturers Bank v. Morgan, 117 U. S. 96.

STATEMENT OF FACTS.

On February 1, 1909, C. S. McMillen executed to appellant a promissory note for the sum of $861.00, due ninety days after date. To secure the payment of the same he endorsed and delivered to appellant as collateral security a note for $1600, secured by vendor's lien on certain property in the town of Herford, Texas, and also a promissory note for $352.00, dated Oct. 1, 1909, made to said C. S. McMillen by J. W. McMillen. McMillen, failing to pay his note to the bank when due, and the vendor's lien note being past due and unpaid, appellant, together with McMillen and his wife, instituted suit in Deaf Smith County, Texas, against W. A. Price, the maker of the note, to foreclose the vendor's lien. May 30, 1910, the Texas court entered judgment, foreclosing the lien, and directing a sale of the property, and ordered that out of the proceeds of the sale there should be first paid to the First National Bank of Clovis the amount owing it by C. S. McMillen, on the promissory note for which the vendor's lien note was pledged as collateral, and directed the payment of the balance to Mrs. McMillen.

Pursuant to the judgment, an order of sale was issued to the Sheriff of Deaf Smith County, June 21, 1910, which, however, was returned unsatisfied on account of the bidder not complying with his bid; thereafter, on the 12th

day of August, 1910, a second order of sale, or execution
was issued, pursuant to which the real estate securing the
vendor's lien note was advertised and sold to the First
National Bank of Clovis, for the sum of $940.00.   The
Sheriff's return, in so far as material, reads as follows:—
    "And on said 6th day of September, A. D. 1910, be-
tween the hours of 10 o'clock A. M. and 4 o'clock P. M.,
at the court house door of said county, in pursuance to
said advertisement, sold said property at public sale to the
First National Bank of Clovis, to whom the same was
struck off for the sum of $940.00, that being the highest
secure bid for the same.   And the said First National
Bank of Clovis having paid the sum so bid by it, I executed
to it a deed for said land.   And after first satisfying the
Sheriff's costs accruing under this writ, amounting to the
sum of $31.30, an itemized bill of which appears below,
and the further sum of $11.05 original court costs, the
remainder, being the sum of $898.20, was paid to cred-
ited on said judgment due said bank by C. S. McMillen
and Laura E. McMillen, whose receipt for the same is
herewith presented and the writ is hereby returned on
this the 7th day of September, A. D. 1910."   ·
    On the same day a deed was executed by the Sheriff to
said bank, which deed was filed for record March 8, 1911,
in the Recorder's office of said Deaf Smith County.   The
deed contained, among other recitals, the following: ·
    Now, therefore, in consideration of the premises afore-
said, and of the payment of the sum of $940.00 by said
purchaser, the receipt of which is evidenced by a credit
of that amount on the judgment against said McMillen,
in favor of the First National Bank of Clovis, all of
which is made clear by reference to the judgment," etc.
    Article 3729, Revised Civil Statutes of Texas, 1911,
which was introduced in evidence upon the trial of this
case in the court below, in so far as pertinent, reads as
follows:—
    "Requisites of an execution.—The style of the execution
shall be, 'The State of Texas.'   It shall be directed to the
sheriff or any constable of the proper county, and shall
be signed by the clerk or justice officially, and sealed with

the seal of the court, if issued out of the district or county court. It shall correctly describe the judgment, stating the court wherein and the time when rendered, the names of the parties, the amount, if it be for money, and the amount actually due thereon, if less than the original amount, the rate of interest, if other than six per cent., and shall have the following requisites: * * * * *

"7. When an alias or pluries execution is issued, it shall show upon its face the number of previous executions which have been issued on the judgment."

The second order of sale did not recite on its face that it was an alias writ, or the number of previous executions. Some ten months after the second sale, the First National Bank of Clovis caused a third execution to issue, in strict compliance with the statute and repurchased the property for $250.00, taking a sheriff's deed therefor.

C. S. McMillen transferred the note executed to him by J. W. McMillen for $352.00 and by him pledged to secure his indebtedness to the First National Bank of Clovis, to the appellee herein. The bank refused to deliver the note, or its proceeds to appellee, claiming that the note for the payment of which it held the same as collateral had not been paid, and that it was entitled to apply the proceeds to the payment of the note. Its contention was upon the assumption that the second execution, under which it purchased the Texas real estate for the sum of $940.00 was void and invalid, and that it acquired no title to the property at the sale thereunder because of such invalidity. That, as it had only bid the sum of $250.00 for the property at the third sale, which strictly complied with the provisions of the statute, such sum did not discharge C. S. McMillen's indebtedness to it.

The trial court held that appellant acquired title by its purchase under the second execution, and was bound by said sale, and gave appellee judgment for the proceeds of the note. From such judgment appellant prosecutes this appeal.

OPINION OF THE COURT.

ROBERTS, C. J.—The vital question in this case, as shown by the facts stated, is, whether the second order of sale was void, because it did not show on its face the number of previous executions which had been issued on the judgment, as required by sub-sec. 7 of article 3729, Revised Civil Statutes of Texas, 1911. If the execution was not void, the sale to appellant resulted in a satisfaction of the judgment, in so far as it directed the sale of the property in question, and a subsequent execution for the sale of the same real estate would be invalid.

"When satisfied, the judgment has fully accomplished its mission, and the preponderance of authority is in favor of disregarding as absolutely void all proceedings taken subsequently to the satisfaction." Freeman on Executions, (3rd ed.) sec. 19.

At the sale, under the second execution, appellant bid in the real estate at an amount sufficient to satisfy the indebtedness owing it by C. S. McMillen, and received a sheriff's deed therefor, and, such amount so bid, after paying in cash the costs, etc., was credited on the judgment. If this was a valid sale, it resulted necessarily in the payment of McMillen's obligation to the bank and he was entitled to the return of the note in question. The subsequent sale, under the third execution, would be invalid and void and would have no effect whatever upon the rights of the parties to this suit.

Appellant relies upon the case of Driscol v. Morris, 2 Tex. Civ. App. 602, 21 S. W. 629, where the Court say:—

"Mention of previous executions in a bill of costs attached to an execution is not a compliance with Rev. St. art. 2281, declaring that, when an alias or pluries execution is issued, it shall show 'on its face' the number of previous executions."

A reading of the case, however, will show that the Court approved an instruction, informing the jury that such omission was an irregularity, and also of another instruction advising the jury as follows:—

"But if you find from the evidence that said land did not sell for a grossly inadequate price, or if it did sell for a grossly inadequate price, yet if the irregularities herein before mentioned did not conduce thereto, then you can not find for the intervenor." Thus clearly indicating that the Court did not intend to, nor hold, that such an omission would render a sale under such an execution invalid.

The authorities all agree that mere irregularities in execution and judicial sales do not make the same illegal, but at most make them only voidable, and then only upon prompt action of the injured party. Morris v. Hastings, et al., (Tex. Sup.) 7 S. W. 649; Freeman on Executions, sec. 339.

A later case decided by the Court of Civil Appeals of Texas (Corder v. Steiner, et al., 54 S. W. 277) distinctly

1 holds that a failure to state in the execution the number of executions previously issued does not render the execution void. The Court say:

"Failure to state in the execution the number of executions previously issued did not render the last execution void. It was a mere irregularity."

This question, however, has been settled by the Supreme Court of Texas, contrary to appellant's contention. In the case of Graves v. Hall, 13 Tex. 379, appellant instituted suit to revive a judgment, which appellee resisted on the ground that appellant had not kept the judgment alive by the issuance of executions as required by law; his contention being that the executions subsequent to the first did not purport to be *alias* or *pluries,* etc. The lower court held with appellee, that such executions were nullities, and gave him judgment on his plea of the statute of limitations. The Court say:—

"In support of the judgment we are referred to the cases of Bennett and wife v. Gamble, (1 Tex. R. 124) and Scott & Rose v. Allen, (Id.) 508; neither of these cases, as will be seen, enunciates any such principle as that, where executions have been regularly issued in respect of time. and the judgments and executions are before the court whereby it may be seen that they were so issued, the clerical omission to give them their proper numerical desig-

nation, will warrant their being treated as nullities." The
Court further say:

"Though the excutions in question were irregular in
point of form, they were not nullities. They might have
been amended; and when the Court has before it that
which to amend by, a mere clerical omission will be considered as amended; upon the principle, that, as to mere
matters of form, for the purpose of sustaining right, that
will be considered as done which ought to have been done."

And in the case of Hancock v. Metz, 15 Tex. 205, the
same Court say:—

"However irregular a proceeding may have been, the
title of the purchaser will not be affected by it, unless the
proceeding was absolutely void."

In the case of Morris v. Hastings, supra, the Court
say:—

"When notice of sale has not been properly given, if
objection be made by the defendant in execution without
unnecessary delay, the sale may be set aside. But the notice of sale, being for the benefit of the defendant, will be
considered waived if not made in a reasonable time."

The provisions as to the order of sale and the manner of
making it are for the benefit of the defendant alone and
can be waived by him, and, where there are irregularities
in this regard and he does not move promptly he is considered to have waived them. No one else can assert
2 these rights for him, and it must be apparent that
even the defendant could not have the proceedings set
aside without notice to parties and some regular proceeding authorized by law, and in such manner as to obtain
an order from a court having jurisdiction of the subject
matter.   .

If what has been said above is true, then the issuance
of the second order of sale, the sale of the land thereunder,
the purchase by appellant and the execution of the deed
to it were absolutely binding, and the Clerk and Sheriff,
having performed their regular duties in the execution of
said judgment, had no power to take any further action,
nor did appellant have the right to cause the third execution to issue.

Where a court renders final judgment in a cause, it has
no jurisdiction to proceed further except in carrying
3 out the terms of the judgment, and where that is left
to non-judicial officers, their power is fixed by the
terms of the judgment and when once executed the power
is ended.

We therefore conclude that C. S. McMillen's obligation
to the appellant was discharged by its purchase under the
second execution, and that the third execution issued on
the judgment was invalid and the sale thereunder void.

Appellant, however, contends that this suit is a collateral attack upon the proceedings in the Texas Court, but
in this it is mistaken. Appellee relies upon the judgment,
execution and sale by that Court. He contends that such
proceedings were regular and valid and relies thereon as a
discharge of the indebtedness of his assignor to appellant.

It is true he claims the third execution and sale were
4 void, because of a valid satisfaction of the judgment,
in the amount for which the land sold under the second execution, but this third execution and all proceedings under it we have seen were invalid and void; but it
is clear that every one may disregard proceedings which
are nullities and without jurisdiction.

Appellant further insists that appellee was estopped to
deny that the sale under the second execution was invalid, but we do not understand upon what theory the assumption is based. It is well understood that there
5 are three classes of estoppel, viz:—estoppel by record,
estoppel by deed, and equitable estoppel or estoppel
in pais. There was no attempt made to show that C. S.
McMillen caused the third execution to issue, or that he
had knowledge of its issuance, or acquiesced therein.

For the reasons stated, the judgment of the lower court
will be affirmed, and it is so ordered.

[No. 1614, January 10, 1914.]

E. E. SOUTHARD, Appellee, v. J. H. LATHAM, Appellant.

SYLLABUS (BY THE COURT)

1. The endorsement and delivery of a promissory note operates as an assignment, where the note is non-negotiable; and the assignee, under the statutes of New Mexico, may sue thereon in his own name. Where a note is transferred after maturity it is subject to defenses existing between the payee and payor and the question of its negotiability is immaterial.

P. 507

2. Transfers of property made to innocent third parties, in violation of a restraining order, are not void nor voidable, because made in disregard of such order.

P. 507

3. A surety, on a promissory note is not discharged from liability by an extension of time granted the principal, where the makers are not precluded from paying the note prior to the expiration of such an extension and the extension granted was without consideration.

P. 508

4. An exception to findings of fact made by the trial court must specify the particular finding or findings objected to, where more than one finding is made, and a general objection is insufficient to present any question for review unless all the findings are incorrect and an objection to a finding, where no requested finding on the proposition is asked, which points out counsel's theory or contention, should clearly indicate the claimed error.

P. 510

Appeal from the District Court of Sierra County: Merritt C. Mechem, District Judge; affirmed.

EDWARD D. TITTMAN, Hillsboro, N. M., for appellant.

Error in overruling defendant's demurrer to complaint.
4 A. & E. Enc. 95; Smith v. Crane, 22 N. W. 633; 1 Parsons on Notes, 30; Smith v. Maryland, 59 Ia. 645; Read
v. McNulty, 78 Am. Dec. 467; Hughitt v. Johnson, 28
Fed. 865; 7 Cyc. 595, note 71; Davis v. Brady, 97 N. W.
719; Hegeler v. Comstock, 45 N. W. 331; Jones v. Ra-
batz, 27 Minn. 240; Lamb v. Story, 45 Mich. 488; Garret-
son v. Purdy, 178.

Error in sustaining plaintiff's demurrer to answer. 8
Cyc. 43; Ginsberg v. Sheman, 128 N. Y. Sup. 653; 8 Cyc.
55, note 90; Campbell v. Gilman, 26 Ill. 120; Bryan v.
Saltenstall, 3 Marsh. 672; Kingston v. Walters, 14 N. M.
368; Sec. 2540, C. L. 1897.

Error in sustaining plaintiff's objection to evidence regarding endorsements on the note. Laws 1907; Duncan
v. Lawrence, 6 Abbottts Practice, N. Y. 304; Roberts v.
Glenn, 4 Ohio Dec. (reprint) 269.

Findings of fact or refusal to make findings are subject
to review, if there was no substantial evidence to support
such findings. Puritan Co. v. Toti, 14 N. M. 426; 16 Cyc.
1087; Kimball v. Odell, 122 N. Y. Sup. 755; Ham v.
R. R. Co., 149 Mo. App. 200; Schwitzer v. Hamburg
Amer. P. A. G., 149 App. Div. 900; 134 N. Y. Sup. 812.

Error in refusing and adopting findings. Brooks v.
Wright, 13 Allen 72; Davis v. Graham, 29 Ia. 514; Lime
Rock Bank v. Mallett, 34 Me. 56; Dubuisson v. Folks, 30
Miss. 432; Randolph on Commercial Paper, vol. 2, p. 652;
Fawcett v. Freshwater, 31 Ohio St. 637; Chute v. Pattee,
37 Me. 102; Pierce v. Goldsberry, 13 Ind. 52; Keim v.
Andrews, 59 Miss. 39; Abel v. Alexander, 45 Ind. 523;
Lee v. Field, 9 N. M. 435.

Error in refusing defendant's proposed conclusion of
law No. 2. French v. Bush, 194 Fed. 574; 31 Cyc. 350,
notes 34 and 35; Feiselman v. Manchester Fire Ins. Co.,
19 So. 540; Creek v. McManus, 32 Pac. 675.

Error in refusing defendant's proposed conclusion of
law No. 2. French v. Bush, 194 Fed. 574; 31 Cyc. 350,
Daniel's Negotiable Instr., vol. 2, p. 328; Thompson on
Bills. 390; National Bank v. McKay, 86 Hun. 365; Gist
v. Feist, 61 N. W. 621; Hoffman v. Butler, 105 Ind. 372;

Fisher v. Denver National Bank, 45 Pac. 440; 1 A. & E. Enc. of Law, 364; Anthony v. Fritz, 16 Vroom. 1.

Defense in equity. Guild v. Butler, 127 Mass. 386.

Defense at common law and statute. New York, Pennsylvania, Alabama, Colorado, Kansas, Arkansas, 1884 Dig stats. No. 6389; Georgia, 1892, Code No. 2156; Illinois, 1885, Starr & C. Ann. Stats. 2372; Indiana, 1881, R. S. No. 1210; Iowa, 1880 R. C. No. 2108; Kentucky, G. S. 797; Mississippi, 1880 R. C. No. 997; Missouri, 1879 R. S. No. 3896; N. Carolina, 1883, Code No. 2097; Ohio, 1880 R. S. No. 5833; Tennessee, 1884, Code No. 2725; Texas, 1879 R. S., art. 3660; Virginia, 1873 Code 993; West Virginia, 1884 Ann. Code, ch. 101, No. 1; Randolph on Comm. Paper, vol. 2, p. 610, No. 931.

The change in the principal's liability discharging the surety has been made an equitable defense. (England) 17 and 18 Vict. C. 125.

An extension by a holder with notice that a person is an accommodation maker, discharges. Chopper v. Union Bank, 7 Harr. & J. 92; Rules on Bills, 249; Randolph on Comm. Paper, vol. 2, 582, (ed. 1888); Barron v. Cady, 40 Mich. 259; Stillwell v. Aaron, 69 Mo. 539; Champion v. Robertson, 4 Bush. 17; Mariners Bank v. Abbott, 28 Me. 280; Wallace v. Souther, 2 Can. Sup. Court 598; Day v. Billingsly, 3 Bush. 157; Harrington v. Wright, 48 Vt. 427; Megget v. Baum, 57 Miss. 22.

H. A. WOLFORD, Hillsboro, N. M., for appellee.

The finding of a trial court based upon conflicting evidence is conclusive upon appeal. Riverside Land & Cement Mfg. Co. v. Hardwick, 120 Pac. (N. M.) 123; Doughert yv. Van Riper, 120 Pac. (N. M.) 333; Hamilton v. Havercamp, 130 Pac. (N. M.) 159.

The transferee of accommodation paper, even after maturity, and with notice that it is accommodation paper, takes it discharged of all defenses that might have existed against the accommodated party. Naef v. Potter, 11 L. R. A. (N. S.) 1034.

The extension must be definite and binding and upon a

valid consideration; and as to what would be such an agreement and such a consideration, see 45 Pac. 402; 14 Ohio 348 and annotations; 7 Cyc. 899; 7 Cyc. 900.

Where the uncertainty or indefiniteness of the amount can be cured by reference to some other part of the note, its back or its face, the paper will be treated as negotiable. Tiedeman on Commercial Paper, sec. 28, p. 66; Id., sec. 242, p. 399.

Defendant waived any objection to the ruling of the court when he answered to the merits. Ross v. Berry, 124 Pac. (N. M.) 342.

An injunction against the transfer of a note with a notice of lis pendens and a decree for the surrender of the note will not affect a subsequent purchaser without notice. Randolph, vol. 3, sec. 1687.

Where, after the sustaining of a demurrer to an answer, the pleader elects to amend, he waives the right to allege error on the ruling. Western College of New Mexico v. Turknett, 125 Pac. (N. M.) 1086; Bremen Mining Co. v. Bremen, 13 N. M. 111, 79 Pac. 806.

Court did not err in sustaining the plaintiff's objection to evidence regarding endorsements on the note. Session Laws, 1907, p. 296, sub-sec. 308.

OPINION OF THE COURT.

ROBERTS. C. J.—On the 5th day of January, 1907, the appellant, Frank D. Morgans, and H. L. Roper executed a promissory note payable to Ed Patten, for $2,000, bearing interest at 12 per cent per annum payable sixty days after date. The note was in the usual form, with the exception of the following stipulation, viz:—

"A failure to pay any of said interest when due shall cause the whole note to be counted as principal at the option of the holder of the note."

In 1912, for a valuable consideration, Patten transferred the note to the appellee by the following indorsement written on the back of the note, viz:—

"Pay to the order of E. E. Southard, Ed. Patton."
which endorsement was accompanied by a delivery of the note.

This action was instituted in the court below, to recover from Latham the balance due on the note.

To the complaint appellant demurred on the ground that the note was not negotiable under the laws of this State, hence, a failure to state a cause of action. The demurrer was overruled, which is assigned as error.

The note having been transferred after maturity, would be subject to defenses existing between the payee and payors, and the question as to whether the note was negotiable or non-negotiable is immaterial. The indorsement and delivery of the note operated as an assignment, even though the note should be treated as non-negotiable, (Merchants' National Bank v. Gregg, 107 Mich. 146) and appellee had the right, under our statute to sue thereon in his own name. This being true, the court properly sustained the demurrer.

One ground of defense, set up by the defendant in his answer was, that the original payee of the note, Patten, had been, prior to the negotiation of the note to appellee, enjoined by the District Court of Sierra County from transferring or selling any of his property; that the negotiation of the note to appellee was in violation of such restraining order. To this paragraph of answer a demurrer was sustained. The action of the court in sustaining the demurrer is assigned as error. But clearly the fact alleged constituted no defense. Appellee was not a party to the injunction proceedings, and is not shown to have had notice thereof. The remedy for the violation of a restraining order is punishable for contempt of court. Transfers of property made to innocent third parties, in violation of a restraining order, are not void nor voidable because made in disregard of such an order. The facts set up in the above paragraph of the answer constituted no defense and the demurrer was properly sustained.

On the back of the note in question appeared an indorsement, "For collection, pay to F. A. Hodges or order, without recourse on me. Ed. Patton." Appellant asked appellee if this indorsement was on the note at the time he purchased it, to which inquiry the court sustained an

objection. Of this ruling appellant complains, but he has
failed to point out in what manner his rights were prejudiced thereby. Where a party complains of an erroneous ruling by the court, in excluding or admitting evidence, it is incumbent upon him to show injury thereby.

Appellant's assignments of error 4, 5, 6, 7, 8, 11, 12,
and 13, will all be considered together, because in so far
as any of said assignments merit consideration they question the sufficiency of the proof to support the findings
made by the court. The note in question was a joint and
several obligation and was signed by Latham, Morgans
and Roper; appellant contends that he was surety for
Roper; that such fact was known to Patten; that Patten
agreed with Roper to extend the time of payment of the
note, and that said agreement was based upon a sufficient
consideration and that he was thereby discharged. Waiving the question, as to whether Latham was principal or
surety, and the knowledge of Patten as to his status,
which, upon the evidence would seemingly, necessarily be
resolved against appellant, we will proceed to inquire into
the effect of the extensions granted by Patten to Roper,
for, it will be seen that as such extensions, so granted, did
not release the surety, if Latham be treated as such, it becomes immaterial as to whether Latham was the principal
promisor, or only a surety for Roper. Memorandums of
extensions of time for the payment of the note were indorsed upon the back thereof in four instances, all, however, of the same tenor. We quote the last extension so
indorsed: "I herewith extend the time of payment on
this note to the 15th day of April, 1910. Ed. Patten."
This extension, it will be noted, was a mere forbearance on
the part of Patten, not to exact payment until a certain
date. The makers of the note were not precluded
3 from paying it at any time. No consideration for the
extension was stated, and the evidence did not disclose
any. The trial court found there was no consideration
therefor. There was no new agreement even to pay the
same rate of interest stipulated in the note. Under practically all the authorities such an extension would not
release the surety. Even had Roper agreed to pay the

same rate of interest provided for by the note, as a consideration for the extension, such a promise would not support the stipulation, according to the weight of authority, both English and American. (Daniel on Negotiable Instruments, 5th ed., sec. 1317a; Abel v. Alexander, 45 Ind. 523; Reynolds v. Ward, et al., 5 Wend. 502; Tatum v. Morgan, 108 Ga. 336; Fanning v. Murphy, 126 Wis. 538; 5 Am. & Eng. Ann. Cas. 435; Olmstead v. Latimer, 158 N. Y. 313, 43 L. R. A. 685. In the case of Fanning v. Murphy, supra, the following memorandum was indorsed upon the note:

"This note, by mutual agreement, is extended for one year from April 15, 1893, at eight per cent, payable semi-annually, interest having been paid to April 15, 1893, and all coupons surrendered." The note provided for eight per cent interest. The Court say:—

"A debtor's promise to pay interest on an existing contract and according to its terms during a period of delay in the enforcement thereof, is a promise to do precisely what he is bound to do without a promise. 'If the debtor's promise to pay interest creates no additional obligation it is no consideration for a contract to delay.' Sully v. Childers, 106 Tenn. 109, 60 S. W. Rep. 499; Howell v. Seiver, 1 Lea. (Tenn.) 360; Tatum v. Morgan, 108 Ga. 336, 33 S. E. Rep. 940; Harburg v. Kumpf, 151 Mo. 16, 52 S. W. Rep. 19; La Belle Savings Bank v. Taylor, 69 Mo. App. 99. All elementary writers, as before stated, so far as we can discover, are in harmony with these authorities. 1 Brandt, Suretyship, (3rd ed.) sec. 388; 2 Randolph Com. Paper, (2nd ed.) sec. 678; 2 Daniel Neg. Inst. (5th ed.) sec. 1317a."

In the case of Olmstead v. Latimer, supra, the agreement for the extension was reduced to writing and signed by the payee. It was subject to the terms and rate of interest specified in the original undertaking. The Court, in an opinion written by Chief Justice Parker, held that the extension of the time for payment of a mortgage, made by a written agreement which is not based on any consideration, is invalid. In this opinion the New York cases are reviewed and shown to be in accord on the proposition. From the above it will be seen that a further discussion of the subject would be fruitless; that there was no valid agreement for the extension of the time of payment; that the debtor, by the agreement, was not precluded from paying the note during the term of the extension, and, therefore, the surety, if Latham be treated as such, was not discharged.

Appellant complains of the findings made by the court as to the amount due on the note, as interest, and the attorney's fee allowed. These questions, however, were not called to the attention of the trial court, either by requested findings or objection and exception to the findings made, and this Court will, therefore, not consider the alleged errors. We have determined that the findings made by the court, as to the liability of Latham, were cor-
4 rect. This being true, all the findings were not in-
     correct, and a general objection to such findings is not sufficient to present for review, objections to particular findings. The rule is thus stated in 8 Am. Ency. Pl. & Pr., 276:

"The exception must specify the particular finding or findings objected to. A general objection will be insufficient, unless all the findings are incorrect, or unless the finding contains only one proposition; and the objection should suggest in what respect the proof is deficient."

Finding no error in the record, the judgment of the lower court is affirmed, and it is so ordered.

[No. 1616, January 10, 1914.]

M. J. FAGGARD & COMPANY, Appellee, v. MRS. C. CUNNINGHAM, Appellant.

SYLLABUS (BY THE COURT)

1. Under sections 3305 and 3365, C. L. 1897, a defendant may appeal from a default judgment rendered and entered against him by a Justice of the Peace.

P. 512.

Appeal from the District Court of Roosevelt County;

John T. McClure, District Judge; reversed and remanded.

GEORGE L. REESE, Portales, N. M., for appellant.

It is not necessary to enter an appearance in the Justice Court in order to be entitled to appeal to the District Court. Right to appeal from the Justice Court. C. L. 1897, secs. 3305, 3306, 3307, 3308, 3309, 3365, and 3317; Douthit v. Bailey, 14 N. M. 534, 99 Pac. 342; 6 Enc. Pl. & Pr. 227; St. Louis & S. F. R. R. Co. v. Couch, (Okla.) 114 Pac. 694.

The District Court is not a court for the correction of errors committed in the trial of cases in the Justice Court, where such Justice Court has original jurisdiction of the case tried. C. L. 1897, sec. 3317; Archibeque v. Miera, 1 N. M. 162; 13 Cyc. 786; Territory v. Lowitski, 6 N. M. 237, 27 Pac. 496; State v. O'Brien, (Mont.) 10 Ann. Cas. 1008.

T. E. MEARS, Portales, N. M., for appellee.

There can be no appeal from a default judgment. C. L. 1897, secs. 3255, 3257, 3260, 3266; 24 Cyc. 651; Wiggins v. Henderson, 36 Pac. 459; Whipple v. Southern Pac. Co., 55 Pac. 975; State ex rel., etc., v. Superior Court of Jefferson Count, et al., 41 Pac. 895; Clendenning v. Crawford, 7 Neb. 474.

OPINION OF THE COURT.

ROBERTS, C. J.—A default judgment was entered against appellant by a Justice of the Peace in precinct No. 1, Roosevelt County, from which he appealed to the District Court. In that court a motion was interposed to dismiss the appeal, upon the ground that no appeal could be taken from a default judgment, entered by a Justice of the Peace, which was sustained. The sustaining of this motion presents the only question for review.

Section 3305, C. L. 1897, provides:

"Any person aggrieved by any judgment rendered by

any Justice of the Peace, may appeal by himself, his agent or attorney, to the District Court of the County where the same was rendered," etc.

While section 3365 reads:

"In all cases before a Justice of the Peace in which judgment shall be rendered against any party, either party may take his appeal to the District Court "

The above sections, it will be observed, confer the right **1** of appeal upon "any person aggrieved" by any judgment, and the right is extended to "all cases." This being true, a defendant would have the right to appeal from a default judgment, unless some other section of the statute expressly or impliedly denies the right. Appellee has not called our attention to any provision of the statute in any way limiting or restricting the above sections in this regard. Under section 3317, all cases appealed to the District Court are tried *de novo*.

"A statute allowing an appeal from 'all final judgments' includes and authorizes an appeal from a judgment by default." 6 Ency. Pl. & Pr. 227.

Section 3305, supra, was construed by the Territorial Supreme Court in the case of Douthitt v. Bailey, 14 N. M. 530. The Court say:

"There is no restriction as to what cases can be appealed; the statute is mandatory and says in direct words that 'any person aggrieved by any judgment rendered by any justice may appeal,' consequently any person even if he enters the plea of guilty before a Justice of the Peace has the right to appeal, and on his filing the proper bond, the Justice is bound to grant the appeal to the District Court, where the case is tried *de novo*."

Appellee relies upon the cases of Clendenning v. Crawford & McLaughlin, 7 Neb. 474; State v. Oliver (Wash.) 41 Pac. 895; Wiggins v. Henderson, (Nev.) 36 6Pac. 459; Whipple v. Southern Pacific Co., (Ore.) 55 Pac. 975, but an examination of the statutes upon which the decision in each case was based, will disclose entirely different provisions respecting the right of appeal, from those in force in this jurisdiction.

For the reasons stated, the judgment and order are

therefore reversed, and the cause remanded for further proceedings not inconsistent with this opinion.

[No. 1617, January 10, 1914.]

STATE OF NEW MEXICO, Appellee, v. John CABODI, Appellant.

SYLLABUS (BY THE COURT)

1. Assuming the meaning to be plain, false grammar or wrong spelling will not render an indictment insufficient.

P. 516

2. A question, not jurisdictional, cannot be raised the first time on appeal.

P. 517

3. Where the name, Dewey Dimon, appears upon the roll of jurors empanelled to try a cause, and the verdict is signed "DeWitt Dimon, Foreman," and no objection to the variance is made in the trial court, the Supreme Court, on appeal, where the question is first raised, is warranted in assuming that no substitution in the personnel of the jury was made and that Dewey Dimon named on the jury roll signed the verdict as DeWitt Dimon.

P. 517

4. Where a complaining party is aware at the time, that the interpretation of the evidence, by an interpreter, is not correct, it is incumbent upon him to call the court's attention to such erroneous translation, and ask to have it corrected; and, where he has not such knowledge at the time, but afterwards becomes aware of the fact, he must set out all the facts in his motion for a new trial, pointing out therein specifically the evidence erroneously translated, and support such contention by affidavit or proof, so that the trial court can pass intelligently upon the question.

P. 518

5. Under the provisions of section 14, art. II of the State Constitution, the defendant is entitled to have the testimony interpreted to him in a language which he understands. While such right cannot be denied a defendant, it is incumbent upon him to, in some appropriate manner, call the attention of the trial court to the fact that he does not understand the languge in which the testimony is given.

P. 519

6. The word "charge" used in section 14, article II of the State Constitution, in the clause "to have the charge and testimony interpreted to him in a language that he understands," refers to the indictment or information, and not the instructions given to the jury by the court.

P. 520

Appeal from the District Court of McKinley County; Herbert F. Raynolds, District Judge; affirmed.

D. J. THOMAS, Gallup, N. M., for appellant.

Indictment does not charge the crime of murder in the first degree. Session Laws, 37th Legislative Assembly, ch. 36, sec. 1.

No person, who is not a member of 'the jury, may be present during their deliberations. State v. Sherbourse, 1 Dudley (Ga.) 28; Starling v. Thorne, 87 Ga. 513; Welch v. Taverner, 87 Ia. 207; Tarkington v. State, 72 Miss. 731; McElrath v. State, 2 Swan. (Tenn.) 382; Clapp v. State, 94 Tenn. 186; Wright v. State, 17 Tex. App. 152; State v. Cartwright, 20 W. Va. 32.

The testimony of certain witnesses was not interpreted into Italian. Constitution of N. M., art. II, sec. 14; Ralph v. State, 52 S. E. 297; State v. Haines, 36 S. Car. 504; Queenan v. Oklahoma, 61 L. R. A. 324; Hopt v. Utah, 110 U. S. 262; 1 Bl. Comm. 133; Lewis v. United States, 1012, par. 374; Dyson v. State, 26 Miss. 362.

Waiver of rights by accused. 1 Bishop Crim. Pro., par. 266; Territory v. Ortiz, 8 N. M. 154; State v. Belvel, 27 L. R. A. 846.

State v. Cabodi, 18 N. M. 513.

Ira L. Grimshaw, Assistant Attorney General, Santa
Fe, N. M., for appellee.

No error in sustaining appellant's motion in arrest
based upon the claim that the indictment was defective in
that it used the word "effect" instead of the statutory
word "affect." 1 Bishop, New C. P., sec. 354; 22 Cyc.
291, note 63; Smith v. Territory, (Okla.) 77 Pac. 187;
State v. Hedge, 6 Ind. 350; State v. Earp, 41 Tex. 487;
Hudson v. State, 10 Tex. App. 215; State v. Meyers, 85
Tenn. 203; Summerville v. State, 6 Tex. App. 433; Stinson v. State, 5 Tex. App. 31; Witten v. State, 4 Tex. App.
70; Grant v. State, 55 Ala. 201; Koutz v. State, 41 Tex.
570; Thomas v. State, 2 Tex. App. 293; Brumley v.
State, 11 Tex. App. 114; Lefter v. State, 122 Ind. 206.

No questions can be raised for the first time on appeal,
unless they are questions of jurisdiction. U. S. v. Cook,
15 N. M. 127; Duncan v. Holder, 15 N. M. 332; State v.
Duffield, 49 W. Vaa. 274.

No affidavits were filed to show an incorrect interpretation of the testimony in or with the motion for a new trial.
Bare statement of counsel for appellant is insufficientt.
Territory v. Hicks, 6 N. M. 603; Territory v. Yee Dan,
7 N. M. 441.

Contention that defendant was deprived of his constitutional right of having the testimony interpreted to him
in the language he understands, is not well taken. Const.
N. M., art. II, sec. 14.

"Charge," as used in section 14 of article II of the
Constitution, refers only to arraignment.

OPINION OF THE COURT.

ROBERTS, C. J. Appellant, John Cabodi, was convicted in the District Court of McKinley County, of murder in the first degree and was sentenced to death. From
the judgment he appeals to this Court and presents five
propositions upon which he relies for a reversal of the
cause. The errors relied upon will be considered in the
order presented.

The Session Laws of 1907, as compiled and printed by

the Secretary of the Territory, defines murder in the first degree as follows:—

"All murder which shall be perpetrated by means of poison or lying in wait, torture, or by any kind of wilful, deliberate and premeditated killing, or which is committed in the perpetration of or attempt to perpetrate any felony, or perpetrated from a deliberate and premeditated design unlawfully and maliciously to AFFECT the death of any human being, or perpetrated by any act greatly dangerous to the lives of others, and indicating a depraved mind regardless of human life, shall be deemed murder in the first degree."

In preparing the indictment in this case, the pleader used the word "EFFECT" instead of the word "AFFECT" found in the printed volume of the Session Laws. Because of this, appellant moved in arrest of judgment, which motion was overruled by the Court. This ruling is presented as the first ground of error.

The enrolled copy of the act in the office of the Secretary of State, uses the word "EFFECT," and this word also appears in the original bill. The word "EFFECT," was, therefore, properly used in the indictment. However,

1   had the correct word been "AFFECT," the motion was not well taken, for as stated in Bishop's New C. P., section 354,

"Assuming the meaning to be plain, false grammar or wrong spelling * * * * will severally not render the indictment insufficient."

In the case of Smith v. Territory, (Okla.) 77 Pac. 187, the identical question arose. There the statute used the word "Effect" and the indictment "Affect" in charging murder in the first degree. The Court say:

"This was clearly a mistake of the pleader, a clerical error, and where a defect in an indictment is merely technical and the indictment being sufficient in all other respects, we are unable to see how the substantial rights of the defendant are affected by such mistake."

The motion in arest of judgment was, therefore, properly overruled.

It is next contended that the verdict was returned by a

person as foreman, named DeWitt Dimon, who was not a member of the panel of jury, trying the cause. The record shows that a man named Dewey Dimon was one of the jurors accepted to try the cause. The verdict of the **2** jury was signed "DeWitt Dimon, Foreman." This question, however, was not raised in any manner in the court below. It does not go to the jurisdiction, either of the person of the defendant, or the subject of the prosecution. It has been uniformly held by the Territorial Supreme Court that a question, not jurisdictional, cannot be raised the first time on appeal. U. S. v. Cook, 15 N. M. 127.

Had this question been called to the attention of the trial court, the signature of the foreman to the verdict could and would probably have been corrected. Appellant does not undertake to show that some unauthorized person was present and participated in the deliberations of the jury. Had such a showing been made, of course the verdict would be set aside by the trial court, or by this Court on appeal. The only objection urged is that one of the jurors did not use the same Christian name, as appeared upon the jury roll, when he signed the verdict, as foreman. In the case of State v. Duffield, 49 W. Va. 274, a similar question arose. The record there showed that "Henry Hunt" was one of the jurors empanelled and sworn to try the cause. The verdict was signed "W. H. Hunt," and the Court held that the variance did not affect the verdict. The Court say:

"There was but one Hunt on the jury and it is not at all probable that, after the jury was sworn, that Henry Hunt got out of the jury box and W. H. Hunt, another and different person, took his place in the presence of the court and its officers."

In this case a person named Dimon was empanelled on the jury and a person whose last name was Dimon signed the verdict as the foreman of that jury. It is impossible **3** to believe that Dewey Dimon was a person other than DeWitt Dimon. If such had been the case, appellant could readily and easily have made it appear to the District Court, which he made no attempt to do. This

Court therefore is warranted in assuming that no substitution in the personnel of the jury was made and that Dewey Dimon named on the jury roll signed the verdict as De-Witt Dimon.

It is next urged that the trial court erred in not sustaining appellants' motion for a new trial, wherein he alleged that the interpretation was not literal or correct, from Italian into English, and vice versa.

Upon the trial no objection was interposed by appellant to the interpretation of the evidence, and in the motion for new trial no attempt was made to show that the interpretation was incorrect by affidavit or otherwise, except the mere allegation of such fact in the motion. The trial court decided the question adversely to appellant, by a denial of the motion, and this Court cannot go into the question of fact as to whether the interpretation was, or was not literal. The record fails to disclose any inability of the interpreter, or that the interpretation was not literal.

4   In such a case where it appears that the complaining party is aware at the time, that the interpretation of the evidence is not correct, it is incumbent upon him to call the court's attention to such erroneous translation and ask to have it corrected, and where he has not such knowledge at the time, but afterward becomes aware of the fact, he must set out all the facts in his motion for a new trial, pointing out therein specifically the evidence erroneously translated, and support such contention by affidavit or proof, so that the trial court can intelligently pass upon the question. Territory v. Hicks, 6 N. M. 596; Territory v. Yee Dan, 7 N. M. 439.

It is next assigned as error that appellant was deprived of his constitutional right "to have the * * * testimony interpreted to him in a language that he understands." This assignment is based upon the fact that two witnesses, Stafer and Dugan, testified in the English language, and the evidence so given was not interpreted in Italian. Section 14, art. II of the Constitution provides: ·

"No person shall be held to answer for a capital, felonious or infamous crime unless on a presentment or indictment of a grand jury except in cases arising in the militia when in actual service in time of war or public danger. In all criminal prosecutions the accused shall have the right to appear and defend himself in person, and by counsel; to demand the nature and cause of the accusation; to be confronted with the witnesses against him; to have the charge and testimony interpreted to him in a language that he understands; to have compulsory process to compel the attendance of necessary witnesses in his behalf, and a speedy public trial by an impartial jury of the county or district in which the offense is alleged to have been committed."

Under this provision the defendant is entitled to have the testimony interpreted to him in a language which **5** he understands. The right cannot be taken from a defendant, but it certainly is incumbent upon him, in some appropriate manner, to call to the attention of the trial court the fact that he does not understand the language in which the testimony is given. If such were not the case, it would be possible for a defendant to remain silent throughout the trial, and upon conviction, for the first time bring to the knowledge of the court the fact that he did not understand the language in which the testimony was given. In other words, he could remain silent, and take his chance of a favorable verdict, failing in which he could secure a new trial upon the ground that he did not understand the language in which the testimony was given. The statement of the proposition demonstrates its absurdity. The record in this case fails to disclose that the appellant did not understand the English language, or that the inability of appellant to understand that language was in any manner called to the attention of the trial court. It is true, appellant stated that he preferred to testify through an interpreter, but this statement does not imply that he did not understand English. In this jurisdiction, it is quite common for persons of Spanish descent, who are thoroughly conversant with the English language, to testify in Spanish rather than in English. It is only natural that one should prefer to express himself in his native tongue, rather than an acquired language. The record in this case, however, in-

dicates that the appellant did understand the English language, how thoroughly, however, does not appear.

It is next urged as error, that the charge of the court to
the jury was not interpreted into Italian. This is based
upon the assumption that the word "charge," used in the
constitutional provision, refers to the instructions given
to the jury by the court. The clause reads, "to have the
charge and testimony interpreted to him in a language
that he understands." (See above for section in full.) It
is apparent that the word "charge" refers to the in-
6 dictment or information, and not to the instructions
given to the jury upon the trial.

No question is raised by appellant as to the sufficiency
of the evidence to warrant the verdict rendered. We have,
however, reviewed the same and are satisfied that the verdict was fully warranted thereby. Nothing appearing in
the record to the contrary, we are convinced that the appellant was fairly tried and justly convicted, and the
judgment of the trial court must be affirmed, and the
judgment and sentence of the court shall be executed on
Friday, the 6th day of February, 1914, and it is so ordered.

(No. 1586, January 12, 1914.)

MARY BELLE WHITEHILL, Appellee, v. VICTORIO
LAND & CATTLE COMPANY, Appellant.

SYLLABUS (BY THE COURT)

1. An attempted exercise of jurisdiction by the land department in the acceptance of an entry, including lands reserved from entry by the government, where the reservation
from entry appears as a matter of record in the land office,
is void, as to the lands reserved, for the reason that it is an
assumption of power in excess of its jurisdiction, and the
same can be shown by a defendant in an action at law.

P. 531

Appeal from the District Court of Luna County; Colin
Neblett, District Judge; reversed and new trial granted.

WILSON & WALTON, Silver City, N. M., for appellant.

Court erred in refusing to instruct the jury that plaintiff could not recover for injuries to that portion of the
land covered by plaintiff's desert entry which was cancelled   Scott v. Carew, 196 U. S. 100; Doolan v. Carr,
125 U. S. 618; Burfenning v. Chicago, etc., Ry. Co., 163
U. S. 321; Morton v. Nebraska, 21 Wall. 660; Lake Superior, etc., Co. v. Cunningham, 155 U. S. 354; Grisar v.
McDowell, 6 Wall. 363; Kraus v. Congdon, 161 Fed.
Rep. 18.

JAMES S. FIELDER, Deming, N. M., for appellee.

Fencing of lands.   Session Laws 1909, chap. 70.
Fencing laws have no application where cattle are
driven upon unfenced land in order that they may feed
there.   Light v. United States, 220 U. S. 537; Lazarus v.
Phelps, 152 U. S. 81; Monroe v. Cannon, 24 Mont. 316;
St Louis Cattle Co. v. Vaught, 1 Tex. App. 388; Union
Pac v. Rollins, 5 Kans. 165.

The granting or refusal of a motion for new trial, being addressed to the sound discretion of the trial court,
will not, unless it plainly appears that such discretion has
been abused, be reviewed on appeal.   Duncan v. Holder,
15 N. M. 323.

Appellate court will not disturb a verdict where there
is substantial evidence to support it.   Territory v. Clark,
13 N. M. 353.

An entry of land, valid upon its face, constitutes such
an appropriation and withdrawal of the land as to segregate it from the Public Domain, and appropriate it to private use; and even though the entry may be in fact invalid, no lawful entry or settlement can be made on the
land by another person.   32 Cyc. 808, et seq.; Holy v.
Murphy, 207 U. S. 407; McMichael v. United States, 197
U. S. 304; 32 Cyc. 818; U. S. v. Waddell, 112 U. S. 76;

Stearns v. U. S., 152 Fed. 900; Wormouth v. Gardner, 105 Cal. 149; Hodges v. Colcord, 12 Okla. 313.

Until the entryman has become entitled to a patent, he has no vested rights in the land as against the United States, such as will deprive Congress of the right to dispose of the land otherwise than by a patent to him. 32 Cyc. 817: Campbell v. Wade, 132 U. S. 34.

As against defendant, plaintiff's title was perfect at the time of the trespass committed by defendant. Holt v. Murphy. 207 U. S. 407; McMichael v. Murphy, 197 U. S. 304; Hartman v. Warren, 70 Fed. 946; Germania Iron Co. v. James, 89 Fed. 811.

STATEMENT OF FACTS.

This was an action brought by Mary Belle Whitehill, appellee, against the Victorio Land & Cattle Company, appellant, in the District Court of Luna County, for the recovery of damages for trespass by cattle upon certain lands claimed by appellee, in Grant County, under a desert land entry. The desert entry being for the Southeast Quarter of the Northwest Quarter, and the Southeast Quarter of Section Twelve, in Township Twenty, South of Range Twelve West, and Lots numbered Three and Four in Section Seven, and Lot numbered One in Section Eighteen, in Township Twenty South, Range Eleven West, (being 318.25 acres.)

The complaint alleged residence of the plaintiff, corporate capacity, domicile and place of business of the defendant, and appellant herein, and further alleged possession of the lands described by plaintiff; that the defendant between July 20 and August 4, 1911, did wrongfullly and without right or authority and against the will and protest of the plaintiff, cause and allow a large number of its cattle to go upon the lands described, and tread down, eat and destroy grass then growing thereon, to the damage of the plaintiff in the sum of $3200, for which she prayed judgment.

The defendant, appellant here, answering, denied knowledge or information, sufficient to form a belief, as to the ownership and right to the possession in plaintiff of the lands described, and denial of the trespass alleged; and further answering, set up that the lands were unfenced, that the defendant had no knowledge of plaintiff's claim to the land, and was the owner of a large number of cattle then ranging upon the public domain of the United States. Plaintiff, by way of reply, denied all new matter in the defendant's answer.

The cause being tried to a jury, resulted in a verdict for plaintiff, assessing her damages at $1591.25.

The testimony showed that on May 6, 1911, plaintiff, Mary Belle Whitehill, filed her desert entry declaration in the United States Land Office, at Las Cruces, New Mexico, for the land within described, at which time a portion of said land, to-wit: the Northeast Quarter of the Northeast Quarter, being lot One in Section Eighteen, Township Twenty South, Range Eleven West, had been reserved by the government of the United States, for which reason this portion of the desert land entry was subsequently cancelled by letter of October 17, 1911. The trespass complained of in the complaint, and for which damages was sought according to the testimony, occurred between the 20th day of July and the 4th day of August, 1911.

OPINION OF THE COURT.

HANNA, J.—The first error assigned and presented for the consideration of this Court is based upon a refusal of the District Court to instruct the jury that plaintiff could not recover for injuries to that portion of the land, covered by plaintiff's desert entry, which was subsequently cancelled. It appears from the record that, prior to the time when plaintiff filed her desert land entry declaration in the local land office, a forty-acre tract included in her entry had been reserved from entry by the government. Subsequent to her entry, plaintiff was cited to show cause why that portion of her entry should not be cancelled, and failing to make a showing, the entry was cancelled as to the forty acres in question, but not until after the trespass complained of in this action.

It is contended by the appellant that the sub-division

of plaintiff's entry not being subject to entry, the receiving and allowing of entry by officers of the local land office was without authority, and, therefore, void.

On the other hand,. appellee contends that an entry of land valid on its face, constitutes such an appropriation and withdrawal of the land as to segregate it from the public domain, and appropriate it to private use; and even though the entry may be in fact invalid, no lawful entry or settlement can be made on the land by another person.

With this contention we agree, and we find the principle supported by the following well considered authorities: James v. Ger. Iron Co., 107 Fed. 597; Hasting & Etc. Railroad Co. v. Whitney, 132 U. S. 357; Parsons v. Venzke, 164 U. S. 89; Hodges v. Colcord, 193 U. S. 192; McMichael v. Murphy, 197 U. S. 304; Holt v. Murphy, 207 U. S. 407.

We do not overlook appellant's contention' that the rule, referred to, is applicable only to cases where the entries or filings are valid when made, or at least are only voidable by reason of facts not apparent upon the records; and, that, in the case under present consideration, the same records by which were proved the making of the entry showed a portion of the land included therein had been theretofore reserved, for which reason the land was not subject to entry and as to the portion reserved the entry was void.

The record in this case is not clear as to the character of reservation, or withdrawal from entry, which the sub-division of land included within the desert entry had been subjected to.

The language is that the land had been reserved from entry by the government of the United States. We are not to consider the question as one arising between the government and the entryman, but as affecting the status of the entry at the time of the alleged trespass by appellant. It would seem to turn upon the point of whether a portion of the entry was void or only voidable, by reason of the pre-existing reservation. It is apparent that the officials of the land office have, in the matter of the cancellation of that portion of the entry cancelled, pursued a course which it may be argued recognized the entry as one of prima facie validity. The withdrawal of the land was a fact peculiarly within the knowledge of the officials of the land office. The fact that the officers of the land office were in error in overlooking an order of withdrawal of the land from entry, would not, as a matter of first impression, make the entry void, but rather voidable, upon the question being raised by the party entitled to raise it, i. e., the government.

The cases cited, supra, are those where latent defects exist. The entry being so far as could be known, at the time of its making, prima facie valid, but investigation subsequently developing that the entryman was disqualified to make the entry, or had perpetrated fraud, conditions to be discovered by evidence dehors the record, and being essentially questions of fact.

It has long been settled that as to matters of fact, within the scope of the authority of the officers of the Land Department of the United States, their findings must be taken as conclusive in the absence of fraud and mistake, upon the principle of estoppel by former adjudication. Johnson v. Towsley, 13 Wall. 72; Moore v. Robbins, 96 U. S. 530. Smelting Co. v. Kemp, 104 U. S. 936; Sanford v. Sanford, 19 Or. 3, 13 Pac. 602.

If the reservation of the land in question from entry is a question of fact to be determined by the land officials, then the District Court would be concluded by the findings of the officials, as evidenced by the acceptance of the entry, and no error could now be predicated upon the refusal of that court to instruct the jury that plaintiff could not recover for injuries to that portion of the land reserved from entry.

If the reservation from entry, however, deprived the officials of all jurisdiction over the land, and left them devoid of authority to consider a filing upon the land reserved, then the acceptance of the entry would be without jurisdiction and absolutely void, all of which could be inquired into in an action at law.

No cases in point have been cited, nor have we been able to find any, where the facts were analogous to those now before us. Appellant has cited the case of Burfenning v Chicago, St. P., etc., Ry. Co., 163 U. S. 321, 16 Sup. Ct. 1018, 41 L. Ed. 176, where the United States Supreme Court, speaking by Mr. Justice Brewer, said:

"It has undoubtedly been affirmed over and over again that in the administration of the public land system of the United States questions of fact are for the consideration and judgment of the land department, and that its judgment thereon is final. Whether, for instance, a certain tract is swamp land or not, saline land or not, mineral land or not, presents a question of fact not resting on record, dependent on oral testimony; and it cannot be doubted that the decision of the Land Department, one way or the other, in reference to these questions is conclusive and not open to relitigation in the courts, except in those cases of fraud, etc., which permit any determination to be re-examined. Johnson v. Towsley, 13 Wall. 72; Smelting Company v. Kemp, 104 U. S. 636; Steel v. Smelting Company, 106 U. S. 447; Wright v. Roseberry, 121 U. S. 488; Heath v. Wallace, 138 U. S. 573; McCormick v. Hayes, 159 U. S. 332.

"But it is also equally true that when by Act of Congress a tract of land has been reserved from homestead and preemption, or dedicated to any special purpose, proceedings in the Land Department in defiance of such reservation or dedication, although culminating in a patent, transfer no title, and may be challenged in an action at law. In other words, the action of the Land Department cannot override the expressed will of Congress, or convey away public lands in disregard or defiance thereof. Smelting Co. v. Kemp, 104 U. S. 636-646; Wright v. Roseberry, 121 U. S. 488, 519; Doolan v. Carr, 125 U. S. 618; Davis' Admr. v. Weibbold, 139 U. S. 507, 529; Knight v. U. S. Land Assn., 142 U. S. 161."

It is to be noted that the illustrations given of the rule by Mr. Justice Brewer, were specifically limited to cases not presenting facts resting on record, which is not a condition in the present case, the records of the land office, in this instance, showing a reservation. Were the present case one where a reservation had been made by Act of

Congress, there would be no question but the authorities last cited would be analogous and controlling upon this Court. What distinction can there be, however, as a matter of principle, between a reservation from homestead of certain lands by Act of Congress and a reservation from entry of lands by executive proclamation or departmental withdrawal? Is not the jurisdiction of the Land Department as effectively cut off in the one case as in the other?

In the case of the New Dunderberg Min. Co. v. Old, 79 Fed. 602, speaking of the jurisdiction of the Land Department, the Court said:

"Jurisdiction of the subject matter is the power to deal with the general abstract question. The test of jurisdiction is whether or not the tribunal has power to enter upon the inquiry, not whether its conclusion in the course of it is right or wrong."

Our inquiry is thus limited to the question of the power of the local land office officials to accept and give validity to an entry upon lands reserved from entry by the government, where the reservation is shown upon the records of the land office. A case more nearly in point than all others we have examined, is Morton v. Nebraska, 21 Wall. 660, cited in the Burfenning case, where the facts disclose that patent had issued for saline lands, noted as such on the field books, although the notes thereof had not been transferred to the register's general plats. It is true that known salines were reserved from entry by Act of Congress, but the character of the land was a matter of record in the land office as the fact of the reservation in this case was a matter of the record.

The Supreme Court said in the case last cited, (Morton v. Neb.),

"It does not strengthen the case of the plaintiffs that they obtained certificates of entry, and that patents were subsequently issued on these certificates. It has been repeatedly decided by this Court that patents for lands which have been previously granted, reserved for sale, or appropriated, are void. The executive officers had no authority to issue a patent for the lands in controversy, because they were not subject to entry, having been previously reserved,

and this want of power may be proved by a defendant in an
action at law."

The Supreme Court of the United States, in the Burfenning case, supra, said, in commenting on the Morton
v. Neb. case:

"It will be observed that the records disclosed that the
lands were saline lands when the proceedings in the Land
Department were had. So the case was not one in which
the department determined a fact upon parol evidence,
but one in which it acted in disregard of an established
and recorded fact."

Thus it is to be observed that if the decision as to
whether lands were salines rested upon parol evidence the
first principle and rule should apply and the conclusion of
the land officers would be final, whereas if the character
of the lands had been determined and was disclosed by the
record there would be a failure of jurisdiction and a want
of power which might be proved by a defendant in an action at law.

In another case, Davis' Administrator v. Weibbold, 139
U. S. 507-529, we find an expression of opinion by Mr.
Justice Field as to the conclusiveness of the patents of the
Land Department when assailed collaterally in actions at
law. Justice Field said:

"We have had occasion to assert their unassailability in
such cases in the strongest terms, both in Smelting Co. v.
Kemp, 104 U. S. 636, 640-646, and in Steel v. Smelting
Co., 106 U. S. 447, 451, 452. They are conclusive in such
actions of all matters of fact necessary to their issue, where
the department had jurisdiction to act upon such matters,
and to determine them; but if the lands patented were not
at the time public property, having been previously disposed of, or no provision had been made for their sale, or
other disposition, or they had been reserved from sale, the
department had no jurisdiction to transfer the land, and
their attempted conveyance by patent is inoperative and
void, no matter with what seeming regularity the forms of
law have been observed." See, also, Knight v. U. S. Land
Ass'n, 142 U. S. 161-176.

While it is true we are not concerned with a patent, in

this case, we do not consider that an entry can be held to
have any greater validity than would a patent which might
be subsequently issued and based upon such entry.

Judge Sanborn, in the case of United States v. Winona
& St. P. R. Co., 67 Fed. 948, 959, after reviewing numerous authorities illustrating the distinction between the
case in which the Land Department has acted upon a subject matter within and one without its jurisdictioon, said:

"A careful study and analysis of these decisions will
show that none of them are inconsistent with the following
rules: (1) A patent or certificate of the land department
to land, over which that department has no power of disposition and no jurisdiction to determine the claims of
applicants for, under the acts of Congress, is absolutely
void, and conveys no title whatever. Land the title to
which had passed from the government to another party
before the claim on which the patent was based was initiated, land reserved from sale and disposition for military
and other like purposes, land reserved by a claim under a
Mexican or Spanish grant *sub judice,* and land for the
disposition of which the acts of Congress have made no
provision, is of this character. Polk v. Wendal, 9 Cranch.
87, and cases cited under it supra. (2) A patent or certificate of the Land Department to land over which that
department has the power of disposition and the jurisdiction to determine the claims of applicants for, under the
Acts of Congress, is impregnable to collateral attack,
whether the decision of the department is right or wrong,
and it conveys the legal title to the patentee or to the party named as entitled to that title in the patent or certificate. Minter v. Crommelin, 18 How. 87, 89, and cases
cited under it supra. (3) A court of equity may, in a direct proceeding for that purpose, set aside such a patent or
certificate, or declare the legal title under it to be held
in trust for one who has a better right to it, in cases
in which the action of the Land Department has resulted
from fraud, mistake, or erroneous views of the law. Bogan
v. Mortgage Co., 11 C. C. A. 128, 63 Fed. 192, 195; Cunningham v. Ashley, 14 How. 377; Barnard's Heirs v. Ashley's Heirs, 18 How. 43; Garland v. Winn, 20 How. 6;

Lytle v. State, 22 How. 193; Lindsey v. Hawes, 2 Blank 554, 562; Johnson v. Towsley, 13 Wall. 72, 85; Moore v. Robbins, 96 U. S. 538; Bernier v. Bernier, 147 U. S. 242, 13 Sup. Ct. 244; Mullan v. U. S., 118 U. S. 271, 278, 279, 6 Sup. Ct. 1041; Moffat v. U. S., 112 U. S. 24, 5 Sup. Ct. 10."

The question now under consideration was referred to by Mr. Justice Field in Smelting Co. v. Kemp, 104 U. S. 636, at 641, where he said:

"Of course, when we speak of the conclusive presumptions attending a patent for lands, we assume that it was issued in a case where the department had jurisdiction to act and execute it; that is to say, in a case where the lands belonged to the United States, and provision had been made by law for their sale. If they never were public property, or had previously been disposed of, or if Congress had made no provision for their sale, or had reserved them, the department would have no jurisdiction to transfer them, and its attempted conveyance of them would be inoperative and void, no matter with what seeming regularity the forms of law have been observed. The action of the department would in that event be like that of any other special tribunal not having jurisdiction of a case which it had assumed to decide. Matters of this kind, disclosing a want of jurisdiction, may be considered by a court of law. In such cases the objection to the patent reaches beyond the action of the special tribunal, and goes to the existence of a subject upon which it was competent to act."

In a proceeding, entitled "John Campbell," before the Secretary of the Interior, (6 L. Dec. 317), it was held that

"The President is vested with general authority in the matter of reserving land for public uses, and land so set apart is not subject to disposition under the public land laws during the existence of such reservation." See also John C. Irwin, 6 L. D. 585.

It is a settled rule of decision in the Federal courts that so long as an executive withdrawal of public lands continues in force, the lands covered thereby are not subject

to entry, and no lawful settlement on them can be acquired. Wolsey v. Chapman, 101 U. S. 768; Bullard v.
Railroad, 122 U. S. 167; Spencer v. McDougal, 159 U. S.
62.

In conclusion, therefore, we are of the opinion that an
attempted exercise of jurisdiction by the Land De-
1 partment in the acceptance of an entry, including
lands reserved from entry by the government, where
the reservation from entry appears as a matter of record
in the land office, is void, as to the lands reserved, for
the reason that it is an assumption of power in excess of
its jurisdiction, and the same can be shown by a defendant in an action at law.

We conclude that the District Court committed error
in refusing the instruction asked by appellant. Our conclusion makes it unnecessary to pass upon the remaining
assignment of errors.

The judgment of the lower court is, therefore, reversed,
and a new trial granted.

[No. 1635, February 5, 1-914.]

THE SOUTH SPRING RANCH & CATTLE CO., et
al., Plaintiffs, v. THE STATE BOARD OF EQUAL-
IZATION OF THE STATE OF NEW MEXICO,
Defendant.

SYLLABUS (BY THE COURT)

1. The State Board of Equalization has power to equalize
the valuations of property for taxation purposes by classes,
both as between classes in the same county and as between
counties throughout the state, and the fact that the action
taken results in the increase or decrease of total valuations
in the state is immaterial.

P. 572

SYLLABUS BY THE PACIFIC REPORTER.

2. Where a statute empowers a state board to equalize val-

uations for taxation, but does not point out the mode, any reasonable and efficient mode may be adopted to accomplish the end in view.

P. 543

3. The statute fixing the time and place of a meeting of the State Board of Equalization is notice to the taxpayers that the board will meet and perform only lawful acts and not that it will do illegal things.

P. 567

4. As used in Laws 1913, ch. 84, section 23, providing that the District Attorney shall, on complaint, submit an assessment to the District Court for correction to avoid injustice to the taxpayer, the word "injustice" is apparently the broadest term that could have been employed in the connection, and applies to any over valuation of the property of a taxpayer.

P. 569

5. So long as the taxpayer is not assessed more than the law provides, and there is no well-defined scheme of discrimination or fraudulent action, he cannot complain on certiorari of an action of the State Board of Equalization.

P. 572

Original petition for certiorari in the Supreme Court by the South Spring Ranch & Cattle Company, a corporation, and others, to review an action of the State Board of Equalization; petition and writ dismissed.

JAMES M. HERVEY, CHARLES A. SPIESS, EDWARD R. WRIGHT and HARRY S. BOWMAN, for plaintiffs.

Validity of the order promulgated by the Board of Equalization of the State of New Mexico for the year 1913. Session Laws 1913, ch. 81, secs. 1, 3, 4, 5, 7; Laws 1913, ch. 84, sec. 12.

What the term "to adjust and equalize the assessment

Ranch & Cattle Co. v. Board of Equalization, 18 N. M. 531.

rolls" means. 37 Cyc. 1076, 1077, 1078; Desty on Taxation, vol. 1, p. 505.

Powers conferred upon the Board of Equalization. Wells Fargo & Co. v. Board of Equalization, 56 Cal. 194; Const. of California, art. XIII, sec. 9; People v. Lothrop, 3 Colo. 428; Const. of California, art. X, sec. 15; People v. Ames, 60 Pac. 346, (Colo.); State v. Vaile, 26 S. W. 672; State v. Thomas, 50 Pac. 615; C. L. 1897, (N. M.) sec. 4048; Lead Co. v. Sims, 18 S. W. 906; Wallace v. State Board of Equalization, 46 Pac. 266, (Mont.); State v. Thomas, (Utah) 50 Pac. 615; M., K. & T. Ry. Co. v. Miami Co. Commrs., 73 Pac. 103; Wallace v. Bullen, 52 Pac. 954, and 54 Pac. 974; Orr v. State Board, 28 Pac. 416; Hacker v. Howe, 101 N. W. 255; Poe v. Howell, (N. M.) 67 Pac. 65; Territory v. First National Bank, 10 N. M. 283; Appeal of McNeal, 128 Pac. 285, (Okla.)

FRANK W. CLANCY, Attorney General; and IRA L. GRIMSHAW, Assistant Attorney General, Santa Fe, N. M., for defendant.

The office of the writ of certiorari is to inquire into and determine only whether the lower tribunal had jurisdiction. Const. of N. M., art. VI, sec. 3; Spelling on Ext. Remedies, sec. 1949; 6 Cyc. 759; In re Lewisohn, 9 N. M. 102; Leyba v. Armijo, 11 N. M. 437.

' The Court cannot consider the merits of the order or the case, and cannot examine into the evidence nor matters de hors the record. 2 Spelling on Extr. Rem., sec. 2018; 6 Cyc. 823; 2 Cooley on Taxation, 1400 to 1405; Floyd v. Gilbreath, 27 Ark. 676; 2 Spelling on Extr. Rem., sec. 2022; 49 N. J. L. 169; Shelby County v. Miss. Railroad Co., 1 S. W. 82; In re Henriquez, 5 N. M. 178.

The record returned by defendant is conclusive and cannot be controlled by any matters not appearing therein. 2 Cooley on Taxation, 1410; 6 Cyc. 827; 2 Spelling on Extra. Rem., sec. 2018; Id., pp. 1747, 1751-2; Id., sec. 2010; Id., 1739; People ex rel., etc., v. County Commrs., 27 Colo. 88; Low v. R. R., 18 Ill. 325; Commissioners v.

Darby, 27 Ill. 140; Charleston v. County Commrs., 109 Mass. 270.

The Court cannot inquire into the assessment to determine whether it is excessive or not. 2 Cooley on Taxation, 1405-6; 2 Spelling on Extra. Rem., sec. 1967.

Every lawful intendment is made in favor of the determination and its regularity. 6 Cyc. 532; 2 Spelling on Extra. Rem., p. 1759; Hannible R. R. Co. v. State Board of. Equalization, 64 Mo. 297; Taylor v. Louisville Railroad Co., 88 Fed. 350.

The defendant had power and was acting within its statutory rights in making a percentage increase of values for taxation in real property. Const. of N. M., art. VIII, sec. 5, 9; C. L. 1897, sec. 2635; Laws 1907, ch. 103, sec. 1; Laws 1901, ch. 16; C. L. 1897, sec. 2636; Laws 1903, ch. 88, sec. 1; Laws 1909, ch. 124; Laws 1913, ch. 81; Laws 1913, ch. 84.

All laws prior to 1913 were impliedly repealed, because the latter laws made radical changes in the leading parts of the old system. Sutherland Stat. Const., sec. 146; C. L. 1897, sec. 2636; Territory v. Bank of Albuquerque, 10 N. M. 296.

Territorial Board of Equalization had power to adjust and equalize the assessment rolls by raising or lowering the valuation of certain classes of property. Territory v. Bank of Albuquerque, 10 N. M. 296.

Defendant had power by law to make the order of October 1, 1913, in so far as it pertained to personal property. Laws 1913, ch. 84, sec. 13; Territory v. Bank, 10 N. M. 296; Washington County v. St. Louis R. R. Co., 58 Mo. 372-376.

OPINION OF THE COURT.

PARKER, J.—This is a proceeding by certiorari to review the action of the State Board of Equalization in attempting to equalize the valuation of property for the purposes of taxation. It is admitted by counsel on both sides that the proceeding by certiorari in this jurisdiction is confined within the common-law limits; there being no statute enlarging the scope of the remedy. The question.

then, is whether the Board of Equalization had power or jurisdiction to do what it has done. If the board had the power and jurisdiction to do what was done, it will be assumed in this discussion that the action was correct, at least that it is not subject to review for mere error.

The state board made an order attempting to equalize the valuation of property throughout the State for the purposes of taxation. The order made decreases valuations in every County in the State save one; said decreases aggregating $1,585,590. They made increases in every County in the State; the said increases amounting to $9,233,673. This leaves a net increase of valuation of $7,648,083. The details of said action, in so far as they relate to increases, are best shown by the following table, viz.:

It is ordered by the board that the following raises be made on different classes of taxable property in the various Counties of the State; such percentage or raise being upon the valuation of properties now appearing upon the tax roll as follows:

Ranch & Cattle Co. v. Board of Equalization, 18 N. M. 531.

County	%	Agricultural Lands Amount	Imps. Amount	%	Grazing Lands Amount	Imps. Amount	%	Timber Lands Amount	%	Coal Lands Amount	%	City and Town Lots Amount	Imps. Amount	%	Carriages & Wagons Amount
Bernalillo	20	$56,859	$19,254	20	$44,604	$1,366	0	$	0	$	20	$298,082	$303,200	20	$4,571
Chaves	25	395,892	59,774	20	74,103	33,298	0		0		25	141,512	212,180	20	4,910
Colfax	25	124,537	26,243	30	293,042	45,416	0		0		20	61,059	144,500	20	3,122
Curry	20	102,047	38,616	0			0		0		0			20	2,465
Dona Ana	0			0			0		0		0			20	5,646
Eddy	10	113,234	9,647	0			0		0		0			20	2,845
Grant	0			0			0		0		0			20	2,292
Gua dalpe	0			0			0		0		0			20	1,286
Lincoln	20	58,285	6,670	0			0		0		0			20	2,092
Luna	0			0			0		0		10	22,854	22,031	20	662
McKinley	0			20	93,055	3,609	10	4,500	0		10	8,821	17,482	20	971
Mora	25	82,926	8,412	20	64,264	5,695	10	342	0		0			20	2,073
Otero	0			0			0		0		0			20	1,134
Quay	0			10	62,094	12,776	10	3,962	0		0			20	2,664
Rio Arriba	20	140,774	20,391	20	83,241	47	0		0		10	11,319	8,523	20	1,928
Roosevelt	0			0			0		0		0			20	1,298
Sandoval	0			0			0		0		0			20	1,850
San Juan	0			20	79,911	2,315	20	1,082	0		0			20	2,215
San Miguel	30	204,724	15,875	25	174,813	6,189	10	2,100	0		20	67,374	135,877	20	2,507
Santa Fe	20	46,201	20,281	0			0		0		20	37,359	76,672	20	3,927
Sierra	0			0			0		0		0			20	1,297
Socorro	0			20	109,666	12,987	15	884	0		0			20	2,628
Taos	25	66,128	12,608	20	50,821	1,879	0		20	733	10	485	303	20	1,951
Torrance	0			0			0		0		0			20	1,746
Union	0			0			0		0		0			20	3,075
Valencia	0			20	147,940	1,836	10	18,931	0		0			20	1,069
		$1,391,604	$237,668		$1,276,104	$127,213		$31,801		$733		$648,865	$920,568		$62,339

County	Saddles & Horses Amount (20%)	Merchandise Amount (20%)	Amount (50%)	Watches & Clocks Amount (100%)	Amount (50%)	Musical Instruments Amount (20%)	Household Goods Amount (20%)	Amount (50%)	Other Property Amount (50%)
Bernalillo .20	1,138	52,638	4,421	703	1,040	3,733	20,966	11,538	35,417
Chaves .20	2,562	37,678	3,112	2,372	9,025	1,167	7,855	24,910	75,085
Colfax .20	1,522	35,243	5,697	911	1,553	6,710	11,621	6,775	1,464
Curry .20	652	13,667	707	195	1,963	9,945	6,494		37,793
Dona Ana .20	1,229	14,774	1,441	460	1,505	3,457	5,387		12,924
Eddy .20	1,232	20,015	2,388	284	700	4,939	7,345		28,317
Grant .20	1,010	35,882	4,335	305	47	3,920	8,289		20,657
Guadalupe .20	486	10,199	550	263	330	542	2,193		5,049
Lincoln .20	364	8,258	414	208		786	786		17,285
Luna .20	168	7,888	898	41		1,871	2,153		7,878
McKinley .20	307	15,323	2,068	460	217	2,370	3,126	1,076	34,074
Mora .20	864	9,620	366	155	813	648	2,888		23,747
Otero .20	409	6,229	1,007	239	137	1,096	3,207		8,090
Quay .20	827	14,438	2,192	432	248	2,729	2,369		2,268
Rio Arriba .20	1,035	9,297	320	84	33	574	5,084		10,506
Roosevelt .20	352	6,249	962	517	215	1,761	3,439		28,680
Sandoval .20	886	3,430	295	73	40	244	1,983		
San Juan .20	755	8,331	1,153		309	2,681	2,000		28,524
San Miguel .20	823	29,515	4,042	463	811	3,282	3,719	5,384	13,857
Santa Fe .20	1,357	16,582	2,095	803	1,782	3,302	7,948	6,678	7,608
Sierra .20	529	6,283	544	113	260	662	14,601		713
Socorro .20	760	15,343	730	50	153	793	1,549		1,699
Taos .20	1,283	7,098	620	425	91	91	4,360		23,212
Torrance .20	783	8,464	80	376		725	2,768		90,048
Union .20	1,139	12,053	1,151	245	287	1,920	2,542		13,171
Valencia .20	762	10,561	223	123	195	498	3,896		
Total	$23,214	$415,008	$42,311	$11,219	$22,053	$70,496	$150,776	$56,361	$528,616

An analysis of this table discloses that the state board raised valuations of property according to classes, and by means of certain percentages in each instance. In the case of about half in number of the different classes of property, the valuations were raised in some counties, and not raised in others. For instance, in the Counties of Dona Ana, Grant, Guadalupe, and Lincoln, no raises were made upon agricultural lands, grazing lands, timber lands, coal lands, and city town lots, while in most of the other Counties the valuation of these classes of property, or some of them, were raised in considerable amounts. The valuation of other classes of property was raised in every County in the State where any of said property had been returned and appeared on the tax rolls. This appears to be the case in regard to carriages and wagons, saddles and harness, merchandise, saloon and office fixtures, watches, clocks, jewelry, musical instruments, household goods, automobiles, and a general class listed as "other property."

These raises of valuation are from 20 to 100 per cent. This evidently presents two fundamental bases upon which the action of the board must have been taken, viz: First, the board raised the valuation of a particular class of property in a given County, or Counties, to the same valuation at which it was listed for taxation, in some other given County; second, the board raised the valuation of given classes of property to the same comparative valuation of other classes of property, both in the same County and elsewhere throughout the State. This must be taken as the true effect of what the board did. For instance, when they raised the valuation of agricultural lands 20 per cent. in Bernalillo, Chaves, Colfax, Curry, Eddy, Luna, Mora, Roosevelt, San Miguel, Santa Fe, and Taos Counties, and failed to raise the valuation of the same classes of property in the Counties of Dona Ana, Grant, Guadalupe, Lincoln, McKinley, Otero, Quay, Rio Arriba, Sandoval, San Juan, Sierra, Socorro, Torrance, Union, and Valencia, it is to be assumed that said raise in said valuation was to equalize the valuation of said class of property in the Counties first named, with its valuation in the other Counties named. But when the board raised the valuation of carriages and wagons 20 per cent. in every County in the State, it necessarily did so for the purpose of equalizing the valuation of this class of property with the valuation by it put upon agricultural lands, for instance, throughout the State.

We have, then, a case where the board has equalized the valuation of property between classes, and having fixed thereby a comparative standard of valuation, they have attempted to bring up to that same standard all other classes of property in the State. Whether this is exactly the method employed by the board in arriving at this con· clusion does not specifically appear in the return, but, at any rate, this is the necessary consequence of what was done.

This state of affairs would seem to present two questions for discussion, viz: (1) Has the State Board of Equalization power to adjust and equalize the valuation of property by classes for the purposes of taxation? (2) If so, and the action results in increasing the total valuation in Counties or in the State at large, is the action justified?

We do not understand counsel on either side of this case to rely upon any of the provisions of legislation prior to the adoption of the State Constitution, and the passage of two acts at the session of the State Legislature of 1913.

The pertinent constitutional provisions are as follows:

"Section 1. The rate of taxation shall be equal and uniform upon all subjects of taxation."

"Sec. 5. A State Board of Equalization is hereby created which shall consist of the Governor, Traveling Auditor, State Auditor, Secretary of State and Attorney General. Until otherwise provided, said board shall have and exercise all the powers now vested in the Territorial Board of Equalization."

"Sec. 9. All property within the territorial limits of the authority levying the tax, and subject to taxation, shall be taxed therein for State, County, municipal and other purposes: Provided, that the State Board of Equalization shall determine the value of all property of railroad, express, sleeping car, telegraph, telephone and other transportation and transmission companies, used by such companies in the operation of their railroad, express, sleeping car, telegraph, or telephone lines, or other transportation or transmission lines, and shall certify the value thereof as so determined to the County and municipal taxing authorities." Const., art. 8.

At the session of 1913, the State Legislature passed two acts, which are chapters 81 and 84 of that session. Section 1 of chapter 81 follows the constitutional provision heretofore quoted, and confers power upon the state board to fix values upon transportation and transmission companies, and adds banks and trust companies, and live stock. Section 3 of that act directs the state board to fix the valuation of the property mentioned in section 1, a one-third of the true value thereof, for taxation purposes. Section 4 of that act expressly confers power upon boards of County commissioners to fix values upon all taxable property, except that mentioned in section 1, and is as follows: "The boards of County commissioners of the several Counties shall meet on the second Monday in February of each year and shall proceed in like manner as the State Board of Equalization to ascertain the true value of property of different classes subject to taxation within their respective Counties other than property mentioned in section one hereof, and shall fix a valuation thereof for taxation purposes of thirty-three and one-third per centum of the true value so ascertained." Section 5 of that act directs the assessors of the respective Couties to extend upon the tax rolls the values so fixed by said boards and to list all other property, the valuation of which shall not have been specifically fixed by such County boards, at the same proportionate and uniform valuation as fixed by said boards upon other property. Section 7 of that act confers upon the State board and County boards the same powers and duties of equalization as formerly possessed under the Territorial and State laws.

Chapter 84, passed one day later than chapter 81, is a more comprehensive act than the latter, and deals more in detail with the assessment, levy equalization, and collection of taxes. Section 1 of that act repeals most of the previous legislation under the Territorial government.

Section 2 of the act reiterates the duty of the assessor to fix the valuation for purposes of taxation in accordance with the standards fixed by the County board. Section 12 of that act provides for an appeal from the action of the assessor to the County board, sitting as a board of equalization, and for an appeal from said County board to the State Board of Equalization for the re-examination and revision of the assessment of any taxpayer. Section 13 of the act confers the powers upon the State Board of Equalization, and is as follows: "The State Board of Equalization shall at its said meeting on the first Monday in July examine the assessment roll of each County of the State, for the purpose of ascertaining the rate of assessment and valuation of property therein, and the board shall have the power to adjust and equalize the said assessment rolls so that the valuation of property for purposes of taxation shall be of substantial uniformity throughout the State. Such board at this meeting shall also have power to hear and determine any appeals taken as hereinbefore provided, and any other appeals from the action of any County board, which may be taken by the State, or by any County, or by not less than ten taxpayers of any County, acting through a District Attorney; and in case of any such appeal the appellant must file with the secretary of said board a complete transcript of the appeal case in time for consideration by said board at said meeting in July." Section 14 confers the power on the state board to prescribe the form of assessment books. Section 15 requires the assessors to forward one copy of the completed assessment book or roll to the seat of government for examination by the State board. Section 19 requires the State Auditor, at the conclusion by the State board of its duties as to the revision and correction of the assessment books, and the hearing and determination of appeals, to make the levy of said taxes and to certify the same to the County boards. Section 20 requires the County boards, as soon as practicable after receiving the Auditor's certificate, to make all levies of necessary taxes for the ensuing fiscal year, and to certify the same and the rates thereof to the County Assessor.

Before proceeding to an examination of the specific objections urged by petitioners to the action of the State Board of Equalization, a correct interpretation of our taxing laws will be sought, and in that connection certain fundamental considerations may first be mentioned.

It is to be seen, from the foregoing provisions of the Constitution and statutes, that uniformity throughout the State of the burdens of taxation is to be maintained. In fact, it would be an anomaly in America if discrimination in taxation were to be contemplated in Constitution or statute. This consideration, it seems to us, should be constantly borne in mind in determining the true intent and meaning of the legislation involved.

The second consideration, of equal importance, is the fact that the basis of taxation has been clearly fixed by the statute, viz., the actual value of property. The statute provides that one-third of this actual value shall be taken as the sum upon which the tax of each taxpayer in the State shall be computed. It therefore becomes the duty of each of the three taxing agencies of the State, viz., assessors, board of County commissioners, and the State Board of Equalization, in exercising any of their respective powers, to adhere at all times to this standard of valuation. Any departure therefrom is a violation of the letter and spirit of the taxing laws.

Another consideration, likewise important, is the fact that the taxing statutes authorize and require the classification of property for the purposes of taxation. The state board is granted the power to prescribe the forms of the tax rolls, which necessarily includes the power to provide that property shall be listed for taxation in such classes as may be prescribed in these forms. The boards of county commissioners are specifically required to meet before the tax lists are actually returned by the taxpayer, and proceed in the same manner as the state board is to proceed, to ascertain the true value of property of different classes subject to taxation, within their respective Counties, and to fix a valuation thereof for taxation purposes. Section 4, c. 81, Laws of 1913. The assessors are required by section 5 of the same act to extend these valuations on the tax rolls, and to list other property, the value of which has not been so fixed, at the same proportionate valuation. It is therefore clear that the taxation in this State was intended to be by classes of property within Counties, and that valuations for taxation purposes were not otherwise to be ascertained and fixed, at least as to property which by its nature is susceptible of classification.

Another consideration is the fact that the precise manner of the exercise of the power of equalization by the state board is not pointed out in the statute. It is

2 therefore fair to assume the legislative intent to have been to confer upon the board an efficient power of equalization so that the burdens of taxation may be equally distributed throughout the State, and upon all of her citizens. An efficient power of equalization cannot be exercised by the state board unless it has power to deal with classes of property, because the valuations are based upon classification. Justice cannot be done by the state board, by way of equalization, as between citizens of the State, unless it has the power to equalize valuations of classes of property, both of different kinds in the same County and of different classes as between Counties throughout the State. It would seem clear, therefore, that unless the power of the state board is lacking or restrained by reason of the terms of the legislation, considered as a whole, the state board ought to have, and has, the power to deal with classes of property, both within any given County and between Counties throughout the State. To hold otherwise is to defeat the express intent of the taxing laws. If the valuations in Counties can only be increased or decreased as a whole, then the state board has no power to adhere to the fundamental principle of taxation prescribed in the act, namely, that the basis of valuation shall be actual value. If a given class of property in a County is correctly valued, and another given class in the same County is undervalued, and the state board decreases the total valuation in that County, it necessarily departs from the correct standard of valuation as to the first-named class of property. If it increases the valuation of the County as a whole, it necessarily imposes an unjust burden upon the owners of the class of property which had theretofore been properly valued.

Another consideration is the fact that the power to equalize taxation necessarily includes the power to value property. Taxation consists of three things, viz., assessment, levy, and collection of the tax. Asessment consists of two things, viz., the listing of the property and the valuing of the same for taxation purposes. When the valuations are fixed in the first instance by county boards,. on given classes of property, as agricultural or grazing lands, for instance, it is the exercise of one part of the assessing power. When the county board sits as a board of equalization, and fixes values, it is still in the exercise of the same assessing power, and when the state board equalizes the valuation of property throughout the State, either by classes or by Counties, increasing or decreasing the said valuation, this same part of the assessing power is necessarily exercised. It is true that boards of equalization, either County or State, ordinarily have no power to perform one of the powers of assessment, namely, the finding and listing of the property belonging to the individual taxpayer. This part of the power, under our system, devolves upon the assessors or, in some contingencies, upon the collectors. But it is nevertheless true that whenever valuations are fixed by any taxing agency, whether originally or by way of equalization, the other portion of the assessing power is exercised.

In this connection it is to be observed that there is no reference in the taxing laws to the question of increase or decrease of the total valuation in the State, by reason of the action of the state board. Its plain duty is stated to be to equalize the burdens of taxation throughout the State, and whether that action results in increase or decrease of valuations would seem to be entirely immaterial, and to have been so regarded by the legislative department. To hold that the state board has power only to adopt some intermediate standard to which all valuations must be brought, both from above and below it, is to compel the exercise by the Board of Equalization in a manner contrary to the letter and spirit of the taxing laws.

As before stated, the basis of taxation is actual value of property. To bring the valuations of classes of property in any County, or the total value in said County, which has been properly fixed, down to some intermediate line, to which line valuation in other Counties should be raised, would defeat the expressed object of the taxing laws and compel the state board to depart from its plain duty in this regard.

If the preceding statement is fully warranted, as we believe it to be, it becomes unnecessary, perhaps, to discuss another important consideration, viz., the rule of interpretation of taxing laws. If the power to equalize includes, without limitations, the power to assess values, then there is no question concerning the application of the so-called strict or liberal rule of interpretation to our taxing statutes. The power is necessarily included under either rule. But if the power to value property is not necessarily included in the power to equalize valuations, and may or may not be included, according to whether a strict interpretation of the terms used is applied, it then becomes important to determine the true rule of interpretation in such cases.

It is frequently said in the reported cases and by the text-writers that taxes are involuntary contributions, levied by the sovereign upon the citizen for the support of government, and that laws for such purposes, consequently, should be construed strictly in favor of the taxpayer. This is upon the theory that the taxation, in case the tax is not paid, may result in a forfeiture of the citizen's property. It is further often said that the legislature is always at hand to express, in terms requiring no interpretation, its intent as to the extent and manner of exercise of the powers of taxation by the several taxing agencies which may be established by law. In this connection it is further sometimes said that the legislature, having plenary power over the subject, will be deemed to have expressly refrained from granting powers not specifically enumerated. Therefore it is frequently held that no tax shall be laid, and no power shall be exercised, unless the same is within the express letter, as well as the spirit of the taxing statutes.

As applied to questions as to whether a tax shall be laid on any given class of property or any given occupation of a citizen, there is reason for the rule of strict construction. The legislature has plenary power, and, if it has declined to speak, it is presumed that it is intended that the tax shall not be laid. But no such proposition is involved in this case. The laws being considered are the general tax laws of the State for raising the necessary revenues to support the state government. Every subject of taxation which was dealt with by the state board was clearly within the letter and spirit of the taxing laws. It taxed no property which was not admittedly subject to taxation. Nor is any question of the visiting of penalties upon the taxpayer involved. In such cases there is clearly reason for strict construction. But this case involves the simple question of the administration of the general taxing laws, to the end that the burdens of taxation may be equally distributed among the people. In such case there is no reason for strict interpretation and narrow and technical definitions of terms. In this connection we cannot do better than to quote somewhat at length from Cooley, the great judge and author, as follows:

"The underlying principle of all construction is that the intent of the legislature should be sought in the words employed to express it, and that when found it should be made to govern, not only in all proceedings which are had under the law, but in all judicial controversies which bring those proceedings under review. Beyond the words employed, if the meaning is plain and intelligible, neither officer nor court is to go in search of the legislative intent; but the legislature must be understood to intend what is plainly expressed, and nothing then remains but to give the intent effect. If the words of the law seem to be of doubtful import, it may then, perhaps, become necessary to look beyond them in order to ascertain what was in the legislative mind at the time the law was enacted; what the circumstances were, under which the action was taken; what evil, if any, was meant to be redressed; what was the leading object of the law; and what the subordinate and relatively unimportant objects." Cooley on Taxation (3rd ed.) 450.

"The question regarding the revenue laws has generally been whether or not they should be construed strictly. To express it in somewhat different language, the question is whether, when a question of doubt arises in the application of a statute to its subject-matter or supposed subject-matter, the doubt is not to be solved in favor of the citizen, rather than in favor of the State upon whose legislation the doubt arises, and whether such solution is not most in accord with the general principles applied in other cases. Strict construction is the general rule in the case of statutes which may divest one of his freehold by proceedings not in the ordinary sense judicial, and to which he is only an enforced party. It is thought to be only reasonable to intend that the legislature, in making provision for such proceedings, would take unusual care to make use of terms which would plainly express its meaning, in order that ministerial officers might not be left in doubt in the exercise of unusual powers, and that the citizen might know exactly what were his duties and liabilities. A strict construction in such cases seems reasonable, because presumptively the legislature has given, in plain terms, all the power it has intended should be exercised. It has been very generally supposed that the like strict construction was reasonable in the case of tax laws." Id. 453.

"There may and doubtless should be a distinction taken in the construction of those provisions of revenue laws which point out the subjects to be taxed, and indicate the time, circumstances, and manner of assessment and collection, and those which impose penalties for obstructions and evasions. There is no reason for peculiar strictness in construing the former. Neither is there reason for liberality. The difference in some cases is exceedingly important. The one method squeezes everything out of the statute which the unyielding words do not perforce retain; the other reaches out by intendment, and brings the statute whatever can fairly be held embraced in its beneficent purpose. The one narrows the statute as it is studied; the other expands it. Every lawyer knows how much easier it is to find a remedy in a statute than an offense. There must surely be a just and safe medium between a view of the revenue laws which treats them as harsh enactments to be circumvented and defeated if possible, and a view under which they acquire an expansive quality in the hands of the court, and may be made to reach out and bring within their grasp, and under the discipline of their severe provisions, subjects and cases which it is only conjectured may have been within their intent. Revenue laws are not to be construed from the standpoint of the taxpayer alone, nor of. the government alone. Construction is not to assume either that the taxpayer, who raises the legal question of his liability under the laws, is necessarily seeking to avoid a duty to the State which protects him, nor, on the other hand, that the government, in demanding its dues, is a tyrant, which, while too powerful to be resisted, may justifiably be obstructed and defeated by any subtle device or ingenious sophism whatsoever. There is no legal presumption either that the citizen will, if possible, evade his duties, or, on the other hand, that the government will exact unjustly or beyond its needs. All construction, therefore, which assumes either the one or the other, is likely to be mischievous, and to take one-sided views, not only of the laws, but of personal and official conductt. The government in its tax legislation is not assuming a hostile position towards the citizen, but, as we have elsewhere said, is apportioning, for and as the agent of all, a duty among them; and the citizen, it is to be presumed, will perform that duty when it is clearly made known to him, and when the time of performance has arrived." Id. 460, 461.

"If there should be any leaning in such cases, it would seem that it should be in the direction of the presumption that everything is expressed in the tax laws which was intended to be expressed. The laws are framed by the government for its own needs, and, if imperfections are found to exist, the legislature, in the language of Mr. Dwarris, 'is at hand to explain its own meaning, and to express more

clearly what has been obscurely expressed.' But there
can be no propriety in construing such a law either with
exceptional strictness amounting to hostility, or with exceptional favor.beyond that accorded to other general laws.
It is as unreasonable to sound a charge upon it as
an enemy to individual and popular rights as it is to
seek for sophistical reasons for grasping and holding by
its authority every subject of taxation which the dragnet of
the official force has brought within its supposed com-
pass. The construction, without bias or prejudice, should
seek the real intent of the law; and, if the leaning is to
strictness, it is only because it is fairly and justly pre-
sumable that the legislature, which was unrestricted in
its authority over the subject, has so shaped the law as,
without ambiguity or doubt, to bring within it everything
it was meant should be embraced." Id. 463. See, also,
37 Cyc. 768.

Judge Cooley cites with approval the case of Cornwall
v. Todd, 38 Conn. 443, 447. In that case the question
was whether a statute which imposes a personal tax on
"persons who are residents" of the taxing districts could
be applied to the personalty belonging to the estate of a
deceased person. The Court said: "The greatest, and
perhaps the only, objection that can be urged against this
rule is that we cannot say in strictness that the deceased
or his estate is a resident of the district. This objection
assumes that the statute is to be strictly construed. But
we do not think that the doctrine of strict construction
should apply to it. Statutes relating to taxes are not
penal statutes, nor are they in derogation of natural
rights. Although taxes are regarded by many as burdens.
and many look upon them even as money arbitrarily and
unjustly extorted from them by government, and hence
justify themselves and quiet their consciences in resorting
to questionable means for the purpose of avoiding taxation, yet, in point of fact, no money paid returns so good
and valuable a consideration as money paid for taxes laid
for legitimate purposes. They are just as essential and
important as government itself, for without them, in some
form, government could not exist. The small pittance we

thus pay is the price we pay for the preservation of all our property, and the protection of all our rights. But there is not only a necessity for taxation, but it is eminently just and equitable that it should be as nearly equal as possible. Hence it is the policy of the law to require all property, except such as is specially exempted, to bear its proportion of the public burdens. Not only so, but the law manifestly contemplates that property rated in the list shall be liable for all taxes, town and school district taxes alike. This is evident from the provision that the district taxes shall be laid on the town list, with special provision for certain changes rendered necessary in order to tax all the real estate situated within the district, and none situated without, and also to assess the tax in each instance upon the right person. In construing statutes relating to taxes, therefore, we ought, where the language will permit, so to construe them as to give effect to the obvious intention and meaning of the legislature, rather than to defeat that intention by a too strict adherence to the letter." Id. 462.

In Singer Mfg. Co. v. Wright, 97 Ga. 114, 121, 25 S. E. 249, 251 (35 L. R. A. 497), the Court, in applying the above rule of construction, says: "While, as a general rule, tax laws must be strictly construed as to their operation upon those to be thereby affected, it will not do, in every instance, to confine words to their literal and ordinary signification."

In Big Black Creek Improvement Co. v. Commonwealth, 94 Pa. 450, it is said: "Statutes are to be construed so as may best effectuate the intention of the makers, which sometimes may be collected from the cause or occasion of passing the statute, and, where discovered, it ought to be followed with judgment and discretion in the construction, though that construction may seem contrary to the letter of the statute." See, also, Chicago Dock Co. v. Garrity, 115 Ill. 155, 3 N. E. 448.

In London & Northwest American Mortg. Co. v. Gibson, 77 Minn. 394, 399, 80 N. W. 207, the question was whether the maxim, "De minimis non curat lex," should be applied to a tax sale which had been had for an amount slightly over the legal tax, and the Court said: "However, assuming the general rule to be that tax laws must be strictly construed as to their operation upon those thereby affected, we are not disposed to confine in every case the words and phrases of the statute to their literal and ordinary signification. Statutes are to be construed so as best to effectuate the intention of those who made them, and such intent should not be defeated by a too strict adherence to the very letter of the law."

In Salisbury v. Lane, 7 Idaho, 370, 63 Pac. 383, the question was whether the improvements upon unpatented mining claims were exempt under the statutes of that Territory, and the Court said: "We are not in accord with the position taken by counsel for respondent that, in construing statutes in pari materia, we must follow the word, and not the purpose, of the law. All statutes pertaining to revenue are to be construed most strictly in favor of the object of the statute; that is, in favor of the purpose of the statute."

In Aggers v. People, 20 Colo. 348, 38 Pac. 386, the statute provided that property omitted from the tax list might be assessed for back taxes, and the property had not been omitted, but one of the taxes to which it was subject had not been extended and charged upon the property. And the Court said: "The purpose of the statute evidently is to prevent property from escaping taxation through oversight, omission or mistake, and to enable the taxing officers to impose upon all property its just and equal proportion of the public burden. The strict construction contended for by counsel for respondent would prevent the accomplishment of this object and purpose. We think rather that the rule of construction that should be adopted is as stated in Cornwall v. Todd, 38 Conn. 443, quoted with approval by Cooley in his * * * work or Taxation. * * * "

In State v. Taylor, 35 N. J. Law, 184, 190, without disclosing in the opinion just what was involved in regard to which the statement was made, the report lays down the rule as follows: "A liberal construction must therefore, be given to all tax laws for public purposes, not

only that the officers of the government may not be hin
dered, but also that the rights of all taxpayers may be
equally preserved."

In White v. Walsh, 62 Misc. Rep. 423, 427, 114 N. Y
Supp. 1015, 1017, the statute imposed a tax upon every
"mortgage," and the plaintiff resisted a tax because his
mortgage was in the form of a deed, but was intended as
a mortgage, and the Court says: "The law does not favor
the ingenious scrivener, but looks to the legislative inten
tion as the only guide in interpreting tax laws. The Court
cannot extend the fair meaning of the law so as to include things not named or described as subjects of taxation; neither will it permit parties to give new names to
old forms and thus escape the letter of the law."

In Baltimore, C. & A. Ry. Co. v. Com'rs., 93 Md. 113,
123, 48 Atl. 853, 856, the question was as to the powers
of county commissioners as to the levy of taxes upon
property liable to assessment but not assessed, and the
Couort said: "The object to be accomplished by conferring these powers is to give all possible practical effect to
the fundamental principle embodied in our bill of rights
* * * that 'every person in the State, or person holding
property therein, ought to contribute his proportion of
public taxes for the support of the government, according
to his actual worth in real or personal property.' The
reason, therefore, why the power of the county commissioners, in respect to the annual levy of taxes and to the
assessmentof property for taxation in connection therewith, should not receive a 'strict and severe,' but rather a
'reasonable and liberaal,' construction is quite obvious."

These cases and many others which might be cited, as
well as the text of Judge Cooley, would seem to establish
clearly the proper rule of construction of taxing statutes,
to the effect that a reasonable and fair construction
whereby the intent of the legislature is fully carried out
should be adopted, and that neither a so-called strict construction nor, perhaps, a liberal construction should be
adopoted. As stated by Judge Cooley, it is more properly
a middle ground which should be taken, fair alike to the
citizen and to the State. Under such a rule, the powers

of the State Board of Equalization, to adjust and equalize the burdens of taxation throughout the State, would seem to authorize the definition of those terms as including the power to value property, if, indeed, it is not necessarily in-cluded within those terms..

In view of what has been heretofore stated, there would seem to be no difficulty in concluding that the ac-tion of the state board is entirely justifiable in so far as it has dealt with classes of property. Its action is pre-sumed to be intended to equalize the burdens of taxation throughout the State, and all of its acts would seem to fall plainly within the terms of its grant of power.

When the state board took the tax rolls of the several Counties for examination, it found them to contain a list of the property of the respective Counties arranged by classification, as provided by law. When it raised the val-uation of a given class of property in certain Counties and did not raise the valuation of the same class of prop-erty in other Counties, it simply equalized the valuations of that class of property in all the Counties of the State. When the state board raised the valuation of certain classes of property in every County in the State, it simply equalized the valuation of those classes of property with the valuation upon other classes of property throughout the State. In this action the state board was adhering to its plain duty, namely, to value property at one-third of its actual value for taxation purposes. In no instance, so far as appears, did the state board increase the valua-tion of any class of property in any County beyond one-third of its actual value, or beyond what some one or more classes of property in some one or more Counties had been valued by the County taxing authorities. The question, then, as to whether the state board has power to revise and correct the tax rolls, as they come up from the various Counties, and, as an original proposition, to value all of the property in the State at what it deems to be one-third of its actual value, is not involved in this case. The state board has simply brought up to a stand-ard, which had been fixed by the taxing authorities of some Counties in the State upon some classes of property, the valuation of all other classes of property in the State. In so doing, it has pursued its power in the only efficient and intelligent manner possible under our law, and has, it is to be presumed, accomplished the purpose for which it was created, namely, to equalize the burdens of taxation upon all of the citizens. While it is alleged in the petition for the writ in this case, that the property of the petitioners had already been fully valued, and had been assessed at one-third thereof for taxation purposes, and that the action of the state board in increasing said valuations resulted in an overvaluation of the property of petitioners, still in this proceeding, as we have before seen, this fact must be deemed not to be established. The state board are necessarily presumed to have acted upon evidence and to have reached a correct result, and their judgment is not open to review.

A construction fair to the taxpayer, and fair to the State, neither unduly strict nor unduly liberal, authorizes the holding that it was the intention of the legislature that the State Board of Equalization should have the power which it has attempted to exercise, at least in so far as it relates to the increase of valuation of classes of property throughout the State. As against this conclusion, counsel for petitioners present the following propositions: (1) The action of the state board is not authorized because it amounts to assessment by increasing the total valuation of property in the State; (2) even if the board has powers of assessment, the power has been illegally exercised in acting upon classes of property. The argument in support of these propositions proceeds upon several grounds. It is first argued that the word "equalization" has a well-defined meaning throughout the country, which has necessarily excluded all asserting power. In support of the argument, several cases are cited.

Poe v. Howell, 67 Pac. 62, is a case decided by Judge D. H. McMillen, on the district bench in Chaves County, in December, 1901. In that case the territorial board had determined that real estate and improvements and stocks of merchandise, in incorporated cities, towns, and villages, and stocks of merchandise outside of such cities,

towns, and villages, had been undervalued throughout the
Territory, as compared with the valuations of other classes
of property in the Territory, and had ordered the valuations of the same to be increased 10 per cent. in one instance and 15 per cent. in the other. A proceeding was
brought by a taxpayer to enjoin the collector from extending on the tax rolls the amounts of these raises. The
learned judge held in that case that the action of the territorial board was unauthorized, viz.: First, under the
statute then in force, the territorial board dealt with Counties as units only; second, and principally, that the power
of equalization necessarily excluded all assessing powers,
and therefore the territorial board had no power to increase the total valuations in the Territory, not in terms,
but in effect, that some intermediate line must be adopted,
to which valuations in Counties must be brought, both
from above and below, leaving the total valuations of the
Territory the same. The statute under which this decision was rendered is section 2636, C. L. 1897, and contains the following language: "It shall be the duty of
the Auditor of the Territory at such meeting to furnish
said board with the assessment roll of each County of
the Territory for their inspection and examination, for
the purpose of ascertaining the rate of assessment and
value of property therein, and whenever they are satisfied
that the scale of valuation has not been made with reasonable uniformity by the different County Assessors, the
said board shall adjust and equalize the said assessment
rolls by raising or lowering the valuation thereof, so that
the same shall be of a uniform value throughout the Territory."

In comparison with this language, we again quote the
language from section 13, c. 84, Laws 1913, as follows:
"The State Board of Equalization shall at its said meeting on the first Monday in July, examine the assessment
roll of each County of the State, for the purpose of ascertaining the rate of assessment and valuation of property
therein, and the board shall have the power to adjust and
equalize the said assessment rolls so that the valuation

of property for purposes of taxation shall be of substantial uniformity throughout the State."

It may be argued with some force that, under the language of section 2636, C. L. 1897, the territorial board was required to deal with Counties as units, although this was denied by the Territorial Supreme Court, in Territory v. Bank, 10 N. M. 283, 65 Pac. 172, which will be noticed later. The language of the section mentions the assessment rolls, and provides for the raising or lowering of the valuations thereof. The language of section 13 of chapter 84, Laws of 1913, supra, with which we are con· cerned, is vastly different. It provides for the equaliza· tion of the valuations of property in the State, not assessment rolls.

Judge McMillen's second proposition, that "equalization" has a well-defined meaning throughout the country and necessarily excluded all forms of assessing power, however, is more doubtful.

We have therefore pointed out that to equalize the valuation of one thing, which has been undervalued, with that of another, which has been truly valued, necessarily included a portion of the assessing power. If an increase in total valuations results from the action, it is merely incidental, and, as we have before seen, would seem to be immaterial and to have been so considered by the legislature.

Previously, in August, 1900, the Territorial Supreme Court, in Territory v. Bank, 10 N. M. 283, 65 Pac. 172, had held differently. The Territorial Board of Equalization, under the powers conferred by section 2636, C. L. 1897, raised the valuation of bank stock of a number of banks in the Territory to 60 per cent. of its par value. The Court in that case, in an opinion by Mr. Justice Mc-Fie, held that even under section 2636, C. L. 1897, the territorial board had power to equalize the valuation of property by classes, and that no notice of such action was required; the statute itself, by its provision for an annual meeting on a certain day, being a sufficient notice to the taxpayer. The Court also necessarily held that the Territorial Board of Equalization, under said section 2636, C.

L..1897, had power to increase the total valuations in the State, because it appears, from the opinion in that case, that an increase of valuations was made upon the bank stock of a large number of banks in the Territory, and none appear to have been decreased.

In Poe v. Howell, supra, Judge McMillen attempted to distinguish that case from the case of Territory v. Bank, supra, in that in the latter it did not appear that the action of the territorial board resulted in any increase of valuations in the Territory as a whole. In this we think he was in error, because it appears, at least inferentially, from the statement of the facts in the case, that the action taken must have resulted in increase of valuations.

Poe v. Howell was never appealed to the Supreme Court of the Territory. Territory v. Bank, 10 N. M. 283, 65 Pac. 172, was cited and approved in Bank v. Albright, 13 N. M. 514, 86 Pac. 548. This case was affirmed by the Supreme Court of the United States. See 208 U. S. 548, 28 Sup. Ct. 349, 52 L. Ed. 614. Bank v. Perea, 5 N. M. 664, 25 Pac. 776, was affirmed in 147 U. S. 87, 13 Sup. Ct. 194, 37 L. Ed. 91. Neither of these cases are pertinent to this part of the discussion. These are all of the decisions in this jurisdiction.

The holding in Territory v. Bank, 10 N. M. 283, 65 Pac. 172, is not without support, in principle, by cases in other jurisdictions, under similar statutes.

In Chamberlain v. Walter (C. C.) 60 Fed. 788, the question was not the same as here; it being a question as to when courts may relieve against discrimination in taxation. But in that case railroad property had been raised several thousand dollars per mile, which valuation was all, or more than, the actual value of the property, while all other property in the State was valued for taxation at from 50 to 60 per cent. of its value. The state board had power there to equalize by raising the valuation of railroad property which was undervalued, and by decreasing such as was overvalued, but there was no aggregate value to be maintained, so far as the requirements of the statute were concerned. The Court held that, as there was no aggregate to be maintained, to equalize was to se-

cure equality, and the increase in total valuations resulting from the action of the board was ignored.

In Appeal of McNeal, 35 Okla. 17, 128 Pac. 285, there
is a review of all of the Oklahoma decisions, and it is
chiefly valuable for this reason, because the statute under
which the decision was rendered is different from ours,
in that it expressly authorizes the state board to deal with
classes of property and to equalize all property to conform to the fair cash value thereof. The former decisions in Oklahoma were rendered under the following statutory provision: "It shall be the duty of said board to
examine the various County assessments and to equalize
the same, and to decide upon the rate of territorial tax
to be levied for the current year, together with any other
general or special territorial taxes required by law to be
levied, and to equalize the levy of such taxes throughout
the Territory. And shall therefrom find the percentage
that must be added to or deducted from the assessèd value
of each County, and shall then order the percentage so
found to be added to or subtracted from the assessed
values of each of the various Counties of the Territory,
and shall notify the various County Clerks of the percentage so ordered to be added to or subtracted from the
valuation of property in their respective Counties."

Under this statute it was held in Gray v. Stiles, 6 Okla.
455, 49 Pac. 1083, that the sole power of the state board
was to equalize by increasing the valuation in some of
the Counties and decreasing that of others, the aggregate
amount in the Territory to remain the same as fixed by
the local taxing agencies, except such slight variations as
might necessarily occur in the process of equalization.
Previously, under the same statute, in Wallace·v. Bullen,
6 Okl. 17, 52 Pac. 954, it was pointed out that the basis
of taxation was fixed by statute at actual value of
property, and the state board had taken a standard fixed
in one County (Kingfisher) as the true standard. and had
brought all other Counties up to that same standard. The
Court said: "We hold that the statute creating the Territorial Board of Equalization conferred upon that board
authority to review and correct the valuations of prop-

erty for taxation returned to them by the County Clerks
of the several Counties of the Territory, and to equalize
such valuation upon the basis of the true cash value of
the property, and that they may lawfully increase the aggregate of valuation of property in the several Counties of
the Territory returned by the said several Clerks of the several Counties; that the several acts of said board complained of in the petition in this cause were within the
jurisdiction of the said board, and authorized by law."
On rehearing of this case (6 Okl. 757, 54 Pac. 974), Gray
v. Stiles was expressly overruled, and the former opinion was adhered to; the Court added: "And under the
provisions of our statutes relating to the assessment and
valuation of property for revenue purposes, and defining
the power of the several officers and boards, we hold that
the Territorial Board of Equalization, in exercising its
powers to equalize the assessments of the various Counties
for purposes of taxation, may, from all the returns made
from the various Counties, determine which of such returns in the judgment of the board most nearly represents an assessment based upon the true cash value of the
property in such County, and may adopt such return as
the standard or basis for equalization, and may add to or
deduct from all the remaining returns such per cent. as
will be required to cause the various other Counties to
conform to such standard or basis of assessed valuation,
notwithstanding such action may result in increasing or
diminishing the aggregate valuation as shown by the returns made by the several County Clerks."

In Bardrick v. Dillon, 7 Okl. 535, 54 Pac. 785, this
same doctrine is applied to equalization by county boards.
The Court said: "The statute points out no manner in
which this power is to be executed and duty performed,
and there is no limitation upon the manner in which the
equalization shall be done, except that property shall not
be valued above its true cash value. Our statute contemplates that all taxable property shall be valued for purposes of taxation at its fair cash value; and all assessing
officers and equalizing boards are bound, when performing the duties imposed on them, to keep this fact in view,

and not fix such values or make such additions for purposes of equalization as will increase the property beyond its fair cash value."

These Oklahoma cases are certainly authority for one phase of our holding in the case at bar, viz., that the result of increase or decrease of total valuations is immaterial in defining the power of the equalization under a statute quite similar to ours.

In State v. Nichols, 29 Wash. 159, 69 Pac. 771, the Washington Supreme Court discussed one phase of this same question. They have there express statutory authority to deal with property by classes, but no power is given in terms to increase the total valuations in the State. The same argument against the power to increase total valuations was there made as is made here, but the Court overruled the same, declined to follow the Colorado, Montana, and California cases which were urged upon them, and relied upon the Oklahoma cases, and a case from Utah (State v. Thomas, 16 Utah, 86, 50 Pac. 615.)

In Utah they had a constitutional provision providing for the valuation of property for taxation purposes at its actual value, and for the equalization of values in Counties by county boards and in the State by state boards.

In Salt Lake City v. Armstrong, 15 Utah, 472, 49 Pac. 641, the Utah Supreme Court held that county boards had the power to equalize, notwithstanding such action resulted in the increase of totoal valuations in the County. The argument of the Court was based somewhat on the fact that the mode of equalization was not pointed out in the Constitution, and that therefore the county board might exercise the power in such reasonable and efficient manner as it might determine.

In State v. Thomas, 16 Utah, 86, 50 Pac. 615, the Court went further and held that increase in total valuations in Counties was not objectionable. It applied the same principle to the action of the state boards. It is true that in Utah they had a statute supplementing the constitutional provision, expressly empowering the state board to equalize vaulations to the actual value of property, and in this jurisdiction we have no such statute. But it is nevertheless true that here, as heretofore pointed out, and as stated in the Oklahoma cases above quoted, the duty to reach actual value as a basis for taxation is constantly before each taxing agency of the State by the provisions of our statute now being considered.

In Arizona the same question has been considered. There they had no statute specifically authorizing equalization by classes of property, but, like ours, their statute required the listing of property by classes. They had no express statutory authority to increase the total valuations within the Territory nor to equalize valuations to actual value. Their statute, while not in the exact terms of ours, gives the territorial board no more or different powers than is possessed by our state boards. The Arizona Court, in Copper Queen M. Co. v. Territorial Board of Equalization, 9 Ariz. 383, 84 Pac. 511, affirmed 206 U. S. 474, 27 Sup. Ct. 695, 51 L. Ed. 1143, held two things, viz.: First, that increasing the total valuations by equalization was allowable, distinguishing and rather criticising Poe v. Howell, supra; second, that the Board of Equalization had power to equalize by classes of property, citing and approving Territory v. Bank, 10 N. M. 283, 65 Pac. 172, supra, counsel attempting to distinguish the Arizona case by saying that the Arizona statute gave county boards no power to equalize by classes, but limited them to dealing with individuals, while the territorial board was given power to make classification of property. Even so, it still remains true that no specific power to equalize by classes or to increase totals in the Territory was conferred, and the action of the territorial board was justified on the ground that it had exercised its powers in the only fair, reasonable, and efficient manner it could to secure uniformity of tax burdens.

Counsel for petitioners rely principally upon the Colorado, Montana, and California cases, aside from Poe v. Howell, supra. The leading case in Colorado, and a much cited case elsewhere, is People v .Lothrop, 3 Colo. 428. This case is often cited to both of the propositions involved in the case at bar, namely, increase of total valuations, and dealing with property by classes instead of dealing with Counties as units. In this case the Board of Equalization of the State of Colorado has raised the aggregate valuations of property in several of the Counties and diminished such aggregate valuations in other Counties, and in some Counties they had made no change. The net increase of valuation was over $5,000,000. The Constitution under which the board acted provided "the duties of the said Board of Equalization shall be to adjust and equalize the valuation of real and personal property among the several Counties of the State." They also had the constitutional provision that "all taxes shall be uniform upon the same class of subjects within the territorial limit of the authority levying the tax." They had a statute that the board was required to "examine the various assessments as far as regards the State tax and equalize the rate of assessments in the various Counties whenever they are satisfied that the scale of valuation has not been adjusted with reasonable uniformity by the different assessors." The board was also required to ascertain whether the "valuation of real estate in each County bears a fair relation or proportion to the valuation of all other Counties in the State, and on such examination they may increase or diminish the aggregate valuation of real estate in any County as much as in their judgment may be necessary to produce a just relation between all the valuations of real estate in the State, but in no instance shall they reduce the aggregate valuation of all the Counties below the aggregate valuation as returned by the Clerks of the several Counties." The statute further provided that "all taxable property shall be listed and valued each year, and shall be assessed at its full cash value."

They had a constitutional provision in Colorado creating the office of County Assessor. The decision of this case is made to turn largely upon this last mentioned provision of the Constitution. The Court says: "The Constitution provides (section 8, art. 14) for the election in each County, each alternate year, of a County Assessor. He is thus a constitutional officer, and, though his duties are left unprescribed, the essential duties of an assessor must be presumed to have been contemplate.l. Is there not here a plain intention on the part of the people to preserve local control over the valuation of property for purposes of taxation? This local control existed under the territorial form of government under which they had been living, and is this not an effort to secure it beyond contingency? In view of this provision and of other constitutional limitations, it may be gravely doubted whether it is competent for the legislative authority to take from County Assessors the substantial control of valuations of property for State taxation, and vest it in a central authority."

It thus clearly appears that the Colorado Court believed that all assessing power had been vested in the County Assessors by the Constitution of the State itself, and that therefore the State Board of Equalization could necessarily exercise no such power. The Court further says: "The Assessor is thus made an integral part of the revenue system which not only thus specifies and defines his duties, but assigns to other officers and boards equally well-defined and separate duties. The Assessor shall list and value. The board of commissioners shall equalize, adjust, increase and diminish, supply omissions, and correct errors, and hear complaints. The County Clerk shall prepare assessment rolls and compute and extend the tax therein. The State Board of Equalization shall adjust and equalize valuations, and, lastly, the County Treasurer shall collect the tax."

As before stated, this case is much relied upon throughout the western country. But we must say that in our opinion it is not authority for what it is often cited. The substance and effect of this case is that, by reason of the constitututional provisions of the State, it was not competent for the State legislature to confer the assessing power upon any other person or body than Assessors, as provided for in the Constitution, and that, in view of such constitutional provisions, the sections of the statute which were under consideration were given a more limited and restricted interpretation than they would have been given, had they been considered purely as a statute standing

alone. The Court also founded its argument somewhat
upon the fact that they had a limitation upon the rate of
taxation in their Constitution in Colorado, and that, if
the power to increase valuations existed in the state board,
this limitation might be easily annulled. The Court says:
"Under this construction of the statute the efforts of the
people to establish and maintain legitimate restraints on
the power to tax will have been unavailing, and the checks
and guards which they have embodied in their Constitution to that end cease to be of practical force or value.
The spirit of the law and not 'the letter which destroys'
must prevail. We cannot believe that any such grant of
power of the State Board of Equalization was within the
intent of the legislative authority." Just how the taxing
power in the hands of the state board is more unsafe than
in the hands of the Assessors is not pointed out, nor can
we understand.

In People v. Ames, 27 Colo. 126, 60 Pac. 346, a new
statute had been passed in 1899, which repealed previous
legislation, and which provided that the State Board of
Equalization should adjust and equalize the valuation of
real and personal property among the several Counties of
the State, and that it should have power to either increase
or diminish the aggregate valuation of all taxable property
not to exceed in any year 5 per cent. of such valuation,
and only as an incident to such equalization. The same
constitutional provision existed as when the case of People
v. Lothrop, supra, was decided. The State Board of Equalization had increased and diminished the valuations of
certain kinds and classes of property in Arapahoe County,
varying from 2 to 54 per cent. in increase. The Court adhered to its former decision, and emphasizes the importance of the constitutional provision in determining the
powers of their State Board of Equalization. The Court
says: "Each is a constitutional body, with powers defined and limited by the fundamental law of the State,
the respective authority of which is essentially different.
The former shall equalize and adjust the property values
among the several Counties of the State; the latter shall
equalize and adjust such values within the respective

Counties. The language employed with respect to the authority of each is different. That values should be equitably adjusted among the several Counties of the State was necessary, because, without a power lodged somewhere to effect this result, great inequality might prevail in the valuation of the different Counties, and the burden of supporting the State government would be inequitably distributed. For a like reason, it was necessary that property values be adjusted and equalized within the respective Counties, so that the taxes for County purposes would be uniform. The state board has no authority to revise the work of the county board. Therefore it has no power to equalize valuations between classes or kinds of property in the respective Counties, for that is a matter which the Constitution confides to the county board."

Thus it clearly appears that the Colorado decisions interpreting their statute are largely based upon the fact that the three taxing agencies, viz., Assessors, county boards, and state board, are all constitutional offices or bodies, and have granted to them certain specific powers which prevent the legislature from extending to the state board any part of the assessing power.

The constitutional provisions of Montana are copied from Colorado. Two cases from Montana are cited. State v. Board of Equalization, 18 Mont. 473, 480, 46 Pac. 266, and State v. Fortune, 24 Mont. 158, 60 Pac. 1086. The Montana Court follows the decision in Colorado, but in the latter case the Chief Justice concurred solely upon the ground of stare decisis and states that, if the question were an open one, he would favor a departure from the Colorado doctrine as demonstrably wrong.

In Wells Fargo & Co. v. State Board of Equalization, 56 Cal. 194, the state board had undertaken to pass upon individual assessments and to raise or lower the valuation thereof. The Constitution of California provided that the duty of the state board was "to equalize the valuation of the taxable property of the several Counties in the State for the purpose of taxation," and that the duty of the county boards was "to equalize the valuation of the taxable property in the County for the purposes of taxa-

tion." Those two provisions were followed by a proviso
which was ambiguous in terms, for the reason that the
power to raise or lower the entire assessment roll, or any
assessment contained therein, was apparently given to
both the County and the State boards.   The Court construed the proviso distributively, reddendo singula singu-
lis, giving to the county boards power to deal with individual assessments, and the state board power to deal with
the rolls as a whole.

In Orr v. State Board of Equalization, 3 Idaho, (Hasb.)
190, 28 Pac. 416, the state board had increased the valuations by classes of property, and the action was challenged
upon that ground.   The statute in Idaho · provided the
manner of the exercise of the powers by the state board as
follows: "(1) They shall add to the aggregate valuation
of real and personal property in each County, which they
believe to be valued below its proper valuation, such percentage in each case as will raise the same to its proper
valuation."   The Court held that the state board had no
such power, because of the terms of the statute, which
prescribed the mode of the exercise of the power.   Other
cases have been cited and relied upon by counsel, which
we have examined, but we have found nothing in them to
change our views, as heretofore expressed.   We appreciate
that little aid is to be obtained from the cases in the other
States on account of the diversity of the statutory provisions.   We think, however, that certain principles, fairly deducible from all of the authorities, are accepted in all
of the cases, as follows:

The power of the state boards to equalize the burdens
of taxation includes the power to deal with classes of
property, unless, by reason of the terms of the taxing statute, or constitutional provisions, the power is restrained.
Where the mode of the exercise of the power of equalization is pointed out in the statute, it must, of course, be
followed.   Where the mode is not pointed out, any reasonable and efficient mode may be adopted to accomplish
the end in view.   Unless controlled by statutory terms,
the power to equalize includes the power to increase or
decrease valuations, and such result is immaterial.

If we are correct in our deductions from the authorities, there would seem to be no difficulty in sustaining the action of the state board, in so far as they dealt with classes or property and increased total valuations in the State. Even if these deductions from the cases are not wholly warranted, we believe the considerations mentioned in the earlier part of this opinion amply justify our conclusions that under our statutes, and considering them as a whole, such action of the state board was justified.

The strongest argument, apparently, against the power of the state board, is the fact that no provision is made for notice to those affected by the action. Counsel do not **3** claim that this fact renders the action void as being an invasion of the constitutional rights of the taxpayer. But the fact that no such provision is made is suggested as strongly persuasive of the legislative intent not to confer the power which has been assumed by the state board. The argument, apparently strong, may be plainly and effectively answered. The statute fixing the time and place of meeting of the state board is itself notice to all taxpayers. Territory v. Bank, 10 N. M. 283, 65 Pac. 172, and cases cited. But this notice is notice only that the state board will meet and perform such acts as it may lawfully perform. It is notice to the taxpayer owning property of a certain class which has been grossly undervalued that the state board may raise the valuation of that class of property to its true valuation for taxation purposes. But it is no notice to the taxpayer whose property is already fully valued, and who has already passed the Assessor and county commissioners without harm, that the state board, by reason of its action, will impose upon him an overvaluation amounting to an illegal assessment. The notice of the statute is notice that the state board may do legal things but not illegal things. As is pointed out in Territory v. Bank, 10 N. M. 283, 65 Pac. 172, it is not contemplated that the taxpayer shall actually come to the State Capitol and attend the meetings of the state board, as the expense would be intolerable and absurd. This notice, while it is due process of law in the tax proceedings, is not intended to be actual notice. But it is sufficient notice to all who are not wronged; it is no notice to those who are wronged by the imposition of an illegal tax. The taxpayer thus wronged has actual notice only after the action has been taken which inflicts the injury. The injury is not intentional on the part of the state board, but it is accidental as a result of a general order affecting all alike in some general class. The state board does not investigate the comparative valuations of the property of individuals in the same class, but compares classes of property with other classes. The relation, therefore, of the assessed valuations of the property of any given individual to the actual value of his property is not examined and passed upon by the state board. The taxpayer, then, must presume such remedies as the law provides.

We have a statute covering the matter as follows: "The assessment book, when delivered to the County collector of taxes, properly verified by the affidavit of the County Assessor, and properly certified by the county commissioners, as required by law, shall constitute his authority to collect the taxes therein set forth, and he shall not be held liable for any irregularity or illegality in any of the proceedings prior to his receiving said assessment book; and the amounts to be paid as taxes as shown by said assessment book, shall not be altered, reduced or in any manner changed, except by direction of the District or Supreme Court; but this prohibition shall not extend to the correction of obvious clerical errors in names, description of property, or computation of amount of taxes. If the collector shall discover any errors of other kinds in said assessment book by which any injustice would be done to any taxpayer, it shall be his duty to report the same to the District Attorney, and any taxpayer complaining of any such injustice may submit his complaint to the District Attorney; and if the District Attorney is satisfied that correction or change should be made so as to avoid injustice to the taxpayer, it shall be his duty to submit the matter to the District Court and ask for an order of that court that such change or correction should be made, without cost to the taxpayer injuriously affected." Chapter 84, par. 23, Laws 1913.

It is to be noticed that the word "injustice" to the taxpayer is employed in this section. The word "injustice" would seem to be the broadest term which the legislature could have employed in this connection. Any case of overvaluation of the property of the taxpayer would seem clearly to be an injustice within the meaning of the act. It is to be further noticed that an injustice which is discovered after the tax rolls come into the hands of the collector is to be relieved against, under the terms of the section. Therefore, it would seem clear that the fact that the state board had increased the assesed valuation of property of any particular class would not deprive any taxpayer in that class from seeking the relief provided for. In other words, the action of the State Board of Equalization is not final as against the claims of any taxpayer in the

4 State. The section requires the taxpayer to submit any claim of injustice to the District Attorney of the proper County, and if the District Attorney is satisfied that injustice has been done to the taxpayer, it is his duty to submit the matter to the District Court and ask for an order correcting the injustice without cost to the taxpayer. In this way relief is afforded to each individual taxpayer, without any cost or expense to him. If he can show that, by reason of the action taken by the state board, he is compelled to pay taxes upon more than one-third of the actual value of his property, it is to be assumed that the District Attorney will promptly present the matter to the District Court and secure the relief to which the taxpayer is entitled. It is true that the section provides that the District Attorney must be satisfied of the injustice before he will be required to make application to the District Court. This provision may make the District Attorney one of the taxing officers of the State, and there seems to be no appeal from his refusal to present the complaint of the taxpayer to the District Court. It does not follow, however, that his judgment upon the matter is necessarily final. To tax the citizen on more than one-third of the actual value of his property is illegal, under the taxing laws of this State. If it is illegal, and the taxpayer resorts to all the means provided by law to correct the injustice, it

stocks of merchandise, and in 12 of the Counties certain named persons were assessed by the board on stocks of merchandise at various amounts. In one of the Counties a large number of persons and corporations had returned various areas of land as grazing land at $1.80 per acre, and the state board made an order changing the classification of these lands from grazing lands to coal lands, and fixed the valuation thereof at $12 per acre. This action was clearly in the nature of original assessment of property.

The action of the state board in regard to the change in classification of property is not involved in this case. Nor do we understand how the petitioners in this case can question the action of the state board in any of the other particulars mentioned. They are not among the persons who were specifically raised in valuations or specifically added to the lists and thereby subjected to original assessment. All that was done by the state board, which af-

1   fects petitioners, was the raising of valuations of classes of property of which they allege they are the owners. As before seen, we cannot assume in this proceeding that any of the property of the petitioners is assessed at more than its actual value divided by three.

5   If this is so, no injustice has been done them. So long as the taxpayer is not assessed more than the law provides, and in the absence of some well-defined and established scheme of discrimination, or some fraudulent action, he has no cause of complaint, and the courts have no power to review the action of the various taxing agencies established by law. 37 Cyc. 1263; Cooley on Taxation (3rd ed.) 1459; Albuquerque Bank v. Perea, 5 N. M. 664, 25 Pac. 776; Bank v. Albright, 13 N. M. 514, 86 Pac. 548. First National Bank v. Albright, 208 U. S. 548, 28 Sup. Ct. 349, 52 L. Ed. 614.

As before stated, the action of the state board in making original assessments of individuals and exempting others from general orders affecting classes of property would seem to be questionable. The power to deal with individuals would seem to be conferred exclusively on the County taxing officers by the various provisions of the statute, except in cases of direct appeal to the state board. But we cannot decide this question because it is not involved. We simply decide that petitioners are not in a position to raise the question.

There is no error in the action of the State Board of Equalization of which the petitioners can complain in this proceeding, and, for the reasons stated herein, the petition and writ of certiorari will be dismissed, and it is so ordered.

[No. 1572, February 11, 1914.]

STATE OF NEW MEXICO, Appellee, v. CANDIDO PADILLA, Appellant.

SYLLABUS (BY THE COURT)

1. The correctness of instructions given by the trial court will not be reviewed by the Supreme Court, unless exception is taken to the giving of such instructions at the time they were given.

P. 576

2. The failure of the court to instruct the jury on all of the law applicable to the case cannot be taken advantage of, unless excepted to at the time the jury is instructed.

P. 576

3. A variance between the allegations in the indictment and the proofs at the trial cannot be raised on a motion for a new trial and cannot be assigned as error in this Court unless the question was raised at the trial of the case and the court trying the same given an opportunity to pass upon the question.

P. 577

4. Where there is substantial evidence to support a verdict the appellate court will not disturb it.

P. 578

5. A new trial on the ground of newly discovered evidence
will not be granted for evidence that was known to defendant
at the time of the trial.

P. 578

Appeal from the District Court of Colfax County;
Thomas D. Leib, District Judge; affirmed.

J. LEAHY, Raton, N. M., for appellant.

Proof of burglary is without foundation. Little v. Commonwealth, 152 S. W. 569.

Court invaded the province of the jury because it precluded from the jury the consideration of any defence, except that of alibi. Court should have requested instruction as to how the defendant came into possession of the
property. 6 Cyc. 254; State v. Dashman, 55 S. W. 69;
Torres v. State, 55 S. W. 828; Hayes v. State, 35 S. W.
983; William v. State, 33 S. W. 371; Eley v. State, 13
S. W. 998; Considine v. U. S., 112 Fed. 342; Robertson
v. State, 26 S. E. 728; Bond v. State, 4 S. W. 580.

Court should have submitted every explanation offered
by defendant touching his possession of any of the property. 6 Cyc. 255; Knight v. State, 65 S. W. 88; Alvin v.
State, 60 S. W. 551; Williams v. State, 33 S. W. 371;
McCoy v. State, 81 S. W. 46; Wheeler v. State, 30 S. W.
913; People v. Land, 76 Pac. 232; State v. Scott, 19 S.
W. 89; Cornwall v. State, 18 S. E. 154; Falvey v. State,
11 S. E. 607; C. L. 1897, sec. 1111.

The breaking and entering as alleged should have been
defined and complete instructions given on the evidence
touching the same. Timmons v. State, 32 Am. Rep. 376;
Dennis v. People, 27 Mich. 151; State v. Reid, 20 Ia. 413;
Harris v. People, 38 Am. Rep. 267; State v. Yohe, 53 N.
W. 1088; State v. Fleming, 12 S. E. 131.

The time of the offense should have been fully covered by
the instructions. People v. Bielfus, 26 N. W. 771; Berger-
son v. State, 74 N. W. 253; State v. Morris, 47 Conn. 179.

Breaking must be affirmatively proved as charged. Jones
v. State, 7 S. W. 669.

State v. Padilla, 18 N. M. 573.

No essential fact can be presumed. People v. Griffin, 19 Cal. 578; State v. Gray, 46 Pac. 801; State v. Frahm, 35 N. W. 451; Levine v. State, 3 S. W. 660.

Variance. State v. Teeter, 27 N. W. 485; Green v. State, 19 S. W. 1055.

Defendant's possession alone is wholly insufficient to rest a verdict, judgment or sentence upon. Fuller v. State, 48 Ala. 273; Lester v. State, 32 S. E. 335; Dawson v. State, 25 S. W. 21; Mangham v. State, 13 S. E. 55, 40 Am. St. R. 791.

There was no direct evidence of burglary having been committed, and the evidence could only support a verdict of guilty of larceny. Sullen, et al. v. Board of Commissioners, 47 Pac. 165; People v. Barry, 29 Pac. 1026.

HARRY S. CLANCY, Assistant Attorney General, Santa Fe, N. M., for appellee.

Objections to instructions given, or for refusal to give requested instructions, must be made at the time the alleged erroneous instructions were given, or instructions refused, or the objections cannot be raised on appeal State v. Eaker, 17 N. M. 379; State v. Lucero, 17 N. M. 484.

There was no error in the refusal of the court to grant a new trial upon the ground of newly discovered evidence. 12 Cyc. 735; 29 Cyc. 896; Hardin v. State, 33 S. E. 700; State v. Foley, 46 N. W. 746; Parsley v. State, 64 S. W. 257; Frickie v. State, 51 S. W. 394; Moore v. State, 53 S. W. 862; Tanner v. State, 44 S. W. 489; Butts v. State, 33 S. W. 866.

OPINION OF THE COURT.

NEBLETT, D. J.—Appellant was indicted by the grand jury of Colfax County for breaking and entering the shop of Max Karlsruher in the night time with intent to commit larceny therein, and was tried in the District Court of said County and found guilty as charged in the indictment and sentenced by the court to imprisonment in the State penitentiary for not less than two years nor more than three years and to pay the costs of his prosecution.

It is urged by appellant in his brief that instructions numbered 6 and 7 given by the court of its own motion at the trial of this case are erroneous. The record in this case nowhere shows that exceptions were taken to the giving of these instructions by the court at the time they were given, nor does counsel set up as error the giving of such instructions in his motion for a new trial. It is a

1 well settled rule of this Court, decided in numerous cases, that this Court will not review any alleged error in instructions given by the trial judge unless exceptions are saved at the time of the giving of same and an opportunity given the trial court to correct the error. The most recent cases decided by this Court sustaining this view are State v. Eaker, 131 Pac. 489; State v. Lucero, 131 Pac. 491.

It is assigned as error by appellant in his motion for a new trial that the trial court failed to fully and suffi-

2 ciently instruct the jury on the law of the case and the issues raised at the trial. An examination of the record discloses that no instructions covering defendant's views of the issues raised in this case by the evidence were submitted by the defendant to the court to be given to the jury. Without passing upon the question as to whether or not the instructions given by the trial judge in this case covered all the issues raised, it is well settled that the non-direction by the court to the jury of a material issue raised by the evidence cannot be reviewed on appeal unless proper instructions covering the issues are submitted by the defendant and refused by the court. In the case of Territory v. Gonzales, (N. M.) 68 Pac. 925, this Court said: "Where counsel are of the opinion that the court's instructions do not fully cover the issues in the case, it is the duty of counsel to submit proper instructions covering omissions claimed in the trial court; and if counsel fail to do so, he is not in position to assign error upon such grounds in this Court." This principle, as laid down in the Gonzales case, was upheld and followed in the case of Territory v. Watson, 12 N. M. 419.

It is provided by the laws of New Mexico, chap. 57, Laws of 1907, sec. 37, "Exceptions to the decisions of the court upon any matter of law arising during the progress of a cause must be taken at the time of such decision and no exceptions shall be taken in any appeal to any proceedings in a District Court except such as shall have been expressly decided in that court. * * * * This statute is a re-enactment in exact words of sec. 3139 and sec. 3145 of the Compiled Laws of New Mexico, 1897. It was held by this Court in the case of Territory v. Watson, supra, that section 3145 of the Compiled Laws of 1897 is applicable in criminal cases as well as in civil cases.

The indictment in this case alleges that the shop of Max Karlsruher, was burglarized, and the testimony offered in this case was as to the breaking and entering of the store of Max Karlsruher. Counsel for appellant claims that this is a fatal variance between the allegation in the indictment and the proof offered on the trial. It is provided by statute, chapter 57, sec. 37, Sessions Laws of
3 1907, quoted above, that only such questions of law as are passed upon by the trial court can be assigned as error and reviewed in this Court. "The record does not disclose that this question was raised during the trial of this case in the court below; and it is not, therefore, properly before this Court for review and cannot be reviewed by this Court, as it is not a question which was directly passed upon by the trial judge at the time of the trial and no assignment of error by the trial judge can be made where he was not given an opportunity to and did not specifically pass upon the question raised. It was the duty of the defendant to raise this question before verdict either by motion to dismiss on the grounds of a variance between the allegations of the indictment and the proofs offered at the trial or by a request for an instruction of not guilty."

Even though this question was properly before this Court for consideration, there is nothing in appellant's contention that there is a variance. The building from which the goods were stolen, being a place for the sale of goods, was rightfully denominated a shop in the indict-

ment and is in conformity with the definitions of the word
shop by lexicographers generally. The New Mexico statute has not prescribed any punishment for burglary in a
store. The fact that the witness in testifying termed the
building a store was unimportant. Whatever name the
witness might have given the building, it is nevertheless
a shop. Commonwealth v. Riggs, 77 Amer. Dec. 333, 80
Mass. (14 Gray), 376.

Appellant urges as a ground of error in this case that
the evidence introduced at the trial was insufficient upon
which to base a verdict. We have read the record of
4   the evidence and find that there is evidence from which
the jury could properly infer that the building mentioned in the indictment was entered in the night time,
and it is a well settled rule of law fully upheld by decisions
of this Court that if there is any substantial evidence to
support a verdict, the same will not be disturbed on appeal.

We will now consider the action of the court in refusing to grant a new trial on the ground of newly discovered
evidence. The rule of law as to granting a new trial
5   on the ground of newly discovered evidence was fully
discussed and settled in this State in the case of Ter-
rtiory v. Claypool & Lueras, 11 N. M. 568; Hancock v.
Beasley, 14 N. M. 239, in this case, the Court said:

"Newly discovered evidence, in order to be sufficient,
must fulfill all the following requirements, to-wit: (1).
It must be such as will probably change the result if a
new trial is granted; (2) it must have been discovered
since the trial; (3) It must be such as could not have
been discovered before the trial by the exercise of due diligence; (4) It must be material to the issue; (5) It must
not be merely cumulative to the former evidence; (6) It
must not be merely impeaching or contradicting the former evidence." We think that the rule adopted in said
case fully and correctly states the law, and we see no reason to depart from the holding of the Court in that case.
The affidavits filed by appellant in support of his motion
for a new trial on the ground of newly discovered evidence admits that the evidence which he claims as newly
discovered was within his knowledge at the time of the trial

of this case in the lower court, and the same could not therefore have been newly discovered since the trial. If the defendant had exerted such diligence as the law requires the evidence could have been produced at the hearing. For these reasons we think the lower court committed no error in refusing to grant a new trial on this ground.

Finding no error in the record, the judgment of the lower court is affirmed, and it is so ordered.

[No. 1570, February 12, 1914.]

MARY DUNCAN, Appellant, v. MARY BROWN, Appellee.

SYLLABUS (BY THE COURT)

1. Judicial decisions, affecting title to real estate, presumptively acquired in reliance upon such decisions, should not be disturbed or departed from except for the most cogent reasons; doubts as to the soundness of such decisions, without other and graver considerations, do not warrant a departure.

P. 585

2. Whenever a question fairly arises in the course of a trial, and there is a distinct decision of such question, the ruling of the court in respect thereto cannot be called mere dictum.

P. 588

Appeal from the District Court of McKinley County; Herbert F. Raynolds, District Judge; affirmed.

B. F. ADAMS, Albuquerque; SAM BUSHMAN, Gallup, N. M., for appellant.

A deed signed by the wife alone, conveying community property to the husband, was absolutely void under the laws of New Mexico at the time the deed is alleged to have been made. Elliot v. Piersol, 1 Pet. 338; 7 L. Ed. 169.

Husband must join her in the deed. Rhea v. Rhenner, 1 Pet. 109, 7 L. Ed. 73.

Statute required certain manner and form of conveyance. Edgar v. Baca, 1 N. M. 620.

Statute must be strictly complied with. 21 Cyc. 1330-3.

Wife could convey through some third person only. 21 Cyc. 1664.

Wife has no power of disposal over the community property. 21 Cyc. 1668; (b.)

Power to contract does not carry with it the power to convey real estate. C. L. 1897, sec. 1511; Jasper v. Wilson, 14 N. M. 482.

A statute inconsistent with the common law repeals it in so far as it is inconsistent. Lewis Suth. Stat. Con. (2nd ed.) 572.

Words of a statute are to be taken in their natural and ordinary signification. Lewis Suth. Stat. Con. (2nd ed.) sec. 358, p. 684.

Statutory enactments. Laws 1901, p. 113, sec. 1; C. L. 1897, sec. 1511; Laws 1852, ch. 44; C. L. 1897, secs. 3939-3970; Laws 1884, ch. 14.

Deed was void. Edgar v. Baca, 1 N. M. 619; Graham v. Struwe, 13 S. W. 381.

Property was community property. Bal. Comm. Prop., sec. 80, 116, 75 and sec. 90; Whetstone v. Coffey, 48 Tex. 269; Kirkwood v. Domnan, 16 S. W. 429; Kirchner v. Murray, 54 Fed. 624; Arnett v. Reade, 220 U. S. 311, (N. M.), 55 L. Ed. 480.

Where absolute decree is granted the spouses become tenants in common. 14 Cyc. 728; Wait v. Wait, 4 N. Y. 95; Reynolds v. Reynolds, 24 Wend. 193; Barrett v. Failing, 111 U. S. 523, 28 L. Ed. 506; C. L. 1897, sec. 1512; Godey v. Godey, 39 Cal. 157; Whetstone v. Coffey, 48 Tex. 269; Hughs v. Doe, 45 Pac. 1068; Philbrick v. Andrews, 35 Pac. 359; Biggi v. Biggi, 98 Cal. 35, 35 Am. St. R. 141, 32 Pac. 803; Hayes v. Horton, 46 Ore. 597, 81 Pac. 386; 2 Bishops Marr. & Div. (5th ed. sec. 716; Freeman, Co-tenancy, (2nd ed.) sec. 76; Stelz v. Shreck, 128 N. Y. 263, 13 L. R. A. 325, 26 Am. St. R. 475, 28 N. E. 510;

Russell v. Russell, 122 Mo. 235, 43 Am. St. R. 581, 26 S.
W. 55, 23 L. R. A. 806.

A judgment is conclusive only upon the issues presented by the pleadings. Bank of Visalia v. Smith, 146 Cal.
398, 81 Pac. 542; Kirchner v. Dietrich, 110 Cal. 502, 42
Pac. 1064; Coats v. Coats, 118 Pac. 445.

Decree of divorce left the realty undisposed of.   Tabler
v. Peverill, 88 Pac. 997; Ball, Comm. Prop., sec. 209-10;
McKay on Community Property, sec. 413.

Conveyance after becoming discovert.   Tied. Real Prop.,
sec. 794.

A statute allowing a married woman to "convey and de-
vise" real estate does not remove the incapacity which prevents her from contracting.   Todd v. Lee, 15 Wis. 400;
Grapengether v. Fejervary, 9 Ia. 163; Mayo v. Hutchinson, 57 Me. 546; Cummings v. Sharpe, 21 Ind. 331; Major
v. Symmes, 19 Ind. 117; Miller v. Newton, 23 Cal. 554;
Glass v. Warwick, 40 Pa. St. 140; Willard v. Eastham, 15
Gray 328; Perkins v. Eliiott, 22 N. J. Eq. 127; Cozzens v.
Whitney, 3 R. I. 79; Jones v. Crosthwaite, 17 Ia. 393;
Maguire v. Maguire, 3 Mo. App. 458; Hodson v. Davis,
43 Ind. 258; Catterton v. Young, 2 Tenn. Ch. 768; Nel-
son v. Miller, 52 Miss. 410; Maclay v. Love, 25 Cal. 368;
Veal v. Hurt, 63 Ga. 728; Saulsbury v. Weaver, 59 Ga.
254; Robertson, 1 Lea, 633; Bank v. Scott, 10 Neb. 83;
Harris v. Finberg, 46 Tex. 79; Stiles v. Lord, 11 Pac. 316;
Holyoke v. Jackson, 3 Pac. 843; McKee v. Reynolds, 26
Ia. 582; White v. Wager, 25 N. Y. 332.

H. B. JAMISON, Albuquerque, N. M., for appellee.

Equity upholds a deed from the wife to the husband in
absence of statute where there is reasonable consideration.
21 Cyc. 1291; Turner v. Shaw, 9 Am. St. R. 321.

In 1889, under New Mexico statutes, a married woman
could convey to her husband, subject to same limitations
as if she was unmarried.   C. L. 1897, sec. 1510; Id., sec.
1511; C. L. 1897, sec. 3951.

The divorce obtained by appellant on May 16, 1901,
was res judicata as to her rights in property involved in

this suit. Barnett v. Barnett, 9 N. M. 205; Barrett v. Failing, 111 U. S. 523, 28 L. Ed. 505; (Cases of De Godey v. De Godey, 39 Cal. 157; Whetstone v. Coffey, 48 Tex. 269, and Wait v. Wait, 4 N. Y. 95, have distinguishing statutes or circumstances); Greathead v. Bromley, 7 T. R. 455; Broom, Max. (4th ed.) 324; 2 Taylor Evidence, sec. 1513; Henderson v. Henderson, 3 Hare, 115; City of Aurora v. West, 74 U. S. 82, 19 L. Ed. 49; Beloit v. Morgan, 74 U. S. 619, 19 L. Ed. 205; Brandernagle v. Cocks, 19 Wend. 207; Le Guen v. Gouverneur, 1 Johns. Cas. 491; Bates v. Spooner, 45 Ind. 493; Thompson v. Thompson, 31 N. E. 530; Fischli, 12 Am. Dec. 251; Kamp v. Kamp, 59 N. Y. 212; Hardin v. Hardin, 38 Tex. 617; Roe v. Roe, 35 Pac. 809; Greene v. Greene, 2 Gray, 361; Homer v. Fish, 1 Pick. 441; Stahl v. Stahl, 114 Ill. 375; Patton v. Loughridge, 49 Ia. 218; Mott v. Mott. 82 Cal. 413.

Rule of Stare Decisis should be applied. Laws 1901, ch. 62, sec. 31; Klock v. Mann, 16 N. M. 211.

STATEMENT OF FACTS.

This action was instituted by appellant in the court below to quiet her title to an undivided one-half interest in and to certain real estate in the town qf Gallup, County of McKinley, State of New Mexico. The facts in the case are undisputed, and may be stated briefly as follows:

On November 28, 1898, appellant was united in marriage with John D. Heindl, now deceased. In February, of the next year, John D. Heindl purchased the real estate over which this litigation arose and paid for the same with money earned after his marriage to appellant.

On September 20, 1899, appellant, by quit claim deed conveyed to her said husband all her right, title and interest in and to the real estate. Shortly before the execution of the deed by appellant to her husband they had ceased to live together as husband and wife, and in June thereafter a decree was entered by the District Court of McKinley County granting to Mary Heindl an absolute divorce from her said husband.

Sometime in the year 1907, John D. Heindl died, the

record owner, and in possession of the real estate in controversy. His will was duly probated, by the terms of which he devised the said real estate to his brother Joseph Heindl. Thereafter, in December, 1907, Joseph Heindl, by warranty deed conveyed the real estate to the appellee herein, who took possession of the same, which she has ever since retained.

The judgment of the court, granting the divorce to appellant, was silent as to all property rights, and this action was instituted by appellant to quiet her title to an undivided one-half interest in and to the real estate mentioned, upon the theory that the property being community property and the decree not having adjudicated the rights of the parties therein she still retained her interest in the said real estate.

Upon the issues framed and the facts as stated, the court stated the following conclusions of law, viz.:

1. "That the quit claim deed recorded in Book C, page 39, records of McKinley County, New Mexico, executed by the plaintiff, conveyed to John Heindl and to his heirs and assigns all right, title and interest of plaintiff in and to the land described in the complaint."

2. "That the decree of divorce between plaintiff and John Heindl determined their property rights and was and is res adjudicata and barred plaintiff from any right, title or interest in the property described in the complain of the plaintiff."

Judgment was entered for the appellee, from which this appeal is prosecuted.

OPINION OF THE COURT.

ROBERTS, C. J.—We will first discuss the second assignment of error, viz.: that "The court erred in holding as a conclusion of law that the decree of divorce between plaintiff and John D. Heindl determined their rights and was and is res adjudicata and barred plaintiff from any right, title or interest in the property described in the complaint," for, if this assignment be not well taken, the effect of the quit claim deed and the right of a wife to convey real estate directly to her husband become of no

importance in this case. Nor would a determination of the
questions serve any useful purpose, for since 1901, by sec.
5, chap. 62, S. L. 1901, and sec. 4, chap. 37, S. L. 1907.
she has an unquestioned right to convey real estate directly to her husband, subject to the general rules of the common law which control the actions of persons occupying
confidential relations with each other.

Was the divorce decree obtained by appellant May 16,
1900, res adjudicata as to her rights in the property involved in this suit? That it was so, was held by the Territorial Supreme Court in an opinion written by Chief
Justice Smith in 1897, in the case of Barnett v. Barnett,
reported in 9 N. M. 205. Appellant contends, however,
(1) that the decision in the Barnett case was wrong in
principle and contrary to the weight of authority, and (2)
that the point was not involved in that case and therefore
what was said by the Court upon the question was obiter
dictum, and therefore should not control the judgment
in a subsequent suit when the very point is presented for
decision. Admitting for the sake of argument, without
so deciding, however, that the holding in the Barnett case
is contrary to the weight of authority and were the matter
presented to this Court as an original proposition a different result might be reached; the fact remains, however, that at the time the divorce was granted, and at the
time appellee bought the property in question, the law as
adjudicated in Barnett v. Barnett was the declared law in
this jurisdiction on the subject. This being true, the
question arises as to whether we should overrule this decision and inflict the consequences of overruling it upon
the appellee.

The decision in that case does not affect the property
rights of husband and wife under any decree of divorce
entered after March 20, 1901, for by sec. 31, chap. 62, S.
L. 1901, it is specifically provided that,

"The failure to divide the property on divorce shall not
affect the property rights of either husband or wife, either
may subsequently institute and prosecute a suit for division and distribution thereof, or with reference to any

JANUARY TERM, 1914.   585

Duncan v. Brown, 18 N. M. 579.

other matter pertaining thereto, which could have been litigated in the original suit for divorce."

But prior to the enactment of this statute, and subsequent to the decision of that case, it was the declared law in this jurisdiction that "The marital status having ceased absolutely, no rights which accrued in or by virtue of such relations, and were not asserted in the proceedings for dissolution can be subsequently maintained." In other words, that a decree of divorce was res adjudicata as to all rights which were, or could have been litigated and determined in the divorce proceedings, and, as the parties in that proceeding could have litigated the question of property rights and a division thereof, the question could not thereafter be adjudicated in another independent action.

When Mary Brown bought this property from Jooseph Heindl, Barnett v. Barnett was a rule of property upon which she could rely for her title. If the opinion of a competent attorney had been sought by her, he evidently would have advised her that her title was good under the rule announced in that case. Can the appellant, then, knowing the law at the time she obtained her divorce to be as laid down in that case, come into this Court and ask that this rule of property be set aside in her favor and against a purchaser of that property, who relied upon Barnett v. Barnett?

"It must be a very strong case, indeed, and one where mistake and error had evidently been committed, to justify this Court, after the lapse of five years, in reversing its own decision; thereby destroying rights of property which may have been purchased and paid for in the meantime, upon the faith and confidence reposed in the judgment of this court." Goodtitle v. Kibbe, 9 How. 471.

Judicial decisions, affecting title to real estate presump-
1 tively acquired in reliance upon such decisions, should not be disturbed or departed from except for the most cogent reasons, certainly not because of doubts as to their soundness. If there should be a change, the legislature can make it, as the legislature in this jurisdiction did, with infinitely less derangement of titles than would follow a

new ruling of the Court, for the statutory regulations operate only in the future.   Should we overturn the rule announced in the Barnett case, the result would be to open
up the subject of property rights between husband and
wife in every decree of divorce granted subsequent to the
decision in that case and prior to the enactment of the
statute of 1901, and cast a cloud upon the title of all real
estate transferred by either the divorced husband or wife,
the title to which was not adjusted in the decree.

In the case of Propeller Genesee Chief v. Fitzhugh, 12
How. 443, Mr. Justice Tenney, speaking for the Court,
says:

"The case of Thomas Jefferson did not decide any
question of property, or lay down any rule by which the
right of property should be determined.   If it had, we
should have felt ourselves bound to follow it notwithstanding the opinion we have expressed.   For every one
would suppose that after the decisions of this Court, in a
matter of that kind, he might safely enter into contracts,
upon the faith that rights thus acquired would not be disturbed.   In such a case, STARE DECISIS is the safe and
established rule of judicial policy, and should always be
adhered to."

The rule was stated in the following language by the
Supreme Court of California, in the case of Smith v. Mc-
Donald, 42 Cal. 484,

"When a rule, by which the title to real property is to
be determined, has become established by positite law or
by deliberative judicial decision, its inherent correctness
or incorrectness, its justice or injustice in the abstract,
are of far less importance than that it should, itself be
constant and invariable.   We should not disturb such a
rule of property here, even though we be satisfied that we
could substitute another preferable in theory, or better calculated by its operation to promote the purpose of justice."

In the case of McVay's Admr. v. Ijams, 27 Ala. 238,
the Alabama Court say:

"When, however, a rule of property has been adopted
by judicial decision, and may reasonably be supposed to
have entered into the business transactions of the coun-

try, it is our duty to adhere to it, lest we should overturn titles founded upon it. In such case, it is better to leave the corrective to the legislature."

For the reasons stated we decline to re-examine the grounds of the decision in Barnett v. Barnett, and with out intimating any opinion as to the correctness or incorrectness of the conclusions attained, must adhere to it in this case on the principle of STARE DECISIS, if the point was involved in that case and presented to the court for determination.

In the Barnett case the parties were divorced in 1894, the decree being silent as to all property rights. During the marriage state a large amount of real estate had been acquired, deeds to which were taken in the husband's name. Two years after the decree was entered the wife instituted suit for partition or division of all the real and personal property standing in the name of or owned by her husband at the time the decree was entered and alleged to be community property, and acquired during the existence of the marriage relation. The trial court decided in favor of the wife and awarded partition of the property. Upon appeal several grounds of error were assigned, the fifth being, "The court committed error in holding that the decree divorcing appellant from the appellee was not a complete bar to any claim of property rights made under the bill of complaint filed in this case." Chief Justice Smith discusses and decides several questions, and then says:

"We realize that we might have foreborne the foregoing investigation, as we do not doubt that the plaintiff in error is impregnable in his defense of res adjudicata, but we have deemed it due to counsel to consider with care their respective contentions." The Chief Justice then proceeds to discuss the question raised by the fifth assignment of error, and holds that the property rights of the parties should have been litigated in the divorce proceeding, and that the decree therein entered was res adjudicata, not only as to all questions actually litigated, but as to all questions which could have been, but were not therein adjudicated. The larger part of the opinion is devoted to a dicsussion of this question. It is true the Court also held, that under the civil law, the wife lost her matrimonial gains, when she had been guilty of adultery, but that it did so, does not militate against the effect of its decision

2 on other points presented by the record and decided by the Court. Whenever a question fairly arises in the course of a trial, and there is a distinct decision of such question, the ruling of the Court in respect thereto cannot be called mere dictum. As was said by the Supreme Court of the United States, in the case of Union Pacific Co. v. Mason, City, etc., R. Co., 199 U. S. 160:

"Of course, where there are two grounds, upon either of which the judgment of the trial court can be rested, and the appellate court sustains both, the ruling on neither is OBITER, but each is the judgment of the Court and of equal validity with the other. Whenever a question fairly arises in the course of a trial, and there is a distinct decision of that question, the ruling of the court in respect thereto can, in no just sense, be called mere dictum. Railroad Companies v. Schutte, 103 U. S. 118, 26 Ed. 327, in which this Court said: 'It cannot be said that a case is not authority on one point because, although that point was properly presented and decided in the regular course of the consideration of the cause, something else was found in the end which disposed of the whole matter. Here the precise question was properly presented, fully argued and elaborately considered in the opinion. The decision on this question was as much a part of the judgment of the Court as was that on any other of the several matters on which the case as a whole depended.' "

The above excerpt is a complete answer to appellant's contention in this regard. The question was presented by the assignments of error, fully argued by counsel and decided by the court. It might as well be argued that what the court said as to the rights of a wife, condemned as an adulteress, in the property of the community was obiter, because the court also decided that the matter was res adjudicata.

Such being the case, it follows that the rule of STARE DECISIS applies to this case, and under the rule an-

nounced in the case of Barnett v. Barnett, the case must
be affirmed, and it is so ordered.

[No. 1632, February 12, 1914.]

THE BOWMAN BANK & TRUST COMPANY, a cor-
poration, Appellee, v. THE FIRST NATIONAL
BANK OF ALBUQUERQUE, a corporation; THE
REGENTS OF THE NEW MEXICO COLLEGE OF
AGRICULTURE AND MECHANIC ARTS, Ap-
pellants.

SYLLABUS (BY THE COURT)

1. In an interpleader suit, the amount due cannot be the
subject of controversy, and where such controversy exists it
presents an insuperable objection to its prosecution.

P. 598

2. Where a party, holding a certificate of deposit issued
by a bank, is entitled to collect the same, and makes demand
upon the bank for its payment, which is refused, he becomes
entitled, as a matter of law, to interest on the deposit, at
the statutory rate, from the time of such demand. In such
case ,where suit is brought against the bank to recover the
amount of such certificate and interest thereon from the
time demand was made, the bank cannot interplead and pay
the money into court, and escape liability, unless it tenders
the sum which the plaintiff is entitled to recover at the
time the tender is made, should it prevail.

P. 598

3. Where a demurrer is interposed and sustained to an
answer and interpleader, and the interpleading defendant
thereupon takes leave to answer, and by his answer filed,
pursuant to leave granted, takes issue with plaintiff upon
the merits, and abandons his impartial attitude assumed in
his interpleader, and takes up the cudgel for the other claimant of the fund, he thereby waives his interpleader, and can-

not predicate error upon the action of the court in sustaining the demurrer.

P. 599

4. An incumbent in office is not ousted by the mere election or appointment of his successor, where the statute requires such official to qualify for the office by doing certain
acts; his right to the office not being complete until he has
qualified for the same as directed.

P. 601

5. Where the statute creating a board of regents for the
Agricultural College and Experiment Station provides for the
election of one of the members of said board as secretary
and treasurer, and also provides that such secretary and
treasurer shall continue in office until his successor shall be
elected and qualified, the incumbent is not ousted from the
office of secretary and treasurer by the appointment of a new
board of regents, but continues as such until a new secretary
and treasurer has been elected and has qualified as directed
by the statute.

P. 602

6. The treasurer of such board, in the absence of direction from the board of regents ,assuming the power of such
board so to do, has the right to reposit the funds in his hands
in such bank or banks as he chooses, and to withdraw such
funds at his pleasure, being liable, of course, at all times
under his bond "to account for and pay over to the person
or persons entitled thereto" such moneys.

P. 603

Appeal from the District Court of Dona Ana County;
Edward L. Medler, District Judge; affirmed.

A. B. McMILLEN, Albuquerque, N. M., for appellants.

Appellant's interpleader complied in every respect with
the requirements of law, and the facts show a proper case
for interpleader, and the court was in error in refusing to

permit appellant to pay the amount of the certificate of deposit, with interest, into court. Puterbaugh's Ch. Pleading, p. 279, and authorities cited; Story Eq. Pleading, sec. 291, and cases cited; Louisiana State Lottery Co. v. Clark, 16 Fed. 20; McWhirtes v. Halstead, 24 Fed. 828; Griggs v. Thompson, 1 Ga. Dec. 146; Strange v. Bell, 11 Ga. 103; Adams v. Dickson, 19 Ga. 513, 65 Am. Dec. 608; Barton v. Black, 32 Ga. 53; Davis v. Davis, 96 Ga. 136, 21 S. E. 1002; National Park Bank v. Lanahan, 60 Md. 477; Monks v. Miller, 13 Mo. App. 363; Orr Water Ditch Co. v. Larcomb, 14 Nev. 53; Farley v. Blood, 30 N. H. 354; Mt. Holly Turnpike Co. v. Ferree, 17 N. J. Eq. 117; North Pac. Lbr. Co. v. Lang, 28 Ore. 246. 52 Am. St. R. 780; Greene v. Mumford, 4 R. I. 313; Wabash Ry. Co. v. Flannigan, 95 Mo. App. 477, 75 S. W. 691; Nixon v. Malone, 95 S. W. 577; Woodmen of the World v. Wood, 100 Mo. App. 655; School District v. Weston, 31 Mich. 85; Board of Education v. Scoville, 13 Kans. 17; Nat. Iivestock Bank v. Platte Valley St. Bank, 54 Ill. App. 483, 155 Ill. 250.

This applies with particular force to money in bank or other depository. City Bank of N. Y. v. Skelton. Federal Cases No. 2739, 2 Blatch. 14; Foss v. First National Bank, 3 Fed. 185; James v. Sams, 90 Ga. 404, 17 S. E. 962; Livingstone v. Bank of Montreal, 50 Ill. App. 562; People's Savings Bank v. Look, 95 Mich. 7, 54 N. W. 629; Wayne Co. Savings Bank v. Airey, 95 Mich. 520, 55 N. W. 355; Fletcher v. Troy Savings Bank, 14 How. 383; Smith v. Emigrant Industrial Sav. Bank, 2 N. Y. Supp. 617; Harrisburg Nat. Bank v. Hiester, (Pa.) 2 Pears. 255; Dickeschief v. Exchange Bank, 28 W. Va. 340; Harris Bank. Co. v. Miller, 190 Mo. 640; Wells v. Com. Ex. Bank, 87 N. Y. S. 480; Helene v. Com. Ex. Bank, 89 N. Y. S. 310; Continental Sav. Bank v. McClure, 104 Tenn. 607, 58 S. W. 240.

In case of interpleader the stakeholder is entitled to his costs and to the allowance of a reasonable attorney fee. Morse v. Stearns, 131 Mass. 389; Christian v. National I. Ins. Co., 62 Mo. App. 35; Franco-American Loan, etc., Assn. v. Joy, 56 Mo. App. 433; German Ex. Bank v. Excise Commissioners, 6 Abb. N. Cas. 394; Daniel v. Fain, 5 Lea. 258; Stevens v. Germanis L. Ins. Co., 26 Tex. Civ. App. 156, 62 S. W. 824; Bolin v. St. Louis, etc., Ry. Co., (Tex. Civ. App.) 61 S. W. 444; Florida Internal Imp. Fund v. Greenough, 105 U. S. 527; La. State Lottery Co. v. Clark, 16 Fed. 20; McCall v. Walter, 71 Ga. 287; Glasser v. Priest, 29 Mo. App. 1; McNamara v. Prov. Sav. O. A. Co., 114 Fed. 910; Loring v. Thorndike, 87 Mass. 257; Nixon v. Malone, 95 S. W. 577.

Vincent B. May, even while secretary and treasurer, had no lawful power to negotiate and deal in bills payable and other securities of the New Mexico College of Agriculture and Mechanic Arts. C. L. 1897. sec. 3553; Id., sec. 3556; Id., sec. 3575; Cook on Corporations, sec. 717, and cases cited.

Upon the appointment of the new board of regents, the sole duty of Vincent B. May was to turn over the funds to his successor. Conklin v. Cunningham, 7 N. M. 486, 38 Pac. 170; Eldodt v. Territory, 10 N. M. 141, 61 Pac. 107; C. L. 1897, sec. 3574.

WADE & WADE, Las Cruces, N. M., for appellee.

Defendant bank was not entitled to its costs and attorneys' fees in view of its conduct. 11 Enc. Pl. & Pr., 480-1

The fund in question was under May's control. He could deposit it in any bank he saw fit. C. L. 1897, sec. 3574; Maloy v. Board of Co. Comm'rs., 10 N. M. 638; C. L. 1897, sec. 3556.

May was treasurer until his successor qualified. He had full power to demand and receive payment of the certificate of deposit. C L. 1897. sec. 3574

STATEMENT OF FACTS.

On July 17, 1911, Vincent B. May was the duly elected, qualified, and acting treasurer of the board of regents of the New Mexico College of Agriculture and Mechanic Arts, and under bond to account for all moneys coming into his hands as such official. On said day he had in his hands, of the permanent funds of said institution derived from lands sold, theretofore granted the State by the United States government, for the use of said institution, (Act June 21, 1898, c. 489, 30 Stat. 485) the sum of $21,-656.76, which he deposited with the Bank of Commerce of Albuquerque, receiving from said bank the following certificate: "The Bank of Commerce of Albuquerque, $21,-656.76. Albuquerque, N. M., July 17, 1911. Vincent B. May, Secy. & Treas., has deposited in this bank twenty-one thousand six hundred fifty-six dollars and 76-100 dollars payable to his order on the return of this certificate properly endorsed. This certificate is payable six or twelve months after date with interest at five per cent. per annum for a stated period only. No interest after maturity. F. R. Harris, A Cashier. Certificate of deposit not subject to check" The appellant First National Bank of Albuquerque thereafter took over the business of said Bank of Commerce and assumed the liability on said certificate.

On July 5, 1912, said Vincent B. May, purporting to act as secretary and treasurer of said board of regents, in dorsed over to the appellee bank said certificate of deposit, taking in exchange therefor a certificate of deposit issued by said appellee bank; the purpose of the action being to secure an advancement from the appellee bank of the interest to become due on said certificate from the appellant bank on July 17th, for the purpose of providing funds to meet some outstanding accounts, or to protect an overdraft representing money advanced by appellee for such purpose

On June 11th preceding, an entire new board of regents of said institution was appointed by the Governor of the State, consisting of Morgan O. Llewellyn, James H. Paxton, Francis E. Lester, A. H. Hudspeth and Hiram Hadley; but said board did not meet, organize, and the members assume their duties until the forenoon of July 5th. At that time James H. Paxton was elected president and Morgan O. Llewellyn was elected secretary and treasurer; but said Llewellyn did not qualify as treasurer, by executing the necessary bond. until some time in August thereafter.

On July 9, 1912, Morgan O. Llewellyn, sent appellant

the following telegram, which was received by it: "Las Cruces, N. M., July 9, 1912. First National Bank of Albuquerque, N. M. You are instructed not to pay out any moneys on deposit belonging to New Mexico College of Agriculture & Mechanic Arts except upon the order of M. O. Llewellyn, secretary and treasurer of the board of regents. Money was deposited with Bank of Commerce [Signed] M. O. Llewellyn, Secretary and Treasurer Board of Regents."

On July 17th, the above certificate of deposit was presented to appellant for payment for the account of plaintiff. Whereupon appellant notified said Llewellyn and received a second telegram from him, directing the bank to refuse payment and notifying appellant bank he had succeeded May as secretary and treasurer on the 5th inst. Appellant bank thereupon refused payment and notified Llewellyn that it held the certificate pending an adjustment of the matter, and further stated that it desired to avoid any complications in connection with the transaction.

No further action was taken by any of the parties connected with the transaction, until, on the 7th day of October, 1912, the appellee filed its complaint in the District Court of Dona Ana County against the appellant to recover the amount due on said certificate of deposit, principal and interest, on July 17, 1912, and interest on said sum at the rate of 6 per centum per annum from said date until said money should be paid. Thereafter, on the 4th day of November, appellant filed its answer and interpleader, setting up the controversy between the College and its officers on the one hand and the appellee on the other; the notice not to pay; its efforts to adjust the mat ter; its readiness and willingness to pay; that it had no interest in the controversy or the success of either party thereto; that it could not safely pay appellee over the objection of the secretary and treasurer of said board, and tendered into court the amount of said certificate, together with the stipulated interest thereon to July 17. 1912, to abide the order of the court. But appellant did not tender or offer to pay the interest and damages claimed

by appellee in its complaint by reason of appellant's refusal to pay said certificate of deposit upon its demand
made July 17th, when the same became due and payable.
The answer and interpleader further alleged that the interpleader was not filed by collusion with either of the
claimants to said deposit, and prayed that the board of
regents be made parties and required to interplead with
plaintiff; that upon payment of said amount tendered into
court that appellant be discharged and recover its costs,
together with reasonable attorney's fee; and that the appellee be enjoined from further prosecuting its suit against
appellant. To this answer and interpleader plaintiff demurred upon several grounds; one being as follows: "That
the tender by the defendant to pay into court moneys stipulated to be paid in and by the said certificate of deposit
is not sufficient in this, that it does not cover the full liability of the defendant to the plaintiff in the event that
the plaintiff shall prevail." The demurrer was sustained
generally and the order sustaining the same recites that:
"The defendant electing to stand upon the facts as alleged in said interpleader, it is ordered by the court that
said interpleader be and the same is hereby dismissed, to
which said ruling and order of the court defendant excepts. It is further ordered that the defendant be allowed
to file an amended answer and to otherwise plead or defend against the action set forth in plaintiff's complaint
as it may be advised." Pursuant to the leave given, appellant filed an answer to the merits, denying any right
whatever in appellee to recover the money represented by
said certificate of deposit; alleging that it held the fund,
subject to the order of the New Mexico College of Agriculture and Mechanic Arts, through its secretary and treasurer; that the transfer of the certificate by Vincent B.
May to appellee, as secretary and treasurer, was without
value received; and that appellee was not a bona fide
holder 'hereof. The answer further alleged that Vincent
B. May had ceased to be a member of the board of regents,
and the secretary and treasurer thereof, at the time he
transferred the certificate of deposit to appellee, and that
at that time he had no right to control said fund or to

indorse said certificate. To this answer a reply was filed by appellee denying all the material allegations of the an-swer, but admitting that appellant had received the notices from M. O. Llewellyn not to pay said certificate of de-posit upon the order of Vincent B. May. Upon motion the board of regents of said College were permitted to in-tervene and become parties to said suit. An answer to the appellee's complaint was filed by the board, in which it al-leged that the funds in controversy belonged to the per-manent fund of said College, and as such was subject to the control of the board of regents;. denied that May had any authority to indorse said certificate of deposit; alleged that he had ceased to be a member of the board of regents at the time of his attempted transfer of the fund, and that he had likewise ceased to be the secretary and treas-urer of said board. To this answer appellee filed a reply, denying all the material allegations of the answer.

Upon the issues thus framed, the evidence was heard by the court, findings of fact made, and conclusions of law stated. The facts so found were in accord with the facts stated by this court and need not be repeated. Upon the facts found, conclusions of law were stated by the court as follows: "(1) That at the time of the transaction be-tween the plaintiff and Vincent B. May, and at the time of the maturing of the certificate of deposit, the said Vin-cent B. May was responsible under his official bond for the safe-keeping of the funds under consideration and lia·ble to account therefor and was the proper custodian there-of and authorized to determine the bank or other place in which the same might be kept on deposit; and that while the said Vincent B. May was not required to keep the said funds on interest upon a certificate of deposit in the absence of a specific direction from the said board of re-gents, his having done so, and the said Agricultural Col-lege having received the benefit of such interest, the board of regents is now estopped from complaining. (2) That the said M. O. Llewellyn did not become qualified to take over the funds under consideration, or otherwise perform the duties of secretary and treasurer of the board of re-gents of the Agricultural College of New Mexico until on

or after the 21st day of August, A. D. 1912, and had no
power or authority to direct the disposition of the funds
in question at the time he undertook so to do. (3) That
the intervening petition of the regents of the Agricultural
College of New Mexico should be dismissed. (4) That the
plaintiff is entitled to recover of and from the defendant
bank the sum of $21,656.76, with interest thereon at the
rate of 5 per cent. per annum from the 17th day of July,
A. D. 1911, to the 17th day of July, A. D. 1912, and with
interest thereon at the rate of 6 per cent. per annum from
the 17th day of July, A. D. 1912, to this date, together
with its costs to be taxed." Judgment was entered in accordance with the conclusions of law stated, from which
judgment the First National Bank of Albuquerque and
the board of regents appeal.

OPINION OF THE COURT.

ROBERTS, C. J. (after stating the facts as above).—
The first alleged error is predicated upon the action of
the court in sustaining the demurrer to the answer and
interpleader of the First National Bank of Albuquerque.
As shown in the preceding statement of facts, one ground
of the demurrer was that the tender was insufficient to
cover the full liability of the appellant bank to the appellee in the event the appellee should prevail. If the demurrer was well taken on this ground, no error was committed in sustaining it.

In its complaint the appellee set forth facts, which, if
true, entitled it to recover not only the face value of the
certificate of deposit and interest thereon from July 17,
1911, to Juyl 17, 1912, but interest on said sum at the
rate of 6 per cent. per annum from the time of its demand
upon appellant bank for the payment thereof, which was
July 17, 1912, to the time the same was actually paid or
judgment therefor entered. If, in fact, appellee was lawfully entitled to the money, it was entitled to interest
thereon from the time of its demand upon the bank for
payment and its refusal to pay, and this, as a matter of
law. At the time appellant filed its interpleader, if appellee was entitled to recover, there was due it from the

appellant bank, as interest, more than $400, not included within or provided for by the tender. If it succeeded in the action, the fund thus tendered would be insufficient to pay the amount of the judgment to which it was entitled.

"The amount due cannot be the subject of controversy in an interpleader suit, and this difference between the debt claimed by the defendant, and the sum which

1 the plaintiff is willing to pay, presents an insuperable objection to its prosecution." Baltimore & Ohio R. Co. v. Arthur, 90 N. Y. 234.

By its answer and interpleader the appellant bank sought to relieve itself from the liability which appellee was seeking to impose upon it by its complaint, by paying into court the amount of the fund, to the extent of its liability, and by bringing into court. another claimant of the fund, compel the two claimants to litigate their rights

at their own expense, and thus protect itself from all

2 vexation and responsibility. But, in order for it to interplead, there must be no question as to the amount due, and where, as in this case, the interpleader raised a question as to the amount which was the subject of the interpleader, by contradicting and taking issue with appellee's complaint on this question, the interpleader was demurrable.

"The rule is that when a question is raised as to the amount which is the subject of the interpleader such question prevents the right of the interpleader. The mere fact of there being a dispute as to the amount of the fund is always fatal to the bill. Moore v. Usher, 7 Simon's Rep. 384; Diplock v. Hammond, 28 Eng. L. & Eq. 202; President, etc., v. Bangs, 2 Paige (N. Y.) 570; Chamberlain v. O'Connor, 8 How. Prac. (N. Y.) 245." Clasner v. Weisberg, 43 Mo. App. 214.

Here appellant was asking that it be permitted to step out of the litigation, and that plaintiff be enjoined from prosecuting its suit against it, and this, in spite of the fact that appellee was claiming as against it a liability which it did not admit.

In the case of Helene v. Corn Exchange Bank, et al.,

96 App. Div. 392, 89 N. Y. Supp. 310, almost the same identical question was presented. In that case the trial court sustained the motion for interpleader and permitted the bank to pay into court the amount of the deposit, with accrued interest thereon only to the time of demand, but did not require the payment of the interest accruing as a matter of law after the demand made. The Court say: "The difficulty with the present order lies in the fact that the bank is not required to protect Wells to the full extent of his claim. If, when he made his demand upon the bank for the payment of the money, he was entitled thereto, the bank was in duty bound to pay it to him, and by its refusal to pay it subjected itself to the payment of interest until it should comply with the demand. The judgment which Wells demands in his complaint is for the amount of the fund on deposit, with interest thereon from the 30th day of January, 1904, and, if entitled to the money, he is entitled to interest thereon as well as the principal, not as a matter of discretion, but as a matter of law. Mansfield v. New York Cent. & H. R. R. Co., 114 N. Y. 331, 21 N. E. 735, 1037, 4 L. R. A. 566. By the order of interpleader the bank is discharged upon paying over and depositing with the chamberlain of the city of New York the sum on deposit, $304.80, and no more. If Wells succeeds in the action, the fund thus directed to be deposited will be insufficient to pay the amount of the judgment to which he is entitled ,or to pay the amount which he was entitled to receive at the time the order directing the interpleader and the payment was made. The bank cannot be discharged from liability without paying the sum which the party is entitled to recover at the time when the order for interpleader is granted. This it has not been required to do." See, also, Bridesburg Mfg. Co.'s Appeal, 106 Pa. 275.

No error was committed in sustaining the demurrer to the answer and interpleader; but, even if the demurrer had been erroneously sustained, appellant waived its

3 interpleader when it answered to the merits. The general doctrine is that interpleader lies, "where two or more persons claim the same thing, under different titles, or in separate interests, from another person, who, not claiming any title or interest therein, and not knowing to which of the claimants he ought of right to render the duty claimed, or to deliver the property claimed, is either molested by an action or actions brought against him, or fears he may suffer injury, from the conflicting claims of the parties against him. He therefore applies to a court of equity to protect him, not only from being compelled to pay or deliver the thing claimed, to both claimants, but also from the vexation attending upon suits, which are, or possibly may be, instituted against him." 2 Story's Equity Jur., sec. 806; Burton v. Black, 32 Ga. 53.

"It is * * * * of the essence of an interpleader suit that the" plaintiff shall be and continue "entirely indifferent between the conflicting claims" (11 Ency. Pl. & Pr. 455), and, "not only must he be disinterested when he brings his bill, but he must continue to be disinterested— his position must be one of 'continuous impartiality.'" (Wing, Adm'r, v. Spaulding, et al., 64 Vt. 83, 23 Atl. 615.) "All the text-writers agree that the first essential of a bill of interpleader is that the complainant must be a mere naked stakeholder without any interest in the fund, and without any controversy of his own to be settled in the cause" (Bridesburg Mfg. Co. Appeal, supra), and "an interpleader is allowed for the protection of a defendant who admits that he has the subject of the action, and makes no claim to it himself and is ready and willing to pay or dispose of it as the court may direct, and says that a third party without collusion claims it. He cannot take issue with the plaintiff, and at the same time have the benefit of an interpleader. The two are inconsistent, and he must elect between them. He cannot have both. By filing his answer, the defendant in error waived and abandoned his interpleader." Johnson v. Oliver, 51 Ohio St 6, 36 N. E. 458. In this case, after the demurrer had been sustained to its interpleader, the appellant bank, instead of standing upon its interpleader, asked leave to answer or further plead, and, pursuant to the leave granted it, laid aside the impartial attitude assumed in its interpleader and took up the cudgel for the board of regents.

By its answer, it said in effect that the plaintiff had no
right, title, or interest in or to the fund; denied that it
was the owner thereof, or that it had any claim whatever
upon the deposit; and alleged that the fund was the property of the intervening defendant and that it held the
same subject to its order. When the appellant bank elected
to litigate with the plaintiff, the question of its right to
the fund, and departed from its impartial attitude, theretofore assumed in its interpleader, it waived and abandoned its interpleader and cannot, in view of that fact,
question the propriety of the court's ruling thereon.

Appellant's next contention is that upon the appointment of the new board of regents, June 11, 1912, Vincent
B. May ceased to be a member of the board of regents, and
for the same reason ceased to be its secretary and treasurer or to have any power as such; his sole duty being to
turn over the funds to his successor.

As to the first proposition it is sufficient to say that
there is nothing in the record to show that the board of
regents appointed June 11th qualified by taking the oath
of office prescribed in section 1 of article XX of the Constitution, and it certainly could not be contended that
4 the mere appointment or election of an official, without his qualification, would oust an incumbent from
office. Appellants cite the cases of Conklin v. Cunningham, 7 N. M. 445, 38 Pac. 170, and Eldodt v. Territory,
10 N. M. 141, 61 Pac. 105, as sustaining the proposition
that "the appointment of an officer by the Governor is
complete on delivery of the commission, and gives the appointee prima facie title to the office," but an examination
of these cases will show that in each instance the officer
demanding the office had qualified for the same, by giving
bond where one was required and taking the oath of office.
There is nothing in the record to show that the new board
of regents attempted to act officially on any matter until
July 5, 1912, or that the members thereof qualified as
such before that date. But as we view the matter, it is
immaterial as to the time of the qualification of the new
board, for, in view of the provisions of section 3574, C. L.
1897, the treasurer of the board would still continue as

such until the election and qualification of his successor, notwithstanding the fact that he had ceased to be a member of the board. This section provides for the election of a secretary and treasurer, and other officials, and **5** continues, "all other officers so elected shall hold their offices until their successors are duly elected and qualified," thus clearly providing against a vacancy in office. It is true, the secretary and treasurer, under the statute, must be, when elected, a member of the board of regents, but that his right to hold until the appointment and qualification of his successor is not dependent upon his continuing to be a member of the board is clear, otherwise the legislature would not have provided for his continuance in office until his successor was elected and qualified. The purpose of this provision was to guard against a vacancy in the office. Even without the statutory provision he would be continued in office by virtue of section 2, art. XX, of the Constitution, which provides: "Every officer, unless removed, shall hold his office until his successor has duly qualified." Under this provision there can be no doubt as to his right to hold the office until his successor has qualified. In this case the newly elected treasurer did not qualify until some time in August; consequently May was the treasurer of the board of regents on July 5th, when he transferred the certificate of deposit in question. Even if it should be held that May had no right to hold the office of treasurer, after he ceased to be a member of the board of regents, his right to the office could not be questioned collaterally; it could be done only in a direct proceeding for that purpose. Case, et al., v. State ex rel. Mann. 69 Ind. 46. He would be an officer de facto, and his acts, as it respects third persons, would be valid. McGregor v. Balch, 14 Vt. 428, 39 Am. Dec. 231.

But it is contended that May, even while secretary and treasurer, had no power to transfer the certificate of deposit in question, because section 3553, C. L. 1897, provides all "the disbursements and expenditures of all moneys provided for by this act, shall be vested in a board of five regents," and by section 3556 it is provided "the board of regents shall direct the disposition of any moneys belonging to or appropriated to the Agricultural College and Experiment Station established by this act;" but it is not contended in this case that the board of regents had directed the deposit of the money in this case originally with the Bank of Commerce, or that it had ever attempted to provide for its disposition.

Section 3574, C. L. 1897, provides: "The person so elected as secretary and treasurer shall, before entering upon the discharge of his duties as such, execute a good and sufficient bond to the Territory of New Mexico, with two or more sufficient sureties, residents of this Territory, in the penal sum of not less than twenty thousand dollars, conditioned for the faithful performance of his duties as such secretary and treasurer, and that he will faithfully account for and pay over to the person or persons entitled thereto all moneys which shall come into his hands as such officer," etc.

In the absence of any direction from the board of regents, assuming for the sake of argument that the board **6** had the power to direct and control the disposition, deposit or investment of the funds in the hands of the treasurer, it could hardly be contended that it was not the duty of the treasurer to safely preserve and keep such funds. This being true, he could deposit such funds in any bank he saw fit, or keep them in his own possession, liable of course at all times under his bond "to account for and pay over to the person or persons entitled thereto" such moneys. Suppose that he should, in the absence of direction, deposit such funds in an insolvent bank and a loss should occur, would he not be liable nevertheless? Again, suppose he had distributed the funds among several banks, and he expected to be called upon by his successor, within the near future to turn over to him the moneys in his hands, would he not have the power to assemble the funds, to procure the actual cash, in order that he might turn it over to his successor? In the present case, May could have been in an anomalous situation, should appellant's contention be sound, if he had been required to account to his successor on the 5th day of July, and the incoming official had refused to accept as cash the certificate of deposit in ques-

tion. The new treasurer had the right to demand that the
actual cash should be turned over to him. Now, if May
did not have the authority to withdraw the money from the
First National Bank of Albuquerque, or to indorse the certificate of deposit, it would have been impossible for him to
produce the money.

The funds in question were placed in May's hands by
the Territorial officials. He took them under his official
bond. He became absolutely responsible for these moneys.
and so long as he accounted for the same and paid the
money over to the person or persons entitled thereto, as
provided in his bond, he could deposit the fund with any
bank or banks he desired. Maloy v. Board of Commissioners of Bernalillo County, 10 N. M. 638, 62 Pac. 1106, 52
L. R. A. 126. In the absence of direction from the board,
assuming its power to direct, May alone had the right to
select a place of deposit. The fact that he deposited the
money on time deposit, at 5 per cent interest, does not
alter the case. The College received the benefit of the
interest accumulations. The certificate was payable to
May. It was issued for his protection, so that he could
demand the money when he desired, and as evidence of the
deposit. He had the right to transfer over the certificate
of deposit to the appellee, and the appellee was lawfully
entitled to the money represented by such certificate at
the time it demanded payment from the appellant bank.
This being true, and payment having been refused, it was
entitled to interest thereon, under the statute at the rate
of 6 per centum per annum. The newly appointed treasurer, who had not qualified, had no right to interfere in
the matter. When he was lawfully entitled to call the old
treasurer to account, he could require him to pay over to
him the actual cash represented by such certificate, or
such as had not been lawfully paid out by May. In this
case it is not contended that May was acting in bad faith,
or that he was insolvent, or that his sureties were not amply able to respond for the full amount of the bond, or that
any attempt was made to defraud the College.

The board of regents joined in the appeal and adopted
the assignments of error and brief filed by the appellant

bank. What we have said has disposed of all the questions raised in the case, and further discussion as to the rights of the board is unnecessary.

What might have become a serious question in this case, had it been raised, is as to the right of the board of regents or the secretary and treasurer to the posession and control of moneys derived from the sale of lands granted to the Territory and confirmed to the State in view of the provisions of section 10 of the Enabling Act, which, it might be argued, makes the State Treasurer the custodian of such fund, and charges him with the duty, subject to the approval of the Governor and Secretary of State, of investing the same in safe interest-bearing securities.

Finding no error in the record, the judgment of the lower court is affirmed, and it is so ordered.

[No. 1615, February 14, 1914.]

IN THE MATTER OF THE APPLICATION OF B. S. EVERMAN FOR A WRIT OF HABEAS CORPUS.

SYLLABUS (BY THE COURT)

1. The district local option law, chap. 78, S. L. 1913, is a complete enactment in itself and requires nothing further to give it validity; it depends upon the popular vote for a determination only of the territorial limits of its operation, and is a valid and constitutional exercise of the legislative power.

P. 607

2. A license to retail intoxicating liquor is neither a property right nor a contract. It is in no sense a contract made by the State with a party holding the license; it is a mere permit subject to be modified or annulled at the pleasure of the legislature.

P. 610

3. The creation or designation of the district, as required by sections 1 and 2, chap. 78, C. L. 1913, is an administrative act and not legislative.

P. 612

Original Application for Writ of Habeas Corpus

J. H. CRIST, Santa Fe; H. D. TERRILL, Clovis, N. M.,
for petitioner.

IRA L. GRIMSHAW, Assistant Attorney General, Santa
Fe, N. M., for State.

OPINION OF THE COURT.

ROBERTS, C. J.—The petitioner was the holder of a
license issued by the board of county commissioners of
Roosevelt County, authorizing him to sell intoxicating liquors at Taiban, an unincorporated village in said County.
After the issuance of said license, and while the same was
in full force and effect, and unexpired, the qualified voters
of Taiban and contiguous territory petitioned the board
of county commissioners of said County, in accordance
with the provisions of chap. 78, S. L. 1913, commonly
called the "district prohibition law," to submit to the
qualified voters within the named district the question "of
whether or not the barter, sale or exchange of intoxicating
liquors shall be prohibited therein as provided by this
act." (Sec. 1, chap. 78, supra.) Upon the filing of said
petition, the district was designated by the board of county
commissioners, in accordance with sec. 2, of the Act, and
the election was called and held pursuant to said Act. At
said election a majority of the votes cast were in favor of
prohibiting the sale, barter or exchange of intoxicating
liquors within said district. Sec. 14, of the Act, provides
for the refund, to the holder of a license authorizing the
sale of intoxicating liquors, the unused portion of the license, at the time prohibition goes into effect. Petitioner
did not apply for such refund, but continued to sell intoxicating liquors at Taiban, notwithstanding the result
of the election and the provisions of said act making it
unlawful to do so. Upon complaint filed against him, he
was arrested and detained by the sheriff of said County,
under a warrant issued upon such complaint, and he
brings this action to obtain his release. His right to be
discharged by the writ of habeas corpus is predicated upon

the assumption that said chapter 78, S. L. 1913, is unconstitutional.

The act in question does not differ materially from similar laws, found in many of the other States of the
1   Union, except in one particular, viz:—the act in question provides for the creation and designation of the
district wherein the question is to be submitted to the
voters, by the board of county commissioners, upon petition signed by 25% of the qualified electors residing within such proposed district; the submission of the question
to the voters of such district so created, and, upon a majority of the votes cast at such election being in favor of
prohibition, prohibit the sale, barter or exchange of intoxicating liquors within such district for four years absolutely,
and thereafter, until and unless upon petition the question
is again submitted to the voters of such district and the
majority shall vote in favor of licensing the sale of intoxicating liquors, whereas: all similar laws which we have
been able to find in other States, provide for the submission of the question to the voters of some district, or sub-
division of the County.theretofore created by the board of
county commissioners, or by law, for some other object or
governmental purpose.

The constitutionality of "local option" legislation is no
longer an open question in American jurisprudence, and
such laws are almost universally upheld. While some of
the early cases, it is true, held such laws unconstitutional
and void, because based on a contingency, and, in effect
delegated legislative powers to the people, (Parker v. Commonwealth, 6 Penn. St. 507; Rice v Foster, 4 Harr. (Dela.)
497), there is today practically no State holding to the
contrary with the possible exception of Tennesee.   See
Wright v. Cunningham, 115 Tenn. 445.)   Pennsylvania.
Iowa, Indiana and California have all departed from the
contrary doctrine, first announced by the courts of those
States, as the cases hereafter cited will show.

Woolen & Thornton on Intoxicating Liquors, vol. 1,
page 231, section 155, contains a full discussion on the
history of local option laws and citing authorities says
that by the "great weight of judicial decision now," such

laws do not violate the constitutional provision that the power to make laws is vested in the legislature, but that such laws are constitutional and valid.

"The constitutional objection to such a law is met, if the act, when it came from the legislature, received the Governor's approval, was properly published and was, of itself, a complete and perfect enactment. In such case the popular will is expressed under and by virtue of a law that is in force and effect and the people neither make nor repeal it. By this vote, petition or remonstrance, as the case may be, they only determined whether a certain thing shall be done under the law and not whether the law shall take effect. * * * As a result a different regulation, of a police nature, may under such a law exist in one town, city or county from that which exists in another. In such case, the maxim delagata potestas non potest delegari has no application." See section 156 to the same effect, et seq. In Commonwealth v. Weller, 14 Bush (Ky.), 218, the act prohibited the sale of liquor in a certain County. The Act was conditioned upon a ratification by a majority of the voters of that County. The constitutionality thereof was attacked upon the same grounds as in the case at bar. The Court held that "the popular will expressed for or against the provisions of the law does not, in any manner, destroy or affect the legislative intent," and that as the law was "perfect in all its parts and could be enforced without any other legislation" the objections urged were not well taken, and the Court, on page 224, said:

"We see no reason why, in a case like this involving a question of local interest and of mere police regulation, the popular will should not ·be consulted and on a question made the subject of this enactment, it is eminently just and proper.

In Schulher v. Bordeaux, 64 Miss. 59, a case wherein the local option law was attacked, the Court held that the question of the right to make an act of the legislature depend, for its operation, on a future contingency has been established by oft-repeated examples, and such action does not violate the constitution.

In Boyd v. Bryant, 35 Ark. 69, the prohibition law was again upheld.

In Caldwell, et al., v. Barrett, et al., 73 Ga. 604, the local option law was declared constitutional. The Court in that case said that the practice in that State, for more than half a century, had been to leave local questions, such as location of county sites, etc., to the vote of the people, to be effected thereby and that such laws had never been thought to be unconstitutional.

To the same effect, see Commonwealth v. Bennett, 108 Mass. 27.

In the case of State v. Pond, 93 Mo. 606, the local option law of that State was declared constitutional. The town of Trenton, by a majority vote, under the terms of the local option statute, held an election, which resulted in a majority of the votes being cast against the sale of intoxicating liquor. The relator thereafter applied for a license to keep a dram shop in that town. The application was refused and thereupon a mandamus was filed to compel the County Court to grant him such license. The Court on page 622 said:

"While this local option act provides that any County, or town, or city of the class named, may, by a majority vote, put such County, town, or city under the operation of the law, it does not refer to them the question of passing a law; that the legislature had already done, and only called upon them to decide by a vote whether they would accept the provisions of a law regularly enacted by both houses of the General Assembly and approved by the Governor, By its provisions the law and not the vote extended its influence over the locality voting against the sale of intoxicants. It was the law that authorized the vote to be taken, and when taken the law, and not the vote, declared the result that should follow the vote. The vote was the means provided to ascertain the will of the people, not as to the passage of the law, but whether intoxicating liquors should be sold in their midst. If the majority voted against the sale, the law, and not the vote, declared it should not be sold. The vote sprang from the law, and not the law from the vote. By their vote the electors declared no conse-

quences, prescribed no penalties, and exercised no legislative function. The law declared the consequences, and
whatever they may be they are exclusively the result of
the legislative will."

See also State of Iowa v. Forkner, 94 Ia. 1, which fully
discusses the constitutionality of this class of laws.
Groesch v. State, 42 Ind. 447; State v. Wilcox, 42 Conn.
365; State v. Kline, 50 Oregon (1907) 426; Sanford v.
County of Morris, 13 Am. Rep. 422; Paul v. Gloucester,
50 N. J. Law 585; Glovernell v. Howell, 70 N. Y. 287;
Ex Parte Handler, 176 Mo. 383; Ex Parte Lynn, 19 Tex.
A. 294; Cain v. Comm'rs., 86 N. C. 8; Bancroft v. Dumas,
21 Vt. 456, 114 Sta. Rep. 324, and authorities thereunder;
Ex Parte Beck, (Cal.) 124 Pac. 543.

And it is also well settled, were our statute not authority on it, that a person has no interest in a license
2 which cannot properly be revoked. It is neither a
property right nor a right of contract, but is a mere
license revocable under certain conditions.

In the case of State of Minn. v. Cooke, 24 Minn. 247,
the defendant attempted to justify the sale of liquor in a
prohibited district by giving in evidence a license authorizing him to sell liquor for a period of twelve months
from its date. He claimed that he had never received any
notice of the revocation of his license. The question of
the delegation of the law-making power was also involved.
The Court held that the effect of the local option act was
to make the vote of a majority of the voters against licenses a prohibition and that the penalty for selling liquor within that prohibited district provided for an effectual revocation of outstanding licenses by the vote of
electors. It is plain, therefore, that in that case the license was revoked by reason of the action of the voters.

In Fell v. State, 42 Md. 71, the Court held "there can
be no question of the power of the legislature to fix the
time when a law shall go into effect; nor can it be doubted
that the legislature has power to prohibit the sale of spirituous or fermented liquors in any part of the State; notwithstanding a party to be affected by the law may have
procured a license under the general license laws of the

State which has not yet expired. Such a license is in no
sense a contract made by the State with a party holding the
license; it is a mere permit subject to be modified or annulled at the pleasure of the legislature, who have the
power to change or repeal the law under which the license
was granted."

Also see Freund on Police Power, sec. 564, page 591.

Section 8 of chapter 78 of the laws of 1913, makes it
unlawful to engage in the liquor business in prohibited
districts. Section 14 of the same act provides for a refund
of the amount of the uunsed license, where the licensee was
doing business before the district became a prohibited district. These two sections, without doubt, revoked the license of the petitioner in this case, and he can claim no
benefits under it. If this is not an express repeal, it surely
and clearly was an intention on the part of the legislature
to revoke licenses when these events have happened and in
law is an implied repeal, which is as effective in the case
at bar as though it were express.

Therefore, it seems that the main contention of peti
tioner is: The legislature in empowering twenty-five per
centum of the people of a proposed area or district to petition the board of county commissoners to call an election
in that district to determine whether or not the local option law shall be adopted, delegates its legislative powers
and functions to these twenty-five per centum of the people of the district.

The district is created by the statute upon the filing of
the petition with the board of county commissioners in
compliance therewith. The board must then designate its
boundaries upon the minutes. If a majority of the votes
cast be in favor of prohibition, intoxicating liquor may
not lawfully be sold within the district, except in certain
cases for enumerated purposes, not involved in this case,
until the question is again resubmitted to the voters and a
majority of the votes cast are favorable to the licensing and
sale of intoxicating liquors, which question cannot be submitted for four years after the previous election. On the
other hand, if a majority of the votes cast are not in favor
of prohibition, the sale of liquor within the district may

be licensed, in accordance with law. In either event the
question may not be resubmitted for a period of four years
The district remains in existence, as designated in the
petition and upon the minutes of the board of county commissioners, whatever may be the result of the election, and.
under the law, in the event a majority of the votes cast
at the election are in favor of prohibition, the law which
prohibits the sale of intoxicating liquors applies to the dis
trict; while, on the other hand, if the vote be not in favor
of prohibition, the law which licenses the sale is in force.
The act calls for no legislation on the part of the people
of any district, and the vote of the electors thereof does
not make the law. The electors thereof perform no legislative functions whatever. As said by the Supreme Court
of California, in the case of Ex Parte Beck, supra:

"The act is wholly one of the State legislature, in force
all over the State so far as the rights of the people of the
respective localities mentioned to avail themselves thereof
is concerned; the only thing left to the electors of each such
locality to determine being whether they will avail themselves of the prohibitions contained therein. This we have
seen, involves no delegation by the legislature or exercise
by the electors of legislative power, or the exercise of any
power of local government by the district specified."

There is no merit in petitioner's contention, that, because the law provides for the designation of the district
by the board of county commissioners, upon petition of
twenty-five per cent. of the qualified voters, resident within the proposed district, the legislature has delegated its
legislative powers and functions to these twenty-five per
centum of the people of the district.

The creation, or designation of the district is an administrative act and not legislative. It is created pur-
3 suant to the provisions and upon the conditions prescribed by the legislature. The law points out how
it shall be formed, designated and created. In carrying out
the provisions of the Act, the qualified electors and board
of county commissioners are administering the law; they
are not assuming to make law. Were this not true, boards

of county commissioners, in creating precincts, election districts, etc., would be exercising legislative power.

The act in question can not properly be held violative of any provisions of our Constitution that has been called to our attention, and we see no reason to doubt its validity. This being so, we are compelled to uphold it as a valid enactment of the State legislature. This being so, it necessarily follows that the petitioner is not entitled to be discharged upon the showing made.

For the reasons stated, the writ is discharged and the petitioner remanded to custody.

[No. 1643, February 23, 1914.]

JAMES R. SMITH, et al., Appellees, v. THE CITY OF RATON, et al., Appellants.

SYLLABUS (BY THE COURT)

1. Sub-sections 6 and 67, section 2402, C. L. 1897, examined; Held, that the first paragraph of sub-section 6, authorizing the issuance of municipal bonds for certain purposes, and providing the procedure therefor, which portion of said sub-section was enacted as a part of sec. 14, chap. 39, S. L. 1884, was not repealed, modified or amended by sub-section 67, enacted as sec. 1 of chap. 70, S. L. 1897.

P. 620

2. The first paragraph of sub-section 6 of section 2402, C. L. 1897, is not inconsistent with any provisions of the State Constitution and was therefore continued as a law of the State by virtue of section 4 of article XXII of our Constitution.

P. 622

3. Under the power granted to cities and towns by sub-section 5, sec. 2402, C. L. 1897, to erect all needful buildings for the use of the city or town, such municipalities are limited to the erection of such needful buildings as may be required for public uses, or for municipal uses and purposes

and contradistinguished from private or quasi-public uses,
and, if the primary object of a building to be constructed is a
municipal purpose, the fact that it may be incidentally used
for theatrical purposes, may not have the effect of rendering
the action in erecting it invalid; but where the paramount
purpose and object is for other than strictly municipal purposes, legislative authority is lacking in this State, for the
erection of such buildings by cities and towns.

P. 623

Appeal from the District Court of Colfax County;
Thomas D. Leib, District Judge; affirmed.

E. C. CRAMPTON, HUGO SEABERG, O. L. PHILLIPS, R
C. ALFORD, Raton, N. M.; CHARLES A. SPIESS, E. Las
Vegas, N. M., for appellees.

Appellants failed to file with the proper officer of the
city of Raton, prior to the election, an estimate of the approximate cost of the proposed improvements, and therefore the proceedings initiated for the incurring of the indebtedness in erecting the so-called municipal building,
and for the issuance of bonds therefor, were illegal and
void. C. L. 1897, sec. 2402, sub-sec. 67; Laws 1897, ch.
70; Const. of N. M., art. IX, secs. 12 and 13.

Constitutional provisions and statutes are subject to the
same rule of construction with reference to amendment,
repeal, intent and meaning. Prouty v. Stover, 11 Kans.
285, 26 Pac. 183; Prohibitory Amendment cases, 24
Kans. 700, 30 Pac. 499; Franklin v. Westfall, 27 Kans.
619, 31 Pac. 614; Cleveland v. Spartanburg, 54 S. Car.
83, 31 S. E. 871; C. L. 1897, sec. 2900; Butts v. Woods,
4 N. M. 349; Laws 1884, ch. 39, sec. 14; Lanigan v. Gallup, 131 Pac. 997.

The Constitution preserved in force all laws of the Territory of New Mexico not inconsistent with its provisions.
Const. N. M., art. XXII, sec. 4.

The provisions of the statute requiring an estimate to
be filed before election are mandatory. Moore v. Matton,
45 N. E. 567; City of Booneville v. Stevens, 95 S. W.

314; Moss v. City of Fairbury, 92 N. W. 721; City of Dallas v. Ellison, 30 S. W. 1128; City of Dallas v. Atkins, 32 S. W. 780; Edwards v. Cooper, 79 N. E. 1049; Leibole v. Frankston, 83 N. E. 781; McLauren v. Tatum, 67 N. E. 561; Kirksville v. Coleman, 77 S. W. 120; Lippincott v. Pana, 92 Ill. 24; Manhattan Co. v. Ironwood, 74 Fed. Rep. 535, and cases cited; McClure v. Township of Oxford, 74 U. S. 429, 24 L. Ed. 129; sec. 14, ch. 39, Laws 1884, was repealed by ch. 70, Laws 1897.

Where a later act covers the whole subject matter of an earlier act, and embraces new provisions, it operates by implication to repeal the prior act. Koons v. Cluggish, et al., (Ind. App.) 34 N. E. 651; Lowe v. Board of Commissioners, 51 Pac. 579; Board v. Shoemaker, 27 Kans. 77; Stetson, etc., v. Brown, 59 Pac. 507; Missouri Pac. Ry. Co. v. Park, 71 Pac. 586; Baca v. Board of Commissioners, 10 N. M. 438, 62 Pac. 979; Petitti v. State, 121 Pac. 278.

Right of appellees to bring suit at this time. Crampton v. Zabriskie, 101 U. S. 601, 25 L. Ed. 1070; Bayle v. New Orleans, 23 Fed. 843; Harrington v. Plainview, 6 N. W. 777; Willard v. Comsaock, 17 N. W. 401; Wilkerson v. Van Orman, 30 N. W. 495; Bradford v. San Francisco, 44 Pac. 912; Fowler v. City of Superior, 54 N. W. 805; Winamac v. Huddleston, 31 N. E. 561; Dillon on Municipal Corps. (5th ed.) vol. 4, secs. 1579-1585; Id., vol. 1, sec. 215, and cases cited.

It was not within the power of the city council to appropriate public money to the use of building an opera house, or a building whose main object was that of an opera house. Water Supply Co. v. City of Albuquerque, 128 Pac. 77; In re Mayor, 99 N. Y. 569, 99 N. E. 642; Sun Publishing Co. v. Mayor, 152 N. Y. 257, 46 N. E. 499, 47 L. R. A. 788; Dibble v. Town of New Haven, 56 Conn. 199; Dunham v. Hyde Park, 75 Ill. 371; Mitchell v. Board of Co. Commrs., 132 Ind. 540; Torrent v. Muskegon, 47 Mich .115; Parker v. Concord, 71 N. H. 468; Greeley v. People, 60 Ill. 19; Clark v. Brookfield, 81 Mo. 503; Attorney General v. Burrell, 31 Mich. 25; Bates v. Bassett, 60 Vt. 530; City of Denver v. Hallett, 34 Colo.

393; State v. Barnes, 22 Okla. 191, 97 Pac. 997; Brooks
v. Brooklyn, 124 N. W. 668, 26 L. R. A. (N. S.) 425;
Sugar v. Monroe, 108 La. 677, 59 L. R. A. 723; 32 So.
961; Wheelock v. Lowell, 196 Mass. 220, 124 Am. State
Rep. 543, 81 N. E. 977, 12 Am. & E. Ann. Cas. 1109;
Stetson v. Kempton, 13 Mass. 272, 7 Am. Dec. 145; King-
man v. Brockman, 153 Mass. 255, 11 L. R. A. 123, 26 N.
E. 998; Spaulding v. Lowell, 23 Pick. 71; Opinion of the
Justices, 182 Mass. 605, 66 N. E. 25, 60 L. R. A. 592;
White v. Stamford, 37 Conn. 586; McQuillan on Corps.,
vol. 3, sec. 1117; State v. Gilbert, 56 Ohio St. 575, 47 N.
E. 551, 38 L. R. A. 519; State v. Lynch, 102 N. E. 670;
Fiske, Civil Gov. in the United States, p. 31; Worden v.
New Bedford, 131 Mass. 24, 41 Am. R. 185; Mead v.
Acton, 139 Mass. 341, 1 N. E. 413; Jenkins v. Andover,
103 Mass. 94; Greenbanks v. Boutwell, 43 Vt. 207; Egan
v. City and County of San Francisco, decided in Califor-
nia, June 11, 1913.

Municipal corporations have only the powers expressly
conferred and such as are necessarily incident to·those expressly granted or essential to the declared objects and
purposes of the corporation. Dillon Municipal Corps.,
(5th ed.) sec. 357; Von Schmidt v. Widber, 105 Cal. 151;
Gassner v. McCarthy, 160 Cal. 82.

H. L. BICKLEY, J. LEAHY, H. M. RODRICK, Raton, N
M.; PERSHING & TITSWORTH, Denver, Colo.; ALBERT T
ROGERS, JR., E. Las Vegas, N. M., for appellants.

Sub-section 67, of sec. 2402, C. L. 1897, became void
and inoperative by the adoption of the Constitution of
New Mexico. Art. IX, sec. 12.

It was not the intention of the legislature, in adopting
said sub-sec. 67, to repeal sub-sec. 6; Laws 1897, ch. 70,
sec. 1; Laws 1884, ch. 39, par. 14; C. L. 1897, sec. 2402,
sub-sec. 6.

Municipal officers should be allowed freedom, and should
not be restricted by judicial construction of statutes, in
the expenditure of money simply for those purposes nec-

essary for the physical existence of such city. Dissenting opinion in the case of State v. Lynch, 102 N. E. 670.

STATEMENT OF FACTS.

Plaintiffs below, appellees here, brought this action in the District Court of Colfax County, as residents and tax-payers of the City of Raton, seeking to enjoin the defend-ants, below, the City of Raton and its officers, from con-structing a so-called municipal building, and issuing bonds for that purpose. By an ordinance adopted March 15, 1912, the question of authorizing the city council to contract an indebtedness on behalf of the city by issuing its said bonds therefor "in an amount not exceeding $25,-000, for the purpose of erecting public buildings in and for the City of Raton," was submitted to the qualified elec-tors of the city at the general election of April 2, 1912, at which election the proposed bond issue was aushorized by the requisite majority of the qualified electors. There-after, the municipal authorities caused to be prepared cer-tain plans and specifications, which were approved by the building committee and the city council, it being the in-tention of the said city council to construct the building according to said plans and specifications if they could pay for it.

A preliminary restraining order was issued by the Dis-trict Court and was subsequently made permanent, the opinion of the District Court being based upon the fol-lowing propositions, to-wit., 1st, that appellants failed to file with the proper officer of the City of Raton, prior to said election, a carefully prepared estimate of the approxi-mate cost of the proposed improvement, as specified in chapter 70 of the Session Laws of 1897, the same being sub-section 67 of section 2402 of the Compiled Laws of 1897; 2nd, that the municipal building sought to be built under the proceedings herein, was about to be erected for an opera house; that the main object of said building, as shown by the plans and specifications introduced in evi-dence, was an opera house, and all other purposes or uses sought to be made of said building were incidental. Both of which propositions were fully covered by findings of fact, appearing in the final decree of the District Court, in substantially the language quoted, supra.

OPINION OF THE COURT.

HANNA, J.—Our first inquiry is directed to the validity of the election of April 2, 1912, upon the proposed bond issue by the City of Raton, notwithstanding the absence of a sworn estimate of the approximate cost of the proposed building, which was required by sub-section 67 of section 2402, C. L. 1897, defining powers of municipalities.

It has been decided by this Court in Lanigan v. Town of Gallup, 17 N. M. 627, 131 Pac. 997, that sections 12 and 13 of article IX, of the Constitution, limiting the powers of municipalities in the creation of debt, are not self-executing. Appellants concede this and contend that full and ample legislative authority for the issuance of the bonds in question is to be found in sub-section 6, of section 2402, (C. L. 1897), with the provisions of which sub-section the City of Raton has fully complied.

Under the provisions of this sub-section, all municipalities were authorized to contract an indebtedness and issue bonds for specified purposes, including the erection of public buildings, provided, no debt be created, except for supplying the city or town with water, unless the question of incurring the same shall, at a regular election of officers for the city, be submitted to a vote of such qualified electors as shall have, in the preceding year, paid a property tax, and a majority of those voting shall vote in favor of creating such debt. Sub-section 6 of section 2402, C. L. 1897, as compiled, is derived from two sources. The first paragraph of the sub-section was a part of section 14, chapter 39, S. L. 1884, entitled, "An Act to incorporate Cities and Towns." The second paragraph of the sub-section was enacted as section 4, of chapter 46, S. L. 1893, and provides for special elections to vote upon issuing bonds "for the construction of sewers, or other public improvements."

Sub-section 67 of section 2402, (C. L. 1897) was enacted by the legislature of 1897, as section 1, of chapter

70, entitled, "An Act Relating to Municipal Corporations."
This sub-section (67) in terms provided that any incorporated city, town or village having a population of at
least one thousand, should have power to erect and operate
water works, etc.; to construct public buildings, etc.; to
issue bonds for the purposes mentioned, limited, however,
as to a total bonded indebtedness of not to exceed four
per centum of the value of taxable property therein; provided, before such bonds could be issued a special election
be held, upon notice prescribed in the act, and that two-
thirds of the legal votes cast at such election be in favor
of the issue of the bonds; that a special tax be levied each
year to provide a sinking fund and to pay the interest on
the bonds; that a carefully prepared estimate of the approximate cost of the proposed improvement must be filed
with the clerk, or other proper officer, and no bonds issued
in excess of such estimate. The act further provided for
the execution of the bonds; the denominations thereof;
the term thereof and the interest thereon; and sale at not
less than par, with other minor details' not necessary to
this discussion.

This act, somewhat in detail, defined the powers of municipalities upon the subject of borrowing money and issuing bonds for four purposes, viz.: constructing public
buildings, sewers, waterworks and gas works, all of which
powers had been conferred by the act of 1884, compiled as
the first paragraph of sub-section 6 of section 2402, C. L.
1897.

The essential differences between the two sub-sections is
as follows:—Sub-section 6 provides for a vote upon the
issuance of the bonds at a *regular* election and an authorization by a majority of the qualified electors, who have
paid a property tax the preceding year, while sub-section
67 provides for a special election and authorization of the
bond issue by an affirmative vote of two-thirds of all legal
votes cast at such election. It is also worthy of note that
sub-section 67 conferred upon municipalities power to
borrow money and issue bonds to provide means for protection from fire, and, to lay off and improve streets and
alleys; failing, however, to cover certain powers conferred

by sub-section 6, viz.: the purchase of water works, construction of canals, purchase of canals, purchase of gas works, purchase of illuminating gas and to pay deficiency in the treasury.

From the fact that sub-section 67 did not cover all the purposes of sub-section 6, and provided for special elections as distinguished from regular elections, and the further fact that 67 in terms provided that the municipalities within the purview of the act "shall have all powers now given by law to icorporated towns," it is earnestly contended by counsel for appellants, that it was not the intention of the legislature, in adopting sub-section 67, to repeal sub-section 6. The repealing clause of the Act, including sub-section 67, did not specifically repeal sub-section 6, but contained the usual formula, "all acts or parts of acts in conflict with this act are hereby repealed."

In this connection it is ably contended by counsel for appellees that both sub-sections 6 and 67 are complete bonding acts, in which all necessary requirements are provided and that sub-section 67 impliedly repeals sub-section 6, so far as repugnant.

It is so generally recognized that courts should give such construction to statutes, apparently in conflict, that both may stand, that citation of authority is unnecessary. Likewise it is universally conceded that repeals by implication are not favored and are not to be indulged in unless it is evident that the legislature so intended.

It is to be presumed that the legislature had in mind all existing laws upon the same subject at the time it gave consideration to and passed a statute. If there be no express reference to the existing statute, or apparent intention on the part of the legislature to repeal the same,

1 it is to be concluded, and it is a sound canon of construction, that the legislature did not intend to abrogate the former law, relating to the same matter, unless the later act is clearly repugnant to the prior one, or completely covers and embraces the subject matter thereof, or unless the reason for the prior act is removed.

In this case appellees contend that the later act covers the former act, but a careful study of both does not warrant such conclusion. Not only are several purposes of the earlier act not included within the later act, but the later act may well be considered as intended simply to enlarge the powers conferred by the first act and provide for special elections in addition to a general election as provided by the Act of 1884.

In this connection our discussion is limited to that portion of sub-section 6 as passed by the legislature in 1884. The latter portion of the sub-section, adopted in 1893, is probably repugnant to the provisions of sub-section 67, and, therefore, repealed by that sub-section. This portion of sub-section 6 is not involved in the present case and it is, therefore, not necessary for us to pass upon the question of its repeal at this time.

Other than as thus qualified we are of the opinion that sub-sections 6 and 67, while dealing with the same subject matter in a general way, were not necessarily repugnant, but were designed to effect different objects, i. e., the method of holding the election upon the question, and, except as qualified, are both to be considered as existing statutes of the Territory at the time of its admission as a State.

Therefore, in view of our conclusion that both sub-sections 6 and 67 were existing laws of the Territory of New Mexico at the time of its admission as a State, except so far as the second paragraph of sub-section 6 may be repugnant to the provisions of sub-section 67, it only remains necessary for us to consider whether either, or both, of the sub-sections referred to were inconsistent with the provisions of the Constitution, and for that reason were not carried forward under statehood, because of the provisions of the Constitution set forth in section 4 of article XXII, which provides as follows:

"All laws of the Territory of New Mexico in force at the time of its admission into the Union as a State not inconsistent with this Constitution, shall be and remain in force as the laws of the State until they expire by their own limitations or are altered or repealed."

In this connection it becomes quite evident that the
first paragraph of sub-section 6 is in full conformity
2 with and not in any way inconsistent with section 12
of article IX of the Constitution. And this being the
law under which the City of Raton attempted to conduct
its election, and there being no controversy as to the compliance with this section, the question is clearly disposed
of, and it does not seem necessary to us at this time to
consider the effect of the Constitution upon sub-section
67. It might be argued that the provisions of sub-section
67 inconsistent with the Constitution, would be inoperative by reason of the repugnance of inconsistency, but that
the provisions of the Constitution in this respect, being
self-executing, would supplement the provisions of sub-
section 67, and constitute a comprehensive law upon the
subject, when read together with the self-executing provisions of the Constitution. This aspect of the question has
not been presented for our consideration, and it is unnecessary for the purposes of this case to now decide that sub-
section 67 is in force in whole or in part, or affected by
reason of self-executing provisions of the Constitution
which might be read into the act, or considered in connection with it, for which reason we deem it best not to pass
upon the question of the status of sub-section 67, at this
time.

For the reasons heretofore given, we are of the opinion
that the absence of the sworn estimate of the approximate
cost of the proposed improvement, prescribed by the terms
of sub-section 67, did not constitute an omission which
would invalidate the election of April 2, 1912, and that
the decree of the honorable District Judge in this respect
is therefore erroneous.

We, therefore, pass to the consideration of the second
phase of the question, namely, that the court erred in holding that the so-called municipal building, sought to be
built under the proceedings had, was to be erected as and
for an opera house, that the main object of said building,
as shown by the plans and specifications introduced in evidence, was an opera house, and all other purposes or uses
sought to be made of the building, were incidental, and

that it is not within the power of the city council to appropriate public money to the use of the building of an opera house, or of a building whose main object was that of an opera house.

It appears from the evidence in the case, that plans and specifications for a proposed municipal building had been approved, and that it was the intention of the city council to construct a municipal building in accordance with such plans and specifications, provided the city had the funds available for the construction of the building, and that there was a divergence in the evidence as to the probable cost of the building constructed in accordance with such plans and specifications. It is conceded that the cost must not exceed the funds lawfully available for the purpose, and that if no other funds be available except the proceeds of the proposed bond issue, then the cost should not exceed $25,000. It is also conceded by appellants to be their desire to construct a municipal building containing not only suitable offices for the officials, but a public hall, or auditorium of sufficient capacity to accommodate public meetings of the people of Raton, and of such character as to afford facilities for public entertainments, theatrical or otherwise. In this connection it is pointed out by appellees and evidently borne out by the facts, and certainly by the finding of the District Judge, that a very large portion of the building would be devoted to such an auditorium, equipped as an opera house, with stage, boxes and seating accommodations, even dressing rooms having been provided by the architect.

Numerous authorities have been cited by both appellants and appellees, but we do not desire to make this opinion unduly lengthy by a consideration of the numerous decisions, all of which have been examined and carefully considered.

After thorough consideration of all the authorities cited in the briefs of counsel, we have reached the conclusion that, if the primary object of a building to be constructed is a municipal purpose, the fact that it may be incidentally used for theatrical purposes may not have the effect of rendering the action in erecting it invalid.

3

Bates v. Bassett, 60 Ver. 530, 15 Atl. 200, 1 L. R. A. 166; Jones v. Camden, 44 S. C. 319, 23 S. E. 141, 15 Am. St. 819.

It is, of course, well settled that a municipal corporation has such powers, and such only, as are, first, expressly granted, or, second, such as are fairly and necessarily implied from those granted; or third, such as are essential to the declared purpose of the incorporation. Brooks v. Brooklyn, 124 N. W. 668, 26 L. R. A. (N. S.) 425.

By appellants it is contended that the City of Raton clearly had the power to erect the building contemplated, under, and by virtue of, the provisions of sub-sections 5, 56, and 6, of section 2402, C. L. 1897, which sub-sections are as follows:

"5. To erect all needful buildings for the use of the city or town.

"56. To provide for the erection and care of all public buildings necessary for the use of the town.

"6. To contract an idebtedness by borrowing money or of issuing bonds for the purpose of ferecting public buildings."

It is not our desire to put a strict construction on the grant of statutory power to municipalities, nor is it our intention to judicially legislate upon the question of the power granted in this instance. It is doubtless true that the power can be given to municipalities to construct opera houses, or other buildings of like character. We fully appreciate that municipalities are called upon in the present day and age for the exercise of powers not heretofore considered necessary to be exercised by municipalities. But notwithstanding this fact, we believe that it is for the legislature and not for the courts to extend the powers of municipalities to meet modern conditions, and after careful consideration of the statutes quoted, we are constrained to believe that the powers therein conferred must be limited to the erection of such needful buildings as may be required for public uses, or for municipal uses and purposes as contradistinguished from private or quasi-public uses, such as the one under consideration. In considering this phase of the present case, we must bear in mind that the learned District Judge found as a matter of fact, and incorporated in his decree, the conclusion that the particular building here in question was about to be erected by the said City of Raton, "as and for an opera house; that the main object of said building, as shown by the plans and specifications introduced in evidence, was an opera house, and all other uses sought to be made of such building were merely incidental."

Thus we find that the issue as presented to the District Court was resolved by him as clearly showing a paramount use of the building for other than strictly municipal purposes. It is contended that the courts cannot control the discretion of the municipal authorities said to exist because it is urged that it is for the city council, or city authorities, to determine what is or what is not a municipal or public purpose. While we concede the general rules with regard to the discretion of municipal officers in the exercise of certain functions of government, we do not think this is a case where the rule can be applied. In the present instance, the question under consideration is rather one of whteher the use to which the money of the taxpayer is to be applied is a public one, which becomes a question of law as limited and defined by the statutes upon the subject, and to be resolved and considered in the light of the rules of construction, which, in our opinion, are the outgrowth of a disposition on the part of the courts to arrive at not only a reasonable rule of construction, but one not tending to cast upon the taxpayer obligations which his citizenship in the community do not necessarily impose.

We do not disagree with the views of the Supreme Court of Massachusetts, as announced in the case of Kingman v. Brockton, 153 Mass. 255, 11 L. R. A. 123, that it is not incompetent for a city to appropriate public money for the erection of the building which is larger than its present needs for municipal purposes require. We agree that the municipality may allow such portions of such building to be used for other purposes than municipal, either for a stipulated rent, or price, or gratuitiously, and that in erecting a public building a city need not limit the size to actual existing needs but may make reasonable provision for probable future needs.

In concluding this opinion, we desire to observe that appellants have here contended that the relief afforded to plaintiffs below in this case, should not go to the extent of a prohibition against the issuance of municipal bonds for the purpose of constructing a public building in the City of Raton, of a reasonable character. In other words, that the injunction granted should be directed to the character and plan of the proposed building rather than a general prohibition. In support of this view of the matter it is urged that the city council had not undertaken to adopt final plans and specifications, nor had it attempted to let a contract for any particular kind of building; that until it did so, the court was necessarily, in granting the relief, striking at a mere conjecture. While it is true that the record discloses evidence that it was the intention of the city council to proceed in the erection of the building in accordance with the plans and specifications which had been approved, provided the city found itself possessed of sufficient funds to do so, there would seem to be some merit in the contention of appellants, and we believe it is clear from the foregoing opinion that we hold that the election and authorization of the bonds was in full conformity with our statutes governing such matters. We are also clear in our opinion that this Court is bound by the finding of the District Court that the paramount purpose of this building was for other than municipal uses and purposes.

Therefore, the injunction granted by the District Court, in our opinion, was properly issued so far as this phase of the question is concerned.

While it appears from the examination of the final decree that the District Court found that the estimate of the approximate cost of the proposed improvement had not been filed with the proper officer in the City of Raton, as required by chapter 70 of the Session Laws of 1897, which appears as sub-section 67 of section 2402, C. L. 1897, with which conclusion of the District Court as to a necessity therefor, we are unable to agree, nevertheless it appears that the injunction was directed against the erection of the particular building referred to in the complaint, and the plans and specifications. There is substantial evidence to support the finding that the city council was about to erect a building in conformity with such plans and specifications, and such as referred to in the complaint, and in view of the fact that the District Court had an opportunity of hearing the witnesses and considering this phase of the question, and can therefore better judge concerning the weight of this evidence, for which reason we are not disposed to disturb the finding.

Wherefore, inasmuch as the permanent injunction was limited in its effect to a restraint upon the authorities in the matter of the erection of this particular building, we consider that the injunction was proper, and the decree of the lower court should be affirmed, and it is so ordered.

[No. 1624, February 23, 1914.]

STATE OF NEW MEXICO, ex rel. JACOBO CHAVEZ, Appellee, v. WILLIAM G. SARGENT, State Auditor, Appellant.

SYLLABUS (BY THE COURT)

1. The office of Superintendent of Insurance, created by chapter 5, Laws of 1905, which was amended by chapter 48, Laws 1909, was not abolished by section 6 of article XI of the Constitution. The latter is not self-executing except as to those powers specifically conferred upon the Corporation Commission therein. It requires legislation to carry the section into effect in regard to some of the powers therein conferred on the Corporation Commission, among which are many of the powers now exercised by the Superintendent of Insurance. The Superintendent of Insurance was continued in office by section 9 of article XXII of the Constitution, until superseded by the Corporation Commission, and he has not been fully so superseded, by reason of the lack of legislation to carry the constitutional provision into effect. He

Memorandum Brief for Appellee.

Is the office of Superintendent of Insurance abolished? Const. N. M., art. XI, sec. 6; Id., art. XXII, sec. 4; Laws 1905, ch. 5; Laws 1909, ch. 48; Id., sec. 6; Mitchell, et al., v. National Surety Co., 206 Fed. 807.

OPINION OF THE COURT.

PARKER, J.—This is a proceeding by mandamus by the relator, as Superintendent of Insurance, against the respondent, as State Auditor, to compel the approval of a warrant drawn by him on the Insurance fund for the sum of $1400 in favor of relator, as Superintendent of Insurance for salary from the 1st day of December, 1912, to the 1st day of July, 1913.

The respondent defended upon the ground that there was no appropriation of the legislature for any salary of the Superintendent of Insurance after December 1, 1912, and that, therefore, he had no authority to pay the salary. The District Court found against the respondent, and he appeals to this Court.

The question is one of statutory construction. The insurance department was organized by chapter 5 of the laws of 1905. Section 4 of that act is as follows:

"Such superintendent of insurance shall receive a salary of two thousand four hundred dollars per annum, which shall be paid out of the insurance fund hereinafter provided for."

Section 12 of that act creates an Insurance fund out of which all the salaries and expenses of the department are to be paid, upon the warrant of the Superintendent of Insurance, approved by the State Auditor. This act was amended by chapter 48 of the laws of 1909. Section 11 of chapter 5 of the laws of 1905, as amended by section 2 of chapter 48 of the laws of 1909, requires,

"All insurance companies, partnerships or associations engaged in the transaction of the business of insurance in this Territory shall annually on or before the 1st day of February in each year, pay to the Superintendent of Insurance two per centum on the gross amount of premiums received, less returned premiums within this Territory.

during the year ending the previous 31st day of December."

Section 16 of the Act of 1905, as amended by section 4 of the Act of 1909, provides that,

"No insurance company organized by any other author- ity than the Territory of New Mexico shall, directly or in- directly issue policies, take risks or transact business in the Territory until it shall have first appointed, in writ- ing, the Superintendent of Insurance to be the true and lawful attorney of such company in and for this Territory, upon whom all lawful processes in any action or proceed- ings against the company may be served with the same effect as if the company existed in this Territory. Said power of attorney shall stipulate and agree upon the part of the company, that any lawful process against the com- pany which (when) served on said attorney shall be of legal force and validity as if served upon the company and that the authority shall continue in force so long as any liability remains outstanding against the company in this Territory. A certificate of such appointment. duly certi- fied and authenticated, shall be filed in the office of the Superintendent of Insurance, and copy certified by him shall be deemed sufficient evidence; service upon such at- torney shall be deemed sufficient service upon the prin- cipal."

Section 6 of the Act of 1909, provides,

"That in this act, unless the context otherwise requires, 'Company' or 'Insurance Company' shall include all cor- porations, associations, partnerships or individuals engaged as principals in the insurance business, excepting frater- nal and benevolent orders and societies."

Section 25 of the Act of 1905, as amended by section 41, laws 1909, requires all fraternal, benevolent or relig- ious societies or associations, whether operating under the lodge system or otherwise, to designate the Superintend- ent of Insurance as its attorney upon whom processes may be served, and requires all such societies to make annual reports to the Superintendent of Insurance, and to pay an annual fee of $5.00, but otherwise they are expressly ex- empted from all the provisions of the two acts.

The two acts contain quite a comprehensive system of inspection and regulation, both of foreign and domestic insurance companies, with power in the Superintendent of Insurance to revoke the authority of any company to do business in the State.

This was the state of the law at the adoption of the Constitution. By that instrument it was provided in section 6, of article XI, as follows:

"Subject to the provisions of this Constitution, and of such requirements, rules and regulations as may be prescribed by law, the State Corporation Commission shall be the department through which shall be issued all char ters for domestic corporations and amendments or extensions thereof, and all licenses to foreign corporations to do business in this State; and through which shall be carried out all the provisions of this Constitution relating to corporations and the laws made in pursuance thereof. The commission shall prescribe the form of all reports which may be required of corporations by this Constitution or by law, and shall collect, receive and preserve such reports, and annually tabulate and publish them. All fees required by law to be paid for the filing of articles of incorporation, reports and other documents, shall be collected by the commission and paid into the State treasury. All charters, papers and documents relating to corporations on file in the office of the Secretary of the Territory, the Commissioner of Insurance and all other territorial offices, shall be transferred to the office of the commission."

It appears from this section of the Constitution that an an entire transfer of all of the powers of the supervision and control of insurance corporations from the Superintendent of Insurance to the Corporation Commission was contemplated. The Superintendent of Insurance is required to transfer to the Corporation Commission all charters, papers and documents relating to corporations on file in his office. The Corporation Commission is declared to be the agency through which all of the provisions of the Constitution, or laws made in pursuance thereof, shall be carried out.

Section 4, article XXII, of the Constitution, brought

forward such laws of the Territory as were not inconsistent with the Constitution. There is nothing inconsistent between insurance laws of the Territory and the State Constitution in regard to the regulation of insurance companies, except that the powers of regulation shall be exercised by the Corporation Commission instead of the Superintendent of Insurance. But this provision of the Constitution is not self-executing. It announces a general principle or rule which requires legislation to make it effective. This is at once apparent. Had the section provided that the chairman of the Corporation Commission or any member thereof should have and exercise until otherwise provided by law, all the powers exercised by the Superintendent of Insurance under the Territorial laws, and that each insurance company should appoint said chairman or member its attorney in fact to receive service of process as now required in regard to the Superintendent of Insurance, then the section would be self-executing and no legislation would be required to carry it into effect. Then the Corporation Commission might investigate insurance companies and might cancel permits or licenses to do business, and might receive service of process for insurance companies, and otherwise do and perform all of the functions of the office of Superintendent of Insurance, and insurance companies would be compelled to appoint said Corporation Commission as attorney in fact to receive such service of process, and pay the two per centum to the commission. But such is not the case, and no legislation has been had in aid of the constitutional provision. Chapter 78, laws 1912, the only act of the State legislature in this regard, refers to the procedure before the Corporation Commission in cases involving transportation and transmission companies, and no mention is made of insurance corporations.

Section 9, of article 22 of the Constitution, provides as follows:

"All courts existing, and all persons holding offices or appointments under authority of said Territory, at the time of the admission of the State, shall continue to hold and exercise their respective jurisdictions, functions, offices and appointments until superseded by the courts, officers, or authorities provided for by this Constitution."

We have then the anomalous situation of the Constitution providing a general rule for the regulation of the insurance corporations by the Corporation Commission, but no legislation to carry it into effect, and we have a territorial officer charged by the laws with the regulation of insurance corporations and unincorporated associations, and who was continued in office by the Constitution until "superseded by the * * * authorities provided for by this Constitution."

Under such circumstances, evidently the office of Superintendent of Insurance has not been abolished. The Corporation Commission has not "superseded" the Superintendent of Insurance, because it has not been clothed with the necessary powers by legislation to carry into effect the constitutional provision. Certain powers are specifically conferred by the Constitution, section 6, article 11.
1 supra, and such the Corporation Commission may exercise without legislation. But the larger portion of the powers over insurance companies and associations still remain with the Superintendent of Insurance.

The question as to whether the office of Superintendent of Insurance has been abolished and whether he might still receive service of process for insurance companies, was considered by our own Federal Court, and Judge Pope reached the same conclusion. Mitchell v. National Surety Co., 206 Fed. 807.

It would seem that such a state of affairs could hardly have arisen anywhere, but it has in Kansas, Michigan, and Florida.

In Kansas the territorial legislature was in session when the State was admitted on January 29, 1861. This legislature passed an act on January 31, 1861, which was the subject of controversy in State v. Meadows, 1 Kan. 91. The language of the schedule of the Kansas Constitution was:

"The governor, secretary and judges, and all other officers, both civil and military, under the territorial government, shall continue in the exercise of the duties of their respective departments until the said officers are superseded under the authority of this Constitution."

The Court said: "It was, without doubt, competent for the Constitution, by its terms, to provide against an inter· regnum, by adopting the territorial officers and machinery, and making the existing functionaries of the Territory the officers of the State for the time being, to secure the means of preserving by legal steps the enforcement of the laws. That they designed so to do, and to fill every department of the State government in this ·way until superseded by the action of the State government, provided for elsewhere in the Constitution, would seem to be apparent from the language above quoted. The expression, 'all other officers,' is very broad and comprehensive. It could hardly have been made more so. Members of the legislature, not only in the common use and acceptation, but in the technical and legal sense of the term, are officers of the government.

"The legislature of the State could, by no process of reasoning, be considered as superseding the territorial legislature before the issuing of the proclamation of the governor convening them."

The Florida case was one where a territorial court exercised jurisdiction of a Federal cause after the admission of the State into the Union. The Supreme Court of the United States, in Benner v. Porter, 9 How. 235, held that all Federal jurisdiction in territorial courts ceased on admission of the State, but in comment on the transition from the territorial to State government, said:

"It will be seen, therefore, under this ordinance of the Constitution, that, on the admission of Florida as a State into the Union, the organization of the government under the new Constitution became complete, as every department became filled at once by the adoption of the territorial functionaries for the time being. The convention being the fountain of all political power, from which flowed that which was embodied in the organic law, were, of course, competent to prescribe the laws and appoint the officers under the Constitution, by means whereof the government could be put into immediate operation, and thus

avoid and interregnum that must have intervened if left to
an organization according to the provisions of that instrument. This was accomplished by a few lines adopting the
machinery of the territorial government for the time being, and until superseded by the agency and authority of
the Constitution itself."

In Michigan the territorial government was organized
in 1805, but under the Ordinance of 1787 for the government of the Northwest Territory, Michigan had a right to
form a State government at any time whenever the Territory should contain sixty thousand free white male inhabitants. This was done, and, prior to March 26, 1836, a
full State government was in operation, although Congress
did not formally admit the State into the Union until
January 26, 1837. In the meantime a corporation was
formed under the laws of the new State, and received the
conveyance from the board of governors and judges, who,
besides performing the ordinary functions of government
of the Territory, were granted certain powers of conveyance of government land in and about Detroit, of which
the land in controversy was a part. The Court held that
the State government was lawfully established and its acts
were valid before the State was formally admitted by
Congress, and further said:

"Were the powers and duties of the Governor and Judges
such as we have seen them to be, under these various acts
of Congress referred to, superseded by the organization of
the State government? And were these offices absolutely
and for all purposes, vacated and determined by that
event?

"If determined at what time? The change, from a
territorial to a State government, was not, and from necessity could not be, instantaneous. Indeed, our Constitution itself contemplated that there could be no such sud-
den transition, for the fifth section of the Schedule (of
just as high authority as the Constitution) declares, that
'all officers, civil and military, now holding their offices
and appointments in this Territory, under the authority
of the United States, or under the authority of this Territory, shall continue to hold and exercise their respective

offices and appointments, until superseded under this Constitution.' The act of the State legislature providing for the appointment of Judges of the Supreme Court of the State, did not take effect, nor did such Judges enter upon the term of their offices, until after July 4, 1836. The Judges of the Territory, therefore, continued to hold their offices, and to discharge the duties thereof, until after that time." Scott v. Detroit Young Men's Society, 1 Doug. (Mich.) 119, 143.

It seems plain, therefore, that the Superintendent of Insurance, a territorial officer, still remains in office and may exercise all the functions of his office, except such as are specifically transferred to the Corporation Commission by the Constitution.

As before seen, the Act of 1905 created the office of Superintendent of Insurance, and provided a permanent salary for him. This amounted to a continuing appropriation out of the Insurance fund, and required no subsequent appropriations by the legislature. State, ex rel Fornoff, v. Sargent, 136 Pac. 602.

The legislature of 1907 made no appropriation for the salary of Superintendent. The legislature of 1909, however, made a specific appropriation of $2400 for salary of the Superintendent, $1400 for clerk and $600 for contingent expenses, per year, for the 61st and 62nd fiscal years, and extended appropriations, together with all others, from year to year until another appropriation bill should be passed. Chap. 127, secs. 4 and 11, Laws 1909.

The State legislature of 1912 made no appropriation for the officers of the Insurance department, and, on the other hand, diverted all of the surplus moneys in the Insurance fund and attempted to provide that all moneys received in the future by the Insurance department should be covered into the State Salary fund. Chapter 83, sections 18 and 21, Laws 1912.

These two sections were considered in State, ex rel. Delgado, v. Sargent, 134 Pac. 218, in which we held that the last paragraph of section 18 was unconstitutional because general legislation, and that section 21 diverted only such portion of the Insurance fund as was not required to meet existing appropriations. While we held the last paragraph of section 18 unconstitutional because it antagonized section 16 of art. IV of the Constitution, the fact nevertheless remains that by the passage of the paragraph, there was clearly manifested a legislative intent to discontinue and abolish the Insurance fund, and to cover all funds received in the future into the State Salary fund. The legislature failed, not by reason of want of intent, but by reason of constitutional restriction, to accomplish its purpose.

The legislature of 1913, by section 9 of chapter 83 of that session, appropriated out of the general funds of the State, and up to March 15, 1913, for salary of Superintendent $700, and for salary of clerk, $406 and for contingent expenses, $175. This clearly indicates legislative intent to pay the Superintendent by appropriation, and not out of the Insurance fund, and to stop all pay after March 15, 1913. It is true this item was vetoed by the Governor, but the fact remains that the legislature attempted to accomplish this result.

We shall not attempt to define what effect in interpretation or construction of prior statutes the passage of an unconstitutional provision or a provision which may be vetoed by the executive may have. By reason of the provisions of another act, of the session of 1909, it becomes unnecessary to do so. We deem the latter act controlling.

It will be remembered that under the Act of 1905, sec. 12, all expenses of the Insurance department, including salaries, were to be paid out of the Insurance funds, "on warrants drawn on such fund by the Superintendent of Insurance and approved by the Territorial Auditor." In direct conflict with this provision, chapter 40, laws of 1909, provides that the Territorial Treasurer shall pay out no funds which shall come into his hands "except on warrant of the Territorial Auditor." The warrant of the Superintendent of Insurance on the Insurance fund, approved by the Auditor, is not the warrant of the Auditor. This provision alone is decisive of this case adverse to the relator. He is seeking to compel the approval of his warrant on the Insurance fund by the Auditor, which, as is seen, is now prohibited by law. Chapter 40, laws of 1909, was not called to our attention on argument, nor was it relied upon by respondent in his answer. He relied, as before seen, upon the fact that the salary of the Superintendent of Insurance was now payable out of specific appropriations, and there being none, he was not authorized to approve warrants for the same. But even so, the legislative intent to depart permanently from the policy of paying the Superintendent of Insurance on his own warrants, out of the Insurance fund is made certain by the chapter.

In this connection it is to be noted that, since the passage of the Act of 1909, the Superintendent of Insurance has never drawn his salary from the Insurance fund. He continued to draw his salary under the general appropriation bill of 1909 until December 1, 1912. The Superintendent of Insurance and the Territorial Auditor immediately interpreted the Act of 1909 as a departure from the theory of the Act of 1905, and the Auditor issued his warrants on the Salary fund, not the Insurance fund, and the Superintendent of Insurance accepted the same, and discontinued drawing warrants on the Insurance fund.

It is to be regretted that this anomalous condition exists. We have here a faithful public servant, charged with the duty of performance of the major portion of the powers in regard to the supervision and regulation of insurance companies, and there is no other officer properly clothed with power to perform the same. And yet there is no provision of law whereby he can be paid. This is due, no doubt, to mistake on the part of the legislature in assuming that the constitutional provision is fully self-executing, and that the Corporation Commission has succeeded to all the powers of the Superintendent of Insurance. But he is in no worse position than are all of the County officers of the State, owing to the differences of opinion between the legislative and executive departments of the State. It may not be unreasonable to assume that both those departments will realize that relator is entitled to his salary and that they will provide the same at the next session of the legislature.

Canavan v. Canavan, 18 N. M. 640.

For the reasons stated, the judgment of the court below
will be reversed and the cause remanded with instructions
to dismiss the writ of mandamus, and it is so ordered.

]No. 1562, February 23, 1914.[
STEPHEN CANAVAN, et al., Plaintiffs in Error, v.
KATE CANAVAN, Defendant in Error.

SYLLABUS (BY THE COURT)

1. The proceedings examined and held to be proceedings
as for civil contempt.

P. 642

2. A final decree dissolves a preliminary injunction which
is ancillary to the main case unless the same is specially continued by the decree, and thereafter a litigant cannot be punished as for civil contempt for violation of the preliminary
injunction prior to its dissolution.

P. 645

Error to the District Court of McKinley County; Herbert F. Raynolds, District Judge; reversed and remanded.

E. W. DOBSON, Albuquerque; CHARLES A. SPIESS, Las
Vegas, and MANN & VENABLE, Albuquerque, N. M., for
plaintiff in error.

The order adjudging Canavan in contempt was made
after final decree and after the restraining order had
ceased to be effective. It not being carried forward by the
final decree. Gardner v. Gardner, 87 N. Y. 14; People,
ex rel. Morris, v. Randall, 73 N. Y. 416; State against
Bruce, et al., 45 S. E. 153; Sweeney v. Hanley, 126 Fed.
197; 10 Enc. Pl. & Pr. 1029; Beach on Injunction, sec.
109; Gompers v. Buck Stove & Range Co., 221 U. S. 446,
55 L. Ed. 809.

Upon the entry of the final decree the temporary injunction came to an end. Gardner v. Gardner, 87 N. Y.

14; Eureka Con. Min. Co. v. Richmond Min. Co., 5 Sawy. 121; Fed. Cas. No. 4549; 10 Enc. Pl. & Pr. 1029; Buffington v. Harvey, 95 U. S. 99, 24 L. Ed. 381.

If a temporary order is violated, the court has no jurisdiction after the dissolution of the injunction to punish for its violation as for contempt. Moat v. Holbein, 2 Edw. Chan. 188; Clark's Case, 12 Cush. 320; State v. Rive, 67 S. C. 236, 45 S. E. 153; Peck v. Yorks, 32 How. Pr. 408; U. S. v. Price, 1 Alaska, 204; Smith v. McQuade, 13 N. Y. Sup. 63; Ex Parte Maulsby, 13 Md. 625; In re Fanning, 40 Minn. 4; Robertson v. Bingley, 1 McCord Eq. (S. C.) 333; State v. Matthews, 49 S. E. 199, 27 S. E. 52; Rapalje on Contempt, sec. 50; Taber v. Manhattan Ry. Co., 35 N. Y. Sup. 465.

This is a civil and not a criminal contempt. 9 Cyc. 6; In re Wilson, 17 Pac. 608; Wyatt v. The People, 28 Pac. 961; Holbrook v. Ford, 153 Ill. 633, 27 L. R. A. 324; People v. Oyer & Term., 101 N. Y. 245; Gompers v. Buck Stove & Range Co., 221 U. S. 446, 55 L. Ed. 809; In re Nevitt, 54 C. C. A. 622, 117 Fed. 451; Bessette v. Conkey Co., 194 U. S. 324, 48 L. Ed. 997; Rapalje on Contempts, sec. 21.

Being a civil contempt and the object of the contempt proceedings being to afford relief to the complainant, the final decree is a bar to any relief not awarded therein. 23 Cyc. 1108; In re Ambrose, 72 Cal. 378, 14 Pac. 33; Randall v. Dusenberry, 41 N. Y. Sp. Ct., (9 Jones & S. 456.)

The judgment committing appellant to jail for contempt amounts to an imprisonment for debt in a civil action, and is in conflict with section 21 of the Bill of Rights contained in the Constitution of New Mexico. In re Jaramillo, 8 N. M. 600; Bill of Rights, Const. N. M., sec. 21.

VIGIL & JAMISON and A. T. HANNETT, Albuquerque, N. M., for defendant in error.

OPINION OF THE COURT.

PARKER, J.—This is an appeal from a judgment in a contempt proceeding. The appellant has been before the Court on two former occasions. See Ex Parte Canavan,

130 Pac. 248, and Canavan v. Canavan, 131 Pac. 493. The facts sufficiently appear in those cases, and will not be here repeated. The first case was a habeas corpus proceeding upon a partial and imperfect record. It did not appear from the record in that case that the Court was without jurisdiction, and we held that habeas corpus was not a proper remedy. In the second case, we refused to review the judgment in the contempt proceeding because it was rendered after the final decree in the divorce case, and was, consequently, not reviewable on appeal from the final decree. In this case, however, the appeal is brought directly from the judgment in the contempt proceeding. The question now is as to whether the judgment in the contempt proceeding was erroneous.

Counsel for appellant relied upon several propositions, two of which only will be considered.

It is first asserted that the alleged contempt is a civil contempt. This was practically assumed in Canavan v. Canavan, supra, and is now so decided. Counsel have alleged, in support of this conclusion, first, that all of the affidavits, motions and orders of the court in the contempt proceeding are entitled and filed in the original divorce proceeding. While this fact may not always be controlling, it is always a strong circumstance tending to show that the proceeding is civil and not criminal. Second, counsel urge that the form of the prayer of the plaintiff to the effect that the court commit appellant to jail until he turns over the $19,000 decreed to the plaintiff, is controlling. This fact we deem of the highest importance and determinative of the character of the proceeding. Third, counsel suggests that the judgment in contempt itself in adjudging costs to the plaintiff, characterizes the proceeding as civil. It must be apparent that if the proceeding were criminal, no costs could be awarded the plaintiff. Costs in such a case would go into the public treasury. Fourth, counsel urges that the coercive nature of the judgment itself fixes the character of the proceeding. It clearly appears from the judgment that the object sought to be attained thereby was to secure the payment of the decree to the plaintiff. With all of these sug-

1

gestions we agree and they are undoubtedly the law on the subject.

Gompers v. Buck Stove & Range Co., 221 U. S. 418, 34 L. R. A. (N. S.) 874.

Our own Territorial Court has pointed out the true rule on this subject in Costilla Land & Investment Co. v. Allen, 15 N. M. 528, 110 Pac. 874, where it is said:

"The border line between what may be termed civil and what criminal contempt is, as has been pointed out by many authorities, exceedingly indistinct and narrow, leaving it often a question of extreme refinement as to whether the act was one or the other. Of course all judgments for contempt are in a sense punitive since the sentence imposed, even if simply to preserve private rights and even if the so-called fine go to the litigant purely by way of reimbursement, has the effect to punish the recalcitrant and to declare the purpose of the court that its orders shall not be trifled with. The authorities, however, draw a distinction between those contempts where the protection of the court and a vindication of its dignity are the main objects of the proceeding and those where a mere effective remedy to private litigants is after all the purpose of what is done."

Counsel for appellant take the second position as follows: The injunction, for the alleged violation of which appellant was committed, was a preliminary injunction, and was merged into or dissolved by the final decree of divorce which made no reference to the same; this being true, it is asserted, there remains no power in the court to punish for civil contempt after merger or dissolution of the injunction, even if the same was in fact violated while it was in force.

The first half of the proposition seems to be well established, and to be uniformly recognized. Thus Mr. High states the rule as follows:

"But when the injunction is merely ancillary to the principal relief sought and is in terms granted until further order of the court, it is regarded as abrogated by the final judgment of the court granting the principal relief sought by the action and making no provision for continuing the injunction." High on Injunctions, (4th ed.) section 1503.

See also 22 Cyc. 981, where it is said: "The entry of a final decree in the injunction suit renders a temporary injunction ineffective." See also Sweeney v. Hanley, 126 Fed. 99, wherein it is said:

"It will be noticed that by this final decree the injunction theretofore granted was not continued in force. Upon the entry of the final decree the temporary injunction came to an end. Gardner v. Gardner, 87 N. Y. 14; Eureka Con. Mining Co. v. Richmond Min. Co., 121 Fed. Cases 45-49: Ency. 24, L. E. 381. A motion was subsequently made on behalf of the defendants to the suit for an order dissolving the preliminary injunction, which motion the court below denied. Whether or not it was the real reason for that action of the court, it is a sufficient reason therefore that no such injunction was then in force, it having come to an end by the entry of the final decree in the cause, making no provision for the injunction."

This must be so. The final decree always represents the determination of the court upon all the issues between parties, unless some of them are expressly reserved or excepted therefrom. It must of necessity require some special reservation, exception or continuance of the court to preserve an anterior ancillary order in the form of an injunction issued for the purpose of preserving the status of property *pendente lite*.

The second half of the proposition is of more difficulty. On principle it would seem that a party to an equity proceeding who has been enjoined from removing the estate which is the subject of litigation from the jurisdiction, and who has violated the injunction and who has thereby defeated his antagonist from collecting the amount of the decree which has been awarded against him, certainly should be punishable by the coercive remedy of a proceeding as for civil contempt, until he shall pay the judgment. One's sense of right and wrong would seem to sanction the proposition. But when examined more carefully, it would seem not to be sound. It is to be remembered that an injunction is a rule of conduct merely imposed for the

time being, upon a litigant by the properly constituted authority. But for the injunction the acts against which it is directed may be lawfully performed. If the litigant
2 violates the injunction during its existence, he may be punished as for civil or criminal contempt, or both. But if the injunction be dissolved, what was unlawful when it was in force, because prohibited by it, becomes lawful and no basis remains upon which to predicate a proceeding in contempt. The principle runs through other branches of the law. For instance, if a statute prohibits the doing of any given act, the citizen may be punished for doing it so long as the statute remains in force. But if the statute be repealed and the legislature fails to provide that the statute shall remain in force as to all prior violations of the act, that which was unlawful has become lawful, and no prosecutions can be had. While the criminal in morals is still a criminal, in legal contemplation the law has released him from his criminality. Just so with injunctions. A person violating an injunction and thereby defrauding his adversary of the fruits of his cause of action, is still guilty in morals, but in legal contemplation the law has dicsharged him of his offense.

A different principle would seem to govern in case of criminal contempt, but we will not discuss the same, it not being involved. In actions for civil contempt the duty commanded by the injunction no longer exists after the dissolution. In order to punish for a civil contempt it would seem that there must be a present rule of conduct subsisting and in force together with the acts violating the same.

Comparatively little satisfactory authority is to be found on the subject. It is said in Spelling on Injunctions and Extraordinary Legal Remedies, section 1129, that this is the correct rule, and he cites one case, that of Moat v. Holbein, 2 Edw. Ch. (N. Y.) 188. The opinion is by the Vice-Chancellor, and is not at all satisfactory in its discussion of the proposition, but it seems to be the earliest case to be found.

In Peck v. Yorks, 32 How. Pr. (N. Y.) 408, the same doctrine is announced and a very well considered opinion is rendered by the Court, in which it is said:

State v. Armijo, 18 N. M. 646.

"An injunction, which is but an order of the court, can have no more force or extended operation after it is set aside or modified than a statute repealed or modified, in regard to acts previously done. In either case, the rule being abolished, the infraction of it is abolished also, and nothing remains on which a conviction can be based."

See also Tabor v. Manhattan Ry. Co., 35 N. Y. S. 465, to the same effect.

In Gompers v. The Buck Stove & Range Co., supra, while the exact point was not involved which is involved here, a similar proposition. was involved and the court held that by reason of the settlement of the main case, the ancillary proceedings by way of injunction had come to an end, and that, therefore, no proceedings for civil contempt could be maintained.

We, therefore, hold that the proceeding in this case, be- ing a proceeding as for civil contempt, and being a proceeding for a violation of a preliminary injunction after the same had been merged and dissolved, and for acts alleged to have been committed prior to its dissolution, is not maintainable.

It follows from what has been said, that the judgment of the court below is erroneous and the same will be reversed, and the cause remanded to the District Court with directions to proceed in accordance with this opinion.

]No. 1519, April 20, 1914.[

STATE OF NEW MEXICO, Appellant, v. LOLA CHAVES de ARMIJO, Appellee.

SYLLABUS (BY THE COURT)

1. The right to hold a public office is not a natural right. It exists, where it exists at all, only because and by virtue of some law expressly or impliedly conferring it.

P. 650

2. The right may be conferred by act of the legislature, or exist by virtue of the common law, in those jurisdictions

where the common law is in force, and no statute expressly or impliedly denies the right.

P. 650

3. Section 1 of chapter 134, S. L. 1909, which provides that "No person prevented by the Organic Act of the Territory of New Mexico * * * * shall be entitled to vote or hold public office in this Territory," refers to the original act of Congress creating the Territory of New Mexico, and the only limitations thereby imposed upon the right to vote or hold public office are that such rights shall be exercised only by citizens of the United States, including those recognized as citizens by the treaty with the Republic of Mexico, etc.

P. 652

4. The statutory law of the Territory of New Mexico neither expressly conferred or denied the right of women to vote or hold public office, hence we must look to the common law, if it was in force in the Territory, to ascertain and determine the right of women to vote and hold public office.

P. 653

5. The common law is the rule of practice and decision in New Mexico, by virtue of section 2871, R. S. 1897, except where modified by statute.

P. 654

6. The office of State Librarian is in ministerial office.

P. 656

7. Under the common law, a woman was eligible to hold a purely ministerial office, whatever might be the nature of the office, if she was capable of performing the duties thereof, and there was no incompatibility between the nature and character of the duties of the office and their due performance by a woman, where, in so doing, she was not called upon to exercise judgment and discretion.

P. 656

8. Such political rights as were recognized by the com-

mon law, and not in conflict with our established laws, institutions and customs, and suitable to our conditions was
carried into the body of our law.

P. 659

9. The appellee, being rightfully in office at the time of
the adoption of the Constitution, she was continued in .office
by virtue of section 9, article XXII of the Constitution.

P. 666

Appeal from the District Court of Santa Fe County;
Edmund C. Abbott, District Judge; affirmed.

Renehan & Wright, Santa Fe, N. M., for appellee.

Laws of Territory, not inconsistent with the Constitution, shall remain in force. Const. N. M., art. XXII, sec.
4; Id., sec. 9.

Women may hold the office of notary public and such
other appointive offices as may be provided by law. Const.
(N. M.), art. XX, sec. 77.

In all the courts of this Territory, the common law as
recognized in the United States of America, shall be the
rule of practice and decision. C. L. 1897, sec. 2871;
Browning v. Browning, 3 N. M. 671; sec. 1823, C. L. 1884.

Right of women to hold office. Robinson's Case, 131
Mass. 376; Bradwell's Case, 55 Ill. 535; 62 Me. 597;
Mechem on Public Officers, sec. 73; 66 N. H. 207; 73 N.
H. 621; Opinion of the Justice, 115 Mass. 602: Wright v.
Noll, 16 Kans. 602; Huff v. Cook, 44 Ia. 639: State, ex
rel., v. Hoffstetter, 137 Mo. 636, 38 L. R. A. 208; Id.,
note.

Office of State Librarian is a ministerial office. C. L.
1897, Tit., 23.

"As may be provided by law" is equivalent to the ex-
pression "as may have been provided by law." Vol. 5,
Words & Phrases, p. 4449: Griggs v. City of St. Paul, 56
Minn. 150, 57 N. W. 461.

The office is appointive and not elective. Const. (N.
M.) art. VII, secs. 1 and 2; Territory v. Maxwell, 2 N.

M. 268-9; Browning v. Browning, 3 N. M. 674; Kirchner
v. Laughlin, 4 N. M. 394; Childers v. Talbott, 4 N. M.
336; Territory v. Ashenfelter, 4 N. M. 109; Eberle v. Carmichael, 8 N. M. 698; Byerts v. Robinson, 9 N. M. 431;
Albright v. Territory, 13 N. M. 133; Ry. Co. v. Cazier,
13 N. M. 133; Sandoval v. Albright, 14 N. M. 349; Rad-
cliff v. Chavez, 15 N. M. 264.

FRANK W. CLANCY, Santa Fe, Attorney General; FELIX
LESTER and SUMMERS BURKHART, Albuquerque, N. M.,
for appellant.

RENEHAN & WRIGHT, for appellee; supplemental brief
on re-argument.

Revised Statutes of U. S., secs. 1859-60.
Can a State office be a local office? Vol. 7, Words &
Phrases, title "State Officers;" People v. Nixon, 158 N. Y.
221; State v. Dillon, 90 Mo. 229; State v. Burns, 38 Fla.
367; In re Board of Health, 60 N. Y. Supp. 27.
Effect of sections 1859 and 1860 of the Revised Statutes
of the United States; and the effect of sec. 2871, C. L.
1897, upon the provisions of sections 1859 and 1860 of the
Rev. Stat. of U. S.; Ex Parte DeVore, 18 N. M. 246.
Distinction between Civil and Political Rights. Fletcher
v. Tuttle, 151 Ill. 41, 42 Am. St. Rep. 220; State, ex rel.
v. Quible, 125 N. W. 619; State v. Cones, 15 Neb. 444,
19 N. W. 682.
Right of a woman to hold office at Common Law. State,
ex rel. Hostetter, 137 Mo. 636, 38 L. R. A. 208, and note:
State ex rel. v. Quible, 125 N. W. 619.
Specific statute making women eligible to appointive of-
fices. Laws 1913, ch. 60; Constitution of N. M., art.
XXII, sec. 9.

OPINION OF THE COURT.

ROBERTS, C. J.—This is a quo warranto proceeding
to oust the respondent from the office of State Librarian.
The sole basis for the proceeding is the fact of the alleged
ineligibility of the respondent to hold the office on account

of sex, she being a woman. The District Court held that the respondent was eligible and dismissed the petition, and the State appealed.

A discussion of the matter involved would seem naturally to present the following inquiries, viz:—

1. What is the nature of the right to hold public office, and what is the source of that right?

2. What provision, either statutory or common law, or both, had been made in this jurisdiction in that regard prior to the adoption of the State Constitution?

3. What effect, if any, did the Constitution have upon the right?

It may be stated that the right to hold a public office is not a natural right. It exists, where it exists at all,

1   only because and by virtue of some law expressly or impliedly conferring it. Mechem on Public Officers, sec. 64, 29 Cyc. 1375. It may be conferred by act of the legislature, as is usually the case, or exist by virtue of the common law, in those jurisdictions where the common

2   law is in force, and no statute expressly or impliedly denies the right. In the latter case recourse must of course be had to the common law to determine the limitations upon, and extent of the right.

It therefore becomes necessary to examine the condition of the law in this jurisdiction in regard to the right of women to hold office. The Territory of New Mexico was organized by the Act of Congress of September 9, 1850. Section 6 of that act provides:—

"That every free white male inhabitant, above the age of twenty-one years, who shall have been a resident of said Territory at the time of the passage of this act, shall be entitled to vote at the first election, and shall be eligible to any office within said Territory; but the qualifications of voters and of holding office at all subsequent elections, shall be such as shall be prescribed by the legislative assembly; *Provided*, that the right of suffrage, and of holding office, shall be exercised only by citizens of the United States, including those recognized as citizens by the treaty with the Republic of Mexico, concluded February second, eighteen hundred and forty-eight."

The provisions of this section appear in R. S. U. S. of 1878, as sections 1859 and 1860, in somewhat different language, but in the view we take of the case such revised sections are of no, importance in determining the issues involved herein.

By an act of the Territorial legislature, approved July 20, 1851, which will be found on page 196 of the Session Laws of 1851, a complete election law was enacted. Section 19 of the act defined the qualifications of voters and of holding elective office as follows:—

"Sec. 19. Every white male citizen of the United States, over twenty-one years of age, who shall have resided in the Territory one year, and in the county in which he offers to vote, for three months shall be entitled to vote and be elected to office in any election provided for in this act, unless in the cases hereinafter specified."

By this section it will be observed that the right to vote is limited to white *male* citizens of the United States, who possess the required qualifications as to residence. Likewise, by the section no one could be "elected to office, in any election provided for in this act," unless he possessed the required qualifications. Under this section a woman was debarred from voting and could not be elected to any office, at any election held under the act in question. Section 21 of the same act reads as follows:

"Section 21. No person prevented by the organic law of the Territory, no officer or soldier in the United States army, and no person included in the term 'camp followers' of the United States army shall be entitled to vote or hold office in this Territory." It will be observed that the latter section is broader in its scope than section 19. It denies the right to hold office, either elective or appointive, to any person "prevented by the organic law of. the Territory." Section 19, insofar as it prescribed the qualification of voters, was evidently superseded by the registration law, which required all voters to be registered, and prescribed the qualifications required for registration, which will be found as sec. 1703, C. L. 1897, and permitting all registered voters to vote; sec. 1706, C. L. 1897, section 21, supra, however, was carried into the compilation of 1897 in its original form, as section 1647. It will, therefore, be seen that sec. 19, of the original act is of no importance, in this case, except as an aid to the proper construction of section 21. Section 21, supra, was amended by chapter 21, S. L. 1907, and again by chapter 134, S. L. 1909. The amendment of 1907, need not be set out, as it is, insofar as material, in the same identical language as sec. 1, of chapter 134, S. L. 1909, which, insofar as pertinent, reads as follows:

"Sec. 1. No person prevented by the organic act of the Territory of New Mexico, * * * * shall be entitled to vote or hold public office in this Territory; * * * * ."

It will be observed that the original section used the term "organic law," whereas the amendment refers to the "organic act," thus clearly meaning the original Act of Congress, creating the Territory, and not the section of the Revised Statutes of 1878, hereinbefore referred to. It is

3 evident, therefore, that we must look to the terms of the organic act to determine who were prevented from holding office, by its terms. It prescribes the right of suffrage and of holding office at the first election, and then provides that the qualifications of voters and of holding office at all subsequent elections shall be prescribed by the legislative assembly, and concludes with the following proviso: *"Provided,* That the right of suffrage, and of holding office, shall be exercised only by citizens of the United States, including those recognized as citizens by the treaty with the Republic of Mexico ,concluded, etc." From a reading of the section, it would appear to the legal mind that the proviso was a limitation upon legislative power and that it was intended to operate directly upon the right of suffrage. But in what light did the legislative assemblies regard the proviso when they referred to the limitations upon the right of suffrage and of holding office contained in section 21 of the original act and the amendments thereto? It is clear that they treated it as an independent section, and as a limitation upon the right itself, rather than a legislative limitation. The only limitations upon the right, or the only reference to the sub-

ject, in the organic act, are found in the section above
quoted.   It must be apparent that the legislature did not
refer to the limitations upon the right of suffrage and of
holding office at the first election, for to so hold would
present insurmountable absurdities.   For instance, at the
first election the right was confined to "free white male
inhabitants."   Now is it to be presumed that the legislature
in 1907 and 1909 would attempt to violate the Fifteenth
Amendment of the Constitution of the United States, and
the Act of Congress making such amendment applicable
to territories?   Again the section limits the right of suffrage and of holding office, at the first election to free
white male inhabitants "who shall have been a resident of
said Territory at the time of the passage of this act," consequently, should we hold that the limitations referred to,
were those prescribed for the first election, it would necessarily result that the legislature, as late as 1909 was attempting to deny the right of suffrage to all those, who
were not residents of New Mexico in 1850.   Such, of
course, was never the intention, and, therefore, the legislature necessarily must have had in view the limitations contained in the proviso, and intended that the right of suffrage and of holding office should be exercised only by citizens of the United States, including those recognized as
citizens by the treaty with the Republic of Mexico, etc.

"The Supreme Court of the United States, in Minor v.
Happersett, 21 Wall. 162, has held that the word 'citizen,'
as used in the Constitution and Laws of the United States,
has uniformly conveyed the idea of membership of a nation, and nothing more, and hence include either sex
alike."   Cronly v. City of Tucson, 56 Pac. 876, (Arizona.)

Hence, from a review of the statute law of the Territory,
it will be seen that there was no express denial of the right
of suffrage, or of holding office, to women, neither was
4   the right granted in terms.   In this connection it is
to be remembered that the civil law of Spain and Mexico was in force in this Territory at the time of the original enactment by the territorial legislature, under which
women had no such right as is contended for, and this re-

mained the situation until January 7, 1876, when the
5 act was passed by the legislature, adopting the common
law in this jurisdiction. This appears as section
2871, R. S. 1897, and reads as follows:

"In all the courts in this Territory the common law as
recognized in the United States of America, shall be the
rule of practice and decision."

There being no statute, either denying or conferring the
right of suffrage and of holding office upon a woman, it is
clear that we must look to the common law, if the above
section adopted it in New Mexico, to ascertain and determine the right of women to vote and hold office. Under
the common law, the right of women to vote, was, of course,
never recognized, and such right is not involved in this
case, but merely the right to hold an appointive office,
which is purely ministerial. Before discussing the right
of a woman to hold such an office, under the common law,
it will be necessary to dispose of appellant's contention,
viz.: That the civil law and not the common law, is in
force here, except where modified by statute. In support
of the contention, Ward v. Broadwell, 1 N. M. 85; Chaves
v. McKnight, 1 N. M. 147; Ilfeld v. Baca, 14 N. M. 65,
are cited and relied upon. The first two cases cited were
decided long prior to the passage of the Act of January 7,
1876, and at the time such decisions were rendered the
civil law was in force in New Mexico, except where changed
by statute, or abrogated by the organic act. No such point
was involved in the last case cited. On the other hand, as
early as 1886, in the case of Browning v. Est. of Browning,
3 N. M. 659, the Supreme Court of New Mexico construed
the above statute and held:—

"The legislature intended by the language used in that
section to adopt the common law, or *Lex non scripta,* and
such British statutes of a general nature not local to that
kingdom, nor in conflict with the Constitution or laws of
the United States, nor of this Territory, which are applicable to our condition and circumstances, and which were
in force at the time of our separation from the mother
country."

This construction of the effect of the above statute has

been consistently adhered to by the courts of the Territory for more than a quarter of a century. (Territory v. Ashenfelter, 4 N. M. 93; Dye v. Crary, 12 N. M. 160; Sandoval v. Albright, 14 N. M. 345.)

Adopting the construction of sec. 2871, supra, in the Browning case as correct, it is, therefore, necessary to inquire into the right of a woman, under the common law of England, at the time of our separation from that country, to hold such an office as Librarian of the State Library. Before reviewing the common law, however, it would perhaps be well to consider the statutes of the Territory, creating the office and defining the duties of the librarian, in order to determine the nature of the office, for, as we shall later see, under the common law, women were only permitted to hold certain offices, and their right to so hold such offices depended, to a large degree, upon the nature and duties of the office.

The statutes relating to the Territorial library, the custody and management thereof, will be found under section 2187, to and including section 2215, C. L. 1897. Under said sections the management of the library is placed in the hands of a board of trustees, and said board is given the power to adopt rules for the conduct and management thereof. All books must be purchased by the board. The act defines the duties of the Territorial Librarian, which may be briefly summarized as follows: (a) Such librarian has the care and custody of the library, (b) is to keep same in a room in the Capitol building provided for that purpose, and to provide for the safe keeping therein of all things belonging or appertaining thereto, (c) has charge of all books, maps, etc., belonging to the library or directed to be deposited therein, (e) must keep the library open during certain hours, (f) not to permit books to be removed from the library, except by certain officials, and to take a receipt for all books removed, (g) to prepare an alphabetical catalogue of the library, (h) to label each book in the library in a specified manner, (i) to report to the Governor, when required, a list of books missing and the fines collected, and to report to the legislature, (j) to institute suit, in the name and use of the Territory, for the recovery of certain penalties, for the unauthorized removal from the library of any books, etc.   From a review of the statutes upon the subject it will be found that the librarian is not required to exercise his or her judgment in any respect.   The duties are precsribed by statute or defined by rules adopted by the board of trustees. The office is purely ministerial.

6

"Ministerial offices, it is said, are those which give the officer no power to judge of the matter to be done, and which require him to obey some superior."   State v. Loechner, 65 Neb. 814, 59 L. R. A. 115.

Under the statute in question, the librarian was required to conform to the rules adopted by the board of trustees. He was given no initiative as to any matter, or power to determine any question.   He was to perform the duties prescribed by the act, and the rules of the board, in the manner directed.

"A ministerial act is defined to be 'one which a person performs in a given manner, in obedience to the mandate of legal authority, without regard to or or the exercise of his own judgment upon the propriety of the act being done.' "   Fornney v. Jefferson Vello, 17 Ind. 169, 79 Am. Dec. 468.

An officer, performing only ministerial acts, is, of course, only a ministerial officer.

The office, being purely ministerial, it remains to determine the right of a woman to hold such an office under the common law.   From a review of the American cases, where the common law rights of women to hold public office have been considered, there appears to be a decided conflict of authority upon the subject.   We have, however, been referred to no case, where the duties were so purely ministerial, in which the right to exercise the duties of the office have been denied to women.

7

In Opinion of Justices, 107 Mass. 604, the right of a woman to hold the office of Justice of the Peace was denied.   But this office, under the Constitution of that State, was a judicial office, the duties of which must be exercised by the incumbent in person.   The case cannot, therefore, be considered in point in this case, where the office is ministerial.

Again, in Lelia J. Robinson's case, 131 Mass. 376, the same court denied the right of a woman to be admitted as an attorney and counsellor of the court. The Court say:

"An attorney at law is not, indeed, in the strictest sense, a public officer. But he comes very near it. As was said by Lord Holt, 'The office of an attorney concerns the public, for it is for the administration of justice.'"

In the opinion, the Court evidently treats an attorney at law as an officer, and denies the right of a woman to be admitted thereto, because under the common law a woman was not permitted to hold any office that concerned the administration of justice, where she was required to exercise the duties of the office in person.

The same Court, later, in Opinion of Justices, 136 Mass. 578, held, that under the statutes of 1879, c. 291, sec. 2, which provided that the Governor, with the advice and consent of the council, should appoint nine persons, who should constitute a state board of health, lunacy, and charity, it was competent to appoint a woman member of the board. While the Court does not, in terms, base the right upon the common law, it does say:

"The duties of the board are mostly administrative, and are such as may well be performed by women. There is no incompatibility between the nature and character of the duties and their due performance by women," thus recognizing the common law limitations upon the right, and implying, that under the statute, a contrary doctrine would have been announced were the office under consideration one, which at common law, a woman would have no right to hold.

In an earlier case, the same Court, in Opinion of Justices, 115 Mass. 602, held, that under the Constitution a woman might be a member of a school committee. The Constitution was silent upon the question of the right, and the Court, in discussing the right of a woman to hold such an office, under the common law, say:—

"The common law of England, which was our law upon the subject, permitted a woman to fill any local office of an administrative character, the duties attached to which were such that a woman was competent to perform them."

The Supreme Court of Michigan, in the case of Attorney General v. Abbott, 121 Mich. 540, 47 L. R. A. 92, 80 N. W. 372, held that a woman could not be elected to the office of prosecuting attorney, under an article of the Constitution of that State which provided that such officers shall be "chosen by the electors," in the absence of an express provision conferring the right to hold such an office on women. The Court say:

"There being no express provision of the Constitution or laws of the State conferring upon respondent the right to hold this office, the question must be determined by the principles of the common law, and the manner in which those principles have been construed in this State for the past years. * * * * There can be no question of the common law rule that a woman cannot hold a general public office in the absence of express constitutional or statutory authority conferring upon her such right."

The opinion of the Court was based chiefly upon the exposition of the common law right of women to hold office. By Chief Justice Gray, in Robinson's case, supra. It will be noted from the above quotation, that the Court say, that at common law, a woman could not hold "general public office." The Court does not undertake to define the meaning of "general public office," but it will be seen from the concurring opinion of Mr. Justice Hooker, that the Court had in view the disqualification of women under the common law, to hold general public office, connected with the administration of justice, where she was compelled to perform in person the duties of the office, calling for the exercise of personal discretion and judgment. The Justice says:—

,"It remains to inquire whether the office of prosecuting attorney is such a ministerial office as to render a woman ineligible." Thereby implying that women would be eligible to hold certain ministerial offices, even though they might fall within the meaning of the term "general public office." Certainly the criterion, is not whether the office be a State, District or County office, for the Supreme Court of Massachusetts, in the Opinion of Justices, 136 Mass. 578, recognized the right of women to be appointed to, and hold, the office of member of the State board of health lunacy and charity, which clearly would make her a State officer. It would seem, that under the common law, a woman was not capable of holding a public office, connected with the administration of justice, or the legislative department of the government, for her powers could not be delegated and in either position she would be called to exercise judgment and discretion, and, it was generally supposed, in that period of the history of the world, when the common law had its birth, that women were incapable mentally of exercising judgment and discretion and were classed with children, lunatics, idiots and aliens insofar as their political rights were concerned, but we have been cited to no English case which denies the right of a woman under the common law, to hold a purely ministerial office,

8   whatever might be the nature of the office, if she was capable of performing the duties thereof, and in so doing was not called upon to exercise judgment and discretion. The Michigan Court evidently recognized this distinction in the case of Attorney General v. Abbott, supra, for Justice Hooker says, in discussing the inquiry suggested as to the nature of the office of prosecuting attorney:

"That, I think, is settled by one of our own decisions, the case of Eagle v. Chipman, 51 Mich. 524, 16 N. W. 886. It was there held that a prosecuting attorney could not delegate his powers; that he was vested with a personal discretion as a minister of justice. He might perhaps employ assistants when authorized by law, but could not delegate his official discretion. It seems clear that this judicial discretion takes the office out of the class recognized by the common law, and the cases, both English and American, as within the right of women to hold."

Even in the above case, where the official was "vested with a personal discretion as a minister of justice," a strong dissenting opinion was filed by Justice Moore, wherein he contended that a woman was eligible to that office.

The Supreme Court of Oregon, In re Leonard's Applica-

State v. Armijo, 18 N. M. 646.

tion to be admitted as an attorney, 12 Ore. 93, denied the
right of a woman to be admitted as a member of the bar.
The opinion was based entirely upon the Robinson case,
supra.   The Massachusetts Supreme Court denied the
right of a woman to be appointed a notary public.   See
Women as Notaries Public, 6 L. R. A. 842; Opinion of
Justices, 165 Mass. 599.

The New Hampshire Supreme Court, In re Opinion of
Justices, 62 Atl. 969, 5 L. R. A. (N. S.) 415, denied the
right of a woman to hold the office of notary public on the
ground that the office was "public and governmental," and
could not, at common law, be held by a woman.

On the other hand, many courts have recognized the
right of women to hold various offices, where no statute or
constitutional provision existed, either expressly or impliedly denying the right.   Thus, in the case of Wright v.
Noell, 16 Kan. 601, in an opinion by Justice Brewer, the
Supreme Court of Kansas held that a woman in that State,
was eligible to hold the office of Superintendent of Schools.
Likewise, the Supreme Court of Washington announced
the same doctrine in the case of Russell v. Guptill, 13 Wash.
361.   The Supreme Court of Indiana, in the case of In re
Leach, 134 Ind. 665, held that a woman could be admitted
to practice law.   As did the Supreme Court of Connecti-
cut ,in the case Matter of Hall, 50 Conn. 131.   The Indiana Court say:—

"We have searched in vain for an expression from the
common law excluding women from the profession of the
law."

The Supreme Court of Michigan, in the case of Wilson
v. Newton, 87 Mich. 493, held that a woman could be appointed deputy County Clerk, as the office of County Clerk
was wholly ministerial.   A woman was held eligible to
election as County Clerk, under a constitutional provision.
which provided that no person shall be chosen to an office,
"who is not a citizen of the United States, and who shal!
not have resided in this State one year."   State, ex rel.
Crow, v. Hostetter, 137 Mo. 636, 38 L. R. A. 208.

The Supreme Court of Nebraska, in the case of State,
ex rel. Jordan, v. Quible, 86 Neb. 417, 125 N. W. 619, 27

State v. Armijo, 18 N. M. 646.

L. R. A. (N. S.) 531, held that a woman was eligible to the office of County Treasurer.

The Court say:—

"No constitutional or statutory provision inconsistent with the right of a woman to hold that office has been found. A familiar legislative enactment, however, adopts 'so much of the common law. of England as is applicable, and not inconsistent' with the Federal and State Constitutions and the statutes of this State. This Court, in its early history, announced that the common law thus adopted permitted women to hold office administrative in character, the duties of which they were competent to discharge." See also Opinion of Justices, 57 Southern, 351, (Fla.) Exhaustive notes on the right of women to hold office generally will be found appended to the cases of State, ex rel. Crow, v. Hostetter, 38 L. R. A. 208, and State, ex rel. Jordan, v. Quibble, 27 L. R. A. (N. S.) 531. From a review of the cases it will be found that the courts in this country are by no means agreed upon the rights of women under the common law to hold office. The right, as to many offices, has has been denied by some courts and upheld by others. We do not believe, however, that an American case can be found expressly denying the right of a woman to hold a purely administrative, ministerial office, such as the one here in question. On the other hand, many cases affirm their right to hold offices, even where judgment and discretion must be exercised by the incumbent. A review of the English cases will show that women have held many important offices in that country, some by appointment, others by inheritance. Her right to hold a purely ministerial office, so far as we have been able to ascertain, was never denied by the English courts, and her eligibility to judicial office sometimes was made to depend upon whether the duties of the office could be performed by a deputy. Eleanor was appointed Lord Keeper of England. 1 Campbell, L. L. Ch. 134. An unmarried woman was held to be eligible to appointment as arbitrator, 8 Edw. 4; 1 Br. 37. A woman was chosen sexton, by election, and her right to the office upheld; Olive v. Ingram, 2 Str. 1114.

In King v. Stubbs, 2 T. R. 395, it was held that a woman could be elected to and hold the office of overseer of the poor. Counsel, in arguing against the right, said:—

"Wherever it is said that a woman may hold any particular office, it is either because the office is ministerial, or because, though partly judicial, it is hereditary, and then she may appoint a deputy."

The Court say:

"The only question then is, whether there be anything in the nature of the office that should make a woman incompetent and we think there is not. There are many instances where, in offices of a higher nature, they are held not to be disqualified; as in the case of the office of High Chamberlain, High Constable and Marshal; and that of a common constable, which is both an office of trust, and likewise, in a degree judicial. So in the case of the office of sexton."

Other English cases will be found cited in the note in 38 L. R. A. 208, and note to Schuchardt v. People, 39 Am. R. 34. We shall not attempt to review them all. The common law rule upon the subject, deducible from the cases, may be stated as follows:—that while women did not generally hold public office, and the question of their competency was not well settled, they did hold various offices, some of which were of great importance; some were appointive and some hereditary; that their right to hold a purely ministerial office was never denied, and has been upheld; that they were ineligible to hold any office, which called for the exercise of judgment and discretion, unless the duties of the office could be exercised by deputy, it being generally supposed that women, from the nature of the sex, and their inexperience, were incapable of exercising that judgment and discretion which was necessary to properly discharge the duties of the office. Another consideration was, that there must be incompatibility between the nature and character of the duties of the office and their due performance by women; if the duties of the office could be performed by a deputy she was held capable of holding the office. It is worthy of note, as stated by the Annotator of the case note, in 38 L. R. A. 208, "That in every instance in which a woman's right to any office was questioned, prior to the present generation, she was held to be competent, although the courts often took occasion to say that women were not competent to hold all offices."

The office of State Librarian is clearly such an office as a woman might hold under the common law of England, at the time of our separation from that country. The office is purely ministerial and called for the exercise of neither judgment nor discretion, and the duties of the office are not incompatible with the ability of a woman to perform.

Another argument, were it needed, might be advanced in favor of such a construction of the law by the courts, viz:—the long-continued executive construction of the law upon the subject. Since the year 1905, the Governor, in whom, by the act creating the Territorial library, the appointing power was vested, has uniformly appointed women to fill this office. Such appointments have been confirmed by the legislative council of the Territory without question as to the right of a woman to fill the office. Governor Otero, in 1905, appointed Mrs. Anita Chapman as librarian, and she was promptly confirmed by the council. The present incumbent was twice appointed to the office by Governor Curry, and the present Governor of the State nominated a woman for the office, whose appointment, however, failed of confirmation by the senate, but not because of the fact that the appointee was a woman. Other instances might be cited where the executive authority of the Territory recognized the right of women to fill various offices. Women were appointed notaries public, and served without question, even prior to the Act of 1909, which distinctly authorized their appointment. The people, in various parts of the State, have elected women to the office of County Superintendent of Schools, and their right to hold such offices has never been questioned. The Supreme Court of the Territory, in 1908, admitted a woman to practice law in the Territory, and twenty-five years ago a woman was admitted to the bar at Las Vegas. The people of the Territory, the chief executive of the Territory, and the courts, have long recognized the right of women to hold various offices and the office in question having been acceptably filled for many years by women, it is clear that this Court should not oust a woman from the office, because of her sex solely, unless it is clearly and unmistakably demonstrated that she holds the office without right or lawful authority. The most that can be said against her right to so hold, is that the statute does not, in terms, make her eligible. This is true, but on the other hand it does not deny such right. Under the common law, no case has been cited denying the right of a woman to hold the particular office in question, nor, on the other hand, have we found a case affirming the right. But on principle, deducible from the old English cases, we are of the opinion, that under the common law she could have held the office, and no statute of the Territory denying her the privilege, she was rightly in office at the time of the adoption of the State Constitution.

But it is insisted, that the right to hold the office is a political right, which was not carried into the law of the Territory by the statute adopting the common law of England. It is sufficient answer to this contention to say, that we adopted all of the common law, or *Lex non scripta* of England and such British statutes as were of a general nature and not local to that kingdom, in force at the time of our independence, in so far as the same did not conflict with the Constitution or laws of the United States and the organic act of the Territory and the legislative enactment thereof, which were applicable to our conditions and circumstances and our form of government. Many of the political rights recognized by the common law were in conflict with our customs and institutions and not suited to our conditions and, of course, were not brought into our law, but such as were recognized by the common law, and not in conflict with our established laws, institutions and customs, and suitable to our conditions, were, of course, carried into the body of our law. That the common law is applicable to the question involved in this case, in the absence of a statute upon the subject, has never been denied by an American court, even in those cases which denied woman the right to hold office.

State v. Armijo, 18 N. M. 646.

It is also suggested, that at the time of the adoption of the common law, the legislature did not have in view, or contemplation the fact that a woman would claim the right thereunder to hold office. This is doubtless true. But it is also probable that the question was not considered by the legislature. This can be no argument against the right of a woman to hold office under that law. Since the adoption of the common law in New Mexico, it is as much the rule of decision in this State, as in those States in which it was the law from the beginning of their political existence. Swayne v. Lone Acre Oil Co., 98 Tex. 597. Again, innumerable rights, privileges and immunities were conferred, recognized, protected, preserved and en forced by the common law, and it is hardly imaginable that the legislative assembly when it adopted the common law in the Territory, had in mind each particular right or privilege which would be claimed under that law. The legislature adopted it all, to the extent hereinbefore stated, and the courts will not deny a right asserted under that law, on the ground that the legislature did not have the particular right or remedy in view at the time of the adoption of the law.

The question as to the right of a woman to be appointed to such an office under the Constitution of the State, is not involved in this case. It is conceded that if the present incumbent was rightfully in office, at the time of the adoption of the Constitution, she was continued in office by virtue of sec. 9, article XXII, of. the Constitution, which provided :—

"All courts existing, and all persons holding offices or appointments under authority of said Territory, at the time of the admission of the State, shall continue to hold and execute their respective jurisdictions, functions, offices, and appointments until superseded by the courts, officers, or authorities provided for by this Constitution."

This clause was for the purpose of continuing in office those legally entitled thereto at the time of the adoption of the Constitution, until succeeded by their successors, appointed or elected according to law. It did not, of course, divest the courts of the power given them by law to remove officers for the causes prescribed by law, or to oust intruders from such offices. If the appellee was rightfully in office at the time of the adoption of the Constitution, she was continued therein by the above clause, until her successor was appointed and qualified, according to law, subject only to removal for legal cause prior to that time.

Appellee, rightfully holding the office at the time of the adoption of the Constitution, was entitled to retain the office at the time of the institution of this suit, and
9 the judgment of the lower court sustaining the demurrer to the information will be sustained, and it is so ordered.

CONCURRING OPINION.

PARKER, J.—I have had great difficulty in agreeing with some of the propositions upon which the opinions of my associates are based. Upon first examination of the case, I was convinced that women were prohibited from holding office by reason of the condition of the statute law on the subject. My conclusion was reached as follows:—The organic act prescribed the qualification of voters and office holders at the first territorial election, and limited the same to males, thereby excluding females; it granted power to the legislature to prescribe the qualification of voters and office holders for the future, but restricted the power so that only citizens of the United States might receive the right; the legislature at its session in 1851 prescribed the qualification of electors and elective office holders, and limited the same to males; it further restricted office holding generally to such persons as were not prevented by the terms of the organic law. This was the state of the specific statute law on the subject at the time appellee was appointed as Territorial Librarian.

As a conclusion from the foregoing facts, I was of the opinion that Congress in the organic act, and the Territorial legislature in its acts on the subject, having extended these rights to males only, when dealing with the subject, should be held, under the doctrine of *expressio*

unius est exclusio alterius, to have, in legal contemplation, denied these rights to women, as effectually as if the
denial had been express; that this denial of the right to
women, being specific, and in a statute dealing specifically
with this subject, it was not controlled by the Act of 1876,
which was a statute of a most general character, and which
adopted the common law as the rule of practice and decision in this jurisdiction, and did not purport to deal specifically with the right to hold office. This position was
disclaimed by counsel for the State on re-argument and,
after repeated conferences and discussions with the other
members of the Court,, and upon more mature consideration, I am convinced that this conclusion is not warranted.

In this connection it is to be noted that there is no express grant of a right to hold appointive office in either
the organic act or the Territorial legislation to either males
or females. Section 19 of the Act of 1851 is complete on
the subject of the right to vote and hold elective office,
and it follows perfectly the restriction contained in the
organic act. Section 21 of the Act of 1851 must, therefore, be held to relate to offices other than elective offices;
otherwise its provisions are meaningless and unnecessary,
being fully covered by the provisons of section 19, insofar
as the restriction to citizens of the United States is concerned. It must, therefore, relate to appointive offices.
This section is negative in form and would appear to be a
limitation upon, rather than a grant of, the right to hold
office. But while negative and restrictive in form, it is
permissive, at least, if not positive and creative in substance. The section prohibits aliens from holding appointive office, but impliedly authorizes citizens of either
sex, to hold such office. If the legislature of 1851, in the
exercise of the powers conferred by the organic act, had
simply provided that "no person not a citizen of the United States shall vote or hold office," the implication would
be irresistible that it intended thereby to grant that right
to citizens. Just so in the present case. It provided that
no person not a citizen, (that is, no person prohibited by
the organic law) might hold appointive office, thereby impliedly granting that right to citizens. Women are, of

there is no statutory grant to women of the right to hold appointive office. This contention has been disposed of. Second, the common law, which was adopted by the Act of 1876, clearly excludes a woman from such an office as State Librarian. With the latter contention of counsel I cannot agree. If this question had arisen in England, just prior to the separation of the ,Colonies, I feel convinced that the right of a woman to hold this office would have been upheld. The question at common law, in case of appointive offices, was whether the office was ministerial and, consequently, did not involve the exercise of judgment or discrteion, of which women were not supposed to be possessed. If so, a woman could be appointed to and hold the same, if it was not unsuited to her ability to perform its duties. This office is a ministerial office. Not a single duty exists which is not subject to control by either the board of trustees of the library, or the letter of the statute creating the office. Nothing is left to discretion. The restriction to local officers by the Massachusetts Court in 115 Mass. 602, is engrafted on the law, and is not warranted by the English cases.

For the raesons stated, I concur in the result reached by Judge Roberts.

DISSENTING OPINION.

HANNA, J.—I find I cannot concur in the majority opinion of the Court in its conclusion that under the common law a woman was eligible to hold a purely ministerial office, if she was capable of performing the duties thereof and was not called upon to exercise judgment and discretion.

My reasons therefor are: First, that the right to hold office under our political system is not a natural right, but exists only because and by virtue of some law expressly or impliedly creating or conferring it. Mechem on Public Officers, sec. 64. And it has been held that women, although citizens of the United States in the broad sense have, under our political system, no political power, and cannot, except under an enabling statute, be considered eligible to hold office.

Minor v. Happersett, 21 Wall. 162; Mechem on Public Officers, sec. 73.

This is doubtless the law of the case, unless our legislature by the adoption of the common law, (sec. 2871, C. L.) as the rule of practice and decision in our courts, have enlarged the right so far as women are concerned. Can it, therefore, be said that the right to hold an office, such as the one in question, had been conferred upon women by the common law, assuming for the present that if the right existed, as a common law right, and our Constitution or legislation did not prohibit it, a woman may hold the office under consideration.

Our inquiry is made a difficult one by reason of the fact that no office similar to the one under consideration, i. e., librarian, was ever referred to in the English reports; so we will give a general consideration to the early English cases, where the right of a woman to hold office was considered.

The cases, decided prior to April 21, 1788, are collected in the case of Rex v. Stubbs, reported in 2 T. R. (D. & E.) 395. It was there contended by counsel that "woman is capable of serving almost all of the offices in the kingdom; such as those of queen, marshal, great chamberlain, and constable of England, the champion of England, commissioner of sewers, governor of the workhouse, sexton, keeper of the prison, of the gate house of the dean and chapter of Westminster, returning offices for members of Parliament, and constable, the latter of which is in some respects judicial." Opposing counsel contending as follows:

"With respect to all the instances cited in which women have served other offices; no argument whatever can be drawn from them to show that a woman is competent to serve this office, there being not the least similarity between the nature of the respective offices. As to the Queen of England, it is sufficient to say, that of all other stations, there is not one perhaps which requires less personal exertion than this. And it was even doubted whether the regal office in this kingdom was hereditary in a female. In consequence of which the statute 1 M. St. 3, c. 2 was passed, purposely to declare that a female was capable of inheriting. The reason why a female may hold the office of constable of England, is because she may appoint a deputy; now that reason is an admission that if she could not appoint a deputy she could not hold the office. The same reason is given why Lady Russell might hold the office of the custody of the castle of Dunningham, because the office was granted to be exercised *per se vel deputatum suum*. Cro. Jac. 18. So the offices of great chamberlain, marshal. and champion of England, are hereditary; they are granted to a man and his heirs. With respect to the instance of a commissioner of sewers; it is merely an opinion of Callis, for which he gives an absurd reason, that Semiramis governed Syria. As to the case of the sexton, which is said to be only a private office of trust, to take care of the church, etc., and therefore a woman may serve it; it is also said there, that if there were any thing to be done by the sexton, not proper for a woman, it would be otherwise. With respect to the case of the constable, it is only the opinion of Serjeant Hawkins, that a custom to serve by rotation is good, because he thought that a woman might procure a deputy; now this admits that she cannot serve in person; and if she cannot serve by deputy, the custom could not be supported. In answer to these cases, it is not necessary to consider how far they are authorities to show that in certain cases a woman may appoint a deputy, but for this part of the argument it is sufficient if they prove the incompetency of females to serve those offices in person. Wherever it is said that a woman may hold any particular office, it is either because the office is ministerial, or because, though partly judicial, it is hereditary, and then she may appoint a deputy. So a woman, who is a forester in fee, cannot execute the office herself, but she may appoint a deputy, the office being ministerial. The incompetency of women extends to a variety of cases; they cannot serve on juries; vote for members of parliament; in particular, the case in 16 Vin. Abr. 415, is decisive to show that a woman is incompetent to serve it. There a woman was rejected as unfit; and Powell, Jr., said, 'a woman cannot be an overseer of the poor, and there can be no· custom of the parish to appoint her, because it is an office created by act of parliament.' Secondly, an officer, who acts merely ministerially, may appoint a deputy but a judicial officer cannot; neither can a deputy be appointed where the office is (strictly speaking) neither ministerial or judicial, but an office of trust and discretion and the office of overseer of the poor is of that description. It is said in Bro. Abr. tit. Deputie, pl. 9.—tit. Graunt, pl. 108. —tit. Patent, pl. 66, and Sir W. Jones, 113, that an office of trust cannot be assigned; neither can it be executed by deputy, unless power be expressly given for that purpose. Co., Litt. S. 379. A steward cannot appoint a deputy without power. 9 Co. 48. Nor the clerk of the papers. Freem. 429. The office of high constable of England is expressly granted to be exercised by himself, or his sufficient deputy. And the offices of earl marshal, great chamberlain, and the champion of England, are hereditary; that they are to the grantees and their heirs; so that according to the terms of those grants power is given to appoint a deputy. All of the offices mentioned on the other side (except one) are either ministerial or hereditary; in both which cases a deputy may be appointed. The instance indeed of a constable's appointing a deputy, if it be the law, forms an exception to the general rule."

In the Stubbs case the office involved was overseer of the poor, it being contended that in the Stat. 43 Eliz., c. 2, prescribing that the office should be served by "substantial householders," there was no reference to sex, and the defendant, Stubbs, a woman, was eligible to appointment. The Court disposed of the question in the following language:

"As to the second objection, we think that the circumstance of one of the persons appointed being a woman does not vitiate the appointment. The only qualification required by Eliz. is that they shall be substantial householders; it has no reference to sex. The only question, then, is whether there be anything in the nature of the office that should make a woman incompetent? and we think there is not. There are many instances where, in offices of the higher nature, they are held not to be disqualified; as in the case of the office of high chamberlain, high constable,

and marshal; and that of a common constable, which is
both an office of trust, and likewise, in a degree, judicial;
So in the case of the office of sexton. As to the case in
Vin. tit. Poor. 415, that is no conclusive authority. It is
to be collected from the case that there were other persons
in the parish proper to serve; and if so, the Court held
that the justices had not acted improperly in refusing to
approve of a woman; where there are a sufficient number
of men qualified to serve the office, they are certainly more
proper; but that is not the case here, and therefore, if
there be no absolute incapacity, it is proper in this instance from the necessity of the case. And there is no
danger of making of making it a general practice; for as
the justices are invested with a discretionary power of approbation, it is not likely that they will approve of such
an appointment when there are other proper subjects."

So that we find that the English courts had not affirmatively determined the rights of women in the matter of
the holding of office, in 1788.

In the Stubbs case, while the woman was conceded to be
a substantial householder, and as a result came within the
terms of the statute, the Court said it was proper that she
serve "from the necessity of the case," and that "there is
no danger of making it a general practice."

Turning to the American cases in which the common
law was considered as affecting the rights of a woman to
hold an office, we find a conflict of opinion. Our inquiry
is necessarily limited to those States where the power to
hold office has not been conferred expressly upon women
by Constitution or statute. It has been held that a woman
cannot hold a judicial office, i. e., that of Justice of the
Peace. Opinion of the Justices, 107 Mass. 604.

The reason assigned in this case was that the office was
a judicial one and must be exercised by the officer in person, and a woman, whether married or unmarried, cannot
be appointed to such an office. In a later opinion from the
same Court, the Court said:

"The common law of England, which was our law upon
the subject, permitted a woman to fill any local office of
an administrative character, the duties attached to which

were such that a woman was competent to perform." Opinion of the Justices, 115 Mass. 602.

This opinion of the Court was announced without citing authority, and would be of some importance in determining what the common law, upon the subject, has been interpreted to be, by American courts, had not the same court in a later opinion (Robinson's case, 131 Mass. 376) which carefully considered all the English authorities, arrived at a somewhat different conclusion. It is unnecessary to quote at length from this opinion, which is a careful review of the English cases and authorities, and I will only quote the conclusion reached, in the following language:

"And we are not aware of any public office, the duties of which must be discharged by the incumbent in person, that a woman was adjudged to be competent to hold, without express authority of statute, except that of overseer of the poor, a local office of an administrative character, in no way connected with judicial proceedings. The King v. Stubbs, 2 T. R. 395."

As to the one exception referred to by the Massachusetts Court, in this opinion, we have observed that the English Court based its decision upon the necessity of the case and that the statute, impliedly at least, by fixing the qualification of "sugstantial householders," had conferred the right to fill the office upon women, by legislative grant.

The Court of Appeals of Kentucky, in the case of Atchison v. Lucas, 83 Ky. 465, said: "At common law, a woman could not hold any public office," and denied to a woman the right of filling the office of jailor. The Court further said in this decision:

"We do not mean to adjudge that offices of legislative creation may not be filled by women, or the right of suffrage granted them in certain cases; but, on the contrary, such rights may be conferred."

By the statements, quoted, the Court clearly took the position that the right to hold office was to be controlled by legislation creating, or conferring the right, and in the absence of enabling legislation must be considered as withheld, and further that no right arose by virtue of the common law. This may seem to conflict with the English cases, referred to, where women filled certain offices, through deputies, but the very fact that her right was so limited to offices where she might appoint a deputy would indicate that otherwise she did not possess the right.

So we find the rulé proclaimed in Comyns' Digest, vol. 5, p. 202, under title "Grant of an Office," (B2) as follows:

"To a woman: (What offices a woman may execute;) So, the grant of an office of government, which may be exercised by a substitute or deputy, to a woman, will be good; as a woman may be made regent of the kingdom. Cal. 201."

Likewise in Ohio, it was held, that in the absence of constitutional or statutory provision on the subject, a woman could not hold the office of director of a workhouse. State v. Rust, 4 Ohio Cir. Ct. 329.

It is also contended that the Massachusetts Court in "Opinions of the Justices," 136 Mass. 578, recognized a woman's right to serve as a member of the board of health, lunacy an dcharity because the duties of the board are mostly administrative and are such as may well be performed by a woman, thus recognizing what it is contended are the common law limitations upon the right of woman to fill an office.

I cannot agree with this contention. The Court simply passed upon a statute providing that the board should consist of nine "persons" appointed by the Governor and held that "the word 'persons' clearly included women." This Court expressly referred to its previous decision in Robinson's case, (131 Mass. 376) and said that there was no conflict between the two cases. The distinction between the two is obvious, the one being based upon the common law of the subject (Robinson's case) and the other upon the construction of a statute plainly intending to continue women as qualified incumbents for positions, which by previous legislative enactments women had been designated as qualified to fill.

The New Hampshire Supreme Court, in a case involving the question of the right of a woman to fill the office of notary public, said:

"Because of our common law women are disabled from holding public office, and because the place of notary public is a public governmental office, and because we are unable to find any evidence of legislative purpose or intention to change the common law of this State in this respect, if such power exist, a point not considered, we are compelled to answer in the negative the question submitted." Re Opinion of Justices, 62 Atl. 969, 5 L. R. A. (N. S.) 418.

The rule laid down in this case is the prevailing doctrine in this country upon the subject, as applied to the office of notary public.

It may be argued that the office of notary public is a judicial one, but the reasons assigned for the disqualification of women is not put upon that ground.

It has been held in Massachusetts that none of the acts which a notary is called upon to perform are judicial, but that the office is a public one, the duties of which must be performed personally and cannot be performed by deputy. Women as Notaries Public, 6 L. R. A. 842.

In the Michigan case of Attorney General v. Abbott, 121 Mich. 540, 47 L. R. A. 92, 80 N. W. 372, it was stated as the opinion of the Court, by Long, J., that:

"There can be no question of the common law rule that woman cannot hold general public office in the absence of express constitutional or statutory authority conferring upon her such right."

It is argued that because Hooker, J., in a special concurring opinion, in the Michigan case, conceded that there were instances "where it had been held that they (women) could hold local offices of little importance, where the duties were wholly ministerial," is was to be implied that women could be eligible to hold certain ministerial offices, even though they might fall within the term "general public office."

This is a legitimate argument to be drawn from the opinion, but I believe that a careful consideration of this opinion better justifies a different conclusion. In commenting upon those instances of "local offices" ministerial in nature and of little importance, which women had held, Justice Hooker said:

"But while these cases support the claim that women might hold some offices, they reinforce the authorities which deny the general right contended for here."

The right contended for was "that inasmuch as the Constitution is silent upon the subject of the qualifications requisite to this office, we must recognize the right of everyone to hold it."

It is worthy of note that the opinion in this case, while apparently pointing out that local ministerial offices of little importance had been held by women, did not give any authority as a basis for the conclusion that such statement might be the rule of common law. We are more inclined to believe that the common law rule is correctly stated by the editor of the note to the case of State v. Hostetter, (Mo.) reported in 38 L. R. A. 208, at 215, in the following language:

"It may be said to be the general doctrine now held both in England and America that women are ineligible to any important office except when made so by enactment It is usually said that this is the common law of the subject."

It is also argued that many courts have recognized the right of women to hold various offices, where no statute or constitutional provision existed denying the right. The Hostetter case, 137 Mo. 636, 38 L. R. A. 208, is cited as an instance. It is to be found, however, in this case that the Supreme Court of Missouri had under consideration a statute defining the qualifications for the particular office, among other things, to be that of citizenship of the United States, and a former statute, with respect to the same of-had previously provided that the citizenship should be restricted to "free white male citizens." The Court said:

"The dropping of the word 'male' in describing the qualifications for such offices, has value as a guide to the legislative purpose in enacting the present law on this subject."

The effect of the opinion was to hold that the legislature intended to remove the disqualification, and qualify women for this office, which, in passing, it is worthy of note, was held to be a ministerial office, admitting of the use of a deputy and the duties of which were said to be not of such a nature as to be incompatible of discharge by a woman.

A legislative intent to make women eligible was looked for and found by this Court. I do not disagree with this view but consider that it is for the legislature to grant the right or withhold it, within constitutional limitations, and that the alleged common law rights have not been so definitely defined as to be worthy of consideration as sufficient rules now to be applied.

Wright v. Noell, 16 Kan. 601, is another case cited in support of the rule, last referred to. Justice Brewer in this case based his opinion upon the rule announced by the Supreme Court of Massachusetts, (Opinion of Justices, 115 Mass. 602), which Court, a few years later in a lengthy opinion reviewing all of the English authorities (Robinson's case, 131 Mass. 379), materially qualified its opinion

The Washington case of Russell v. Guptill, 13 Wash. 361, followed the Kansas case (16 Kan. 601), and Massachusetts case (115 Mass. 602.) In re Leach, 134 Ind. 565, and In the Matter of Mary Hall, 50 Conn. 131, are cases involving the construction of statutes, and in each case it was held that the term "persons" used in the statute, necessarily included women.

The case of Wilson v. Newton, 87 Mich. 493, was also cited, but is not in point and only declared and affirmed the common law rule (2 Bl. Com. 36) that a ministerial officer may appoint a deputy and, that under a statute, which was silent as to qualification of deputies, his choice was not limited to any race, sex, color or age.

The case of State v. Quibble, 86 Neb. 417, 125 N. W. 619, 27 L. R. A. (N. S.) 531, is also cited, but this as well as all the other American cases, which seem to be in point, relies upon the Massachusetts case (115 Mass. 602.) An earlier case in Nebraska, Crosby v. Cones, 15 Neb. 444. followed the Massachusetts case, and the later case followed the earlier one without question or consideration of authority.

After a careful consideration of the English and American cases, I conclude as follows: That, if there was any common law rule defining the rights of women, in the matter of holding public office, it was so indefinite and uncertain as to be of no value in sustaining a contention that our legislature adopted it and put it into force by adopting the common law. It is apparent that the women of England had, prior to 1776, asserted rights to public offices in a few instances, but as stated by the Massachusetts Supreme Court, no case is to be found, prior to 1776, where any public office, the duties of which must be discharged by the incumbent in person, that a woman was adjudged by the English courts to be competent to hold without express authority of statute. This being true, it would seem to be for the legislature to enlarge the rights of women, which our recent legislature has done, (chap. 60, S. L. 1913) by providing that women may hold any appointive office in this State. Can we properly hold that she had the right prior to this legislation of 1913? In doing so, I believe we invade the province of the legislature.

It may be said that the office of State Librarian is one that permits of the appointment of a deputy and is therefore not within the application of the limitations herein pointed out.

It is true that the Librarian has a right to appoint a deputy in instances specified by the statute, but the limitation of such right would preclude any general power to so appoint. I cannot concur in the opinion that importance is to be attached to the executive construction referred to in the majority opinion, because I believe that no statute attempting to define the rights of women to this, or other similar office, is involved, and that the right was not declared by the common law, therefore, the right fails to exist because never granted, and there can, therefore, be no law to construe. The so-called executive construction has doubtless grown up under the assumption that there being no prohibition, there was no disqualification, entirely overlooking the principle, enunciated by Mr. Mechem, that the right to hold a public office under our political system is not a natural right, and exists, where it exists at all, only by virtue of some law expressly or impliedly creating and conferring it. Mechem on Public Officers, sec. 64.

For the reasons indicated, I dissent.

[No. 1626, April 20, 1914.]

OSCAR C. SNOW, Appellant, v. FRANCISCO ABA LOS et al., Appellees.

SYLLABUS (BY THE COURT)

1. Chapter 1, S. L. 1895, "An act in regard to community ditches and acequias," was purely administrative, and while section 1 of said act makes community acequias corporations, "for the purpose of this act," the legislature did not confer upon the organization thus created the power to acquire or hold title to water rights. Such corporations have no powers not expressly or impliedly granted them by the act creating them.

P. 692

2. The history of community acequias considered.

P. 692

3. In New Mexico, the "Colorado Doctrine," as it is termed, of prior appropriation prevails. Such doctrine was established or founded by the custom of the people, and grew out of the conditions of the country and the necessities of the people. It was recognized by the courts of the Territory and became the settled law.

P. 693

4. An appropriator of water does not acquire a right to specific water flowing in the stream, but only the right to take therefrom a given quantity of water, for a specified purpose.

P. 693

5. The intention to apply water to beneficial use, the di-

version works, and the actual diversion of the water, all precede the actual application of the water to the use intended, but it is the application of the water, or the intent to apply, followed with due diligence toward application, and ultimate application, which gives to the appropriator the continued and continuous right to take the water.

P. 694

6.　Under a community ditch, each water user, by application of the water to a beneficial use, acquires a right to take water from the public stream or source of supply, which right is a several right, owned and possessed by the individual user, notwithstanding the fact that the ditch through which the water is carried to his land may have been constructed by the joint labor and money of the individual appropriator, in conjunction with others similarly situated, and the act of 1895, supra, did not change the status of the individual consumer.

P. 694

7.　While a ditch, through which water is carried for the irrigation of lands owned by the constructors in severalty is owned and possessed by the parties as tenants in common, the water rights acquired by the parties are not attached to the ditch, but are appurtenant to the lands irrigated, and are owned by the parties in severalty.

P. 695

8.　While section 1, chap. 1, S. L. 1895, makes all community acequias corporations, for the purpose of that act, such law did not divest the individual water users of any rights of property which he theretofore owned or possessed.

P. 698

9.　The right to divert and utilize water acquired by the individual water user under a community acequia, being a several right, such individual consumer is a proper and necessary party in an action for the adjudication of water rights, utilized through such community acequia.

P. 699

10. The fact that a water user may have entered into a contract, by which he agrees, at some future time, to convey his water right to another party, does not militate against his right to maintain an action for the adjudication of his right to the use of the water.

P. 701

ADDITIONAL SYLLABUS (BY PACIFIC REPORTER)

11. The "appropriation of water" consists in the taking or diversion of it from some natural stream, or other source of water supply, pursuant to law, with intent to apply it to some beneficial use, which intent is consummated within a reasonable time by the actual application of all of the water to the use designed, or to some other useful purpose.

P. 693

Appeal from the District Court of Dona Ana County; Edward L. Medler, District Judge; reversed with directions.

HOLT & SUTHERLAND, Las Cruces, N. M., for appellant.

On demurrer: None of the points raised or attempted to be raised by the demurrer can be reached, when considered in the light of the allegations of plaintiff's complaint, and can be raised only by answer. Authorities on the two theories as to the appropriation of water: Wiel on Water Rights in Western States, sec. 1338; Wheeler v. Northern Irr. Company, 10 Colo. 583; Wiel on Water Rights, sec. 398; Sowards v. Meagher, 108 Pac. 1113; Hagerman Irr. Co. v. McMurray, 113 Pac. 833; City of Pocatello v. Bass, 96 Pac. 120; Conley v. Dyer, 43 Colo. 22; Kinney on Irrigation & Water Rights, (2nd ed.) sec. 1573; Combs v. Farmers, etc., Co. 88 Pac. 396; Kinney, pp. 2853-4; Clark v. Smith, 13 Peter, 195; Howland v. Chellen, 110 U. S. 15; Ames Realty Co. v. Big Indian Mining Co., 146 Fed. 166; Kinney on Irr. & Water Rights,, secs. 1573-1577; 1475; Wyett v. Laramer, etc., Co., 18 Colo. 298; Albuquerque, etc., Co. v. Gutierrez, 10 N. M. 177, 188 U. S. 545; Farmers, etc., Co. v. Brumbach-

81 Neb. 641; Farmers' Co-op. D. Co. v. Riverside Ir. Co.,
94 Pac. 761; Kinney, sec. 1481; sec. 8, C. L. 1897; Candelario et al. v. Vallejos et al., 13 N. M. 147; Elmor v.
Drainage Com., 135 Ill. 269; Rodgers v. Pitt et al., 129
Fed. 932; Farnham on Waters and Water Rights, sec.
668; Wiel, sec. 1345; Montezuma Co. v. Smithville Co.,
218 U. S. 374; Whitehead v. Cavin, 55 Ore. 98; Huff v.
Porter, 102 Pac. 728; Kinney, secs. 1544, 1545; Lytle
Creek Water Co. v. Perdew, 4 Calif. 426; Wiel, secs. 1338,
1340.

Under statute of New Mexico suit for adjudication of
water rights may be instituted by the Attorney General, if
not begun by private parties. Sec. 20, ch. 49, L. 1907;
sec. 23, ch. 49, L. 1907.

On Demurrer of Defendant F. J. D. Westell:

Hulsman v. Todd, 31 Pac. 39; Sisk v. Caswell, 112
Pac. 185; Farmers', etc., Co. v. Southworth, 21 Pac. 1028;
Church v. Stillwell, 54 Pac. 295.

MARK B. THOMPSON, Las Cruces, N. M., for appellees,
W. W. Cox and F. J. D. Westell.

Lux v. Hagin, 65 Calif. 329; Blacks Pomeroy on Water
Rights, sec. 62; St. Anthony Fall Water Power Co. v.
City of Minneapolis, 43 N. W. 56; Blacks Pomeroy Water
Rights, sec. 63; Bladly v. Harkness, 26 Calif. 69; Lytle
Creek Water Co. v. Perdew, 65 Calif. 447; McGillivray
v. Evans, 27 Calif. 92.

YOUNG & YOUNG, Las Cruces, N. M., for appellee, The
Las Cruces Community Ditch.

31 Cyc. 572; Turner v. Great Northern Ry. Co., 55 Am.
St. R. 883; Vol. 3, A. & E. Pl. & Pr. 523; Carpenter
v. Gookin, 21 Am. Dec. 556; Riddle v. Gage, 75 Am. Dec.
151; 3 Cyc. 325, and cases cited.

M. B. THOMPSON, for appellee; Supplemental Brief.

Sec. 21, C. L. 1887; sec. 13, C. L. 1897; sec. 36, C. L. 1897; sec. 14, C. L. 1897; 11 A. & E. Pleading & Practice; Bliss v. Rice, 17 Pick. 23; Webster v. Vanderventer, 6 Gray, 429; Stinson v. Fernall, 77 Me. 576; Nevada Ditch Co. v. Bennett, 30 Ore. 59; Hargrave v. Cook, 108 Cal. 72; Pomeroy on Code Remedy, sec. 808; Candelario v.. Vallejos, 13 N. M. 147; Secs. 25, 26 and 27, C. L. 1897.

STATEMENT OF THE CASE.

This action was instituted by appellant in the District Court of Dona Ana County, for the purpose of securing an adjudication of the rights of all water users, taking water from the Rio Grande river below the Elephant Butte dam, in that portion of New Mexico embracing what is known as the "Rio Grande or Elephant Butte Irrigation Project." The purpose of the action is to secure a judicial determination of the priorities of all the existing rights to the use of water within said district, in advance of the completion of said dam by the United States government. Some 7,000 claimants, or alleged claimants, are made parties defendant. The complaint, briefly summarized, was as follows:

Alleged residence of plaintiff in Dona Ana County, and his ownership in fee simple of 966.95 acres of land, which was specifically described.

Paragraph 2 alleged that such lands could not be successfully cultivated without the application of water from sources other than from natural rainfall.

Paragraph 3 alleged that the Rio Grande river is a natural stream, flowing in such manner that such waters might be diverted and made to flow to and upon the lands of plaintiff.

Paragraph 4 alleged that: "In the year 1850 the then owners and occupants of the lands of plaintiff hereinabove described, they being the predecessors in interest of plaintiff, diverted, and caused to be diverted from said Rio Grande river, sufficient of its unappropriated waters to irrigate the aforesaid lands by making a reasonable use of such waters, and which quantity was requisite and necessary for the proper irrigation of such lands, to-wit., an

aggregate of 690 inches, miner's measurement, as defined
by chapter 49 of the Acts of the Thirty-seventh Legislative
Assembly of New Mexico, continuous flow, delivered on
such lands. And thereupon and thereafter, by means of
headgates, an irrigation ditch and other works constructed
by such predecessors in interest of plaintiff and other owners of land in said County of Dona Ana similarly situated,
who organized and composed and thereafter continuously
maintained, operated, and utilized for the purposes aforesaid, what was then, ever since has been, and now is, known
as the 'Mesilla Community Ditch,' plaintiff's said predecessors in interest caused the waters, so appropriated and diverted as aforesaid, to flow and otherwise to be conducted
to and upon the aforesaid lands of plaintiff, whereby said
lands were irrigated and rendered productive of valuable
crops; that plaintiff's said predecessors in interest thereafter continued so to divert and cause to be diverted, and
to conduct and cause to be conducted, said quantity of
water from said Rio Grande river, requisite and necessary
for the proper irrigation of the hereinbefore described
lands, and did continuously utilize said water in irrigating
said lands, and thereby produce valuable crops thereon;
that immediately therefrom and continuously thereafter,
and claiming through said original owners, plaintiff and
his mesne grantors from said original owners have, ever
since said year 1850, continuously diverted, and caused to
be diverted, from said Rio Grande river the aforesaid
quantity of water, requisite and necessary for the proper
irrigation of said lands, and have continuously conducted,
and caused same to be conducted, to and upon said lands
in the manner and by the means aforesaid, and there used
the same for the irrigation and benefit of said lands ever
since the said year 1850, by reason and by means whereof
valuable crops have been and are being produced thereon."
Paragraph 5 alleged adverse claims by defendants.
Paragraph 6 alleged, in substance, that the lands referred to are situated within the district, the irrigation of
which is contemplated by means of the irrigation system
commonly known and designated as the "Rio Grande Project," contract covering the construction of which has

heretofore been entered into between the United States and the Elephant Butte Water Users' Association.

In paragraph 7 plaintiff asked leave of the court to insert the names of, and to make additional parties defendant, any other persons, firms, or corporations subsequently discovered to the claimants of any right adverse to the aforesaid rights of plaintiff.

Plaintiff prayed that his right to divert the quantity of water mentioned might be established, and that the several defendants be barred and forever estopped from having or claiming any right or title in or to the use of such waters adverse to the plaintiff, and that the respective rights of the several parties defendant in and to the waters of said river might in like manner be ascertained, fixed, declared, and established. Plaintiff also asked for general relief.

Among the defendants are divers community ditches, one thereof being the Mesilla Community Ditch.

W. W. Cox, one of the individual defendants, interposed a demurrer upon the grounds: "(1) That there is a defect in the parties plaintiff, in that the complaint shows upon its face that plaintiff has not been, and is not now, nor have his predecessors in interest been, appropriating or diverting any waters from the Rio Grande river in any quantity whatever, but it appears on the face of the complaint that whatever right or interest in and to any diversion or appropriation of waters of the Rio Grande river the plaintiff may now have, or he or his predecessors in interest may have had, is by reason of and by virtue of certain appropriations and diversions of the waters of the said Rio Grande river made by the Mesilla Community Ditch. (2) That it appears on the face of the complaint that the Mesilla Community Ditch, being a corporation under and by virtue of the laws of the State of New Mexico, and being trustee for the plaintiff, is the real party in interest in any cause or action to determine and adjudicate any rights that plaintiff may have by reason of the beneficial use of any waters appropriated and diverted as alleged in the complaint. (3) That it appears on the face of the complaint that no cause or reason exists to maintain the action; it not appearing that he has demanded of the said Mesilla Community Ditch that the action be commenced for the benefit of him, the said plaintiff, and others similarly situated."

F. J. D. Westell, another of the individual defendants, filed a demurrer upon the grounds: "(1) That the complaint does not show by what right plaintiff's alleged predecessors in interest diverted the waters of the Rio Grande river, nor that any such right to divert ever existed in favor of said alleged predecessors in interest, nor that plaintiff is now the bona fide holder or owner of any right, or has any right to the present use of any of the alleged diverted water, nor what amount of water was diverted from the Mesilla Community Ditch. (2) That there is a defect in parties plaintiff, in that the complaint shows upon its face that plaintiff's alleged right to divert waters of the Rio Grande river was transferred to the Mesilla Community Ditch, and that the complaint fails to show any right to divert any water from the irrigation system of said Mesilla Community Ditch, nor that plaintiff is now the owner or bona fide holder of any such right, and therefore is not the real party in interest."

The demurrers were sustained.

The Las Cruces Community Ditch filed a motion to make the complaint more definite and certain upon 17 specific points. The motion was sustained as to the first, second, fourth, sixth, seventh, eighth, twelfth, and fifteenth of such points, which were as follows:

"First. Whether the said Mesilla Community Ditch mentioned and referred to in paragraph 4 of the said complaint is a corporation authorized and existing under the laws of the State of New Mexico governing community acequias, or ditches, and if the said Mesilla Community Ditch is such a corporation, whether or not the plaintiff is a member of the same.

"Second. Whether the water claimed by the plaintiff for the irrigation of his said land was appropriated by the plaintiff or any predecessor or predecessors in interest of the plaintiff individually, or whether the appropriation made by the plaintiff or any predecessor or predecessors in

interest was as a member or members of the said Mesilla
Community Ditch."

"Fourth. Whether the plaintiff is an independent and
individual owner of any water right in the said Rio Grande
river for the irrigation of his said lands, and, if not such
an individual owner, under what rules, regulations, and
conditions the plaintiff is entitled to use water appropriated by the said Mesilla Community Ditch for the irrigation of his said lands."

"Sixth. What is the nature and character of the Elephant Butte Water Users' Association of New Mexico mentioned in paragraph 6 of the said complaint?"

"Seventh. Whether or not the plaintiff is a member of
the said Elephant Butte Water Users' Association of New
Mexico, and, if such a member, whether the plaintiff has
executed any contracts or agreement with the said Elephant Butte Water Users' Association of New Mexico,
whereby the plaintiff has agreed to surrender the control
and distribution of all the waters heretofore appropriated
by him or his predecessors in interest from the said Rio
Grande river to the said Elephant Butte Water Users' Association."

"Eighth. Whether the plaintiff and all of the defendants in this action, save and except the several community
ditches made defendants herein, have entered into any
agreement or agreements touching the surrender to the
said Elephant Butte Water Users' Association of the
waters from the Rio Grande river claimed by the defendants, and, if so, the nature, character, and purport of the
said agreement."

"Twelfth. How and by what means the water from the
Rio Grande river, heretofore used by the plaintiff, for the
irrigation of his said lands, has been distributed to the
plaintiff."

"Fifteenth. If the plaintiff is a member of the said Mesilla Community Acequia, what is the area of lands irrigated by the said Mesilla Acequia, and what proportion
do the lands of the plaintiff bear to the total area of lands
irrigated by the Mesilla Community Acequia?"

Plaintiff elected to stand upon the complaint, and declined to plead further; thereupon judgment was rendered dismissing the case at plaintiff's costs as to the defendant named in the motion and as to the defendants who filed the respective demurrers. From the judgment thus rendered this appeal is prosecuted.

OPINION OF THE COURT.

ROBERTS, C. J.—We will first consider the action of the District Court in sustaining the demurrers, as our conclusions upon the legal questions raised by the demur · rers will necessarily determine many of the questions raised by the motion interposed by the Las Cruces Community Ditch.

The principal contention of the demurring defendants is that the suit at bar cannot be maintained by the plaintiff for the reason that he is not the real party at interest, but that he Mesilla Community Ditch is the real party in interest, because, it is claimed by the defendants, that the said Mesilla Community Ditch was the original appropriator of the waters, the right to the exclusive use of which is claimed by the plaintiff, and by virtue of the further fact that said community ditch is the trustee for plaintiff, and that plaintiff has failed to allege demand upon said community ditch to prosecute the action for the benefit of himself and others similarly situated. Appellant claims that none of the points raised by the demurrer can properly be reached, when considered in the light of plaintiff's complaint, and can be raised only by answer; nevertheless, in view of the importance of the litigation and the desirability of obtaining an early decision of the main questions involved, we are asked to consider the questions raised upon the merits, and will therefore treat all the points discussed as properly before us for determination, without further inquiry.

Sections 20 and 21, c. 49, S. L. 1907, provides for the adjudication of the rights to the use of the water of any stream system, by an appropriate action in any District Court which has jurisdiction to hear and determine the same.

In order to dispose of the questions raised by the demur-

rer it will be necessary to consider the history, nature, and
character of community ditches, and the relations
which exist between the consumer, or members of such
community corporations, and the corporation. Also
the nature and character of the right to the use of the
water of the public streams of New Mexico. Briefly stated,
the question is whether the appropriation of the water was
made by the community acequia, or the individual consumer.

The community irrigating ditch or acequia is an institution peculiar to the native people living in that portion
of the Southwest which was acquired by the United
States from' Mexico. It was a part of their system of
agriculture and community life long before the American occupation. After the Territory of New Mexico
was organized, the legislature, by the act of January 7,
1852 (Laws 1851-51, p. 276), provided for the government
of community acequias, and doubtless incorporated into
the written law of the Territory the customs theretofore
governing such communities. Under the act in question,
elections were to be called and held by justices of the peace
of the various precincts of the Territory, at which all the
owners or tenants of lands to be irrigated therefrom were
permitted to vote for overseers of such ditches. It was
made the duty of such overseers to superintend the repairs and excavations on such ditches, to apportion the
persons or number of laborers to be furnished by the proprietors, to regulate them according to the quantity of
land to be irrigated by each one from said ditch, to distribute and apportion the water in the proportion to which
each was entitled, taking into consideration the nature of
the seed, crops, and plants cultivated, and to conduct and
carry on said distribution with justice and impartiality.
Further provision was made as to the repair of ditches,
the calling out of laborers, the punishment of overseers
for neglect of duty and of all persons obstructing or interfering with the flow of water in a community acequia.
Thereafter, at almost every session of the legislature, laws,
either general or special, were enacted relative to such acequias, but no important change was made until 1895,

when, by section 1, chap. 1, S. L. 1895, the legislature provided that "All community ditches or acequias, now constructed or hereafter to be constructed in this Territory.
shall for the purposes of this act be considered as corporations or bodies corporate, with power to sue or to be sued
as such." The act in question was purely administrative.

    It did not confer upon the organization, in its corpor-
1 ate capacity thus created, the power to acquire or hold
    title to water rights. The words "for the purposes of
this act" are words of express limitation, and such corporations, so created, have and possess no powers not thereby,
either expressly or impliedly, granted them. This being
true, we are compelled to resort to a consideration of the
history, nature, and character of such associations, for the
purpose of determining the relation of the consumer to the
corporation, and the nature 'and character of the right to
the use of water which he acquired by virtue of his membership therein.

New Mexico being in the arid region, the early settlements were established along the banks of perennial rivers,
or in the mountain valleys where water from springs and
creeks was reasonably certain to be available for irrigation
at the needed times. As a protection against Indians, settlements were made in communities, and the people built
their houses and established their towns and plazas close
together, and cultivated the lands in small tracts adjacent
    to the settlement. When a settlement was established,
2 the people by their joint effort would construct an irri-
    gation ditch, sufficiently large to convey water to their
lands for the irrigation of crops. Each individual owned
and cultivated a specific tract of land, sufficient to provide
food for the needs of his family, and from the main ditch
laterals were run to the various tracts of land to be watered.
The distribution of the water and the repair of the ditch
was in charge of a mayordomo, or officer elected by the
water users under the ditch. This official would require the
water users to contribute labor toward the repair of the
ditch and its maintenance, and also distributed the water
to the various irrigators equitably, in proportion to the
land to be irrigated, as his necessities required. When a

landholder under a community acequia conveyed his real
estate, his right to the use of water as a member of the
community passed with the real estate.

In New Mexico, the "Colorado doctrine," as it is termed,
of prior appropriation prevails.   Established or founded
by the custom of the people, it grew out of the condi-
3 tion of the country and the necessities of its citizens.

The common law doctrine of riparian right was not
suited to an arid region, and was never recognized by the
people of this jurisdiction.   When the question came before
the courts for adjudication, (Albuquerque L. & I. Co. v.
Gutierrez, 10 N. M. 197, 61 Pac. 357), the doctrine of
prior appropriation was recognized by the courts and became the settled law of the Territory.   The judicial declaration, however, did not make the law; it only recognized
the law as it had been established and applied by the people, and as it had always existed from the first settlement
of this portion of the country.   This construction of the
law by the courts has been consistently adhered to by the ·
legislature of the Territory, as the various acts upon the
subject will show.

The latest definition of the term "appropriation of
water" under the Arid Region Doctrine of Appropriation
by Kinney, in his work on Irrigation and Water Rights,
(2nd ed.) section 707, is as follows: "The appropriation
of water consists in the taking or diversion of it from
11 some natural stream or other source of water supply,
in accordance with law, with the intent to apply it to
some beneficial use or purpose, and, consummated, within
a reasonable time, by the actual application of all of the
water to the use designed, or to some other useful purpose."

The water in the public stream belongs to the public.
The appropriator does not acquire a right to specific water
flowing in the stream, but only the right to take therefrom
a given quantity of water, for a specified purpose.   He acquires this right as above stated.   Necessarily he must have
some suitable ditch, or other device, to enable him to
4 take the water from the stream.   In other words, the
water must be captured before it can be applied to a
beneficial use.   In order to apply the water, and thereby

invest the appropriator with a right to continue to take
and use the same, he must have suitable appliances for
conducting the water to the place of use, otherwise he
would not be able to use the same.

The intention to apply to beneficial use, the diversion
works, and the actual diversion of the water necessarily all
precede the application of the water to the use intended,
but it is the application of the water, or the intent to apply,
followed with due diligence toward application and ultimate application, which gives to the appropriator the continued and continuous right to take the water. All the
steps precedent to actual application are but prelimin-
5   ary to the same, and designed to consummate the actual application. Without such precedent steps no application could be made, but it is the application to a
beneficial use which gives the continuing right to divert
and utilize the water.

Applying these principles to a community acequia, and
the question raised by the demurrers in this case become
easy of solution. A number of people settle in a given
community, each owning lands capable of being irrigated
from a natural stream. A., for example, conceives the idea
of irrigating his farm. He finds that his neighbors like
wise desire to irrigate their lands. They agree to construct
a common ditch to the source of supply. Each individual
contributes his labor and money, and the ditch is constructed, capable of carrying a sufficient amount of water
to irrigate the lands of all the parties. They appoint a
mayordomo or superintendent, whose business it is to di
vert the waters from the stream into the irrigating ditch.
This mayordomo is but the agent of the individual owners
of the lands under the ditch, and when he turns the water
in he is acting for them. The water flows down the ditch
and A. takes therefrom the water to irrigate his farm. He
has applied the water to a beneficial use, and by reason of
such application he has acquired the right to continue to
divert from the public waters a sufficient amount to irrigate his lands. The people under the community sys-
6   tem, as stated, have no right to any specific water flowing in the river, but by the completed appropriation

each has the right to continue to divert therefrom water
sufficient for the purpose for which it is used.

The ditch, or carrier system, having been constructed by
the joint labors of all the water users, is owned by them as
tenants in common; each having a common interest in the
same. While this is true, each has a several right to take
water from the stream system for the irrigation of his
lands. After the water, the right to divert which, as stated,
is vested in the several parties, has been actually diverted
under such several rights, into the ditch, and reduced to
possession, and by such diversion becomes intermingled,
such waters are probably owned by the parties as ten-
7 ants in common. Under such community systems, the
water commissioners or mayordomo had general charge
of the ditch and distributing system; it was his duty to
keep it in repair, assessing the labor upon the parties using
the ditch. He diverted the water into the ditch, but only
by virtue of rights acquired by individual users, by completed appropriations, or rights acquired to divert water.
He distributed the waters equitably to the several users, in
proportion to the lands irrigated, taking into consideration
the nature of the crops and quantity required. No one is
entitled to waste water. When his requirements have been
satisfied, he no longer has a right to the use of water, but
must permit others to use it.

Such being the case, we are of opinion, that prior to the
enactment of the statute of 1895, supra, making such community acequias corporations, for certain purposes, each
individual water user under a community acequia was the
owner of a right to take water from the public stream or
source from which it was drawn, which right was divorced
from and independent of the right enjoyed by his co-con-
sumer; that the fact that such water was diverted into a
ditch, owned in common with other water users, did not
give such other users any interest in, or control over, the
right to take water, or water right, which each individual
consumer possessed; that the right to divert water, or the
water right, is appurtenant to specified lands, and inheres
in the owner of the land; that the right is a several right
owned and exercised by the individual, and, the officers of

the community acequia, in diverting the water act only as the agents of the appropriator.

Section 44, c. 49, S. L. 1907, provides: "All water used in this Territory for irrigation purposes, except as otherwise provided in this act, shall be considered appurtenant to the land upon which it is used." This provision was, we believe, but a recognition of the law relative to waters used for irrigation, established by general custom. Where land is owned in severalty, to which a water right is appurtenant, which water right is of course only a right to take from the public stream a sufficient amount of water to properly irrigate the land, we fail to understand how such a right could be owned in common with other water users.

Appellees have cited us to section 62, Black's Pomeroy on Water Rights, where the author says: "Whenever ditches or other structures for diverting or appropriating water belong to two or more proprietors, such owners are. in the absence of special agreements to the contrary, tenants in common of the ditch, and of the water rights connected therewith, and their proprietary rights are governed by the rules of law regulating tenancy in common"—and also refer to the cases of St. Anthony Falls Water Power Co. v. City of Minneapolis, 41 Minn. 270, 43 N. W. 56; Bradley v. Harkness, 26 Cal. 69; Lytle Creek Water Co. v. Perdew, 65 Cal. 447, 4 Pac. 426. The learned author and the courts, we believe, erroneously consider the water rights attached to the ditch, which of course is owned by the parties constructing it as tenants in common, whereas said water rights are appurtenant to the lands owned in severalty by the parties. The ditch is simply the carrier. or agency employed by the parties, to conduct the water, the right to which is appurtenant to the land, to be irrigated. Suppose, for example, that two farmers each owned a farm; their lands being contiguous. In order to reach their lands they should jointly construct a wagon road to the same. The road would be owned by the parties jointly or as tenants in common. Each would have the right to use the road. The fact that they haul their produce raised on the farm over the wagon road thus constructed would not make them tenants in common of the crops so hauled. However, if they should, for instance. mix their grain together, for the purpose of hauling it to market, they would of course be tenants in common of the grain so commingled.

In the case of Norman v. Corbley, 32 Mont. 195, 79 Pac 1069, this principle is applied by the Supreme Court of Montana. The Court say: "To constitute a tenancy in common there must be a right to the unity of possession (17 Am. & Eng. Enc. L, [2nd ed.] 651, and cases), and if this right is destroyed, the tenancy no longer exists. With respect to a water right this unity must extend to the right of user, for the parties can have no title to the water itself."

In the case of City of Telluride v. Davis, 33 Colo. 355, 80 Pac. 1051, 108 Am. St. Rep. 101, the Colorado Supreme Court considered a similar question. There two parties constructed a ditch for the purpose of conveying water to mining claims, each owning a separate claim. The waters were carried through the ditch to the claims, where each party utilized one-half of the water. The trial court held that the appropriation made by the parties was a joint appropriation, and was owned and held by them as tenants in common and that neither could, without the consent of the other, divide the water at any other point than where they had theretofore divided it, nor divert or take his water through a different headgate. The Court say: "We think the court below erred in holding that the appropriation made by Brown and Davis invested them with a joint ownership of the water appropriated. While it is true that they acted together in making the appropriation and in constructing the ditch, it was their understanding that each was to be entitled to one-half of the water so appropriated, and such share was to be applied on the separate estate and land of each; and, while there was a unity of possession in the water while it was being carried through the ditch, yet, when it reached the Ohio placer, the property of Mr. Brown, such unity of possession ceased, and one-half of the water was diverted to his individual use; while the remaining one-half was continued on till it

reached the Kokomo placer, the separate and individual
property of appellee. The water was not used, or to be
used, upon any land jointly owned by them, but as stated
above, was to be used upon each one's separate and individual land. In these circumstances, the right to a unity
of possession necessary to constitute a tenancy in common
did not extend to the right of user, which is essential to
the existence of such a tenancy in a water right. Norman
v. Corbley, 32 Mont. 195, 79 Pac. 1059."

Did the act of 1895 change the status, in this regard, of
the right acquired by the individual to divert and utilize
    water from a public stream? This question was ap-
8   parently fully answered by the Territorial Supreme
    Court, in the case of Candelario v. Vallejos, 13 N. M.
147, 81 Pac. 589, where it enunciated the doctrine that
the organization of such an association in no manner involved the surrender of individual property rights. The
Court say: "We are of opinion that under that system he
remained as any other citizen vested with full rights of
property, sacred against any alienation except by his con·
sent or by due process of law. * * * * The corporation
thus created * * * has only the powers expressly or by
necessary implication granted to it by the act creating it
and no more. It belongs to the class of corporations—
citing Elmore v. Drainage Commissioners, 135 Ill. 269-
273, 25 N. E. 1010, 25 Am. St. Rep. 363. * * * This was
no voluntary organization; the owners of these lands and
the water rights appurtenant thereto were not given leave
to incorporate, as a preliminary to which they deeded their
several holdings to the corporation. On the contrary, the
legislature, for the purpose purely of more conveniently
and economically distributing the water upon such lands,
and thus perhaps of leaving by such economical use, an
overplus for new appropriations, decided to make corporations out of each of the ditches. The legislature did not
take away or diminish any property rights previously held
by the several owners, nor could it do so. * * * * As it
could not by its fiat confiscate the property of its citizens,
it could not by creating a corporation and officers thereof

confide to such corporation the power to confiscate property. * * * * "

The words, " 'that such officers shall have general charge of all affairs pertaining to the same,' * * * do not disturb property rights as they previously existed in the various co-partners; they do not disturb or destroy priorities as they existed before the statute of incorporations; they do not give the power to take away from one the water belonging to him and to give it to another."

The act in question was administrative only, and for convenience gave a legal status to such organizations, in order to facilitate the distribution of the water and the maintenance of the ditches and laterals. It did not attempt to interfere with the rights theretofore owned by the individual. It could not, had it so desired, have arbitrarily divested the individual of his right to divert and utilize water and invest the same in the corporation by it created. That it did not attempt to do so is plain.

If our conclusion is sound, and the right to divert and utilize water, acquired under a community ditch, is a several right, vested in the individual appropriator, it neces·
9 sarily follows that the individual is a proper and necessary party in an action for the adjudication of water rights, where such rights are exercised through a community ditch. If it be true that the individual is the owner of the right to divert water, it would necessarily follow that he would only be bound by decree, in a suit, to which he was a party.

Appellees contend that the appellant necessarily would not have any priority of right over his co-water users under the Mesilla Community Ditch. Admitting for the purpose of argument only that this contention is sound, it does not militate against his right to maintain this action. He has the right to have all the priorities adjudicated and settled by a decree of the court, even though such rights would be held co-ordinate and equal with his own. It was the evident design of the legislature, by chapter 49, S. L. 1907, to have adjudicated and settled by judicial decree all water rights in the State, to have determined the amount of water to which each water user was entitled, so that the distribution of water could be facilitated, and the unappropriated water to be determined, in order that it might be utilized.

The only remaining ground of demurrer, not disposed of by what has been above said, is ground No. 1 in the demurrer interposed by F. J. D. Westell, viz.: "That the complaint does not show by what right plaintiffs alleged predecessors in interest diverted the waters of the Rio Grande river, nor that any such right to divert ever existed in favor of said alleged predecessors in interest, nor that plaintiff is now the bona fide holder or owner of any right, or has any right to the present use of any of the alleged diverted water, nor what amount of water was diverted from the Mesilla Community Ditch." A reading of the complaint, and construing the law relative to such water rights as above applied, will clearly demonstrate the lack of merit in this ground of the demurrer. Our conclusion is that the District Court erred in sustaining each of said demurrers.

We are also of the opinion that the motion to make the complaint more definite and certain, interposed by the Las Cruces Community Ditch, should not have been sustained, as to the grounds set forth in the statement of facts.

The first ground of the motion, which was sustained by the court, was that the plaintiff be required to allege whether or not the Mesilla Community Ditch is a corporation, and whether the plaintiff is a member of the same. In view of our conclusion as to the nature and character of such corporations it is evident that such an allegation is wholly unnecessary. However, the facts alleged in paragraph 4 of the complaint clearly show the organization and existence of an association such as was declared by the act of 1895 to be a corporation for certain specified purposes, and the complaint further shows that the plaintiff is a member of such association.

The second, fourth, twelfth, and fifteenth grounds of the motion sustained by the court have been disposed of by what we have said in discussing the demurrers, and further argument is unnecessary. These grounds of the motion were predicated upon the assumption that the Mesilla

Community Ditch was the proper party to institute the action, and that a member of such a community corporation could not maintain the action in his own name, and were designed to require plaintiff to allege facts in his complaint more clearly establishing the fact that he acquired his rights as a member of such a community association or corporation. This, as we have seen, would not militate against his right to maintain the action, and such allegations would add nothing material to the complaint.

The sixth, seventh, and eighth grounds of the motion were designed to require plaintiff to allege whether he had entered into an agreement, to convey his water rights to the Elephant Butte Water Users' Association, and to require him to state the nature and character of such association. The fact that he had entered into an agree-
10 ment to, in the future, convey his rights to another party would not preclude him from maintaing the suit. He alleged in his complaint that he was the owner of the right. Until the title to such right passed from him he would have the right to maintain the suit. We fail to perceive how it was in any way material to the cause of action to allege the required facts. By sustaining the motion upon these grounds the court required plaintiff to plead facts which were foreign and not relevant to the cause of action set forth in the complaint, and facts which, if they existed, could properly be raised, if at all, only by answer.

For the reasons stated, the cause is reversed, with directions to the District Court to overrule the demurrer, and the motion to make the complaint more definite and certain; and it is so ordered.

great bodily harm will justify the taking of life in those
cases where an illegal arrest is attempted.

Territory v. Lynch, p. 15. 6. 34

ASSESSMENT—Taxation—Real Owner.

It is impracticable for the assessor to obtain the name
of the real owner of a tract of land, from the official county
records, as available for his inspection, and, in the absence
of fraud, an assessment against unknown owners is not invalid, because of the fact that the assessor might have ascertained the name of the real owner from the records or
conveyances in the office of the county recorder, in th.se
cases where the owner has failed to list his property for
taxation.

Daughtry v. Murry, p. 35. 1. 41

ASSESSOR—Duty—Presumption.

It must be presumed, in the absence of a showing to
the contrary, that the assessor did his duty, and that inasmuch as he made the assessment to unknown owners, it was
impracticable to obtain the real owner's name.

Daughtry v. Murry, p. 35. 2. 42

ASSESSOR—Unknown Owners.

It must be presumed, in the absence of a showing to
the contrary, that the assessor did his duty, and that inasmuch as he made the assessment to unknown owners, it was
impracticable to obtain the real owner's name.

Daughtry v. Murry, p. 35. 2. 42

ASSIGNMENTS OF ERROR—Findings.

Where assignments of error questioned the correctness
of findings of fact, appellant having brought up the record
proper only, the appellee was justified in bringing up the
transcript by certiorari, and the cost thereof could be taxed
by the clerk of the Supreme Court as provided by laws 1907,
c. 57, sec. 34.

State Ex. Rel. v. Bd. of Ed., p. 286. 1. 288

ASSIGNMENTS OF ERROR—Copies.

Where the assignment of errors is copied into appellant's brief, and the brief served upon appellee's counsel,
service of a separate copy of the said assignment of errors
is not necessary.

Palmer v. Allen, p. 237. 3. 239

ASSIGNMENTS OF ERROR—Review.

Assignments of error that "the court below erred in
affirming the decision of the Board of Water Commissioners," and that "the court below erred in rendering judgment herein in favor of said appellee, affirming the said

the party applying for a continuance to show the materiality
of the facts which he claims the absent witness will substantiate.

State v. Analla, p. 294. 2. 298

AFFIRMANCE—Default—Showing.

A cause affirmed, upon motion of appellee, for failure
of appellant to file and serve briefs within the time required
by rule of court XIII, will not be reinstated upon the docket
and the affirmance vacated, where the only showing made
excusing such default and failure to apply for an extension
of time within which to file briefs was, that appellant's local
attorney in this state sent the brief to its general counsel
for examination and approval. Appellant should have applied for an extension of time, within the time limit for filing
briefs, when it became apparent that it would not be able
to comply with the rule.

Deal v. Western C. & G. Co., p. 70. 2. 72

AGREEMENT—Tax Payer—Actions.

A tax payer has no such direct interest in an agreement
between a municipality and a corporation for supplying water
as will allow him to sue ex contractu for breach, or ex delicto
for violation of the public duty thereby assumed.

Braden v. Water Co., p. 173. 1. 179

AGRICULTURAL COLLEGE—Treasurer.

Where the statute creating a board of regents for the
Agricultural College and Experiment Station provides for the
election of one of the members of said board as secretary
and treasurer, and also provides that such secretary and
treasurer shall continue in office until his successor shall be
elected and qualified, the incumbent is not ousted from the
office of secretary and treasurer by the appointment of a new
board of regents, but continues as such until a new secretary
and treasurer has been elected and has qualified as directed
by the statute.

Trust Co. v. Bank, p. 589. 5. 602

ALIBI—Witnesses—Evidence.

Upon cross examination the State has the right to expose to the jury the relations existing between the witnesses
testifying and the defendant, and the fact that the witnesses
have been frequently used by the defendant to establish an
alibi was proper to go to the jury for the purpose of weakening the evidence given by the witnesses on their direct
examination.

State v. Lumpkin, p. 480. 3. 485

ALLEGATION—Answer.

An allegation in the answer of what the parties intended

APPEAL—Cost Bond—Waiver.

Where a cost bond is required by statute, on appeal or writ of error, only for the protection of the adverse party, failure to give the same may be waived.

Canavan v. Canavan, p. 468.   2. 471

APPEAL—Certificate.

In order to recover on appeal costs incurred in the District Court, they must be taxed prior to the filing of the transcript on appeal or writ of error, and the transcript must include a certificate of the clerk of the District Court as to such costs.

State Ex. Rel. v. Bd. of Ed., p. 286.   3. 289

APPEAL—Certiorari—Notice.

A person against whom a Justice of the Peace has rendered a judgment void for want of jurisdiction, is not bound to appeal or remove the same by writ of certiorari, even though he have actual notice of the existence of the judgment.

Pickering v. Palmer, p. 473.   2. 478

APPEAL—Transcript—Costs.

In order to recover on appeal costs incurred in the District Court, they must be taxed prior to the filing of the transcript on appeal or writ of error, and the transcript must include a certificate of the clerk of the District Court as to such costs.

State Ex. Rel. v. Bd. of Ed., p. 286.   3. 289

APPEAL—Decisions—Exceptions.

Exceptions to the decisions of the court upon any matter of law arising during the progress of a cause must be taken at the time of such decision and no exceptions shall be taken in any appeal to any proceeding in a District Court except such as shall have been expressly decided in that court.

State v. Armijo, p. 262.   6. 271

APPEAL—District Court—De Novo.

On appeal to the District Court from a Justice of the Peace a cause is triable de novo.

Rogers v. Lumber Co., p. 300.   1. 302

APPEAL—Judgment—Default.

Under sections 3305 and 3365, C. L. 1897, a defendant may appeal from a default judgment rendered and entered against him by a Justice of the Peace.

Faggard Co. v. Cunningham, p. 510.   1. 512

APPELLANT—Interest—Trial Court.

Where the appellant has no interest in a sum of money, an assignment of error that the tral court erred in its disposition of such sum, will not be considered on appeal.

Edwards v. Fitzhugh, p. 424. 2. 426

APPELLEE—Office—Continued.

The appellee, being rightfully in office at the time of the adoption of the Constitution, she was continued in office by virtue of section 9, article XXII of the Constitution.

State v. Armijo, p. 646. 9. 666

APPELLATE COURT—Showing—Review.

In the absence of a showing of abuse of discretion vested in the trial judge by sec. 12, chapter 116, Session Laws 1905, the appellate court will not review the action of the court in returning to the jury box the names of veniremen, drawn to complete the panel.

State v. Analla, p. 294. 3. 293

APPELLATE COURT—Evidence—Verdict.

The appellate court will not weigh the evidence, but will examine it to ascertain whether or not the verdict of the jury is supported by substantial evidence.

Lyons v. Kitchell, p. 82. 3. 90

APPELLATE COURT—Verdict.

Where there is substantial evidence to support a verdict the appellate court will not disturb it.

State v. Padilla, p. 573. 1. 578

APPEARANCE—Practice—Proceeding.

An appearance, in practice, is a coming into court as a party to a suit, whether as plaintiff or defendant, and is a formal proceeding by which a defendant submits himself to the jurisdiction of the court.

Childers v. Lahann, p. 487. 1. 490 .

APPEARANCE—Waiver.

A general appearance, without objecting to the failure to file a cost bond, operates as a waiver.

Canavan v. Canavan, p. 468. 3. 472

APPEARED—Jurisdiction—Record.

The question as to whether a party has appeared and submitted himself voluntarily to the jurisdiction of the court should be tried by the record and not by other evidence.

Childers v. Lahann, p. 487. 2. 491

great bodily harm will justify the taking of life in those cases where an illegal arrest is attempted.

Territory v. Lynch, p. 15.   6. 34

ASSESSMENT—Taxation—Real Owner.

It is impracticable for the assessor to obtain the name of the real owner of a tract of land, from the official county records, as available for his inspection, and, in the absence of fraud, an assessment against unknown owners is not invalid, because of the fact that the assessor might have ascertained the name of the real owner from the records or conveyances in the office of the county recorder, in those cases where the owner has failed to list his property for taxation.

Daughtry v. Murry, p. 35.   1. 41

ASSESSOR—Duty—Presumption.

It must be presumed, in the absence of a showing to the contrary, that the assessor did his duty, and that inasmuch as he made the assessment to unknown owners, it was impracticable to obtain the real owner's name.

Daughtry v. Murry, p. 35.   2. 42

ASSESSOR—Unknown Owners.

It must be presumed, in the absence of a showing to the contrary, that the assessor did his duty, and that inasmuch as he made the assessment to unknown owners, it was impracticable to obtain the real owner's name.

Daughtry v. Murry, p. 35.   2. 42

ASSIGNMENTS OF ERROR—Findings.

Where assignments of error questioned the correctness of findings of fact, appellant having brought up the record proper only, the appellee was justified in bringing up the transcript by certiorari, and the cost thereof could be taxed by the clerk of the Supreme Court as provided by laws 1907, c. 57, sec. 34.

State Ex. Rel. v. Bd. of Ed., p. 286.   1. 288

ASSIGNMENTS OF ERROR—Copies.

Where the assignment of errors is copied into appellant's brief, and the brief served upon appellee's counsel, service of a separate copy of the said assignment of errors is not necessary.

Palmer v. Allen, p. 237.   3. 239

ASSIGNMENTS OF ERROR—Review.

Assignments of error that "the court below erred in affirming the decision of the Board of Water Commissioners," and that "the court below erred in rendering judgment herein in favor of said appellee, affirming the said

GENERAL INDEX.

A.

ABSTRACT QUESTION—Academic.

An abstract question, disconnected with the granting of relief in a case, and the determination of which would not affect the result, becomes an academic question which this Court will not consider.

Nursery Co. v. Mielenz, p. 417.   1. 422

ACEQUIA—Water Rights—Consumer.

The right to divert and utilize water acquired by the individual water user under a community acequia, being a several right, such individual consumer is a proper and necessary party in an action for the adjudication of water rights, utilized through such community acequia.

Snow v. Abalos, p. 681.   9. 699

ACEQUIAS—Considered.

The history of community acequias considered.

Snow v. Abalos, p. 681.   2. 692

ACEQUIAS—Constructed.

Chapter 49, laws of 1907, does not regulate community acequias constructed prior to the passage of the act as to the right to change the point of diversion from the stream into such acequias.

Pueblo of Isleta v. Tondre & Picard, p. 388.   1. 391

ACTION—Broker—Commissions.

In an action for a broker's commissions for effecting an exchange of real estate where the complaint states the making of a valid written contract of exchange between the principal and the customer procured by the broker, the complaint need not further state that the customer was able, ready and willing to complete the exchange on the terms of the contract; or that he made any effort to that end; or the refusal of the principal to complete it.

Keinath & Co. v. Reed, p. 358.   7. 370

ACTION—Damages—Adequate Remedy.

An action for damages for trespass under a void judgment and execution issued thereunder, is not such a plain, speedy and adequate remedy at law, as will bar an action to enjoin the enforcement of the judgment.

Pickering v. Palmer, p. 473.   4. 480

ACTION—Written Contract.

In an action based upon a written contract which is admitted by the answer, the intentions of the parties as to what should be the effect of the contract is to be decided by the Court upon an inspection of the contract.

Keinath & Co. v. Reed, p. 358.   8. 370

ADMISSION—Material Fact.

The admission by a party to a suit, of a material fact which in and of itself is sufficient to defeat or authorize a recovery, affords substantial evidence, sufficient to support a verdict based thereon, in the appellate court.

Lyons v. Kitchell, p. 82.   4. 91

ADMISSION—Confession—Hope.

The admission in evidence of a confession by the accused is to be determined by the fact of whether the same was made freely and without hope of benefit to his cause.

State v. Armijo, p. 262.   1. 267

ADVERSE PARTY—Knowledge.

Neither the rule to the effect that where the facts required to be shown are of a negative character, the burden of evidence may sometimes be sustained by proof rendering probable the existence of the negative facts, nor the rule to the effect that where knowledge or means of knowedge are almost wholly with the party not having the burden of proof, when all the evidence within the power of the moving party has been produced, the burden of evidence may sometimes shift to the party having the knowledge or means of knowledge, excuses the party having the burden of evidence from showing, no matter with what difficulty, sufficient facts, necessarily inconsistent with the position of the adverse party, to cause the court to say that a prima facie case has been made out requiring explanation, in which event, such showing, in connection with silence of the adverse party, may be sufficient to produce positive conviction in the mind of the court or jury.

Young v. Woodman, p. 207.   1. 211

ADVERSE PARTY—Examination.

Where, on cross examination, a witness is asked a question the answer to which calls for an explanation, the adverse party has the right, on redirect examination, to ask the witnes to explain the same.

State v. Lumpkin, p. 480.   6. 487

AFFIDAVIT—Continuance.

Nothing is to be presumed in aid of an affidavit in support of a motion for a continuance, and it is incumbent upon

the party applying for a continuance to show the materiality
of the facts which he claims the absent witness will substantiate.

State v. Analla, p. 294. 2. 298

AFFIRMANCE—Default—Showing.

A cause affirmed, upon motion of appellee, for failu; e
of appellant to file and serve briefs within the time required
by rule of court XIII, will not be reinstated upon the docket
and the affirmance vacated, where the only showing made
excusing such default and failure to apply for an extension
of time within which to file briefs was, that appellant's local
attorney in this state sent the brief to its general counsel
for examination and approval. Appellant should have applied for an extension of time, within the time limit for filing
briefs, when it became apparent that it would not be able
to comply with the rule.

Deal v. Western C. & G. Co., p. 70. 2. 72

AGREEMENT—Tax Payer—Actions.

A tax payer has no such direct interest in an agreement
between a municipality and a corporation for supplying water
as will allow him to sue ex contractu for breach, or ex delicto
for violation of the public duty thereby assumed.

Braden v. Water Co., p. 173. 1. 179

AGRICULTURAL COLLEGE—Treasurer.

Where the statute creating a board of regents for the
Agricultural College and Experiment Station provides for the
election of one of the members of said board as secretary
and treasurer, and also provides that such secretary and
treasurer shall continue in office until his successor shall be
elected and qualified, the incumbent is not ousted from the
office of secretary and treasurer by the appointment of a new
board of regents, but continues as such until a new secretary
and treasurer has been elected and has qualified as directed
by the statute.

Trust Co. v. Bank, p. 589. 5. 602

ALIBI—Witnesses—Evidence.

Upon cross examination the State has the right to expose to the jury the relations existing between the witnesses
testifying and the defendant, and the fact that the witnesses
have been frequently used by the defendant to establish an
alibi was proper to go to the jury for the purpose of weakening the evidence given by the witnesses on their direct
examination.

State v. Lumpkin, p. 480. 3. 485

ALLEGATION—Answer.

or did not intend the contract should effectuate, raises a question of law to be decided by the Court.

Keinath & Co. v. Reed, p. 358.   9.   370

ALTERATION—Interlineation—Parties.

Alteration of an instrument by interlineation by one who was acting as a friend of both parties, and who drev the original instrument at a time prior to his becoming interested in behalf of either party, was not a fatal alteration.

Lohman v. Reymond, p. 225.   4   255

AMENDMENT—New Cause of Action.

In permitting amendments, upon the trial, the Court is limited by sub-sec. 82 of the Civil Code to such amendments as do not change "substantially the claim or defense." Held that the trial court was without authority, in an action in ejectment, to permit the filing of a trial amendment for specific performance of a contract to convey real estate, as such amendment introduced a new cause of action.

Literary Society v. Garcia, p. 318.   1.   324

ANNUAL FEE—License.

Chapter 28, Session Laws of 1912, fixing an annual fee of $10 for a license fee for operating an automobile, is not unconstitutional, as a property tax imposed without regard to the value of the property on which it is made, but is a license tax, since the character of the tax is not determined by the mode adopted in fixing its amount.

State v. Ingalls, p. 211.   9.   224

ANSWER—Interpleader—Waiver.

Where a demurrer is interposed and sustained to an answer and interpleader, and the interpleading defendant thereupon takes leave to answer, and by his answer filed, pursuant to leave granted, takes issue with plaintiff upon the merits, and abandons his impartial attitude assumed in his interpleader, and takes up the cudgel for the other claimant of the fund, he thereby waives his interpleader, and cannot predicate error upon the acton of the court in sustaining the demurrer.

Trust Co. v. Bank, p. 589.   3.   599

ANSWER—Question of Fact.

An allegation in the answer of what the parties intended or did not intend the contract should effectuate, raises a question of law to be decided by the Court.

Keinath & Co. v. Reed, p. 358.   9.   370

APPEAL—Application.

All the facts, entitling the person, not a party to the record, to appeal should be stated in the application for appeal.

Bass v. Insurance Co., p. 282.   2.   285

APPEAL—Judgment—Reversal.

Error or irregularities in the course of the proceedings at or anterior to the trial, which, if presented to an appellate court by way of appeal or writ of error, must necessarily result in the reversal of the judgment, are not sufficient, for that reason, as grounds for the release of a prisoner upon application for a writ of habeas corpus.

Habeas Corpus, p. 452.   2. 456

APPEAL—Jurisdictional Question.

A question, not jurisdictional, cannot be raised the first time on appeal.

State v. Cabodi, p. 513.   2. 517

APPEAL—Transcript—Exceptions.

A bill of exceptions will be stricken from the transcript on appeal, upon motion therefor, when no notice has been given the adverse party of the time and place of its proposed settlement and signing, as required by sec. 26, chap. 57, S. L. 1907.

Palmer v. Allen, p. 237.   1. 239

APPEAL—Prosecution—Malicious.

Upon such appeal the burden is upon the State to show that the prosecution was instituted maliciously, or without probable cause.

State v. Coats, p. 314.   3. 318

APPEAL—Record—Silent.

When a party takes an appeal in open court he must see that the record affirmatively shows that it was taken in open court, and where the record is silent upon the question the presumption is that the appeal was not so taken, and in such case it is incumbent upon the appellant to cause citation to be issued and served upon appellee.

Childers v. Lohman, p. 487.   3. 491

APPELLANT—Briefs—Notice.

Where an appellant fails to file briefs within the time limited by subdivision 4 of rule XIII, the order of dismissal or affirmance goes as a matter of course, upon motion of the appellee, and no notice need be given the appellant, or his attorney.

Deal v. Western C. & G. Co., p. 70.   1. 71

APPELLANT—Affirmance—Dismissal.

The appellant has no right to dismiss his appeal in the face of a motion for affirmance well taken.

Hubbell v. Armijo, p. 68.   l. 69

APPROPRIATION OF WATER.

The "appropriation of water" consists in the taking or diversion of it from some natural stream, or other source of water supply, pursuant to law, with intent to apply it to some beneficial use, which intent is consummated within a reasonable time by the actual application of all of the water to the use designed, or to some other useful purpose.

Snow v. Abalos, p. 681.   11. 693

APPROPRIATION—Mounted Police.

Held, that the Act of 1905 (chap. 9) creating a force of Mounted Police, fixing salaries of its members, and providing for payment thereof, was repealed by the act of the legislature of 1909, (chap. 127, sec. IV) insofar as it provided for salaries and membership of the force, and that, therefore, a writ of mandate directed to the State Auditor requiring him to make a levy to pay such salaries is not issuable, because the appropriation by the Act of 1905 has ceased to be a continuing appropriation, and the legislature has failed to make appropriation for the present fiscal year.

State Ex. Rel. v. Sargent, p. 272.   3. 280

APPROPRIATIONS—Insurance Moneys.

Chap. 135, Laws of 1909, interpreted and held, that the appropriations carried by that Act were limited to the insurance moneys mentioned in the title.

State Ex. Rel. v. Auditor, p. 131.   1. 135

APPROPRIATION—Water—Rights.

An appropriator of water does not acquire a right to specific water flowing in the stream, but only the right to take therefrom a given quantity of water, for a specified purpose.

Snow v. Abalos, p. 681.   1. 693

APPROPRIATOR—Purpose—Stream.

An appropriator of water does not acquire a right to specific water flowing in the stream, but only the right to take therefrom a given quantity of water, for a specified purpose.

Snow v. Abalos, p. 681.   4. 693

ARREST—Illegal—Manslaughter.

Where the arrest is illegal, the offense is reduced to manslaughter, unless the proof shows express malice toward the deceased.

Territory v. Lynch, p. 15.   1. 33

ARREST—Justify.

Nothing short of an endeavor to destroy life or inflict

great bodily harm will justify the taking of life in those cases where an illegal arrest is attempted.

Territory v. Lynch, p. 15.   6.   34

ASSESSMENT—Taxation—Real Owner.

It is impracticable for the assessor to obtain the name of the real owner of a tract of land, from the official county records, as available for his inspection, and, in the absence of fraud, an assessment against unknown owners is not invalid, because of the fact that the assessor might have ascertained the name of the real owner from the records or conveyances in the office of the county recorder, in those cases where the owner has failed to list his property for taxation.

Daughtry v. Murry, p. 35.   1.   41

ASSESSOR—Duty—Presumption.

It must be presumed, in the absence of a showing to the contrary, that the assessor did his duty, and that inasmuch as he made the assessment to unknown owners, it was impracticable to obtain the real owner's name.

Daughtry v. Murry, p. 35.   2.   42

ASSESSOR—Unknown Owners.

It must be presumed, in the absence of a showing to the contrary, that the assessor did his duty, and that inasmuch as he made the assessment to unknown owners, it was impracticable to obtain the real owner's name.

Daughtry v. Murry, p. 35.   2.   42

ASSIGNMENTS OF ERROR—Findings.

Where assignments of error questioned the correctness of findings of fact, appellant having brought up the record proper only, the appellee was justified in bringing up the transcript by certiorari, and the cost thereof could be taxed by the clerk of the Supreme Court as provided by laws 1907, c. 57, sec. 34.

State Ex. Rel. v. Bd. of Ed., p. 286.   1.   288

ASSIGNMENTS OF ERROR—Copies.

Where the assignment of errors is copied into appellant's brief, and the brief served upon appellee's counsel, service of a separate copy of the said assignment of errors is not necessary.

Palmer v. Allen, p. 237.   3.   239

ASSIGNMENTS OF ERROR—Review.

Assignments of error that "the court below erred in affirming the decision of the Board of Water Commissioners," and that "the court below erred in rendering judgment herein in favor of said appellee, affirming the said

decision of the Board of Water Commissioners," are not
sufficiently specific to present any question for review.

Development Co. v. Land & Irrigation Co., p. 1.   1.   6

ATTORNEY—Client—Services.

In the absence of a contract, express or implied, between
attorney and client, fixing the stipulated percentage which
the payee is entitled to recover from the payor, in case of
default and the placing of the note in the hands of an attorney for collection as the compensation which the attorney
is to receive, the attorney is only entitled to recover from
his client the reasonable value of his services.

Rogers v. Lumber Co., p. 300.   2.   203

ATTORNEY—Engaged—Good Cause.

The fact that appellant's attorney has been busily engaged with other matters does not constitute "good cause"
for failure to file and serve assignment of error as required
by Sec. 31, C. 57, S. L. 1907.

Hubbell v. Armijo, p. 68.   2.   70

AUTOMOBILE—License—Property Tax.

Chapter 28, Session Laws of 1912, fixing an annual fee
of $10 for a license fee for operating an automobile, is not
unconstitutional, as a property tax imposed without regard to
the value of the property on which it is made, but is a license
tax, since the character of the tax is not determined by the
mode adopted in fixing its amount.

State v. Ingalls, p. 211.   9.   224

AUTOMOBILE—Revenue Measure.

Sec. 3 of chapter 28, Session Laws of 1912, imposing license fee for automobiles, in excess of the expense of administering the act, is a revenue measure, and as such is a
valid exrcise of power by the legislature.

State v. Ingalls, p. 211.   5.   222

AUTOMOBILE—Regulation—Legislation.

The law regulating the use of automobiles alone, of all
the vehicles which use the highway, is not invalid special
legislation.

State v. Ingalls, p. 211.   4.   221

B.

BANK—Certificate of Deposit.

Where a party, holding a certificate of deposit issued
by a bank, is entitled to collect the same, and makes demand
upon the bank for its payment, which is refused, he becomes
entitled, as a matter of law, to interest on the deposit, at
the statutory rate, from the time of such demand. In such

case, where suit is brought against the bank to recover the amount of such certificate and interest thereon from the time demand was made, the bank cannot interplead and pay the money into court, and escape liability, unless it tenders the sum which the plaintiff is entitled to recover at the time the tender is made, should it prevail.

Trust Co. v. Bank, p. 589.　　　　　　　　　2.　59S

BANK—Legislative Power.

Said Joint Resolution No. 14, insofar as it requires the deposit of these funds in banks, is beyond legislative power and void.

State v. Marron, p. 426.　　　　　　　　　3.　449

BANK—Trust Funds.

When trust funds have been commingled with the general funds of a bank, before a trust upon such general funds can be imposed, as against creditors of the bank, it must appear that the trust fund in some form still exists and came into the hands of the receiver of the insolvent bank.

Daughtry v. Bank, p. 119.　　　　　　　　2.　127

BILLS OF EXCEPTION—Settled—Signed.

A bill of exceptions, in a case tried to a jury, must be settled and signed by the judge of the court in which the case was tried, and where the record fails to show that such bill of exceptions was signed by the judge it will be stricken from the files, upon motion.

Palmer v. Allen, p. 237.　　　　　　　　　2.　239

BILLS OF EXCEPTION—Notice—Stricken.

A bill of exceptions will be stricken from the transcript on appeal, upon motion therefor, when no notice has been given the adverse party of the time and place of its proposed settlement and signing, as required by sec. 26, chap. 57, S. L. 1907.

Palmer v. Allen, p. 237.　　　　　　　　　1.　239

BILLS OF SALE—Acknowledgment.

The form of execution and authentication of bills of sale for the transfer of title to live stock, except sheep, is prescribed by section 119, C. L. 1897, which requires such bills of sale to be acknowledged by some officer authorized to take acknowledgments of conveyances of real estate, and which section, in that regard, repeals by necessary implication, the provisions of section 75, C. L. 1897.

Williamson v. Stevens, p. 204.　　　　　　　1.　206

BILLS OF SALE—Live Stock—Officer.

The form of execution and authentication of bills of sale for the transfer of title to live stock, except sheep, is

prescribed by section 119, C. L. 1897, which requires such
bills of sale to be acknowledged by some officer authorized to
take acknowledgments of conveyance of real estate, and which
section, in that regard, repeals, by necessary implication, the
provisions of section 75, C. L. 1897.

Williamson v. Stevens, p. 204.   1. 206

BONDS—Building Contract.

The surety on a bond for the faithful performance by the
contractor of a building contract is absolutely discharged
from liability when the obligee fails to retain not less than
fifteen (15%) per cent of the value of all work performed
and material furnished in the performance of said contract
in accordance with the terms of said bond, said surety not
having consented to such alteration.

Salmon v. Morgan, p. 72.   ·. 80

BOND—Supersedeas—Costs.

Under section 14, chapter 57, S. L. 1907, the giving of
a bond for costs, where no supersedeas bond is given, is essential to perfect an appeal or writ of error, and where a
plaintiff in error has failed to file a cost bond, within thirty
days from the time he sues out his writ of error, and advantage is taken of such default, by defendant in error, before
it is cured, the writ of error will be dismissed.

Devl. Co. v. Land Co., p. 138.   1. 140

BROKER—Customer—Contract.

Under an employment to sell or exchange the property
of his principal, a broker has fully performed his undertaking
when he procures a customer, with whom the principal makes
a valid contract of sale or exchange.

Keinath & Co. v. Reed, p. 358.   3. 367

BROKER—Commissions—Contract.

In an action for commissions earned by a broker in effecting an exchange of property of his principal, where the
complaint pleaded a written contract of employment of the
broker by the principal to make an exchange and a written
contract of exchange between the principal and a customer
procured by the broker; an answer which alleged (a) that the
principal had not accepted the property of the customer; (b)
that the principal had not accepted the customer as a proper
party with whom to make an exchange other than on the
terms of the written contracts entered into by them; (c) that
the written contracts of exchange were intended by the parties to be merely stipulations by which an exchange of property might be effected and not a valid, binding and enforceable contract of exchange; (d) that the broker had not done
all he was required to do in order to earn his commissions;

(e) that the customer had failed to perform his part of the contract; tendered issues of law and not of fact.

Keinath & Co. v. Reed, p. 358. 1. 367

BROKER—Customer—Sale.

Under an employment to sell or exchange the property of his principal, a broker has fully performed his undertaking when he procures a customer, with whom the principal makes a valid contract of sale or exchange.

Keinath & Co. v. Reed, p. 358. 8. 367

BUILDING CONTRACT—Alteration.

Any material alteration in a building contract will release non-consenting sureties upon a bond given to guarantee the faithful performance of the same; and where a contract provides for the retention by the owner of a stated percentage of the estimate, or stated amount, at the time of each payment to the contractor, prior to completion of the building, and the owner fails to comply therewith and pays the contractor in excess of the stipulated amount without the consent of the sureties, such overpayment is a breach of the contract by the owner, and the bond given to secure the same cannot be enforced against the sureties.

Lyons v. Kitchell, p. 82. 1. 8×

BUILDING CONTRACT—Performance.

The surety on a bond for the faithful performance by the contractor of a building contract is absolutely discharged from liability when the obligee fails to retain not less than fifteen (15%) per cent of the value of all work performed and material furnished in the performance of said contract in accordance with the terms of said bond, said surety not having consented to such alteration.

Salmon v. Morgan, p. 72. 1. 80

BUILDING & LOAN—Funds—Homes.

Corporations or associations doing business by collecting monthly installments of dues for the accumulation of funds out of which to loan those contributing to such fund amounts for the purchase of homes, are subject to the provisions of chapter 72, Session Laws of 1899, entitled "An act relating to building and loan associations, as doing business in a form and character similar to that authorized to be done by building and loan associations organized under the provisions of said act."

State Ex. Rel. v. Corp. Comm., p. 166. 1. 173

C.

CERTIFICATE OF DEPOSIT—Interest.

Where a party, holding a certificate of deposit issued by a bank, is entitled to collect the same, and makes demand upon the bank for its payment, which is refused, he becomes entitled, as a matter of law, to interest on the deposit, at the statutory rate, from the time of such demand. In such case, where suit is brought against the bank to recover the amount of such certificate and interest thereon from the time demand was made, the bank cannot interplead and pay the money into court, and escape liability, unless it tenders the sum which the plaintiff is entitled to recover at the time the tender is made, should it prevail.

Trust Co. v. Bank, p. 589.　　　　　　　　　2.　593

CITY—Municipal Purpose.

Under the power granted to cities and towns by subsection 5, sec. 2402, C. L. 1897, to erect all needful buildings for the use of the city or town, such municipalities are limited to the erection of such needful buildings as may be required for public uses, or for municipal uses and purposes and contradistinguished from private or quasi-public uses and, if the primary object of a building to be constructed is a municipal purpose, the fact that it may be incidentally used for theatrical purposes, may not have the effect of rendering the action in erecting it invalid; but where the paramount purpose and object is for other than strictly municipal purposes, legislative authority is lacking in this State, for the erection of such buildings by cities and towns.

Smith v. City, p. 613.　　　　　　　　　3.　623

CITY ORDINANCE—Violation.

Where a city ordinance is not before the Court, and where a judgment for violation of the same is an ordinary judgment for money in the amount of a fine, and where no imprisonment is imposed, and where the nature of the act charged against the defendant is not criminal in character and is not punishable by any general law of the State, but relates solely to a local regulation of the city for the safety and welfare of its inhabitants, the proceeding will be treated by this Court as a civil and not a criminal proceeding.

City v. Belmore, p. 331.　　　　-　　　3.　339

CITY ORDINANCE—Fine—Civil.

Where a city ordinance is not before the Court, and where a judgment for violation of the same is an ordinary judgment for money in the amount of a fine, and where no imprisonment is imposed, and where the nature of the act charged against the defendant is not criminal in character and is not punishable by any general law of the State, but

relates solely to a local regulation of the city for the safety and welfare of its inhabitants, the proceeding will be treated by this Court as a civil and not a criminal proceeding.
City v. Belmore, p. 331. 3. 339

CITATION—Default—Cause Shown.

Where good cause is shown for the failure to cause citation to be issued and served upon appellee as, and within the time, required by statute, the appellate court can extend the time for serving the citation and will permit a citation to be issued and served at any time before the end of the term of the appellate court to which the appeal was properly returnable.
Childers v. Lahann, p. 487. 1. 493

CITIZEN—Public Office—Rights.

Section 1 of chapter 134, S. L. 1909, which provides that "No person prevented by the Organic Act of the Territory of New Mexico * * * * shall be entitled to vote or hold public office in this Territory," refers to the original act of Congress creating the Territory of New Mexico, and the only limitations thereby imposed upon the right to vote or hold public office are that such rights shall be exercised only by citizens of the United States, including those recognized as citizens by the treaty with the Republic of Mexico, etc.
State v. Armijo, p. 646. 3. 652

CHAPTER 84, LAWS 1913—Construed.

Chapter 84, Laws of 1913, as construed to authorize the sale of property for taxes delinquent previous to the time the act became effective. Held not to operate retrospectively in respect to such taxes.
Crane v. Cox, p. 377. 2. 380

CHILD—Court—Discretion.

This Court will not review the discretion of the trial court in the matter of permitting a child of tender years to be sworn, as a witness, under the provisions of sec. 3016, Comp. Laws of 1897, except in a clear case of abuse of such discretion.
State v. Armijo, p. 262. 5. 270

CLERK—Writ of Error—Practice.

Where the Supreme Court, upon statehood, appointed the clerk of the former Territorial Court to be clerk of the Supreme Court and allowed him to continue to issue writs of error, as had been the practice before statehood, writs of error, so issued, with the knowledge and acquiescence of the Supreme Court and the justices thereof, must be taken to be issued at their direction within Const., art. VI, sec. 3, providing for that manner of issuing writs of error.
Wood-Davis v. Sloan, p. 290. 2. 293

COLLECTOR—Sale—Authority.

Section 34, chapter 84, Laws 1913, directs the collector to offer for sale "each parcel of property upon which any taxes are delinquent as shown by the tax rolls." Held, to authorize the sale of property for taxes which had become delinquent prior to the year 1913.

.Cox v. Crane, p. 377.   1. 381

COLORADO DOCTRINE—Water Rights.

In New Mexico, the "Colorado Doctrine," as it is termed, of prior appropriation prevails. Such doctrine was established or founded by the custom of the people, and grew out of the conditions of the country and the necessities of the people. It was recognized by the courts of the Territory and became the settled law.

Snow v. Abalos, p. 681.   3. 693

COMMISSIONS—Broker.

In an action for commissions earned by a broker in effecting an exchange of property of his principal, where the complaint pleaded a written contract of employment of the broker by the principal to make an exchange and a written contract of exchange between the principal and a customer procured by the broker; an answer which alleged (a) that the principal had not accepted the property of the customer; (b) that the principal had not accepted the customer as a proper party with whom to make an exchange other than on the terms of the written contracts entered into by them; (c) that the written contracts of exchange were intended by the parties to be merely stipulations by which an exchange of property might be effected and not a valid, binding and enforceable contract of exchange; (d) that the broker had not done all he was required to do in order to earn his commissions; (e) that the customer had failed to perform his part of the contract; tendered issues of law and not of fact.

.Keinath & Co. v. Reed, p. 356.   1. 367

COMMITMENT—Surplusage.

Where a District Court is without power to suspend the execution of the judgment in a criminal cause, or to withhold the commitment, an order so made, attempting to do so, is null and void and without force and effect, and amounts to surplusage.   .   .

In re Juan Lujan, p. 310.   1. 312

COMMON LAW—Penalties.

While common law crimes are recognized and punished in this state, common law penalties are not inflicted, but the punishment therefor is prescribed by sec. 1054, C. L. 1897.

Ex Parte De Vore, p. 246.   6. 261

COMMON LAW—Recognized Practice.

Such political rights as were recognized by the common law, and not in conflict with our established laws, institutions and customs, and suitable to our conditions, were carried into the body of our laws.
State v. Armijo, p. 646.　　　　　　　8. 653

COMMON LAW—Practice.

The common law is the rule of practice and decision in New Mexico, by virtue of section 2874, R. S. 1897, except where modified by statute.
State v. Armijo, p. 646.　　　　　　　5. 654

COMMON LAW—Modified—Office.

The statutory law of the Territory of New Mexico neither expressly conferred or denied the right of women to vote or hold public office, hence we must look to the common law, if it was in force in the Territory, to ascertain and determine the right of women to vote and hold public office
State v. Armijo, p. 646.　　　　　　　4. 653

COMMON LAW—Statutes—Modified.

The word "recognize," used in the above section, is given various significations by the lexicographers. Webster, among other definitions, defines its meaning to be "to avow knowledge of." Century Dictionary, "to know again." Webster defines the meaning of the verb "know" to be, among others given, "to recognize." In the above section the word "recognized" was used in the sense of "known," and as used was intended to adopt the common law of crimes, as known in the United States and the several states of the Union, which was the common law, or lex non scripta of England, as it existed at the time of the Independence of the United States, supplemented and modified by such British statutes as were of a general nature and not local to that kingdom.
Ex Parte De Vore, p. 246.　　　　　　　2. 256

COMMUNITY ACEQUIAS—Condemnation.

Said chapter authorizes the enlarging of an old community acequia by condemnation proceedings.
Pueblo of Isleta v. Tondre & Picard, p. 388.　　3. 335

COMMUNITY DITCHES—Water Rights.

Chapter 1, S. L. 1895, "An act in regard to community ditches and acequias," was purely administrative, and while section 1 of said act makes community acequias corporations, "for the purpose of this act," the legislature did not confer upon the organization thus created the power to acquire or hold title to water rights. Such corporations have no powers not expressly or impliedly granted them by the act creating them.
Snow v. Abalos, p. 681.　　　　　　　1. 692

CONDEMNATION—Proceedings.

Said chapter authorizes the enlarging of an old community acequia by condemnation proceedings.

Pueblo of Isleta v. Tondre & Picard, p. 388.   2. 395

CONFESSION—Admission—Evidence.

The admission in evidence of a confession by the accused is to be determined by the fact of whether the same was made freely and without hope of benefit to his cause.

State v. Armijo.   1. 267

CONFESSION—Voluntary.

The court may, even after it has admitted a confession in evidence, rule it out if satisfied that the confession was not free and voluntary, by subsequent evidence.

State v. Armijo, p. 262.   1. 267

CONSIDERATION—Contract—Inadequacy.

Mere inadequacy of consideration is not sufficient, in and of itself, to avoid a contract.

Frazer v. Bank, p. 340.   4. 356

CONSTITUTION—Language.

The word "charge" used in section 14, article II, of the State Constitution, in the clause "to have the charge and testimony interpreted to him in a language that he understands," refers to the indictment or information, and not the instructions given to the jury by the court.

State v. Cabodi, p. 513.   6. 520

CONSTITUTION—Interpretation.

Under the provisions of section 14, art. II, of the State Constitution, the defendant is entitled to have the testimony interpreted to him in a language which he understands. While such right cannot be denied a defendant, it is incumbent upon him to, in some appropriate manner, call the attention of the trial court to the fact that he does not understand the language in which the testimony is given.

State v. Cabodi, p. 513.   5. 519

CONSTITUTION—General Legislation.

The last paragraph of sec. 18, chapter 83, Laws 1912, held to be void as violative of section 16 of article IV of the Constitution, which prohibits general legislation in appropriation bills.

State Ex. Rel. v. Auditor.   3. 138

CONSTITUTION—Taxing Power.

Whether the word "securities" as used in the enabling act and the Constitution is not limited to public obligations for the payment of which the taxing power is available, is

not decided because its decision is not necessary to a determination of this case, and is not discussed by counsel.
State v. Marron, p. 426. 2. 439

CONSTITUTION—Supreme Court—Power

The Constitution, sec. 3, art. VI, having conferred upon the Supreme Court the power to issue writs of error and providing for the issuance of the writ by "direction of the court or by any justice thereof," such writ can only be issued in the manner therein provided.
Devl. Co. v. Land Co., p. 138. 2. 141

CONSTITUTION—Amendment.

Chapter 57, S. L. 1907, should be read, as if amended by section 3, art. VI, of the Constitution.
Devl. Co. v. Land Co., p. 138. 3. 142

CONSTITUTION—Office—Created.

Where the Constitution of a State creates an office and prescribes the salary for such office, the necessity for legislative appropriation for such office is dispensed with on the ground that such provision in a State Constitution is proprio vigore an appropriation.
State Ex. Rel. v. Sargent, p. 272. 1. 278

CONSTITUTION—General Legislation—Void.

The last paragraph of sec. 18, chapter 83, Laws 1912, held to be void as violative of section 16 of article IV of the Constitution, which prohibits general legislation in appropriation bills.
State Ex. Rel. v. Auditor, p. 131. 3. 138

CONTEMPT—Injunction—Violation.

A final decree dissolves a preliminary injunction which is ancillary to the main case unless the same is specially continued by the decree, and thereafter a litigant cannot be punished as for civil contempt for violation of the preliminary injunction prior to its dissolution.
Canavan v. Canavan, p. 640. 1. 642

CONTEMPT—Civil—Proceeding.

The proceedings examined and held to be proceedings as for civil contempt.
Canavan v. Canavan, p. 640. 1. 642

CONTINUANCE—Materiality.

Nothing is to be presumed in aid of an affidavit in support of a motion for a continuance, and it is incumbent upon the party applying for a continuance to show the materialty of the facts which he claims the absent witness will substantiate.
State v. Analla, p. 294. 2. 298

CONTRACT—Attorney—Services.

In the absence of a contract, express or implied, between attorney and client, fixing the stipulated percentage which the payee is entitled to recover from the payor, in case of default and the placing of the note in the hands of an attorney for collection as the compensation which the attorney is to receive, the attorney is only entitled to recover from his client the reasonable value of his services.

Rogers v. Lumber Co., p. 300.   2. 303

CONTRACT—Deviation—Nullifies.

It is the deviation from the terms of the contract that operates to release the surety and not the injury or damage done by such departure, and the breach of the contract ipso facto nullifies it as to the sureties.

Lyons v. Kitchell, p. 82.   2. 89

CONTRACT—Executory—Damages.

In the case of a breach of an executory contract for the sale of goods, by vendee, before title has passed the vendor, as a general rule, cannot recover on the contract price, but his right is limited to an action for damages.

Nursery Co. v. Mielenz, p. 417.   2. 422

CONTRACT—License—Permit.

A license to retail intoxicating liquor is neither a property right nor a contract. It is in no sense a contract made by the State with a party holding the license; it is a mere permit, subject to be modified or annulled at the pleasure of the legislature.

Habeas Corpus, p. 605.   2. 610

CONTRACT—Oral—Statute of Frauds.

The statute of frauds is no bar to an action for the price of land actually conveyed, where the deed has been accepted or title has otherwise passed, although the grantor could not have been compelled to convey, or the grantor to accept, a deed, because the contract was oral.

Harris v. Hardwick, p. 303.   2. 309

CONTRACT—Option—Declaration.

Held, further, that a declaration of the fact that the party had elected to exercise his option to cancel the contract should have been made to the first party, and until it was made, the option was not exercised and the contract continued in full force and effect.

Beck v. Chambers, p. 53.   2. 60

CONTRACT—Partnership.

Where parties to a contract construe it as having created a partnership relation, and act upon such construction, the Court will not, after rights have accrued thereunder, by reason of such construction, give to the contract a different construction, which would be at variance with the understanding of the parties to it.

Frazer v. Bank, p. 340. 5. 357

CONTRACT—Principal—Broker.

In an action by a broker for commissions earned by him in effecting an exchange of the property of his principal, where the complaint pleads a valid and enforceable written contract between the principal and a customer procured by the broker, to exchange property, it was not necessary for the complaint to allege that the customer was "in a position and able to convey a perfect title to the property which he proposed to exchange."

Keinath & Co. v. Reed, p. 358. 4. 363

CONTRACT—Exchange—Customer.

In such a case the principal by entering into a contract of exchange with the customer produced by the broker, accepted the customer as able, ready and willing to make the exchange.

Keinath & Co. v. Reed, p. 358. 5. 368

CONTRACT—Surety.

The surety on the note of a minor, given in payment for real estate, is discharged from liability thereon, where the minor on becoming of age, disaffirms the contract and restores the property purchased.

Evants v. Taylor, p. 371. 1. 375

CONTRACT—Title—Price.

In the case of a breach of an executory contract for the sale of goods by vendee before title has passed, the vendor, as a general rule, cannot recover on the contract price, but his right is limited to an action for damages.

Nursery Co. v. Mielenz, p. 417. 2. 422

CONTRACTOR—Labor—Party.

The fact that a water user may have entered into a contract, by which he agrees, at some future time, to convey his water right to another party, does not militate against his right to maintain an action for the adjudication of his right to the use of the water.

Snow v. Abalos, p. 681. 10. 701

CONTRACT—Water User.

Where a county has contracted with a party to construct a court house and jail, and a tax payer seeks to enjoin the board of county commissioners from paying said contractor for work and labor performed, and to be performed, under

said contract, the contractor is an indispensable party to the
suit, and where such contractor was not made a party, the
court properly dismissed the petition.

    Walrath v. Co. Com., p. 101.   `.. 107

CONTRACTOR—Overpayment—Sureties.

Any material alteration in a building contract will release non-consenting sureties upon a bond given to guarantee
the faithful performance of the same; and where a contract
provides for the retention by the owner of a stated percentage of the estimate, or stated amount, at the time of each
payment to the contractor, prior to completion of the building, and the owner fails to comply therewith and pays the
contractor in excess of the stipulated amount without the
consent of the sureties, such overpayment is a breach of the
contract by the owner, and the bond given to secure the
same cannot be enforced against the sureties.

    Lyons v. Kitchell, p. 82.   l. 88

CONVICTION—Evidence—Burden.

Neither the rule to the effect that where the facts required to be shown are of a negative character, the burden
of evidence may sometimes be sustained by proof rendering
probable the existence of the negative facts, nor the rule :o
the effect that where knowledge or means of knowledge are
almost wholly with the party not having the burden of proof,
when all the evidence within the power of the moving party
has been produced, the burden of evidence may some times
shift to the party having the knowledge or means of knowledge, excuses the party having the burden of evidence from
showing, no matter with what difficulty, sufficient facts, necessarily inconsistent with the position of the adverse party,
to cause the court to say that a prima facie case has been
made out requiring explanation, in which event, such showing, in connection with silence of the adverse party, may be
sufficient to produce positive conviction in the mind of the
court or jury.

    Young v. Woodman, p. 207.   l. 211

CORPORATION—Water Supply.

A tax payer has no such direct interest in an agreement
between a municipality and a corporation for supplying water
as will allow him to sue ex contractu for breach, or ex delicto
for violation of the public duty thereby assumed.

    Braden v. Water Co., p. 173.   l. 179

CORPORATIONS—Funds.

Corporations or associations doing business by collecting
monthly installments of dues for the accumulation of funds
out of which to loan those contributing to such fund amounts
for the purchase of homes, are subject to the provisions of

are required to divide their counties into three road districts, which shall be the same as the county commissioner
districts of the county.

State v. Byers & Buehl, p. 92.   1. 100

COUNTY COMMISSIONERS—Mandamus.

The board of county commissioners, in determining the
fact as to whether liquor is being sold outside of the locality
for which the license was granted, acts only in a ministerial
capacity; and, where the facts upon which it acts are not
disputed, mandamus is the proper remedy to compel the cancellation of a liquor license, where liquor is being sold thereunder outside of the locality for which such license was
granted.

Lorenzino v. James, p. 240.   3. 244

COURT—Abstract Question.

An abstract question, disconnected with the granting
of relief in a case, and the determination of which would not
affect the result, becomes an academic question which this
Court will not consider.

Nursery Co. v. Mielenz, p. 417.   1. 422

COURT—Amendments—Civil Code.

In permitting amendments, upon the trial, the Court is
limited by sub-sec. 82 of the Civil Code to such amendments
as do not change "substantially the claim or defense." Held,
that the trial court was without authority, in an action in
ejectment, to permit the filing of a trial amendment for specific performance of a contract to convey real estate, as
such amendment introduced a new cause of action.

Literary Society v. Garcia, p. 318.   1. 324

COURT—Confession—Rule.

The court may, even after it has admitted a confession
in evidence, rule it out if satisfied that the confession was
not free and voluntary, by subsequent evidence.

State v. Armijo, p. 262.   3. 268

COURT—Evidence—Ultimate Facts.

The Court is only required to find the ultimate facts in
controversy, raised by the issues in the case, and is not
required, nor is it proper, to set out the evidence upon which
it relies in determining such ultimate facts.

Frazer v. Bank, p. 340.   1. 350

COURT—Jury—Instructions.

The failure of the court to instruct the jury on all of
the law applicable to the case cannot be taken advantage of,
unless excepted to at the time the jury is instructed.

State v. Padilla, p. 573.   2. 576

COURT—Jurisdiction—Evidence.

A defendant, by answering over, upon demurrer over-ruled, waives all objections to the petition of the plaintiff, except to the jurisdiction of the court and the failure of the petition to state a cause of action, and, where a defendant raises by demurrer the question of a defect of parties plaintiff, and, upon such demurrer being overruled answers to the merits, he cannot thereafter raise the same question by objecting to the introduction of evidence.

Baca v. Baca, p. 63.   1. 67

COURT—Jurisdiction—Judgment.

Where, in a judgment covering several cases, by inadvertence or otherwise, one or more cases are included over which the court had no jurisdiction to render judgment, this Court has jurisdiction, under section 38 of chapter 57 of the Laws of 1907, to modify the judgment by eliminating such case, or cases, from the judgment.

City v. Belmore, p. 331.   2. 338

CRIMES—Practice—Decision.

Common law crimes are recognized and punished in New Mexico, by virtue of sec. 3422, C. L. 1897, which provides, "In criminal cases, the common law as recognized by the United States and the several states of the Union shall be the rule of practice and decision."

Ex Parte De Vore, p. 246.   1. 253

CRIMINAL CAUSE—Commitment.

Where a District Court is without power to suspend the execution of the judgment in a criminal cause, or to withhold the commitment, an order so made, attempting to do so, is null and void and without force and effect, and amounts to surplusage.

In re Juan Lujan, p. 310.   1. 313

CRIMINAL PROSECUTION—Motive.

In a criminal prosecution the State is not required to prove a motive for the crime, if without this the evidence is sufficient to show that the act was done by the accused.

State v. Alva, p. 140.   5. 151

CROSS-COMPLAINT—Assignment.

Where, in a suit to compel an accounting by trustees, cross-complainant, at the time of filing his cross-complaint for appointment of a receiver, was justified from the record in believing that he would only be required to present and prove his title to claims transferred to him in the receivership proceeding, and for that reason only set up the assignment of such claims to his capacity to join in the suit to compel the trustees to account, his cross-complaint was not based on the instrument of assignment; and hence the assignment, when offered in evidence, was not objectionable because such instrument, or a copy thereof, was not filed in compliance with Code Civ. Proc., sub-sec. 307, (Laws 1907, c. 107), providing that, when any instrument of writing on which the action or defense is found is referred to in the pleadings, the original or a copy shall be filed with the pleading, if within the power or control of the party wishing to use the same, and if the original or a copy be not filed or a sufficient reason given for the failure to file it, the instrument may not be admitted in evidence.

Lohman v. Reymond, p. 225.   1. 231

CROSS EXAMINATION—Redirect—Evidence.

Where, on cross examination, a witness is asked a question the answer to which calls for an explanation, the adverse party has the right, on redirect examination, to ask the witness to explain the same.

State v. Lumpkin, p. 480.   6. 487

D.

DAMAGES—Adequate Remedy.

An action for damages for trespass under a void judgment and execution issued thereunder, is not such a plain, speedy and adequate remedy at law, as will bar an action to enjoin the enforcement of the judgment.

Pickering v. Palmer, p. 473.   1. 480

DECISION—Trial—Dictum.

Whenever a question fairly arises in the course of a trial, and there is a distinct decision of such question, the ruling of the court in respect thereto cannot be called mere dictum.

Duncan v. Brown, p. 579.   2. 588

DEFAULT—Showing.

A cause affirmed, upon motion of appellee, for failure of appellant to file and serve briefs within the time required by rule of court XIII, will not be reinstated upon the docket and the affirmance vacated, where the only showing made excusing such default and failure to apply for an extension of time within which to file briefs was, that appellant's local attorney in this state sent the brief to its general counsel for examination and approval. Appellant should have applied for an extension of time, within the time limit for filing briefs, when it became apparent that it would not be able to comply with the rule.

Deal v. Western C. & G. Co., p. 70.   2. 72

DEFAULT—Rules of Court—Briefs.

Where a party who is in default, having failed to file

briefs within the time limited by the rules of the court, tenders such briefs for filing at the same time that a motion to affirm the judgment because of such default is tendered, the motion to affirm will be denied.

McMillen v. Bank, p. 285.   1. 286

DEFENDANT—Counter Claim.

A defendant may not as a matter of right introduce a new cause of action by way of counter claim by means of a trial amendment.

Candelaria v. Miera, p. 107.   1. 115

DEMAND—By Mail—Proof.

Proof that "demand was made by mail" implies a prepayment of postage and a deposit of the demand in a United States postoffice, but that the letter was properly addressed to the addressee at the place where he resides or receives his mail, is not thereby implied, and proof of that fact must be had before the receipt of the letter by the addressee, will be inferred.

Silberberg Co. v. McNeil, p. 44.   1. 49

DEMURRER—Answering Over.

A defendant, by answering over, upon demurrer overruled, waives all objections to the petition of the plaintiff, except to the jurisdiction of the court and the failure of the petition to state a cause of action, and, where a defendant raises by demurrer the question of a defect of parties plaintiff, and, upon such demurrer being overruled, answers to the merits, he cannot thereafter raise the same question by objecting to the introduction of evidence.

Baca v. Baca, p. 63.   1. 67

DEMURRER—Answer—Interpleader.

Where a demurrer is interposed and sustained to an answer and interpleader, and the interpleading defendant thereupon takes leave to answer, and by his answer filed, pursuant to leave granted, takes issue with plaintiff upon the merits, and abandoned his impartial attitude assumed in his interpleader, and takes up the cudgel for the other claimant of the fund, he thereby waives his interpleader, and cannot predicate error upon the action of the court in sustaining the demurrer.

Trust Co. v. Bank, p. 589.   3. 599

DEPOSIT—Drafts—Proof.

Where a person, as soon as he learned of an unauthorized deposit of his funds in a bank, drew drafts on the same in order to immediately withdraw them, he will not be held to have ratified the deposit in the absence of proof of his assent to the deposit.

Daughtry v. Bank, p. 119.   1. 126

DIMINUTION—Record—Costs.

After the filing of the supplemental transcript, and the argument and submission of the case, it is too late for appellee to suggest a diminution of the record, to include in the transcript a certificate of the taxation of costs in the District Court.

State Ex. Rel. v. Bd. of Ed., p. 286.　　　　　1. 289

DISTRICT—Administrative.

The creation or designation of the district, as required by sections 1 and 2, chap. 78, C. L. 1913, is an administrative act and not legislative.

Habeas Corpus, p. 605.　　　　　2. 612

DISTRICT ATTORNEY—Complaint.

As used in Laws 1913, chap. 84, section 23, providing that the District Attorney shall, on complaint, submit an assessment to the District Court for correction to avoid injustice to the taxpayer, the word "injustice" is apparently the broadest term that could have been employed in the connection, and applies to any over-valuation of the property of a taxpayer.

Ranch & Cattle Co. v. Bd. of Equal., p. 531.　　4. 569

DISTRICT ATTORNEY—Assessment.

As used in Laws 1913, chap. 84, section 23, providing that the District Attorney shall, on complaint, submit an assessment to the District Court for correction to avoid injustice to the taxpayer, the word "injustice" is apparently the broadest term that could have been employed in the connection, and applies to any over-valuation of the property of a taxpayer.

Ranch & Cattle Co. v. Bd. of Equal., p. 531.　　4. 569

DISTRICT COURT—Appeal—De Novo.

On appeal to the District Court from a Justice of the Peace a cause is triable de novo.

Rogers v. Lumber Co., p. 300.　　　　　1. 302

DISTRICT COURT—Probable Cause.

In such a case, where the prosecuting witness appeals from a judgment of the Justice of the Peace taxing him with the costs, the District Court is required to try the question as to whether the prosecution was instituted maliciously, or without probable cause de novo, and must enter its own independent judgment in the case. In such case the discretion conferred by the statute upon the Justice of the Peace is necessarily transferred to the District Court.

State v. Coats, p. 314.　　　　　2. 317

DISTRICT COURT—Costs—Appeal.

Costs in the District Court can not be taxed on appeal, where no cost bill is filed in the Supreme Court showing the taxation of such costs.

State Ex. Rel. v. Bd. of Ed., p. 286.　　　　2. 289

DISTRICT COURT—Judgment—Affirmed.

The judgment of the District Court is affirmed upon the authority of State v. Romero, 124 Pac., 649, and State v. Romero, 125 Pac., 617, decided by this Court on March 23, 1912.

Herbert v. Co. Comrs., p. 129.　　　　1. 131

DISTRICT COURT—Judgment—Sentence.

Where a defendant, duly sentenced by a District Court to serve a definite term in the State penitentiary, is permitted to go and remain at large, under a void order of the Court, he may be taken into custody and compelled to serve the term fixed in the judgment, even though a longer period of time than that for which he was sentenced has elapsed since the sentence was imposed.

In re Juan Lujan, p. 310.　　　　2. 314

DISTRICT COURT—Judgment—Notice.

In this State, where a Justice of the Peace has no power to set aside his judgments or grant a new trial, and where upon appeal or certiorari to the District Court, the cause is triable de novo only, one against whom a void judgment has been rendered by a Justice of the Peace, is not, though with actual notice thereof, guilty of laches and negligence sufficient to bar his right to an equitable remedy against such judgment, because he fails to appeal or sue out a writ of certiorari.

Pickering v. Palmer, p. 473.　　　　3. 479

DIVERSION—Acequias—Change.

Chapter 49, Laws of 1907, does not regulate community acequias constructed prior to the passage of the act as to the right to change the point of diversion from the stream into such acequias.

Pueblo of Isleta v. Tondre & Picard, p. 388.　　　　1. 391

DIVERSION—Natural Stream.

The "appropriation of water" consists in the taking or diversion of it from some natural stream, or other source of water supply, pursuant to law, with intent to apply it to some beneficial use, which intent is consummated within a reasonable time by the actual application of all of the water to the use designed, or to some other useful purpose.

Snow v. Abalos, p. 681.　　　　11. 693

DOUELE TAXATION—Prohibited.

Double taxation in the objectionable and prohibited sense exists only where the same property is taxed twice when it ought to be taxed but once, and to consider such double taxation the second tax must be imposed upon the same property by the same state or government during the same taxing period.

State v. Ingalls, p. 211.   6.   22:

E.

ELECTION—General Election—Meaning.

An election which is general within the meaning of the term "general election," as used in sec. 4138, C. L. 1897, is one that is held throughout the entire state or territory.

Territory v. Ricordati, p. 10.   1.   14

ENGINEER—Discretion—Review.

Under chap. 49, S. L. 1907, from any act or refusal to act of the state engineer, the aggrieved party may appeal to the Board of Water Commissioners, and may likewise appeal from the decision of said board to the District Court. The statute contemplates a hearing or trial de novo before each board or tribunal, and not a review of the order or decision of the inferior tribunal. An assignment of error, in such a proceeding, upon appeal from a judgment of the District Court, that "the court below erred in finding and adjudging that the said Board of Water Commissioners had and was possessed of the right, warrant and authority to review the discretion of the said state engineer in the matter of the approval of permits to appropriate," is therefore not well taken, because the record in this case fails to show that the District Court so held, or that any such issue was presented, or could have been involved in the case.

Development Co. v. Land & Irrigation Co., p. 1.   1.   6

ENLARGING—Acequia—Condemnation.

Said chapter authorizes the enlarging of an old community acequia by condemnation proceedings.

Pueblo of Isleta v. Tondre & Picard, p. 388.   2.   395

ENTRY—Reservation—Action at Law.

An attempted exercise of jurisdiction by the land department in the acceptance of an entry, including lands reserved from entry by the government, where the reservation from entry appears as a matter of record in the land office, is void, as to the lands reserved, for the reason that it is an assumption of power in excess of its jurisdiction, and the same can be shown by a defendant in an action at law.

Whitehill v. Cattle Co., p. 520.   1.   531

EQUALIZATION—State Board—Power.

The State Board of Equalization has power to equalize the valuations of property for taxation purposes by classes, both as between classes in the same county and as between counties throughout the state, and the fact that the action taken results in the increase or decrease of total valuations in the state is immaterial.

Ranch & Cattle Co. v. Bd. of Equal., p. 531.　　1.　572

EQUITABLE REMEDY—Void Judgment.

In this State, where a Justice of the Peace has no power to set aside his judgments or grant a new trial, and where upon appeal or certiorari to the District Court the cause is triable de novo only, one against whom a void judgment has been rendered by a Justice of the Peace, is not, though with actual notice thereof, guilty of laches and negligence sufficient to bar his right to an equitable remedy against such judgment, because he fails to appeal or sue out a writ of certiorari.

Pickering v. Palmer, p. 473.　　3.　479

ERRORS—Brief—Service.

Where the assignment of errors is copied into appellant's brief, and the brief is served upon appellee's counsel, service of a separate copy of the said assignment of errors is not necessary.

Palmer v. Allen, p. 237.　　3.　239

ERRONEOUS TRANSLATION—Knowledge.

Where a complaining party is aware at the time that the interpretation of the evidence, by an interpreter, is not correct, it is incumbent upon him to call the court's attention to such erroneous translation, and ask to have it corrected; and, where he has not such knowledge at the time, but afterwards becomes aware of the fact, he must set out all the facts in his motion for a new trial, pointing out therein specifically the evidence erroneously translated, and support such contention by affidavit or proof, so that the trial court can pass intelligently upon the question.

State v. Cabodi, p. 513.　　4.　513

ESCROW—Contract—Good Faith.

A stipulation that "both parties hereunto have this day deposited in escrow with K., S. & H. this contract and a copy of the original contract, his demand note for $1,000.00 as evidence of good faith and as a forfeit in event either party hereto fails or refuses to comply with the terms of the contract as therein provided," held to be a penalty.

Keinath & Co. v. Reed, p. 358.　　6.　360

ESTOPPED—Appellee—Knowledge.

Appellee was not estopped to deny the invalidity of the proceedings had under the third execution, where it is not shown that he caused such execution to issue, or had knowledge of its issuance, or acquiesced therein.

McMillen v. Bank, p. 494. 3. 502

EVIDENCE—Conflict—Instructions.

If there be a conflict of evidence and the court is not satisfied that the confession was voluntary, the confession may be submitted to the jury, under instructions to disregard it if, upon all the evidence, they believe it was involuntary.

State v. Armijo, p. 262. 4. 263

EVIDENCE—Confession.

If there be a conflict of evidence and the court is not satisfied that the confession was involuntary, the confession may be submitted to the jury, under instructions to disregard it if, upon all the evidence, they believe it was involuntary.

State v. Armijo, p. 262. 1. 263

EVIDENCE—Cross Examination.

Evidence that a witness for the State expects to receive a reward upon conviction of the accused, can properly be elicited upon cross examination of such witness for the purpose of showing his interest in the result of the prosecution.

State v. Lumpkin, p. 480. 4. 486

EVIDENCE—Instructions.

Where there is any evidence tending to show such a state of facts as may bring the homicide within the grade of manslaughter, defendant is entitled to an instruction on the law of manslaughter, and it is a fatal error to refuse it.

Territory v. Lynch, p. 15. 9. 35

EVIDENCE—Judgment—Reversed.

A judgment will be reversed where there is no evidence to support the verdict upon which it is based.

Spencer v. Timber Co., p. 191. 1. 194

EVIDENCE—New Trial.

A new trial on the ground of newly discovered evidence will not be granted for evidence that was known to defendant at the time of the trial.

State v. Padilla, p. 573. 5. 578

EVIDENCE——Guilt—Admissions.

Corroborative evidence, whether consisting of acts or admissions, must at least be of such a character and quality as tends to prove the guilt of the accused by connecting him with the crime.

State v. Alva. p 143. 2. 147

EVIDENCE—Erroneous Translation.

Where a complaining party is aware at the time, that the interpretation of the evidence, by an interpreter, is not correct, it is incumbent upon him to call the court's attention to such erroneous translation, and ask to have it corrected; and, where he has not such knowledge at the time, but afterwards becomes aware of the fact, he must set out all the facts in his motion for a new trial, pointing out therein specifically the evidence erroneously translated, and support such contention by affidavit or proof, so that the trial court can pass intelligently upon the question.

EXCEPTIONS—Certificate—Court.

Where the certificate of the trial judge to an alleged bill of exceptions is not certified to by the clerk of the court, and is not shown to have been filed in the clerk's office, neither the alleged bill of exceptions to which it relates, nor the said certificate, will be considered by this Court.

EXCEPTIONS—Time.

Exceptions to the decisions of the court upon any matter of law arising during the progress of a cause must be taken at the time of such decision, and no exceptions shall be taken in any appeal to any proceeding in a District Court except such as shall have been expressly decided in that court.

EXCESS—Sentence—Void.

A sentence is legal so far as it is within the provisions of law and the jurisdiction of the court over the person and the offense, and only void as to the excess, when such excess is separable and may be dealt with without disturbing the valid portion of the sentence.

EXECUTION—Alias—Irregularity.

Under the decisions of the Supreme Court of Texas, a failure to indorse upon an alias or pluries execution the number of previous executions which have been issued on the judgment, as required by section 7, article 3729, Rev. Civ. Stat. Tex. 1911, is merely an irregularity, which does not render the execution and sale thereunder void.

EECUTORY CONTRACT—Trees—Damages.

Where an executory contract provides for the manufacture of an article after a particular pattern or style, so that it would be useless, or practically useless, to anyone except

the person for whom made, or in the case of trees prepared
for planting, upon breach by the vendee before delivery, the
measure of damages is the whole contract price.

Nursery Co. v. Mielenz, p. 417.   3.   422

EXECUTOR—Fraud—Report.

Where the report of an executor is so imperfect, partial and misleading as to amount to a fraud in law, items in
said report may be re-examined by a court of equity notwithstanding the prior approval of the Probate Court.

Candelaria v. Miera, p. 107.   3.   118

EXECUTOR——Moneys—Sales.

Moneys received from th esales of possessory rights to
real estate, even if said sales were void, must be accounted
for by the Executor.

Candelaria v. Miera, p. 107.   1.   113

F.

FIDELITY BOND—Contract.

Where a surety on a fidelity bond undertakes to respond upon condition that demand be first made upon the
principal, such demand is a part of the contract and must
be alleged and proved.

Feder-Silberberg Co. v. McNeil, p. 44.   2.   52

FINAL JUDGMENT—Appeal.

Section 1, chap. 57, S. L. 1907, gives to "Any person aggrieved by any final judgment," etc., the right of appeal. Under this statute the right of appeal is not confined to a
party to the suit, but any person directly interested and injuriously affected by the judgment may appeal.

Bass v. Insurance Co., p. 282.   1.   284

FINDINGS—Construction.

Findings are not to be construed with the strictness of
special pleadings. It is sufficient if from them all, taken together with the pleadings, the Court can see enough upon a
fair construction to justify the judgment of the trial court,
notwithstanding their want of precision and the occasional
intermixture of matters of fact and conclusions of law.

Frazer v. Bank, p. 340.   2.   351

FINDINGS—Judgment—Pleadings.

An exception to findings of fact made by the trial court
must specify the particular finding or findings objected to,
where more than one finding is made, and a general objection is insufficient to present any question for review unless
all the findings are incorrect and an objection to a finding.
where no requested finding on the proposition is asked.

which points out counsel's theory or contention, should clearly indicate the claimed error.

Southard v. Latham, p. 503. 1. 510

FINDINGS—Insufficient—Objection.

Findings are not to be construed with the strictness of special pleadings. It is sufficient if from them all, taken together with the pleadings, the Court can see enough upon a fair construction to justify the judgment of the trial court, notwithstanding their want of precision and the occasional intermixture of matters of fact and conclusions of law.

Frazer v. Bank, p. 340. 2. 351

FORECLOSURE—Erroneous Calculation.

A's property was sold under foreclosure judgment, to satisfy the mortgages of B Senior and C Junior mortgages; C at the sale bid in the property for the sum of the mortgage debts, interest, and costs as shown by the judgment. After the sale B discovered that he had been overpaid. Such overpayment was caused by an erroneous calculation of interest. B paid the excess into court. Held, that as long as the judgment remained in force, the sum paid by B into court is not a surplus of the foreclosure sale, remaining after the mortgage debts were satisfied, and as such the property of A as mortgagor and owner of the equity of redemption.

Edwards v. Fitzhugh, p. 424. 1. 426

FORFEITURE—Optional—Time.

A contract for the exchange of land provided "in the event that the party of the first part shall fail to comply with the terms thereof, within the time herein limited, the said second party may at his option declare this contract void, in which event all rights and liabilities hereunder shall cease and determine." Held, that the forfeiture of the contract was made optional with the second party, and if he did not see fit to exercise his option and declare the forfeiture, the contract continued in full force and effect.

Beck v. Chambers, p. 53. 1. 60

FUNDS—Accumulation—Loans.

Corporations or associations doing business by collecting monthly installments of dues for the accumulation of funds out of which to loan those contributing to such fund amounts for the purchase of homes, are subject to the provisions of chapter 72, Session Laws of 1899, entitled "An act relating to building and loan associations, as doing business in a form and character similar to that authorized to be done by building and loan associations organized under the provisions of said act."

State Ex. Rel. v. Corp. Comrs., p. 166. 1. 173

G.

GOOD CAUSE—Citation—Time.

Where good cause is shown for the failure to cause citation to be issued and served upon appellee as, and within the time, required by statute, the appellate court can extend the time for serving the citation and will permit a citation to be issued and served at any time before the end of the term of the appellate court to which the appeal was properly returnable.

Childers v. Lahann, p. 487.   4.   493

GOOD CAUSE—Required—Attorney.

The fact that appellant's attorney has been busily engaged with other matters does not constitute "good cause for failure to file and serve assignment of error as required by Sec. 31, C. 57, S. L. 1907.

Hubbell v. Armijo, p. 68.   2.· 70

GOVERNMENT—Reservation—Power.

An attempted exercise of jurisdiction by the land department in the acceptance of an entry, including lands reserved from entry by the government, where the reservation from entry appears as a matter of record in the land office. is void, as to the lands reserved, for the reason that it is au assumption of power in excess of its jurisdiction, and the same can be shown by a defendant in an action at law.

Whitehill v. Cattle Co., p. 520.   1.   531

H.

HABEAS CORPUS—Application—Discharge.

Where petitioner, in his application for the writ of habeas corpus, sets forth certain grounds for his discharge, which his counsel fail to discuss in their brief, or upon the argument of the case, the court assumes that such points are waived and will not consider the same.

Ex Parte DeVore, p. 246.   7.   262

HABEAS CORPUS—Appealable.

An order in habeas corpus proceedings discharging petitioner is not appealable, in the absence of a statute granting such right.

Notestine v. Rogers, p. 462.   1.   466

HABEAS CORPUS—Functions—Perverted.

The writ of habeas corpus is not a writ of error, nor does it, except when perverted, discharge the functions of a writ of error.

Habeas Corpus, p. 452.   1.   456

HABEAS CORPUS—History.

The history of community acequias considered.
Snow v. Abalos, p. 681.   2. 692

HABEAS CORPUS—Iregularities.

Error or irregularities in the course of the proceedings at or anterior to the trial, which, if presented to an appellate court by way of appeal or writ of error, must necessarily result in the reversal of the judgment, are not sufficient, for that reason, as grounds for the release of a prisoner upon application for a writ of habeas corpus.
Habeas Corpus, p. 452.   2. 456

HABEAS CORPUS—Writ of Error.

The writ of habeas corpus is not a writ of error, nor does it, except when perverted, discharge the functions of a writ of error.
Habeas Corpus, p. 452.   1. 456

HABEAS CORPUS—Petitioner—Discharge.

Where petitioner, in his application for the writ of habeas corpus, sets forth certain grounds for his discharge, which his counsel fail to discuss in their brief, or upon the argument of the case, the court assumes that such points are waived and will not consider the same.
Ex Parte De Vore, p. 246.   7. 262

HABEAS CORPUS—Recognized—Common Law Crimes.

Common law crimes are recognized and punished in New Mexico, by virtue of sec. 3422, C. L. 1897, which provides, "In criminal cases, the common law as recognized by the United States and the several states of the Union shall be the rule of practice and decision."
Ex Parte De Vore, p. 246.   1. 253

HOMICIDE—Arrest—Authority.

Where persons have authority to arrest and are resisted and killed, in the proper exercise of such authority, the homicide is murder in all who take part in such resistance.
Territory v. Lynch, p. 15.   3. 33

I.

IDEM SONANS—Sounds—Spelling.

If two names spelled differently necessarily sound alike, the court may, as a matter of law, pronounce them to be idem sonans, but if they do not necessarily sound alike, the question of whether they are idem sonans is a question for the jury.
State v. Alva, p. 143.   8. 150

courdt trying the same given an opportunity to pass upon the question.

State v. Padilla p. 573.   3.   577

INDICTMENT—Warrant—Authorized.

As to the sufficiency of a warrant, it should appear on its face to have duly proceeded from an authorized source. It need not set out the crime with the fulness of an indictment, but it should contain a reasonable indication thereof.

Territory v. Lynch, p. 15.   7.   34

INFANT—Disaffirmance.

Where an infant purchased real estate, and upon coming of age, disaffirms the sale, he must in order to make the disaffirmance effectual restore the property, if he has title to it, to his vendor, and in such case the duty to restore becomes a right to restore, which the vendor may not defeat by refusing to take back the property.

Evants v. Taylor, p. 371.   2.   376

INHABITANTS—Highways—Taxes.

The inhabitants of incorporated cities and towns are subject to the provisions of chapter 124, Session Laws of 1905, as amended by chapter 53, Laws of 1907, relative to labor upon public highways, or payment of road taxes in lieu of such labor.

State v. Byers & Buehl, p. 92.   3.   98

INJUNCTION—Final Decree—Contempt.

A final decree dissolves a preliminary injunction which is ancillary to the main case unless the same is specially continued by the decree, and thereafter a litigant cannot be punished as for civil contempt for violation of the preliminary injunction prior to its dissolution.

Canavan v. Canavan, p. 640.   2.   645

INJUNCTION—Sale—Taxes.

A preliminary injunction will not be granted to restrain the sale of property for taxes, unless the tax payer first pays so much of the tax as he admits is just.

Crane v. Cox, p. 377.   3.   386

IMPRISONMENT—Mittimus—Legality.

Where a party is confined in prison the legality of the imprisonment does not rest upon the mittimus, but upon the judgment, and a prisoner who has been legally and properly sentenced to prison can not obtain his discharge simply because there is an imperfection, or error, in the mittimus.

Ex Parte De Vore, p. 246.   5.   259

INNOCENT THIRD PARTIES—Voidable.

Transfers of property made to innocent third parties, in

violation of a restraining order, are not void nor voidable, because made in disregard of such order.

Southard v. Latham, p. 503. 2. 507

IRREGULARITIES—Not Sufficient.

Error or irregularities in the course of the proceedings
at or anterior to the trial, which, if presented to an appellate
court by way of appeal or writ of error, must necessarily result in the reversal of the judgment, are not sufficient, for
that reason, as grounds for the release of a prisoner upon
application for a writ of habeas corpus.

Habeas corpus, p. 452. 2. 456

IRRIGATION—Lands—Tenants in Common.

While a ditch, through which water is carried for the
irrigation of lands owned by the constructors in severalty is
owned and possessed by the parties as tenants in common,
the water rights acquired by the parties are not attached to
the ditch, but are appurtenant to the lands irrigated, and are
owned by the parties in severalty.

Snow v. Abalos, p. 681. 7. 695

INSTRUCTIONS—Error—Objection.

Appellant can not avail himself of alleged errors by
the trial court in giving, or refusing to give, instructions
where he interposed no objection to the action of the court
and failed to save exceptions.

State v. Analla, p. 294. 1. 299

INSTRUCTIONS—Exception—Court.

The correctness of instructions given by the trial court
will not be reviewed by the Supreme Court, unless exception
is taken to the giving of such instructions at the time they
were given.

State v. Padilla, p. 573. 1. 576

INSTRUCTIONS—Exception—Specific.

Exceptions to instructions must be specific.

State v. Alva, p. 143. 9. 152

INSTRUMENT—Assignment—Release.

An instrument in the form of a release of claims of
three creditors of an insolvent against the insolvent's trust
estate to L., together with the oral testimony explaining the
same, might be properly held to amount to an assignment of
such claims to L.

Lohman v. Reymond, p. 225. 3. 234

INSURANCE—Superintendent—Salary.

The office of Superintendent of Insurance, created by
chapter 5, Laws of 1905, which was amended by chapter 48,
Laws 1909, was not abolished by section 6 of article XI of

the Constitution. The latter is not self-executing except as to those powers specifically conferred upon the Corporation Commission therein. It requires legislation to carry the section into effect in regard to some of the powers therein conferred on the Corporation Commission, among which are many of the powers now exercised by the Superintendent of Insurance. The Superintendent of Insurance was continued in office by section 9 of article XXII of the Constitution, until superseded by the Corporation Commission, and he has not been fully so superseded, by reason of the lack of legislation to carry the constitutional provision into effect. He may still exercise such functions of his office as were not specifically transferred to the Corporation Commission.

State Ex. Rel. v. Sargent, p. 627.   p. 634

INSURANCE FUND—Salary Fund.

Under sec. 21, of chap. 83, Laws of 1912, only the surplus monies in the Insurance fund, over and above the amounts required to meet the appropriations under chapter 135, Laws 1909, were diverted to the State Salary fund.

State Ex. Rel. v. Auditor,   2. 136

INTENTION—Water Application.

The intention to apply water to beneficial use, the diversion works, and the actual diversion of the water, all precede the actual application of the water to the use intended, but it is the application of the water, or the intent to apply, followed with due diligence toward application, and ultimate application, which gives to the appropriator the continued and continuous right to take the water.

Snow v. Abalos, p. 681.   5. 694

INTERPLEADER—Amount Due.

In an interpleader suit, the amount due cannot be the subject of controversy, and where such controversy exists it presents an insuperable objection to its prosecution.

Trust Co. v. Bank, p. 589.   1. 598

INVESTMENT—Interest Bearing.

The deposit of the Permanent School Fund of the State in interest-bearing deposits in banks, under the provisions of Joint Resolution No. 14, Laws of 1913, is an investment of the same.

State v. Marron, p. 426.   1. 426

J.

JUDGE—Confession—Evidence.

The judge, and as a preliminary without which no confession can go to a jury, determines, on testimony laid before him, both for and against, whether or not to admit the confession; the burden being on the prosecuting power that tenders it. His decision covers, besides the law, the fact, as to which it is not ordinarily to be disturbed or reviewed; and the jury can pass merely on the effect of the confession in evidence.

State v. Armijo, p. 262.   2. 268

JUDGE—Discretion—Abused.

In the superintendence of the process of empaneling the jury, a large discretion is necessarily confided to the judge, which discretion will not be revised on error or appeal, unless it appears to have been grossly abused or exercised contrary to law.

Territory v. Lynch, p. 15.   l. 29

JUDGE—Decision—Reviewed.

The judge, and as a preliminary without which no confession can go to a jury, determines, on testimony laid before him, both for and against, whether or not to admit the confession the burden being on the prosecuting power that tenders it. His decision covers, besides the law, the fact, as to which it is not ordinary to be disturbed or reviewed; and the jury can pass merely on the effect of the confession in evidence.

State v. Armijo, p. 262.   2. 268

JUDGE—Exceptions—Stricken.

A bill of exceptions, in a case tried to a jury, must be settled and signed by the judge of the court in which the case was tried, and where the record fails to show that such bill of exceptions was signed by the judge it will be stricken from the files, upon motion.

Palmer v. Allen, p. 237.   2. 239

JUDICIAL DECISIONS—Doubts.

Judicial decisions, affecting title to real estate, presumptively acquired in reliance upon such decisions, should not be disturbed or departed from except for the most cogent reasons; doubts as to the soundness of such decisions, without other and graver consideration, do not warrant a departure.

Duncan v. Brown, p. 579.   l. 585

JUDICIAL POWERS—Irregularities.

A ministerial officer acting under process fair on its face, issued from a tribunal or person having judicial powers, with apparent jurisdiction to issue such process, is justified in obeying it against all irregularities and illegalities except his own.

Territory v. Lynch, p. 15.   l. 34

JUDICIAL PROCEEDINGS—Nullities.

Every person may disregard judicial proceedings which are nullities and without jurisdiction.

McMillen v. Bank, p. 494.   1. 502

JUDGMENT—Aggrieved—Appeal.

Section 1, chap. 57, S. L. 1907, gives to "any person aggrieved by any final judgment," etc., the right to appeal. Under this statute the right of appeal is not confined to a party to the suit, but any person directly interested and injuriously affected by the judgment may appeal.

Bass v. Insurance Co., p. 282.   1. 284

JUDGMENT—Collateral Assault.

As to jurisdictional questions, a judgment under which the prisoner is held is aided by the same presumptions as in other cases of collateral assault. If the record is silent as to jurisdictional facts, jurisdiction is presumed.

Habeas corpus, p. 452.   3. 457

JUDGMENT—District Court—De Novo.

In such a case where the prosecuting witness appeals from a judgment of the Justice of the Peace taxing him with the costs, the District Court is required to try the question as to whether the prosecution was instiued maliciously, or wihout probable cause de novo and must enter its own independent judgment in the case. In such case the discretion conferred by the statute upon the Justice of the Peace is necessarily transferred to the District Court.

State v. Coats p. 314.   2. 317

JUDGMENT—Default—Briefs.

Where a party who is in default, having failed to file briefs within the time limited by the rules of the court, tenders such briefs for filing at the same time that a motion to affirm the judgment because of such default is tendered, the motion to affirm will be denied.

McMillen v. Bank, p. 285.   1. 286

JUDGMENT—Erroneous Calculation.

A's property was sold under foreclosure judgment, to satisfy the mortgages of B Senior and C Junior mortgages, C at the sale bid in the property for the sum of the mortgage debts, interest, and costs as shown by the judgment. After the sale B discovered that he had been overpaid. Such overpayment was caused by an erroneous calculation of interest. B paid the excess into court. Held that as long as the judgment remained in force, the sum paid by B into court is not a surplus of the foreclosure sale, remaining after the mortgage debts were satisfied, and as such the property of A as mortgagor and owner of the equity of redemption.

Edwards v. Fitzhugh, p. 424.   1. 426

JUDGMENT—Evidence—Verdict.

A judgment will be reversed when there is no evidence to support the verdict upon which it is based.

Spencer v. Timber Co., p. 191.   1. 194

JUDGMENT—Issues at Law—Pleadings.

Where the answer raises issues of law only, the case is ripe for judgment on the issues of law involved and a motion for judgment on the pleadings is properly entertained.

Keinath & Co. v. Reed, p. 358.   2. 367

JUDGMENT—Officers—Powers.

Where a court renders final judgment in a cause, it has no jurisdiction to proceed further except in carrying out the terms of the judgment, and where that is left to non-judicial officers, their power is fixed by the terms of the judgment, and, when once executed, the power is ended.

McMillen v. Bank, p. 494.   3. 502

JUDGMENT—Justice of the Peace—Void.

A judgment rendered by a Justice of the Peace, before the return day of the summons, is void. as being without jurisdiction.

Pickering v. Palmer, p. 473.   1. 477

JUDGMENT—Imperfections—Discharge.

Where a party is confined in prison, the legality of the imprisonment does not rest upon the mittimus, but upon the judgment, and a prisoner who has been legally and properly sentenced to prison can not obtain his discharge simply because there is an imperfection, or error, in the mittimus.

Ex Parte De Vore, p. 246.   5. 259

JUDGMENT—Review—Decision.

Assignments of error that "the court below erred in affirming the decision of the Board of Water Commissioners," and that "the court below erred in rendering judgment herein in favor of said appellee, affirming the said decision of the Board of Water Commissioners," are not sufficiently specific to present any question for review.

Development Co. v. Land & Irrigation Co., p. 1   1. 6

JUDGMENT—Inadvertence.

Where, in a judgment covering several cases, by inadvertence or otherwise, one or more cases are included over which the Court had no jurisdiction to render judgment, this Court has jurisdiction, under section 38 of chapter 57 of the Laws of 1907, to modify the judgment by eliminating such case, or cases, from the judgment.

City v. Belmore, p. 331.   2. 333

JUDGMENT—Default—Appeal.

Under sections 3305 and 3365, C. L. 1897, a defendant

may appeal from a default judgment rendered and entered against him by a Justice of the Peace.
Faggard Co. v. Cunningham, p. 510. 1. 512

JUDGMENT—Sale—Execution.

Under the decisions of the Supreme Court of Texas, a failure to indorse upon an alias or pluries execution the number of previous executions which have been issued on the judgment, as required by sec. 7, art. 3729, Rev. Civ. Stat. Tex. 1911, is merely an irregularity, which does not render the execution and sale thereunder void.
McMillen v. Bank, p. 494. 1. 500

JURISDICTION—Practice.

An appearance, in practice, is a coming into court as a party to a suit, whether as plaintiff or defendant, and is a formal proceeding by which a defendant submits himself to the jurisdiction of the court.
Childers v. Lahann, p. 487. 1. 490

JURISDICTION—Certiorari—Notice.

A person against whom a Justice of the Peace has rendered a judgment void for want of jurisdiction, is not bound to appeal or remove the same by writ of certiorari, even though he have actual notice of the existence of the judgment.
Pickering v. Palmer, p. 473. 2. 478

JURISDICTION—Cost Bond.

Under section 14, chapter 57, S. L. 1907, a cost bond is required, on appeal or writ of error, only for the protection of the appellee or defendant in error, and is not essential in order to confer jurisdiction upon this Court.
Canavan v. Canavan, p. 468. 1. 470

JURISDICTION—Court—Writs of Error.

Const., art. VI, sec. 3, providing that the Supreme Court shall have jurisdiction to issue writs of error which may be issued by the direction of the Court or any justice thereof, repealed Laws 1907, c. 57, sec. 3, providing for the issuance of writs of error by the clerk of the Court.
Wood-Davis v. Sloan, p. 290. 1. 292

JURISDICTION—Judgment—Power.

Where a court renders final judgment in a cause, it has no jurisdiction to proceed further except in carrying out the terms of the judgment, and where that is left to non-judicial officers, their power is fixed by the terms of the judgment, and, when once executed, the power is ended.
McMillen v. Bank, p. 494. 3. 502

JURISDICTION—Land Department—Entry.

An attempted exercise of jurisdiction by the land de-

partment in the acceptance of an entry, including lands reserved from entry by the government, where the reservation
from entry appears as a matter of record in the land office,
is void, as to the lands reserved, for the reason that it is an
assumption of power in excess of its jurisdiction, and the
same can be shown by a defendant in an action at law.
Whitehill v. Cattle Co., p. 520.   1. 531

JURISDICTION—Parties—Merits.

A defendant, by answering over, upon demurrer overruled, waives all objections to the petition of the plaintiff, except to the jurisdiction of the court and the failure of the petition to state a cause of action, and, where a defendant raises
by demurrer the question of a defect of parties plaintiff, and,
upon such demurrer being overruled answers to the merits, he
cannot thereafter raise the same question by objecting to
the introduction of evidence.
Baca v. Baca, p. 63.   1. 67

JURISDICTION—Presumed—Collateral Assault.

As to jurisdictional questions, a judgment under which
the prisoner is held is aided by the same presumption as in
other cases of collateral assault. If the record is silent as
to jurisdictional facts, jurisdiction is presumed.
Habeas corpus, p. 452.   3. 457

JURISDICTION—Record—Evidence.

The question as to whether a party has appeared and
submitted himself voluntarily to the jurisdiction of the court
should be tried by the record and not by other evidence.
Childers v. Lahann, p. 487.   2. 491

JURISDICTION—School Officers.

A school teacher has no fixed tenure of office by provision of law in this jurisdiction and his rights are measured
by the terms of his contract with the school officers.
State v. Board of Education p. 183.   2. 190

JURISDICTIONAL QUESTIONS—Record.

As to jurisdictional questions, a judgment under which
the prisoner is held is aided by the same presumptions as in
other cases of collateral assault. If the record is silent as
to jurisdictional facts, jurisdiction is presumed.
Habeas Corpus, p. 452.   3. 457

JURORS—Challenge for Cause—Peremptory.

Within reasonable limits, each party has a right to
put pertinent questions to show, not only that there exists
proper grounds for a challenge for cause, but to elicit facts
to enable him to decide whether or not he will exercise his
right of peremptory challenge.
Territory v. Lynch, p. 15.   2. 31

JURORS—Empaneled—No Substitution.

Where the name Dewey Dimon, appears upon the roll of jurors empaneled to try a cause, and the verdict is signed "DeWitt Dimon, Foreman," and no objection to the variance is made in the trial court, the Supreme Court, on appeal, where the question is first raised, is warranted in assuming that no substitution in the personnel of the jury was made and that Dewey Dimon named on the jury roll signed the verdict as DeWitt Dimon.
State v. Cabodi, p. 513. 3. 517

JURORS—Selection—Special Venire.

Sections 995, 997, 1001 and 1002, R. S. 1897, construed. and held to require the selection of jurors, summoned upon a special venire, by lot.
Territory v. Prather, p. 195. 3. 204

JURY—Empaneled—Sworn.

The jury must be selected, empaneled and sworn in the manner required by the statute, and a material departure from the statutory method, by which a party is deprived of a substantial right, is ground for reversal.
Territory v. Prather, p. 195. 1. 199

JURY—Instructions—Failure to Instruct.

The failure of the court to instruct the jury on all of the law applicable to the case cannot be taken advantage of, unless excepted to at the time the jury is instructed.
State v. Padilla, p. 573. 2. 576

JURY—Selected by Lot—Prejudicial.

Where the statute requires the jury to be selected by lot, all other methods are impliedly prohibited, and the right to have the jury so selected is a substantial right, the deprivation of which must be presumed to be prejudicial to a party.
Territory v. Prather, p. 195. 2. 201

JURY—Statutory Method—Reversal.

The jury must be selected, empaneled and sworn in the manner required by the statute, and a material departure from the statutory method, by which a party is deprived of a substantial right, is ground for reversal.
Territory v. Prather, p. 195. 1. 199

JURY—Verdict—Evidence.

The verdict of a jury will not be set aside on appeal when it is supported by substantial evidence.
State v. Lumpkin, p. 480. 2. 485

JUSTICE OF THE PEACE—Judgment—Void.

A judgment rendered by a Justice of the Peace, before

the return day of the summons, is void, as being without
jurisdiction.

Pickering v. Palmer, p. 473.   1.   477

JUSTICE OF THE PEACE—Prosecuting Witness—Docketing Case.

Where a Justice of the Peace, under sec. 3, chap. 57,
S. L. 1907, finds that a criminal prosecution has been instituted "maliciously, or without probable cause," and taxes the
costs against the prosecuting witness, and the prosecuting
witness appeals from such judgment, the case should be
docketed as the State v. The Prosecuting Witness, and not
as originally entitled.

State v. Coats, p. 314.   1.   316

L.

LAND—Contract—Forfeiture.

A contract for the exchange of land provided "in the
event that the party of the first part shall fail to comply
with the terms thereof, within the time herein limited, the
said second party may at his option declare this contract
void, in which event all rights and liabilities hereunder shall
cease and terminate." Held that the forfeiture of the contract was made optional with the second party, and if he did
not see fit to exercise his option and declare the forfeiture,
the contract continued in full force and effect.

Beck v. Chambers, p. 53.   1.   60

LAND DEPARTMENT—Acceptance of Entry—Void.

An attempted exercise of jurisdiction by the land department in the acceptance of an entry including lands reserved from entry by the government, where the reservation
from entry appears as a matter of record in the land office.
is void, as to the lands reserved, for the reason that it is an
assumption of power in excess of its jurisdiction, and the
same can be shown by a defendant in an action at law.

Whitehill v. Cattle Co., p. 520.   1.   531

LARCENY—Animal—Ownership—Appellate Court.

Where appellant relies upon a failure of proof as to
ownership of an alleged stolen animal, it is incumbent upon
him to present a complete transcript of all the evidence adduced in the trial court. Failing to do so, the appellate
court will presume that the facts necessary to support the
verdict were disclosed by evidence not incorporated in the
bill of exceptions.

State v. Analla, p. 291.   1.   296

LARCENY—Animal—Prosecution.

Where, in a prosecution instituted for a violation of
sec. 79, C. L. 1897, the indictment charges that the defend-

ants "then and there, unlawfully and feloniously did take, steal and knowingly drive away, etc.," the animal in question, it is not necessary to further allege that the owner was thereby deprived of the immediate possession of the animal.
State v. Lumpkin, p. 480.   1. 483

LAWS—1909—Interpreted—Appropriations.

Chap. 135, Laws of 1909, interpreted and held, that the appropriations carried by that Act were limited to the insurance monies mentioned in the title.
State Ex Rel. v. Auditor.   1. 135

LAWS 1912—Surplus Monies.

Under sec. 21, of chap. 83, Laws of 1912, only the surplus monies in the Insurance fund, over and above the amounts required to meet the appropriations under chapter 135, Laws 1909, were diverted to the State Salary fund.
State Ex Rel. v. Auditor.   2. 136

LEGISLATURE—Common Law—Statute.

The right may be conferred by act of the legislature, or exist by virtue of the common law, in those jurisdictions where the common law is in force, and no statute expressly or impliedly denies the right.
State v. Armijo, p. 646.   2. 650

LEGISLATURE——Criminal Act—Intent.

The legislature may forbid the doing of an act and make its commission criminal without regard to the intent of the doer, and if such legislative intent appears, the courts must give it effect although the intention of the doer may have been innocent.
State v. Alva, p. 143.   4. 151

LEGISLATION—Privilege—Restrictions.

The right of redemption is created by statute and the beneficiary of such legislation must take the privilege burdened with all its restrictions.
Mining Co. v. Mining Co., p. 153.   2. 165

LEGISLATIVE POWER—DEPOSIT—BANKS.

Said Joint Resolution No. 14, insofar as it requires the deposit of these funds in banks, is beyond legislative power and void.
State v. Marron, p. 426.   3. 440

LIBRARIAN—Office—Ministerial.

The office of State Librarian is a ministerial office.
State v. Armijo p. 646.   .   6. 656

LICENSE—Cancellation—Liquor.

Section 4129, C. L. 1897, construed, and held not to authorize the cancellation of a liquor license.
Lorenzino v. James, p. 240.   1. 245

LICENSE—Cancellation—County Commissioners—Discretion.

Under section 4, chapter 115, S. L. 1905, where liquor is being sold "outside of the locality for which such license was granted," it is the duty of the board of county commissioners to cancel the license, and such board has no discretion in the matter, where the facts exist, which authorize the cancellation.

Lorenzino v. James, p. 240.   1. 244

LICENSE—Liquor—Contract.

A license to retail intoxicating liquors is neither a property right nor a contract. It is in no sense a contract made by the State with a party holding the license; it is a mere permit subject to be modified or annulled at the pleasure of the legislature.

Habeas corpus, p. 605.   2. 610

LICENSE—Liquor—Locality.

Under section 4, chapter 115, S. L. 1905, where liquor is being sold "outside of the locality for which such license was granted," it is the duty of the board of county commissioners to cancel the license, and such board has no discretion in the matter, where the facts exist, which authorize the cancellation.

Lorenzino v. James, p. 240.   1. 244

LICENSE FEES—AUTOMOBILES.

Sec. 3 of chapter 28. Session Laws of 1912, imposing license fees for automobiles, in excess of the expense of administering the act, is a revenue measure; and as such is a valid exercise of power by the legislature.

State v. Ingalls, p. 211.   5. 222

LOCAL OPTION—Popular Vote—Valid.

The district local option law, chap. 78, S. L. 1913, is a complete enactment in itself and requires nothing further to give it validity; it depends upon the popular vote for a determination only of the territorial limits of its operations, and is a valid and constitutional exercise of the legislative power.

Habeas corpus, p. 605.   1. 607

M.

MANDAMUS—Alternative Writ—Issuance.

The alternative writ of mandamus in this case examined, and found to be inadequate to justify the issuance of a peremptory writ.

State v. Marron, p. 426.   5. 443

MANDAMUS—Cancellation—Liquor License.

The board of county commissioners, in determining the fact as to whether liquor is being sold outside of the locality for which the license was granted, acts only in a ministerial capacity; and, where the facts upon which it acts are not disputed, mandamus is the proper remedy to compel the cancellation of a liquor .license, where liqpor is being sold thereunder outside of the locality for which such license was granted.

Lorenzino v. James, p. 240. 3. 244

MANDAMUS—Contract—Ministerial Duty.

Mandamus cannot be maintained to compel reinstatement of a school teacher who has been removed by the school officers and whose relation to the school authorities rests wholly in contract. It is only where the teacher, by positive provision of law, has a fixed tenure of office, or can be removed only in some prescribed manner, and where, consequently, it is the plain ministerial duty of the school board to retain him, that mandamus can be maintained.

State v. Board of Education, p. 183. 1. 187

MANDAMUS—Discretion——Control.

The Governor, Secretary of State and Attorney General have power to eliminate by means of disapproval any given form or forms of investment, and thereby bring the State Treasurer to one single form of investment, and in such event, he is subject to mandamus to perform all acts necessary to accomplish the same. Whether he does not possess discretion, as to the safety of the investment, which he may exercise independent of control by mandamus, not decided, because not involved.

State v. Marron, p. 426. 1. 441

MANDAMUS—Peremptory Writ.

The alternative writ of mandamus in this case examined, and found to be inadequate to justify the issuance of a peremptory writ.

State v. Marron, p. 426. 5. 443

MANDAMUS—School Teacher—Contract.

Mandamus cannot be maintained to compel reinstatement of a school teacher who has been removed by the school officers and whose relation to the school authorities rests wholly in contract. It is only where the teacher, by positive provision of law, has a fixed tenure of office, or can be removed only in some prescribed manner, and where, consequently, it is the plain ministerial duty of the school board to retain him, that mandamus can be maintained.

State v. Board of Education, p. 183. 1. 187

MAIL—Receipt—Proof.

Proof that "demand was made by mail" implies a prepayment of postage and a deposit of the demand in a United States postoffice but that the letter was properly addressed to the addressee at the place where he resides or receives his mail is not thereby implied, and proof of that fact mus⁺ be had before the receipt of the letter by the addressee will be inferred.

Silberberg Co. v. McNeil p. 44.   1. 49

MAIN SUBJECT—TAXATION—UNCONSTITUTIONAL.

If there be more than one subject mentioned in the act, if they be germane or subsidiary to the main subject or if relative directly or indirectly to the main subject, having a mutual connection, and are not foreign to the main subject, or so long as the provisions are of the same nature and come legitimately under one general denomination or subject the act is not unconstitutional.

State v. Ingalls, p. 211.   3. 220

"MAY"—"Shall"—Statute.

The word "may" as used in the statute, is employed in the sense of "shall."

Lorenzino v. James, p. 240.   2. 244

MINISTERIAL OFFICE—Justified.

A ministerial officer acting under process fair on its face, issued from a tribunal or person having judicial powers, with apparent jurisdiction to issue such process, is justified in obeying it against all irregularities and illegalities except his own.

Territory v. Lynch, p. 15.   8. 34

MINOR—Surety—Liability.

The surety on the note of a minor, given in payment for real estate, is discharged from liability thereon, where the minor on becoming of age, disaffirms the contract and restores the property purchased.

Evants v. Taylor, p. 371.   1. 375

MORTGAGE—Foreclosure—Purchaser.

A agreed with B that he would procure a mortgage on land owned by A to be foreclosed and sold on execution. B agreed to become a purchaser of the land at such sale, and to pay to A the difference between the price he was required to pay for the land less than $3500.00. The contract was fully performed, and B was placed in possession of the land, under a deed executed to him under such foreclosure proceedings. He refused to pay A the agreed difference of $925.00. Held, that the vendor could recover the stipulated price.

Harris v. Hardwick, p. 303.   1. 310

MORTGAGE—Foreclosure—Stipulated Price.

A agreed with B that he would procure a mortgage on land owned by A to be foreclosed and sold in execution. B agreed to become a purchaser of the land at such sale, and to pay to A the difference between the price he was required to pay for the land less than $3500.00. The contract was fully performed, and B was placed in possession of the land, under a deed executed to him under such foreclosure proceedings. He refused to pay A the agreed difference of $925.00. Held, that the vendor could recover the stipulated price.

Harris v. Hardwick, p. 303. 1. 310

MORTGAGE—Foreclosure—Surplus.

A's property was sold under foreclosure judgment, to satisfy the mortgages of B Senior and C Junior mortgages; C at the sale bid in the property for the sum of the mortgage debts, interest, and costs as shown by the judgment. After the sale B discovered that he had been overpaid. Such over-payment was caused by an erroneous calculation of interest. B paid the excess into court. Held that as long as the judgment remained in force, the sum paid by B into court is not a surplus of the foreclosure sale, remaining after the mortgage debts were satisfied, and as such the property of A as mortgagor and owner of the equity of redemption.

Edwards v. Fitzhugh, p. 424. 1. 426

MOTION—Dismiss—Affirmance.

The appellant has no right to dismiss his appeal in the face of a motion for affirmance well taken.

Hubbell v. Armijo, p. 68. 1. 69

MOUNTED POLICE—Salaries—Membership.

Held, that the Act of 1905 (chap. 9) creating a force of Mounted Police, fixing salaries of its members, and providing for payment thereof, was repealed by the Act of the legislature of 1909, (chap. 127, sec. IV) insofar as it provided for salaries and membership of the force, and that, therefore, a writ of mandate directed to the State Auditor requiring him to make a levy to pay such salaries is not issuable, because the appropriation by the Act of 1905 has ceased to be a continuing appropriation, and the legislature has failed to make an appropriation for the present fiscal year.

State Ex Rel. v. Sargent, p. 272. 3. 280

MUNICIPAL BONDS—Issuance—Procedure.

Sub-sections 6 and 67, section 2402, C. L. 1897, examined: Held, that the first paragraph of sub-section 6, authorizing the issuance of municipal bonds for certain purposes, and providing the procedure therefor, which portion of said sub-section was enacted as a part of sec. 14, chap. 39, S. L. 1884, was not repealed, modified or amended by sub-section 67, enacted as sec. 1 of chap. 70, S. L. 1897.

Smith v. City, p. 613. 1. 626

MUNICIPAL BONDS—Purpose.

Sub-sections 6 and 67, section 2402, C. L. 1897, exam
ined: Held, that the first paragraph of sub-section 6, authorizing the issuance of municipal bonds for certain purposes,
and providing the procedure therefor, which portion of said
sub-section was enacted as a part of sec. 14, chap. 39, S. L.
1884, was not repealed, modified or amended by sub-section
67, enacted as sec. 1 of chap. 70, S. L. 1897.

MUNICIPALITIES—Municipal Purpose.

Under the power granted to cities and towns by sub-
section 5, sec. 2402, C. L. 1897, to erect all needful buildings
for the use of the city or town, such municipalities are limited to the erection of such needful buildings as may be required for public uses, or for municipal uses and purposes
and contradistinguished from private or quasi-public uses,
and, if the primary object of a building to be constructed is a
municipal purpose, the fact that it may be incidentally used
for theatrical purposes, may not have the effect of rendering
the action in erecting it invalid; but where the paramount
purpose and object is for other than strictly municipal purposes, legislative authority is lacking in this State, for the
erection of such buildings by cities and towns.

Smith v. City, p. 613.   3.   623

MURDER—Illegal Arrest.

If the outrage of an attempted illegal arrest has not
excited the passions, a killing will be murder.

Territory v. Lynch, p. 15.   5.   33

N.

NEW MEXICO—Prior Appropriation.

In New Mexico, the "Colorado Doctrine," as it is termed,
of prior appropriation prevails. Such doctrine was estab-
ished or founded by the custom of the people, and grew out
of the conditions of the country and the necessities of the
people. It was recognized by the courts of the Territory and
became the settled law.

Snow v. Abalos, p. 681.   3.   693

NEW TRIAL—Equitable Remedy.

In this State, where a Justice of the Peace has no
power to set aside his judgments or grant a new trial, and
where upon appeal or certiorari to the District Court the
cause is triable de novo only, one against whom a void judgment has been rendered by a Justice of the Peace, is not,
though with actual notice thereof, guilty of laches and negligence sufficient to bar his right to an equitable remedy
against such judgment, because he fails to appeal or sue out
a writ of certiorari.

Pickering v. Palmer, p. 473.   3.   479

take acknowledgments of conveyance of real estate, and which
section, in that regard, repeals, by necessary implication, the
provisions of section 75, C. L. 1897.
Williamson v. Stevens, p. 204.					1 206

OFFICIALS—Investment—Disapproval.

The Governor, Secretary of State and Attorney General
have power to eliminate by means of disapproval any given
form or forms of investment, and thereby bring the State
Treasurer to one single form of investment, and in such
event, he is subject to mandamus to perform all acts necessary to accomplish the same. Whether he does not possess
discretion, as to the safety of the investment, which he may
exercise independent of control by mandamus, not decided,
because not involved.
State v. Marron, p. 426.					l. 441

OPTION—Local—Legislative Power—Validity.

The district local option law, chap. 78, S. L. 1912, is a
complete enactment in itself and requires nothing further to
give it validity; it depends upon the popular vote for a determination only of the territorial limits of its operation, and
is a valid constitutional exercise of the legislative power.
Habeas Corpus, p. 605.

ORGANIC ACT—Territory of New Mexico—Citizens.

Section 1 of chapter 134, S. L. 1909, which provides that
"No person prevented by the Organic Act of the Territory of
New Mexico * * * * shall be entitled to vote or hold public
office in this Territory," refers to the original act of Congress
creating the Territory of New Mexico, and the only limitations thereby imposed upon the right to vote or hold public
office are that such rights shall be exercised only by citizens
of the United States, including those recognized as citizens
by the treaty with the Republic of Mexico, etc.
State v. Armijo, p. 646.					5. 652

ORTHOGRAPHY—Idem Sonans.

It matters not how two words are spelled, what their
orthography is; they are idem sonans within the meaning of
the books, if the attentive ear finds difficulty in distinguishing
them when pronounced, or common and long continued usage
has by corruption or abbreviation made them identical in
pronunciation.
State v. Alva, p. 143.					6. 150

OWNERSHIP—Animal—Transcript——Verdict.

Where appellant relies upon a failure of proof as to
ownership of an alleged stolen animal, it is incumbent upon
him to present a complete transcript of all the evidence adduced in the trial court. Failing to do so, the appellate
court will presume that the facts necessary to support the

verdict were disclosed by evidence not incorporated in the bill of exception.

P.

Where parties to a contract, construe it as having created a partnership relation, and act upon such construction, the Court will not, after rights have accrued thereunder, by reason of such construction, give to the contract a different construction, which would be at variance with the understanding of the parties to it.

PLEADING—Defect—Demurrer.

A defective allegation in a pleading can only be raised by a demurrer distinctly specifying the defect as a ground of objection. Sub-sec. 36, sec. 2685, C. L. 1897.

POLITICAL RIGHTS—Common Law—Recognized.

Such political rights as were recognized by the common law, and not in conflict with our established laws, institutions and customs, and suitable to our conditions was carried into the body of our law.

PRACTICE—Decision—Common Law.

The common law is the rule of practice and decision in New Mexico, by virtue of section 2871, R. S. 1897, except where modified by statute.

PRESUMPTION—Record—Appeal.

When a party takes an appeal in open court he must see that the record affirmatively shows that it was taken in open court, and where the record is silent upon the question the presumption is that the appeal was not so taken, and in such case it is incumbent upon the appellant to cause citation to be issued and served upon appellee.

PRINCIPAL—Contract—Customer.

In such a case the principal by entering into a contract of exchange with the customer produced by the broker, accepted the customer as able, ready and willing to make the exchange.

PRINCIPAL—Surety—Demand.

Where a surety on a fidelity bond undertakes to respond upon condition that demand be first made upon the principal, such demand is a part of the contract and must be alleged and proved.

Feder, Silberberg Co. v. McNeil, p. 44.

PROBABLE CAUSE—Burden—Prosecution.

Upon such appeal the burden is upon the State to show that the prosecution was instituted maliciously, or without probable cause.

State v. Coats, p. 314.   3.   318

PROBATE COURT—Report—Re-examined.

Where the report of an executor is so imperfect, partial and misleading as to amount to a fraud in law, items in said report may be re-examined by a court of equity notwithstanding the prior approval of the Probate Court.

Candelaria v. Miera, p. 107.   3.   113

PROMISSORY NOTE—Assignment—Endorsement.

The endorsement and delivery of a promissory note operates as an assignment, where the note is non-negotiabe; and the assignee, under the statutes of New Mexico, may sue thereon in his own name. Where a note is transferred after maturity it is subject to defenses existing between the payee and payor and the question of its negotiability is immaterial.

Southard v. Latham, p. 503.   ʹ.   507

PROMISSORY NOTE—Extension—Consideration.

A surety, on a promissory note is not discharged from liability by an extension of time granted the .principal, where the makers are not precluded from paying the note prior to the expiration of such an extension and the extension granted was without consideration.

Southard v. Latham, p. 503.   3.   508

PRONUNCIATION—Spelling—Rule.

Pronunciation and not spelling is the test in the application of the rule.

State v. Alva, p. 143.   7.   150

PROSECUTING WITNESS—Probable Cause—Docketing.

Where a Justice of the Peace, under sec. 3, chap. 57. S. L. 1907, finds that a criminal prosecution has been instituted "maliciously, or without probable cause" and taxes the costs against the prosecuting witness, and the prosecuting witness appeals from such judgment, the case should be docketed as the State v. The Prosecuting Witness, and not as originally entitled.

State v. Coats, p. 314.   1.   316

PUBLIC OFFICE—Not a Natural Right—Law.

The right to hold a public office is not a natural right. It exists, where it exists at all, only because and by virtue of some law expressly or impliedly conferring it.

State v. Armijo, p. 646.   1.   650

PUBLIC OFFICE—Salary—Payment.

This rule has been extended to a general law fixing the salary of a public officer and prescribing its payment at particular periods.

State Ex Rel. v. Sargent, p. 272.   2. 279

PUBLIC STREAM—Appropriator—Joint Labor.

Under a community ditch, each water user, by application of the water to a beneficial use, acquires a right to take water from the public stream or source of supply, which right is a several right, owned and possessed by the individual user, notwithstanding the fact that the ditch through which the water is carried to his land may have been constructed by the joint labor and money of the individual appropriator, in conjunction with others similarly situated, and the act of 1895, supra, did not change the status of the individual consumer.

Snow v. Abalos, p. 681.   6. 694

PUNISHMENT—Common Law Crimes.

While common law crimes are recognized and punished in this state, common law penalties are not inflicted, but the punishment therefor is prescribed by sec. 1054, C. L. 1897.

Ex Parte De Vore, p. 246.   6. 261

R.

REAL ESTATE—Decisions.

Judicial decisions, affecting title to real estate, presumptively acquired in reliance upon such decisions, should not be disturbed or departed from except for the most cogent reasons; doubts as to the soundness of such decisions, without other and graver considerations, do not warrant a departure.

Duncan v. Brown, p. 579.   1. 585

REAL ESTATE—Exchange—Complaint.

In an action for a broker's commission for effecting an exchange of real estate where the complaint states the making of a valid written contract of exchange between the principal and the customer procured by the broker, the complaint need not further state that the customer was able, ready and willing to complete the exchange on the terms of the contract; or that he made any effort to that end; or the refusal of the principal to complete it.

Keinath & Co. v. Reed, p. 358.   7. 370

REAL ESTATE—Infant—Disaffirmance.

Where an infant purchased real estate, and upon coming of age, disaffirms the sale, he must in order to make the disaffirmance effectual restore the property, if he has title to it, to his vendor, and in such case the duty to restore becomes a right to restore, which the vendor may not defeat by refusing to take back the property.

Evants v. Taylor, p. 371.   2. 375

REAL OWNER—Taxation—Impracticable.

It is impracticable for the assessor to obtain the name of the real owner of a tract of land, from the official county records, as available for his inspection, and, in the absence of fraud, an assessment against unknown owners is not invalid, because of the fact that the assessor might have ascertained the name of the real owner from the records of conveyances in the office of the county recorder, in those cases where the owner has failed to list his property for taxation.

Daughtry v. Murry, p. 35.   1. 41

"RECOGNIZE"—"Know."

The word "recognize," used in the above section, is given various significance by the lexicographers. Webster, among other definitions, defines its meaning to be "to avow knowledge of." Century Dictionary, "to know again." Webster defines the meaning of the verb "know" to be, among others given, "to recognize." In the above section the word "recognized" was used in the sense of "known," and as used was intended to adopt the common law of crimes, as known in the United States and the several states of the Union, which was the common law, or lex non scripta of England, as it existed at the time of the Independence of the United States, supplemented and modified by such British statutes as were of a general nature and not local to that kingdom.

Ex Parte De Vore, p. 246.   2. 256

RECORD—Appeal—Party.

All the facts, entitling the person, not a party to the record, to appeal should be stated in the application for appeal.

Bass v. Insurance Co., p. 282.   -   2. 285

RECORD—Diminution—Costs.

After the filing of the supplemental transcript, and the argument and submission of the case, it is too late for appellee to suggest a diminution of the record, to include in the transcript a certificate of the taxation of costs in the District Court.

State Ex Rel. v. Board of Education, p. 286.   4. 289

REDEMPTION—Statute—Beneficiary.

The right of redemption is created by statute and the beneficiary of such legislation must take the privilege burdened with all its restrictions.

Mining Co. v. Mining Co., p. 153.   2. 165

REGENTS—Board of—Treasurer—Successor.

Where the statute creating a board of regents for the Agricultural College and Experiment Station provides for the election of one of the members of said board as secretary and treasurer, and also provides that such secretary and treasurer shall continue in office until his successor shall be elected and qualified, the incumbent is not ousted from the office of secretary and treasurer by the appointment of a new board of regents, but continues as such until a new secretary and treasurer has been elected and has qualified as directed by the statute.

Trust Co. v. Bank, p. 589. 5. 602

REGENTS—Treasurer—Banks.

The treasurer of such board, in the absence of direction from the board of regents, assuming the power of such board so to do, has the right to deposit the funds in his hands in such bank or banks as he chooses, and to withdraw such funds at his pleasure, being liable, of course, at all times under his bond "to account for and pay over to the person or persons entitled thereto" such moneys.

Trust Co. v. Bank, p. 589. 6. 603

RELEASE—Condition—Issue.

Where cross-complainant alleged that a certain release of claims against an insolvent's estate was made only on one condition, while defendant charged that the release was made on the same and also on another condition, such allegations presented a complete issue, and no reply was necessary.

Lohman v. Reymond, p. 225. 5. 235

REPEAL—Statute—Common Law.

Where a statute does not specifically repeal or cover the whole ground occupied by the common law, it repeals it only when, and so far as directly and irreconcilably opposed in terms.

Ex Parte De Vore, p. 246. 4. 259

REPEAL—Intention of Legislature.

When a statute professes to repeal absolutely a prior law, and substitutes other provisions on the same subject, which are limited only till a certain time, the prior law does not revive after the repealing statute is spent, unless the intention of the legislature to that effect be expressed.

State Ex Rel. v. Sargent, p. 272. 4. 280

REPEAL—Prior Law—Revival.

When a statute professes to repeal absolutely a prior law, and substitutes other provisions on the same subject, which are limited only till a certain time, the prior law does not revive after the repealing statute is spent, unless the intention of the legislature to that effect expressed.

State Ex Rel. Sargent, p. 272. 4. 280

REVENUE—Constitution.

The requirement of equality and uniformity, in taxation applies only to taxes in the proper sense of the word levied with the object of raising revenue for general purposes, and not such as are an extraordinary and exceptional kind, and is, under a constitutional provision providing for equality in taxation, to be restricted to taxes on property, as distinguished from such as are levied on occupations, business or franchises, and as distinguished also from exactions imposed in the exercise of the police power rather than that of taxation.

State v. Ingalls, p. 211.   8.   224

REWARD—Witness—Conviction.

Evidence that a witness for the State expects to receive a reward upon conviction of the accused can properly be elicited upon cross examination of such witness for the purpose of showing his interest in the result of the prosecution.

State v. Lumpkin, p. 480.   4.   486

RIGHT—Conferred—Statute.

The right may be conferred by act of the legislature, or exist by virtue of the common law, in those jurisdictions where the common law is in force, and no statute expressly or impliedly denies the right.

State v. Armijo, p. 646.   2.   659

ROAD TAX—Person—Notice.

The person subject to road tax must be notified to appear, at such time and place and with such tools as may be designated, to perform the work in lieu of road tax.

State v. Byers & Buehl, p. 92.   2.   101

RULE—Means of Knowledge—Explanation.

Neither the rule to the effect that where the facts required to be shown are of a negative character, the burden of vidence may sometimes be sustained by proof rendering probable the existence of the negative facts, nor the rule to the effect that where knowledge or means of knowledge are almost wholly with the party not having the burden of proof, when all the evidence within the power of the moving party has been produced, the burden of evidence may sometimes shift to the party having the knowledge or means of knowledge, excuses the party having the burden of evidence from showing, no matter with what difficulty, sufficient facts, necessarily inconsistent with the position of the adverse party, to cause the court to say that a prima facie case has been made out requiring explanation, in which event, such showing, in connection with silence of the adverse party, may be sufficient to produce positive conviction in the mind of the court or jury.

Young v. Woodman, p. 207.   1.   211

8.

SALARY—Appropriation—Office.

Where the constitution of a State creates an office and prescribes the salary for such office, the necessity for legislative appropriation for such office is dispensed with on the ground that such provision in a State constitution is proprio vigore an appropriation.

State Ex Rel. v. Sargent, p. 272.   1. 278

SALARY—General Law—Rule.

This rule has been extended to a general law fixing the salary of a public officer, and prescribing its payment at particular periods.

State Ex Rel. v. Sargent, p. 272.   1. 278.

SALES—Accounts—Moneys.

Moneys received from the sales of possessory rights to real estate, even if said sales were void, must be accounted for by the executor.

Candelaria v. Miera, p. 107.   1. 113

SALES—Irregularities—Waiver.

Statutory provisions as to the order of sale and the manner of making it are for the benefit of the defendant alone, and can be waived by him, and, where there are irregularities in this regard, and he does not move promptly, he is considered to have waived them.

McMillen v. Bank, p. 494.   2. 501

SECURITIES—Public Obligations.

Whether the word "securities" as used in the enabling act and the constitution is not limited to public obligations for the payment of which the taxing power is available, is not decided because its decision is not necessary to a determination of this case, and is not discussed by counsel.

State v. Marron, p. 426.   2. 439

SENTENCE—Jurisdiction—Excess—Separable.

A sentence is legal so far as it is within the provisions of law and the jurisdiction of the court over the person and the offense, and only void as to the excess, when such excess is separable and may be dealt with without disturbing the valid portion of the sentence.

Habeas Corpus, p. 452.   4. 460

SENTENCE—Remain at Large—District Court.

Where a defendant, duly sentenced by a District Court to serve a definite term in the State penitentiary, is permitted to go and remain at large, under a void order of the court, he may be taken into custody and compelled to serve the term fixed in the judgment, even though a longer period of time than that for which he was sentenced has elapsed since the sentence was imposed.

In re Juan Lujan, p. 310. 2. 314

SCHOOL FUND—Deposit—Investment.

The deposit of the Permanent School Fund of the State in interest-bearing deposits in banks, under the provisions of Joint Resolution No. 14, Laws of 1913, is an investment of the same.

State v. Marron, p. 426. l. 437

SCHOOL TEACHER—Tenure of Office—Contract.

A school teacher has no fixed tenure of office by provision of law in this jurisdiction and his rights are measured by the terms of his contract with the school officers.

State v. Board of Educ., p. 183. 2. 190

SPECIAL VENIRE—Jurors—Summoned.

Sections 995, 997, 1001 and 1002, R. S. 1897, construed. and held to require, the selection of jurors, summoned upon a special venire, by lot.

Territory v. Prather, p. 195. 3. 201

STATUTE—Common Law.

As a general rule, where an act is prohibited, and made punishable by statute, the statute is to be construed in the light of the common law, and the existence of a criminal intent is essential.

State v. Alva, p. 143. 3. 151

STATUTE—Construction—Legislative Intent.

Penal statutes are to be strictly construed, but are not to be subjected to a strained or unnatural construction in order to work exemptions from their penalties. Such statutes are to be interpreted by the aid or the ordinary rules for the construction of statutes and with the cardinal object of ascertaining the legislative intention.

Ex Parte De Vore, p. 246. 3. 254

STATUTE—Cost Bond—Adverse Party.

Where a cost bond is required by statute, on appeal or writ of error, only for the protection of the adverse party, failure to give the same may be waived.

Canavan v. Canavan, p. 468. 2. 471

STATUTES—Penal—Strict Construction.

Penal statutes are to be strictly construed, but are not to be subjected to a strained or unnatural construction in order o work exemptions from their penalties. Such statutes are to be interpreted by the aid of the ordinary rules for the construction of statutes, and with the cardinal object of ascertaining the legislative intention.

Ex Parte De Vore, p. 246. 3. 254

STATUTE—Repeal—Irreconcilable.

Where a statute does not specifically repeal or cover the whole ground occupied by the common law, it repeals it only when, and so far, as directly and irreconcilably opposed in terms.

Ex Parte De Vore, p. 246.   4. 259

STATUTE—Taxation—Equalization.

Where a statute empowers a state board to equalize valuations for taxation, but does not point out the mode, any reasonable and efficient mode may be adopted to accomplish the end in view.

Ranch & Cattle Co. v. Bd. of Equal., p. 531.   2. 545

STATUTE—Validity—Title—Notice.

The true test of the validity of a statute, alleged to contain two subjects, one of which is not clearly expressed in the title, in conformity with Sec. 16 of Art. IV of the Constitution, is whether the title fairly gives reasonable notice of the subject matter of the statute itself.

State v. Ingalls, p. 211.   l. 219

STATUTE OF FRAUDS—Deed—Contract.

The statute of frauds is no bar to an action for the price of land actually conveyed, where the deed has been accepted or title has otherwise passed, although the grantor could not have been compelled to convey, or the grantor to accept a deed, because the contract was oral.

Harris v. Hardwick, p. 303.   2. 309

STIPULATION—Parties—Penalty.

A stipulation that "both parties hereunto have this day deposited in escrow with K., S. & H., this contract and a copy of the original contract, his demand note for $1,000.00 as evidence of good faith and as a forfeit in event either party hereto fails or refuses to comply with the terms of the contract as therein provided," held to be a penalty.

Keinath & Co. v. Reed, p. 358.   6. 369

SUBJECT—Germane—Unconstitutional.

If there be more than one subject mentioned in the act, if they be germane or subsidiary to the main subject, or if relative directly or indirectly to the main subject, having a mutual connection, and are not foreign to the main subject, or so long as the provisions are of the same nature and come legitimately under one general denomination or subject the act is not unconstitutional.

State v. Ingalls, p. 211.   3. 220

SUFFIX—"Jr"—Immaterial.

The addition or omission of the suffix "Jr." is immaterial in either a civil or criminal proceeding. The person so styled is presumed, in the absence of some proof to the contrary, to be the same person referred to whenever his name appears with, or without, the suffix.

City v. Belmore, p. 331.   1. 337

SUIT—Claims—Review.

Where, in a suit to compel trustees to account, the trial court did not hear all of the witnesses testify, an assignment that the court erred in finding that certain claims has been assigned to cross-appellant L. required a review on appeal of all the evidence in the case.

Lohman v. Reymond, p. 225.   2. 234

SUIT—Controversy—Objection.

In an interpleader suit, the amount due cannot be the subject of controversy, and where such controversy exists it presents an insuperable objection to its prosecution.

Trust Co. v. Bank, p. 589.   1. 598

SUPERINTENDENT OF INSURANCE—Salary—Warrant.

State ex rel. Fornoff v. Sargent, 136 Pac. 602, and State ex rel. Delgado v. Sargent, 134 Pac. 218, approved. Sections 4 and 11 of Chapter 127, Laws 1909, and Chapter 40, Laws 1909, interpreted and construed, and held to repeal by necessary implication, Section 12 of Chapter 5, Laws 1905, in so far as the same authorizes the payment of the salary of the Superintendent of Insurance out of the Insurance Fund upon the warrant of the Superintendent of Insurance approved by the State Auditor. The Superintendent of Insurance, after the act of 1909, was to be paid his salary out of the general salary fund of the Territory, and was so paid until December 1, 1912, when the appropriation therefor ceased.

State ex rel. vs. Sargent, p. 627.   6. 639

SUPREME COURT—Assumption—No Substitution.

Where the name, Dewey Dimon, appears upon the roll of jurors empanelled to try a cause, and the verdict is signed "DeWitt Dimon, Foreman," and no objection to the variance is made in the trial court, the Supreme court, on appeal, where the question is first raised, is warranted in assuming that no substitution in the personnel of the jury was made and that Dewey Dimon named on the jury roll signed the verdict as DeWitt Dimon.

State v. Cabodi, p. 513.   3. 517

SUPREME COURT—Clerk—Discretion.

Where the Supreme court, upon statehood, appointed the clerk of the former Territorial Court and allowed him to continue to issue writs of error, as had been·the practice before statehood, writs of error so issued, with the knowledge and acquiescence of the Supreme court and the justices thereof, must be taken to be issued at their direction within Const .

ness and at the same time a tax on the property employed in the business.

State v. Ingalls, p. 211.   7. 223

TAX—Delinquent.

Chapter 84, Laws of 1913, as construed to authorize the sale of property for taxes delinquent previous to the time the act became effective. Held, not to operate retrospectively in respect to such taxes.

Crane v. Cox, p. 377.   2. 386

TAXATION—Board of Equalization.

The State Board of Equalization has power to equalize the valuations of property for taxation purposes by classes, both as between classes in the same county and as between counties throughout the state, and the fact that the action taken results in the increase or decrease of total valuations in the state is immaterial.

Ranch & Cattle Co. v. Bd. of Equal., p. 531.   . 572

TAXATION—Board—Reasonable Mode.

Where a statute empowers a state board to equalize valuations for taxation, but does not point out the mode, any reasonable and efficient mode may be adopted to accomplish the end in view.

Ranch & Cattle Co. v. Bd. of Equal., p. 531.   2. 543

TAXATION—Delinquent—Sale of Property.

Section 34, Chapter 84, Laws 1913, directs the collector to offer for sale, "each piece of property upon which any taxes are delinquent as shown by the tax rolls." Held, to authorize the sale of property for taxes which had become delinquent prior to the year 1913.

Crane v. Cox, p. 377.   1. 381

TAXATION—Equal—Uniform.

The requirement of equality and uniformity in taxation applies only to taxes in the proper sense of the word levied with the object of raising revenue for general purposes, and not to such as are an extraordinary and exceptional kind, and is, under a constitutional provision providing for equality in taxation, to be restricted to taxes on property, as distinguished from such as are levied on occupations, business or franchises, and as distinguished also from exactions imposed in the exercise of the police power rather than that of taxation.

State v. Ingalls, p. 211.   8. 224

TAXPAYER—Admits—Injunction.

A preliminary injunction will not be granted to restrain the sale of property for taxes, unless the taxpayer first pays so much of the tax as he admits is just.

Crane v. Cox, p. 377.   3. 386

TAXPAYER—Discrimination.

So long as the taxpayer is not assessed more than the law provides, and there is no well-defined scheme of discrimination or fraudulent action, he cannot complain on certiorari of an action of the State Board of Equalization.

Ranch & Cattle Co. v. Bd. of Equal., p. 531.   5. 572

TAXPAYER—Fraudulent Action—Certiorari.

So long as the taxpayer is not assessed more than the law provides, and there is no well-defined scheme of discrimination or fraudulent action, he cannot complain on certiorari of an action of the State Board of Equalization.

Ranch & Cattle Co. v. Bd. of Equal., p. 531.   5. 572

TAXPAYER—State Board—Meetings—Notice.

The statute fixing the time and place of a meeting of the State Board of Equalization is notice to the taxpayers that the board will meet and perform only lawful acts and not that it will do illegal things.

Ranch & Cattle Co. v. Bd. of Equal., p. 531.   5. 567

TENDER—Amount——Conditions.

A tender by a debtor to a creditor (who in good faith asserts that the amount tendered is insufficient) is not good as a tender if it be coupled with such conditions that the acceptance of the same will involve an admission by the creditor that no more is due.

Mining Co. v. Mining Co., p. 153.   1. 165

TESTIMONY—Interpreted—Own Language.

Under the provisions of Section 14, Art. II of the State Constitution, the defendant is entitled to have the testimony interpreted to him in a language which he understands. While such right cannot be denied a defendant, it is incumbent upon him to, in some appropriate manner, call the attention of the trial court to the fact that he does not understand the language in which the testimony is given.

State v. Cabodi, p. 513.   5. 519

TITLE—Generality of—Act of Legislature.

The generality of a title to an act of the legislature is no objection to it so long as it is not made a cover to legislation incongruous in itself, and which by no fair intendment can be construed as having a necessary or proper connection.

State v. Ingalls, p. 211.   2. 220

TRANSFERS—Restraining Order—Voidable.

Transfers of property made to innocent parties, in violation of a restraining order, are not void nor voidable, because made in disregard of such order.

Southard v. Latham, p. 503.   2. 507

TREASURER—Board of Regents—Deposit—Funds.

The treasurer of such board, in the absence of direction from the board of regents, assuming the power of such board so to do, has the right to deposit the funds in his hands in such bank or banks as he chooses, and to withdraw such funds at his pleasure, being liable, of course, at all times under his bond, "to account for and pay over to the person or persons entitled thereto" such moneys.

Trust Co. v. Bank, p. 589.   6.   603

TREES—Delivery—Breach.

Where an executory contract provides for the manufacture of an article after a particular pattern or style, so that it would be useless, or practically useless, to anyone except the person for whom made, or in the case of trees prepared for planting, upon breach by the vendee before delivery, the measure of damages is the whole contract price.

Nursery Co. v. Mielenz, p. 417.   3.   422

TRESPASS—Damages—Remedy.

An action for damages for trespass under a void judgment and execution issued thereunder, is not such a plain, speedy and adequate remedy at law, as will bar an action to enjoin the enforcement of the judgment.

Pickering v. Palmer, p. 473.   4.   480

TRIAL—Decision—Not Dictum.

Whenever a question fairly arises in the course of a trial, and there is a distinct decision of such question, the ruling of the court in respect thereto cannot be called mere dictum.

Duncan v. Brown, p. 579.   2.   583

TRIAL—Merits—Waiver of Rights.

By going to trial on the merits and not objecting to evidence, defendant waived any right he may have had consequent on cross-complainant's failure to reply to defendant's answer.

Lohman v. Reymond, p. 225.   6.   236

TRIAL COURT—Child—Discretion.

This court will not review the discretion of the trial court in the matter of permitting a child of tender years to be sworn, as a witness, under the provisions of Sec. 3016, Comp. Laws of 1897, except in a clear case of abuse of such discretion.

State v. Sanchez, p. 262.

TRIAL COURT—Evidence—Weight.

Where the trial court hears all the witnesses testify and is thus able to observe their manner and demeanor while testifying, the Appellate court will not review the evidence further than to determine whether or not the findings are supported by substantial evidence; in the absence of such an overwhelming weight of evidence against such findings as would clearly show that the trial court erred in its conclusions drawn therefrom, and, in an equity case, where the court hears the witnesses ore tenus, there is no reason for a departure from the rule.

Frazer v. Bank, 340.   3. 352

TRIAL COURT—Instructions—Exceptions.

Appellant can not avail himself of alleged errors by the trial court in giving, or refusing to give, instructions, where he interposed no objection to the action of the court and failed to save exceptions.

State v. Analla, p. 294.   4. 299

TRIAL COURT—Interest—Disposition on Appeal.

Where the appellant has no interest in a sum of money, an assignment of error that the trial court erred in its disposition of such sum, will not be considered on appeal.

Edwards v. Fitzhugh, p. 424.   3. 426

TRIAL JUDGE—Clerk—Certificate.

Where the certificate of the trial judge to an alleged bill of exceptions is not certified to by the clerk of the court, and is not shown to have been filed in the clerk's office, neither the alleged bill of exceptions to which it relates, nor the said certificate will be considered by this court.

City v. Belmore, p. 331.   4. 340

TRIAL JUDGE—Discretion—Veniremen.

In the absence of a showing of abuse of discretion vested in the trial judge by Sec. 12, Chapter 116, Session Laws 1905, the Appellate court will not review the action of the court in returning to the jury box the names of veniremen, drawn to complete the panel.

State v. Analla, p. 294.   3. 293

TRUSTEE—Accounting—Receiver.

Where, in a suit to compel an accounting by trustees, cross-complainant at the time of filing his cross-complaint for appointment of a receiver, was justified from the record in believing that he would only be required to present and prove his title to claims transferred to him in the receivership proceedings, and for that reason only set up the assignment of such claims to his capacity to join in the suit to compel the trustees to account, his cross-complaint was not based on the instrument of assignment; and hence the assignment, when offered in evidence, was not objectionable because such instrument, or a copy thereof, was not filed in compliance with Code Civ. Proc., Sub-Sec. 307 (Laws 1907,

c. 107), providing that, when any instrument of writing on which the action or defense is found is referred to in the pleadings, the original or a copy shall be filed with the pleading, if within the power or control of the party wishing to use the same, and if the original or a copy be not filed or a sufficient reason given for the failure to file it, the instrument may not be admitted in evidence.

Lohman v. Reymond, p. 225.   1.   231

TRUSTEE—Testamentary—Negligent—Responsible.

A testamentary trustee, where he is negligent or unfaithful, is responsible for the amount the property coming into his hands ought to have yielded.

Candelaria v. Miera, p. 107.   2.   117

TRUST FUNDS—In Existence—Insolvent Bank.

When trust funds have been commingled with the general funds of a bank, before a trust upon such general funds can be imposed, as against creditors of the bank, it must appear that the trust fund in some form still exists and came into the hands of the receiver of the insolvent bank.

Daughtry v. Bank, p. 119.   2.   127

U.

ULTIMATE FACTS—Evidence.

The court is only required to find the ultimate facts in controversy, raised by the issues in the case, and is not required, nor is it proper, to set out the evidence upon which it relies in determining such ultimate facts.

Frazer v. Bank, p. 340.   1.   350

UNAUTHORIZED DEPOSIT—Drafts—Ratified.

Where a person, as soon as he learned of an unauthorized deposit of his funds in a bank, drew drafts on the same in order to immediately withdraw them, he will not be held to have ratified the deposit in the absence of proof of his assent to the deposit.

Daughtry v. Bank, p. 119.   1.   126

V.

VARIANCE—Allegations—Proofs.

A variance between the allegations in the indictment and the proofs at the trial cannot be raised on a motion for a new trial, and cannot be assigned as error in this court unless the question was raised at the trial of the case and the court trying the same given an opportunity to pass upon the question.

State v. Padilla, p. 573.   3.   577

VERDICT—Substantial Evidence.

The verdict of a jury will not be set aside on appeal when it is supported by substantial evidence.

State v. Lumpkin, p. 480.   2. 485

Where there is substantial evidence to support a verdict the Appellate court will not disturb it.

State v. Padilla, p. 573.   l. 57S

W.

WATER—Appurtenant to Lands.

While a ditch, through which water is carried for the irrigation of lands owned by the constructors in severalty, is owned and possessed by the parties as tenants in common, the water rights acquired by the parties are not attached to the ditch, but are appurtenant to the lands irrigated, and are owned by the parties in severalty.

Snow v. Abalos, p. 681.   7. 695

WATER—Diversion—Intention.

The intention to apply water to beneficial use, the diversion works, and the actual diversion of the water, all precede the actual application of the water to the use intended, but it is the application of the water, or the intent to apply, followed with due diligence toward application, and ultimate application, which gives to the appropriator the continued and continuous right to take the water. ·

Snow v. Abalos, p. 681.   5. 694

WATER COMMISSIONERS—Board—Trial de Novo.

Under Chap. 49, S. L. 1907, from any act or refusal to act of the state engineer, the aggrieved party may appeal to the Board of Water Commissioners, and may likewise appeal from the decision of said board to the District court. The statute contemplates a hearing or trial de novo before each board or tribunal, and not a review of the order or decision of the inferior tribunal. An assignment of error, in such a proceeding, upon appeal from a judgment of the District court, that "the court below erred in finding and adjudging that the said Board of Water Commissioners had and was possessed of the right, warrant and authority to review the discretion of the said state engineer in the matter of the approval of permits to appropriate," is therefore not well taken, because the record in this case fails to show that the District court so held, or that any such issue was presented, or could have been involved in the case.

Development Co. v. Land & Irrigation Co., p. 1.   2. 7

WATER RIGHTS—Consumer—Acequia.

The right to divert and utilize water acquired by the individual water user under a community acequia, being a several right, such individual consumer is a proper and nec-

essary party in an action for the adjudication of water rights
utilized through such community acequia.

Snow v. Abalos, p .681.   9. 699

WATER USER—Corporations—Acequia.

While Section 1, Chap. 1, S. L. 1895, makes all communi-
ity acequias corporations, for the purpose of that act, such
law did not divest the individual water users of any rights of
property which he theretofore owned or possessed.

Snow v. Abalos, p. 681.   .   8. 698

WATER USER—Convey Water Rights.

The fact that a water user may have entered into   a
contract by which he agrees, at some future time, to convey
his water right to another party, does not militate against
his right to maintain an action for the adjudication of his
right to the use of the water.

Snow v. Abalos, p. 681.   10. 701

WITNESSES—Alibi—Relations.

Upon cross examination the state has the right to expose to the jury the relations existing between the witnesses
testifying and the defendant, and the fact that the witnesses
have been frequently used by the defendant to establish an
alibi was proper to go to the jury for the purpose of weakening the evidence given by the witnesses on their direct
examination.   .

State v. Lumpkin, p. 480.   3. 485

WITNESSES—Manner and Demeanor.

Where the trial court hears all the witnesses testify and
is thus able to observe their manner and demeanor while
testifying, the Appellate court will not review the evidence
further than to determine whether or not the findings   are
supported by substantial evidence; in the absence of such an
overwhelming weight of evidence against such findings as
would clearly show that the trial court erred in its conclusions
drawn therefrom, and, in an equity case, where the court
hears the witnesses ore tenus, there is no reason for a departure from the rule.

Frazer v. Bank, p. 340.   3. 352

WITNESSES—Reward—Interest.

Such witness, however, cannot be interrogated as   to
a reward offered for the arrest and conviction of parties other
than the defendants, or in which the witness had   no prospective interest.

State v. Lumpkin, p. 480.   5. 486

WOMEN—Eligible—Public Office.

Under the common law, a woman was eligible to hold
a purely ministerial office, whatever might be the nature of

the office, if she was capable of performing the duties there-of, and there was no incompatibility between the nature and character of the duties of the office and their due performance by a woman, where, in so doing, she was not called upon to exercise judgment and discretion.

State v. Armijo, p. 646.   7. 656

WOMEN—Statutory Law.

The statutory law of the Territory of New Mexico neither expressly conferred or denied the right of women to vote or hold public office, hence we must look to the common law, if it was in force in the Territory, to ascertain and determine the right of women to vote and hold public office.

State v. Armijo, p. 646.   4. 653

WRIT OF ERROR—Supreme Court—Issuance.

Const., Art. VI, Sec. 3, providing that the Supreme Court, shall have jurisdiction to issue writs of error which may be issued by the direction of the court or any justice thereof, repealed Laws 1907, Ch. 57, Sec. 3, providing for the issuance of writs of error by the clerk of the court.

Wood-Davis v. Sloan, p. 290.   7. 292

WRITTEN CONTRACT—Effect.

In an action based upon a written contract which is admitted by the answer, the intentions of the parties as to what should be the effect of the contract is to be decided by the court upon an inspection of the contract.

Keinath & Co. v. Reed, p. 358.   8. 370

Lightning Source UK Ltd.
Milton Keynes UK
UKHW020828201218
334296UK00009B/1152/P